THE POEMS
OF CHARLES
CHURCHILL

VOL. ONE

THE BRUISER, C. CHURCHILL (once the Rev.d) in the Character of a Russian Hercules, Regaling himself after having Kill'd the Monster Caricatura that so sorely Gall'd his Virtuous friend the Heaven born WILKES.

— But he had a Club this Dragon to Drub, — Or he had ne'er don't I warrant ye. — Dragon of Wantley.

Designed and Engraved by W.m Hogarth. Price 1.s 6.d — Published according to Act of Parliament August 1.st 1763.

HOGARTH'S REPLY TO CHURCHILL

POEMS

OF

CHARLES CHURCHILL

EDITED BY

J A M E S   L A V E R

VOLUME ONE

BARNES & NOBLE, INC.

NEW YORK

PUBLISHERS · BOOKSELLERS · SINCE 1873

First published in two volumes, 1933
This edition (2 volumes in 1) published, 1970
Barnes & Noble SBN 389 03962 4
Methuen SBN 416 17420 5/35

POEMS

OF

CHARLES CHURCHILL

EDITED BY
JAMES LAVER

VOLUME ONE

MCMXXXIII

THE POEMS
OF CHARLES
CHURCHILL

CONTENTS

VOLUME ONE

	PAGE
PREFATORY NOTE	vii
INTRODUCTION	xiii
THE ROSCIAD	I
THE APOLOGY	48
NIGHT	62
THE GHOST : BOOK I	73
BOOK II	91
BOOK III	114
BOOK IV	152

VOLUME TWO

THE PROPHECY OF FAMINE	211
AN EPISTLE TO WILLIAM HOGARTH	231
THE CONFERENCE	252
THE AUTHOR	265
THE DUELLIST : BOOK I	278
BOOK II	285
BOOK III	293
GOTHAM : BOOK I	308
BOOK II	324
BOOK III	344
THE CANDIDATE	361
THE FAREWELL	388
THE TIMES	404
INDEPENDENCE	428
THE JOURNEY	447
FRAGMENT OF A DEDICATION	453
INDEX	461

PLATES

CHURCHILL	*facing p.* xiii
HOGARTH'S REPLY TO CHURCHILL	*facing title page* VOL. II

PREFATORY NOTE

Churchill left all his papers to John Wilkes, and the latter, in the first flush of enthusiasm, announced that he proposed to spend the rest of his life in bringing out a completely annotated edition of his friend's works. Had he done so, the labour of later editors might have been spared, for Wilkes not only knew much about Churchill's life, but he could have pointed every allusion in the satires and filled in every blank.[1] But Wilkes was no literary man. He could write a slashing article in The North Briton, *but the labours of conscientious editing and of thorough annotation were forever beyond him.*

He did indeed make an attempt to carry out his promise and the results of his labours have come down to us,[2] but they are not very helpful. He is both too scanty and too diffuse. He leaves a thousand points in ' The Duellist ' unelucidated and contents himself with writing a Wilkite pamphlet on the single line :

' And Innocence with Holland sleeps.'

Indeed he regarded the annotating of Churchill simply as a platform for himself; and as a note to a line in ' The Ghost ' which points at Lord Talbot, takes the opportunity of inserting the entire correspondence between himself and that nobleman, with regard to their duel, as well as an elaborate recital of the whole matter in a letter to Lord Temple. His account of Medmenham,

[1] *Perhaps not every blank, for in a letter to Churchill from Paris (Aug. 27, 1764) he says : ' I have been so many months absent from the great theatre of London, I begin to find obscurities in your late pieces '—and in the same letter he makes a proposal, which had it been carried out, would have shed light on many a dark passage. ' I believe I mentioned before the permission I have to print whatever I please here. You may avail yourself of this as much as you please. It is an observation of Swift that out of the bills of mortality nobody understands stars, feign'd names, or hints. I believe you would give double pleasure to the public if, after any new piece, you would take the trouble of a few short explanatory notes, and let the names be printed at length, like the Key to the Dispensary, Dunciad, etc. I can do this for you here, at no expense to you, and could send you any number of copies you please. The notes might be in the form of a letter from Martinus Scriblerus, guessing at names, telling little anecdotes, heightening passages a damn'd Mansfield keeps down, etc., etc.' (Brit. Mus. Add. MS. 30,878, f. 48, 49.)*

[2] *See* The Correspondence of the late John Wilkes, *etc., by John Almon, vol. III., 1805. The notes were originally printed in an appendix to the folio edition of* The North Briton, *1769.*

in a note to ' The Candidate,' is valuable, as he was himself a member of the fraternity, and his notes on ' The Dedication to Warburton' clear up more obscure points, but his remarks on ' Night,' ' Gotham,' ' The Conference' and ' The Epistle to Hogarth' add almost nothing to our information.

When Churchill set out on his ill-fated journey to France, he took with him, to show to Wilkes, the proof-sheets of his latest poems. These, with the crease-marks which they acquired in the pocket of Wilkes still plainly visible, are now in the British Museum. Wilkes made a few notes in the margins (which have been incorporated in the present edition) and filled in some of the blanks. But his declared intention of dedicating the rest of his life to his friend's memory was soon forgotten.

There is, in the Dyce collection in the Victoria and Albert Museum, a bound volume of Churchill's various poems. Before it came into the possession of Dyce it belonged to Mitford, and it contains ' MS. notes transcribed from Gray's Copy of Churchill in the possession of Mr. Penn of Stoke Park.' These notes, where suitable, have likewise been drawn upon by the present editor. Through the kindness of Mr. Iolo Williams (whose Seven XVIIIth Century Bibliographies, London, 1924, contains a valuable one of Churchill) it was possible to consult a bound volume of Churchill's poems formerly in the possession of the famous eighteenth century book collector M. Wodhull. Wodhull made some notes on the fly-leaves of the volume, and although some of his suggestions are wide of the mark, others are extremely useful.

A modern editor of Churchill is fortunate in being able to consult the valuable Wilkes-Churchill correspondence, now in the British Museum.[1] A bound volume contains the greater part of the letters which passed between the two during the years 1762 to 1764. The letters (highly seasoned as some of them are) have never been published in their entirety, and they throw a flood of light on the relationship of the two friends. Unfortunately, while Wilkes' letters are very well preserved and are written in his admirably clear hand, those of Churchill show a brown water-stain extending over almost half the surface of the paper and sometimes making the writing quite illegible. Churchill's hand, also, is difficult to read, as Wilkes himself was driven to complain. ' I wish [he remarks] you wou'd learn to write a good hand. Nature's

---

[1] Add. MS. 30,878.

chief masterpiece is writing well ; and you are microscopical.'
These letters have been largely drawn upon in the Introduction
for the present volume, and, where suitable, in the Notes.

Among other contemporary sources should be mentioned the
letters of Horace Walpole, and of the poet Gray; and a certain
amount of information (mostly hearsay) is to be gleaned from the
commonplace book of William Cole,[1] the antiquary. The files of
periodicals, especially The North Briton and The Gentleman's
Magazine for the years 1761 to 1764 have been of great assistance.
Acknowledgment should also be made to the biographies of
Churchill's friends, especially Wilkes[2] and Lloyd[3]. The satirical
verses produced in enormous number in answer to Churchill are of
value as showing the hostility he aroused, but they are naturally
not overweighted with exact information.

A memoir of Churchill appeared in The Whitehall Evening
Post for December 8th, 1764. This was reprinted in several other
newspapers and in The Annual Register for 1764. The so-
called Genuine Memoir of Mr. Charles Churchill appeared,
anonymously, in 1765. Kippis used this in his article in the
Biographia Britannica and added to it a certain amount of in-
formation derived from Wilkes. The poems were reprinted
several times, with a memoir : in Bell's edition of The Poets of
Great Britain, 1779 ; in Johnson's Works of the English Poets,
1790, and in A Complete Edition of the Poets of Great Britain,
(R. Anderson), 1794, but the first attempt to produce a complete
critical apparatus was reserved for W. Tooke.

W. Tooke was a worthy solicitor about whom very little is
known, save that, according to his own account, he had ' an
intimate acquaintance with several of the friends and contempor-
aries of the poet.' It became known that he was collecting materials
for annotating Churchill, and Flexney,[4] Churchill's publisher,
handed over to him ' several MSS. relating to the Life and
writing of the Satirist, in the handwriting of the Rev. William
Churchill, his brother.' A modern editor would have printed
these documents in their entirety, and it is much to be regretted
that Tooke did not do so.

The first edition of The Poetical Works of Charles Churchill

[1] Brit. Mus. Add. MS. 5832, *vol.* 31.
[2] *By Almon,* 1805.
[3] *Memoir by Kenrick preferred to edition of Lloyd's Works,* 1774.
[4] *Who died on January 7th, 1808, aged 77.*

with explanatory notes and an authentic account of his life *came out anonymously in 1804, and was favourably received. Forty years later he brought out a second and revised edition and this, falling into the hands of John Forster, was criticised by him in* The Edinburgh Review[1] *in the true bludgeoning style of that redoubtable journal. Forster had little patience with the rambling irrelevancies of Churchill's editor, and he remarks, with some justification, if a little harshly, that ' our business is with Churchill, and not with the London University, or with the Society for the Diffusion of Useful Knowledge, or with the Reform Bill, or with the Penny Postage Bill, or with the Dissenters' Marriage Act, or with the Whigs in general, or with Lord Campbell in particular, or with the Popish Ascendancy, or with the voters of Metropolitan Boroughs, or with the members who represent them in Parliament. . . . It would be difficult to imagine a worse biographer than Mr. Tooke . . . nor is he a more lively hand at a Note. . . . Whether he praises or blames, Mr. Tooke has the rare felicity of never making a criticism that is not a mistake. Nothing of this kind, committed forty years back, has he cared to correct, and every note added has added something to the stock of blunders.'*

This is much too severe. Some of Tooke's notes on obscure characters mentioned in ' The Ghost ' would be very difficult to replace, and, as a solicitor, he was able to throw light on one or two obsolete legal points which would give a modern non-legal editor an infinity of trouble.

Yet it must be admitted that his system of annotation (if system it can be called) is a singularly irritating one. A single instance will suffice. In ' The Rosciad ' (line 653 et seq.) we read that Shuter:

> ' *At Islington, all by the placid stream*
> *Where City swains in lap of Dulness dream . . .*
> *Secret as night with Rolt's experienced aid,*
> *The plan of future operations laid, etc.'*

Tooke's only comment is to tell us that the ' placid stream ' means ' the new river, as it was named, before similar works were denominated canals, to be since superseded by railways.' But the whole point of the passage is that the poet is speaking of

---

[1] The Edinburgh Review, *January*, 1845. *Forster's essay was reprinted in his* Biographical Essays, 1858, *and in* The Traveller's Library, *vol.* 16, 1856.

Sadler's Wells Theatre which stood by the Islington canal and was directed by Richard Rolt. The editor who does not tell the reader that tells him nothing.

Numerous blanks occur in Churchill's lines and some of these are very difficult to fill in with certainty, but Tooke should at least have made the attempt. He refused altogether to annotate ' The Times' with the remark that ' If the Times were really as depraved when the poet wrote as he represents them to have been, we should have cause to rejoice in the ameliorated condition of our countrymen at this period. But we are persuaded that Englishmen never merited the general execration, so nervously bestowed upon them in this poem. A depraved few have occasionally imported from abroad crimes at the mention of which every good man must shudder ; but neither rank nor fortune have been able to shield them from the indignation and abhorrence of all ranks of people.

' In this poem we have abstained from elucidating the obscurities that occur ; we should deem ourselves inexcusable were we, in an attempt to gratify the curiosity of our readers, to fix a stain upon the memory of persons, who have either been the victims of the most injurious calumny, or, if guilty, have appeared before that tribunal, the judgments of which neither wealth nor influence can evade.'

This is all very well, but the duty of an editor is to elucidate his text, even at the cost of pursuing through the quagmires of contemporary scurrility the traces of those crimes at the mention of which every good man must shudder.

The most useful example of such scurrilous writings is perhaps an anonymous attack on Foote, entitled ' Sodom and Onan.' Some of the blanks in Churchill can be filled in with some confidence from this work.

As a result of Forster's criticisms, in a subsequent edition of Churchill's works,[1] Tooke's notes were largely cut down and his errors corrected from Forster's marked copy of the previous issue. Tooke's memoir was omitted and a new one by James L. Hannay substituted. But no new notes were added, and certain passages in Churchill remained as obscure as before. Later accounts of Churchill, such as that of Mr. Beresford Chancellor in his Lives

[1] The Poems of Charles Churchill (*The Aldine Edition of the British Poets*), 2 vols., London, 1866. *Meanwhile, there had appeared an Edinburgh edition with memoir, critical dissertation and explanatory notes . . . by G. Gilfillan, 1855.*

of the Rakes, *and that of Mr. Iolo A. Williams in* Seven XVIIIth Century Bibliographies, *are naturally not concerned with the actual annotation of the poems. The present editor wishes to record his grateful acknowledgment to previous workers in the same field, to record his debt to the Gabrielle Enthoven collection of playbills in the Victoria and Albert Museum, and to Mrs. Enthoven and her assistants for their kindness in elucidating some obscure points in dramatic history, and to thank Mr. Carl Winter for an expert reading of the proofs.*

CHURCHILL

from an engraving by Burford
after a portrait by Schaak

INTRODUCTION

CHARLES CHURCHILL, the eldest son of the Reverend Charles Churchill, was born in February, 1731, in Vine Street, Westminster. His mother was a Scot, but nothing more is known about her, and even that solitary fact can only be deduced from one vague reference in her son's writings. His father was an impecunious clergyman, Rector of Rainham in Essex. It was not until two years later that he became curate and lecturer at St. John's, Smith Square, Westminster. These lectureships were pious foundations, and the ' lecturer ' was usually expected to deliver a mid-week sermon, or a sermon in addition to those preached by the regular clergy of the parish.

Even before his appointment to St. John's, Churchill Senior seems to have had the house in Vine Street ; how else should his son be born there ? We know almost nothing about this early period except a vague reference in Churchill's poems to ' an old house and an older aunt.' It would seem that Churchill's mother—since he barely mentions her—died when he was still very young, and that the house was kept by a sister of hers or of her husband's. Churchill had a sister named Patty, and two younger brothers : William who became a clergyman, and John who was brought up as a physician. At least part of his childhood was passed at Rainham—so much can be deduced from the acquaintance with rural things which he displays in ' Gotham,' although it is evident in very few passages in his other writings, and he may possibly—although this seems unlikely—have picked up his knowledge while he was curate at Cadbury. When he was eight years old Churchill was sent to school at Westminster, then under the charge of Dr. Nichols. Dr. Pierson Lloyd was usher of the fourth form and his son, Robert Lloyd, a scholar at Westminster, became Churchill's closest friend. Bonnell Thornton, another close friend in later life, was some years Churchill's senior, but among his more immediate contemporaries were several boys after-wards to be as famous : George Colman, Richard Cumberland and Warren Hastings. William Cowper was a timid, shrinking junior when Churchill had already reached the upper forms.

In spite of the wilfulness of his disposition, Churchill did not waste all his time at school, and when in his fifteenth year he offered himself as a candidate for the Westminster foundation, he went in head of the election. Destined as he was for ordination, and with the school reputation of being a sound scholar, it was natural that he should be entered for one or other of the two Universities. The whole episode of his University career is very obscure and accounts differ widely. He is said to have been entered at Trinity College, Cambridge, in 1749, but never to have gone into residence. Tooke declared that he stood for a postmastership (*i.e.* a scholarship) at Merton College, Oxford, at the age of eighteen. The *Cambridge Chronicle* [1] stated that he ' was admitted to St. John's College in this University under a Tutor of great Eminence : a Day or two after his Admission he requested his leave to go & meet some Friends at Ely : but this being refused, he took the Liberty of making his Exit without Leave, & never returned again to College.'

Another cause must have contributed to his unpopularity with the authorities : their discovery that this undisciplined young man was already married. The strength of his passions and his natural imprudence had indeed already hurried him into a state he had so little prospect of supporting, for at the age of seventeen he had contracted a ' Fleet ' marriage with a girl named Scot who, like himself, lived at Westminster. Churchill's father, although distressed by his son's rashness, so far forgave him as to take the young couple into his own house, and there Churchill lived until he could be launched on his clerical career, burdened with a wife and without the advantage of a University degree.

That Churchill never wished to take orders at all is evident both from his subsequent career and the clearly expressed opinion of the poems. But his father had been so considerate, and was so anxious that his eldest son should follow his own profession that the young man was almost compelled to bow to his wishes. Forster saw in his acceptance of the career mapped out for him the tragedy of Churchill's life, and without going so far—for Churchill was a man of strong natural desires and the temptations of the town were equally open to laymen —we may agree that the years spent in an uncongenial profession, in which he was compelled, to some extent, to play the

---

[1] December 15th, 1764. Quoted by William Cole, the antiquarian Rector of Bletchley, in his commonplace-book. (*Brit. Mus. Add. MS.* 5832.)

hypocrite, sharpened his appetite for debauchery when the moment of release arrived. His movements during the next few years are difficult to trace. Tooke, who had the advantage of whatever oral tradition may have persisted, declares that he retired to the north of England until 1753, when he returned to London in order to take possession of a small property inherited by his wife. He also says that he had at one time a curacy in Wales at thirty pounds a year and that he eked out his income by opening a cider cellar.

On reaching the canonical age he was ordained deacon by Bishop Willis of Bath and Wells and obtained the curacy of South Cadbury in Somersetshire, under Bailey, a friend of his father. Here he performed his duties with sufficient regularity if with little inward zeal; but the occupations of a country curate and the cares of a narrow household could not entirely engage his thoughts. He began a rambling poem directed against superstition, of which he himself seems to have had no trace whatever. This work was entitled 'The Fortune Teller.' It was laid aside for some years and only after its author had become famous did he take it from a drawer and issue it to the public, with numerous additions and corrections, as the first book of 'The Ghost.' It was Churchill's habit to make additions to his poems with every new edition, and we may be sure that many lines were added to 'The Fortune Teller' before it ever came to be printed. It is, however, possible, and by no means uninteresting, by deducting from the first book of 'The Ghost' all the political allusions and all references to events which had not happened when 'The Fortune Teller' was written, to arrive at some idea of the contents of the original manuscript.

Churchill was evidently much interested in the Elizabeth Canning affair which was filling the newspapers in 1753, first with an account of Betsy's misfortunes and then with the tale of her conviction for perjury and her transportation. We can also name with probability some of the books—presumably on the shelves of Mr. Bailey—which Churchill was reading at the time : works on classical antiquities, the 'Life of Bamfylde Moore Carew' and Defoe's account of Campbell, the deaf and dumb Scottish fortune-teller. Also, as is natural enough, his constant scriptural readings have left their mark on the poem. In no other work of his are there so many references to

Gideon's Fleece, the Plagues of Egypt and other events recorded in the Old Testament.

We do not know that Churchill ever tried to find a publisher for this first offspring of his talent, but if he had he would almost certainly have been unsuccessful. The poem is written in the octosyllabic measure which he never handled so well as the heroic couplet, and the lines themselves show little trace of the rude vigour of his later writing.

Other matters absorbed his attention. In 1756 he was ordained priest by Sherlock, Bishop of London, and he took his father's curacy at Rainham. For two years father and son worked together, but in 1758 his father died. He had lived and died a clergyman of the old school, hostile to the new ' enthusiasm,' but good-living, quiet and attentive to his duties. His parishioners liked and respected him and, as his son seemed likely to tread in the father's footsteps, they were quite willing to make him their spiritual shepherd. More important still, the parishioners of St. John's, Westminster, elected Churchill to his father's lectureship.

This circumstance, which compelled him to travel frequently to London, was the cause both of Churchill's moral ruin and of his literary success. Had he been compelled to spend the rest of his life in a country parsonage, he would no doubt have continued to write, but he might never have won the ear of the public and he would certainly never have been caught up into the whirl of politics. He might also have escaped four years of reckless dissipation and an untimely death.

His affairs, after his father's death, were far from prosperous. He had two young sons. His wife was as careless and extravagant as himself, and he was already completely tired of her. He saw himself compelled to labour at an uncongenial task on a very small salary, and he lacked altogether the patience and persistence (not to say the saintliness) which might have made such a lot in life tolerable. He had several small children to provide for, and in an endeavour to do so he opened a school. To a man of Churchill's temperament this was unrelieved drudgery. It was, moreover, unavailing, for his debts mounted steadily.

From such an existence his visits to London to lecture at St. John's must have been a welcome relief, and another circumstance soon occurred to make these visits more frequent.

He succeeded in obtaining a post as tutor to the famous girls' school in Queen Square, Bloomsbury. This establishment, known as ' The Ladies' Eton,' had been founded about the middle of the century by Mrs. Dennis, sister of Sir Peter Dennis, Bart., Vice-Admiral of the Red, and it attracted a fashionable clientèle. The young ladies were trained in all polite accomplishments, and an amusing insight into the high tone of the seminary is afforded by the story of how ' the pupils, in order to learn getting in and out of a coach properly, went to St. George the Martyr's Church (only across the square) in a stately old vehicle in relays.' [1] The uncouth, burly figure of Churchill must have been singularly out of place in such an atmosphere of genteel formality. However, he continued for a little while to instruct the young ladies in English literature, and the task was probably a more congenial one than teaching the country lads at home. We may imagine him, when his duties were done, turning with relief from the rarefied air of Bloomsbury and lumbering off to the Strand for a friendly bottle and a little masculine conversation. In the coffee-houses and taverns he renewed his old friendship with Lloyd, also a schoolmaster, for on his father's promotion to the second mastership of Westminster, the son had obtained his former place as usher. The two friends discussed their troubles and their hopes, their hatred of teaching, their financial difficulties, their literary aspirations. Each helped to unsettle the other, and Churchill returned to Rainham after each visit more discontented than ever and the poorer by the cost of several bottles of wine.

The inevitable crash could not long be delayed. In his distress Churchill had only one friend to whom he could turn : Dr. Pierson Lloyd, his old schoolmaster. The good man called a meeting of the creditors and persuaded them to accept five shillings in the pound. Even this Churchill was unable to furnish and Dr. Lloyd provided the funds himself. This extraordinary kindness Churchill never forgot, and Dr. Lloyd became for him the very symbol of disinterested goodness. The old man had troubles enough of his own. His son,

---

[1] Godfrey Heathcote Hamilton, in a letter to *The Times*, January 13th, 1931. The site of the school, on the east side of Queen Square, is now occupied by the National Hospital for Diseases of the Nervous System.

Robert, was as improvident as Churchill, and only awaited his chance to abandon school-mastering for what seemed the easier paths of literature. If Dr. Lloyd hoped, by helping Churchill, to reconcile his son to his position at Westminster, he was sadly mistaken. Robert Lloyd gave up his post soon after Churchill's bankruptcy and tried to support himself by writing for the booksellers. He had also more ambitious designs. He wrote verse with great facility and soon produced a series of what can hardly be called satires ; they are rather moral dissertations in rhymed couplets, marked by ease of manner, good sense and a total absence of inspiration. ' The Author's Apology ' made no great stir but was well received, and ' The Actor,' which was a plea for naturalism on the stage, established his modest reputation. His agreeable manners made him welcome among the wits of the coffee-houses, and the harassed clergyman must have envied his pleasant and apparently carefree existence.

Churchill resolved to follow his example as soon as he could. His life with Mrs. Churchill had become intolerable and a formal separation (which took effect in February, 1761) was arranged between them. He began, like Lloyd, to write for the journals, and earned a few shillings by contributing scraps to a periodical called *The Library*. Then, like Lloyd, he produced a poem. It was entitled ' The Bard ' and was written in Hudibrastic verse. As not a line has come down to us, it is impossible to say whether it was satirical in intention or not, but the choice of metre and Churchill's persistent leaning to satire suggest that it was. He offered it to a bookseller named Waller, who rejected it with contempt, but Churchill was not the man to be discouraged by a single repulse. He set to work on another poem immediately. He had, we may well imagine, already been in trouble with his ecclesiastical superiors. Such seems the only explanation of the subject chosen for his satire ' The Conclave,' written to ridicule the Dean and Chapter of Westminster. Dr. Zachariah Pearce, Bishop of Rochester and Dean of Westminster, was peculiarly obnoxious to him. The good doctor had translated Longinus and it is under that name that he appears in the poem. Tooke, in a footnote,[1] has pre-

---

[1] ' The Ghost,' Book II., line 457. Characteristically Tooke does not say how he came by the fragment nor whether he knew of the existence in manuscript of the whole poem.

served the opening lines, written in a metre which Churchill was never to adopt again :

> ' The Conclave was met, and Longinus the Pope,
> Who leads a great number of fools in a rope,
> Who makes them get up, and who makes them sit still ;
> Who makes them say yea or nay, just as he will ;
> Who a critic profound does all critics defy,
> And settles the difference 'twixt *Beta* and *Pi* ;
> Who forgiveness of faults preaches up to another,
> But forbids it to come near himself or his brother . . .'

The last two lines certainly seem to contain a hint that Churchill had at some time been admonished by the bishop, and cherished against him a personal rancour to which his later works give occasional expression.

He hawked ' The Conclave ' round the shops of the book-sellers. Some of them liked it ; its rough swashbuckling verses seemed to promise sales. But its satire was too particu-lar, too obviously directed against a body by no means power-less to retaliate. The satirist was advised to write something less dangerous, something which would gratify the malice of the public, without any risk for the author and publisher. Churchill was compelled to cast about for another subject.

He was not long in finding what he sought. He had long had a passion for the theatre, and on his visits to London had paid many surreptitious visits to the rival houses, presumably in the company of Lloyd, whose ' Actor ' shows at least that the theatre of the day was well known to him. Churchill resolved to follow his example and in the winter of 1760-61 attended the theatre assiduously. The players, when they stepped to the footlights to declaim the more heroic portions of their parts, or when they came before the curtain to receive the applause of the audience, may or may not have noticed in the front row of what was then the pit, separated from the orchestra by a row of iron spikes, the big burly figure in the ' black scratch wig ' and shabby clothes, who gazed at them with so much surly attention. But if they did, they little sus-pected the mine he was preparing to explode under their feet.

The poem which, like all Churchill's works, was written very rapidly, was finished in February, and the author, forti-fied by the approval of his friends, hawked it round the booksellers' shops. He wanted £20 for it, but no one could be found to offer him more than £5.[1] It says much both for Churchill's obstinacy and his belief in himself that he refused to accept less than the sum he had asked and, failing this, determined to publish the work at his own expense.

'The Rosciad,' for that was the title, appeared in March, 1761. Its success was immediate, that is to say, the poem sold an enormous number of copies, but the reviewers of the day were by no means so eager to salute the rise of genius as they have since become. Chief among them was Smollett, then editor of the influential *Critical Review*, although he afterwards denied having written the paper which gave so much offence to Churchill. The critical reviewer, whoever he was, admitted that the poem was written in ' tolerable good rhyme,' but hinted that the author's opinions were ' not new, being indeed no more than the echo of the critics in every coffee-house.' The writer ridiculed the anonymity of the poet, declaring roundly that he who praised Lloyd so warmly could be none other than Lloyd himself. ' We will not pretend, however, absolutely to assert that Mr. Lloyd wrote this poem, but we may venture to affirm that it is the production jointly or separately of the new triumvirate of wits (Colman, Lloyd, and Thornton) who never let an opportunity slip of singing their own praises.' The publisher and printer wrote immediately to the papers to deny that Lloyd had had any hand in the matter and Colman sent a similar denial. Lloyd indeed, in spite of the praise which had been lavished upon him, was not too well pleased by the success of ' The Rosciad,' a success so much greater than that of ' The Actor.' However, he was an almost excessively good-natured man. He recognised the greater vigour of Churchill's verse and resigned himself cheerfully enough to his friend's superiority.

> ' Pleas'd I behold superior genius shine,
> Nor ting'd with envy wish that genius mine,
> To Churchill's muse can bow with decent awe,
> Admire his mode, nor make that mode my law :
> Both may, perhaps, have various pow'rs to please,
> Be his the Strength of Numbers, mine the Ease.'

[1] This is Tooke's account. Cowper says that he only demanded £5 and could not obtain even that.

The two men became greater friends than ever even to the extent of pooling their resources in a common fund.

Apart from the author himself, those most interested in the success or failure of ' The Rosciad ' were, naturally, the actors. They saw the poem everywhere, heard it quoted on all hands, and reflected ruefully that it could not have appeared at a more unfortunate time : the end of the season, the period of their ' benefits.'

To say that they were startled is to underestimate the effect of Churchill's bombshell ; they were outraged. Lloyd's ' Actor ' had been a mild philosophic discussion of the principles of their art ; ' The Rosciad ' was as personal as a smack in the face, as definite as a hiss from the pit. They threatened every kind of violence against the person of the author, should he ever become known.

Churchill's reply to the contempt of the reviewers and the fury of the actors was to order his name to be printed upon the title page of the second edition. Then, arming himself with a stout cudgel, he walked boldly into the Bedford coffee-house and, seating himself and drawing off his gloves, called loudly for a dish of coffee and ' The Rosciad.' No one present dared risk an encounter with an author at once so burly and so self-confident. In the Rose Tavern, Churchill was nearly involved in a duel with knives with the actor Yates, but the latter's courage failed at the last moment, and henceforward the poet was unmolested. He continued to visit the theatres, and the performers on the stage grew nervous and forgot their lines whenever they saw his bull-like face, glowering at them over the spikes of the pit.

Thomas Davies, one of the sufferers, has left an account[1] of the resentment and consternation it caused among his fellow actors. ' The author,' he says, ' soon found that he had no occasion to advertise his poem in the public prints ; the players spread its fame all over the town ; they ran about like so many stricken deer ; they strove to extract the arrow from the wound, by communicating the knowledge of it to their friends. The public, so far from being aggrieved, enjoyed the distress of the players ; they thought ' The Rosciad ' a pleasant and

---

[1] In his *Life of Garrick*, Chap. xxviii. Davies was an author and bookseller as well as an actor, but is now chiefly remembered for having been the means of introducing Boswell to Johnson.

reasonable retaliation for the mirth which the stage had continually excited at their expense. It was observed by the laughers that the players who were most hurt pretended to be the least sensible of their own injuries, but were extremely warm in their feelings for the obloquy thrown upon others. ' Why,' said one of these disinterested persons, ' should this man attack Mr. Havard ? I am not at all concerned for myself ; but what has poor Billy Havard done that he must be treated so cruelly ? ' ' And pray,' said a gentleman who was present at this mock declaration of benevolence, ' what has Mr. Havard done, that he cannot bear his misfortunes as well as another . . .'

' It would be unjust to insinuate that all the actors felt themselves equally hurt by Churchill's satire. Some of them took no notice of the poem ; others wisely endeavoured to profit by his comment on their faults. Barry, Woodward, and Mossop, who were most severely handled, were at that time in Ireland, and owed their first knowledge of the rank which they held in ' The Rosciad ' to a Dublin edition of it. Havard was more offended than became a man so calm and dispassionate. Ross pleaded guilty, and laughed at his punishment over a glass with his friend, Bonnell Thornton. Sparks was too much a man of the world to be hurt by a poetical arrow. King was displeased, but King kept his temper. Shuter, out of revenge, got very merry with the poet. Foote, who lived by degrading all characters, was outrageously offended.'

Among the male actors of the period only Garrick was untouched by Churchill's satire. His position, none the less, was extremely awkward. No one knew better than he how precarious is the popularity of an actor, and no one realized better the difficulties of an actor-manager among other members of his touchy profession. The satirised actors came to him with their complaints of Churchill's hard usage and Garrick could hardly avoid at least the appearance of sympathy. His own immunity from attack he thought it prudent to explain by suggesting that Churchill flattered him in order to be given the freedom of his theatre. This was balm to the wounded actors, but, of course, one of them repeated the conversation, and it came to the ears of Churchill.

He was already meditating a new satire, and had chosen as his subject those critical reviewers who had given to ' The

Rosciad ' so very lukewarm a welcome. He resolved to give
Garrick, too, a sharp rap over the knuckles. ' The Apology '
was primarily an attack on Smollett, but Churchill took the
opportunity of ridiculing the confusion he had caused among
the actors, and his treatment of the whole profession was much
more contemptuous than it had been in ' The Rosciad.'
Garrick was pointed at quite plainly in the lines beginning :

> ' Let the vain tyrant sit amid his guards,
> His puny green-room wits and venal bards,
> Who meanly tremble at the puppet's frown,
> And for a playhouse freedom lose their own.'

Garrick, whose only desire was to be on good terms with
everybody, took the alarm at once. He wrote a very careful
letter to Lloyd, professing himself Churchill's great admirer,
and the good-natured Lloyd arranged a meeting and a recon-
ciliation between them. The friendship thus begun cost Gar-
rick considerable trouble and some hard cash to preserve, but
he did preserve it until Churchill's death.

Churchill made between £750 and £1000 by his two first
poems, and the money thus gained allowed him for the first
time to gratify his tastes. These tastes were neither extrava-
gant nor refined ; he cast off his previous suit of rusty black
and put on a blue coat and a hat edged with gold, but he wanted
no fine house, he had no wish to travel (the war would, in any
case, have made it difficult) ; he desired nothing but a bottle, a
woman and the conversation of his friends.

The Dean of Westminster once more remonstrated with
him on his behaviour and for devoting his talents to such
secular subjects. Churchill replied with a somewhat irrelevant
gibe at Dr. Pearce's translation of Longinus, whereupon the
Dean requested him to resume clerical dress. This Churchill
refused to do, but he did not resign his lectureship at St.
John's, in spite of the outcry of the parishioners, until 1763.

He seems, however, to have been conscious of the public
disapproval excited by his new mode of life, and his next poem,
' Night,' was written with the view of justifying his conduct.
It appeared in October, 1761. A poem entitled ' Day ' by
John Armstrong had just been published, and may have sug-
gested Churchill's title, although it did not suggest his subject
matter. The theme of Churchill's poem is the paradoxical

proposition that poor and honest men must stay up late because of the innumerable wealthy upstarts who strut about by day.

> ' Rogues justified, and by success made bold,
> Dull fools and coxcombs sanctified by gold,
> Freely may bask in fortune's partial way,
> And spread their feathers opening to the day ;
> But threadbare Merit dares not show the head
> Till vain Prosperity retires to bed,
> Misfortunes, like the owl, avoid the light ;
> The sons of Care are always sons of Night.'

Churchill's merit could not have been very threadbare at that moment, whatever Lloyd's might be. The rest of the poem propounds the doctrine that there is no vice but hypocrisy, and although it contains some excellent incidental satire, the poem as a whole is somewhat unconvincing. More important, it did not sell.

The public was not interested in the reasons, philosophic or otherwise, which kept Churchill up all night. What was wanted was personal satire, and in this the new poem was conspicuously lacking. It involved him, however, in a new quarrel. Churchill was a most touchy mortal and he never forgot a real or fancied injury. Someone mentioned ' Night ' to Dr. Johnson who allowed little merit either to that or to Churchill's other poems. Churchill came to hear of this and henceforward Johnson was his enemy, to be gibbeted whenever occasion offered.

Such occasion was not long delayed. At the beginning of the year 1762 the ' town ' was much excited by ' Scratching Fanny,' or the ' Cock Lane Ghost.' [1] Cock Lane was an obscure turning between Newgate Street and West Smithfield, and to the poor-class lodging in the by-street in which the manifestations were supposed to take place flocked all the nobility and gentry, including the Duke of York and Horace Walpole, and all the philosophers and wits, including Doctor Johnson. Johnson was always interested in the supernatural and seized the opportunity eagerly, but, as soon as he suspected imposture, he took every means to have it exposed, and it was largely due

---

[1] For a fuller account of the matter see ' The Ghost,' Book II, note on line 246.

to his account of the matter in *The Gentleman's Magazine* that the excitement died down.

The occasion seemed a good one to Churchill to refurbish his old poem of ' The Fortune Teller,' and the verses which he had made at Cadbury were expanded to form the first book of ' The Ghost.' The second book followed almost at once and in this Johnson is satirised as :

> ' Pomposo,—insolent and loud,
> Vain idol of a scribbling crowd,
> Whose very name inspires an awe,
> Whose every word is sense and law ;
> For what his greatness hath decreed,
> Like laws of Persia and of Mede,
> Sacred through all the realm of Wit
> Must never of repeal admit,' etc.

Johnson took the blow with great dignity, remarking only that he had thought Churchill a blockhead before and had seen no reason to alter his opinion. Certainly ' The Ghost ' was not likely to increase Churchill's reputation. It is a most rambling poem with enormous parentheses. It is completely formless and jumps from one subject to another in the most erratic fashion, turning aside now to administer a drubbing to the Laureate, Whitehead, now to make fleeting reference to the news of the day—the elopement of Miss Hunter with the Earl of Pembroke, or obscure happenings at the funeral of George II. Obscurity indeed is the poem's winding sheet, for few modern readers can have the patience to disentangle all the allusions. Churchill crammed into the poem whatever appeared in the news before him, or whatever came into his head. He even introduced an elaborate parody of Pope's tale of Lodona and Pan and made laboured fun of the Lord Mayor's show.[1]

However, a new influence was now to enter Churchill's life and to give his pen renewed scope for satire. How he became acquainted with John Wilkes is not known,[2] but the two men,

---

[1] The fourth book did not appear until November, 1762, and is even longer and more tedious than the preceding ones.

[2] Fitzgerald, in his *Life of Wilkes*, declares roundly that ' he made his acquaintance in an odd way. One Armstrong, a military doctor, with literary tastes, had published a complimentary poem addressed to

seemingly so ill-assorted, were soon on intimate terms, and henceforward their lives are so closely intertwined that it is impossible to understand Churchill's poems, and a great part of his motives in writing them, without constant reference to the affairs of Wilkes.

It is possible that a common hostility to Smollett brought the two men together. Wilkes and Smollett had recently been on good if not exactly intimate terms, and as late as March, 1762, we find Smollett writing to Wilkes to profess his ' warmest regard, affection and attachment.' However, when Bute became First Lord of the Treasury on May 29th, 1762, he engaged a number of writers to defend his measures. Among these was Smollett, and in no long time the ' obliged, humble servant' of Wilkes was declaring in *The Briton* that : ' such a caitiff should not escape unpunished ; he does not deserve to enjoy the protection of the law, far less the privilege of a

Wilkes, whom he styles ' gay Wilkes,' and in which he attacked Churchill.

' Wilkes' attention was thus at once drawn to Churchill, and he sought his acquaintance forthwith, disdaining the incense thus offered to him.'

On the face of it the story is unlikely, and an examination of the facts prove it to be unfounded. John Armstrong had in 1760 received the post of physician to the army in Germany, probably through Wilkes' influence. On November 3rd of that year he wrote to Wilkes enclosing a poetical epistle entitled ' Day ' which Wilkes published in 1761, probably without the author's knowledge or consent. Armstrong indeed did not know of its publication until October of the following year. It is unlikely that Armstrong, when he wrote ' Day,' had ever heard of Churchill, and as A. H. Bullen remarks, very justly, in the *Dictionary of National Biography*, ' the reader must be extraordinarily lynx-eyed to discover any allusion to Churchill in Armstrong's epistle.' Bullen, however, is surely mistaken in supposing that Churchill's attack on Armstrong in ' Night ' was inspired by Wilkes. ' Night ' was published in January, 1762. It is doubtful if Churchill knew Wilkes at that time. The first dated letter which has come down to us was written on June 15th, and is very formal in style, as if they had not known one another long. Wilkes, moreover, complimented both Churchill and Armstrong in the mock ' Dedication of Mortimer ' to the Earl of Bute, which was published early in 1763. Armstrong, who was born in Scotland, objected to Wilkes' attacks upon his countrymen in *The North Briton* and wrote to him on September 17th, 1763 : ' I cannot with honour or decency associate myself with one who has distinguished himself by abusing my country.' (*Brit. Mus. Add. MS.* 30,867, f. 216.)

Henceforward Churchill's hostility to Armstrong was reinforced by that of Wilkes and the poet lost no opportunity of ridiculing the author of ' Day.'

native Briton ; he does not deserve to breathe the free air of heaven ; but ought to be exiled from every civilized society.'

Even if the friendship of Wilkes and Churchill were at first purely convivial, the former must soon have perceived how powerful an ally Churchill might become in the war against the Ministry. Churchill was honest ; Churchill was profoundly shocked by abuses which moved Wilkes to a merely superficial indignation ; Churchill regarded Wilkes as the heaven-sent champion of liberty, and he was, moreover, possessed of a style of vigorous invective hardly known in English literature since the death of Dryden.

Wilkes attacked the Ministerial journal *The Briton* in a paper purporting to be written entirely by Scotsmen and bearing the ironical title of *The North Briton*. This famous periodical made its first appearance on June 5th and, while preserving its name, soon abandoned even the ironical pretence of supporting Bute. Wilkes had so many occupations that he was unable to give much time to it, but Churchill threw himself into the venture with all the enthusiasm of friendship. It is estimated that at least half the numbers were written by him and, by the sworn testimony of the printers, he received all the profits.

The story of their relationship can be pieced together from the valuable Wilkes-Churchill correspondence in the British Museum.[1] The first letter in the collection is particularly important for it proves that, when it was written, Wilkes and Churchill were already friendly, but not yet intimate, and that both were admitted to the rites of Medmenham Abbey, presided over by Sir Francis Dashwood. It also shows that the collaboration in *The North Briton* had begun and that Churchill was busy with his poem of ' The Ghost.' It is dated from Winchester, Tuesday, June 15th, (1762).[2]

The mention of Medmenham is sufficient to prove how completely Churchill had thrown off the restraints of clerical life. That he was a frequent visitor may be doubted, for the break-up of the Abbey followed hard upon the cementing of his friendship with Wilkes. Besides, the flummery of the

---

[1] *Add. MS.* 30,878.

[2] ' My dear Sir, As the Devil would have it/no contrivance of mine would answer till now to send you/*The North Briton*. . . . Pray remember the ghost for me to-night/and next Monday we meet at Medmenham. I am, my dear Churchill, Your affectionate humble servant, JOHN WILKES.

' Franciscans ' cannot have been much to Churchill's taste. He was not a blasé man of the world in need of exotic rites to make vice attractive. It was all too attractive already, and it must be admitted that his letters to Wilkes make anything but edifying reading. The bottle and the bed, and his contempt of those who profess to despise them, are the staple themes of his discourse.

Churchill's dissipations, indeed, were often to prove an embarrassment to Wilkes, who subordinated even love-making to his ambition. Of that ambition Churchill had not a trace, and his more energetic and mercurial friend had frequently to speed him on to greater activity in the Cause. It was not so much that Churchill did not take his politics seriously ; indeed, he took them far more seriously than Wilkes, but he was a heavy man, inclined to corpulence, and indolent by nature. Wilkes left the drudgery of bringing out *The North Briton* in his hands and he frequently found it irksome. A letter of his dated July 13th, 1762, throws a vivid light both on his temper and on his relationship with Wilkes.

' Dear Wilkes,' he writes, ' I wish it was in my power to send you the next Saturday's *N.B.* according to your desire, but tho' I expected you would depend on me I have not as yet wrote a letter of it, according to my usual maxim of putting everything off till the last. You may be certain, however, of its being done in time. I have the cause too much at heart to let it be out of my head.

' Where is the Ghost ? I cannot tell—the Flesh has engrossed so much of my care that I have never once thought of the Spirit. I am sorry I cannot meet you at Aylesbury, or come to you at Winchester, but that which I at first considered merely as the amusement of a trifling hour, is become the serious attention and delight of my days, it has already been so three weeks, and is likely to continue as much longer. . . . When we meet, which I flatter myself will be soon, you will be amazed to see how I am altered. Breakfast at nine—two dishes of tea and one thin slice of bread and butter—Dine at three—eat moderately—drink a sober pint—Tumble the bed till four—Tea at six—Walk till nine—Eat some cooling fruit and to bed. There is regularity for you—And will ye not ye old Scripture pumping Divines, ye mercenary preceptmongers . . . Will ye not allow me the indulgence of sense in that

interval, or will ye declare me unworthy of Absolution ? Keep
it to yourselves ye worthy descendants of the Scribes and
Pharisees—Could you see her with her eyes half shut or the
whites of them turn'd up, you would yourselves follow the
example if you could, or . . . (illegible) at Providence if you
could not. By the way, my dear Wilkes, did you ever know a
man, who rail'd at Fornication unless he was old or impotent.
. . . In yours you tell me you are engaged with ——. I could
not understand it, my Lindamira says it must be with Old
Scratch. . . . I rather think you meant it a hint for me to
fill up a blank, and she seems to like the interpretation, and
looks towards the Bed. . . .

' Last Saturday I heard the Trial of the Conspirators relative
to Miss Fanny and was much entertained. . . .

' You say nothing when you shall be in Town. I hope soon.
. . . Notwithstanding my boasted sobriety you shall see when
you come to Town that my reformation is not universal, and
tho' I will not get drunk with ev'ry Fool, I am above being
thoroughly sober with an honest fellow like you. I am, my
Dear Wilkes, Yours most sincerely, C. CHURCHILL.'

Wilkes was not quite so honest as his friend believed, and
we may safely assume, from our knowledge of the poet's
character, that it was without his knowledge that Wilkes now
engaged in an attempted negotiation with the very Minister
whom he and his assistants were so vehemently attacking in
The North Briton. Dining one evening with Richard Rigby,
he asked him to intercede on his behalf with the Duke of
Bedford and to get the latter to approach Bute with the sug-
gestion that he (Wilkes) should be made Governor of Canada.
Rigby asked what guarantee the favourite could have that Lloyd
and Churchill would not continue their attacks once Wilkes
was out of the way, to which Wilkes replied that he would take
both Lloyd and Churchill with him to America, the one as his
secretary, the other as his chaplain. It is interesting to
speculate whether Churchill's friendship would have resisted
the strain of such a proposal, but he was never to be tempted
to abandon either his friend or his principles, for the project
came to nothing.

It seems strange that Bedford should ever have approached
Bute with the proposal, but apparently he did so. Bute, how-
ever, declined to deal, and Wilkes returned to the attack. In

No. 31 of *The North Briton* he even assails Rigby, whom he suspected of having held out promises which he was unable, or unwilling, to fulfil.

Wilkes seems to have had for Churchill a genuine affection, subordinated, as always, to his own interests ; while Churchill had for Wilkes a deeper love, as well as the admiration of a poor and somewhat uncouth man for a brilliant and influential friend. But his idleness and his dissipations did not make writing easy. The letters of both are very characteristic. Wilkes writes often. He is anxious for his friend's health—and spurs him on to greater activity. He fears that Churchill is overworking—and entreats him in the next line to ' take care of Saturday's *North Briton.*' He is ecstatic that ' the Scottish eclogue ' (*i.e.* ' The Prophecy of Famine ') is to be inscribed to him—and begs that Churchill will correct the proof which Kearsley, the printer, has been ordered to bring to him. Even when half his letter is about women Wilkes does not forget to mingle business with pleasure.[1]

Churchill writes more seldom. He lacked his friend's power of rapid recovery after a debauch. In love-making, too, he had none of Wilkes' rapidity of attack and retreat, and all too frequently he is constrained to offer excuses for his neglect of *The North Briton.* ' Yours of the 25th came not to hand till this morning. That of the 26th I received on Thursday, when a particular Engagement which took me up the whole day and kept me in bed till Eleven the next morning, was the Occasion of the *N.B.* being as it was.'

Truly a somewhat unsatisfactory collaborator for one who had so many irons in the fire as Wilkes : for to his duties as a militia officer and his activities as a pamphleteer were added the excitements of his duel with Lord Talbot. In this Wilkes behaved with so much spirit that his popularity was greatly increased and he wrote exultantly to Churchill : ' I am surfeited with caresses. A sweet girl, whom I have sighed for unsuccessfully these few months, now tells me she will trust her

[1] As, for example, in an undated note in the British Museum :

' My dear Churchill, I am just summon'd about my house and my girl—I shall return in less than an hour—If you will wait, you shall kiss the (sweetest) *lips* . . . of this hemisphere—I expect the proof by eleven and am infinitely desirous of your revising it—It is I fear very very incorrect. Ever yours, JOHN WILKES.'
' Friday ten.'

honour to a man who takes so much care of his own. Is not that prettily said ? Pray look me out *honour* in the dictionary, as I have none here, that I may understand the dear creature—but, by God, I will not wait for answer. Adieu.'

Churchill's amours were somewhat more sordid. He frequented brothels and even appeared in a box in the theatre in the company of women of the town. When Wilkes at last got a letter out of him, it is indeed full of poetry (the new ' Scottish Eclogue ' which was to turn into ' The Prophecy of Famine ') but as a postscript Churchill adds : ' I have just received Mrs. Borewell's[1] favour. I long for the fray.' The result of all this was only too certain. When Wilkes returned to London in November, Churchill had disappeared. Wilkes wrote to him several times, presumably to his lodgings ' at Mrs. Horners in Tothill Street, Westminster ' but could get no reply. The explanation was simple. Churchill had contracted syphilis. When Wilkes knew the truth he wrote a characteristic letter apologising for his impatience. ' I am sorry that the Lord has visited you in David's way. . . . I did not know till your letter of yesterday that you had implor'd the aid of the quicksilver god. I hop'd that you had only retir'd to some gentle purgations and purifications.'

Churchill's enforced leisure—he had probably retired on this, as on a subsequent occasion, to ' Mrs. Kier's Vaux Hall '[2]— gave him an opportunity of finishing ' The Prophecy of Famine.' The poem appeared in January, 1763, and was an immediate success. Churchill's satire, before somewhat erratic or else aimed at objects in which the public took little interest, had now found a target. The unpopularity of the Scottish followers and pensioners of Bute was at its height, and Churchill's ridicule of the entire nation doubly welcome. Happy the satirist whose attack coincides with a violent wave of public opinion. Churchill's reputation, which had been

---

[1] The name (it can hardly be a genuine name) is interesting as showing that Churchill had already read, no doubt in manuscript, the famous ' Essay on Woman.'

[2] Mr. Beresford Chancellor (in *The Lives of the Rakes*, IV, p. 118) suggests that this was a relation of the Miss Carr with whom Churchill subsequently eloped. This seems to me excessively unlikely. What respectable tradesman would have a house at Vauxhall to which gentlemen afflicted with venereal disease could retire for a cure ? See note on p. xxxviii.

shaken by the comparative failure of 'Night' and 'The Ghost,' was once more re-established. Even the Scottish papers were impressed, in spite of themselves, and 'The Prophecy of Famine' was favourably reviewed in Edinburgh itself. *The Scots Magazine*,[1] while deploring its tendency to 'the widening national breaches, and fermenting (? fomenting) divisions' praised it highly as a poem, and in a subsequent issue[2] printed the work in its entirety with the remark that 'this epistle is by no means inferior with regard to its poetical merit, to the other productions of this ingenious writer.'

The poem is indeed one of Churchill's happiest efforts. It opens in an amusing vein of mock pastoral, principally directed against Mason and Lord Lyttelton, and then, in a strong manly rhythm of its own, turns with furious invective against the Scots. The natural images of the poem are vividly seen and freshly described, and the picture of the Cave of Famine is a model of vivid imagination and energetic language. It is difficult for a modern reader not to be slightly horrified by Churchill's ridicule of Scottish poverty, or to gloat with him over the shepherd's five brothers who had perished in the Rebellion of '45. But to contemporaries it was just this ferocious partisanship which made the poem attractive. Their jealousy of the success of Scottish immigrants, their political prejudices against the Stuarts, their hatred of Bute, himself a Scotsman, a Stuart, and a King's favourite, helped to point every allusion in Churchill's satire, and to mark him out as a hard-hitting champion of English liberty.

Churchill was delighted with the success of his poem and with grim humour dressed his younger son in Highland costume and paraded him about the town. The boy, when questioned on the meaning of his garb, replied: 'Sir, my father hates the Scotch, and does it to plague them.' Were not Armstrong and Smollett both Scots, and, even more important, were they not the enemies of Wilkes? They had both once been his friends, but Wilkes never hesitated to sacrifice private friendship to politics. The next victim was Hogarth, and as Churchill was to devote the whole of his forthcoming satire to settling the account, the facts of the quarrel are worth setting out in some detail.

[1] February, 1763.   [2] May, 1763.

Hogarth had been friendly with both Wilkes and Churchill and had paid at least one visit to Medmenham ; but, whether the fact was known to Wilkes or not, he had been patronised by Bute for some years before the death of George II. On the accession of Bute to power, Hogarth was made serjeant-painter to George III, and, moved perhaps by gratitude to his patron, he resolved to bring out a caricature ridiculing Bute's opponents, Pitt and Temple. Wilkes was warned by a friend of what was afoot and immediately protested to Hogarth, who replied that he meant no offence to Wilkes, but only intended to attack the two fallen ministers. Wilkes warned him that such an assault would immediately be avenged by a paper in *The North Briton*, but Hogarth took no notice, and on September 7th, 1762, the print entitled ' The Times ' appeared. This represented the ' World ' public-house on fire, Pitt exciting the flames and Bute's efforts to put them out frustrated by Wilkes, Churchill and Lord Temple. The satire is laboured and the details of it now unintelligible, but it excited the violent hostility of the ' Popular ' party.

Garrick was terribly distressed. Churchill having just sent him (as he frequently did) a request for a loan, the worthy manager took the opportunity of trying to make peace.

' Dear Churchill,'[1] he wrote, ' I sent to you last night but could not hear of you—I cannot conveniently this week obey your commands but I will ye latter End of ye Next—I have made a purchase that has beggar'd Me, however should you be greatly press'd I'll strain a point before that time, tho I suppose it is ye same thing to you. . . .

' I must entreat of you by ye Regard you profess for Me, that You don't tilt at my Friend Hogarth before you see Me— You cannot sure be angry at his Print ? there is surely very harmless, tho very Entertaining stuff in it. He is a great and original Genius : I love him as a Man and reverence him as an Artist—I would not for all ye Politicks and Politicians in ye Universe, that you two should have the least Cause of Illwill to Each other. I am sure you will not publish against him if you think twice—I am very unhappy at ye thought of it, pray make Me quiet as soon as possible by writing to me at Hampton or seeing Me here.'

[1] The actual letter is to be found in the Garrick correspondence, Forster Collection, Victoria and Albert Museum.

Garrick's plea was unavailing. Wilkes made a violent on-slaught on Hogarth in No. 17 of *The North Briton,* and he prompted Churchill, if the poet needed any prompting, to attack their former friend in a full-length satire. For the moment, however, Hogarth was forgotten, for Wilkes was engaged with more redoubtable opponents. His attacks upon the Ministry became steadily more outrageous, and the wonder is not so much that the authorities struck at last, but that they waited so long. Bute had been in supreme power for less than a year, and during that period had been subjected to a torrent of abuse such as has been directed against no other Prime Minister in English history.[1] He resigned on April 8th, 1763 ; and *The North Briton* exulted in his fall and claimed the chief credit for having brought it about. But Wilkes was not yet satisfied. He prepared a violent onslaught on the King's Speech which announced the newly concluded peace with France. He showed the paper to Churchill who was strongly opposed to its publication. Wilkes, however, insisted, and the famous ' No. 45 ' of *The North Briton* appeared on April 23rd.

Grenville, the new Prime Minister, determined to prosecute. He took legal advice, but even before he had received it, a general warrant for the arrest of all concerned in *The North Briton* had been made out and dated. On April 29th it was placed in the hands of the King's Messengers. Churchill, arriving at Great George Street on an early visit to Wilkes, found the house full of King's Messengers and their assistants bent on arresting Wilkes under the General Warrant. Their verbal orders were to arrest Churchill also and only Wilkes' presence of mind saved him. Before Churchill could speak, Wilkes said quickly : ' Good morrow, Mr. Thomson, How does Mrs. Thomson do to-day ? Does she dine in the country ? ' Churchill seized his meaning, replied that Mrs. Thomson was even then waiting for him, hurried home, secured his papers and retired from London.

No further effort seemed to have been made to molest Churchill, although the authorities knew from the evidence of Kearsley the printer that he had received the profits from *The North Briton* and was, therefore, at least as likely as Wilkes to have written any particular paper. But having secured Wilkes

[1] Except, perhaps, that directed by Junius against Grafton.

they probably thought that his assistants could be dealt with at leisure.

The following week Churchill returned to town in time to attend the hearing of Wilkes' case before the Court of Common Pleas. Hogarth also attended, for he saw his chance of revenge, and, concealing himself behind a pillar, made a drawing of Wilkes which he immediately etched and published. It can hardly be called a caricature, for Wilkes, with his squint and his leer, was admittedly ugly, but its hostile intention was manifest. Four thousand copies were sold. The second round of the contest was won by Hogarth. He had still to reckon with Churchill who, although again indisposed, and for the same reason,[1] returned to his satire with renewed venom. ' An Epistle to William Hogarth ' appeared in July, 1763, and was as eagerly purchased as ' The Prophecy of Famine.'

Meanwhile Wilkes had won a great triumph. Following the judgment of Lord Chief Justice Pratt he had been released from prison and, borrowing some money from Lord Temple, had hurried over to Paris to see his daughter and to dissipate a little. His devotion to Miss Wilkes was almost the strongest emotion of which he was capable, but equally sincere was his delight in the charms of all those ladies who were willing to bestow their favours on a man so witty and celebrated, albeit so ugly also.

Churchill had embarked upon a more lasting attachment and spent the Summer of 1763 touring Wales with his new mistress. He was present at Oxford for Commemoration and listened to enough University scandal to swell one of his later satires. Hogarth had been terribly shaken by the ' Epistle ' and almost immediately launched his reply. This took the form of a caricature. In his haste Hogarth did not stop to engrave an entire new plate ; he took the copper of his own portrait, burnished out the central figure and substituted for it a representation of ' The Bruiser, C. Churchill (once the

---

[1] ' Wilt not Thou, Man of Politics, wilt not Thou another time believe Orthodoxy. I am most confoundedly —— [illegible] confin'd to my room with an *Eruptio Venerio* where I am likely to remain some days ; Your company when you have a moment to spare at Mrs. Kier's at Vaux Hall will be an agreeable relief. Ye Scots Pastoral arose from a Pox but this will be rather of a milder Nature, and Hogarth —— [illegible] much obliged to the agreeable Mrs. J. (?) for being so merciful [in] her distributions. . . .' (*Brit. Mus. Add. MSS.* 30,878.)

Reverend !) in the Character of a Russian Hercules, regaling himself after having kill'd the Monster *Caricatura* that so sorely galled his virtuous friend, the Heaven-born Wilkes.' The print, although widely circulated, and reproduced in the journals, does not seem to have had all the effect that the artist intended.[1] Churchill was quite unmoved by it. He wrote to Wilkes : [2]

[1] The *Scots Magazine*, in its issue of September, 1763, reproduced the print and printed a description of it, but added an ' Ironical Explanation,' turning the laugh against Hogarth.
   ' The principal figure is a Russian bear (*i.e.* Mr. Churchill) with a club in his left paw, which he hugs to his side, and which is intended to denote his friendship for Mr. Wilkes. On the notches of the club are written, *lye* 1, *lye* 2, etc., signifying the falsities in *The North Briton*. In his other paw is a gallon-pot of porter, of which (being very hot) he seems going to drink. Round his neck is a clergyman's band, which is torn, and seems intended to denote the bruiser.—The other figure is a pug-dog, which is supposed to mean Mr. Hogarth himself, pissing with the greatest contempt on the epistle wrote to him by Charles Churchill. In the centre is a prison begging-box, standing on a folio, the title of which is *Great George-street*. *A list of the subscribers to The North Briton*. Under it is another book, the title of which is, *A new way to pay old debts, a comedy, by Mesnager* (*i.e.* Massinger, spelt Massenger in Hogarth's print). All of which alludes to Mr. W's debts, which the engraver would insinuate are to be defrayed by the subscriptions to *The North Briton*.
   ' *Ironical Explanations.*
   ' As the print called *The Bruiser*, published in Mr. Hogarth's name, seems to be generally misunderstood, permit me to give what I think a true explication of its meaning ; by which I make no doubt of proving to the satisfaction of every accurate and impartial observer that this is done by some sly enemy to Mr. Hogarth, as it contains many compliments to Mr. Churchill, and repeats verbatim the accusation urged by him in his epistle to Mr. Hogarth.
   ' The print exhibits Mr. Churchill under the figure of a bear, in allusion to his *uncourtly* principles. His love for his country and its produce, the painter has signified by his holding forth with apparent delight, a foaming pot of porter, in preference to either French claret, or whisky. With his left paw he grasps, or rather leans upon, a club, or trunk of a tree, with the branches lopt off ; on their stumps is wrote *lye* 1, *lye* 2, &c., &c., showing that . . . he scorns to support his cause, or use a weapon, without first having cleaned it from all manner of untruths, even to the smallest shoot of fallacy.
   ' His ragged band, and begging-box, express his contempt of imprisonment, and preference of an honest poverty to his becoming rich or great by servile adulation. By the book inscribed ' Great George-street, &c.' Mr. W——s is brought in for a share of the compliment, as a brother-champion in the same cause : his popularity is marked by the large volume of subscribers to his publication. The other book, entitled, *A new way to pay old debts, by Mesnager* [*sic*], points to the above gentleman's imprisonment in the tower, and the seizure of his

'That I am a lazy dog need I say? If Wilkes knows any-
thing, he knows that. That I am a drunken dog, all men know,
and that I am an honest dog few but you will believe . . . I
take it for granted you have seen Hogarth's Print—Was ever
anything so contemptible. . . . I intend an Elegy on him,
supposing him dead, but my Dear —— [illegible] who is this
instant at my elbow, and towards whom I feel my spirit stir,
and my bowels yearn, tells me that he will be really dead before
it comes out; Nay, she . . . tells me with a kiss that I have
kill'd him, and begs I will never be her enemy. How sweet is
Flattery from the Woman we Love, and how weak is our
boasted strength when opposed to Beauty. . . . How is the
most agreeable G. and (this omit not to tell me at large) how
is my little Muse? How is Miss Wilkes? . . . I have begun
the fourth Book of the Ghost. . . . Is Paris pleasant? Have
the lively Gauls superior attractions to the English? The only
thing I envy France is you. For my own sake I could wish it
was without Pleasure; for yours I could wish every Pleasure
doubled. . . . The Post Chaise waits, and Charlotte cries
away—I beg you will not let me have an opportunity of writing
again. . . .

'I have resolv'd . . . to write an Epic Poem . . . Cul-
loden.'

Wilkes, too, was enjoying himself. He replied: [3]

'The most sensible people here think that the French are
on the eve of some great revolution . . . but Paris is as gay

papers, by way of payment of the arrears due to him as a militia-
officer.

'The dog by the pallet and graver, represents Mr. Hogarth, who
seems terribly frightened at the Russian Hercules, as is particularly
expressed by his losing his retentive faculty; for the attitude is such
that no dog ever made use of for that occasion, except when his water
came involuntarily from him; and as this is what young dogs are
subject to, perhaps the author means to call Mr. Hogarth a puppy, as
being now in his second childhood. Under his feet is placed Mr.
Churchill's epistle, which, as it is universally allowed to be an excellent
performance, I imagine, is to express that hatred to genius of every
sort, with which Mr. Hogarth has been charged.

'But the greatest stroke aimed at the painter of the celebrated
Sigismunda, is the putting his name to this miserable performance;
as it tends directly to prove what Mr. Churchill has asserted in his
epistle, namely, a total decay of that once truly comic genius.' (pp.
497-8) Sept., 1763.

[2] On Sunday 14th (August), 1763.

[3] On Monday, August 29th, 1763.

as ever. I have been in clover for so long that I have almost forgot even Mrs. G——. I am come here to a carnaval. . . . You are read, and admir'd here. My intimate friend, Goy, has almost got you by heart . . .'

And he signs himself : ' Yours most affectionately.'

He was not, however, without his troubles. As he was walking one day in August in the streets of Paris, he was accosted by one Forbes, a Scottish officer in the French service, who insisted that Wilkes had insulted his countrymen and must fight him. It is not necessary to go into the details of the affair. Wilkes professed himself quite ready to meet Captain Forbes as became a man of honour, but pleaded that he had a previous engagement with Lord Egremont. The quarrel came to the notice of the French Court of Marshals, the President of which made them both promise not to fight on French territory. Meanwhile Lord Egremont died, and Wilkes, with charac-teristic recklessness, leaving a note for Forbes, set off for Menin, the first town in the Austrian Netherlands, where he proposed the duel should take place. The note which he scribbled to Churchill[1] is so typical of his profanity and his high spirits that it can hardly be omitted.

' I am here, my dear Churchill,' he wrote, ' in the apostolic bitch's[2] territory on a droll errand. . . . I have seen one of the most charming of our country women at Lille, who has made me amends for leaving Paris.'

Wilkes waited one day at Menin, and as Forbes did not appear, set off post haste ' to Dunkerque, to Calais, to London, and to Churchill.' The letter in which Churchill urged his return did not reach him, but he felt, no doubt, that he had dissipated long enough and that it was time to plunge anew into politics.

He was back in London on September 27th, but Churchill had once more disappeared. Fortunately, or unfortunately, it was only too well known, if not where he had fled, at least why.

The mistress with whom Churchill had been spending the Summer was a certain Elizabeth Carr,[3] the daughter of a

---

[1] Menin, September 21st, 1763.

[2] The Empress Maria Theresa.

[3] William Cole, the antiquary, in his commonplace book, gives the name as Cheere. Sir Henry Cheere (1703-1781) was a statuary and

statuary in Westminster. He had seduced the girl and she had fled with him from her father's house. The affair, naturally enough, created great scandal, for Churchill was a married man and a parson besides, and hearing that he was at Kingston Garden, her father, her brother and a servant went there with loaded pistols to assassinate him. However, Churchill and his mistress had left London and retired to Wilkes' house at Aylesbury, not altogether with Wilkes' approval. The latter was afraid not only of the vengeance of the family, but of legal proceedings against Churchill, and wrote him a letter in great anxiety :

' The family are in the greatest distress, and you are universally condemned for having made a worthy family unhappy. I except Cotes,[1] your brother, and myself. It is known that you are at Aylesbury, therefore I submit to your PRUDENCE, if you choose to continue there. You may command me, my house, servants, etc. I wish you would love yourself half as well as I love you ! I dread Mansfield's warrant. Think of the great card we all have to play ! When you can so nobly assist us in our great parts, ought you to run away to sport in dalliance ? . . . Are you not more private in my place near London than in any country town ? Do not give dull Bishops and others such advantages against you.' The letter continues with some good-natured, if unprintable jests, and Wilkes concludes : ' After all, my best compliments to Betsy.'

Churchill did not make use of his friend's ' place near London.' Instead he returned to town, moved thereto by Wilkes' letter, by the illness of his mistress, and also by genuine compunction. Southey[2] declares that both Churchill and Elizabeth Carr repented of the rash step they had taken ; and that Churchill's repentance was sincere enough may be

the master of Roubiliac. His working premises were at Hyde Park Corner, and he is alluded to as the ' man from Hyde Park Corner' in Colman and Garrick's ' Clandestine Marriage.' Cole remarks that Churchill ' ran away with a young Lady into France, leaving his wife and children to starve. I think the lady was daughter to the celebrated Statuary, Mr. Cheere, who was knighted by the King a few years before.' (*Brit. Mus. Add. MSS.* 5832.) Cole is wrong about the trip to France, and he may also be mistaken in identifying the daughter of Cheere with the Elizabeth Carr who was Churchill's mistress.

[1] A wine-merchant and friend of Wilkes. (See note on ' Independence,' l. 520.)

[2] In his *Life of Cowper.*

gathered from the lines in his next poem, ' The Conference '
in which he refers to his escapade :

> ' 'Tis not the babbling of a busy world,
> Where praise and censure are at random hurl'd,
> Which can the meanest of my thoughts control,
> Or shake one settled purpose of my soul ;
> Free and at large might their wild curses roam,
> If all, if all, alas ! were well at home.
> No—'tis the tale which angry conscience tells,
> When she with more than tragic horror swells
> Each circumstance of guilt, when stern, but true,
> She brings bad actions forth into review,
> And like the dread hand-writing on the wall,
> Bids late remorse arise at reason's call ;
> Arm'd at all points bids scorpion vengeance pass,
> And to the mind holds up reflection's glass,
> The mind which, starting, heaves the heart-felt groan,
> And hates the form she knows to be her own.'

Old Mr. Carr forgave his daughter and took her back into his
house, but her virtuous sister was not so merciful and taunted
Elizabeth so bitterly that the poor girl fled once more and took
refuge with her lover.   Churchill accepted the situation, and
as he was now comparatively wealthy, and his mistress deli-
cate, he lived with her at Richmond for six months and afterwards
took a house in the then rural surroundings of Acton Common.
This was probably the happiest period of his existence.

Meanwhile the happy-go-lucky Lloyd, with whom Churchill
no longer shared a purse in common, was getting deeper and
deeper into debt.   He had hoped to retrieve his fortunes by
conducting the *St. James's Magazine*, and the failure of that
periodical overwhelmed him.   Churchill was not at hand to
help, and as Thornton and his other friends refused to stand
surety for him he was confined in the Fleet prison instead of
being allowed ' the liberty of the Rules '—a kind of parole
under certain restrictions, by which debtors avoided actual
imprisonment.   Churchill, on hearing of the matter, did what
he could to alleviate his friend's misfortune.   He allowed a
guinea a week for his support, and his sister Patty, to whom
Lloyd was vaguely engaged, helped to cheer his confinement.
Lloyd's bills being too great for Churchill to defray out of his

own pocket, he tried to get up a subscription, but this miserably failed, and Lloyd was left in prison.

Wilkes, for the moment, seemed more fortunate. The affair of *The North Briton* was not yet over, but he felt tolerably secure, unaware that he had been watched by Government spies from the moment of his return, and that his enemies (including his old friend, Lord Sandwich, who had succeeded Lord Egremont as Secretary of State) were preparing a new plot against him. Wilkes had been rash enough to have printed on his private press an obscene poem entitled ' An Essay on Woman ' with burlesque notes attributed to Bishop Warburton. A copy of this was obtained by bribery from the printers, and Sandwich read portions of the poem in the House of Lords, where it was pronounced a breach of privilege, in attributing the notes to Warburton, and an obscene and impious libel. On the same day (November 15th) the House of Commons condemned No. 45 of *The North Briton* to be burned by the common hangman as a seditious libel. Wilkes was present in the Commons and, as if he had not enough already on his hands, became involved in yet another quarrel. Samuel Martin, M.P. for Camelford, and Secretary to the Treasury, considering himself insulted by passages in numbers 37 and 40 of *The North Briton*, rose in the House and, looking towards Wilkes, declared that the author of the articles was a malignant, infamous scoundrel, who had stabbed him in the dark. When the session ended Wilkes hurried home and wrote a letter to Martin plainly declaring himself the author. Martin, in reply, sent him a challenge, and the same day (it was now November 16th, Parliament having sat all night) Wilkes fought a duel with Martin in Hyde Park, receiving a wound in the stomach which, however, enabled him to avoid appearing to a citation by the House of Commons.

Wilkes' situation now seemed desperate. His wound was dangerous and he feared other attempts on his life. A Scottish lieutenant of marines was arrested on the night of December 6th in the very act of forcing a way into his house. He resolved, as soon as he should be well enough to travel, to escape once more to France.

Perhaps the authorities were glad to have him out of the way; certainly very little effort seems to have been made to detain him. He was at Dover on the morning of December

25th, 1763, and at Calais the same afternoon. The journey, in his wounded condition, proved very trying both from the state of the roads and the roughness of the sea. He was compelled to rest, and did not reach Paris until four days later, when his spirits began to revive. Lord Hertford called upon him, and David Hume met him at Baron Holbach's. The French were very cordial; indeed, he wrote to his friend, Cotes, ' I am caressed here more than one of my modesty will let me tell you.'

He still thought of returning in order to face the House of Commons, but when the time came his wound was too painful. Instead, he wrote to the Speaker, Onslow, excusing himself and enclosing a certificate from his doctors. He was, indeed, not at all eager to return to England ' for no man in his senses would stand Mansfield's sentence upon the publisher of a paper declared by both houses of parliament, scandalous, seditious, etc.' He began to hope that the Government would not prove implacable, ' and between ourselves,' he confided to Cotes, ' if they would send me Ambassador to Constantinople it is all I should wish.'

Meanwhile, *The North Briton* having come to an end, Churchill had more time to devote himself to verse. Poems poured forth rapidly. ' The Conference,' already referred to, was published in Nov., 1763, and ' The Author,' a defence of satire, in the following month. ' The Duellist,' a violent attack on Martin and other enemies of Wilkes, appeared at the end of December, 1763, or early in the new year.[1] It was very successful and, with ' The Author,' brought Churchill £450. 'Gotham' soon followed. In this poem, which, to the writer, is the most attractive of all Churchill's productions, he seems to escape for a while from the immediate pressure of political resentment. In his rural retreat he had time to look about him, the sights and sounds of the country steal imperceptibly into his verse, and he tries with a calmer mind to oppose to the treachery and incapacity of politicians not mere abuse of their shortcomings but an ideal political system of his own. He imagines a kind of Utopia with himself as king, a king hailed with enthusiasm by his subjects, by flowers of the field, by trees and animals, by seasons and months, by sun and moon and stars.

---

[1] *The Dictionary of National Biography* gives the date of publication as November, 1763, but see *Seven XVIIIth Century Bibliographies*, by I. A. Williams, 1924, p. 198.

' The snow-drop, who in habit white and plain,
Comes on, the herald of fair Flora's train :
The coxcomb crocus, flower of simple note,
Who by her side struts in a herald's coat . . .
All flowers of various names and various forms,
Which the sun into strength and beauty warms,
From the dwarf daisy, which, like infants, clings
And fears to leave the earth from whence it springs,
To the proud giant of the garden race,
Who madly reaching to the sun's embrace,
O'ersteps her fellows with aspiring aim,
Demands his wedded love, and bears his name ;
All, one and all, shall in this chorus join,
And, dumb to others' praise, be loud in mine.'

' Gotham ' has more of what is commonly understood by poetry in it than any of Churchill's other works, but it is not a very valuable contribution to political theory. Indeed, the ideas expressed in it amount to little more than Bolingbroke's ' Idea of a Patriot King '—a notion natural enough in those weary of the confusion and ineffectiveness of politics, but coming a little oddly from Churchill, the friend of Wilkes and the ferocious enemy of all those who were striving to help George III towards a similar ideal.

The train of thought and the kind of writing suggested by ' Gotham ' might have been continued and developed by Churchill, but when Lord Sandwich offered himself, on the death of Lord Hardwicke, as a candidate for the Chancellorship of Cambridge University, the opportunity was too good to be missed. His portrait of Sandwich is one of Churchill's most vigorous pieces of invective, and the form of the poem gave him an opportunity also of settling some old scores against the Universities.

However, with the publication of ' The Candidate,' Churchill's stock of political animosity seems to have run out. His next satire was a purely general one, on a theme already treated by Juvenal. The wide distribution of modern psychological works dealing with sexual perversion has perhaps made it possible to discuss ' The Times,' without any of the exaggerated gestures of repulsion indulged in by previous editors. In a word, the poem deals with homosexual passion, which

Churchill, as is the manner of satirists, considered to be particularly widespread in his own day, the truth being, of course, that it was as familiar to the Greeks and Romans as to the North American Indians, and as frequently to be met with in the Baghdad of Haroun-al-Raschid as in the great cities of modern times.

For Churchill the subject was an excellent one. His own lapses from virtue had been conspicuously normal and he felt a very proper indignation against the perverse corrupters of youth, especially those whose high station increased their opportunity while diminishing the danger of their being punished.

Wilkes was delighted with the poem, which he admired ' almost beyond any ' of Churchill's pieces. ' You have,' he wrote, ' greatly excell'd Juvenal in his own manner. Your apology to the fair at the end saves all, and will leave the modestest virgin unhurt by the boldness of some of the descriptions.'

' The Farewell,' which came out in July, 1764, was more general still, being concerned with the theme of patriotism. ' Independence ', on the well-worn subject of the incorruptibility of satirists, appeared in September, and although Wilkes acknowledged this too with gratitude, it may well have seemed to him that Churchill was beginning to neglect the great end of satire, which was to annoy the enemies of John Wilkes. His restless mind devised a dozen schemes. In his privilege of printing anything he liked in France he saw unlimited possibilities for political blackmail and he wrote to Churchill to make a new proposal: ' When I left England,' he wrote, ' you were very well with old Hanbury. He has an inestimable treasure of letters from Lord Holland, Lord Chesterfield, etc., which I wish the world saw. They cannot be printed in England because of the privilege of their Lordships, but they might here. I wish you wou'd get them of Hanbury. With a little attention I am sure you may. Can you do better than bring them with you to Paris, and print an entire edition under your own eye ? . . . I know there is a single letter of Fox's about the Princess Dowager worth £10,000 . . .'

What Wilkes did not know (in spite of their close acquaintance) was that Churchill, with all his faults, was hardly the man to lend himself to such a scheme. Certainly there is nothing to show that he made the least attempt on the discretion of Sir Charles Hanbury-Williams, and the whole project came to nothing.

Wilkes found it hard to realise that there was an outcrop of granite in the quicksand of Churchill's character. He kept urging him to come to Paris and enjoy life, and painted an enticing picture of its pleasures—half-literary and half-sensual. ' Sterne and I,' he writes, ' often meet, and talk of you. We have an odd party for to-night . . . two lively, young, handsome actresses. . . . Ah, poor Mrs. Wilkes. I am impatient to see you here—I am some days quite philosophical, on others most charmingly dissipated, for Paris has charms to shake even your constancy of soul.'

It was proposed that Churchill should come to Paris with Cotes, and Wilkes was so anxious to see him that he promised to come to Boulogne to meet him, to put him up in Paris, and to provide him with amusement ' unless constancy has chang'd her name to Churchill.' It would seem that it was so. Churchill's feeling for Elizabeth Carr was apparently a deeper one than any other woman had aroused, and we hear nothing of any more escapades.

However, he could not forever resist his friend's entreaties. He put the finishing touches to ' The Journey,' a poem remarkable for the evidence it affords that he considered his work almost done. A note of disillusionment runs through it, and it is, in form, almost an apology for writing so much. Politics seem to be forgotten. He makes a last hit at some of his literary enemies—at Mason, at Murphy, at Foote, at Home, at Armstrong ; refers the reader with sarcastic comments to the works of these writers, and concludes :

' I on my journey all alone proceed.'

His prophecy was truer than he knew. He wrote to Wilkes on October 11th ; Wilkes was at Boulogne to meet him on the 24th of the same month and three days later Churchill left London, leaving a laconic note for his brother : ' Dear Jack, adieu, C. C.'

During the journey he took cold. He arrived at Boulogne miserable and ill, and was compelled to take to his bed. A fever followed and, having no wish to die in France, he persuaded his friends to remove him. The exertion made him worse, and on November 4th he was dead. He was not yet thirty-three. When the news of his death was known all the English ships in Boulogne harbour struck their colours.

Wilkes, as an outlaw, was unable to accompany the corpse of his friend to England, and all the arrangements fell on the shoulders of Cotes. He landed with the body at Dover on December 10th and set out for London. Churchill's coffin, however, remained at Dover and there he was interred in the old cemetery of St. Martin's on Tuesday 13th. Above his grave was placed a stone with the inscription :

HERE LIE THE REMAINS
OF THE CELEBRATED
C. CHURCHILL.

Life to the last enjoy'd, *here* Churchill lies.

The Candidate.

Among Churchill's papers Wilkes found the beginning of a satire on Colman and Thornton, against whom the poet was incensed because of their desertion of Lloyd. This Wilkes destroyed, and as no other copy existed, no trace of the verses remains.

One other work of Churchill has been lost, under mysterious circumstances. The poet, in his hostility to Henry Fox, had seized on the affair of Ayliffe, Fox's steward, who had forged Fox's name to a lease and, in spite of his master's charitable intervention, was hanged. Churchill, believing Ayliffe innocent, meditated a satire on the subject, and is said by Walpole to have obtained from the Rev. Philip Francis (another of Fox's proteges, who resented what he considered inadequate payment for services rendered) a series of letters incriminating Fox. Walpole further declares that Fox bought Churchill off with £500 and Francis by nominating him to the chaplaincy of Chelsea Hospital, but there is no confirmation of the story, and there is nothing in what is known of Churchill's life and character to make it seem probable. Tooke declares that ' Churchill was only prevented by death from publishing a poem he had more than once advertised, entitled " An Elegy, or Ayliffe's Ghost ". A reverend emissary [*i.e.*, the Rev. Philip Francis] was employed by a noble Lord to ward off the threatened blow; but Churchill was not to be bribed, and death alone deprived the world of the promised satire.' For whatever reason, the satire was never published and not a line of it remains.

After Churchill's death a collection of sermons was published, possibly Churchill's own, but generally thought to have been his father's. Prefixed to them, however, was a fragment of an ironical ' Dedication to Warburton', one of the most biting satires Churchill ever wrote, although the propriety of attaching it to a volume of sermons is perhaps doubtful.

The subsequent history of the Churchill family is soon told. His mother lived until 1770. His brother John was a physician ; he attended Wilkes and brought out some editions of Charles Churchill's works. Another brother, William, rector of Orton-on-the-Hill, died in 1804. Of Churchill's two sons, both educated at the expense of Sir Richard Jebb, one, John, made as rash a marriage as his father's and, dying in France, left his widow and daughter destitute. The other, Charles, tried to eke out a living by lecturing, but a long series of begging letters to Wilkes, still in existence,[1] show how little he succeeded. Churchill's offspring seems to have inherited his imprudence without any of his genius.

When the news of Churchill's death was known in London, many a writer and politician breathed more freely. One danger at least was over. Horace Walpole[2] summed up the prevailing opinion in a classical passage which it is indispensable to quote :

' Churchill the poet is dead,—to the great joy of the Ministry and the Scotch, and to the grief of very few indeed, I believe ; for such a friend is not only a dangerous but a ticklish possession. The next revolution would have introduced the other half of England into his satires, for no party could have promoted him, and woe had betided those who had left him to shift for himself on Parnassus ! He had owned that his pen itched to attack Mr. Pitt and Charles Townshend ; and neither of them are men to have escaped by their steadiness and uniformity. This meteor blazed scarce four years ; for his " Rosciad " was subsequent to the accession of the present King, before which his name was never heard of ; and what is as remarkable, he died in nine days after his antagonist, Hogarth. Were I Charon, I should, without scruple, give the best place in my boat to the latter, who was an original genius. Churchill had great powers ; but, besides the facility of outrageous satire, almost all his compositions were wild and

[1] *Brit. Mus. Add. MSS.* 30871-3, 30875.
[2] In a letter to Sir Horace Mann, November 15th, 1764.

extravagant, executed on no plan, and void of the least correction. Many of his characters were obscure even to the present age ; and some of the most known were so unknown to *him* that he has missed all resemblance ; of which Lord Sandwich is a striking instance. He died of a drunken debauch at Calais,[1] on a visit to his friend Wilkes, who is going to write notes to his Works. But he had lived long enough for himself, at least for his reputation and his want of it, for his works began to decrease considerably in vent. He has left some sermons, for he wrote even sermons, but lest they do any good, and for fear they should not do some hurt, he had prepared a Dedication of them to Bishop Warburton, whose arrogance and venom had found a proper corrector in Churchill.'

Johnson had called Churchill a blockhead, but he acknowledged to Boswell in 1763 that he had a better opinion of him than he once had, for he had shown more fertility than Johnson had expected. ' To be sure, he is a tree that cannot produce good fruit : he only bears crabs. But, Sir, a tree that produces a great many crabs is better than a tree which produces only a few.' Boswell, with an independence of judgment with which he has not always been credited, dissented from this severe view. ' It is very true,' he says, ' that the greatest part of it [Churchill's poetry] is upon the topics of the day, on which account, as it brought him great fame and profit at the time, it must proportionably slide out of the public attention as other occasional objects succeed.

' But Churchill had extraordinary vigour, both of thought and expression. His portraits of the players will ever be valuable to the true lovers of the drama, and his strong caricatures of several eminent men of his age, will not be forgotten by the curious. Let me add, that there is in his works many passages which are of a general nature ; and his " Prophecy of Famine " is a poem of no ordinary merit. It is, indeed, falsely injurious to Scotland, but, therefore, may be allowed a greater share of invention.'

The passage is an admirable example of Boswell's shrewdness of judgment and freedom from prejudice.

Cowper's estimate was more generous. He had been Churchill's schoolfellow at Westminster. Churchill was older than he and seems to have been one of the few by whom the

[1] Boulogne.

timid, shrinking Cowper was not bullied. A letter written more than twenty years after Churchill's death[1] is almost entirely devoted to an estimate of his works.

'. . . It is a great thing to be indeed a poet, and does not happen to more than one man in a century. Churchill, the great Churchill, deserved the name of poet : I have read him twice, and some of his pieces three times over, and the last time with more pleasure than the first. The pitiful scribbler of his life[2] seems to have undertaken that task, for which he was entirely unqualified, merely because it afforded him an opportunity to traduce him. He has inserted in it but one anecdote of consequence, for which he refers you to a novel,[3] and introduces the story with doubts about the truth of it. But his barrenness as a biographer I could forgive, if the simpleton had not thought himself a judge of his writings, and under the erroneous influence of that thought, informed his reader that " Gotham," " Independence," and " The Times," were catchpennies. " Gotham," unless I am a greater blockhead than he, which I am far from believing, is a noble and beautiful poem, and a poem with which I make no doubt the author took as much pains as with any he ever wrote. Making allowance, (and Dryden in his " Absalom and Achitophel " stands in need of the same indulgence,) for an unwarrantable use of Scripture, it appears to me to be a masterly performance. " Independence " is a most animated piece, full of strength and spirit, and marked with that bold masculine character which, I think, is the great peculiarity of this writer. And " The Times," (except that the subject is disgusting to the last degree,) stands equally high in my opinion. He is indeed a careless writer for the most part ; but where shall we find in any of those authors who finish their works with the exactness of a Flemish pencil, those bold and daring strokes of fancy, those numbers so hazardously ventured upon and so happily finished, the matter so compressed and yet so clear, and the colouring so sparingly laid on, and yet with such a beautiful effect ? In short, it is not his least praise that he is never guilty of those faults as a writer, which he lays to the charge of others. A proof that he

---

[1] Letter to Rev. William Unwin, 1786.

[2] Presumably the author of the so-called *Genuine Memoir of Mr. Charles Churchill*, 1765.

[3] *Chrysal, or the Adventures of a Guinea.*

did not judge by a borrowed standard, or from rules laid down by critics, but that he was qualified to do it by his own native powers, and his great superiority of genius. For he that wrote so much, and so fast, would through inadvertency and hurry unavoidably have departed from rules which he might have found in books, but his own truly poetical talent was a guide which could not suffer him to err. A racehorse is graceful in his swiftest pace, and never makes an awkward motion though he is pushed to his utmost speed. A carthorse might perhaps be taught to play tricks in the riding-school, and might prance and curvet like his betters, but at some unlucky time would be sure to betray the baseness of his original. It is an affair of very little consequence perhaps, to the well-being of mankind, but I cannot help regretting that he died so soon.'

The excitement about ' Wilkes and Liberty ' over, Hogarth dead, Bute retired into private life, and the trivial absurdities of aldermen completely forgotten, it was natural that the works of Churchill, which dealt so exclusively with these subjects, should, in Boswell's phrase, slide proportionately out of public attention. A new school of poetry, the ' plaintive fops debauched by Gray' (so much disliked by Churchill) and Wordsworth and Coleridge (so much disliked by Churchill's editor Tooke), rose steadily in popular estimation. Churchill, in spite of numerous re-issues of his works, became a somewhat remote figure belonging to a previous age, and Byron visiting his tomb at Dover in 1816 could only make of it the theme of a meditation on ' The Glory and the Nothing of a Name.'

Byron, in his earlier work, at least, belonged to the same tradition as Churchill and was well fitted to appreciate his work, but as the nineteenth century advanced the satirical element in English poetry grew smaller and smaller. It has not yet recovered its place therein, for the satirist needs both irreverence and strong moral conviction, and the Victorian age had the second without the first, while the modern period has the first without the second.

It is a pity. Satire is a healthy element in literature, and might save us on the one hand from the gradual shrinking of poetry to a few ' nature-notes,' and on the other from the tortured obscurities of the new metaphysical school. Churchill for all his carelessness and his topicality had something of the large masculine utterance of his master Dryden. It would be well if that largeness and that masculinity could inspire English verse anew.

CHURCHILL'S POEMS

VOLUME ONE

THE ROSCIAD

THE APOLOGY

NIGHT

THE GHOST

THE ROSCIAD*

Unknowing and unknown, the hardy muse
Boldly defies all mean and partial views ;
With honest freedom plays the critic's part,
And praises, as she censures, from the heart.

R oscius deceased, each high aspiring player
Push'd all his interest for the vacant chair.
The buskin'd heroes of the mimic stage
No longer whine in love, and rant in rage ;
The monarch quits his throne, and condescends
Humbly to court the favour of his friends ;
For pity's sake tells undeserved mishaps,
And, their applause to gain, recounts his claps.
Thus the victorious chiefs of ancient Rome,
To win the mob, a suppliant's form assume,   10
In pompous strain fight o'er the extinguish'd war,
And show where honour bled in every scar.
    But though bare merit might in Rome appear
The strongest plea for favour, 'tis not here ;
We form our judgment in another way,
And they will best succeed, who best can pay :
Those, who would gain the votes of British tribes,
Must add to force of merit, force of bribes.
    What can an actor give ? in every age
Cash hath been rudely banish'd from the stage ;   20

* First published anonymously in March, 1761. 'Printed for the
Author, and sold by W. Flexney.' In the first edition the poem
extended to 730 lines, in the second and third editions to 836 lines.
The final length was 1,090 lines.

[1] Quintus Roscius, the greatest of Roman comic actors, was a native
of Solonium, near Lanuvium. He was the friend of Cicero, who
defended him against a charge of fraud. Having amassed a great
fortune, he acted during the latter years of his life for nothing, and died
about 62 B.C.

[10] ' It was the custom for those who pretended to offices and dig-
nities among the Romans, to solicit and caress the people at their
general assemblies, clad only in a loose gown, without any coat under
it, either to promote their supplications the better, by suing in such an
humble habit, or that such as had received wounds in the war might
thus more readily demonstrate the visible tokens of their fortitude.'
(Tooke.)

Monarchs themselves, to grief of every player,
Appear as often as their image there ;
They can't, like candidate for other seat,
Pour seas of wine, and mountains raise of meat.
Wine ! they could bribe you with the world as soon,
And of Roast Beef, they only know the tune :
But what they have they give ; could Clive do more,
Though for each million he had brought home four ?
   Shuter keeps open house at Southwark fair,
And hopes the friends of humour will be there ;   30
In Smithfield, Yates prepares the rival treat

[27] Clive left India for the second time in February, 1760 ; he was an extremely wealthy man, having £30,000 a year from Mir Jaffier, and a personal gift from the same potentate of £200,000, as well as other emoluments.

[29] Edward Shuter (*c.* 1728-1776) was born in Vine Street, St. Giles's, London. His humour attracted the attention of Chapman, an actor at Drury Lane, and in 1744 he appeared in ' Richard III.' at Chapman's Theatre at Richmond. He then played at both Drury Lane and Covent Garden as well as at Goodman's Fields. In 1747 he obtained a regular engagement with Garrick, but although he played a multitude of comic parts he did not make a ' hit ' with the public until his performance as Master Stephen in ' Every Man in his Humour ' in 1751. In 1753 Shuter became associated with Covent Garden and remained there, except for visits to Ireland and to the Summer Theatre in the Haymarket, for the rest of his acting life. His best part was that of Sir Anthony Absolute in ' The Rivals,' but this was after Churchill's time. Shuter was a comic genius but indolent ; he frequently forgot his part and ' gagged ' outrageously. In his old age he became a follower of Whitefield, which did not prevent him from taking also to gambling and the bottle.

[29] Southwark Fair. A charter for holding a fair at Southwark on 7th, 8th, and 9th days of September was granted by Edward IV. in 1462. It was called Lady Fair and was next in importance to Bartholomew Fair. There is an engraving by Hogarth showing the fair in progress, with two theatrical companies competing for custom. The stage of one of these is in the act of collapsing. Southwark Fair was the cause of great riot and debauchery and was abolished in 1762 by an order of the Court of Common Council.

[31] Richard Yates (1706-1796) was, in Churchill's time, a veteran actor who had been continuously at Drury Lane since 1742. He was a sound comic actor, particularly admired in the parts of Shakespearean clowns. He was also employed in pantomime. (See next note.) His fame is a little overshadowed by that of his second wife, Mary Ann Yates. (See note on line 730.)

[31] The Fair of St. Bartholomew opened on the Eve of the saint's festival, 24th August, and continued for two days after. It was

2

For those who laughter love, instead of meat.
Foote, at Old House, for even Foote will be,
In self-conceit, an actor, bribes with tea ;
Which Wilkinson at second-hand receives,
And, at the New, pours water on the leaves.
   The town divided, each runs several ways,
As passion, humour, interest, party sways.
Things of no moment, colour of the hair,
Shape of a leg, complexion brown or fair,   40
A dress well chosen, or a patch misplaced,
Conciliate favour, or create distaste.

originally a cloth fair held within the precincts of the Priory and was
the only opportunity Londoners had of buying the fine cloth manu-
factured at Bruges, Ghent, and Ypres. With the improvement of
English cloth the serious business of the fair became less important,
and outside the Priory in the open space of West Smithfield grew up a
small town of booths and tents providing every kind of amusement
from drinking and gambling to dramatic entertainments. After the
Restoration the fair was extended from three days to fourteen, but in
1708 was again reduced. In 1769 special constables were appointed to
keep order and the gambling tables and the performance of plays
prohibited. Previously the Drury Lane Company had always sent
down a company of quite respectable actors to play at the fair. Among
these in Churchill's time was Shuter, who played Harlequin, and
Yates, who played Pantaloon. The fair was in decay from the end of
the eighteenth century, and ceased to exist in 1855.

[33] Samuel Foote. (See note on line 396.) In order to evade the
restrictions enforced by the Westminster magistrates Foote announced
his performances at the Haymarket as ' taking a dish of tea.' The
entertainment was supposed to be gratis, only the tea being paid for ;
but no tea was served.

[35] Tate Wilkinson (1739-1803) was the son of the chaplain to the
Savoy Chapel and to Frederick, Prince of Wales. His father was
sentenced to transportation for continuing to solemnize marriages at
the Savoy in defiance of the Marriage Act (26 George II.), but died on
the way. Tate Wilkinson, who had been at Harrow and had many
influential friends, was offered a commission in the Army, but pre-
ferred to go on the stage, where he was not, at first, very successful.
Shuter assisted him, and he appeared at Covent Garden on April 18th,
1757, as the Fine Gentleman in ' Lethe.' Garrick employed him for
a time and, at the end of 1757, he appeared with Foote at Smock Alley
Theatre, Dublin. His imitations of Foote were very popular ; hence
Churchill's remark. He also imitated Garrick, Barry, Sheridan, Mrs.
Woffington, and George Whitefield. He played parts in tragedy also,
and was in management in the provinces, but he is chiefly remembered
as a mimic. He published his ' Memoirs ' in 1790 and, later, other
works of theatrical reminiscence. Churchill's unfavourable opinion
was afterwards modified.

3

From galleries loud peals of laughter roll,
And thunder Shuter's praises ;—he's so droll.
Embox'd, the ladies must have something smart,
Palmer ! oh ! Palmer tops the jaunty part.
Seated in pit, the dwarf with aching eyes
Looks up, and vows that Barry's out of size ;
Whilst to six feet the vigorous stripling grown,
Declares that Garrick is another Coan.   50
　　When place of judgment is by whim supplied,
And our opinions have their rise in pride ;
When, in discoursing on each mimic elf,
We praise and censure with an eye to self ;
All must meet friends, and Ackman bids as fair
In such a court, as Garrick, for the chair.
　　At length agreed, all squabbles to decide,
By some one judge the cause was to be tried ;
But this their squabbles did afresh renew,
Who should be judge in such a trial :—who ?   60
　　For Johnson some ; but Johnson, it was fear'd,
Would be too grave ; and Sterne too gay appear'd ;

---

[46] John Palmer (1742-1798) was the son of a private soldier turned door-keeper at Drury Lane. He made his first appearance on any stage on May 20th, 1762, as Buck in ' The Englishman in Paris.' Churchill, therefore, could only have seen him at the very beginning of his career. In spite of Garrick's unfavourable opinion, Palmer afterwards developed into an excellent actor. As a tragedian he was, according to Foote, ' damned bad ', but he played such parts as that of Joseph Surface in ' The School for Scandal ' better than they have ever been played since. That there was a touch of Joseph Surface in his own character is indicated by his nickname ' Plausible Jack.' (See also note on line 336.)

[48] Spranger Barry. (See note on line 892.) Gray's comment is ' Barry, a tall handsome Irishman. He acted Othello, Romeo and other parts with more applause than merit.'

[50] John Coan, a dwarf, born in Norfolk. He died in 1764. Gray calls him a ' Prussian dwarf ', and it is probable that Coan, like so many other performers before and since, took advantage of the English prejudice in favour of the foreigner. Garrick was a little man.

[55] Ackman was a minor actor at Drury Lane.

[62] The first edition has ' loose ' instead of ' gay,' and a couplet afterwards omitted (lines 67 and 68 being inserted instead) :
　　　　' Some called for M[urph]y, but that sound soon dy'd,
　　　　And Desart Island rang on ev'ry side.'

4

Others for Franklin voted : but 'twas known,
He sicken'd at all triumphs but his own ;
For Colman many, but the peevish tongue
Of prudent Age found out that he was young :
For Murphy some few pilfering wits declared,
Whilst Folly clapp'd her hands, and Wisdom stared.
To mischief train'd, e'en from his mother's womb,

[63] Dr. Thomas Franklin (died 1784), Professor of Greek in the University of Cambridge. He translated Sophocles and other classical authors and adapted several plays from the French.

[65] George Colman, the elder (1732-1794), was born in Florence, where his father was envoy to the Court of Tuscany. On his father's death he was assisted by William Pulteney, afterwards Earl of Bath, by whom he was sent to Westminster School. Here he struck up a friendship with Robert Lloyd, which persisted beyond school-days. In January, 1754, he began a paper called ' The Connoisseur,' in collaboration with Bonnell Thornton, and later in the decade was constantly in the company of his other school-fellows, Churchill and Lloyd. He was also acquainted with Cowper and soon afterwards with Garrick, to whom he dedicated his ' Critical Reflections on the Old English Dramatists.' This not only won him the friendship of the actor but established his reputation as a critic. Hence Churchill's lines. Colman's first dramatic attempt was the farce of ' Polly Honeycomb ' (Drury Lane, December 5th, 1760), and three months later the success of ' The Jealous Wife ' established Colman as a dramatist. He was part owner of Covent Garden Theatre between 1767 and 1774 and of the Haymarket Theatre from 1776 to 1785, and at the former put on the plays of Goldsmith. Towards the end of his life he became feeble-minded and had to be put under restraint.

[67] Arthur Murphy (1727-1805) was the son of a Dublin merchant and himself spent some years in business, but falling in with Foote and others in the London coffee-houses, he commenced author and edited the ' Gray's Inn Journal ' (1752-54). Being disappointed of a legacy he took to the stage, appearing as Othello at Covent Garden (October 18th, 1754) to the Desdemona of George Anne Bellamy. He was successful as an actor, and in 1756 his first farce, ' The Apprentice,' was given at Drury Lane. In 1757 he brought out a periodical called ' The Test ' in support of Henry Fox, and also edited a weekly paper called ' The Auditor ' in opposition to ' The North Briton.' Murphy adapted a number of plays from Voltaire, Molière and Metastasio, but his best work is a comedy ' The Way to keep Him ' (1760), written and acted shortly before the appearance of ' The Rosciad.' In 1761 he brought out ' The Examiner ' (originally called ' The Expostulation '), a satire directed against Churchill and Lloyd, and in the same year an ' Ode to the Naiads of Fleet Ditch,' an angry answer to Churchill's ' Apology,' in which satire Murphy's ' Desert Island,' a dramatic poem imitated from Metastasio, was mercilessly ridiculed.

[69-104] These lines, consisting of a violent attack on Wedderburn, do not occur in the first edition, which appeared before Churchill had

5

Grown old in fraud, though yet in manhood's bloom, 70
Adopting arts by which gay villains rise,
And reach the heights which honest men despise ;
Mute at the bar, and in the senate loud,
Dull 'mongst the dullest, proudest of the proud,
A pert, prim, prater of the northern race,
Guilt in his heart, and famine in his face,
Stood forth ; and thrice he waved his lily hand,
And thrice he twirl'd his tye, thrice stroked his band ;
    ' At Friendship's call ' (thus oft, with traitorous aim,
Men void of faith usurp faith's sacred name)   80
' At Friendship's call I come, by Murphy sent,
Who thus by me developes his intent :
But lest, transfused, the spirit should be lost,
That spirit which in storms of rhetoric toss'd,
Bounces about, and flies like bottled beer,
In his own words his own intentions hear.
    ' Thanks to my friends, but, to vile fortunes born,
No robes of fur these shoulders must adorn.
Vain your applause, no aid from thence I draw ;
Vain all my wit, for what is wit in law ?   90
Twice (cursed remembrance !) twice I strove to gain
Admittance 'mongst the law-instructed train,
Who, in the Temple and Gray's Inn, prepare

become immersed in politics and had learned to hate all the friends of
Bute. Alexander Wedderburn, first Baron Loughborough and first
Earl of Rosslyn, was born at Edinburgh in 1733. Junius called him
' the wary Wedderburn, (who) never threw away the scabbard, or ever
went upon a forlorn hope,' but he was not always so, for he flung off
his advocate's gown in the Scottish court when he was rebuked by the
presiding judge, and the same night set out for London to make his
fortune at the English bar. He was called on November 25th, 1757,
and on the accession to power of his intimate friend Lord Bute rose
rapidly. He was M.P. for the Ayr burghs from 1761 until 1768, and in
the latter year was returned as a Tory for Richmond in Yorkshire.
However, he espoused the cause of Wilkes and felt bound to accept the
Chiltern Hundreds. Another seat having been found for him he
violently opposed Lord North's administration, but became his devoted
partisan when bribed with the Solicitor-Generalship. In 1780 he was
appointed Chief Justice of the Court of Common Pleas and raised to
the peerage. In 1793 he attained his ambition : the Great Seal. He
became Earl of Rosslyn in 1801. Wedderburn was a patron of Murphy,
and when he became Lord Chancellor made him a Commissioner in
Bankruptcy.

For client's wretched feet the legal snare ;
Dead to those arts which polish and refine,
Deaf to all worth, because that worth was mine,
Twice did those blockheads startle at my name,
And foul rejection gave me up to shame.
To laws and lawyers then I bade adieu,
And plans of far more liberal note pursue.   100
Who will may be a Judge—my kindling breast
Burns for that chair which Roscius once possess'd.
Here give your votes, your interest here exert,
And let success for once attend desert.'
  With sleek appearance, and with ambling pace,
And type of vacant head with vacant face,
The Proteus Hill put in his modest plea,—
' Let Favour speak for others, Worth for me.'—
For who, like him, his various powers could call
Into so many shapes, and shine in all ?   110
Who could so nobly grace the motley list,
Actor, Inspector, Doctor, Botanist ?
Knows any one so well—sure no one knows—
At once to play, prescribe, compound, compose ?
Who can—But Woodward came,—Hill slipp'd away,
Melting like ghosts before the rising day.

[107] John Hill (*c.* 1716-1775), calling himself Sir John Hill on the
ground of being a member of the Swedish Order of Vasa, was an
apothecary in St. Martin's Lane. He attempted to act at Covent
Garden and at the Haymarket Theatre but was completely unsuccess-
ful. His attempts to write for the stage were no more acceptable ; and
in 1746 he brought out a monthly journal, ' The British Magazine,'
which continued until 1750. He compiled a great many books, and
obtained a diploma of medicine from the University of St. Andrews,
but was chiefly known as a scurrilous satirical writer. He engaged in
quarrels with the Royal Society, with Fielding, with Christopher
Smart, with Woodward, and with Garrick. Under the patronage of
Bute he commenced in 1759 a monumental work on ' The Vegetable
System,' in twenty-six folio volumes. This was not completed until
1775. Hill lost money on the venture but gained (in 1774) the Swedish
order of knighthood. It is the only one of his works which has any
value, although the complete list of his writings fills several columns
of the ' Dictionary of National Biography.'

[115] In 1752 John Hill printed a letter addressed ' To Woodward,
comedian, the meanest of all characters.' Woodward replied with a
pamphlet, and a paper war followed in which Woodward was completely
successful.

7

With that low cunning, which in fools supplies,
And amply too, the place of being wise,
Which Nature, kind, indulgent parent ! gave
To qualify the blockhead for a knave ;   120
With that smooth falsehood, whose appearance charms,
And reason of each wholesome doubt disarms ;
Which to the lowest depths of guilt descends,
By vilest means pursues the vilest ends,
Wears Friendship's mask for purposes of spite,
Fawns in the day, and butchers in the night ;
With that malignant envy which turns pale
And sickens, even if a friend prevail,
Which merit and success pursues with hate,
And damns the worth it cannot imitate ;   130
With the cold caution of a coward's spleen,
Which fears not guilt, but always seeks a screen,
Which keeps this maxim ever in her view—
What's basely done, should be done safely too ;
With that dull, rooted, callous impudence
Which, dead to shame and every nicer sense,

[117]–[178] These lines refer to Fitzpatrick, the promotor of the Fizzgiggo riots. The passage did not appear until the eighth edition of ' The Rosciad ' (1763) for the very good reason that the events to which they refer did not take place until the January of that year. Davies, in his ' Life of Garrick,' gives a full account of the whole affair. Fitzpatrick was a man of some means and with a taste for the theatre. He spent most of his time at the Bedford coffee-house, and having been introduced to Garrick, was given the freedom of Drury Lane. At first his criticisms in the newspapers were favourable, but upon some fancied slight on the part of Garrick he went out of his way to insult him at a literary society called the Shakespeare Club, of which they were both members. Garrick called upon him but received no satisfaction, and Fitzpatrick's enmity increased, even to the length of publishing a pamphlet entitled ' An Inquiry into the real merit of a certain popular Performer, in a series of Letters . . . to David Garrick, Esq.' Garrick replied with a poem which he called ' The Fribbleriad ' in which Fitzpatrick was ridiculed under the name Fizzgigg. Fitzpatrick waited for revenge and found it, on January 25th, 1763, on the occasion of a performance of the ' Two Gentlemen of Verona ' at Drury Lane. It had been the custom to allow those who waited until the end of the third act to obtain admission to the theatre at half-price, except for new plays and pantomimes. As this was a benefit night Garrick would not allow admission at half-price. Fitzpatrick thereupon collected his friends and made such a riot in the theatre that the performance was abandoned and the money returned. During the disturbance, Moody,

Ne'er blush'd, unless, in spreading vice's snares,
She blunder'd on some virtue unawares ;
With all these blessings, which we seldom find
Lavish'd by Nature on one happy mind,   140
A motley figure, of the Fribble tribe,
Which heart can scarce conceive or pen describe,
Came simpering on ; to ascertain whose sex
Twelve sage, impannell'd matrons would perplex ;
Nor male, nor female ; neither, and yet both ;
Of neuter gender, though of Irish growth ;
A six-foot suckling, mincing in Its gait,
Affected, peevish, prim and delicate ;
Fearful it seem'd, though of athletic make,
Lest brutal breezes should too roughly shake   150
Its tender form, and savage motion spread
O'er Its pale cheeks the horrid, manly red.
    Much did It talk, in Its own pretty phrase,
Of genius and of taste, of players and plays ;
Much too of writings, which Itself had wrote,
Of special merit, though of little note ;
For Fate, in a strange humour, had decreed

one of the actors, prevented a rioter from setting fire to the house.
The next night was the first performance of Mallet's tragedy ' Elvira.'
A riot again arose, and Garrick was compelled to promise to comply
with Fitzpatrick's demands. The latter, however, was still unsatisfied
and asked for an apology from Moody. The Irish actor thought to
put the public in a good humour by saying, with a strong Irish accent,
that ' He was very sorry he had displeased them by saving their lives
in putting out the fire.' This speech only inflamed the rioters the
more, and they demanded that Moody should go down on his knees
and ask their pardon. This Moody refused to do, to the delight of
Garrick, who was, however, compelled to promise that Moody should
not be allowed to appear in his theatre again. Moody, who was a man
of spirit, called on Fitzpatrick, and the latter, either in fear of a duel
or perhaps repenting of his conduct, promised that he and his friends
would lift the ban.
    Fitzpatrick provoked a riot also at Covent Garden, where the
theatre was seriously damaged. Beard, the manager, invoked the law
against the rioters, and Mansfield severely rebuked Fitzpatrick for his
conduct. The latter then changed his tactics and contented himself
with interrupting the play by laughing and hissing, so that, in the end,
Beard as well as Garrick was forced to submit. The affair created
great indignation not only among the actors but among those who
knew that Fitzpatrick's actions proceeded not from public spirit but
from private resentment. Such were the famous Fizzgiggo riots.

That what It wrote, none but Itself should read.
Much, too, It chatter'd of dramatic laws,
Misjudging critics, and misplaced applause ;   160
Then, with a self-complacent jutting air,
It smiled, It smirk'd, It wriggled to the chair,
And, with an awkward briskness not Its own,
Looking around, and perking on the throne,
Triumphant seem'd ; when that strange, savage dame,
Known but to few or only known by name,
Plain Common Sense appear'd, by Nature there
Appointed, with Plain Truth, to guard the chair ;
The pageant saw, and, blasted with her frown,
To Its first state of nothing melted down.   170
    Nor shall the Muse, (for even there the pride
Of this vain Nothing shall be mortified)
Nor shall the Muse (should fate ordain her rhymes,
Fond, pleasing thought ! to live in after-times),
With such a trifler's name her pages blot ;
Known be the character, the thing forgot :
Let It, to disappoint each future aim,
Live without sex, and die without a name !
    Cold-blooded critics, by enervate sires
Scarce hammer'd out when Nature's feeble fires   180
Glimmer'd their last ; whose sluggish blood, half froze,
Creeps labouring through the veins ; whose heart ne'er
    glows
With fancy-kindled heat ;—a servile race,
Who, in mere want of fault all merit place ;
Who blind obedience pay to ancient schools,
Bigots to Greece, and slaves to musty rules ;
With solemn consequence declared that none
Could judge that cause but Sophocles alone :
Dupes to their fancied excellence, the crowd,
Obsequious to the sacred dictate, bow'd.   190
    When, from amidst the throng, a youth stood forth,
Unknown his person, not unknown his worth ;
His look bespoke applause ; alone he stood,
Alone he stemm'd the mighty critic flood :
He talk'd of ancients, as the man became

[191] ' A youth,' *i.e.* Robert Lloyd. (See note on line 232, below.)

10

Who prized our own, but envied not their fame ;
With noble reverence spoke of Greece and Rome,
And scorn'd to tear the laurel from the tomb.
   ' But more than just to other countries grown,
Must we turn base apostates to our own ?   200
Where do these words of Greece and Rome excel,
That England may not please the ear as well ?
What mighty magic's in the place or air,
That all perfection needs must centre there ?
In states, let strangers blindly be preferr'd ;
In state of letters, merit should be heard.
Genius is of no country ; her pure ray
Spreads all abroad, as general as the day ;
Foe to restraint, from place to place she flies,
And may hereafter e'en in Holland rise.   210
May not, (to give a pleasing fancy scope,
And cheer a patriot heart with patriot hope)
May not some great, extensive genius raise
The name of Britain 'bove Athenian praise ;
And, whilst brave thirst of fame his bosom warms,
Make England great in letters as in arms ?
There may—there hath—and Shakspeare's muse aspires
Beyond the reach of Greece ; with native fires,
Mounting aloft he wings his daring flight,
Whilst Sophocles below stands trembling at his height.
   Why should we then abroad for judges roam,   221
When abler judges we may find at home ?
Happy in tragic and in comic powers,
Have we not Shakspeare ?—is not Jonson ours ?
For them, your natural judges, Britons, vote ;
They'll judge like Britons, who like Britons wrote.'
   He said, and conquer'd.—Sense resumed her sway,
And disappointed pedants stalk'd away.
Shakspeare and Jonson, with deserved applause,
Joint judges were ordain'd to try the cause.   230
Mean-time the stranger every voice employ'd,
To ask or tell his name.—Who is it ?—Lloyd.

[205] The first hint of Churchill's invective against the Scottish favourites of Lord Bute.
[232] Robert Lloyd (1733-1764) was the son of Dr. Pierson Lloyd,

Thus, when the aged friends of Job stood mute,
And, tamely prudent, gave up the dispute,
Elihu, with the decent warmth of youth,
Boldly stood forth the advocate of Truth,
Confuted Falsehood, and disabled Pride,
Whilst baffled Age stood snarling at his side.
The day of trial's fix'd, nor any fear
Lest day of trial should be put off here.   240
Causes but seldom for delay can call
In courts where forms are few, fees none at all.
The morning came, nor find I that the sun,
As he on other great events hath done,
Put on a brighter robe than what he wore
To go his journey in the day before.
Full in the centre of a spacious plain,
On plan entirely new, where nothing vain,
Nothing magnificent appear'd, but Art
With decent modesty perform'd her part,   250
Rose a tribunal ; from no other court
It borrow'd ornament, or sought support ;
No juries here were pack'd to kill or clear,
No bribes were taken, nor oaths broken here ;
No gownsmen, partial to a client's cause,
To their own purpose turned the pliant laws ;
Each judge was true and steady to his trust,

master at Westminster School. His relations with Churchill, whose
intimate friend he was, have been dealt with in the Introduction. He
was elected to a Westminster Scholarship at Trinity College, Cam-
bridge, in 1751, and took his degree in 1755. While at Cambridge he
wrote a long poem entitled ' The Progress of Envy ' and contributed
to a journal called ' The Connoisseur,' run by Bonnell Thornton and
George Colman. On leaving Cambridge he became an usher at
Westminster, but soon abandoned an uncongenial post to devote
himself to literature. His poem ' The Actor ' appeared in 1760 and
inspired Churchill to write ' The Rosciad.' From 1761 to 1762 Lloyd
superintended a literary magazine called ' The Library,' and soon
afterwards became editor of the ' St. James's Magazine,' the failure of
which involved him in such difficulties that he was confined to the Fleet.
Here his condition was alleviated by the kindness of Churchill, and the
announcement of the latter's death dealt Lloyd a blow from which he
never recovered. He died on December 15th, 1764, in his thirty-second
year and was buried in the churchyard of St. Bride's, Fleet Street.
Churchill's sister Patty, to whom Lloyd is said to have been engaged,
looked after him during his last illness and died soon afterwards.

As Mansfield wise, and as old Foster just.
   In the first seat, in robe of various dyes,
A noble wildness flashing from his eyes,   260
Sat Shakspeare.—In one hand a wand he bore,
For mighty wonders famed in days of yore ;
The other held a globe, which to his will
Obedient turn'd, and own'd the master's skill :
Things of the noblest kind his genius drew,
And look'd through Nature at a single view :
A loose he gave to his unbounded soul,
And taught new lands to rise, new seas to roll ;
Call'd into being scenes unknown before,
And passing Nature's bounds, was something more.   270
   Next Jonson sat ; in ancient learning train'd,
His rigid judgment Fancy's flights restrain'd ;
Correctly pruned each wild luxuriant thought,
Mark'd out her course, nor spared a glorious fault :
The book of man he read with nicest art,
And ransack'd all the secrets of the heart ;
Exerted penetration's utmost force,
And traced each passion to its proper source ;
Then, strongly mark'd, in liveliest colours drew,
And brought each foible forth to public view :   280
The coxcomb felt a lash in every word,
And fools, hung out, their brother fools deterr'd.
His comic humour kept the world in awe,
And laughter frighten'd folly more than law.

[258] Mansfield. When this poem was written both Churchill and
Lloyd professed the greatest admiration for Mansfield. Compare the
lines in Lloyd's ' The Law Student ' :
      ' O for thy spirit Mansfield ! at thy name
         What bosom glows not with an active flame ?
         Alone from Jargon born to rescue Law,
         From precedent, grave hum, and formal saw !
         To strip chican'ry of its vain pretence,
         And marry Common Law to Common Sense ! '
Churchill's opinion of Mansfield underwent a violent change owing
to the latter's hostility to Wilkes. (See note on ' Epistle to Hogarth,'
line 76.) Sir Michael Foster (1689-1763) was pronounced by Black-
stone to be ' a very great master of the crown law,' and by Lord
Chief Justice De Grey as ' the Magna Charta of liberty of persons as
well as fortunes.' He was appointed a puisne judge of the King's
Bench in 1745.

But, hark !—the trumpet sounds, the crowd gives way,
And the procession comes in just array.
Now should I, in some sweet, poetic line
Offer up incense at Apollo's shrine,
Invoke the muse to quit her calm abode,
And waken memory with a sleeping ode :   290
For how should mortal man, in mortal verse
Their titles, merits, or their names, rehearse ?
But give, kind Dulness ! memory and rhyme,
We'll put off Genius till another time.
First Order came,—with solemn step and slow,
In measured time his feet were taught to go.
Behind, from time to time, he cast his eye,
Lest this should quit his place, that step awry ;
Appearances to save his only care ;
So things seem right, no matter what they are :   300
In him his parents saw themselves renew'd,
Begotten by Sir Critic on Saint Prude.
Then came Drum, Trumpet, Hautboy, Fiddle, Flute ;
Next, Snuffer, Sweeper, Shifter, Soldier, Mute :
Legions of angels all in white advance ;
Furies, all fire, come forward in a dance ;
Pantomime figures then are brought to view,
Fools hand in hand with fools go two by two.
Next came the Treasurer of either House,
One with full purse, t'other with not a sous :   310
Behind, a group of figures awe create,
Set off with all the impertinence of state ;
By lace and feather consecrate to fame,
Expletive kings, and queens without a name.

[290] An allusion to Mason's ' Ode to Memory,' ridiculed by Lloyd in an ' Ode to Oblivion.' Gray, Mason's friend, was ridiculed by Colman in an ' Ode to Obscurity.' (See note on ' The Prophecy of Famine,' line 67.)

[303] The eighteenth-century orchestra consisted in general of flutes, oboes, bassoons, trumpets and drums, in addition to violins.

[304] The stage was lit by chandeliers and, after Garrick's trip abroad (1765), by footlights. Both these required the occasional services of a snuffer. A grenadier stood at the side of the stage to keep the peace.

[310] John Beard's management of Covent Garden was financially very successful. (See note on line 728.)

14

Here Havard, all serene, in the same strains
Loves, hates, and rages, triumphs, and complains :
His easy vacant face proclaim'd a heart
Which could not feel emotions, nor impart.
With him came mighty Davies. On my life,
That Davies hath a very pretty wife :—   320
Statesman all over !—in plots famous grown !—
He mouths a sentence as curs mouth a bone.
Next Holland came,—with truly tragic stalk
He creeps, he flies,—a hero should not walk.

[315] William Havard (*c.* 1710-1778) made his first appearance on the
stage at Goodman's Fields in 1730. He acted subsequently at Drury
Lane and at Covent Garden, taking important but secondary parts
such as that of the King in ' Henry IV.' His acting is said to have
been too stolid but his delivery was good. He wrote three tragedies,
among which his ' King Charles I.' was highly praised when it was
first produced in 1737.

[319] Thomas Davies (*c.* 1712-1785) was a bookseller by trade. He
was well educated at Edinburgh University, but his passion for the
stage led him to appear in 1736 in Lillo's ' Fatal Curiosity ' at the
Haymarket under Fielding's management. After the failure of his
bookselling business he returned to the stage as Pierre in ' Venice
Preserved,' which was performed for his benefit at Covent Garden
(January 24th, 1746). He became a stroller and married the daughter
of a York actor named Yarrow. He performed at Edinburgh and
Dublin and, in 1753, was engaged with his wife at Drury Lane to
understudy the chief actors. ' His wife (says the D.N.B.) was both
beautiful and virtuous.' Churchill's attack, according to Johnson,
drove Davies from the stage, and he again took to bookselling. It was
he who introduced Boswell to Johnson, and the Doctor always liked
him, in spite of certain piratical proceedings. When he became a
bankrupt Johnson collected money for him, induced Sheridan to give
him a benefit at Drury Lane, and encouraged him to write the life of
Garrick. This appeared in 1780 and was very successful. It is a most
valuable repository of theatrical information and has been largely
drawn upon in these notes, and by former editors of Churchill. Tooke
indeed prints in his notes extensive passages from Davies without the
courtesy of inverted commas.

[323] Charles Holland (1733-1769) was the son of a baker in Chiswick
and was himself apprenticed to a turpentine merchant (D.N.B.). He
made his first appearance as an actor at Drury Lane in February, 1755,
in the character of Oroonoko. He remained at Drury Lane until 1769,
when he died of smallpox. Holland was a competent actor and a
worthy man, and has not been handled very kindly by the critics.
Gray calls him ' a Journeyman barber. When he first came on the
stage he could not read, but had got by heart many of Garrick's
principal parts, whose Tones and Gestures he imitated and exag-
gerated. At first, however, he was highly applauded.'

As if with Heaven he warr'd, his eager eyes
Planted their batteries against the skies ;
Attitude, action, air, pause, start, sigh, groan
He borrow'd, and made use of as his own.
By fortune thrown on any other stage,
He might, perhaps, have pleased an easy age :   330
But now appears a copy, and no more,
Of something better we have seen before.
The actor who would build a solid fame,
Must imitation's servile arts disclaim ;
Act from himself, on his own bottom stand ;
I hate e'en Garrick thus at second-hand.
Behind came King.—Bred up in modest lore,

[336] In the first edition this line was followed by six couplets attacking
the personal character of John Palmer. These Churchill subsequently
omitted, and even inserted in ' The Apology ' (lines 330-335) a passage
regretting that his Muse should ' quit the actor to expose the man.'
The deleted lines were :

> That's [Palmer] with a figure form'd to please,
> He wants the graceful elegance of ease ;
> Awkward and stiff he stands, I know not how,
> As always ready to let off a bow.
> Truant to love and false to L[ucia]'s charms,
> He fled ungrateful from her virtuous arms,
> In vain recall'd, renounc'd love's softer claim,
> And hither came to seek the bubble Fame.
> Ah ! to thy L[ucia]'s arms again return ;
> With her in mutual flames of rapture burn ;
> Unequal to this great attempt, remove
> The itch of honour with the p—x of love.

According to Tooke, the Lucia referred to was Lucy Cooper, a woman
of the town. Wodhull remarks that the lines in question were ' said
to be struck out in consequence of Palmer's marrying Miss Pritchard.'
This is a mistake. He married a Miss Burroughes, or Berroughs. (See
also note on line 46.)

[337] Thomas King (1730-1805) was educated at Westminster School.
He was articled to a London solicitor but ran away to become a
strolling player. While playing at Windsor he was seen by Garrick
and engaged for Drury Lane, where he made his début in October,
1748. He appeared in 1750, under Sheridan, at the Smock Alley
Theatre, Dublin, and, except for one season, remained there for eight
years, winning a recognised position as an actor in comedy. He was
back at Drury Lane in October, 1759, and except for one season at
Covent Garden, and various summer engagements, remained there
until 1802, his position for the greater part of the time being a dominant
one. Garrick resigned the part of Lord Ogleby in ' The Clandestine
Marriage ' to King, and the latter was the creator of the part of Sir

Bashful and young he sought Hibernia's shore ;
Hibernia, famed, 'bove every other grace
For matchless intrepidity of face.   340
From her his features caught the generous flame,
And bid defiance to all sense of shame :
Tutor'd by her all rivals to surpass,
'Mongst Drury's sons he comes, and shines in Brass.
    Lo, Yates !—Without the least finesse of art
He gets applause ; I wish he'd get his part.
When hot impatience is in full career,
How vilely ' Hark'e ! Hark'e ! ' grates the ear !
When active fancy from the brain is sent,
And stands on tip-toe for some wish'd event,   350
I hate those careless blunders which recall
Suspended sense, and prove it fiction all.
    In characters of low and vulgar mould,
Where Nature's coarsest features we behold ;
Where, destitute of every decent grace,
Unmanner'd jests are blurted in your face,
There, Yates with justice strict attention draws,
Acts truly from himself, and gains applause ;
But when, to please himself or charm his wife,
He aims at something in politer life,   360
When, blindly thwarting Nature's stubborn plan,
He treads the stage by way of gentleman,
The clown, who no one touch of breeding knows,
Looks like Tom Errand dress'd in Clincher's clothes.
Fond of his dress, fond of his person grown,
Laugh'd at by all, and to himself unknown,
From side to side he struts, he smiles, he prates,

Peter Teazle in ' The School for Scandal.' He was a fairly successful
playwright and was engaged in management at the theatre in King
Street and at Sadler's Wells, and—for short periods—at Drury Lane.
When Churchill wrote King had by no means reached the position he
was afterwards to occupy. He lived to be praised by Hazlitt.

[348] *i.e.* an appeal to the prompter. (See also note on line 31.)

[363] ' Clown ' substituted by Churchill for ' fop,' which appeared in
the earlier editions.

[364] Tom Errand : a comic character in Farquhar's ' The Constant
Couple.' Clincher : a character in the same play, as also in ' Sir
Harry Wildair,' its sequel.

And seems to wonder what's become of Yates.
Woodward, endow'd with various tricks of face,
Great master in the science of grimace,   370
From Ireland ventures, favourite of the town
Lured by the pleasing prospect of renown ;
A speaking Harlequin, made up of whim,
He twists, he twines, he tortures every limb,
Plays to the eye with a mere monkey's art,
And leaves to sense the conquest of the heart.
We laugh indeed, but, on reflection's birth,
We wonder at ourselves, and curse our mirth.
His walk of parts he fatally misplaced,
And inclination fondly took for taste ;   380
Hence hath the town so often seen display'd
Beau in burlesque, high life in masquerade.
　But when bold wits, not such as patch up plays,
Cold and correct, in these insipid days,
Some comic character, strong featured, urge,
To probability's extremest verge ;
Where modest Judgment her decree suspends,
And, for a time, nor censures nor commends ;

[369] Henry Woodward (1714-1777) was the son of a tallow chandler in Southwark. He was educated at Merchant Taylors' School until his father's failure in business led him to take an engagement at Lincoln's Inn Fields in the Lilliputian troupe organised by John Rich. He appeared at Goodman's Fields in 1730 and remained there until 1736, playing a variety of parts, including that of Harlequin. In 1737 he appeared (at Lincoln's Inn Fields, where the company had removed) as Harlequin Macheath in ' The Beggars' Pantomime,' and in 1738 he reached Drury Lane. Here he remained until the season of 1741-42, playing such parts as Slender, Pistol, Sir Andrew Aguecheek, Sir Novelty Fashion, Lord Foppington, etc. He played also at Covent Garden and at Smock Alley Theatre, Dublin. He was back at Drury Lane in 1748 and remained for ten years, playing Lancelot Gobbo, Polonius, Sir Harry Wildair, Falstaff, etc. He was now at the height of his fame, being generally considered as good a comedian as Garrick, although, of course, he did not attempt to compete with him in tragedy. In 1758 he entered with Spranger Barry into an unfortunate attempt to open a new theatre in Dublin. Having lost the greater part of his savings, Woodward reappeared in 1763 at Covent Garden where, with few intervals, he acted until his death. For the last ten years of his life he lived with George Ann Bellamy and his kindness and good humour are described in that lady's confessions. Churchill's unfavourable opinion is not borne out by others. Nevertheless Woodward obtained a great part of his reputation by his performances as Harlequin.

Where critics can't determine on the spot
Whether it is in nature found or not,   390
There Woodward safely shall his powers exert,
Nor fail of favour where he shews desert ;
Hence he in Bobadil such praises bore,
Such worthy praises ; Kitely scarce had more.
   By turns transform'd into all kind of shapes,
Constant to none, Foote laughs, cries, struts, and scrapes :
Now in the centre, now in van or rear
The Proteus shifts, bawd, parson, auctioneer.
His strokes of humour, and his bursts of sport
Are all contain'd in this one word, *Distort.*   400

³⁹³ Bobadil is the bragging captain in Jonson's ' Every Man in his Humour.'

³⁹⁴ Kitely : a character in Jonson's ' Every Man in his Humour,' frequently played by Garrick.

³⁹⁶ Samuel Foote (1720-1777) was born at Truro. One of his uncles having murdered another, Foote inherited a considerable fortune which he dissipated rapidly, first at Worcester College, Oxford, and later in London, where he frequented the coffee-houses and obtained a reputation as a wit. In 1744 he appeared as an actor at the Haymarket under Macklin, but he was a failure, as his real talent lay in mimicry. In 1767 he opened the Haymarket Theatre with a kind of variety entertainment—scenes from farces and an invention of his own entitled ' The Diversions of the Morning.' On the ground that this performance infringed the privileges of the other theatres, the Westminster magistrates forbade Foote to continue. However, he cleverly evaded the law by inviting his friends to take a dish of chocolate at noon, for which tickets could be obtained at George's coffee-house, Temple Bar. It was understood that the entertainment was included for nothing, but the device was a very transparent one, for no chocolate was served at all. Encouraged by his success, Foote instituted an evening entertainment which he called taking ' a dish of tea.' He was very successful also with a series of light comedies, generally satirising known individuals under transparent disguises. In 1766 Foote lost his leg in a riding accident, and the Duke of York, who was present, was moved to obtain for him a licence to open a theatre in Westminster from May 14th to September 14th. Foote purchased his old premises in the Haymarket and built a new theatre, which he opened in 1767. The last years of his life were embittered by the Duchess of Kingston, who, in revenge for Foote's satire, spread rumours of his homosexual practices. Foote was tried, on the evidence of a discharged servant, for criminal assault, and was acquitted. He died the following year.

³⁹⁸ Foote, in his own farce of ' The Minor,' played Shift, Smirke and Mrs. Cole, and, in the epilogue, impersonated George Whitefield, the evangelist, who squinted.

Doth a man stutter, look a-squint, or halt ;—
Mimics draw humour out of Nature's fault ;
With personal defects their mirth adorn,
And hang misfortunes out to public scorn.
E'en I, whom Nature cast in hideous mould,
Whom, having made, she trembled to behold,
Beneath the load of mimicry may groan,
And find that Nature's errors are my own.
   Shadows behind of Foote and Woodward came ;
Wilkinson this, Obrien was that name.   410
Strange to relate, but wonderfully true,
That even shadows have their shadows too !
With not a single comic power endued,
The first a mere mere mimic's mimic stood ;
The last, by Nature form'd to please, who shews,
In Jonson's Stephen, which way genius grows,
Self quite put off, affects with too much art
To put on Woodward in each mangled part ;
Adopts his shrug, his wink, his stare ; nay, more,
His voice, and croaks ; for Woodward croak'd before. 420
When a dull copier simple grace neglects,
And rests his imitation in defects,
We readily forgive ; but such vile arts
Are double guilt in men of real parts.
   By Nature form'd in her perversest mood ;
With no one requisite of art endued,

---

[405] Churchill was no beauty, as can be seen from his portraits. (*Cf.* his own description of his person in ' Independence,' line 149 *et seq.*)

[410] Tate Wilkinson. (See note on line 35.)

[410] William Obrien, or O'Brien (died 1815), was engaged by Garrick in 1758 in place of Woodward. He is said to have had aristocratic connections and he won the praise of Walpole for his elegant bearing on the stage. He played such parts as Lord Foppington in ' The Careless Husband,' Fribble in ' Miss in her Teens,' Lord Trinket in ' The Jealous Wife,' Archer in ' The Beaux' Stratagem,' and Sir Harry Wildair in ' The Constant Couple.' Like Woodward he also played Harlequin. In April, 1764, he made a secret marriage with Lady Susan, eldest daughter of the first Earl of Ilchester and niece of Henry Fox, first Lord Holland. The anger of his wife's relations caused the pair to emigrate to America, upon which the relatives seem to have repented and to have procured him several official posts, first abroad, but later in England.

[416] Stephen : a character in Jonson's ' Every Man in his Humour.'

Next Jackson came.—Observe that settled glare,
Which better speaks a puppet than a player ;
List to that voice—did ever Discord hear
Sounds so well fitted to her untuned ear ?   430
When to enforce some very tender part,
The right hand sleeps by instinct on the heart,
His soul, of every other thought bereft,
Is anxious only where to place the left ;
He sobs and pants to soothe his weeping spouse,
To soothe his weeping mother, turns and bows :
Awkward, embarrass'd, stiff, without the skill
Of moving gracefully or standing still,
One leg, as if suspicious of his brother,
Desirous seems to run away from t'other.   440
   Some errors, handed down from age to age,
Plead custom's force, and still possess the stage.
That's vile—should we a parent's faults adore,
And err, because our fathers err'd before ?
If, inattentive to the author's mind,
Some actors made the jest they could not find,
If by low tricks they marr'd fair Nature's mien,
And blurr'd the graces of the simple scene,
Shall we, if reason rightly is employ'd,
Not see their faults, or seeing, not avoid ?   450
When Falstaff stands detected in a lie,
Why, without meaning, rolls Love's glassy eye ?
Why ?—There's no cause—at least no cause we know—
It was the fashion twenty years ago.
Fashion—a word which knaves and fools may use,

427 John Jackson (*fl.* 1761-1792). Gray calls him ' a very wretched player at Drury Lane.' He first appeared there in October, 1762, and remained three years. He wrote three tragedies and was for a time manager of the Theatre Royal, Edinburgh, and of theatres at Glasgow, Dundee, and Aberdeen. Mrs. Siddons and Master Betty both appeared under his management.

452 James Love (1722-1744), whose real name was James Dance, attracted the attention of Sir Robert Walpole by a poem in his support, but the Minister did little for him and Dance took to the stage. He wrote a poem on ' Cricket,' and a play called ' Pamela.' He acted in Dublin and Edinburgh and in 1762 came to Drury Lane. His theatre at Richmond involved him in great loss. His best part was Falstaff.

Their knavery and folly to excuse.
To copy beauties, forfeits all pretence
To fame—to copy faults, is want of sense.
    Yet (though in some particulars he fails,
Some few particulars, where mode prevails)   460
If in these hallow'd times, when sober, sad,
All gentlemen are melancholy mad ;
When 'tis not deem'd so great a crime by half
To violate a vestal as to laugh,
Rude mirth may hope presumptuous to engage
An Act of Toleration for the stage ;
And courtiers will, like reasonable creatures,
Suspend vain fashion, and unscrew their features ;
Old Falstaff, play'd by Love, shall please once more,
And humour set the audience in a roar.   470
    Actors I've seen, and of no vulgar name,
Who, being from one part possess'd of fame,
Whether they are to laugh, cry, whine, or bawl,
Still introduce that favourite part in all.
Here, Love, be cautious—ne'er be thou betray'd
To call in that wag Falstaff's dangerous aid ;
Like Goths of old, howe'er he seems a friend,
He'll seize that throne you wish him to defend.
In a peculiar mould by Humour cast,
For Falstaff framed—himself the first and last—   480
He stands aloof from all, maintains his state,
And scorns, like Scotsmen, to assimilate.
Vain all disguise ! too plain we see the trick,
Though the knight wears the weeds of Dominic ;
And Boniface disgraced, betrays the smack,
In *anno Domini*, of Falstaff's sack.
    Arms cross'd, brows bent, eyes fix'd, feet marching slow,
A band of malcontents with spleen o'erflow ;
Wrapt in conceit's impenetrable fog,
Which Pride, like Phœbus, draws from every bog,   490

---

[484] ' the weeds of Dominic.' Dominick (a character in Dryden's
' The Spanish Fryar ') is a kind of ecclesiastical Falstaff who helps
Lorenzo in his amour with Elvira the wife of Gomez.
    [485] Boniface, landlord of the inn at Lichfield, a character in Far-
quhar's ' The Beaux' Stratagem.'

22

They curse the managers, and curse the town
Whose partial favour keeps such merit down.
　But if some man, more hardy than the rest,
Should dare attack these gnatlings in their nest,
At once they rise with impotence of rage,
Whet their small stings, and buzz about the stage.
' 'Tis breach of privilege !—Shall any dare
To arm satiric truth against a player ?
Prescriptive rights we plead, time out of mind ;
Actors, unlash'd themselves, may lash mankind.'　　500
　What ! shall Opinion then, of Nature free,
And liberal as the vagrant air, agree
To rust in chains like these, imposed by things
Which, less than nothing, ape the pride of kings ?
No—though half-poets with half-players join
To curse the freedom of each honest line ;
Though rage and malice dim their faded cheek,
What the Muse freely thinks, she'll freely speak ;
With just disdain of every paltry sneer,
Stranger alike to flattery and fear,　　510
In purpose fix'd, and to herself a rule,
Public contempt shall wait the public fool.
　Austin would always glisten in French silks ;
Ackman would Norris be, and Packer Wilks ;
For who, like Ackman, can with humour please ?
Who can, like Packer, charm with sprightly ease ?

491-512 These lines were added in the Second Edition.

513 Austin had been manager of the Chester Theatre and at Drury Lane was Garrick's stage manager, etc. When Garrick died he retired to Ireland, a comparatively wealthy man.

514 Packer and Ackman : minor actors at Drury Lane.

514 Henry Norris (1665-c. 1730), nicknamed Jubilee Dicky from his part in Farquhar's ' The Constant Couple,' was a very capable actor during the period of Betterton and Booth. Churchill, of course, could never have seen him act. Tooke gives the year of his death as 1725.

514 Robert Wilks (c. 1665-1732), a contemporary of Norris, made his first appearance on the stage as Othello at the Smock Alley Theatre, Dublin. After a brief appearance at Drury Lane he per... med in Dublin for five years, returning to Drury Lane in 1696 in the character of Lysippus in 'The Maid's Tragedy.' In 1714 he became joint manager with Cibber and Doggett. His Hamlet was received with much applause, and he was the original Sir Harry Wildair.

Higher than all the rest, see Bransby strut,
A mighty Gulliver in Lilliput !
Ludicrous Nature ! which at once could show
A man so very high, so very low.   520
　If I forget thee, Blakes, or if I say
Aught hurtful, may I never see thee play.
Let critics, with a supercilious air,
Decry thy various merit, and declare
Frenchman is still at top ;—but scorn that rage
Which, in attacking thee, attacks the age.
French follies, universally embraced,
At once provoke our mirth, and form our taste.
　Long from a nation ever hardly used,
At random censured, wantonly abused,   530
Have Britons drawn their sport ; with partial view
Form'd general notions from the rascal few ;
Condemn'd a people, as for vices known,
Which, from their country banish'd, seek our own.
At length, howe'er, the slavish chain is broke,
And Sense, awaken'd, scorns her ancient yoke :
Taught by thee, Moody, we now learn to raise
Mirth from their foibles, from their virtues, praise.
　Next came the legion which our summer Bayes
From alleys, here and there, contrived to raise,   540
Flush'd with vast hopes, and certain to succeed,
With wits who cannot write, and scarce can read.
Veterans no more support the rotten cause,

[517] Bransby, a very tall actor, about whom little is known. As a boy he played Gulliver in Garrick's ' Lilliput.'

[521] Blakes (died 1763) was originally a wig maker. ' He played the Doctor in the Anatomist, and other French characters with great Humor ' (Gray).

[537] John Moody first appeared at Drury Lane in January, 1759, as a substitute for Holland. He made his proper début in May of the same year, and soon after made a hit as Sir Callaghan O'Brallaghan in ' Love à la Mode,' as Captain O'Cutter in ' The Jealous Wife,' and as the Irishman in ' The Register Office.' He showed great spirit in the Fizzgiggo riots (see note on lines 117-178). He retired at the end of the season of 1796.

[539] Bayes is the chief character in ' The Rehearsal,' the farce written by George Villiers, Duke of Buckingham (1671) in ridicule of Dryden. Here Churchill means Foote, who played the part at his Summer Theatre in the Haymarket.

No more from Elliot's worth they reap applause ;
Each on himself determines to rely ;
Be Yates disbanded, and let Elliot fly.
Never did play'rs so well an author fit,
To Nature dead, and foes declared to wit.
So loud each tongue, so empty was each head,
So much they talk'd, so very little said,   550
So wondrous dull, and yet so wondrous vain,
At once so willing, and unfit to reign,
That Reason swore, nor would the oath recall,
Their mighty master's soul inform'd them all.
    As one with various disappointments sad,
Whom dulness, only, kept from being mad,
Apart from all the rest great Murphy came—
Common to fools and wits the rage of fame.
What though the sons of Nonsense hail him Sire,
Auditor, Author, Manager, and Squire !   560
His restless soul's ambition stops not there ;
To make his triumphs perfect dub him Player.
    In person tall, a figure form'd to please,
If symmetry could charm deprived of ease ;
When motionless he stands, we all approve ;
What pity 'tis the Thing was made to move !
    His voice, in one dull, deep, unvaried sound,
Seems to break forth from caverns under ground ;
From hollow chest the low, sepulchral note
Unwilling heaves, and struggles in his throat.   570
    Could authors butcher'd give an actor grace,
All must to him resign the foremost place.
When he attempts, in some one favourite part,

---

544 Ann Elliot (*c.* 1743-1769), the mistress of Murphy, was an un-
educated girl whose natural talent and beauty gained her the public
favour. She played Maria in her lover's farce ' The Citizen,' and was
seemingly launched on a theatrical career which, however, (in Tooke's
discreet phrase) ' she relinquished at the instance of the late Duke of
Cumberland.' After her untimely death Murphy wrote her biography.

557 Murphy. (See note on line 67.) Murphy's farces were acted
at the Summer Theatre in the Haymarket under the joint management
of himself and Foote. ' The Auditor ' was the name of a paper he
edited, famous, like Smollett's ' Briton,' for the defence of Lord
Bute's administration. He also appeared as an actor, playing parts,
such as Othello, for which he was totally unfitted.

To ape the feelings of a manly heart,
His honest features the disguise defy,
And his face loudly gives his tongue the lie.
Still in extremes, he knows no happy mean,
Or raving mad, or stupidly serene.
In cold-wrought scenes the lifeless actor flags ;
In passion, tears the passion into rags.   580
Can none remember ?—Yes—I know all must—
When in the Moor he ground his teeth to dust,
When o'er the stage he Folly's standard bore,
Whilst Common Sense stood trembling at the door.
How few are found with real talents blest !
Fewer with Nature's gifts contented rest.
Man from his sphere eccentric starts astray ;
All hunt for fame, but most mistake the way.
Bred at St. Omer's to the shuffling trade,
The hopeful youth a Jesuit might have made,   590
With various readings stored his empty skull,
Learn'd without sense, and venerably dull ;
Or, at some banker's desk, like many more,
Content to tell that two and two make four,
His name had stood in City annals fair,
And prudent Dulness mark'd him for a mayor.
What then could tempt thee, in a critic age,
Such blooming hopes to forfeit on a stage ?
Could it be worth thy wondrous waste of pains
To publish to the world thy lack of brains ?   600
Or might not reason e'en to thee have shown
Thy greatest praise had been to live unknown ?
Yet let not vanity like thine despair :
Fortune makes Folly her peculiar care.
A vacant throne high-placed in Smithfield view,
To sacred Dulness and her first-born due,
Thither with haste in happy hour repair,
Thy birth-right claim, nor fear a rival there.
Shuter himself shall own thy juster claim,

---

[589] St. Omer, a town in northern France, capital of the department
of Pas-de-Calais. A college of English Jesuits was opened there in
1592.
[605] See note on line 31.

And venal Ledgers puff their Murphy's name ;   610
Whilst Vaughan or Dapper, call him which you will,
Shall blow the trumpet, and give out the bill.
There rule secure from critics and from sense,
Nor once shall Genius rise to give offence ;
Eternal peace shall bless the happy shore,
And little factions break thy rest no more.

From Covent Garden crowds promiscuous go,
Whom the Muse knows not, nor desires to know :
Veterans they seem'd, but knew of arms no more
Than if, till that time, arms they never bore :   620
Like Westminster militia train'd to fight,
They scarcely knew the left hand from the right.
Ashamed among such troops to show the head,
Their chiefs were scatter'd, and their heroes fled.

Sparks at his glass sat comfortably down
To separate frown from smile, and smile from frown.
Smith, the genteel, the airy, and the smart,
Smith was just gone to school to say his part.

[610] ' The Public Ledger,' a newspaper edited by Hugh Kelly.

[611] Thomas Vaughan played the part of Dapper in ' The Alchemist.' He was the author of two farces, ' Love's Metamorphosis ' and ' The Hotel.'

[621] The Westminster Militia was famous for its unmilitary bearing.

[625] Luke Sparks. Very little is known of this actor. ' The Thespian Dictionary ' (1805) declares that he was ' very respectable in tragedy, and a great favourite at Edinburgh, in 1748 : he belonged to Covent Garden, when Mr. Rich was manager. Having acquired a competent fortune, not entirely by acting, he retired from the stage soon after the publication of " The Rosciad," and lived at Brentford. He died about the year 1769.'

[627] William Smith (*c.* 1730-1819), commonly called ' Gentleman Smith,' was educated at Eton and St. John's College, Cambridge. Having been ' sent down,' he came to London and, with the help of Spranger Barry, appeared at Covent Garden in January, 1753. He played a succession of important parts at that theatre until the close of the season of 1773-74, when he announced his retirement from the stage. However, in September, 1774, he appeared at Drury Lane under Garrick. His last professional appearance was as Charles Surface on June 9th, 1788. In 1754 he married Elizabeth, widow of Kelland Courtenay and sister of the notorious Earl of Sandwich, a *mésalliance* which created a tremendous uproar in aristocratic circles. Smith had a passion for hunting and horse-racing, and is said to have stipulated in his theatrical engagement that he should not be called upon to act on Mondays during the hunting season.

Ross, (a misfortune which we often meet)
Was fast asleep at dear Statira's feet ;   630
Statira, with her hero to agree,
Stood on her feet as fast asleep as he.
Macklin, who largely deals in half-form'd sounds,

⁶²⁹ David Ross (1728-1790) was disinherited at the age of thirteen, and in 1749 was playing Clerimont in ' The Miser ' at Smock Alley Theatre, Dublin. He was engaged with Mossop by Garrick and made his first appearance at Drury Lane in 1751 as Young Bevil in ' The Conscious Lovers.' He was very popular, before he lost his figure, as the handsome hero in genteel comedy. He played an immense number of parts at Drury Lane, and on October 3rd, 1757, appeared at Covent Garden in his favourite rôle of Essex. In 1767 he went to Edinburgh and became patentee and manager of the first theatre legally erected in Scotland. Between 1770 and 1778 he performed again at Covent Garden, but broke his leg in the latter year and lived in poverty for some years. He is said to have married Fanny Murray, the cast-off mistress of Lord Spencer, in consideration of an allowance of £200 a year. He was a good actor and agreeable companion, but extravagant and indolent, the latter fault being hinted at in line 630. Davies in his ' Life of Garrick ' says that his defects were ' evidently owing to his great love of ease and his fondness for social pleasure.' Ross's ' Statira ' was Mrs. Palmer, daughter of Mrs. Pritchard. She was a somewhat stolid actress pushed into prominence by her mother.

⁶³³ Charles Macklin (1697-1797) was born in the north of Ireland and was originally a Roman Catholic. He ran away from home and became a servant in a public-house in the Borough frequented by mountebanks. After acting for a while at Bristol he appeared at Lincoln's Inn Theatre about 1725. In 1733 he made his first appearance at Drury Lane. In 1736 he joined Fielding's company at the Haymarket. He was a man of violent temper and killed a fellow actor in the green-room. He was, however, found guilty of manslaughter only. He was at first very friendly with Garrick, but having been made the scapegoat of the latter's quarrel with Fleetwood, manager of Drury Lane, he detested Garrick for the rest of his life. Macklin, dismissed from Drury Lane, began to give lessons in acting and elocution, and continued to do so even when he recommenced acting. His favourite character was Shylock and he has the credit of restoring Shakespeare's version of ' The Merchant of Venice ' to the stage. Macklin appeared in Dublin with Sheridan, and at Covent Garden. At the end of 1753 he quitted the stage and in the following year opened a tavern in the Covent Garden Piazza. In November, 1754, he started, in Hart Street, a lecture and debating society called the British Inquisition. Early in the following year he was declared bankrupt and returned to the stage. In 1761 and 1763 he was in Dublin, where he played in a work of his own. It should be noted that Churchill knew of Macklin chiefly as a lecturer. In 1772, long after Churchill's death, he appeared at Covent Garden as Macbeth, playing the part in Scottish costume instead of the military uniform of his own

Who wantonly transgresses Nature's bounds,
Whose acting's hard, affected, and constrain'd,
Whose features, as each other they disdain'd,
At variance set, inflexible, and coarse,
Ne'er know the workings of united force,
Ne'er kindly soften to each other's aid,
Nor show the mingled powers of light and shade,   640
No longer for a thankless stage concern'd,
To worthier thoughts his mighty genius turn'd,
Harangued, gave lectures, made each simple elf
Almost as good a speaker as himself,
Whilst the whole town, mad with mistaken zeal,
An awkward rage for elocution feel ;
Dull cits and grave divines his praise proclaim,
And join with Sheridan's their Macklin's name.
Shuter, who never cared a single pin
Whether he left out nonsense, or put in,   650
Who aim'd at wit, though levell'd in the dark,
The random arrow seldom hit the mark,
At Islington, all by the placid stream
Where City swains in lap of Dulness dream,
Where, quiet as her strains, their strains do flow,
That all the patron by the bards may know,
Secret as night, with Rolt's experienced aid,

time, as Garrick did. In 1789 Macklin left the stage for ever. For the
remaining eight years of his life he was senile.

⁶⁴⁸ Thomas Sheridan (1719-1788), the biographer of Swift and
father of Richard Brinsley Sheridan, was educated at Westminster, and
took a degree at Trinity College, Dublin. He appeared as Richard III.
in the Smock Alley Theatre in January, 1743, and next year acted at
Drury Lane. He was twice manager of the Dublin theatre, but the
competition of Barry decided him to settle in London. His lectures
on elocution were well received, not only in London but at Bristol,
Bath, Edinburgh, and at Oxford and Cambridge. As an actor his
range was not great. George Anne Bellamy, who acted with
him, declares that he was ' truly capital . . . in all *sententious*
characters.'

⁶⁴⁹ Edward Shuter. (See note on line 29.)

⁶⁵³ ' At Islington,' *i.e.* at Sadler's Wells Theatre, owned by Rosa-
mon, with Richard Rolt as director. The ' placid stream ' was the
new canal.

⁶⁵⁷ Richard Rolt (*c.* 1725-1770) was a miscellaneous writer who
wrote innumerable songs and libretti for Vauxhall, Sadler's Wells, etc.,

The plan of future operations laid,
Projected schemes the summer months to cheer,
And spin out happy folly through the year.   660
    But think not, though these dastard chiefs are fled,
That Covent Garden troops shall want a head ;
Harlequin comes their chief !—See from afar
The hero seated in fantastic car !
Wedded to Novelty, his only arms
Are wooden swords, wands, talismans and charms ;
On one side Folly sits, by some call'd Fun,
And on the other his arch-patron, Lun ;
Behind, for liberty a-thirst in vain,
Sense, helpless captive, drags the galling chain ;   670
Six rude, mis-shapen beasts the chariot draw,

as well as poems, pamphlets, histories, and ' A New Dictionary of
Trade and Commerce.' His writings were without any spark of in-
spiration, but the story (which Tooke repeats) of his having published
in Ireland the works of Akenside as his own, is now discredited. Tooke
seems to have a particular dislike of the man and calls him ' a poor low
creature, by profession a hackney writer to an attorney, and afterwards a
drudge to booksellers,as often as they would trust him with employment.'

    [668] John Rich (*c*. 1682-1761), on the death of his father, Christopher
Rich, in 1714, came into part possession of the new theatre then being
built in Lincoln's Inn Fields. His company consisted of seceders from
Drury Lane, but the latter house still possessed strong enough talent to
remain the better place of entertainment, and Rich was compelled in
1716 to introduce a performance, based on Italian models, which soon
developed into pantomime. In 1716 Rich, under the stage name of
Lun, appeared as Harlequin, Punch and Scaramouch being played by
actors named Shaw and Thurmond. From 1717 till 1760 Rich pro-
duced a pantomime annually and was so successful that Drury Lane
was compelled to imitate him in self-defence. In 1723 both houses
produced a pantomime based on the story of Dr. Faustus, and Rich
later brought out ' Harlequin, a Sorcerer.' The main attraction of these
pieces lay in their ' transformation scenes.' In 1728 Rich had an
enormous success with ' The Beggar's Opera,' and set to work to
build a new theatre in Covent Garden. The house was opened late
in 1732, and became a formidable rival to Drury Lane. Garrick
appeared at Covent Garden during the two seasons of 1746 and 1747,
and then removed to Drury Lane, where he remained for the rest of
his life. On Rich's death he was succeeded as manager of Covent
Garden by his son-in-law John Beard. The peculiarity of Rich's
Harlequinade lay in the abolition of speech. Everything was expressed
by gesture, and in this Rich was unrivalled. Churchill, however,
regarded pantomime as the prostitution of the stage. Rich was an
illiterate and somewhat muddle-headed man, but good company. He
was the founder of the Beefsteak Society.

Whom Reason loaths, and Nature never saw ;
Monsters, with tails of ice and heads of fire ;
' Gorgons, and Hydras, and Chimeras dire.'
Each was bestrode by full as monstrous wight,
Giant, dwarf, genius, elf, hermaphrodite.
The Town, as usual, met him in full cry ;
The Town, as usual, knew no reason why :
But Fashion so directs, and Moderns raise
On Fashion's mould'ring base their transient praise.   680
   Next, to the field a band of females draw
Their force, for Britain owns no Salique law :
Just to their worth, we female rights admit,
Nor bar their claim to empire or to wit.
   First, giggling, plotting, chamber-maids arrive,
Hoydens and romps, led on by General Clive.
In spite of outward blemishes, she shone,
For humour famed, and humour all her own :
Easy, as if at home, the stage she trod,
Nor sought the critic's praise, nor fear'd his rod :   690
Original in spirit and in ease,
She pleased by hiding all attempts to please :
No comic actress ever yet could raise,
On humour's base, more merit or more praise.
   With all the native vigour of sixteen,
Among the merry troop conspicuous seen,

[686] Catherine Clive (1711-1785), better known as Kitty Clive, was
the daughter of William Raftor, an Irish gentleman who had lost his
estates owing to his devotion to James II., and had become a lawyer in
Kilkenny. Catherine was uneducated and somewhat coarse-mannered,
but graceful and high-spirited. She came to the notice of Colley
Cibber and was soon successful at Drury Lane. Her reputation was
completely established in 1731 by her performance of Nell in Coffey's
' The Devil to Pay.' She married a barrister named Clive, but was
soon separated from her husband. However, her private life is
universally admitted to have been exemplary. She played at Drury
Lane until 1741, and in that year was ill-advised enough to play Portia
to Macklin's Shylock, turning the character into a comic part. She
did not realise that she was unfitted for ' genteel comedy ' as well as
for tragedy. She remained with Garrick at Drury Lane from 1746
until 1769, and often tried his temper to the utmost. However, he
had a great respect for her and regretted her retirement. Horace
Walpole delighted in her outspokenness and made her a present of
a house at Strawberry Hill. Johnson declared that ' in the sprightli-
ness of humour I have never seen her equalled.'

See lively Pope advance in jig, and trip
Corinna, Cherry, Honeycomb, and Snip :
Not without art, but yet to Nature true,
She charms the town with humour just, yet new :   700
Cheer'd by her promise, we the less deplore
The fatal time when Clive shall be no more.
   Lo ! Vincent comes—with simple grace array'd,
She laughs at paltry arts, and scorns parade :
Nature through her is by reflection shown,
Whilst Gay once more knows Polly for his own.
   Talk not to me of diffidence and fear—
I see it all, but must forgive it here ;
Defects like these, which modest terrors cause,
From Impudence itself extort applause.   710
Candour and Reason still take Virtue's part ;
We love e'en foibles in so good a heart.
   Let Tommy Arne, with usual pomp of style,

---

[697] Miss Jane Pope (1742-1818) was the daughter of the wigmaker to Drury Lane Theatre, and at fourteen years of age she appeared in Garrick's ' Lilliput ' (December 3rd, 1756). In 1759 she was definitely launched on her career, during the whole of which she remained at Drury Lane. Her last appearance was on May 26th, 1808. Her ' line ' was the pert soubrette, and her most famous part was that of Mrs. Heidelberg in ' The Clandestine Marriage.' Churchill saw the very budding of her comic talent, for she was barely nineteen when ' The Rosciad ' appeared.

[698] Corinna : a character in ' The Confederacy.'
    Cherry : the landlord's daughter in ' The Beaux' Stratagem.'
    Honeycomb : Polly Honeycomb in the farce of that name.
    Snip : a character in ' Harlequin's Invasion,' a speaking pantomime.

[703] Mrs. Vincent, afterwards Mrs. Mills (died 1811). The general opinion was not so favourable as Churchill's. Gray says : ' She had (while she was Miss Burchell) a fine voice, but never learnt to sing well. She was a very poor Actress and particularly in this part ' (*i.e.* as Polly Peachum).

[706] The creator of the part of Polly Peachum in ' The Beggar's Opera' was Miss Fenton, afterwards Duchess of Bolton.

[713] Thomas Augustine Arne (1710-1778), the composer, was the son of an upholsterer in King Street, Covent Garden. His father wished him to be a lawyer but yielded to his obvious vocation for music. Young Arne trained his sister (later Mrs. Cibber) for the operatic stage, and he wrote a number of works for the theatre, including the settings of ' Dido and Æneas ' (1734), ' Comus ' (1738), Congreve's

32

Whose chief, whose only merit's to compile,
Who, meanly pilfering here and there a bit,
Deals music out as Murphy deals out wit,
Publish proposals, laws for taste prescribe,
And chaunt the praise of an Italian tribe ;
Let him reverse kind Nature's first decrees,
And teach e'en Brent a method not to please ;   720
But never shall a truly British age
Bear a vile race of eunuchs on the stage ;
The boasted work's call'd National in vain,
If one Italian voice pollutes the strain.
Where tyrants rule, and slaves with joy obey,
Let slavish minstrels pour the enervate lay ;
To Britons far more noble pleasures spring,
In native notes, whilst Beard and Vincent sing.
    Might figure give a title unto fame,

'Judgment of Paris' (1740) and Mallet's 'Alfred' (1740), the latter containing the famous 'Rule Britannia.' He wrote also an immense number of songs for Vauxhall, Ranelagh, etc., and a number of oratorios. In 1760, having quarrelled with Garrick, he transferred his services to the rival house of Covent Garden.

[718] 'an Italian tribe,' *i.e.* the castrati or eunuch singers in Italian opera. (See note on 'The Times,' line 235.)

[720] Charlotte Brent (died 1802) was Arne's most distinguished pupil and he composed for her a number of bravura airs. She appeared in one of the chief parts of his 'Thomas and Sally,' produced at Covent Garden in 1760, and in his 'Artaxerxes' (1762). In 1766 she became the second wife of Thomas Pinto. She died in poverty.

[723] 'The opera of Artaxerxes was first acted in 1762 under the popular title of an English Opera, the music of it was particularly excellent, although the words were most wretchedly done into English from the Italian of Metastasio. . . . The necessity of introducing two Italian singers . . . gave displeasure to a true born English audience.' (Tooke.)

[728] John Beard (*c.* 1716-1791) was already known as a singer when he appeared as an actor at Drury Lane in 1737. Shortly afterwards he married Lady Henrietta Herbert, only daughter of James, first Earl of Waldegrave, and retired for a while from the stage. She died in 1753, and six years later Beard married Charlotte Rich, daughter of the manager of Covent Garden Theatre. Macheath in 'The Beggar's Opera' was one of Beard's favourite parts and he played it to the Polly Peachum of Mrs. Clive, Miss Macklin and Miss Brent. When Rich died, Beard undertook the management of Covent Garden. He retired in 1767. He was a friendly, popular man, and at one time president of the Beefsteak Club.

What rival should with Yates dispute her claim ?   730
But justice may not partial trophies raise,
Nor sink the actress in the woman's praise.
Still hand in hand her words and actions go,
And the heart feels more than the features show ;
For, through the regions of that beauteous face,
We no variety of passions trace ;
Dead to the soft emotions of the heart,
No kindred softness can those eyes impart :
The brow, still fix'd in sorrow's sullen frame,
Void of distinction, marks all parts the same.   740
  What's a fine person, or a beauteous face,
Unless deportment gives them decent grace ?
Bless'd with all other requisites to please,
Some want the striking elegance of ease ;
The curious eye their awkward movement tires :
They seem like puppets led about by wires.
Others, like statues, in one posture still,
Give great ideas of the workman's skill ;
Wond'ring, his art we praise the more we view,
And only grieve he gave not motion too.   750

[730] Mary Ann Yates (1728-1787), sometimes called Anna Maria Yates, was the daughter of a ship's steward named William Graham. She is said to have attempted the stage unsuccessfully in 1752 when she was engaged by Sheridan in Dublin. She first appeared at Drury Lane in 1753. Her powers developed under the tuition of her husband, Richard Yates, and of Murphy. She remained at Drury Lane until 1767 (*i.e.* beyond the period of Churchill's theatre-going), playing in both tragedy and comedy. Her parts included Mrs. Marwood, Zara, Mrs. Sullen, Cleopatra, Imogen, Desdemona, etc. In October, 1767, she appeared as Jane Shore at Covent Garden, returning to Drury Lane in 1774 as Electra in ' Orestes.' Mrs. Yates was primarily a tragic actress. Her beauty was of the statuesque and ' noble ' type, and some critics found her delivery monotonous. She had indeed been impressed by the French *tirade* as delivered by Mme. Clairon ; yet from the retirement of Mrs. Cibber to the emergence of Mrs. Siddons she was probably supreme in English tragedy. Yates was extremely angry at Churchill's criticism of his wife. Davies says : ' he invited Churchill to a tavern, it was supposed, with an intent either to expostulate with him on his behaviour, or to discuss the matter in a more decisive manner. . . . Mr. George Garrick, hearing what was the purpose of their withdrawing, ran to the place of meeting : he found them extremely enraged ; but by good fortune he reconciled the contending parties with a hearty bottle.'—(' Life of Garrick,' 1780 edition, vol. I., p. 320.)

Weak of themselves are what we beauties call ;
It is the manner which gives strength to all ;
This teaches every beauty to unite,
And brings them forward in the noblest light :
Happy in this, behold, amidst the throng,
With transient gleam of grace, Hart sweeps along.
    If all the wonders of external grace,
A person finely turn'd, a mould of face,
Where, union rare, expression's lively force
With beauty's softest magic holds discourse,   760
Attract the eye ; if feelings void of art
Rouse the quick passions, and inflame the heart ;
If music, sweetly breathing from the tongue,
Captives the ear, Bride must not pass unsung.
    When fear, which rank ill-nature terms conceit,
By time and custom conquer'd, shall retreat ;
When judgment, tutor'd by experience sage,
Shall shoot abroad, and gather strength from age ;
When Heaven, in mercy, shall the stage release
From the dull slumbers of a still-life piece ;   770
When some stale flower, disgraceful to the walk,
Which long hath hung, though wither'd, on the stalk,
Shall kindly drop, then Bride shall make her way,
And merit find a passage to the day ;

[756] Mrs. Hart ' was the daughter of a respectable tradesman in St.
James's, from whose house she eloped with a favoured lover, and
afterwards by the elegance of her figure obtained an engagement at
Covent Garden ; but being possessed of no other claim to public favour,
she grew tired of the insignificance of her theatrical character, and
quitting the stage, took no further pains to support any character at all.'
(' Thespian Dictionary,' 1805.) Tooke continues : ' She then married
one Reddish, an inferior actor, who was induced to take her for the
sake of an annuity of £200, settled on her by a former admirer.'
    [764] Churchill's susceptibility to the beauty of this actress seems to
have blunted his critical faculty. Gray says : ' She was a pretty and
innocent girl ; her principal part was Imogen in Cymbeline.' How-
ever, she did not remain innocent long, for she attracted the attention of
John Calcraft (see note on the ' Epistle to Hogarth,' line 205), the lover
of George Anne Bellamy, and by him had several children. Calcraft
left Miss Bride a large sum of money as well as two annuities, one of
£1,000 and one of £500. The second of these she forfeited by
marrying.
    [771] An allusion to Mrs. Palmer, daughter of Mrs. Pritchard, who
owed her position on the stage entirely to her mother.

Brought into action, she at once shall raise
Her own renown, and justify our praise.
  Form'd for the tragic scene, to grace the stage
With rival excellence of love and rage,
Mistress of each soft art, with matchless skill
To turn and wind the passions as she will ;   780
To melt the heart with sympathetic woe,
Awake the sigh, and teach the tear to flow ;
To put on frenzy's wild, distracted glare,
And freeze the soul with horror and despair ;
With just desert enroll'd in endless fame,
Conscious of worth superior, Cibber came.
  When poor Alicia's madd'ning brains are rack'd,
And strongly imaged griefs her mind distract,
Struck with her grief, I catch the madness too ;
My brain turns round, the headless trunk I view !   790
The roof cracks, shakes, and falls !—new horrors rise,
And Reason buried in the ruin lies.
  Nobly disdainful of each slavish art,
She makes her first attack upon the heart ;
Pleased with the summons, it receives her laws,
And all is silence, sympathy, applause.
  But when, by fond ambition drawn aside,
Giddy with praise, and puff'd with female pride,
She quits the tragic scene, and, in pretence
To comic merit breaks down nature's fence,   800
I scarcely can believe my ears or eyes,
Or find out Cibber through the dark disguise.

[786] Mrs. Susannah Maria Cibber (1712-1766) was the daughter of a Roman Catholic upholsterer in King Street, Covent Garden, and the sister of the celebrated Dr. Arne. She appeared first (in 1732) as a singer in Lampe's ' Amelia,' a serious opera ' set in the Italian manner.' In 1734 she married Theophilus Cibber, whose father, Colley Cibber, trained her as an actress. She came out as Zara in ' The Mourning Bride ' in 1736, and among other parts played Ophelia, Juliet, and Constance. In sprightly comedy and in *grande dame* parts she was a comparative failure, but she was much appreciated by the public in *ingénue* rôles, and she preserved her figure and good looks to the end. Her worthless husband sold her (with her consent) to a wealthy protector with whom she was very happy. She was buried in the cloisters of Westminster Abbey.

[787] Alicia : a character in ' Jane Shore.'

Pritchard, by Nature for the stage design'd,
In person graceful, and in sense refined ;
Her art as much as Nature's friend became,
Her voice as free from blemish as her fame ;
Who knows so well in majesty to please,
Attemper'd with the graceful charms of ease ?
When Congreve's favour'd pantomime to grace,
She comes a captive queen of Moorish race ;   810
When love, hate, jealousy, despair and rage,
With wildest tumults in her breast engage,
Still equal to herself is Zara seen ;
Her passions are the passions of a Queen.
When she to murder whets the tim'rous thane,
I feel ambition rush through every vein ;
Persuasion hangs upon her daring tongue,
My heart grows flint, and every nerve's new strung.
In comedy—' Nay, there,' cries Critic, ' hold ;
Pritchard's for comedy too fat and old :   820
Who can, with patience, bear the gray coquette,
Or force a laugh with over-grown Julett ?
Her speech, look, action, humour, all are just,
But then her age and figure give disgust.'
Are foibles then, and graces of the mind,

[803] Mrs. Hannah Pritchard (died 1768) was acting in the suburban fairs as early as 1733 and soon after had established herself in the regular theatres, creating such important rôles as Selima in ' Zara,' Tag in ' Miss in her Teens,' Mrs. Beverley in ' The Gamester,' and Clarinda in ' The Wedding Day.' She was also very successful as Hecuba, Hermione, Lady Macbeth, Queen Katherine and Queen Gertrude. She was excellent in comedy (her Millamant being particularly admired) but in tragedy she had a tendency to rant. She had been at Drury Lane for nearly ten years before Garrick appeared there, and he was jealous of her success when she played Beatrice to his Benedick. Her final performance was on April 24th, 1768, when she played Lady Macbeth to Garrick's Macbeth. She retired to Bath and died in the following August. She was a coarse, big-boned woman with plain features, but had a clear and well-modulated voice. Her private life was above reproach.

[809] *i.e.* ' The Mourning Bride.'

[813] Zara : a character in Congreve's ' The Mourning Bride.' In her part occur the famous lines :
      ' Hell has no rage like love to hatred turned,
        Nor hell a fury like a woman scorned.'

[822] Julett, Alinda's maid, a character in ' The Pilgrim ' of Beaumont and Fletcher.

In real life, to size or age confined ?
Do spirits flow, and is good-breeding placed
In any set circumference of waist ?
As we grow old, doth affectation cease,
Or gives not age new vigour to caprice ?   830
If in originals these things appear,
Why should we bar them in the copy here ?
The nice punctilio-mongers of this age,
The grand, minute reformers of the stage,
Slaves to propriety of every kind,
Some standard measure for each part should find,
Which when the best of actors shall exceed,
Let it devolve to one of smaller breed.
All Actors, too, upon the back should bear
Certificate of birth ;—time, when ;—place, where ;   840
For how can critics rightly fix their worth,
Unless they know the minute of their birth ?
An audience, too, deceived, may find, too late,
That they have clapp'd an actor out of date.
    Figure, I own, at first may give offence,
And harshly strike the eye's too curious sense ;
But when perfections of the mind break forth,
Humour's chaste sallies, judgment's solid worth ;
When the pure genuine flame by Nature taught,
Springs into sense and every action's thought ;   850
Before such merit all objections fly ;
Pritchard's genteel, and Garrick's six feet high.
    Oft have I, Pritchard, seen thy wond'rous skill,
Confess'd thee great, but find thee greater still ;
That worth, which shone in scatter'd rays before,
Collected now, breaks forth with double power.
The Jealous Wife ! on that thy trophies raise,
Inferior only to the author's praise.
    From Dublin, famed in legends of romance
For mighty magic of enchanted lance,   860
With which her heroes arm'd victorious prove,
And, like a flood, rush o'er the land of Love,

---

[857] ' The Jealous Wife,' by George Colman the Elder, first acted in
1761, is founded upon the episode in Fielding's ' Tom Jones ' where
Sophia takes refuge with Lady Bellaston.

Mossop and Barry came.—Names ne'er design'd
By Fate in the same sentence to be join'd.
Raised by the breath of popular acclaim,
They mounted to the pinnacle of fame ;
There the weak brain, made giddy with the height,
Spurr'd on the rival chiefs to mortal fight.
Thus sportive boys around some basin's brim
Behold the pipe-drawn bladders circling swim ;   870
But if, from lungs more potent, there arise
Two bubbles of a more than common size,
Eager for honour, they for fight prepare,
Bubble meets bubble, and both sink to air.
   Mossop, attach'd to military plan,
Still kept his eye fix'd on his right-hand man ;
Whilst the mouth measures words with seeming skill,
The right hand labours, and the left lies still ;
For he resolved on scripture-grounds to go,
What the right doth, the left-hand shall not know.   880
With studied impropriety of speech
He soars beyond the hackney critic's reach ;

[875] Henry Mossop (*c.* 1729-*c.* 1774) was educated at Trinity College,
Dublin, and being refused by both Garrick and Rich, engaged himself
with Sheridan at Smock Alley, where he appeared on November 28th,
1749, as Zanga in ' The Revenge.' In 1751 he appeared at Drury Lane
as Richard III., in which part he was much applauded. He played
many other tragic parts at Drury Lane during the 'fifties, but having
been estranged from Garrick by Fitzpatrick, he went to Dublin,
played with Barry at Crow Street, and then opened Smock Alley
Theatre in opposition. This resulted in the ruin of both houses.
After the retirement of Barry, Mossop controlled both Dublin theatres,
but with little financial success. Returning to London in 1771, he
was arrested for debt. He was too proud to solicit Garrick's help, and
Mrs. Barry, at Covent Garden, refused to act with him. He died in
1773 or 1774, of a broken heart and in possession of $4\frac{1}{2}d$. Churchill's
opinion is borne out by Davies (' Life of Garrick ') when he says :
' Mossop was rather a powerful speaker than pleasing actor,' but adds,
' With all his defects, Mossop was, after Garrick and Barry, the most
applauded and valuable actor on the stage.' His enemies called him
the ' teapot actor,' in allusion to his habit of standing with one hand on
his hip and the other extended.

[882] The word ' hackney ' was originally applied only to ordinary
riding horses as distinguished from war-horses, draught-horses, or
hunters. A hackney-horse, by a natural transition, came to mean a
horse that could be hired. A hackney critic is therefore a hireling
critic, a hack.

To epithets allots emphatic state,
Whilst principals, ungraced, like lackeys, wait ;
In ways first trodden by himself excels,
And stands alone in indeclinables ;
Conjunction, preposition, adverb, join
To stamp new vigour on the nervous line ;
In monosyllables his thunders roll,
He, she, it, and, we, ye, they, fright the soul.   890
   In person taller than the common size,
Behold where Barry draws admiring eyes !
When labouring passions, in his bosom pent,
Convulsive, rage, and struggling heave for vent,
Spectators, with imagined terrors warm,
Anxious expect the bursting of the storm ;
But, all unfit in such a pile to dwell,
His voice comes forth, like Echo from her cell,
To swell the tempest needful aid denies,
And all adown the stage in feeble murmurs dies.   900
   What man, like Barry, with such pains, can err
In elocution, action, character ?
What man could give, if Barry was not here,
Such well applauded tenderness to Lear ?
Who else can speak so very, very fine,
That sense may kindly end with every line ?

[892] Spranger Barry (1719-1777) was born in Dublin and was brought
up as a silversmith. On his bankruptcy he took to the stage and
appeared at the Theatre Royal in Smock Alley, Dublin, on February
15th, 1744. Barry was very handsome and had a good voice. He
played Lear, Henry V., Orestes, Hotspur, and other important
characters, and was much admired. On October 4th, 1746, he ap-
peared as Othello at Drury Lane, and soon afterwards had the honour
of appearing alternately with Garrick in ' Hamlet ' and ' Macbeth.'
After a quarrel with Garrick in 1750 he migrated to the rival house of
Covent Garden, taking Mrs. Cibber (the Juliet to his Romeo) with him.
Garrick and Barry now competed for public favour in the character
of Romeo, Garrick replacing Mrs. Cibber with the young actress
George Anne Bellamy. The advantage in this contest did not lie
entirely with Garrick. In company with Woodward, Barry went into
management in Dublin but, having lost his money, was compelled to
return to London, where he appeared at the Haymarket under Foote.
In 1768 Barry married Mrs. Dancer and both were engaged by Garrick
at Drury Lane. Both husband and wife, however, went over to Covent
Garden in October, 1774. For the last few years of his life he was
crippled with gout.

Some dozen lines before the ghost is there,
Behold him for the solemn scene prepare :
See how he frames his eyes, poises each limb,
Puts the whole body into proper trim :—   910
From whence we learn, with no great stretch of art,
Five lines hence comes a ghost, and, ha ! a start.
When he appears most perfect, still we find
Something which jars upon and hurts the mind :
Whatever lights upon a part are thrown,
We see too plainly they are not his own :
No flame from Nature ever yet he caught,
Nor knew a feeling which he was not taught :
He raised his trophies on the base of art,
And conn'd his passions, as he conn'd his part.   920
    Quin, from afar, lured by the scent of fame,
A stage leviathan, put in his claim,

[921] James Quin (1693-1766), the illegitimate son of an Irish barrister,
was born in King Street, Covent Garden, but was educated in Dublin.
He made his first appearance on the stage at Smock Alley and may
have acted at Drury Lane as early as 1714. In 1716 he understudied
Mills as Bajazet in ' Tamerlane,' and, his principal falling ill, acted the
part to great applause. After playing a number of important parts at
Drury Lane, he migrated in 1718 to the theatre in Lincoln's Inn Fields,
where he remained for fourteen years, playing Falstaff, King Henry IV.,
Buckingham, Lear, and many other tragic parts. When Covent
Garden opened in 1732 Quin was one of its most important actors, but
in 1734 he removed to Drury Lane, where he played Richard III.,
Antonio in ' The Merchant of Venice,' etc. After a visit to Dublin in
1741 he re-appeared at Covent Garden and remained there for the rest
of his career. In 1746 began his rivalry with Garrick, both playing at
first at Covent Garden. On Garrick's removal to Drury Lane the
rivalry was intensified, Quin representing the old rhetorical school of
acting, wearing plumes and a tragedy costume like a ballet-skirt, while
Garrick was more naturalistic both in dress and delivery. Quin's last
performance as a paid actor was in 1751, after which he retired to Bath,
where he died at the beginning of 1766. Before his death he became
friendly with Garrick and often visited him at Hampton. Quin had
many good qualities. His courage once saved the life of Rich in a
theatre riot, and in his youth he fought two duels with fatal results to
his opponents. His generosity was great, and George Anne Bellamy
has left a pleasing picture of the gruff but good-hearted man who
frequently befriended her. He was very fond of good-living, and had
considerable wit, but was vain and quarrelsome. Churchill, who did
not like him, could only have seen him in performances which he gave
for the ' benefits ' of his friends.

[923] Thomas Betterton (c.1635-1710) is supposed to have begun to
act under Sir William Davenant about 1656, a hundred years before

Pupil of Betterton and Booth. Alone,
Sullen he walk'd, and deem'd the chair his own :
For how should moderns, mushrooms of the day,
Who ne'er those masters knew, know how to play ?
Gray-bearded veterans, who, with partial tongue
Extol the times when they themselves were young ;
Who, having lost all relish for the stage,
See not their own defects, but lash the age,   930
Received, with joyful murmurs of applause,
Their darling chief, and lined his favourite cause.
    Far be it from the candid Muse to tread
Insulting o'er the ashes of the dead ;
But, just to living merit, she maintains,
And dares the test, whilst Garrick's genius reigns ;
Ancients, in vain, endeavour to excel,
Happily praised, if they could act as well.
But, though prescription's force we disallow,
Nor to antiquity submissive bow ;   940
Though we deny imaginary grace,
Founded on accidents of time and place,
Yet real worth of every growth shall bear
Due praise ; nor must we, Quin, forget thee there.
His words bore sterling weight ; nervous and strong,
In manly tides of sense they roll'd along :
Happy in art, he chiefly had pretence
To keep up numbers, yet not forfeit sense ;
No actor ever greater heights could reach
In all the labour'd artifice of speech.   950
    Speech ! is that all ?—And shall an actor found
An universal fame on partial ground ?
Parrots themselves speak properly by rote,
And, in six months, my dog shall howl by note.
I laugh at those who, when the stage they tread,

Churchill frequented the theatre. It is theforore sufficient to say that
he became the first actor of his age, playing Hamlet, Mercutio, Sir
Toby Belch and Macbeth, among many other parts. He produced a
number of dramatic works, mostly adaptations from other authors.
Barton Booth (1681-1733) was engaged by Betterton for the theatre
at Lincoln's Inn Fields, 1700-1704, and accompanied him to the new
Haymarket Theatre in 1705. His best parts were Brutus, Lear,
Henry VIII., Hotspur, and Pyrrhus in Philips's 'Distressed Mother.'

Neglect the heart, to compliment the head ;
With strict propriety their care 's confined
To weigh out words, while passion halts behind :
To syllable-dissectors they appeal ;
Allow them accent, cadence,—Fools may feel ;   960
But, spite of all the criticising elves,
Those who would make us feel, must feel themselves.

His eyes, in gloomy socket taught to roll,
Proclaim'd the sullen ' habit of his soul : '
Heavy and phlegmatic he trod the stage,
Too proud for tenderness, too dull for rage.
When Hector's lovely widow shines in tears,
Or Rowe's gay rake dependent virtue jeers,
With the same cast of features he is seen
To chide the libertine, and court the queen.   970
From the tame scene, which without passion flows,
With just desert his reputation rose ;
Nor less he pleased, when on some surly plan
He was at once the actor and the man.

In Brute he shone unequall'd : all agree
Garrick's not half so great a brute as he.
When Cato's labour'd scenes are brought to view,
With equal praise the actor labour'd too ;
For still you'll find, trace passions to their root,
Small difference 'twixt the Stoic and the Brute.   980
In fancied scenes, as in life's real plan,
He could not, for a moment, sink the man.

---

[962] ' ——Si vis me flere, dolendum est Primum ipsi tibi.'—HORACE,
Ars. Poet., 102, 3.

[964] The part of Zanga in ' The Revenge ' by Dr. Young was a
favourite with Quin, and contains the lines :
    ' Rage on, ye winds ; burst, clouds, and waters, roar.
    You bear a just resemblance to my fortune,
    And suit the gloomy habit of my soul.'

[967] Andromache in ' The Distressed Mother,' adapted by Ambrose
Philips from the ' Andromaque ' of Racine. It was first produced in 1712.

[968] Lothario (' gay Lothario ') in ' The Fair Penitent ' by Nicholas
Rowe (1674-1718).

[975] Sir John Brute, a character in Vanbrugh's ' The Provoked Wife.'

[977] Addison's ' Cato ' was written for the most part as early as 1703
but was not put upon the stage until April 14th, 1713, when it was
acted at Drury Lane with great applause and ran for twenty nights.

In whate'er cast his character was laid,
Self still, like oil, upon the surface play'd.
Nature, in spite of all his skill, crept in :
Horatio, Dorax, Falstaff,—still 'twas Quin.
Next follows Sheridan ;—a doubtful name,
As yet unsettled in the rank of fame :
This, fondly lavish in his praises grown,
Gives him all merit ; that allows him none ;   990
Between them both, we'll steer the middle course,
Nor, loving praise, rob Judgment of her force.
Just his conceptions, natural and great ;
His feelings strong, his words enforced with weight.
Was speech-famed Quin himself to hear him speak,
Envy would drive the colour from his cheek ;
But step-dame Nature, niggard of her grace,
Denied the social powers of voice and face.
Fix'd in one frame of features, glare of eye,
Passions, like chaos, in confusion lie :   1000
In vain the wonders of his skill are tried
To form distinctions Nature hath denied.
His voice no touch of harmony admits,
Irregularly deep, and shrill by fits.
The two extremes appear like man and wife,
Coupled together for the sake of strife.
    His action's always strong, but sometimes such,
That candour must declare he acts too much.
Why must impatience fall three paces back ?
Why paces three return to the attack ?   1010
Why is the right leg, too, forbid to stir,
Unless in motion semicircular ?
Why must the hero with the Nailor vie,
And hurl the close-clench'd fist at nose or eye ?
In royal John, with Philip angry grown,

---

[986] Horatio in 'The Fair Penitent.' Dorax, in Dryden's 'Don Sebastian.'

[987] Thomas Sheridan. (See note on line 648.)

[1013] A prize-fighter of the period.

[1015] ' King John,' with Sheridan in the part of John, and Davies in that of Philip of France, was produced at Drury Lane, December 17th, 1760. (For Davies, see note on line 319.)

I thought he would have knock'd poor Davies down.
Inhuman tyrant ! was it not a shame
To fright a king so harmless and so tame ?
But, spite of all defects, his glories rise,
And art, by judgment form'd, with nature vies.   1020
Behold him sound the depth of Hubert's soul,
Whilst in his own contending passions roll ;
View the whole scene, with critic judgment scan,
And then deny him merit if you can.
Where he falls short, 'tis Nature's fault alone ;
Where he succeeds, the merit's all his own.
   Last Garrick came.—Behind him throng a train
Of snarling critics, ignorant as vain.

[1027] David Garrick (1717-1779), the most famous actor in the history
of the English stage, was the son of an Army captain and was born at
the Angel Inn, Hereford, where his father was quartered. The father
was of French Huguenot extraction, the mother Irish.   David was
educated at Lichfield, was for a time a pupil of Johnson, and travelled
with the latter to London.   Aided by a legacy of £1,000 from an uncle,
he set up as a wine-merchant, but his love of the stage caused him to
take up acting, first as an amateur, then as a professional. After some
success in Gifford's company at Ipswich he appeared (on October
19th, 1741) at Goodman's Fields as Richard III.   His success in this
and other parts was immediate, and in 1742 he appeared (after a short
preliminary engagement at Smock Alley, Dublin) at Drury Lane. Here
he was equally successful, although his estrangement from Macklin
(see note on line 633) was productive of some demonstrations of
hostility.   In 1746, after another season in Dublin, he appeared at
Covent Garden as Hamlet, Richard III., Othello, Macbeth, etc.   In
1747 he became joint-manager of Drury Lane, where he remained until
his retirement in 1776.   In 1749 he married Eva Marie Violetti, a
dancer.   The rivalry of Covent Garden was intense and Garrick's ruin
confidently predicted.   He was indeed compelled to imitate the
Harlequinades at Drury Lane with an entertainment called ' Queen
Mab ' in which Woodward (see note on line 369) played Harlequin.
Garrick's company in 1760, when Churchill was meditating ' The
Rosciad,' included Havard, Palmer, Yates, King, O'Brien, Mrs. Yates,
Mrs. Pritchard, Mrs. Clive and others.   The Fizzgiggo riots (see note
on line 117) disturbed the season of 1762-63, and in September of the
latter year Garrick decided to take a holiday.   He went, with his wife,
to Paris, where he was very well received, and thence to Lyons, Turin,
Rome, Naples, Venice, etc.   He was back in Paris in October, 1764,
and in September, 1765, was acting again at Drury Lane, where he was
received with immense enthusiasm.   In 1769 he projected and carried
out the ill-starred Shakespeare Festival at Stratford.   He took leave of
his public on June 10th, 1776, in his favourite part of Don Felix in
' The Wonder,' and sold his share of the patent to R. B. Sheridan and
others for £35,000.   He died on January 15th, 1779, and was buried in

One finds out,—' He's of stature somewhat low—
Your hero always should be tall you know,—   1030
True natural greatness all consists in height,'
Produce your voucher, Critic.—' Serjeant Kite.'
   Another can't forgive the paltry arts
By which he makes his way to shallow hearts ;
Mere pieces of finesse, traps for applause.—
' Avaunt ! unnatural start, affected pause.'
   For me, by Nature form'd to judge with phlegm,
I can't acquit by wholesale, nor condemn.
The best things carried to excess are wrong ;
The start may be too frequent, pause too long ;   1040
But, only used in proper time and place,
Severest judgment must allow them grace.
   If bunglers, form'd on Imitation's plan,
Just in the way that monkeys mimic man,
Their copied scene with mangled arts disgrace,
And pause and start with the same vacant face,
We join the critic laugh ; those tricks we scorn
Which spoil the scenes they mean them to adorn ;
But when, from Nature's pure and genuine source,
These strokes of acting flow with generous force,   1050
When in the features all the soul's portray'd,
And passions, such as Garrick's, are display'd,
To me they seem from quickest feelings caught,
Each start is nature, and each pause is thought.
   When reason yields to passion's wild alarms,
And the whole state of man is up in arms,
What but a critic could condemn the player
For pausing here, when cool sense pauses there ?
Whilst, working from the heart, the fire I trace,
And mark it strongly flaming to the face ;   1060
Whilst in each sound I hear the very man,
I can't catch words, and pity those who can.

Westminster Abbey. Garrick wrote (or altered and adapted) numerous
plays as well as a great many prologues, epilogues, and occasional
verses.

   [1032] Sergeant Kite : the recruiting sergeant in Farquhar's ' The
Recruiting Officer.' Garrick first played this part at Lichfield at the
age of eleven.

Let wits, like spiders, from the tortured brain
Fine-draw the critic-web with curious pain ;
The gods,—a kindness I with thanks must pay,—
Have form'd me of a coarser kind of clay,
Nor stung with envy, nor with spleen diseased,
A poor dull creature, still with Nature pleased :
Hence to thy praises, Garrick, I agree,
And, pleased with Nature, must be pleased with thee.   1070
   Now might I tell, how silence reign'd throughout,
And deep attention hush'd the rabble rout ;
How every claimant, tortured with desire,
Was pale as ashes, or as red as fire ;
But loose to fame, the Muse more simply acts,
Rejects all flourish, and relates mere facts.
   The judges, as the several parties came,
With temper heard, with judgment weigh'd each claim,
And, in their sentence happily agreed,
In name of both great Shakespeare thus decreed :   1080
  ' If manly sense, if Nature link'd with art ;
If thorough knowledge of the human heart ;
If powers of acting vast and unconfined ;
If fewest faults with greatest beauties join'd ;
If strong expression, and strange powers which lie
Within the magic circle of the eye ;
If feelings which few hearts, like his, can know,
And which no face so well as his can show,
Deserve the preference ;—Garrick ! take the chair,
Nor quit it—till thou place an equal there.'   1090

THE APOLOGY
ADDRESSED TO
THE CRITICAL REVIEWERS*

Tristitiam et Metus
Tradam protervis in mare *Criticum* †
Portare ventis.
HORACE, Od. 26.

L AUGHS not the heart when giants, big with pride,
Assume the pompous port, the martial stride ;
O'er arm Herculean heave the enormous shield,
Vast as a weaver's beam the javelin wield ;
With the loud voice of thundering Jove defy
And dare to single combat—What ?—A fly.
   And laugh we less when giant names, which shine
Establish'd, as it were, by right divine,
Critics, whom every captive art adores,
To whom glad Science pours forth all her stores ;   10
Who high in letter'd reputation sit,
And hold, Astræa-like, the scales of wit,
With partial rage rush forth,—Oh ! shame to tell !
To crush a bard just bursting from the shell ?
   Great are his perils in this stormy time
Who rashly ventures on a sea of rhyme :
Around vast surges roll, winds envious blow,
And jealous rocks and quicksands lurk below :
Greatly his foes he dreads, but more his friends ;
He hurts me most who lavishly commends.   20
   Look through the world—in every other trade
The same employment's cause of kindness made,
At least appearance of good-will creates,
And every fool puffs off the fool he hates :

* First published in April, 1761, 'Printed for the Author, and sold by W. Flexney.'

† So printed in the 2nd, 5th, and 6th 4to editions ; evidently a pun is intended.

¹² Astræa was the goddess of Justice, daughter of the Titan Astræus and Eos, or of Zeus and Themis. In the Age of Bronze she departed from the earth and now shines in the sky as the constellation Virgo.

Cobblers with cobblers smoke away the night,
And in the common cause e'en players unite :
Authors alone, with more than savage rage,
Unnatural war with brother authors wage.
The pride of Nature would as soon admit
Competitors in empire as in wit ;   30
Onward they rush at Fame's imperious call,
And, less than greatest, would not be at all.
    Smit with the love of honour,—or the pence,—
O'errun with wit, and destitute of sense,
Should any novice in the rhyming trade
With lawless pen the realms of verse invade,
Forth from the court, where sceptred sages sit,
Abused with praise, and flatter'd into wit ;
Where in lethargic majesty they reign,
And what they won by dulness, still maintain,   40
Legions of factious authors throng at once,
Fool beckons fool, and dunce awakens dunce.
To Hamilton's the ready lies repair,—
Ne'er was lie made which was not welcome there—
Thence, on maturer judgment's anvil wrought,
The polish'd falsehood's into public brought.
Quick-circulating slanders mirth afford ;
And reputation bleeds in every word.
    A critic was of old a glorious name,
Whose sanction handed merit up to fame ;   50
Beauties as well as faults he brought to view,
His judgment great, and great his candour too ;
No servile rules drew sickly taste aside ;
Secure he walk'd, for Nature was his guide.
But now, O, strange reverse ! our critics bawl
In praise of candour with a heart of gall ;
Conscious of guilt, and fearful of the light,
They lurk enshrouded in the veil of night ;
Safe from detection, seize the unwary prey,
And stab, like bravoes, all who come that way.   60
    When first my Muse, perhaps more bold than wise,
Bade the rude trifle into light arise,

[43] Alexander Hamilton was the printer of ' The Critical Review.'
[59] Some editions have ' detraction ' for ' detection.'

Little she thought such tempests would ensue ;
Less, that those tempests would be raised by you.
The thunder's fury rends the towering oak,
Rosciads, like shrubs, might 'scape the fatal stroke.
Vain thought ! a critic's fury knows no bound ;
Drawcansir-like, he deals destruction round ;
Nor can we hope he will a stranger spare,
Who gives no quarter to his friend Voltaire.   70
  Unhappy Genius ! placed by partial Fate
With a free spirit in a slavish state ;
Where the reluctant Muse, oppress'd by kings,
Or droops in silence, or in fetters sings.
In vain thy dauntless fortitude hath borne
The bigot's furious zeal, and tyrant's scorn.
Why didst thou safe from home-bred dangers steer,
Reserved to perish more ignobly here ?
Thus, when, the Julian tyrant's pride to swell,
Rome with her Pompey at Pharsalia fell,   80
The vanquish'd chief escaped from Cæsar's hand,
To die by ruffians in a foreign land.
  How could these self-elected monarchs raise
So large an empire on so small a base ?
In what retreat, inglorious and unknown,
Did Genius sleep when Dulness seized the throne ?
Whence, absolute now grown, and free from awe,
She to the subject world dispenses law.
Without her license not a letter stirs,
And all the captive criss-cross-row is hers.   90
The Stagyrite, who rules from Nature drew,
Opinions gave, but gave his reasons too.

[68] Drawcansir is a boasting bully in Buckingham's ' The Rehearsal.'
   cf. ' But let not anger with such frenzy grow
      Drawcansir-like, to strike down friend and foe.'
          —R. LLOYD, ' Epistle to Churchill.'
  [70] Smollett superintended the translation of ' The Works of M. de
Voltaire,' in 38 vols., London, 1761-1764. Churchill suggests that the
work was done badly.
  [90] Criss-cross-row, otherwise Christ-cross-row, *i.e.* the alphabet,
so called from the cross prefixed to it in horn books—printed sheets
covered with horn and mounted on wood, for the use of young children.
  [91] Aristotle, who was born at Stagiras, a town in Macedonia.

Our great Dictators take a shorter way—
Who shall dispute what the Reviewers say ?
Their word's sufficient ; and to ask a reason,
In such a state as theirs, is downright treason.
True judgment now with them alone can dwell ;
Like Church of Rome, they're grown infallible.
Dull, superstitious readers they deceive,
Who pin their easy faith on critic's sleeve,   100
And, knowing nothing, every thing believe.
But why repine we that these puny elves
Shoot into giants ?—we may thank ourselves :
Fools that we are, like Israel's fools of yore,
The calf ourselves have fashion'd we adore.
But let true reason once resume her reign,
This god shall dwindle to a calf again.
    Founded on arts which shun the face of day,
By the same arts they still maintain their sway.
Wrapp'd in mysterious secrecy they rise,   110
And, as they are unknown, are safe and wise.
At whomsoever aim'd, howe'er severe,
The envenom'd slander flies, no names appear :
Prudence forbids that step ;—then all might know,
And on more equal terms engage the foe.
But now, what Quixote of the age would care
To wage a war with dirt, and fight with air !
By interest join'd, the expert confederates stand,
And play the game into each other's hand :
The vile abuse, in turn by all denied,   120
Is bandied up and down from side to side :
It flies—hey !—presto !—like a juggler's ball,
Till it belongs to nobody at all.
    All men and things they know, themselves unknown,
And publish every name—except their own.
Nor think this strange—secure from vulgar eyes,
The nameless author passes in disguise ;
But veteran critics are not so deceived,
If veteran critics are to be believed.
Once seen, they know an author evermore,   130
Nay, swear to hands they never saw before.
Thus in the Rosciad, beyond chance or doubt,

51

They by the writing found the writers out.
' That's Lloyd's—his manner there you plainly trace,
And all the Actor stares you in the face.
By Colman that was written—on my life,
The strongest symptoms of the Jealous Wife.
That little disingenuous piece of spite,
Churchill, a wretch unknown ! perhaps might write.'
How doth it make judicious readers smile,   140
When authors are detected by their style !
Though every one, who knows this author, knows
He shifts his style much oftener than his clothes.
    Whence could arise this mighty critic spleen,
The Muse a trifler, and her theme so mean ?
What had I done, that angry heaven should send
The bitterest foe where most I wish'd a friend ?
Oft hath my tongue been wanton at thy name,
And hail'd the honours of thy matchless fame.
For me let hoary Fielding bite the ground,   150
So nobler Pickle stand superbly bound ;
From Livy's temples tear th' historic crown,
Which with more justice blooms upon thine own.
Compared with thee, be all life-writers dumb,
But he who wrote the Life of Tommy Thumb.
Who ever read the Regicide, but swore
The author wrote as man ne'er wrote before ?
Others for plots and under-plots may call,
Here's the right method—have no plot at all.

[133] ' The Rosciad ' having been published anonymously gave rise to
much conjecture concerning its authorship, etc. It was generally sup-
posed that it was written by Colman or Lloyd, or both. Lloyd's poem
' The Actor ' was published in 1760 ; Colman's ' The Jealous Wife '
was produced at Drury Lane in February, 1761.

[150] Henry Fielding was born in 1707 and died in 1754. ' Hoary '
seems therefore a somewhat unsuitable epithet.

[151] ' Peregrine Pickle,' by Smollett, was published in 1751.

[152] Smollett's ' History of England ' had appeared in 1757.

[155] ' Tom Thumb the Great,' a burlesque by Fielding, was pro-
duced in 1730.

[156] ' The Regicide,' founded on the assassination of James I. of
Scotland, was written by Smollett very early in life. It was never
produced on the stage. He has given an account of his theatrical
ventures in the story of Melopoyne in ' Roderick Random.'

Who can so often in his cause engage   160
The tiny pathos of the Grecian stage,
Whilst horrors rise, and tears spontaneous flow
At tragic Ha ! and no less tragic Oh !
To praise his nervous weakness all agree,
And then, for sweetness, who so sweet as he !
Too big for utterance when sorrows swell,
The too big sorrows flowing tears must tell ;
But when those flowing tears shall cease to flow,
Why—then the voice must speak again, you know.
Rude and unskilful in the poet's trade,   170
I kept no Naïads by me ready made ;
Ne'er did I colours high in air advance,
Torn from the bleeding fopperies of France ;
No flimsy linsey-woolsey scenes I wrote,
With patches here and there, like Joseph's coat.
Me humbler themes befit : secure, for me,
Let play-wrights smuggle nonsense duty free ;
Secure, for me, ye lambs, ye lambkins ! bound,
And frisk and frolic o'er the fairy ground :
Secure, for me, thou pretty little fawn !   180
Lick Sylvia's hand, and crop the flowery lawn ;
Uncensured let the gentle breezes rove
Through the green umbrage of the enchanted grove :
Secure, for me, let foppish Nature smile,
And play the coxcomb in the Desert Isle.
The stage I chose—a subject fair and free—
'Tis yours—'tis mine—'tis public property.
All common exhibitions open lie
For praise or censure to the common eye.
Hence are a thousand hackney writers fed ;   190
Hence Monthly Critics earn their daily bread.
This is a general tax which all must pay,

[171] An allusion to Murphy's satire ' The Naïads of Fleet Ditch '
(1761).

[173] Murphy was a notorious plagiarist from the French. (See also
note on ' The Rosciad,' line 67.)

[185] ' The Desert Island,' by A. Murphy (1760). Founded on a
play by Metastasio.

[191] ' The Critical Review ' appeared monthly.

From those who scribble, down to those who play.
Actors, a venal crew, receive support
From public bounty for the public sport.
To clap or hiss all have an equal claim,
The cobbler's and his lordship's right the same.
All join for their subsistence ; all expect
Free leave to praise their worth, their faults correct.
When active Pickle Smithfield stage ascends,   200
The three days' wonder of his laughing friends,
Each, or as judgment or as fancy guides,
The lively witling praises or derides.
And where's the mighty difference, tell me where,
Betwixt a Merry Andrew and a player ?
The strolling tribe, a despicable race !
Like wandering Arabs, shift from place to place.
Vagrants by law, to justice open laid,
They tremble, of the beadle's lash afraid ;
And, fawning, cringe for wretched means of life   210
To Madam Mayoress, or his Worship's wife.
The mighty monarch, in theatric sack,
Carries his whole regalia at his back ;
His royal consort heads the female band,
And leads the heir apparent in her hand ;
The pannier'd ass creeps on with conscious pride,
Bearing a future prince on either side.
No choice musicians in this troop are found
To varnish nonsense with the charms of sound ;
No swords, no daggers, not one poison'd bowl ;   220
No lightning flashes here, no thunders roll ;
No guards to swell the monarch's train are shown ;
The monarch here must be a host alone :

200 Smollett's ' Peregrine Pickle ' seems to have been well known to
Churchill. It appeared in 1751.

205 A ' Merry-Andrew ' was originally a kind of mountebank's
assistant, who copied his tricks with wilful clumsiness. The equivalent
in the modern circus is ' Auguste.'

208 By 17 George II. c. 5, ' All common players of interludes, and all
persons who for hire or reward, act or cause to be acted, any interlude
or entertainment of the stage or any part therein, not being authorised
by law, shall be deemed rogues and vagabonds, and be punished
accordingly.'

No solemn pomp, no slow processions here ;
No Ammon's entry, and no Juliet's bier.
By need compell'd to prostitute his art,
The varied actor flies from part to part ;
And, strange disgrace to all theatric pride !
His character is shifted with his side.
Question and answer he by turns must be,   230
Like that small wit in modern tragedy,
Who, to patch up his fame—or fill his purse—
Still pilfers wretched plans, and makes them worse ;
Like gypsies, lest the stolen brat be known,
Defacing first, then claiming for his own.
In shabby state they strut, and tatter'd robe,
The scene a blanket, and a barn the globe :
No high conceits their moderate wishes raise,
Content with humble profit, humble praise.
Let dowdies simper, and let bumpkins stare,   240
The strolling pageant hero treads in air :
Pleased, for his hour he to mankind gives law,
And snores the next out on a truss of straw.
But if kind fortune, who sometimes we know
Can take a hero from a puppet-show,
In mood propitious should her favourite call
On royal stage in royal pomp to bawl,
Forgetful of himself he rears the head,
And scorns the dunghill where he first was bred.
Conversing now with well-dress'd kings and queens, 250
With gods and goddesses behind the scenes,
He sweats beneath the terror-nodding plume,
Taught by mock honours real pride t'assume.
On this great stage, the world, no monarch e'er

225 ' Ammon's entry.' Probably a reference to the triumphal entry
of Alexander (who claimed descent from Jupiter Ammon and some-
times referred to himself, in English tragedy at least, as ' young
Ammon ') in Nathaniel Lee's ' Rival Queens or the Death of Alexander
the Great.'

236 Churchill seems to have had in mind Hogarth's celebrated print
of ' Strolling Actresses Dancing in a Barn.'

252 By actors of the pre-Garrick school (*e.g.* Quin) tragic parts were
played in a stiff tunic rather like a ballet skirt and in a pseudo-Roman
helmet surmounted by monstrous plumes.

Was half so haughty as a monarch player.
   Doth it more move our anger or our mirth
To see these things, the lowest sons of earth,
Presume, with self-sufficient knowledge graced,
To rule in letters, and preside in taste ?
The town's decisions they no more admit ;   260
Themselves alone the arbiters of wit ;
And scorn the jurisdiction of that court
To which they owe their being and support.
Actors, like monks of old, now sacred grown,
Must be attack'd by no fools but their own.
   Let the vain tyrant sit amidst his guards,
His puny green-room wits and venal bards,
Who meanly tremble at the puppet's frown,
And for a play-house freedom lose their own ;
In spite of new-made laws, and new-made kings,   270
The free-born Muse with liberal spirit sings.
Bow down, ye slaves ! before these idols fall !
Let Genius stoop to them who've none at all !
Ne'er will I flatter, cringe, or bend the knee
To those who, slaves to all, are slaves to me.
   Actors, as actors, are a lawful game,
The poet's right, and who shall bar his claim ?
And if, o'erweening of their little skill,
When they have left the stage they're actors still ;
If to the subject world they still give laws,   280
With paper crowns, and sceptres made of straws ;
If they in cellar or in garret roar,
And kings one night, are kings for evermore ;
Shall not bold truth, e'en there, pursue her theme,
And wake the coxcomb from his golden dream ?
Or if, well worthy of a better fate,
They rise superior to their present state ;
If, with each social virtue graced, they blend

<hr>

[266-27$] These lines were pointed at Garrick in answer to his suggestion that Churchill had praised him so highly in ' The Rosciad ' because he wanted free admission to Drury Lane.

[267] The ' Green Room,' probably so called because it was originally painted green (for reasons unknown), is now obsolete in London theatres. Formerly actors and actresses, when not required on the stage, congregated there.

The gay companion and the faithful friend ;
If they, like Pritchard, join in private life   290
The tender parent and the virtuous wife ;
Shall not our verse their praise with pleasure speak,
Though Mimics bark, and Envy split her cheek ?
No honest worth's beneath the Muse's praise ;
No greatness can above her censure raise ;
Station and wealth to her are trifling things ;
She stoops to actors, and she soars to kings.
   Is there a man, in vice and folly bred,
To sense of honour as to virtue dead,
Whom ties nor human nor divine can bind,   300
Alien from God, and foe to all mankind ;
Who spares no character ; whose every word,
Bitter as gall, and sharper than the sword,
Cuts to the quick ; whose thoughts with rancour swell ;
Whose tongue on earth performs the work of hell ?
If there be such a monster, the Reviews
Shall find him holding forth against abuse.
' Attack profession !—'tis a deadly breach !—
The Christian laws another lesson teach :—

---

²⁹⁰ Mrs. Pritchard's private life was above reproach.

²⁹⁸ ' Is there a man ? ' *i.e.* Smollett. Tobias George Smollett (1721-
1771) came of a Scottish family of considerable influence in Dumbar-
tonshire. He qualified for the medical profession, and during his
apprenticeship composed his tragedy of ' The Regicide,' based upon
the murder of James I. of Scotland. In 1739 he came to London to
seek his fortune, and submitted his play to Lord Lyttelton, the patron
of Thomson and Mallet, but without result. Having obtained a post
as ship's surgeon he sailed in 1740 to the West Indies and served under
Vernon at the siege of Carthagena. In Jamaica he fell in love with ' a
creole beauty,' Nancy Lascelles, whom he married in 1747, some time
after his return to England. He abandoned the Navy in 1744 and
settled as a surgeon in Downing Street. He published several satires,
including a ' Burlesque Ode on the Loss of a Grandmother,' in ridicule
of Lyttelton's ' Monody ' on the death of his wife, and then turned to
prose fiction, basing his manner on that of Le Sage. ' Roderick Ran-
dom ' was produced in 1748 and ' Peregrine Pickle ' in 1751. The
first edition of the latter contained violent attacks upon Garrick,
Cibber, Rich, Akenside, Fielding and Lyttelton. After an ineffectual
attempt to establish himself in a position at Bath he returned to London
and went to live in Chelsea, where he was visited by Johnson, Gold-
smith, Sterne, Garrick, and Wilkes. In 1753 appeared his third novel,
' Ferdinand, Count Fathom,' and two years later his inadequate

Unto the end should charity endure.   310
And candour hide those faults it cannot cure.'
Thus Candour's maxims flow from Rancour's throat,
As devils, to serve their purpose, Scripture quote.
  The Muse's office was by Heaven design'd
To please, improve, instruct, reform mankind ;
To make dejected Virtue nobly rise
Above the towering pitch of splendid Vice ;
To make pale Vice, abash'd, her head hang down,
And, trembling, crouch at Virtue's awful frown.
Now arm'd with wrath, she bids eternal shame,   320
With strictest justice, brand the villain's name ;
Now in the milder garb of Ridicule
She sports, and pleases while she wounds the fool.
Her shape is often varied ; but her aim,
To prop the cause of Virtue, still the same,
In praise of mercy let the guilty bawl ;
When Vice and Folly for correction call,
Silence the mark of weakness justly bears,
And is partaker of the crimes it spares.
  But if the Muse, too cruel in her mirth,   330
With harsh reflections wounds the man of worth ;
If wantonly she deviates from her plan,
And quits the actor to expose the man ;
Ashamed, she marks that passage with a blot,
And hates the line where candour was forgot.
  But what is candour, what is humour's vein,
Though judgment join to consecrate the strain,
If curious numbers will not aid afford,
Nor choicest music play in every word ?
Verses must run, to charm a modern ear,   340

translation of ' Don Quixote.' ' The Critical Review,' of which he had
been placed in charge by the printer Alexander Hamilton, first
appeared in February, 1756, and it was his connection with this
journal which roused the anger of Churchill. His paper criticising
' The Rosciad ' was printed in the number for April, 1761. Smollett's
' History of England ' had appeared at the end of 1757. On January
24th of the same year his farce ' The Reprisal, or the Tars of Old
England,' was produced at Drury Lane. His relations with Garrick were
now cordial and he praised the actor highly in ' The Critical Review.'
  [311] In the eighteenth century ' candour ' meant impartiality rather
than outspokenness.

From all harsh, rugged interruptions clear.
Soft let them breathe, as Zephyr's balmy breeze,
Smooth let their current flow, as summer seas,
Perfect then only deem'd when they dispense
A happy, tuneful vacancy of sense.
Italian fathers thus, with barbarous rage,
Fit helpless infants for the squeaking stage :
Deaf to the calls of pity, Nature wound,
And mangle vigour for the sake of sound.
Henceforth farewell, then, feverish thirst of fame ;   350
Farewell the longings for a poet's name ;
Perish my Muse—a wish 'bove all severe
To him who ever held the Muses dear—
If e'er her labours weaken, to refine,
The generous roughness of a nervous line.

   Others affect the stiff and swelling phrase ;
Their Muse must walk in stilts, and strut in stays ;
The sense they murder, and the words transpose,
Lest poetry approach too near to prose.
See tortured Reason how they pare and trim,   360
And, like Procrustes, stretch, or lop the limb.

   Waller, whose praise succeeding bards rehearse,
Parent of harmony in English verse,
Whose tuneful Muse in sweetest accents flows,
In couplets first taught straggling sense to close.

   In polish'd numbers and majestic sound,
Where shall thy rival, Pope ! be ever found ?
But whilst each line with equal beauty flows,
E'en excellence, unvaried, tedious grows.
Nature, through all her works, in great degree,   370
Borrows a blessing from variety.
Music itself her needful aid requires
To rouse the soul, and wake our dying fires.
Still in one key, the nightingale would tease ;

---

[346] Italian boys were still castrated in infancy in the hope that they
would develop into male *soprani*.

[362] Edmund Waller (1605-1687), English poet.

[367] Churchill preferred the less regular but more vigorous verse of
Dryden. His dislike of Pope was later intensified by his hostility to
Warburton, Pope's friend.

59

Still in one key, not Brent would always please.
　Here let me bend, great Dryden, at thy shrine,
Thou dearest name to all the tuneful nine.
What if some dull lines in cold order creep,
And with his theme the poet seems to sleep ?
Still, when his subject rises proud to view,　　　　380
With equal strength the poet rises too :
With strong invention, noblest vigour fraught,
Thought still springs up and rises out of thought ;
Numbers ennobling numbers in their course,
In varied sweetness flow, in varied force ;
The powers of genius and of judgment join,
And the whole Art of Poetry is thine.
　But what are numbers, what are bards, to me,
Forbid to tread the paths of poesy ?
' A sacred Muse should consecrate her pen ;　　　　390
Priests must not hear nor see like other men :
Far higher themes should her ambition claim :
Behold where Sternhold points the way to fame.'
　Whilst, with mistaken zeal dull bigots burn,
Let Reason for a moment take her turn.
When coffee-sages hold discourse with kings,
And blindly walk in paper leading-strings,
What if a man delight to pass his time
In spinning reason into harmless rhyme,
Or sometimes boldly venture to the play ?　　　　400
Say, where's the crime ?—great man of prudence, say ?
No two on earth in all things can agree ;
All have some darling singularity :
Women and men, as well as girls and boys,
In gew-gaws take delight, and sigh for toys.
Your sceptres and your crowns, and such like things,
Are but a better kind of toys for kings.
In things indifferent Reason bids us choose,
Whether the whim's a monkey or a Muse.
　What the grave triflers on this busy scene,　　　　410
When they make use of this word Reason, mean,

[375] Charlotte Brent. (See note on ' The Rosciad,' line 720.)
[393] Thomas Sternhold (*c.* 1500-1549), joint author with John Hopkins of a metrical version of the Psalms, first published in 1549.

I know not ; but according to my plan,
'Tis Lord Chief-Justice in the court of man,
Equally form'd to rule in age and youth,
The friend of Virtue, and the guide to truth.
To her I bow, whose sacred power I feel ;
To her decision make my last appeal ;
Condemn'd by her, applauding worlds in vain
Should tempt me to take up the pen again :
By her absolved, my course I'll still pursue :   420
If Reason's for me, God is for me too.

NIGHT*

AN EPISTLE
TO ROBERT LLOYD

Contrarius evehor orbi. OVID. Met. Lib. ii.

WHEN foes insult, and prudent friends dispense,
In pity's strains, the worst of insolence,
Oft with thee, Lloyd, I steal an hour from grief,
And in thy social converse find relief.
The mind, of solitude impatient grown,
Loves any sorrows rather than her own.
   Let slaves to business, bodies without soul,
Important blanks in Nature's mighty roll,
Solemnize nonsense in the day's broad glare :
We Night prefer, which heals or hides our care.   10
   Rogues justified, and by success made bold,
Dull fools and coxcombs sanctified by gold,
Freely may bask in fortune's partial ray,
And spread their feathers opening to the day ;
But threadbare Merit dares not shew the head
Till vain Prosperity retires to bed.
Misfortunes, like the owl, avoid the light ;
The sons of Care are always sons of Night.
   The wretch bred up in method's drowsy school,
Whose only merit is to err by rule,   20
Who ne'er through heat of blood was tripping caught,
Nor guilty deem'd of one eccentric thought ;
Whose soul directed to no use is seen,
Unless to move the body's dull machine,
Which, clockwork-like, with the same equal pace,
Still travels on through life's insipid space,
Turns up his eyes to think that there should be,
Among God's creatures, two such things as we ;
Then for his nightcap calls, and thanks the powers

* Although dated 1761, ' Night ' was first published in January,
1762. ' Printed for the Author; and sold by W. Flexney.'

62

Which kindly gave him grace to keep good hours. 30
 Good hours—fine words—but was it ever seen
That all men could agree in what they mean ?
Florio, who many years a course hath run
In downright opposition to the sun,
Expatiates on good hours, their cause defends
With as much vigour as our prudent friends.
The uncertain term no settled notion brings,
But still in different mouths means different things ;
Each takes the phrase in his own private view ;
With prudence it is ten, with Florio two. 40
 Go on, ye fools, who talk for talking's sake,
Without distinguishing, distinctions make ;
Shine forth in native folly, native pride,
Make yourselves rules to all the world beside ;
Reason, collected in herself, disdains
The slavish yoke of arbitrary chains ;
Steady and true each circumstance she weighs,
Nor to bare words inglorious tribute pays.
Men of sense live exempt from vulgar awe,
And Reason to herself alone is law : 50
That freedom she enjoys with liberal mind,
Which she as freely grants to all mankind.
No idol-titled name her reverence stirs,
No hour she blindly to the rest prefers ;
All are alike, if they're alike employ'd,
And all are good if virtuously enjoy'd.
 Let the sage Doctor (think him one we know)
With scraps of ancient learning overflow ;
In all the dignity of wig declare
The fatal consequence of midnight air ; 60
How damps and vapours, as it were by stealth,
Undermine life, and sap the walls of health :
For me let Galen moulder on the shelf ;
I'll live, and be physician to myself.
While soul is join'd to body, whether fate

<hr>

[33] Florio, a fancy name directed at no one in particular. (See ' The Times,' line 481.)

[63] Galen, the famous Greek physician, born at Pergamum, Mysia, about 130 A.D., long regarded as the Aristotle of medicine.

Allot a longer or a shorter date,
I'll make them live, as brother should with brother,
And keep them in good humour with each other.
   The surest road to health, say what they will,
Is never to suppose we shall be ill.   70
Most of those evils we poor mortals know,
From doctors and imagination flow.
Hence, to old women with your boasted rules !
Stale traps, and only sacred now to fools ;
As well may sons of physic hope to find
One medicine, as one hour, for all mankind.
   If Rupert after ten is out of bed,
The fool next morning can't hold up his head ;
What reason this which me to bed must call,
Whose head, thank Heaven, never aches at all ?   80
In different courses different tempers run ;
He hates the moon : I sicken at the sun.
Wound up at twelve at noon, his clock goes right ;
Mine better goes, wound up at twelve at night.
   Then in oblivion's grateful cup I drown
The galling sneer, the supercilious frown,
The strange reserve, the proud, affected state
Of upstart knaves grown rich, and fools grown great.
No more that abject wretch disturbs my rest,
Who meanly overlooks a friend distressed.   90
Purblind to poverty the worldling goes,
And scarce sees rags an inch beyond his nose,
But from a crowd can single out his grace,
And cringe and creep to fools who strut in lace.
   Whether those classic regions are survey'd
Where we in earliest youth together stray'd,
Where hand in hand we trod the flowery shore,
Though now thy happier genius runs before ;

[80] The longevity of men of delicate constitution is well known. Churchill was one of those extremely healthy people who never feel the results of dissipation until it is too late. He died at the age of 33.

[90] Churchill at least never did so. When in the autumn of 1763 he returned to town and found Lloyd a prisoner in the Fleet, he gave a guinea a week towards his support and paid a servant to attend to him. He also tried to raise a subscription to pay Lloyd's debts, but was unable to induce enough people to contribute.

When we conspired a thankless wretch to raise,
And taught a stump to shoot with pilfer'd praise,   100
Who once for reverend merit famous grown,
Gratefully strove to kick his maker down ;
Or if more general arguments engage,
The court or camp, the pulpit, bar, or stage ;
If half-bred surgeons, whom men doctors call,
And lawyers, who were never bred at all,
Those mighty letter'd monsters of the earth,
Our pity move, or exercise our mirth ;
Or if in tittle-tattle, toothpick way,
Our rambling thoughts with easy freedom stray,   110
A gainer still thy friend himself must find,
His grief suspended, and improved his mind.

   Whilst peaceful slumbers bless the homely bed
Where virtue, self-approved, reclines her head ;
Whilst vice beneath imagined horrors mourns,
And conscience plants the villain's couch with thorns,
Impatient of restraint, the active mind,
No more by servile prejudice confined,
Leaps from her seat, as waken'd from a trance,
And darts through Nature at a single glance ;   120
Then we our friends, our foes, ourselves, survey,
And see by Night what fools we are by day.

   Stripp'd of her gaudy plumes and vain disguise,
See where ambition mean and loathsome lies ;
Reflection with relentless hand pulls down
The tyrant's bloody wreath and ravish'd crown.
In vain he tells of battles bravely won,
Of nations conquer'd, and of worlds undone ;
Triumphs like these but ill with manhood suit,
And sink the conqueror beneath the brute.   130

99 ' The Rev. William Sellon, minister of St. James's, Clerkenwell,
and lecturer of St. Andrew's Holborn and of the Magdalen, the person
alluded to in these lines, is again satirised in ' The Ghost,' under the
name of Plausible. ' By the assistance of his clever contemporaries at
Westminster School, Churchill, Lloyd, and Thornton, he contrived to
acquire more reputation there, than his native dullness warranted ; but
on quitting that seminary, he forgot the obligation, and treated his
friends with ingratitude.' (Tooke.) It is by no means clear in what
his ingratitude consisted, or indeed how it is possible for schoolboys to
assist one another to ' reputation.' (See ' The Ghost,' III., line 740.)

But if, in searching round the world, we find
Some generous youth, the friend of all mankind,
Whose anger, like the bolt of Jove, is sped
In terrors only at the guilty head,
Whose mercies, like heaven's dew, refreshing fall
In general love and charity to all,
Pleased we behold such worth on any throne,
And doubly pleased we find it on our own.
   Through a false medium things are shewn by day ;
Pomp, wealth, and titles judgment lead astray.   140
How many from appearance borrow state,
Whom Night disdains to number with the great !
Must not we laugh to see yon lordling proud
Snuff up vile incense from a fawning crowd ?
Whilst in his beam surrounding clients play,
Like insects in the sun's enlivening ray.
Whilst, Jehu-like, he drives at furious rate,
And seems the only charioteer of state,
Talking himself into a little god,
And ruling empires with a single nod ;   150
Who would not think, to hear him law dispense,
That he had interest, and that they had sense ?
Injurious thought ! beneath Night's honest shade,
When pomp is buried, and false colours fade,
Plainly we see, at that impartial hour,
Them dupes to pride, and him the tool of power.
   God help the man condemn'd by cruel fate
To court the seeming, or the real great !
Much sorrow shall he feel, and suffer more
Than any slave who labours at the oar :   160
By slavish methods must he learn to please,
By smooth-tongued flattery, that cursed court-disease
Supple to every wayward mood strike sail,
And shift with shifting humour's peevish gale.
To nature dead he must adopt vile art,
And wear a smile, with anguish in his heart.
A sense of honour would destroy his schemes,

[147] ' And the watchman told, saying . . . the driving *is* like the driving of Jehu the son of Nimshi; for he driveth furiously.' II. Kings, 9, 20.

And Conscience ne'er must speak unless in dreams.
When he hath tamely borne, for many years,
Cold looks, forbidding frowns, contemptuous sneers ; 170
When he at last expects, good easy man !
To reap the profits of his labour'd plan,
Some cringing lackey, or rapacious whore,
To favours of the great the surest door ;
Some catamite, or pimp, in credit grown,
Who tempts another's wife, or sells his own,
Steps 'cross his hopes, the promised boon denies,
And for some minion's minion claims the prize.
  Foe to restraint, unpractised in deceit,
Too resolute, from nature's active heat,   180
To brook affronts, and tamely pass them by,
Too proud to flatter, too sincere to lie ;
Too plain to please, too honest to be great,
Give me, kind Heaven, an humbler, happier state ;
Far from the place where men with pride deceive,
Where rascals promise, and where fools believe ;
Far from the walk of folly, vice, and strife,
Calm, independent, let me steal through life,
Nor one vain wish my steady thoughts beguile
To fear his lordship's frown, or court his smile.   190
Unfit for greatness, I her snares defy,
And look on riches with untainted eye ;
To others let the glittering baubles fall,
Content shall place us far above them all.
  Spectators only, on this bustling stage,
We see what vain designs mankind engage :
Vice after vice with ardour they pursue,
And one old folly brings forth twenty new.
Perplex'd with trifles through the vale of life,
Man strives 'gainst man, without a cause for strife ;   200
Armies embattled meet, and thousands bleed
For some vile spot, where fifty cannot feed.
Squirrels for nuts contend, and, wrong or right,
For the world's empire kings ambitious fight.
What odds ?—to us 'tis all the self-same thing,

[175] Churchill was later to devote a whole satire to the theme of homosexual passion. (See ' The Times.')

A nut, a world, a squirrel, and a king.
Britons, like Roman spirits famed of old,
Are cast by nature in a patriot mould ;
No private joy, no private grief, they know ;
Their soul's engross'd by public weal or woe ;   210
Inglorious ease, like ours, they greatly scorn ;
Let care with nobler wreaths their brows adorn :
Gladly they toil beneath the statesman's pains,
Give them but credit for a statesman's brains.
All would be deem'd, e'en from the cradle, fit
To rule in politics as well as wit.
The grave, the gay, the fopling, and the dunce,
Start up (God bless us !) statesmen all at once.
His mighty charge of souls the priest forgets,
The court-bred lord his promises and debts ;   220
Soldiers their fame, misers forget their pelf,
The rake his mistress, and the fop himself,
Whilst thoughts of higher moment claim their care,
And their wise heads the weight of kingdoms bear.
Females themselves the glorious ardour feel,
And boast an equal or a greater zeal ;
From nymph to nymph the state-infection flies,
Swells in her breast, and sparkles in her eyes.
O'erwhelm'd by politics lie malice, pride,
Envy, and twenty other faults beside.   230
No more their little fluttering hearts confess
A passion for applause, or rage for dress ;
No more they pant for public raree-shows,
Or lose one thought on monkies or on beaus :
Coquettes no more pursue the jilting plan,
And lustful prudes forget to rail at man :
The darling theme Cecilia's self will choose,
Nor thinks of scandal whilst she talks of news.
The cit, a Common-Councilman by place,

224 Churchill was soon, by his association with Wilkes, to be drawn into the political arena himself.
239 The word ' cit ' was originally an abbreviated form of ' citizen,' hence a townsman or ' cockney ' as opposed to a countryman, or a shopkeeper as distinguished from a gentleman.
239 A member of the Common Council of the City of London.

Ten thousand mighty nothings in his face,   240
By situation as by nature great,
With nice precision parcels out the state ;
Proves and disproves, affirms and then denies,
Objects himself, and to himself replies ;
Wielding aloft the politician rod,
Makes Pitt by turns a devil and a god ;
Maintains, e'en to the very teeth of power,
The same thing right and wrong in half an hour :
Now all is well, now he suspects a plot,
And plainly proves, whatever is, is not :   250
Fearfully wise, he shakes his empty head,
And deals out empires as he deals out thread ;
His useless scales are in a corner flung,
And Europe's balance hangs upon his tongue.
    Peace to such triflers, be our happier plan
To pass through life as easy as we can.
Who's in or out, who moves this grand machine,
Nor stirs my curiosity nor spleen.
Secrets of state no more I wish to know
Than secret movements of a puppet-show :   260
Let but the puppets move, I've my desire,
Unseen the hand which guides the master-wire.
    What is't to us, if taxes rise or fall ?
Thanks to our fortune, we pay none at all.
Let muckworms, who in dirty acres deal,
Lament those hardships which we cannot feel.
His grace, who smarts, may bellow if he please,
But must I bellow too, who sit at ease ?
By custom safe, the poet's numbers flow
Free as the light and air some years ago.   270
No statesman e'er will find it worth his pains

[264] Had Churchill lived to-day he might not have been so easy. A profit of £1,000 (or £750) on his two first satires would certainly not have escaped the attention of the Inland Revenue.

[270] A reference to the increase in the window tax. ' By the last act of parliament relative to window lights, the duty, after the 5th day of *April* last is as follows . . . all houses with more than six, and less than 12 windows, pay 1s. a window ; and every house with twelve windows, or upwards, pay one shilling and sixpence a window, besides the house duty.' (' Gentleman's Magazine,' XXXII., 1762, page 352.)

To tax our labours, and excise our brains.
Burthens like these, vile earthly buildings bear ;
No tribute's laid on castles in the air.
Let then the flames of war destructive reign,
And England's terrors awe imperious Spain ;
Let every venal clan and neutral tribe
Learn to receive conditions, not prescribe ;
Let each new year call loud for new supplies,
And tax on tax with double burthen rise ;   280
Exempt we sit, by no rude cares oppress'd,
And, having little, are with little bless'd.
All real ills in dark oblivion lie,
And joys, by fancy form'd, their place supply ;
Night's laughing hours unheeded slip away,
Nor one dull thought foretels approach of day.
    Thus have we lived, and whilst the fates afford
Plain plenty to supply the frugal board ;
Whilst Mirth with Decency, his lovely bride,
And wine's gay god, with Temperance by his side,   290
Their welcome visit pay ; whilst Health attends
The narrow circle of our chosen friends ;
Whilst frank good-humour consecrates the treat,
And woman makes society complete,
Thus will we live, though in our teeth are hurl'd
Those hackney strumpets, Prudence and the World.
    Prudence, of old a sacred term, implied
Virtue, with godlike wisdom for her guide,
But now in general use is known to mean
The stalking-horse of vice, and folly's screen.   300
The sense perverted we retain the name ;
Hypocrisy and Prudence are the same.
    A tutor once, more read in men than books,
A kind of crafty knowledge in his looks,
Demurely sly, with high preferment bless'd,
His favourite pupil in these words address'd :
    ' Wouldst thou, my son, be wise and virtuous deem'd,

[277] ' Alluding to the precautions adopted by government after the
rebellion of 1745, and to some difficulties which occurred in carrying
into effect Mr. Pitt's measure, proposed in 1757, for raising 2,000 men
in the Highlands of Scotland for the British service in America.' (Tooke.)

By all mankind a prodigy esteem'd ?
Be this thy rule ; be what men *prudent* call ;
  Prudence, almighty Prudence, gives thee all.   310
Keep up appearances ; there lies the test ;
The world will give thee credit for the rest.
Outward be fair, however foul within ;
Sin if thou wilt, but then in secret sin.
This maxim's into common favour grown,—
Vice is no longer vice, unless 'tis known.
Virtue indeed may barefaced take the field ;
But vice is virtue when 'tis well conceal'd.
Should raging passion drive thee to a whore,
Let Prudence lead thee to a postern door ;   320
Stay out all night, but take especial care
That Prudence bring thee back to early prayer.
As one with watching and with study faint,
Reel in a drunkard, and reel out a saint.'
  With joy the youth this useful lesson heard,
And in his memory stored each precious word,
Successfully pursued the plan, and now,
' Room for my Lord—Virtue, stand by and bow.'
  And is this all—is this the worldling's art,
To mask, but not amend a vicious heart ?   330
Shall lukewarm caution and demeanour grave
For wise and good stamp every supple knave ?
Shall wretches, whom no real virtue warms,
Gild fair their names and states with empty forms,
While Virtue seeks in vain the wish'd for prize,
Because, disdaining ill, she hates disguise ;
Because she frankly pours forth all her store,
Seems what she is, and scorns to pass for more ?
Well—be it so—let vile dissemblers hold
Unenvied power, and boast their dear bought gold ; 340
Me neither power shall tempt, nor thirst of pelf,
To flatter others, or deny myself ;
Might the whole world be placed within my span,
I would not be that thing, that prudent man.
  ' What ! ' cries Sir Pliant, ' would you then oppose
Yourself, alone, against a host of foes ?
Let not conceit, and peevish lust to rail,

Above all sense of interest prevail.
Throw off, for shame ! this petulance of wit ;
Be wise, be modest, and for once submit :   350
Too hard the task 'gainst multitudes to fight ;
You must be wrong ; the World is in the right.'
    What is this World ?—a term which men have got
To signify, not one in ten knows what ;
A term, which with no more precision passes
To point out herds of men than herds of asses ;
In common use no more it means, we find,
Than many fools in same opinions join'd.
    Can numbers then change nature's stated laws ?
Can numbers make the worse the better cause ?   360
Vice must be vice, virtue be virtue still,
Though thousands rail at good and practise ill.
Wouldst thou defend the Gaul's destructive rage,
Because vast nations on his part engage ?
Though to support the rebel Cæsar's cause
Tumultuous legions arm against the laws ;
Though Scandal would our patriot's name impeach,
And rails at virtues which she cannot reach,
What honest man but would with joy submit
To bleed with Cato, and retire with Pitt ?   370
    Stedfast and true to virtue's sacred laws,
Unmoved by vulgar censure or applause,
Let the World talk, my Friend ; that World, we know,
Which calls us guilty, cannot make us so.
Unawed by numbers, follow Nature's plan ;
Assert the rights, or quit the name of man.
Consider well, weigh strictly right and wrong ;
Resolve not quick, but once resolved, be strong.
In spite of dulness, and in spite of wit,
If to thyself thou canst thyself acquit,   380
Rather stand up, assured with conscious pride,
Alone, than err with millions on thy side.

[370] Pitt and Temple resigned in October, 1761, on the rejection of their proposal for war with Spain. War was, however, declared on January 2nd following.

THE GHOST

BOOK ONE*

WITH eager search to dart the soul,
Curiously vain, from pole to pole,
And from the planets' wandering spheres
To extort the number of our years,
And whether all those years shall flow
Serenely smooth, and free from woe,
Or rude misfortune shall deform
Our life with one continual storm ;
Or if the scene shall motley be,
Alternate joy and misery,   10
Is a desire which, more or less,
All men must feel, though few confess.
Hence, every place and every age
Affords subsistence to the sage
Who, free from this world and its cares,
Holds an acquaintance with the stars,
From whom he gains intelligence
Of things to come some ages hence,
Which unto friends, at easy rates,
He readily communicates.   20
    At its first rise, which all agree on,
This noble science was Chaldean ;
That ancient people, as they fed
Their flocks upon the mountain's head,
Gazed on the stars, observed their motions,
And suck'd in astrologic notions,
Which they so eagerly pursue,
As folks are apt whate'er is new,
That things below at random rove,
Whilst they're consulting things above ;   30
And when they now so poor were grown,
That they'd no houses of their own,

* First published in March, 1762. ' Printed for the Author, and sold
by William Flexney.'

73

They made bold with their friends the stars
And prudently made use of theirs.
   To Egypt from Chaldee it travell'd,
And fate at Memphis was unravell'd :
The exotic science soon struck root,
And flourished into high repute :
Each learned priest, O strange to tell !
Could circles make, and cast a spell ;   40
Could read and write, and taught the nation
The holy art of divination.
Nobles themselves, for at that time
Knowledge in nobles was no crime,
Could talk as learned as the priest,
And prophesy as much at least :
Hence all the fortune-telling crew,
Whose crafty skill mars nature's hue,
Who, in vile tatters, with smirch'd face,
Run up and down from place to place,   50
To gratify their friends' desires,
From Bampfield Carew, to Moll Squires,
Are rightly term'd Egyptians all
Whom we, mistaking, Gypsies call.
   The Grecian sages borrow'd this,

[52] Bamfylde Moore Carew was born in July, 1693, at Brickley near Tiverton in Devonshire. He came of good family, but playing truant from school with some companions, fell in with a company of gypsies and persuaded them to allow him to join their band. After a while he returned to his home to comfort his parents, but longing for the free life of the gypsies finally drove him to throw in his lot with them permanently. He learned their practices and gained their confidence to such purpose that on the death of Clause Patch, 'King of the Mendicants,' Carew was elected in his stead. Having been arrested by a certain Justice Leithbridge, he was tried at Exeter Quarter Sessions and sentenced to transportation for seven years. In America he had many adventures among planters and Indians, finally contriving his return to England, where he resumed his old life. Again he was transported and again he returned, in time to accompany the march of the Young Pretender. Most of his exploits were concerned with begging and obtaining money under false pretences. The year of his death is unknown. (See 'An Apology for the Life of Bamfylde Moore Carew,' London (?) 1750.) In Churchill's time the work had already gone into five or six editions.

[52] Mary Squires, a gypsy at first implicated in the Elizabeth Canning affair, but later proved innocent. (See note on line 461.)

74

As they did other sciences,
From fertile Egypt, though the loan
They had not honesty to own.
Dodona's oaks, inspired by Jove,
A learned and prophetic grove,   60
Turn'd vegetable necromancers,
And to all comers gave their answers.
At Delphos, to Apollo dear,
All men the voice of Fate might hear ;
Each subtle priest on three-legg'd stool,
To take in wise men, play'd the fool ;
A mystery, so made for gain,
E'en now in fashion must remain.
Enthusiasts never will let drop
What brings such business to their shop   70
And that great saint, we Whitefield call,

[59] Dodona's Oaks : Dodona in Epirus was the most ancient oracle
in Greece. The priestess derived her answers from the rustling of the
sacred trees, and the tinkling of bells or pieces of metal suspended
among the branches.

[65] In the centre of the temple at Delphi there was a small opening in
the ground, from which, from time to time, arose an intoxicating
vapour. Over this chasm stood a tripod on which the priestess, called
Pythia, took her seat whenever the oracle was to be consulted. The
words which she uttered were believed to contain the revelation of
Apollo.

[69] ' Enthusiast ' was then a term of abuse. ' The reproach of
Christ,' remarked John Wesley, ' I am willing to bear, but not the
reproach of enthusiasm, if I can help it.' Shaftesbury in his ' Letter on
Enthusiasm ' declared that ' Inspiration is a real feeling of the Divine
Presence, and enthusiasm a false one.'

[71] George Whitefield (1714-1770) was born at the Bell Inn, Glouces-
ter, was educated at St. Mary de Crypt School in the same city, and at
Pembroke College, Oxford, which he entered as a servitor in 1732. He
became acquainted with the Wesleys and entered the Methodist
' Society ' in 1735. In the following year he was ordained deacon and,
after missionary preaching in England, set out, early in 1738, for
Georgia, where he established schools and projected an orphanage. On
his return to England he renewed his acquaintance with the Wesleys
and commenced open-air preaching in 1739. Churchmen began to
look upon him with suspicion. In the same year he sailed again to
America, where his preaching was extremely successful, and where he
won the warm approval of Benjamin Franklin. While in America he
became more and more Calvinistic, finally causing a complete breach
between the followers of Wesley and his own. He returned once more
to the Old World and his preaching in Scotland was the occasion of

Keeps up the humbug spiritual.
Among the Romans, not a bird
Without a prophecy, was heard ;
Fortunes of empires often hung
On the magician magpie's tongue,
And every crow was to the state
A sure interpreter of fate.
Prophets, embodied in a college
(Time out of mind your seat of knowledge,   80
For genius never fruit can bear
Unless it first is planted there ;
And solid learning never falls
Without the verge of college walls)
Infallible accounts would keep
When it was best to watch or sleep,
To eat or drink, to go or stay,
And when to fight or run away ;
When matters were for actions ripe,
By looking at a double tripe ;   90
When emperors would live or die

violent convulsions among his penitents. In 1748 Lady Huntingdon made him one of her domestic chaplains. In 1749 George Lavington published the first part of his ' Enthusiasm of Methodists and Papists Compared,' directed chiefly against Whitefield. Whitefield continued to visit America, but from 1755 to 1763 he was in the United Kingdom attracting large audiences to hear his preaching. His success in having a theatre in Glasgow pulled down in 1753 had prejudiced the wits against him, and in 1760 he was burlesqued in Foote's ' Minor ' under the name of ' Dr. Squintum.' Churchill reflects the common feeling against him, sharpened in his case by the contrast between Whitefield's career in the Church and his own. Whitefield died in America in 1770.

73 Divination by birds. (See note on line 79 below.)

79 The College of Augurs was founded by the ancient kings of Rome, and until 300 B.C. consisted of six members. The number was then increased to nine, and in 104 B.C. to fifteen. Julius Caesar increased the number to sixteen, not including his own membership. The dominance of Augustus and his successors deprived the college of influence, and from the time of Diocletian almost all trace of it is lost. The Auguri were concerned with the interpretation of *natural* signs ; prodigies were regarded as outside their scope. The first and principal method of divination was by observation of the flight of birds, but conclusions were also drawn from meteorological phenomena, from the quickness of fowls to swallow grain, from the movements of quadrupeds or reptiles, and from the examination of the entrails of animals. ' An ass's skull ' (line 92) would hardly be a subject for augury.

They in an ass's skull could spy;
When generals would their station keep,
Or turn their backs, in hearts of sheep,
In matters, whether small or great,
In private families or state
As amongst us, the holy seer
Officiously would interfere;
With pious arts and reverend skill
Would bend lay bigots to his will;   100
Would help or injure foes or friends,
Just as it served his private ends.
Whether, in honest way of trade,
Traps for virginity were laid,
Or if, to make their party great,
Designs were form'd against the state,
Regardless of the common weal,
By interest led, which they call zeal,
Into the scale was always thrown
The will of Heaven to back their own.   110
    England, a happy land we know,
Where follies naturally grow,
Where without culture they arise,
And tower above the common size;
England, a fortune-telling host
As numerous as the stars, could boast;
Matrons, who toss the cup, and see
The grounds of fate in grounds of tea;
Who, versed in every modest lore,
Can a lost maidenhead restore,   120
Or, if their pupils rather choose it,
Can shew the readiest way to lose it.
Gypsies, who every ill can cure
Except the ill of being poor,
Who charms 'gainst love and agues sell
Who can in hen-roost set a spell,
Prepared by arts, to them best known
To catch all feet except their own,
Who as to fortune, can unlock it

[117] A form of divination still half-seriously practised.

As easily as pick a pocket ;   130
Scotchmen, who, in their country's right,
Possess the gift of second sight,
Who, when their barren heaths they quit,
(Sure argument of prudent wit ;—
Which reputation to maintain,
They never venture back again)
By lies prophetic heap up riches,
And boast the luxury of breeches.
    Amongst the rest, in former years,
Campbell, illustrious name ! appears,   140
Great hero of futurity,
Who, blind, could every thing foresee,
Who, dumb, could every thing foretell,
Who, fate with equity to sell,
Always dealt out the will of Heaven
According to what price was given.
    Of Scottish race, in Highlands born,
Possess'd with native pride and scorn,
He hither came, by custom led,
To curse the hands that gave him bread.   150
With want of truth, and want of sense,
Amply made up by impudence,
(A succedaneum, which we find
In common use with all mankind)
Caress'd and favour'd too by those
Whose heart with patriot feelings glows,
Who foolishly, where'er dispersed,
Still place their native country first ;
(For Englishmen alone have sense
To give a stranger preference,   160

---

140 Churchill evidently had in mind : ' The History of the Life and
Adventures of Duncan Campbell, a gentleman who, though deaf and
dumb, writes down any stranger's name at first sight, with their future
fortune,' London, 1720. This was the work of Defoe, who brought out
another edition in 1728 under the pseudonym of W. Bond.

    153 ' A succedaneum ': properly, a substitute for, but sometimes
misused to mean, a remedy.

    160 This extraordinary prejudice in favour of foreign performers of
all kinds has lasted into our own time, and is still potent enough to
compel English dancers to adopt Russian names.

Whilst modest merit of their own
Is left in poverty to groan)
Campbell foretold just what he would,
And left the stars to make it good,
On whom he had impress'd such awe,
His dictates current pass'd for law ;
Submissive, all his empire own'd ;
No star durst smile, when Campbell frown'd.
   This sage deceased, for all must die,
And Campbell's no more safe than I,   170
No more than I can guard the heart,
When Death shall hurl the fatal dart,
Succeeded, ripe in art and years,
Another favourite of the spheres ;
Another and another came,
Of equal skill, and equal fame ;
As white each wand, as black each gown,
As long each beard, as wise each frown,
In every thing so like, you'd swear,
Campbell himself was sitting there :   180
To all the happy art was known,
To *tell* our fortunes, *make* their own.
   Seated in garret,—for you know
The nearer to the stars we go
The greater we esteem his art,—
Fools curious flock'd from every part :
The rich, the poor, the maid, the married ;
And those who could not walk were carried.
   The butler, hanging down his head,
By chambermaid, or cookmaid led,   190
Inquires, if from his friend the moon
He has advice of pilfer'd spoon ?
   The court-bred woman of condition,
(Who to approve her disposition
As much superior, as her birth
To those composed of common earth,
With double spirit must engage
In every folly of the age)
The honourable arts would buy,
To pack the cards, and cog a die.   200

The hero who for brawn and face
May claim right honourable place
Amongst the chiefs of Butcher-row ;
Who might some thirty years ago,
If we may be allow'd to guess
At his employment by his dress,
Put medicines off from cart or stage,
The grand Toscano of the age ;
Or might about the country go
High steward of a puppet-show,   210
Steward and stewardship most meet,
For all know *puppets never eat* ;
Who would be thought (though, save the mark,
That point is something in the dark)
The man of honour, one like those
Renown'd in story, who loved blows
Better than victuals, and would fight,
Merely for sport, from morn to night,
Who treads like Mavors firm ; whose tongue
Is with the triple thunder hung ;   220
Who cries to Fear—stand off—aloof—
And talks as he were cannon proof,
Would be deem'd ready, when you list,
With sword and pistol, stick and fist,
Careless of points, balls, bruises, knocks,
At once to fence, fire, cudgel, box,
But at the same time bears about
Within himself, some touch of doubt,
Of prudent doubt, which hints—that fame
Is nothing but an empty name ;   230
That life is rightly understood

201–320 These lines first appeared in the third edition of the poem.
The italics in lines 210 and 212 make it certain that the satire is directed
against Lord Talbot, the High Steward, who attempted to introduce
some economies into the Royal Household. (See note on Book IV.,
line 924.)

203 ' Butcher-row, a very curious, narrow, timber-built, gable-ended
street that used to run alongside St. Clement's Church in the Strand.'
(Tooke.)

219 Mavors : an alternative form of Mars, in fairly frequent use in
18th century verse.

By all to be a real good ;
That, even in a hero's heart
Discretion is the better part ;
That this same honour may be won,
And yet no kind of danger run,
Like Drugger comes, that magic powers
May ascertain his lucky hours ;
For at some hours the fickle dame,
Whom Fortune properly we name,   240
Who ne'er considers wrong or right,
When wanted most plays least in sight,
And, like a modern court-bred jilt,
Leaves her chief favourites in a tilt :
Some hours there are, when from the heart
Courage into some other part,
No matter wherefore, makes retreat,
And fear usurps the vacant seat,
Whence, planet-struck, we often find
Stuarts and Sackvilles of mankind.   250
    Farther, he'd know (and by his art
A conjurer can that impart)
Whether politer it is reckon'd
To have or not to have a second ;
To drag the friends in, or, alone,
To make the danger all their own ;

[237] Abel Drugger, in Jonson's ' Alchymist,' a favourite part of Garrick's.

[250] Lord George Sackville (1716-1785) was educated at Westminster and Trinity College, Dublin. As Lieutenant-Colonel of the 28th Foot, he distinguished himself at Fontenoy, and rose to be commander of the British contingent with Prince Ferdinand. At Minden he neglected to lead the British cavalry in pursuit of the French, and for this he was court-martialled, dismissed the service, and had his name erased from the Privy Council. This was in 1760, but the accession in the same year of George III, began his restoration to favour. He was immediately admitted to kiss hands, and in 1769 was restored to his rank of Privy Counsellor and appointed one of the Vice-Treasurers of Ireland. He was Secretary of State for the Colonies from 1775-1782, and in the latter year was created Viscount Sackville. The reference to ' Stuart ' in the same line is somewhat obscure. Tooke saw in it an allusion to ' James the Second's dastardly conduct at the battle of the Boyne, and the consternation with which he retreated to Dublin, and from thence to France.'

Whether repletion is not bad,
And fighters with full stomachs mad ;
Whether, before he seeks the plain,
It were not well to breathe a vein ;   260
Whether a gentle salivation,
Consistently with reputation,
Might not of precious use be found,
Not to prevent indeed a wound,
But to prevent the consequence
Which oftentimes arises thence,
Those fevers which the patient urge on
To gates of death, by help of surgeon ;
Whether a wind at east or west
Is for green wounds accounted best ;   270
Whether (was he to choose) his mouth
Should point towards the north or south ;
Whether more safely he might use,
On these occasions, pumps or shoes ;
Whether it better is to fight
By sunshine or by candlelight ;
Or (lest a candle should appear
Too mean to shine in such a sphere ;
For who could of a candle tell
To light a hero into hell ?   280
And lest the sun should partial rise
To dazzle one or t'other's eyes,
Or one or t'other's brains to scorch)
Might not Dame Luna hold a torch ?
    These points with dignity discuss'd,
And gravely fix'd, a task which must
Require no little time and pains,
To make our hearts friends with our brains,
The man of war would next engage
The kind assistance of the sage,   290
Some previous method to direct,
Which should make these of none effect.
    Could he not, from the mystic school
Of art, produce some sacred rule,
By which a knowledge might be got
Whether men valiant were, or not ;

So he that challenges, might write
Only to those who would not fight ?
   Or could he not some way dispense
By help of which (without offence   300
To Honour, whose nice nature's such
She scarce endures the slightest touch)
When he for want of t'other rule
Mistakes his man, and like a fool,
With some vain fighting blade gets in,
He fairly may get out again ?
   Or should some demon lay a scheme
To drive him to the last extreme,
So that he must confess his fears,
In mercy to his nose and ears,   310
And, like a prudent recreant knight,
Rather do any thing than fight,
Could he not some expedient buy
To keep his shame from public eye ?
For well he held, and, men review,
Nine in ten hold the maxim too,
That honour's like a maidenhead,
Which, if in private brought to bed,
Is none the worse, but walks the town,
Ne'er lost, until the loss be known.   320
   The parson, too, (for now and then
Parsons are just like other men,
And here and there a grave divine
Has passions such as yours and mine)
Burning with holy lust to know
When fate preferment will bestow,
'Fraid of detection, not of sin,
With circumspection sneaking in
To conjurer, as he does to whore,
Through some bye alley, or back-door,   330
With the same caution orthodox
Consults the stars, and gets a p——.
   The citizen in fraud grown old,
Who knows no deity but gold,
Worn out, and gasping now for breath,
A medicine wants to keep off death ;

Would know, if that he cannot have,
What coins are current in the grave ;
If, when the stocks (which, by his power,
Would rise or fall in half an hour,   340
For, though unthought of and unseen,
He work'd the springs behind the screen)
By his directions came about,
And rose to par, he should sell out,
Whether he safely might, or no,
Replace it in the funds below.
  By all address'd, believed, and paid,
Many pursued the thriving trade,
And, great, in reputation grown,
Successive held the magic throne,   350
Favour'd by every darling passion,
The love of novelty and fashion,
Ambition, avarice, lust, and pride,
Riches pour'd in on every side.
But when the prudent laws thought fit
To curb this insolence of wit ;
When senates wisely had provided,
Decreed, enacted, and decided
That no such vile and upstart elves
Should have more knowledge than themselves ; 360
When fines and penalties were laid
To stop the progress of the trade,
And stars no longer could dispense,
With honour, farther influence ;
And wizards (which must be confessed
Was of more force than all the rest)
No certain way to tell had got
Which were informers and which not ;
Affrighted sages were, perforce,
Obliged to steer some other course :   370
By various ways, these sons of Chance
Their fortunes labour'd to advance,
Well knowing, by unerring rules,

[355] ' It was by Stat. 17, Geo. II., c. 5, s. 2, enacted that all persons pretending skill in palmistry, telling fortunes, etc., should be deemed rogues and vagabonds, and punished accordingly.' (Tooke.)

Knaves starve not in the land of fools.
Some, with high titles and degrees,
Which wise men borrow when they please,
Without or trouble or expense,
Physicians instantly commence,
And proudly boast an equal skill
With those who claim the *right* to kill.   380
Others about the country roam
(For not one thought of going home)
With pistol and adopted leg,
Prepared at once to rob or beg.
Some, the more subtle of their race,
Who felt some touch of coward grace,
Who Tyburn to avoid had wit,
But never fear'd deserving it,
Came to their brother Smollett's aid,
And carried on the critic trade.   390
Attach'd to letters and the Muse,
Some verses wrote, and some wrote news ;
Those each revolving month are seen
The heroes of a magazine ;
These every morning great appear
In Ledger or in Gazetteer,
Spreading the falsehoods of the day,
By turns, for Faden and for Say ;
Like Swiss, their force is always laid
On that side where they best are paid :   400
Hence mighty prodigies arise,
And daily monsters strike our eyes ;
Wonders, to propagate the trade,
More strange than ever Baker made

[389] Smollett. See note on ' The Apology,' line 298.

[398] Faden was the editor of the *Ledger*, Say of the *Gazetteer*. Faden assisted Kidgell to procure a copy of Wilkes' 'Essay on Woman,' for the Earl of March, in order that portions of the work might be read in the House of Lords.

[399] The Swiss provided most of the mercenary troops of Europe.

[404] Sir Richard Baker (1568-1645) was the author of a 'Chronicle of the Kings of England ' and of various devotional and other works. Most of his literary work was done in the Fleet prison, where he was imprisoned for debts of relatives for whom he had gone surety. He

Are hawk'd about from street to street,
And fools believe, whilst liars eat.
　Now armies in the air engage,
To fright a superstitious age ;
Now comets through the ether range,
In governments portending change ;　　　　　410
Now rivers to the ocean fly
So quick, they leave their channels dry ;
Now monstrous whales on Lambeth shore
Drink the Thames dry, and thirst for more ;
And every now and then appears
An Irish savage, numbering years
More than those happy sages could
Who drew their breath before the flood ;
Now, to the wonder of all people,
A church is left without a steeple ;　　　　　420
A steeple now is left in lurch,
And mourns departure of the church,
Which, borne on wings of mighty wind,
Removed a furlong off we find ;
Now, wrath on cattle to discharge,
Hailstones as deadly fall, and large,

had a predilection for the marvellous, here glanced at by Churchill, and his ' Chronicle,' although highly popular with the country gentry (Sir Roger de Coverley is represented as frequently quoting the ' Chronicle,' which always lay in his hall window), was not much esteemed by the learned. Baker was also the author of a defence of the theatre in reply to Prynne's ' Histrio-Mastix.'

[409] ' A little after six in the evening, a meteor resembling a ball of fire was seen at Whitby. Its direction was from N.E. to S.W., and in its progression it threw off a vast quantity of fire, that formed a train across our hemisphere, which continued a quarter of an hour after the meteor itself had disappeared.' (' Gentleman's Magazine,' Tues., November 3rd, 1761.) ' A comet was discovered from the marine observatory in France. It appeared in the constellation of Camdopardalus, about 15 deg. from the pole.' (*Ibid.*, Sat., June 29th, 1762.)

[413] ' One of the periodical wonders of the metropolis ; but no whale has yet appeared in the river of such monstrous dimensions as that which, on the 9th of July, 1574, shot himself ashore at Broad Stairs.' (Tooke.) The present editor has been unable to find any more exact reference.

[426] ' And Moses stretched forth his rod towards heaven : and the Lord sent thunder and hail, and the fire ran along upon the ground ; and the Lord rained hail upon the land of Egypt.' Exodus ix. 23.

As those which were on Egypt sent,
At once their crime and punishment,
Or those which, as the prophet writes,
Fell on the necks of Amorites,   430
When, struck with wonder and amaze,
The sun suspended, stay'd to gaze,
And, from her duty longer kept,
In Ajalon his sister slept.

But if such things no more engage
The taste of a politer age,
To help them out in time of need
Another Tofts must rabbits breed :
Each pregnant female trembling hears,
And, overcome with spleen and fears,   440
Consults her faithful glass no more
But madly bounding o'er the floor,
Feels hairs o'er all her body grow,
By fancy turn'd into a doe.

Now, to promote their private ends,
Nature her usual course suspends,
And varies from the stated plan
Observed e'er since the world began.
Bodies, (which foolishly we thought,
By custom's servile maxims taught,   450
Needed a regular supply,
And without nourishment must die)

---

430 ' And it came to pass, as they (the Amorites) fled from before
Israel, and were in the going down to Beth-horon, that the Lord cast
down great stones from heaven upon them unto Azekah, and they
died : they were more which died with hailstones than they whom the
children of Israel slew with the sword.'   Joshua x. 11.

432-434 ' Then spake Joshua to the Lord in the day when the Lord
delivered up the Amorites before the children of Israel, and he said in
the sight of Israel, Sun, stand thou still upon Gibeon ; and thou,
Moon, in the valley of Ajalon. And the sun stood still, and the moon
stayed, until the people had avenged themselves upon their enemies.'
Joshua x. 12, 13.

438 Mary Tofts, or Toft (c. 1701-1763) of Godalming, professed to
have given birth, in November, 1726, to a litter of fifteen rabbits. The
affair created enormous public excitement, but the woman soon con-
fessed to an imposture. She afterwards underwent a term of imprison-
ment (in 1740) for receiving stolen goods, and died in obscurity at her
native place.

With craving appetites, and sense
Of hunger easily dispense,
And, pliant to their wondrous skill,
Are taught, like watches, to stand still,
Uninjured, for a month or more,
Then go on as they did before.
The novel takes, the tale succeeds,
Amply supplies its author's needs,   460
And Betty Canning is at least,
With Gascoyne's help, a six months' feast.
  Whilst, in contempt of all our pains,
The tyrant Superstition reigns
Imperious in the heart of man,
And warps his thoughts from Nature's plan ;
Whilst fond Credulity, who ne'er
The weight of wholesome doubts could bear,
To reason and herself unjust,
Takes all things blindly upon trust ;   470
Whilst Curiosity, whose rage
No mercy shews to sex or age,
Must be indulged at the expense
Of judgment, truth, and common sense ;
Impostures cannot but prevail,

[461] Elizabeth Canning (1734-1773) was the daughter of a sawyer and a maid-servant at Aldermanbury. She falsely asserted that she had been kidnapped and kept prisoner by a procuress, from January 1st to 29th, 1753. ' An investigation was set on foot, and having fixed upon a house at Enfield Wash, on the Hertford Road, as the place where she had been confined, one Mrs. Wills who kept it, together with Mary Squires the gypsy, and Virtue Hall, the young woman who lived with Wills, were taken up and committed for trial. . . . Wills and Squires were found guilty, and the latter sentenced to suffer death.' (Tooke.) However, in the following year, Elizabeth Canning was convicted of perjury and sentenced to transportation ; but many believed her innocent, and her case led to a war of pamphlets and great public excitement.

[462] ' Sir Crisp Gascoyne, the Lord Mayor, being dissatisfied with the evidence, took extraordinary pains to unravel the conspiracy, in which he succeeded to his utmost wish. An alibi was clearly made out, and a free pardon granted to Mary Squires. . . . Sir Crisp Gascoyne incurred a great deal of unpopularity by the zeal he displayed in detecting the fraud, but at the expiration of his mayoralty the Common Council did justice to his motives by a special vote of thanks for his conduct on the occasion.' (Tooke.)

And when old miracles grow stale,
Jugglers will still the art pursue,
And entertain the world with new.
    For them, obedient to their will,
And trembling at their mighty skill,   480
Sad spirits, summon'd from the tomb,
Glide glaring, ghastly through the gloom
In all the usual pomp of storms,
In horrid, customary forms,
A wolf, a bear, a horse, an ape,
As fear and fancy give them shape;
Tormented with despair and pain,
They roar, they yell, and clank the chain.
Folly and Guilt (for Guilt, howe'er
The face of Courage it may wear,   490
Is still a coward at the heart)
At fear-created phantoms start.
The priest, that very word implies
That he's both innocent and wise,
Yet fears to travel in the dark,
Unless escorted by his clerk.
    But let not every bungler deem
Too lightly of so deep a scheme;
For reputation of the art
Each Ghost must act a proper part,   500
Observe decorum's needful grace,
And keep the laws of time and place;
Must change, with happy variation,
His manners with his situation;
What in the country might pass down,
Would be impertinent in town.
No spirit of discretion here
Can think of breeding awe and fear,
'Twill serve the purpose more by half
To make the congregation laugh.   510
We want no ensigns of surprise,
Locks stiff with gore, and saucer eyes;
Give us an entertaining sprite,
Gentle, familiar, and polite,
One who appears in such a form

As might an holy hermit warm,
Or who on former schemes refines,
And only talks by sounds and signs,
Who will not to the eye appear,
But pays her visits to the ear,   520
And knocks so gently, 'twould not fright
A lady in the darkest night.
Such is our Fanny, whose good will,
Which cannot in the grave lie still,
Brings her on earth to entertain
Her friends and lovers in Cock Lane.

[523] The excitement over the Cock Lane Ghost was the occasion for Churchill's republishing his old poem, ' The Fortune Teller,' re-named and expanded with a wealth of topical allusion. The story may be briefly summarised. Elizabeth Parsons (1749-1807) was the daughter of the deputy parish clerk of St. Sepulchre's, in the City of London. She was born in an obscure turning named Cock Lane, between Newgate Street and West Smithfield. The family was poor and took in lodgers, among others, a man from Norfolk named William Kent. Kent's wife had died in 1756, three years before his arrival in London, and he was living with his deceased wife's sister, Fanny Lynes. When Kent, on one occasion, was away, Fanny had Elizabeth Parsons, then eleven years old, to sleep with her, and in the night was much disturbed by strange noises, and these noises continued to be heard until Kent and Fanny left Cock Lane for Bartlett Court, Clerkenwell. There Fanny died, on February 2nd, 1760, and her coffin was placed in the vault of St. John's Church.

Parsons owed money to Kent and the latter, at the beginning of 1762, instituted proceedings against him. The strange noises at Cock Lane immediately recommenced, Parsons alleging first that it was a ghost and then that it was the ghost of Fanny Lynes poisoned by Kent with ' red arsenic.' The affair obtained the utmost publicity, and people of all classes crowded to Cock Lane to await further manifestations. (See note on Book II. l. 276.) The Rev. Dr. Aldrich, of St. John's, Clerkenwell, insisted on a séance being held in his own house and, with the help of Dr. Johnson, exposed the imposture. On July 10th, 1762, Parsons and others were convicted of conspiracy and punished. A clergyman named Moore and a tradesman who had lent themselves to the fraud, paid Kent £600 as compensation. The girl Elizabeth was twice married, and died at Chiswick in 1807.

A sacred, standard rule we find,
By poets held time out of mind—
To offer at Apollo's shrine,
And call on one, or all the Nine.
  This custom, through a bigot zeal
Which moderns of fine taste must feel
For those who wrote in days of yore,
Adopted stands like many more ;
Though every cause which then conspired
To make it practised and admired,   10
Yielding to Time's destructive course,
For ages past hath lost its force.
  With ancient bards, an invocation
Was a true act of adoration,
Of worship an essential part,
And not a formal piece of art,
Of paltry reading a parade,
A dull solemnity in trade,
A pious fever, taught to burn
An hour or two, to serve a turn.   20
  They talk'd not of Castalian springs,
By way of saying pretty things,
As we dress out our flimsy rhimes ;
'Twas the religion of the times ;
And they believed that holy stream
With greater force made fancy teem,
Reckon'd by all a true specific
To make the barren brain prolific :
Thus Romish church, (a scheme which bears
Not half so much excuse as theirs)   30
Since Faith implicitly hath taught her,
Reveres the force of holy water.

---

* Published with Book I in March, 1762.

[21] Castalia : a fountain on the slope of Parnassus, sacred to Apollo
and the Muses.

The Pagan system, whether true
Or false, its strength, like buildings, drew
From many parts disposed to bear,
In one great whole, their proper share.
Each god of eminent degree
To some vast beam compared might be ;
Each godling was a peg, or rather
A cramp, to keep the beams together :   40
And man as safely might pretend
From Jove the thunderbolt to rend,
As with an impious pride aspire
To rob Apollo of his lyre.
   With settled faith and pious awe,
Establish'd by the voice of Law,
Then poets to the Muses came,
And from their altars caught the flame.
Genius, with Phœbus for his guide,
The Muse ascending by his side,   50
With towering pinions dared to soar,
Where eye could scarcely strain before.
   But why should we, who cannot feel
These glowings of a Pagan zeal,
That wild enthusiastic force,
By which, above her common course,
Nature, in ecstasy upborne,
Look'd down on earthly things with scorn ;
Who have no more regard, 'tis known,
For their religion than our own,   60
And feel not half so fierce a flame
At Clio's as at Fisher's name ;
Who know these boasted sacred streams
Were mere romantic idle dreams,
That Thames has waters clear as those
Which on the top of Pindus rose,
And that the fancy to refine,
Water's not half so good as wine ;

[62] Clio, the Muse of History.   Catherine (or Kitty) Fisher, a woman
of the town.
  [66] Pindus, a mountain range in Greece, between Thessaly and
Epirus.   It rises to a height of 7,600 feet.

Who know, if profit strikes our eye,
Should we drink Helicon quite dry,   70
The whole fountain would not thither lead
So soon as one poor jug from Tweed ;
Who, if to raise poetic fire
The power of Beauty we require,
In any public place can view
More than the Grecians ever knew ;
If wit into the scale is thrown,
Can boast a Lennox of our own ;
Why should we servile customs choose,
And court an antiquated Muse ?   80
No matter why—to ask a reason
In pedant bigotry is treason.
   In the broad, beaten turnpike-road
Of hacknied panegyric ode,
No modern poet dares to ride
Without Apollo by his side,
Nor in a sonnet take the air,
Unless his lady Muse be there ;
She, from some amaranthine grove,
Where little Loves and Graces rove,   90
The laurel to my Lord must bear,
Or garlands make for whores to wear ;
She, with soft elegiac verse,
Must grace some mighty villain's hearse,
Or for some infant, doom'd by fate
To wallow in a large estate,
With rhymes the cradle must adorn,
To tell the world a fool is born.
   Since, then, our critic Lords expect
No hardy poet should reject   100

[70] Helicon, a mountain range in Bœotia, celebrated as the abode of the Muses.

[78] Charlotte Ramsay, later Mrs. Lennox (1720-1804), was born in New York, the daughter of Colonel James Ramsay, Lieutenant-Governor of that city. She obtained fame as a novelist and poet, among the best known of her productions being ' The Female Quixote ' (1752), ' Shakespeare Illustrated ' (1753-1754) and ' The Sister ' a comedy (acted 1769). She was admired by Dr. Johnson who, at a supper-party, crowned her with a wreath of laurel.

Establish'd maxims, or presume
To place much better in their room,
By nature fearful, I submit,
And in this dearth of sense and wit,
With nothing done, and little said,
(By wild excursive Fancy led
Into a second Book thus far,
Like some unwary traveller,
Whom varied scenes of wood and lawn
With treacherous delight have drawn,   110
Deluded from his purposed way ;
Whom every step leads more astray ;
Who, gazing round, can nowhere spy
Or house or friendly cottage nigh,
And resolution seems to lack
To venture forward or go back)
Invoke some goddess to descend,
And help me to my journey's end ;
Though conscious Arrow all the while
Hears the petition with a smile,   120
Before the glass her charms unfolds,
And in herself my Muse beholds.
   Truth, goddess of celestial birth,
But little loved or known on earth ;
Whose power but seldom rules the heart ;
Whose name, with hypocritic art,
An arrant stalking-horse is made,
A snug pretence to drive a trade,
An instrument, convenient grown
To plant, more firmly, Falsehood's throne,   130
As rebels varnish o'er their cause
With specious colouring of laws,
And pious traitors draw the knife
In the king's name against his life ;
Whether, (from cities far away,
Where Fraud and Falsehood scorn thy sway)
The faithful nymph's and shepherd's pride,

[119] A fancy name for Churchill's mistress of the moment. Not,
presumably, Elizabeth Carr, as Churchill is not known to have taken
up with her until the following summer.

With Love and Virtue by thy side,
Your hours in harmless joys are spent
Amongst the children of Content;   140
Or, fond of gaiety and sport,
You tread the round of England's court,
Howe'er my Lord may frowning go
And treat the stranger as a foe,
Sure to be found a welcome guest
In George's and in Charlotte's breast;
If, in the giddy hours of youth,
My constant soul adhered to truth;
If, from the time I first wrote Man,
I still pursued thy sacred plan,   150
Tempted by Interest in vain
To wear mean Falsehood's golden chain;
If, for a season drawn away,
Starting from virtue's path astray,
All low disguise I scorn'd to try,
And dared to sin, but not to lie;
Hither, O hither! condescend,
Eternal Truth! thy steps to bend,
And favour him, who, every hour,
Confesses and obeys thy power.   160
    But come not with that easy mien
By which you won the lively Dean,
Nor yet assume that strumpet air
Which Rab'lais taught thee first to wear,
Nor yet that arch, ambiguous face
Which with Cervantes gave thee grace;
But come in sacred vesture clad,
Solemnly dull, and truly sad!
    Far from thy seemly matron train
Be idiot Mirth, and Laughter vain!   170
For Wit and Humour, which pretend
At once to please us and amend,
They are not for my present turn;

---

[146] Both George III and his Queen were notable for the purity of
their morals.
[162] Dean Swift (1667-1745).

Let them remain in France with Sterne.
Of noblest City parents born,
Whom wealth and dignities adorn,
Who still one constant tenor keep,
Not quite awake nor quite asleep,
With thee let formal Dulness come,
And deep Attention, ever dumb ;   180
Who on her lips her fingers lays,
Whilst every circumstance she weighs,
Whose downcast eye is often found
Bent without motion to the ground,
Or, to some outward thing confined,
Remits no image to the mind,
No pregnant mark of meaning bears,
But, stupid, without vision stares :
Thy steps let Gravity attend,
Wisdom's and Truth's unerring friend ;   190
For one may see with half an eye,
That gravity can never lie,
And his arch'd brow, pull'd o'er his eyes,
With solemn proof proclaims him wise.
    Free from all waggeries and sports,
The produce of luxurious courts,
Where sloth and lust enervate youth,
Come thou, a downright City Truth :
The City, which we ever find
A sober pattern for mankind,   200
Where man, *in equilibrio* hung,
Is seldom old, and never young,
And from the cradle to the grave,
Not Virtue's friend nor Vice's slave ;
As dancers on the wire we spy,
Hanging between the earth and sky.
    She comes—I see her from afar
Bending her course to Temple-Bar :
All sage and silent is her train,
Deportment grave, and garments plain,   210
Such as may suit a parson's wear,
And fit the headpiece of a mayor.

[174] Laurence Sterne visited France in 1762.

By truth inspired, our Bacon's force
Open'd the way to learning's source ;
Boyle through the works of nature ran,
And Newton, something more than man,
Dived into nature's hidden springs,
Laid bare the principles of things,
Above the earth our spirits bore,
And gave us worlds unknown before.   220
By Truth inspired, when Lauder's spite
O'er Milton cast the veil of night,
Douglas arose, and through the maze
Of intricate and winding ways
Came where the subtle traitor lay,
And dragg'd him, trembling, to the day ;
Whilst he, (O shame to noblest parts !
Dishonour to the liberal arts,
To traffic in so vile a scheme !)
Whilst he, our letter'd Polypheme,   230

[213] A reference to Bacon's ' Advancement of Learning ' (1605) and
' Novum Organum ' (1620).

[215] Robert Boyle (1627-1691), the celebrated chemist and natural
philosopher, the discoverer of the elasticity of air and the author of
' New Experiments,' ' Hydrostatical Paradoxes,' etc.

[216] Sir Isaac Newton (1642-1727). The first book of the ' Principia '
was presented to the Royal Society in April, 1686, and the entire work
was published in 1687.

[221] William Lauder (died 1771), was educated at Edinburgh
University and came to London soon after 1742, when he was already
more than sixty years of age. In 1747 he brought out an article in the
' Gentleman's Magazine ' in which he sought to prove Milton guilty
of plagiarism from a Latin poem, entitled ' Sarcotis ' by Jacobus
Masenius (1654). Under the patronage of Johnson, he published, in
1749, ' An Essay on Milton's Use and Mutation of the Moderns in
his " Paradise Lost." ' However, Warburton and others suspected
fraud, and John Douglas, in 1750, in a pamphlet entitled ' Milton
Vindicated from the Charge of Plagiarism ' proved that Lauder had
inserted in his quotations passages from the Latin version of ' Paradise
Lost.' Johnson dictated to Lauder an abject recantation and com-
pelled him to sign it. Lauder's attempts to reinstate himself in public
opinion failed, and he emigrated to Barbados.

[223] John Douglas (1721-1807), Bishop of Salisbury (1791), exposed
the frauds of William Lauder (see preceding note). He also defended
Lord George Sackville in 1759 against the charge of cowardice at Min-
den, and in 1763 helped, with Johnson, to expose the Cock Lane Ghost.

[230] ' Our letter'd Polypheme ' is Johnson. Churchill's attack was
quite unjustified. (See previous note, line 221).

Who had confederate forces join'd,
Like a base coward skulk'd behind.
By Truth inspired, our critics go
To track Fingal in Highland snow,
To form their own and other's creed
From manuscripts they cannot read.
By Truth inspired, we numbers see
Of each profession and degree,
Gentle and simple, lord and cit,
Wit without wealth, wealth without wit,   240
When Punch and Sheridan have done,
To Fanny's ghostly lectures run.
By Truth and Fanny now inspired,
I feel my glowing bosom fired ;
Desire beats high in every vein
To sing the spirit of Cock Lane ;
To cell (just as the measure flows
In halting rhyme, half verse, half prose)
With more than mortal arts endued,
How she united force withstood,   250
And proudly gave a brave defiance
To Wit and Dulness in alliance.
   This apparition (with relation
To ancient modes of derivation,
This we may properly so call,
Although it ne'er appears at all,
As by the way of innuendo,
Lucus is made *à non lucendo*)
Superior to the vulgar mode,
Nobly disdains that servile road   260
Which coward Ghosts, as it appears,
Have walk'd in, full five thousand years,
And, for restraint too mighty grown,
Strikes out a method of her own.

[234] See note on James Macpherson in ' The Prophecy of Famine,'
line 129.

[241] An allusion to Sheridan's lectures on elocution. (See note on ' The
Rosciad,' line 648.)   The professor is insultingly coupled with Punch.

[242] *i.e.* ' Scratching Fanny,' the Cock Lane Ghost. (See note on
line 276, below.)

Others may meanly start away,
Awed by the herald of the day ;
With faculties too weak to bear
The freshness of the morning air,
May vanish with the melting gloom,
And glide in silence to the tomb :   270
She dares the sun's most piercing light,
And knocks by day as well as night.
Others, with mean and partial view,
Their visits pay to one or two ;
She, great in reputation grown,
Keeps the best company in Town.
Our active, enterprising Ghost
As large and splendid routs can boast
As those, which, raised by Pride's command,
Block up the passage through the Strand.   280
    Great adepts in the fighting trade,
Who served their time on the parade ;
She-saints, who, true to pleasure's plan,
Talk about God, and lust for man ;
Wits who believe nor God nor Ghost,
And fools who worship every post ;
Cowards, whose lips with war are hung ;

[276] The Cock Lane ghost certainly kept good company. Horace
Walpole (in a letter to George Montagu, February 2nd, 1762) has left
a lively account of his own visit :   'We set out from the Opera,
changed our clothes at Northumberland House, the Duke of York,
Lady Northumberland, Lady Mary Coke, Lord Hertford and I, all
in one hackney coach, and drove to the spot ; it rained torrents, yet
the lane was full of mob, and the house so full we could not get in ;
at last they discovered it was the Duke of York, and the company
squeezed themselves into one another's pockets to make room for us.
The house, which is borrowed, and to which the ghost has adjourned,
is wretchedly small and miserable ; when we opened the chamber, in
which were fifty people, with no light but one tallow candle at the end,
we tumbled over the bed of the child to whom the ghost comes, and
whom they are murdering by inches in such insufferable heat and
stench. . . . We had nothing ; they told us, as they would at a
puppet-show, that it would not come that night till seven in the
morning, that is, when there are only 'prentices and old women. We
stayed, however, till half an hour after one.'

[279] A reference to the strings of carriages on their way to the enter-
tainments given by the Duchess of Northumberland, at Northum-
berland House, Charing Cross.

Men truly brave, who hold their tongue ;
Courtiers, who laugh they know not why,
And cits, who for the same cause cry ;   290
The canting tabernacle brother,
(For one rogue still suspects another)
Ladies, who to a spirit fly,
Rather than with their husbands lie ;
Lords, who as chastely pass their lives
With other women as their wives ;
Proud of their intellects and clothes,
Physicians, lawyers, parsons, beaus,
And, truant from their desks and shops,
Spruce Temple clerks and 'prentice fops,   300
To Fanny come, with the same view,
To find her false, or find her true.
    Hark ! something creeps about the house !
Is it a spirit or a mouse ?
Hark ! something scratches round the room !
A cat, a rat, a stubb'd birch broom.
Hark ! on the wainscot now it knocks !
' If thou'rt a Ghost,' cried Orthodox,
With that affected, solemn air
Which hypocrites delight to wear,   310
And all those forms of consequence
Which fools adopt instead of sense ;
' If thou'rt a Ghost, who from the tomb
Stalk'st sadly silent through this gloom,
In breach of nature's stated laws,
For good, or bad, or for no cause,
Give now nine knocks ; like priests of old,
Nine we a sacred number hold.'
    ' Psha,' cried Profound, (a man of parts,
Deep read in all the curious arts,   320
Who, to their hidden springs had traced
The force of numbers rightly placed)
' As to the number, you are right ;
As to the form, mistaken quite.

291 The Tabernacle in Moorfields was a well-known centre of
revivalism of the Whitefield pattern. (See note on Book I, line 71.)
Churchill detested the Methodists.

What's nine ?—Your adepts all agree
The virtue lies in three times three.'
He said ; no need to say it twice,
For thrice she knock'd, and thrice, and thrice.
The crowd, confounded and amazed,
In silence at each other gazed :   330
From Celia's hand the snuff-box fell,
Tinsel, who ogled with the belle,
To pick it up attempts in vain,
He stoops, but cannot rise again.
Immane Pomposo was not heard
T' import one crabbed foreign word :
Fear seizes heroes, fools and wits,
And Plausible his prayers forgets.
At length, as people just awake,
Into wild dissonance they break ;   340
All talk'd at once, but not a word
Was understood or plainly heard.
Such is the noise of chattering geese,
Slow sailing on the summer breeze ;
Such is the language Discord speaks
In Welsh women o'er beds of leeks ;
Such the confused and horrid sounds
Of Irish in potato grounds.
But tired, for even C——'s tongue
Is not on iron hinges hung,   350
Fear and Confusion sound retreat,
Reason and Order take their seat.
The fact confirm'd beyond all doubt,
They now would find the causes out.
For this a sacred rule we find
Among the nicest of mankind ;
Which never might exception brook
From Hobbes e'en down to Bolingbroke,

[335] Pomposo is Dr. Johnson.

[338] Plausible is the Rev. William Sellon. (See note on 'Night,' line 99).

[349] We may agree with Tooke that ' We know not, nor is it now material to ascertain, which of the City magnates or orators was intended by this initial.'

[358] Thomas Hobbes (1588-1679), author of ' Leviathan,' and Henry

To doubt of facts, however true,
Unless they know the causes too.   360
   Trifle, of whom 'twas hard to tell
When he intended ill or well ;
Who, to prevent all farther pother,
Probably meant nor one nor t'other ;
Who to be silent always loath,
Would speak on either side, or both ;
Who led away by love of fame,
If any new idea came,
Whate'er it made for, always said it,
Not with an eye to truth, but credit,—   370
For orators profess'd 'tis known,
Talk not for our sake, but their own,—
Who always shew'd his talents best
When serious things were turn'd to jest,
And under much impertinence
Possess'd no common share of sense ;
Who could deceive the flying hours
With chat on butterflies and flowers ;
Could talk of powder, patches, paint,
With the same zeal as of a saint ;   380
Could prove a Sibyl brighter far
Than Venus or the Morning Star ;
Whilst something still so gay, so new,
The smile of approbation drew,
And females eyed the charming man,
Whilst their hearts flutter'd with their fan ;
Trifle, who would by no means miss
An opportunity like this,
Proceeding on his usual plan,
Smiled, stroked his chin, and thus began :   390
   ' With sheers or scissars, sword or knife,
When the Fates cut the thread of life,
(For if we to the grave are sent,
No matter with what instrument)
The body in some lonely spot,
On dunghill vile, is laid to rot,

St. John, Viscount Bolingbroke (1678-1751), are here mentioned as typical sceptics.

Or sleep among more holy dead
With prayers irreverently read ;
The soul is sent where Fate ordains,
To reap rewards, to suffer pains.   400
   ' The virtuous, to those mansions go,
Where pleasures unembitter'd flow,
Where, leading up a jocund band,
Vigour and Youth dance hand in hand,
Whilst Zephyr, with harmonious gales,
Pipes softest music through the vales,
And Spring and Flora, gaily crown'd
With velvet carpet spread the ground ;
With livelier blush where roses bloom,
And every shrub expires perfume,   410
Where crystal streams meandering glide,
Where warbling flows the amber tide,
Where other suns dart brighter beams,
And light through purer æther streams.
   ' Far other seats, far different state,
The sons of wickedness await,
Justice, (not that old hag I mean
Who's nightly in the Garden seen,
Who lets no spark of mercy rise,
For crimes, by which men lose their eyes :   420
Nor her, who with an equal hand
Weighs tea and sugar in the Strand ;
Nor her, who, by the world deem'd wise,
Deaf to the widow's piercing cries,
Steel'd 'gainst the starving orphan's tears,
On pawns her base tribunal rears ;
But her, who after death presides,
Whom sacred truth unerring guides,
Who, free from partial influence,
Nor sinks nor raises evidence,   430

[418] *i.e.*, Covent Garden, the headquarters of the ' trading justices '
to whom the administration of the police of London was entrusted.
' These men,' remarks Tooke, ' with clerks taken from the lowest
stations, as the fit instruments of their rapacity, levied fines and annual
tributes from those offenders who were rich enough to obtain exemp-
tion from punishment. A specimen of such a justice may be found in
Foote's Minor.'

Before whom nothing's in the dark,
Who takes no bribe, and keeps no clerk)
Justice, with equal scale below,
In due proportion weighs out woe,
And always with such lucky aim
Knows punishments so fit to frame,
That she augments their grief and pain,
Leaving no reason to complain.
  ' Old maids and rakes are join'd together,
Coquettes and prudes, like April weather,   440
Wit's forced to chum with Common Sense,
And Lust is yoked to Impotence.
Professors (Justice so decreed)
Unpaid, must constant lectures read ;
On earth it often doth befal,
They're paid, and never read at all :
Parsons must practise what they teach,
And bishops are compell'd to preach.
  ' She, who on earth was nice and prim,
Of delicacy full and whim ;   450
Whose tender nature could not bear
The rudeness of the churlish air,
Is doom'd, to mortify her pride,
The change of weather to abide,
And sells, whilst tears with liquor mix,
Burnt brandy on the shore of Styx.
  ' Avaro,—by long use grown bold
In every ill which brings him gold,
Who his Redeemer would pull down,
And sell his God for half-a-crown ;   460
Who, if some blockhead should be willing
To lend him on his soul a shilling,
A well-made bargain would esteem it,
And have more sense than to redeem it,—
Justice shall in those shades confine,

[457] Tooke and Wodhull agree in identifying Avaro with Dr. Pearce.
(See note on ' The Prophecy of Famine,' line 128.)

[459] A painted window representing the crucifixion was put up over
the altar in St. Margaret's Church, Westminster. Dr. Pearce, then
Bishop of Rochester and Dean of Westminster, thought it savoured of
popery, and endeavoured to have it removed. (Tooke.)

To drudge for Plutus in the mine,
All the day long to toil and roar,
And, cursing, work the stubborn ore
For coxcombs here who have no brains,
Without a sixpence for his pains :   470
Thence, with each due return of night
Compell'd, the tall, thin, half-starved sprite
Shall earth re-visit, and survey
The place where once his treasure lay,
Shall view the stall where holy Pride,
With letter'd Ignorance allied,
Once hail'd him mighty and adored,
Descended to another lord :
Then shall he, screaming, pierce the air,
Hang his lank jaws and scowl despair ;   480
Then shall he ban at Heaven's decrees,
And, howling, sink to hell for ease.
  ' Those, who on earth through life have past
With equal pace from first to last,
Nor vex'd with passions nor with spleen,
Insipid, easy, and serene ;
Whose heads were made too weak to bear
The weight of business or of care ;
Who, without merit, without crime,
Contrive to while away their time,   490
Nor good nor bad, nor fools nor wits,
Mild Justice, with a smile, permits
Still to pursue their darling plan,
And find amusement how they can.
  ' The beau, in gaudiest plumage drest
With lucky fancy, o'er the rest,
Of air a curious mantle throws,
And chats among his brother beaus ;
Or, if the weather's fine and clear,
No sign of rain or tempest near,   500
Encouraged by the cloudless day,
Like gilded butterflies at play,
So lively all, so gay, so brisk,
In air they flutter, float and frisk.
  ' The belle, (what mortal doth not know

105

Belles after death admire a beau ?)
With happy grace renews her art
To trap the coxcomb's wandering heart ;
And, after death as whilst they live,
A heart is all which beaux can give.   510
     ' In some still, solemn, sacred shade,
Behold a group of authors laid,
Newspaper wits, and sonneteers,
Gentlemen bards, and rhyming peers ;
Biographers, whose wondrous worth
Is scarce remember'd now on earth,
Whom Fielding's humour led astray,
And plaintive fops, debauch'd by Gray,
All sit together in a ring,
And laugh and prattle, write and sing.   520
     ' On his own works, with laurel crown'd,
Neatly and elegantly bound,
(For this is one of many rules,
With writing lords and laureate fools,
And which for ever must succeed
With other lords who cannot read,—
However destitute of wit,
To make their works for bookcase fit)
Acknowledged master of those seats,
Cibber his Birth-day Odes repeats.   530
     ' With triumph now possess that seat,
With triumph now thy Odes repeat ;
Unrivall'd vigils proudly keep,
Whilst every hearer's lull'd to sleep ;
But know, illustrious Bard ! when Fate,

---

[518] See note on ' Gotham,' Book II, line 20.

[530] Colley Cibber (1671-1757) joined the Theatre Royal in 1690,
where he played under the name of ' Mr. Colley.' He was successful
in comedy parts, and in 1696 brought out his first play, ' Love's Last
Shift.' From 1697 to 1732 he was recognised as the leading character
actor on the English stage. In 1733 he retired, but re-appeared at
intervals until 1745, producing a number of comedies during the same
period. In December, 1730, he was appointed Poet Laureate, but his
official odes are quite worthless. On the other hand, his ' Apology for
the Life of Colley Cibber ' (1740) is an admirable autobiography, of
great value to the historian of the stage. Pope, moved by private
pique, made him the hero of ' The Dunciad.'

Which still pursues thy name with hate,
The regal laurel blasts, which now
Blooms on the placid Whitehead's brow,
Low must descend thy pride and fame,
And Cibber's be the second name.'   540
  Here Trifle cough'd, (for coughing still
Bears witness to the speaker's skill,
A necessary piece of art,
Of rhetoric an essential part;
And adepts in the speaking trade
Keep a cough by them ready made,
Which they successfully dispense
When at a loss for words or sense)
Here Trifle cough'd, here paused—but while
He strove to recollect his smile,   550
That happy engine of his art,
Which triumph'd o'er the female heart,
Credulity, the child of Folly,
Begot on cloister'd Melancholy,
Who heard, with grief, the florid fool
Turn sacred things to ridicule,
And saw him, led by whim away,
Still farther from the subject stray,
Just in the happy nick, aloud,
In shape of Moore, address'd the crowd :   560
  ' Were we with patience here to sit,
Dupes to the impertinence of wit,
Till Trifle his harangue should end,
A Greenland night we might attend,
Whilst he, with fluency of speech,
Would various mighty nothings teach.'
Here Trifle, sternly looking down,
Gravely endeavour'd at a frown,
But Nature unawares stept in,
And, mocking, turn'd it to a grin.   570
  ' And when, in Fancy's chariot hurl'd,

[538] William Whitehead succeeded Cibber in Laureateship. (See note on ' The Prophecy of Famine,' line 256.)
[560] The Rev. Mr. Moore, curate of St. Sepulchre's. (See note on Book I, line 523.)

We had been carried round the world,
Involved in error still and doubt,
He'd leave us where we first set out.
Thus soldiers (in whose exercise
Material use with grandeur vies)
Lift up their legs with mighty pain,
Only to set them down again.
    ' Believe ye not (yes, all I see
In sound belief concur with me)   580
That Providence, for worthy ends,
To us unknown, this Spirit sends ?
Though speechless lay the trembling tongue,
Your faith was on your features hung ;
Your faith I in your eyes could see,
When all were pale and stared like me :
But scruples to prevent, and root
Out every shadow of dispute,
Pomposo, Plausible, and I,
With Fanny, have agreed to try   590
A deep concerted scheme—this night
To fix or to destroy her quite.
If it be true, before we've done,
We'll make it glaring as the sun ;
If it be false, admit no doubt,
Ere morning's dawn we'll find it out.
Into the vaulted womb of death,
Where Fanny now, deprived of breath,
Lies festering, whilst her troubled sprite
Adds horror to the gloom of night,   600
Will we descend, and bring from thence
Proofs of such force to common sense,
Vain triflers shall no more deceive,
And Atheists tremble and believe.'
    He said, and ceased ; the chamber rung
With due applause from every tongue :
The mingled sound (now let me see—
Something by way of simile)
Was it more like Strymonian cranes,

[609] The river Strymon in Macedonia, rose in Mount Scomius,
flowed through the Lake Prasias and fell, south of Amphipolis into

Or winds low murmuring when it rains,   610
Or drowsy hum of clustering bees,
Or the hoarse roar of angry seas ?
Or (still to heighten and explain,
For else our simile is vain)
Shall we declare it like all four,
A scream, a murmur, hum, and roar ?
   Let Fancy now, in awful state,
Present this great triumvirate,
(A method which received we find
In other cases by mankind)   620
Elected with a joint consent,
All fools in town to represent.
   The clock strikes twelve—Moore starts and swears ;
In oaths, we know, as well as prayers,
Religion lies, and a church brother
May use at will or one or t'other ;
Plausible from his cassock drew
A holy manual, seeming new ;
A book it was of private prayer,
But not a pin the worse for wear ;   630
For, as we by the bye may say,
None but small saints in private pray.
Religion, fairest maid on earth !
As meek as good, who drew her birth
From that bless'd union, when in heaven
Pleasure was bride to Virtue given ;
Religion, ever pleased to pray,
Possess'd the precious gift one day ;
Hypocrisy, of Cunning born,
Crept in and stole it ere the morn ;   640
Whitefield, that greatest of all saints,
Who always prays and never faints,
(Whom she to her own brothers bore,
Rapine and Lust, on Severn's shore)
Received it from the squinting dame ;

the Aegean Sea. The numerous cranes on its banks are frequently
mentioned by ancient writers.

[645] Whitefield certainly squinted, but it is a little hard on the
evangelist to accuse him of being so nearly related to Lust and Rapine.

From him to Plausible it came,
Who, with unusual care opprest,
Now, trembling, pull'd it from his breast ;
Doubts in his boding heart arise,
And fancied spectres blast his eyes ;   650
Devotion springs from abject fear,
And stamps his prayers for once sincere.
   Pomposo,—insolent and loud,
Vain idol of a scribbling crowd,
Whose very name inspires an awe,
Whose every word is sense and law ;
For what his greatness hath decreed,
Like laws of Persia and of Mede,
Sacred through all the realm of Wit,
Must never of repeal admit ;   660
Who, cursing flattery, is the tool
Of every fawning, flattering fool ;
Who Wit with jealous eye surveys,
And sickens at another's praise ;
Who, proudly seized of learning's throne,
Now damns all learning but his own ;
Who scorns those common wares to trade in,
Reasoning, convincing, and persuading,
But makes each sentence current pass
With puppy, coxcomb, scoundrel, ass ;   670
For 'tis with him a certain rule,
The folly's proved when he calls fool ;
Who to increase his native strength,
Draws words six syllables in length,
With which, assisted with a frown,
By way of club, he knocks us down ;
Who 'bove the vulgar dares to rise,
And sense of decency defies ;
For this same decency is made
Only for bunglers in the trade,   680
And, like the cobweb laws, is still
Broke through by great ones when they will—
Pomposo, with strong sense supplied,
Supported, and confirm'd by Pride,

[653] Pomposo is Dr. Johnson.

His comrades' terrors to beguile
' Grinn'd horribly a ghastly smile : '
Features so horrid, were it light,
Would put the devil himself to flight.
 Such were the three in name and worth,
Whom Zeal and Judgment singled forth 690
To try the sprite on reason's plan,
Whether it was of God or man.
 Dark was the night ; it was that hour
When terror reigns in fullest power ;
When, as the learn'd of old have said,
The yawning grave gives up her dead ;
When Murder, Rapine by her side,
Stalks o'er the earth with giant stride :
Our Quixotes (for that knight of old
Was not in truth by half so bold ; 700
Though Reason at the same time cries,
Our Quixotes are not half so wise,
Since they, with other follies, boast
An expedition 'gainst a Ghost)
Through the dull, deep surrounding gloom,
In close array, towards Fanny's tomb
Adventured forth ; Caution before,
With heedful step, the lanthorn bore,
Pointing at graves ; and in the rear,
Trembling, and talking loud, went Fear. 710
The church-yard teem'd ; th' unsettled ground,
As in an ague, shook around ;
While, in some dreary vault confined,
Or riding on the hollow wind,
Horror, which turns the heart to stone,
In dreadful sounds was heard to groan.
All staring, wild, and out of breath,
At length they reach the place of death.
 A vault it was, long time applied
To hold the last remains of Pride ; 720
No beggar there, of humble race,
And humble fortunes, finds a place,
To rest in pomp as well as ease ;
The only way's to pay the fees.

III

Fools, rogues, and whores, if rich and great,
Proud even in death, here rot in state.
No thieves disrobe the well-dressed dead ;
No plumbers steal the sacred lead ;
Quiet and safe the bodies lie ;
No sextons sell ; no surgeons buy.   730
   Thrice each the ponderous key applied,
And thrice to turn it vainly tried,
Till taught by Prudence to unite,
And straining with collected might,
The stubborn wards resist no more,
But open flies the growling door.
   Three paces back they fell amazed,
Like statues stood, like madmen gazed ;
The frighted blood forsakes the face,
And seeks the heart with quicker pace ;   740
The throbbing heart its fears declares,
And upright stand the bristled hairs ;
The head in wild distraction swims,
Cold sweats bedew the trembling limbs ;
Nature, whilst fears her bosom chill,
Suspends her powers, and life stands still.
   Thus had they stood till now ; but Shame
(An useful though neglected dame,
By Heaven design'd the friend of man,
Though we degrade her all we can,   750
And strive, as our first proof of wit,
Her name and nature to forget)
Came to their aid in happy hour,
And with a wand of mighty power
Struck on their hearts ; vain fears subside,
And, baffled, leave the field to Pride.
   Shall they, (forbid it, Fame !) shall they
The dictates of vile Fear obey ?
Shall they, the idols of the Town,
To bugbears fancy-form'd bow down ?   760
Shall they, who greatest zeal exprest,
And undertook for all the rest,
Whose matchless courage all admire,
Inglorious from the task retire ?

How would the wicked ones rejoice,
And infidels exalt their voice,
If Moore and Plausible were found,
By shadows awed, to quit their ground !
How would fools laugh, should it appear
Pomposo was the slave of fear !   770
' Perish the thought ! though to our eyes
In all its terrors, hell should rise,
Though thousand Ghosts, in dread array,
With glaring eye-balls, cross our way ;
Though Caution, trembling, stands aloof,
Still we will on, and dare the proof.'
They said ; and, without farther halt,
Dauntless march'd onward to the vault.
　　What mortal men, who e'er drew breath,
Shall break into the house of Death   780
With foot unhallow'd, and from thence
The mysteries of that state dispense,
Unless they with due rights prepare
Their weaker sense such sights to bear,
And gain permission from the state,
On earth their journal to relate ?
Poets themselves, without a crime,
Cannot attempt it e'en in rhyme,
But always, on such grand occasion,
Prepare a solemn invocation,   790
A posy for grim Pluto weave,
And in smooth numbers ask his leave.
But why this caution ? why prepare
Rites needless now ? for thrice in air
The spirit of the Night hath sneezed,
And thrice hath clapp'd his wings well-pleased.
　　Descend then, Truth, and guard thy side,
My Muse, my patroness, and guide !
Let others at invention aim,
And seek by falsities for fame ;   800
Our story wants not, at this time,
Flounces and furbelows in rhyme ;
Relate plain facts ; be brief and bold ;
And let the poets, famed of old,

Seek, whilst our artless tale we tell,
In vain to find a parallel.
Silent all three went in ; about
All three turn'd silent, and came out.

BOOK THREE *

It was the hour, when housewife Morn
With pearl and linen hangs each thorn ;
When happy bards, who can regale
Their Muse with country air and ale,
Ramble afield to brooks and bowers,
To pick up sentiments and flowers ;
When dogs and squires from kennel fly,
And hogs and farmers quit their sty ;
When my Lord rises to the chase,
And brawny chaplain takes his place.   10
    These images, or bad or good,
If they are rightly understood,
Sagacious readers must allow
Proclaim us in the country now ;
For observations mostly rise
From objects just before our eyes,
And every lord in critic wit
Can tell you where the piece was writ ;
Can point out, as he goes along,
(And who shall dare to say he's wrong ?)   20
Whether the warmth (for bards, we know,
At present never more than glow)
Was in the town or country caught,
By the peculiar turn of thought.
    It was the hour,—though critics frown,
We now declare ourselves in Town,
Nor will a moment's pause allow
For finding when we came, or how.
The man who deals in humble prose,
Tied down by rule and method goes ;   30

* Published in September, 1762. 'Printed for the Author, and
sold by William Flexney.'

But they who court the vigorous Muse
Their carriage have a right to choose.
Free as the air, and unconfined,
Swift as the motions of the mind,
The poet darts from place to place,
And instant bounds o'er time and space ;
Nature (whilst blended fire and skill
Inflame our passions to his will)
Smiles at her violated laws,
And crowns his daring with applause.   40
   Should there be still some rigid few
Who keep propriety in view ;
Whose heads turn round, and cannot bear
This whirling passage through the air,
Free leave have such at home to sit,
And write a regimen for wit ;
To clip our pinions let them try,
Not having heart themselves to fly.
   It was the hour, when devotees
Breathe pious curses on their knees ;   50
When they with prayers the day begin
To sanctify a night of sin ;
When rogues of modesty, who roam
Under the veil of night, sneak home,
That free from all restraint and awe,
Just to the windward of the law,
Less modest rogues their tricks may play,
And plunder in the face of day.
   But hold,—whilst thus we play the fool,
In bold contempt of every rule,   60
Things of no consequence expressing,
Describing now, and now digressing,
To the discredit of our skill
The main concern is standing still.
   In plays, indeed, when storms of rage
Tempestuous in the soul engage,
Or when the spirits, weak and low,
Are sunk in deep distress and woe,
With strict propriety we hear
Description stealing on the ear,   70

115

And put off feeling half an hour
To thatch a cot, or paint a flower ;
But in these serious works, design'd
To mend the morals of mankind,
We must for ever be disgraced,
With all the nicer sons of taste,
If once, the shadow to pursue,
We let the substance out of view.
Our means must uniformly tend
In due proportion to their end,   80
And every passage aptly join
To bring about the one design.
Our friends themselves cannot admit
This rambling, wild, digressive wit ;
No—not those very friends, who found
Their credit on the self-same ground.
    Peace, my good grumbling Sir ; for once,
Sunk in the solemn, formal dunce,
This coxcomb shall your fears beguile ;
We will be dull—that you may smile.   90
    Come, Method, come in all thy pride,
Dulness and Whitehead by thy side ;
Dulness and Method still are one,
And Whitehead is their darling son :
Not he whose pen, above control,

[92] Whitehead, *i.e.*, William Whitehead. (See note on line 117 below.)

[95] *i.e.*, Paul Whitehead (1710-1774). He was apprenticed to a mercer in the city, but soon abandoned trade to become a law student. His intimacy with Charles Fleetwood, manager of Drury Lane, and his willingness to back a bill for him to the extent of £3,000, resulted in his confinement in the Fleet prison. His first satire, entitled ' The State Dunces,' was published in 1733, and in 1735 he married Ann, daughter of Sir Swinnerton Dyer, who brought him a fortune of £10,000. His satire ' Manners ' appeared in 1739, and for this a writ was served upon him for libel. He became acquainted with the Medmenham Abbey set, and combined the offices of secretary and steward to Sir Francis Dashwood. This alone would account for Churchill's animosity. When Dashwood, now Lord Le Despencer, became Chancellor of the Exchequer, he rewarded Whitehead with the post of Deputy Treasurer of the Chambers, with a salary of £800 a year. He lived quietly at Twickenham for the rest of his life. He bequeathed his heart to his patron, Lord Le Despencer, with £50 for a marble urn in which to place it. Lord Le Despencer had the urn

Struck terror to the guilty soul,
Made Folly tremble through her state,
And villains blush at being great ;
Whilst he himself, with steady face,
Disdaining modesty and grace,   100
Could blunder on through thick and thin,
Through every mean and servile sin,
Yet swear by Philip and by Paul
He nobly scorn'd to blush at all ;
But he, who in the Laureate chair,
By grace, not merit, planted there,
In awkward pomp is seen to sit,
And by his patent proves his wit ;
For favours of the great, we know,
Can wit as well as rank bestow ;   110
And they who, without one pretension,
Can get for fools a place or pension,
Must able be supposed of course
(If reason is allow'd due force)
To give such qualities and grace
As may equip them for the place.
　　But he—who measures, as he goes,
A mongrel kind of tinkling prose,

carried in procession by the Grenadiers of a Yeomanry regiment. It was placed on a marble pillar in the grounds of his estate, and later transferred to the ball of the steeple of the church which Lord Le Despencer had built, (says Wilkes) ' on the top of a very steep hill, for the convenience and devotion of the town at the bottom of it.'

[103] ? by Philip Francis and Paul Whitehead.

[117] William Whitehead (1715-1785) was born at Cambridge, the son of a baker. Through patronage he was educated at Winchester and later became a sizar at Clare Hall, Cambridge. In 1742 he was elected a Fellow of his College, but in 1745 he undertook the private tuition of the future Earl of Jersey and soon after abandoned the fellowship. His tragedy of ' The Roman Father ' was brought out by Garrick in 1750. His unpretentious and not inadequate verse slowly increased his reputation, and on the death of Colley Cibber in 1757, the Duke of Devonshire offered him the laureateship, which had been refused by Gray. The birthday odes which he produced added nothing to his fame. However, his play ' The School for Lovers ' was produced with success in 1762 and he became Garrick's ' reader ' of plays. Churchill's hostility to the Laureate probably dated from the latter's publication in 1762 of his ' Address to Youthful Poets, a poetic Charge,' which taking up the theme of Whitehead's ' Danger of Writing Verse '

And is too frugal to dispense,
At once, both poetry and sense ;   120
Who, from amidst his slumbering guards,
Deals out a charge to subject bards,
Where couplets after couplets creep
Propitious to the reign of sleep ;
Yet every word imprints an awe,
And all his dictates pass for law
With beaus, who simper all around,
And belles, who die in every sound :
For in all things of this relation,
Men mostly judge from situation,   130
Nor in a thousand find we one
Who really weighs what's said or done ;
They deal out censure, or give credit,
Merely from him who did or said it.
    But he—who, happily serene,
Means nothing, yet would seem to mean,
Who rules and cautions can dispense
With all that humble insolence
Which impudence in vain would teach,
And none but modest men can reach ;   140
Who adds to sentiments the grace
Of always being out of place,
And drawls out morals with an air
A gentleman would blush to wear ;
Who, on the chastest, simplest plan,

published twenty years before, may be thought to reflect upon
Churchill in the following lines :

    ' But chief avoid the boist'rous roaring sparks,
    The sons of fire !—you'll know them by their marks.
    Fond to be heard, they always court a crowd,
    And tho' 'tis borrowed nonsense, talk it loud.
    One epithet supplies their constant chime,
    Damn'd bad, *damn'd* good, *damn'd* low, and *damn'd* sublime ! '

    ' Whitehead,' says Tooke, ' adhered to a precept which he had laid
down and made no reply.'   However, Mitford (quoted by D. C.
Tovey in his ' Letters of Thomas Gray ' (London, 1904) declares that
' Mason found among Whitehead's papers some unprinted fragments
of a *counter-scuffle* which the Laureate was preparing, beginning :

    ' So from his common-place when Churchill strings
    Into some motley form his *damned* good things.'

As chaste, as simple, as the man,
Without or character, or plot,
Nature unknown, and art forgot,
Can, with much racking of the brains,
And years consumed in letter'd pains,   150
A heap of words together lay,
And, smirking, call the thing a play ;
Who, champion sworn in virtue's cause,
'Gainst vice his tiny bodkin draws,
But to no part of prudence stranger,
First blunts the point for fear of danger.
So nurses sage, as caution works,
When children first use knives and forks,
For fear of mischief, it is known,
To others' fingers or their own,   160
To take the edge off wisely choose,
Though the same stroke takes off the use.
   Thee, Whitehead, thee I now invoke,
Sworn foe to Satire's generous stroke,
Which makes unwilling conscience feel,
And wounds, but only wounds to heal.
Good-natured, easy creature, mild
And gentle as a new-born child,
Thy heart would never once admit
E'en wholesome rigour to thy wit ;   170
Thy head, if conscience should comply,
Its kind assistance would deny,
And lend thee neither force, nor art
To drive it onward to the heart.
O may thy sacred power control
Each fiercer working of my soul,
Damp every spark of genuine fire,
And languors, like thine own, inspire !
Trite be each thought, and every line
As moral, and as dull as thine !   180
   Poised in mid-air (it matters not
To ascertain the very spot,
Nor yet to give you a relation

_____
[152] Whitehead's ' The School for Lovers,' founded on ' Le Testament ' of Fontenelle.

How it eluded gravitation)
Hung a watch-tower, by Vulcan plann'd
With such rare skill, by Jove's command,
That every word, which whisper'd here
Scarce vibrates to the neighbour ear,
On the still bosom of the air
Is borne, and heard distinctly there ;   190
The palace of an ancient dame,
Whom men as well as gods call Fame ;
A prattling gossip, on whose tongue
Proof of ' perpetual motion ' hung,
Whose lungs in strength all lungs surpass,
Like her own trumpet made of brass ;
Who with an hundred pair of eyes
The vain attacks of sleep defies ;
Who with an hundred pair of wings
News from the farthest quarters brings,   200
Sees, hears, and tells, untold before,
All that she knows and ten times more.

   Not all the virtues which we find
Concenter'd in a Hunter's mind,
Can make her spare the rancorous tale,
If, in one point she chance to fail ;
Or if once in a thousand years
A perfect character appears,
Such as of late with joy and pride
My soul possess'd, ere Arrow died ;   210
Or such as envy must allow
The world enjoys in Hunter now ;
This hag, who aims at all alike,
At virtues e'en like theirs will strike,
And make faults in the way of trade,
When she can't find them ready made.

[204] Catherine (or Kitty) Hunter, who created a great scandal in February, 1762, by eloping with Henry, Earl of Pembroke.   The King was much incensed, deprived Lord Pembroke of his military commands and struck his name from the list of privy counsellors.   Horace Walpole gives an amusing account of the affair in a letter to George Montagu (February 22nd, 1762).   Miss Hunter afterwards married Captain Alured Clarke, who died a Field-Marshal and a Knight in 1832.

[210] Arrow remains unidentified.   (See note on Book II, line 119.)

All things she takes in, small and great,
Talks of a toyshop and a state ;
Of wits and fools, of saints and kings,
Of garters, stars, and leading strings ;   220
Of old lords fumbling for a clap,
And young ones full of prayer and pap ;
Of courts, of morals, and tye-wigs,
Of bears and serjeants dancing jigs ;
Of grave professors at the bar
Learning to thrum on the guitar,
Whilst laws are slubber'd o'er in haste,
And judgment sacrificed to taste ;
Of whited sepulchres, lawn sleeves,
And God's house made a den of thieves ;   230
Of funeral pomps, where clamours hung,
And fix'd disgrace on every tongue,
Whilst Sense and Order blush'd to see
Nobles without humanity ;
Of coronations, where each heart,
With honest raptures, bore a part ;
Of city feasts, where Elegance
Was proud her colours to advance,
And Gluttony, uncommon case,
Could only get the second place ;   240
Of new-raised pillars in the state,
Who must be good, as being great ;
Of shoulders, on which honours sit
Almost as clumsily as wit ;
Of doughty knights, whom titles please,
But not the payment of the fees ;
Of lectures, whither every fool

[231] The funeral procession of George II took place on 11th November, 1760.

[235] The coronation of GeorgeIII took place on 22nd September,1761.

[237] ' Their majesties were entertained by the city at Guildhall, according to custom, on the first Lord Mayor's day after their coronation. The banquet was provided in a style then unprecedented in the civic annals. It cost £6,898. 5. 4.' (Tooke.)

[247] Macklin and Sheridan were both giving lectures on elocution. (See notes on ' The Rosciad,' lines 633 and 648.)

In second childhood goes to school ;
Of grey-beards, deaf to Reason's call,
From Inn of Court, or City Hall,   250
Whom youthful appetites enslave,
With one foot fairly in the grave,
By help of crutch, a needful brother,
Learning of Hart to dance with t'other ;
Of doctors regularly bred
To fill the mansions of the dead ;
Of quacks, (for quacks they must be still,
Who save when forms require to kill)
Who life, and health, and vigour give
To him not one would wish to live ;   260
Of artists who, with noblest view,
Disinterested plans pursue,
For trembling worth the ladder raise,
And mark out the ascent to praise ;
Of arts and sciences, where meet,
Sublime, profound, and all complete,
A set (whom at some fitter time
The Muse shall consecrate in rhyme)
Who, humble artists to out-do,
A far more liberal plan pursue,   270
And let their well-judged premiums fall
On those who have no worth at all ;
Of sign-post exhibitions, raised
For laughter more than to be praised,
(Though by the way we cannot see

254 Hart, a fashionable dancing master.

265 The Society for the Encouragement of Arts, Manufactures and
Commerce was founded in 1753.   It took its origin from an academy
established in the Strand by the landscape painter, William Shipley.
Attention was paid to the application of science to practical purposes.
Exhibitions of pictures by native artists were held, and the first exhi-
bition of the Royal Academy (founded by George III in 1768) took
place in its rooms.

273 'Bonnell Thornton (see note on " Gotham," Book I, line 147),
previous to the annual opening of the Society of Arts on 20th April,
1762, advertised for the same day in the papers an exhibition by the
society of sign painters.   The public, considering it as a mere news-
paper skit, enjoyed the joke ; but the plan was actually carried into
execution in a room in Bow Street, Covent Garden.' (Tooke.)

Why praise and laughter mayn't agree)
Where genuine humour runs to waste,
And justly chides our want of taste,
Censured, like other things, though good,
Because they are not understood.   280
    To higher subjects now she soars,
And talks of politics and whores ;
(If to your nice and chaster ears
That term indelicate appears,
Scripture politely shall refine
And melt it into concubine)
In the same breath spreads Bourbon's league ;
And publishes the grand intrigue ;
In Brussels', or our own Gazette
Makes armies fight which never met,   290
And circulates the pox or plague
To London by the way of Hague,—
For all the lies which there appear
Stamp'd with authority come here ;
Borrows as freely from the gabble
Of some rude leader of a rabble,
Or from the quaint harangues of those
Who lead a nation by the nose,
As from those storms which, void of art,
Burst from our honest patriot's heart,   300
When Eloquence and Virtue (late
Remark'd to live in mutual hate)
Fond of each other's friendship grown,
Claim every sentence for their own ;
And with an equal joy recites
Parade amours and half pay fights,
Perform'd by heroes of fair weather,
Merely by dint of lace and feather,
As those rare acts which Honour taught

287 The family compact between France and Spain concluded in
August, 1761.

289 ' The Brussels Gazette was a notorious vehicle for the experi-
ments of the continental diplomatists on the political credulity of the
public.' (Tooke.)

300 The ' honest patriot ' : Pitt.

123

Our daring sons where Granby fought,   310
Or those which, with superior skill,
Sackville achieved by standing still.
    This hag, (the curious, if they please,
May search, from earliest times, to these,
And poets they will always see
With gods and goddesses make free,
Treating them all, except the Muse,
As scarcely fit to wipe their shoes)
Who had beheld, from first to last,
How our triumvirate had past   320
Night's dreadful interval, and heard,
With strict attention, every word,
Soon as she saw return of light,
On sounding pinions took her flight.
    Swift through the regions of the sky,
Above the reach of human eye,
Onward she drove the furious blast,
And rapid as a whirlwind past,
O'er countries, once the seats of taste,
By time and ignorance laid waste ;   330
O'er lands, where former ages saw
Reason and truth the only law ;
Where arts and arms, and public love,
In generous emulation strove ;
Where kings were proud of legal sway,
And subjects happy to obey,
Though now in slavery sunk, and broke
To superstition's galling yoke ;
Of arts, of arms, no more they tell,
Or freedom, which with science fell :   340
By tyrants awed, who never find
The passage to their people's mind ;
To whom the joy was never known

---

[310] The Marquess of Granby was in command of the second line of cavalry at the Battle of Minden, 1759. His superior officer, Lord George Sackville, refused to obey the command of Prince Ferdinand of Brunswick, commander-in-chief of the allied armies, to advance, and halted Granby who had already begun to move. Sackville, in consequence, was dismissed and was succeeded by Granby. (See also notes on ' The Ghost,' Book I, line 250, and ' Independence,' line 512.)

Of planting in the heart their throne ;
Far from all prospect of relief,
Their hours in fruitless prayers and grief
For loss of blessings they employ
Which we unthankfully enjoy.
   Now is the time (had we the will)
To amaze the reader with our skill,   350
To pour out such a flood of knowledge
As might suffice for a whole college,
Whilst with a true poetic force,
We traced the goddess in her course,
Sweetly describing, in our flight,
Each common and uncommon sight,
Making our journal gay and pleasant,
With things long past, and things now present.
   Rivers—once Nymphs—(a transformation
Is mighty pretty in relation)   360
From great authorities we know
Will matter for a tale bestow :
To make the observation clear
We give our friends an instance here.
   The day (that never is forgot)

359-402 Churchill, never an admirer of Pope, here burlesques the
passage in the latter's ' Windsor Forest,' in which the poet relates how
Lodona, daughter of the River Thames, is pursued by Pan, and
praying Diana for aid, is by her transformed into a stream :

> ' Pan saw and loved, and burning with desire
> Pursued her flight; her flight increased his fire . . .
> Now fainting, sinking, pale, the nymph appears ;
> Now close behind his sounding step she hears ;
> And now his shadow reach'd her as she run,
> His shadow lengthened by the setting sun ;
> And now his shorter breath, with sultry air,
> Pants on her neck, and fans her parting hair . . .
> Faint, breathless, thus she pray'd, nor pray'd in vain :
> " Ah, Cynthia ! Ah—though banish'd from thy train,
> Let me, oh, let me to the shades repair,
> My native shades—there weep, and murmur there."
> She said, and melting as in tears she lay,
> In a soft silver stream dissolved away . . .
> Oft in her glass the musing shepherd spies
> The headlong mountains and the downward skies,
> The watery landscape of the pendant woods,
> The absent trees that tremble in the floods,' etc.

Was very fine, but very hot ;
The nymph (another general rule)
Enflamed with heat, laid down to cool ;
Her hair, (we no exceptions find)
Waved careless, floating in the wind ;   370
Her heaving breasts, like summer seas,
Seem'd amorous of the playful breeze :
Should fond Description tune our lays
In choicest accents to her praise,
Description we at last should find,
Baffled and weak, would halt behind.
Nature had form'd her to inspire
In every bosom soft desire ;
Passions to raise, she could not feel ;
Wounds to inflict, she would not heal.   380
A god, (his name is no great matter,
Perhaps a Jove, perhaps a Satyr)
Raging with lust, a godlike flame,
By chance, as usual, thither came ;
With gloating eye the fair one view'd,
Desired her first, and then pursued :
She, (for what other can she do ?)
Must fly—or how can he pursue ?
The Muse, (so custom hath decreed)
Now proves her spirit by her speed,   390
Nor must one limping line disgrace
The life and vigour of the race.
She runs, and he runs, till at length,
Quite destitute of breath and strength,
To Heaven (for there we all apply
For help, when there's no other nigh)
She offers up her virgin prayer,
(Can virgins pray unpitied there ?)
And when the god thinks he has caught her,
Slips through his hands and runs to water,   400
Becomes a stream, in which the poet
If he has any wit may show it.
    A city once for power renown'd,
Now levell'd even to the ground,
Beyond all doubt is a direction

To introduce some fine reflection.
　　Ah, woeful me ! ah, woeful man !
Ah ! woeful all, do all we can !
Who can on earthly things depend
From one to t'other moment's end ?　　　410
Honour, wit, genius, wealth, and glory,
Good lack ! good lack ! are transitory ;
Nothing is sure and stable found,
The very earth itself turns round :
Monarchs, nay ministers, must die,
Must rot, must stink—ah, me ! ah, why !
Cities themselves in time decay ;
If cities thus—ah ! well-a-day !
If brick and mortar have an end,
On what can flesh and blood depend !　　420
Ah, woeful me ! ah, woeful man !
Ah ! woeful all, do all we can !
　　England, (for that's at last the scene,
Though worlds on worlds should rise between,
Whither we must our course pursue)
England should call into review
Times long since past indeed, but not
By Englishmen to be forgot,
Though England, once so dear to Fame,
Sinks in Great Britain's dearer name.　　430
　　Here could we mention chiefs of old,
In plain and rugged honour bold,
To virtue kind, to vice severe,
Strangers to bribery and fear,
Who kept no wretched clans in awe,
Who never broke or warp'd the law,
Patriots, whom, in her better days,
Old Rome might have been proud to raise ;
Who, steady to their country's claim,
Boldly stood up in Freedom's name,　　440
E'en to the teeth of tyrant Pride,
And, when they could no more, they died.
　　There (striking contrast !) might we place

430 On the union with Scotland in 1707, Great Britain became the official name of the United Kingdoms. ' Dearer ' is, of course, ironical.

127

A servile, mean, degenerate race ;
Hirelings, who valued nought but gold,
By the best bidder bought and sold ;
Truants from honour's sacred laws,
Betrayers of their country's cause,
The dupes of party, tools of power,
Slaves to the minion of an hour,   450
Lackeys, who watch'd a favourite's nod,
And took a puppet for their god.
     Sincere and honest in our rhymes,
How might we praise these happier times !
How might the Muse exalt her lays,
And wanton in a monarch's praise !
Tell of a prince in England born,
Whose virtues England's crown adorn,
In youth a pattern unto age,
So chaste, so pious, and so sage,   460
Who, true to all those sacred bands
Which private happiness demands,
Yet never lets them rise above
The stronger ties of public love.
     With conscious pride see England stand,
Our holy Charter in her hand ;
She waves it round, and o'er the isle
See Liberty and Courage smile.
No more she mourns her treasures hurl'd
In subsidies to all the world ;   470
No more by foreign threats dismay'd,
No more deceived with foreign aid,
She deals out sums to petty states,
Whom Honour scorns, and Reason hates ;
But, wiser by experience grown,
Finds safety in herself alone.
' Whilst thus,' she cries, ' my children stand,
An honest, valiant, native band,

---

[457] George III was born at Norfolk House, St. James's Square,
London, on June 4th, (N.S.) 1738.
     [473] A reference to the system of subsidising Continental armies in
order to leave British troops free for colonial conquests. Prussia,
however, was hardly a ' petty state ' even then.

A train'd militia, brave and free,
True to their king, and true to me,   480
No foreign hirelings shall be known,
Nor need we hirelings of our own :
Under a just and pious reign
The statesman's sophistry is vain ;
Vain is each vile, corrupt pretence :
These are my natural defence ;
Their faith I know, and they shall prove
The bulwark of the king they love.'
    These, and a thousand things beside,
Did we consult a poet's pride,   490
Some gay, some serious, might be said,
But ten to one they'd not be read ;
Or were they by some curious few,
Not even those would think them true ;
For, from the time that Jubal first
Sweet ditties to the harp rehearsed,
Poets have always been suspected
Of having truth in rhyme neglected,
That bard except, who from his youth
Equally famed for faith and truth,   500
By prudence taught, in courtly chime
To courtly ears brought truth in rhyme.
    But though to poets we allow,
No matter when acquired or how,
From truth unbounded deviation,
Which custom calls Imagination,
Yet can't they be supposed to lie
One half so fast as Fame can fly ;
Therefore (to solve this Gordian knot,—
A point we almost had forgot)   510
To courteous readers be it known,
That, fond of verse and falsehood grown,
Whilst we in sweet digression sung,
Fame check'd her flight, and held her tongue,

[495] Jubal was the son of Lamech and Adah. ' He was the father of all such as handle the harp and organ.' (Genesis iv, 21.)

[499] ' That bard,' *i.e.*, Mallet, author of ' Truth in Rhyme.' (See note on ' The Prophecy of Famine,' line 131.)

And now pursues, with double force
And double speed, her destined course,
Nor stops till she the place arrives
Where Genius starves and Dulness thrives ;
Where riches virtue are esteem'd,
And craft is truest wisdom deem'd ;   520
Where Commerce proudly rears her throne,
In state to other lands unknown ;
Where, to be cheated and to cheat,
Strangers from every quarter meet ;
Where Christians, Jews, and Turks shake hands,
United in commercial bands ;
All of one faith, and that to own
No god but Interest alone.
   When gods and goddesses come down
To look about them here in Town,   530
(For change of air is understood
By sons of Physic to be good,
In due proportion, now and then,
For these same gods as well as men)
By custom ruled, and not a poet
So very dull but he must know it,
In order to remain *incog,*
They always travel in a fog.
For if we majesty expose
To vulgar eyes, too cheap it grows ;   540
The force is lost, and, free from awe,
We spy and censure every flaw ;
But well preserved from public view,
It always breaks forth fresh and new ;
Fierce as the sun in all his pride
It shines, and not a spot's descried.
   Was Jove to lay his thunder by,
And with his brethren of the sky
Descend to earth, and frisk about,
Like chattering N—— from rout to rout,   550
He would be found, with all his host,
A nine days' wonder at the most.

[517] The ' place ' referred to is the Royal Exchange.
[550] The present editor has no suggestion.

Would we in trim our honours wear,
We must preserve them from the air ;
What is familiar men neglect,
However worthy of respect.
Did they not find a certain friend
In Novelty to recommend,
(Such we, by sad experience, find
The wretched folly of mankind)   560
Venus might unattractive shine,
And Hunter fix no eyes but mine.
    But Fame, who never cared a jot
Whether she was admired or not,
And never blush'd to shew her face
At any time in any place,
In her own shape, without disguise,
And visible to mortal eyes,
On 'Change, exact at seven o'clock,
Alighted on the weathercock,   570
Which, planted there time out of mind
To note the changes of the wind,
Might no improper emblem be
Of her own mutability.
    Thrice did she sound her trump, (the same
Which from the first belong'd to Fame,
An old, ill-favour'd instrument,
With which the goddess was content,
Though under a politer race
Bagpipes might well supply its place)   580
And thrice, awaken'd by the sound,
A general din prevail'd around;
Confusion through the city pass'd,
And fear bestrode the dreadful blast.
    Those fragrant currents which we meet,
Distilling soft through every street,
Affrighted from the usual course,
Ran murmuring upwards to their source :
Statues wept tears of blood, as fast

---

[562] Kitty Hunter. (See note on line 204.)
[585] The street kennels or gutters filled with highly insanitary refuse.

As when a Cæsar breathed his last :   590
Horses, which always used to go
A foot-pace in my Lord Mayor's show,
Impetuous from their stable broke,
And aldermen and oxen spoke.
   Halls felt the force, towers shook around,
And steeples nodded to the ground ;
St. Paul himself (strange sight !) was seen
To bow as humbly as the Dean :
The Mansion House, for ever placed
A monument of City taste,   600
Trembled, and seem'd aloud to groan
Through all that hideous weight of stone.
   To still the sound, or stop her ears,
Remove the cause or sense of fears,
Physic, in college seated high,
Would any thing but medicine try.

 590   ' Calpurnia here, my wife, stays me at home :
              She dreamt to-night she saw my statua,
              Which, like a fountain with a hundred spouts,
              Did run pure blood.'
                                               JULIUS CÆSAR.

   599 ' When it was first resolved in Common Council to build a
Mansion House for the Lord Mayor, Lord Burlington, zealous in the
cause of the arts, sent down an original design of Palladio, worthy of
its author, for their approbation and adoption.   The first question in
court was not whether the plan was proper, but whether this same
Palladio was a freeman of the city or no.   On this, great debates
ensued, and it is hard to say how it might have gone had not a worthy
deputy risen up, and observed gravely that it was of little consequence
to discuss this point, when it was notorious that Palladio was a papist,
and incapable, of course.   Lord Burlington's proposal was then re-
jected *nem. con.*, and the plan of a freeman and a protestant adopted
in its room.   Dance, the man pitched upon, (who afterwards carried
his plan into execution) was originally a shipwright and, to do him
justice, he appears never to have lost sight of his first profession.
The front of the Mansion House has all the resemblance possible
to a deep-laden Indiaman, with her stern galleries and gingerbread
work.   The stairs and passages within are all ladders and gangways,
the two bulk-heads on the roof fore and aft, not unaptly represent
the binnacle and windlass on the deck of the great north country
Catt.'—*Critical Observations on the Buildings and Improvements of
London*, 1771.

   605 The College of Physicians was situated in Warwick Lane,
Newgate Street.

No more in Pewterers' Hall was heard
The proper force of every word ;
Those seats were desolate become,
And hapless Elocution dumb.   610
Form, city-born and city-bred,
By strict Decorum ever led,
Who threescore years had known the grace
Of one dull, stiff, unvaried pace,
Terror prevailing over Pride,
Was seen to take a larger stride ;
Worn to the bone, and clothed in rags,
See Avarice closer hug his bags ;
With her own weight unwieldy grown,
See Credit totter on her throne ; 620
Virtue alone, had she been there,
The mighty sound unmoved could bear.
 Up from the gorgeous bed, where Fate
Dooms annual fools to sleep in state,
To sleep so sound that not one gleam
Of Fancy can provoke a dream,
Great Dulman started at the sound,
Gaped, rubb'd his eyes, and stared around.
Much did he wish to know, much fear,
Whence sounds so horrid struck his ear, 630
So much unlike those peaceful notes,
That equal harmony, which floats
On the dull wing of city air,
Grave prelude to a feast or fair :
Much did he inly ruminate
Concerning the decrees of Fate,
Revolving, thou to little end,
What this same trumpet might portend.
 Could the French—no—that could not be
Under Bute's active ministry, 640
Too watchful to be so deceived—
Have stolen hither unperceived ?

[607] Pewterers' Hall, Lime Street, the scene of Macklin's lectures on elocution.
[627] Sir Samuel Fludyer, Bart., (died 1768), M.P. for Chippenham, Deputy Governor of the Bank of England, Lord Mayor of London 1761-2.

To Newfoundland, indeed, we know
Fleets of war unobserved may go;
Or, if observed, may be supposed,
At intervals when Reason dozed,
No other point in view to bear
But pleasure, health, and change of air ;
But Reason ne'er could sleep so sound
To let an enemy be found   650
In our land's heart, ere it was known
They had departed from their own.
   Or could his successor (Ambition
Is ever haunted with suspicion)
His daring successor elect,
All customs, rules, and forms reject,
And aim, regardless of the crime,
To seize the chair before his time ?
   Or (deeming this the lucky hour,
Seeing his countrymen in power,   660
Those countrymen who, from the first,
In tumults and rebellion nursed,
Howe'er they wear the mask of art,
Still love a Stuart in their heart)
Could Scottish Charles ?—
                  Conjecture thus,
That mental *ignis fatuus*,
Led his poor brains a weary dance
From France to England, hence to France,
Till Information (in the shape
Of chaplain learned, good Sir Crape,   670
A lazy, lounging, pamper'd priest,

[643] ' In May, 1762, a French squadron escaped out of Brest in a fog, and captured the town of St. John's in Newfoundland ; the garrison surrendered themselves prisoners of war ; and some vessels and stores to a considerable amount, became the prey of the victors. Ministry were much blamed for their negligence, but further enquiry was superseded by the recapture, in the September following, of the settlement by a British force under the command of Lord Colville and Colonel Amherst.' (Tooke.)

[670] Crape is Sir S. Fludyer's chaplain, the Rev. Samuel Bruce. He was also preacher at Somerset Chapel, and, shortly after the publication of this poem, was presented by Fludyer to the vicarage of Inglesham, Wiltshire.

Well known at every City feast,
For he was seen much oftener there
Than in the house of God at prayer;
Who, always ready in his place,
Ne'er let God's creatures wait for grace,
Though, as the best historians write,
Less famed for faith than appetite;
His disposition to reveal,
The grace was short, and long the meal;   680
Who always would excess admit,
If haunch or turtle came with it,
And ne'er engaged in the defence
Of self-denying Abstinence,
When he could fortunately meet
With anything he liked to eat;
Who knew that wine, on Scripture plan,
Was made to cheer the heart of man;
Knew too, by long experience taught,
That cheerfulness was kill'd by thought;   690
And from those premises collected,
(Which few perhaps would have suspected)
That none who, with due share of sense,
Observed the ways of Providence,
Could with safe conscience leave off drinking
Till they had lost the power of thinking;)
With eyes half closed came waddling in,
And, having stroked his double chin,
(That chin, whose credit to maintain
Against the scoffs of the profane,   700
Had cost him more than ever state
Paid for a poor electorate,
Which, after all the cost and rout
It had been better much without)
Briefly (for breakfast, you must know,
Was waiting all the while below)
Related, bowing to the ground,
The cause of that uncommon sound;
Related, too, that at the door

[702] *i.e.*, Hanover, the possession of which helped to involve England
in Continental wars.

135

Pomposo, Plausible, and Moore, 710
Begg'd that Fame might not be allow'd
Their shame to publish to the crowd ;
That some new laws he would provide,
(If old could not be misapplied
With as much ease and safety there
As they are misapplied elsewhere)
By which it might be construed treason
In man to exercise his reason ;
Which might ingeniously devise
One punishment for truth and lies, 720
And fairly prove, when they had done,
That truth and falsehood were but one ;
Which juries must indeed retain,
But their effect should render vain,
Making all real power to rest
In one corrupted, rotten breast,
By whose false gloss the very Bible
Might be interpreted a libel.
      Moore (who, his reverence to save,
Pleaded the fool to screen the knave, 730
Though all who witness'd on his part
Swore for his head against his heart)
Had taken down, from first to last,
A just account of all that pass'd ;
But, since the gracious will of Fate,
Who mark'd the child for wealth and state
E'en in the cradle, had decreed
The mighty Dulman ne'er should read,
That office of disgrace to bear
The smooth-lipp'd Plausible was there ; 740
From Holborn e'en to Clerkenwell,

710 Johnson, Sellon and Moore applied to the Lord Mayor for a
prohibition against the ballad-mongers, who were hawking through
the streets an account of their visit to Fanny's tomb.

728 The reference is to Mansfield, whose interpretation of the law of
libels was most unfavourable to the accused, juries being forbidden to
find a verdict beyond the mere fact of publication. The cases of
Wilkes, Woodfall (the printer of ' Junius '), and others, brought matters
to a head, and by the Libel Act of 1792 the jury were entitled to give a
general verdict on the whole matter at issue.

Who knows not smooth-lipp'd Plausible?
A preacher deem'd of greatest note
For preaching that which others wrote.
  Had Dulman now, (and fools, we see,
Seldom want curiosity)
Consented (but the mourning shade
Of Gascoyne hasten'd to his aid,
And in his hand, what could he more?
Triumphant Canning's picture bore)   750
That our three heroes should advance
And read their comical romance,
How rich a feast, what royal fare,
We for our readers might prepare!
So rich and yet so safe a feast,
That no one foreign, blatant beast,
Within the purlieus of the law,
Should dare thereon to lay his paw,
And, growling, cry, with surly tone,
Keep off—this feast is all my own.   760
  Bending to earth the downcast eye,
Or planting it against the sky,
As one immersed in deepest thought,
Or with some holy vision caught,
His hands, to aid the traitor's art,
Devoutly folded o'er his heart;
Here Moore in fraud well skill'd, should go,
All saint, with solemn step and slow.
O that Religion's sacred name,
Meant to inspire the purest flame,   770
A prostitute should ever be
To that arch-fiend Hypocrisy,
Where we find every other vice
Crown'd with damn'd sneaking cowardice.

[744] Sellon was accused of plagiarising the greater part of the sermon which he had preached at St. Andrew's, Holborn, at St. Giles's and at Clerkenwell, and which he published in 1763. The taunt comes strangely from Churchill, who is generally supposed to have published his father's sermons as his own.

[748] Sir Crisp Gascoyne. (See note on Book I, line 462.)

[750] Elizabeth Canning. (See note on Book I, line 461.)

Bold sin reclaim'd is often seen ;
Past hope that man who dares be mean.
There, full of flesh, and full of grace,
With that fine, round, unmeaning face
Which Nature gives to sons of earth
Whom she designs for ease and mirth, 780
Should the prim Plausible be seen ;
Observe his stiff affected mien ;
'Gainst Nature arm'd by gravity,
His features too in buckle see ;
See with what sanctity he reads,
With what devotion tells his beads !
Now, Prophet, shew me, by thine art,
What's the religion of his heart :
Shew there, if truth thou canst unfold,
Religion centred all in gold ; 790
Shew him, nor fear correction's rod,
As false to friendship as to God.
 Horrid, unwieldy, without form,
Savage as ocean in a storm,
Of size prodigious, in the rear,
That post of honour, should appear
Pomposo ; Fame around should tell
How he a slave to interest fell ;
How, for integrity renown'd,
Which booksellers have often found, 800
He for subscribers baits his hook,
And takes their cash—but where's the book ?
No matter where—wise fear, we know,
Forbids the robbing of a foe ;
But what, to serve our private ends,
Forbids the cheating of our friends ?
No man alive, who would not swear
All's safe, and therefore honest there :

---

784 ' In buckle ' might be used in the eighteenth century for ' in curl ' ; hence, a contorted expression of face.

802 Dr. Johnson's promised edition of Shakespeare—for which he had many years before received subscriptions—had not yet appeared. It is thought that Churchill's attack spurred Johnson on to finish the work, which appeared in 1765.

For, spite of all the learned say,
If we to truth attention pay,   810
The word dishonesty is meant
For nothing else but punishment.
Fame, too, should tell, nor heed the threat
Of rogues, who brother rogues abet,
Nor tremble at the terrors hung
Aloft, to make her hold her tongue,
How to all principles untrue,
Not fix'd to old friends nor to new,
He damns the pension which he takes,
And loves the Stuart he forsakes.   820
Nature (who, justly regular,
Is very seldom known to err,
But now and then in sportive mood,
As some rude wits have understood,
Or through much work required in haste,
Is with a random stroke disgraced)
Pomposo form'd on doubtful plan,
Not quite a beast, nor quite a man ;
Like—God knows what—for never yet
Could the most subtle human wit   830
Find out a monster which might be
The shadow of a simile.
      These three, these great, these mighty three—
Nor can the poet's truth agree,
Howe'er report hath done him wrong
And warp'd the purpose of his song,
Amongst the refuse of their race,
The sons of Infamy, to place
That open, generous, manly mind,
Which we, with joy, in Aldrich find—   840
These three, who now are faintly shown,
Just sketch'd, and scarcely to be known,
If Dulman their request had heard,

[819] See note on ' The Author,' line 254.
[820] Dr. Johnson's sympathy with the Jacobites will be remembered
by all readers of Boswell.
[840] The Rev. Stephen Aldrich, Rector of St. John's, Clerkenwell,
active in exposing the Cock Lane Ghost.

In stronger colours had appear'd,
And friends, though partial, at first view,
Shuddering, had own'd the picture true.
　But had the journal been display'd,
And their whole process open laid,
What a vast, unexhausted field
For mirth must such a journal yield !　　　　　　850
In her own anger strongly charm'd,
'Gainst hope, 'gainst fear, by conscience arm'd,
Then had bold Satire made her way,
Knights, lords and dukes her destined prey.
　But Prudence, ever sacred name
To those who feel not virtue's flame,
Or only feel it, at the best,
As the dull dupes of Interest,
Whisper'd aloud (for this we find
A custom current with mankind,　　　　　　860
So loud to whisper, that each word
May all around be plainly heard ;
And Prudence sure would never miss
A custom so contrived as this
Her candour to secure, yet aim
Sure death against another's fame)
' Knights, lords, and dukes—mad wretch, forbear !
Dangers unthought of ambush there ;
Confine thy rage to weaker slaves,
Laugh at small fools, and lash small knaves,　　870
But never, helpless, mean, and poor,
Rush on, where laws cannot secure ;
Nor think thyself, mistaken youth !
Secure in principles of truth :
Truth ! why, shall every wretch of letters
Dare to speak truth against his betters !
Let ragged Virtue stand aloof,
Nor mutter accents of reproof ;
Let ragged Wit a mute become,
When wealth and power would have her dumb ;　880
For who the devil doth not know
That titles and estates bestow
An ample stock, where'er they fall,

Of graces which we mental call !
Beggars, in every age and nation,
Are rogues and fools by situation ;
The rich and great are understood
To be of course both wise and good ;
Consult then interest more than pride,
Discreetly take the stronger side ;   890
Desert, in time, the simple few
Who Virtue's barren path pursue ;
Adopt my maxims—follow me—
To Baal bow the prudent knee ;
Deny thy God, betray thy friend,
At Baal's altars hourly bend,
So shalt thou rich and great be seen ;
To be great now, you must be mean.'
    Hence, tempter, to some weaker soul,
Which fear and interest control ;   900
Vainly thy precepts are address'd
Where Virtue steels the steady breast.
Through meanness wade to boasted power,
Through guilt repeated every hour ;
What is thy gain, when all is done ?
What mighty laurels hast thou won ?
Dull crowds, to whom the heart's unknown,
Praise thee for virtues not thy own :
But will, at once man's scourge and friend,
Impartial Conscience too commend ?   910
From her reproaches canst thou fly ?
Canst thou with worlds her silence buy ?
Believe it not—her stings shall find
A passage to thy coward mind :
There shall she fix her sharpest dart ;
There shew thee truly, as thou art,
Unknown to those, by whom thou'rt prized,
Known to thyself, to be despised.
    The man who weds the sacred Muse
Disdains all mercenary views ;   920
And he who Virtue's throne would rear
Laughs at the phantoms raised by fear.
Though Folly, robed in purple, shines,

141

Though Vice exhausts Peruvian mines,
Yet shall they tremble, and turn pale,
When Satire wields her mighty flail ;
Or should they, of rebuke afraid,
With Melcombe seek hell's deepest shade,
Satire, still mindful of her aim,
Shall bring the cowards back to shame.   930
   Hated by many, loved by few,
Above each little private view,
Honest, though poor, (and who shall dare
To disappoint my boasting there ?)
Hardy, and resolute though weak
The dictates of my heart to speak,
Willing I bend at Satire's throne ;
What power I have be all her own.
   Nor shall yon lawyer's specious art,
Conscious of a corrupted heart,   940
Create imaginary fear
To damp us in our bold career.
Why should we fear ; and what ? the laws ?
They all are arm'd in virtue's cause ;
And aiming at the self-same end,
Satire is always virtue's friend ;
Nor shall that Muse whose honest rage,
In a corrupt, degenerate age,—
When, dead to every nicer sense,
Deep sunk in vice and indolence,   950
The spirit of old Rome was broke
Beneath the tyrant fiddler's yoke,—
Banish'd the rose from Nero's cheek,
Under a Brunswick fear to speak.
   Drawn by conceit from reason's plan,
How vain is that poor creature, man !
How pleased is every paltry elf
To prate about that thing himself !
After my promise made in rhyme,
And meant in earnest at that time,   960
To jog, according to the mode,

⁹²⁸ George Bubb Dodington, Lord Melcombe. (See note on
' Gotham,' Book I, line 461.)

In one dull pace, in one dull road,
What but that curse of heart and head
To this digression could have led ?
Where plunged, in vain I look about,
And can't stay in, nor well get out.
   Could I, whilst Humour held the quill,
Could I digress with half that skill ;
Could I with half that skill return,
Which we so much admire in Sterne,   970
Where each digression, seeming vain,
And only fit to entertain,
Is found, on better recollection,
To have a just and nice connexion,
To help the whole with wondrous art,
Whence it seems idly to depart ;
Then should our readers ne'er accuse
These wild excursions of the Muse ;
Ne'er backward turn dull pages o'er
To recollect what went before ;   980
Deeply impress'd, and ever new,
Each image past should start to view,
And we to Dulman now come in,
As if we ne'er had absent been.
   Have you not seen, when danger's near,
The coward cheek turn white with fear ?
Have you not seen, when danger's fled,
The self-same cheek with joy turn red ?
These are low symptoms which we find
Fit only for a vulgar mind,   990
Where honest features, void of art,
Betray the feelings of the heart :
Our Dulman with a face was bless'd,
Where no one passion was express'd ;
His eye, in a fine stupour caught,
Implied a plenteous lack of thought ;
Nor was one line that whole face seen in
Which could be justly charged with meaning.

[967] An admirable estimate of Sterne's method, there most studied
when it seems most careless. The same cannot be said of all Church-
ill's digressions in this rambling poem.

To Avarice by birth allied,
Debauch'd by marriage into pride,   1000
In age grown fond of youthful sports,
Of pomps, of vanities, and courts,
And by success too mighty made
To love his country or his trade ;
Stiff in opinion, (no rare case
With blockheads in or out of place)
Too weak and insolent of soul
To suffer reason's just control,
But bending, of his own accord,
To that trim, transient toy, My Lord ;   1010
The dupe of Scots, (a fatal race,
Whom God in wrath contrived to place,
To scourge our crimes, and gall our pride,
A constant thorn in England's side ;
Whom first, our greatness to oppose,
He in his vengeance mark'd for foes ;
Then, more to serve His wrathful ends,
And more to curse us, mark'd for friends) ;
Deep in the state, if we give credit
To him, for no one else e'er said it ;   1020
Sworn friend of great ones not a few,
Though he their titles only knew,
And those, (which, envious of his breeding,
Book-worms have charged to want of reading)
Merely to shew himself polite,
He never would pronounce aright ;
An orator with whom a host
Of those which Rome and Athens boast,
In all their pride might not contend ;
Who, with no powers to recommend,   1030
Whilst Jackey Home and Billy Whitehead,
And Dicky Glover sat delighted,

1000 Wodhull saw in this line a gibe at Fludyer's marriage ' to Miss
Brudenell nearly related to (the) late Duke of Montagu.'

1031 John Home. (See note on ' The Prophecy of Famine,' line 127.)
William Whitehead. (See note on ' The Ghost,' Book III, line 117.)

1032 Richard Glover (1712-1785), began publishing poems as early
as 1728. He was patronised by Frederick, Prince of Wales, and by

144

Could speak whole days in Nature's spite,
Just as those able versemen write,—
Great Dulman from his bed arose ;
Thrice did he spit—thrice wiped his nose—
Thrice strove to smile—thrice strove to frown—
And thrice look'd up—and thrice look'd down—
Then silence broke—' Crape, who am I ? '
Crape bow'd, and smiled an arch reply.   1040
' Am I not, Crape ?—I am, you know,
Above all those who are below.
Have I not knowledge ? and for wit,
Money will always purchase it :
Nor, if it needful should be found,
Will I grudge ten, or—twenty pound,
For which the whole stock may be bought
Of scoundrel wits not worth a groat.
But lest I should proceed too far,
I'll feel my friend the Minister   1050
(Great Men, Crape, must not be neglected)
How he in this point is affected ;
For, as I stand a magistrate
To serve him first, and next the state,
Perhaps he may not think it fit
To let his magistrates have wit.
    ' Boast I not, at this very hour,
Those large effects which troop with power ?
Am I not mighty in the land ?
Do not I sit, while others stand ?   1060
Am I not, with rich garments graced,
In seat of honour always placed ?
And do not Cits of chief degree,
Though proud to others, bend to me ?
    ' Have I not, as a Justice ought,
The laws such wholesome rigour taught,
That Fornication, in disgrace,

Bubb Dodington, through whose interest he was returned to Parliament in 1761. His ' Boadicea ' ran for nine nights at Drury Lane in 1753, and in 1761 he published ' Medea,' a tragedy not intended for the stage, but performed for Mrs. Yates's benefit on three occasions. He also wrote a number of unreadable epics.

Is now afraid to shew her face,
And not one whore these walls approaches
Unless they ride in our own coaches ?   1070
And shall this Fame, an old, poor strumpet,
Without our license sound her trumpet ;
And, envious of our City's quiet,
In broad day-light blow up a riot ?
If insolence like this we bear,
Where is our state ? our office where ?
Farewell all honours of our reign,
Farewell the neck-ennobling chain,
Freedom's known badge o'er all the globe ;
Farewell the solemn-spreading robe,   1080
Farewell the sword, farewell the mace,
Farewell all title, pomp, and place ;
Removed from men of high degree,
(A loss to them, Crape, not to me)
Banish'd to Chippenham or to Frome,
Dulman once more shall ply the loom.'
　　Crape, lifting up his hands and eyes,
' Dulman—the loom—at Chippenham '—cries ;
' If there be powers which greatness love,
Which rule below, but dwell above,   1090
Those powers united all shall join
To contradict the rash design.
　' Sooner shall stubborn Will lay down
His opposition with his gown ;
Sooner shall Temple leave the road
Which leads to Virtue's mean abode ;
Sooner shall Scots this country quit,

[1085] Chippenham was his constituency.

[1085] Fludyer had been a clothier at Frome in Somersetshire. (See also note on line 627 above.)

[1093] William Beckford (1709-1770), Alderman and twice Lord Mayor of London, was born in Jamaica, but came to England in 1723 to be educated. At Westminster he made a lasting friend of Mansfield. In 1747 he became M.P. for Shaftesbury, and in 1754 for the City of London. He was elected Lord Mayor in October, 1762, and was in office during all the agitation concerning Wilkes and No. 45 of *The North Briton*. He was again Lord Mayor in 1768. On his death, he bequeathed to his young son, the future author of ' Vathek,' £1,000,000 in money, and £100,000 a year.

And England's foes be friends to Pitt,
Than Dulman, from his grandeur thrown,
Shall wander outcast, and unknown.   1100
  ' Sure as that cane, (a cane there stood
Near to a table made of wood,
Of dry, fine wood a table made,
By some rare artist in the trade,
Who had enjoy'd immortal praise
If he had lived in Homer's days)
Sure as that cane, which once was seen
In pride of life all fresh and green,
The banks of Indus to adorn,
Then, of its leafy honours shorn,   1110
According to exactest rule,
Was fashion'd by the workman's tool,
And which at present we behold
Curiously polish'd, crown'd with gold,
With gold well wrought ; sure as that cane
Shall never on its native plain
Strike root afresh, shall never more
Flourish in tawny India's shore,
So sure shall Dulman and his race
To latest times this station grace.'   1120
  Dulman, who all this while had kept
His eyelids closed as if he slept,
Now looking steadfastly on Crape,
As at some god in human shape—
' Crape, I protest, you seem to me
To have discharged a prophecy :
Yes—from the first it doth appear
Planted by Fate, the Dulmans here
Have always held a quiet reign,
And here shall to the last remain.   1130
  ' Crape, they're all wrong about this Ghost—
Quite on the wrong side of the post—
Blockheads ! to take it in their head
To be a message from the dead,—
For that by mission they design,
A word not half so good as mine.
Crape—here it is—start not one doubt—

147

A plot—a plot—I've found it out.'
' O God ! ' cries Crape, ' how bless'd the nation,
Where one son boasts such penetration ! '   1140
  ' Crape, I've not time to tell you now
When I discover'd this, or how ;
To Stentor go—if he's not there,
His place let Bully Norton bear—
Our citizens to council call—
Let all meet—'tis the cause of all :
Let the three witnesses attend,
With allegations to befriend,
To swear just so much, and no more,
As we instruct them in before.   1150
  ' Stay—Crape—come back—what, don't you see
The effects of this discovery ?
Dulman all care and toil endures—
The profit, Crape, will all be yours.
A mitre, (for, this arduous task
Perform'd, they'll grant whate'er I ask)
A mitre (and perhaps the best)
Shall, through my interest, make thee blest :
And at this time, when gracious fate
Dooms to the Scot the reins of state,   1160
Who is more fit, (and for your use
We could some instances produce)
Of England's church to be the head,
Than you, a Presbyterian bred ?

[1144] Sir Fletcher Norton (1716-1789), first Baron Grantley, was called to the Bar in 1739, and was for many years leader of the northern circuit. He was appointed Solicitor-General on January 25th, 1762, and knighted on the same day. In 1763, among the duties of his office, he ' exhibited information ' against Wilkes for publishing No. 45 of *The North Briton* and the ' Essay on Woman.' In the same year he became Attorney-General, and continued his hostility to Wilkes. He was later Speaker of the House of Commons, a post which he supported in anything but a calm and judicial manner. He obtained a peerage in 1782. His nickname, Sir Bull-face Double Fee, gives a sufficient indication of the popular opinion of his character and his appearance.

[1164] Thomas Secker (1693-1768), was educated for the dissenting ministry. Having conformed to the Establishment, he became Prebendary of Durham in 1727, Chaplain to George II in 1732, Bishop of Bristol in 1734, of Oxford in 1737, Dean of St. Paul's in 1750, and Archbishop of Canterbury in 1758.

But when thus mighty you are made,
Unlike the brethren of thy trade,
Be grateful, Crape, and let me not,
Like old Newcastle, be forgot.
  ' But an affair, Crape, of this size
Will ask from conduct vast supplies ;   1170
It must not, as the vulgar say,
Be done in hugger-mugger way :
Traitors, indeed, (and that's discreet)
Who hatch the plot, in private meet :
They should in public go, no doubt,
Whose business is to find it out.
  ' To-morrow—if the day appear
Likely to turn out fair and clear—
Proclaim a grand processionade ;
Be all the City-pomp display'd ;   1180
Let the Train-bands '—Crape shook his head ;
They heard the trumpet, and were fled—
' Well '—cries the Knight—' if that's the case,
My servants shall supply their place—
My servants—mine alone—no more
Than what my servants did before—
Dost not remember, Crape, that day,
When, Dulman's grandeur to display,
As all too simple and too low,
Our City friends were thrust below,   1190
Whilst, as more worthy of our love,
Courtiers were entertain'd above ?
Tell me, who waited then ? and how ?
My servants—mine—and why not now ?

1169 ' Lord Bute, principally through the interest of the Duke of
Newcastle, was made Secretary of State on the removal of the Earl of
Holderness. The Thane, as he was then called, soon forgot his
obligations, and by seizing every opportunity to render the Duke's
situation disagreeable, compelled him to resign the place of First Lord
of the Treasury, of which Lord Bute possessed himself on May 29th,
1762. . . . It was observed at the time that though the whole bench
of bishops were of his appointment, Warburton was the only one of
the number who had the gratitude to visit a fallen patron.' (Tooke.)

1178 ' The purpose of this solemn preparation was for the address of
thanks to His Majesty on the conclusion of the peace with France.'
(Tooke.)

In haste then, Crape, to Stentor go—
But send up Hart, who waits below ;
With him, till you return again,
(Reach me my spectacles and cane)
I'll make a proof how I advance in
My new accomplishment of dancing.'　　　　1200
　　Not quite so fast as lightning flies,
Wing'd with red anger, through the skies ;
Not quite so fast as, sent by Jove,
Iris descends on wings of love ;
Not quite so fast as Terror rides
When he the chasing winds bestrides,
Crape hobbled—but his mind was good—
Could he go faster than he could ?
　　Near to that tower, which, as we're told,
The mighty Julius raised of old ;　　　　1210
Where, to the block by Justice led,
The rebel Scot hath often bled ;
Where arms are kept so clean, so bright,
'Twere sin they should be soil'd in fight ;
Where brutes of foreign race are shown
By brutes much greater of our own ;
Fast by the crowded Thames, is found
An ample square of sacred ground,
Where artless eloquence presides,
And nature every sentence guides.　　　　1220
　　Here female parliaments debate
About religion, trade, and state ;
Here every Naiad's patriot soul,
Disdaining foreign, base control,
Despising French, despising Erse,
Pours forth the plain old English curse,
And bears aloft, with terrors hung,
The honours of the vulgar tongue.

[1196] Hart, a dancing master.

[1209] The Tower of London, supposed to have been founded by Julius Caesar.

[1215] Horace Walpole mentions an old lion called Nero in the Tower menagerie.

[1221] ' Female parliaments,' *i.e.,* the fish-wives at Billingsgate.

Here Stentor, always heard with awe,
In thund'ring accents deals out law :　　　1230
Twelve furlongs off each dreadful word
Was plainly and distinctly heard,
And every neighbour hill around
Return'd and swell'd the mighty sound.
The loudest virgin of the stream,
Compared with him would silent seem ;
Thames, who, enraged to find his course
Opposed, rolls down with double force,
Against the bridge indignant roars,
And lashes the resounding shores,　　　1240
Compared with him, at lowest tide
In softest whispers seems to glide.
　　Hither directed by the noise,
Swell'd with the hope of future joys,
Through too much zeal and haste made lame,
The reverend slave of Dulman came.
　' Stentor '—with such a serious air,
With such a face of solemn care,
As might import him to contain
A nation's welfare in his brain—　　　1250
' Stentor '—cries Crape—' I'm hither sent
On business of most high intent,
Great Dulman's orders to convey ;
Dulman commands, and I obey.
Big with those throes which patriots feel,
And labouring for the commonweal,
Some secret, which forbids him rest,
Tumbles and tosses in his breast ;
Tumbles and tosses to get free,
And thus the Chief commands by me :　　　1260
　' To-morrow—if the day appear
Likely to turn out fair and clear—
Proclaim a grand processionade ;
Be all the city-pomp display'd ;
Our citizens to council call—
Let all meet—'tis the cause of all ! '

BOOK FOUR *

Coxcombs, who vainly make pretence
To something of exalted sense
'Bove other men, and, gravely wise,
Affect those pleasures to despise,
Which, merely to the eye confined,
Bring no improvement to the mind,
Rail at all pomp ; they would not go
For millions to a puppet-show,
Nor can forgive the mighty crime
Of countenancing pantomime ;   10
No, not at Covent Garden, where,
Without a head for play or player,
Or, could a head be found most fit,
Without one player to second it,
They must, obeying Folly's call,
Thrive by mere shew, or not at all.
With these grave fops, who (bless their brains !)
Most cruel to themselves, take pains
For wretchedness, and would be thought
Much wiser than a wise man ought   20
For his own happiness, to be ;
Who what they hear, and what they see,
And what they smell, and taste, and feel,
Distrust, till Reason sets her seal,
And, by long trains of consequences
Ensured, gives sanction to the senses ;
Who would not, Heaven forbid it ! waste
One hour in what the world calls Taste,
Nor fondly deign to laugh or cry,
Unless they know some reason why,—   30
With these grave fops, whose system seems

* Published in November, 1763. 'Printed for J. Coote . . . .
W. Flexney . . . . G. Kearsley . . . . T. Henderson . . . . J. Gardner
. . . . and J. Almon.'

[10] It was the policy of Rich at Covent Garden to attract the public
by means of spectacular pantomimes ; Garrick, at Drury Lane, was
compelled by the success of Rich to follow his example.

To give up certainty for dreams
The eye of man is understood
As for no other purpose good
Than as a door, through which, of course,
Their passage crowding objects force ;
A downright usher, to admit
New-comers to the court of Wit :
(Good Gravity ! forbear thy spleen,
When I say wit, I wisdom mean)   40
Where, (such the practice of the court,
Which legal precedents support)
Not one idea is allow'd
To pass unquestion'd in the crowd,
But ere it can obtain the grace
Of holding in the brain a place,
Before the chief in congregation
Must stand a strict examination.

   Not such as those, who physic twirl,
Full fraught with death, from every curl ;   50
Who prove, with all becoming state,
Their voice to be the voice of Fate,
Prepared with essence, drop, and pill,
To be another Ward or Hill,
Before they can obtain their ends,
To sign death-warrants for their friends,
And talents vast as theirs employ,
Secundum artem to destroy,
Must pass (or laws their rage restrain)
Before the chiefs of Warwick Lane :   60

[54] ' Joshua Ward. He began life in partnership with his brother William, a drysalter, in Thames Street. About the year 1733, on returning from a long residence abroad, he began to practise physic, and in time was called in to attend King George the Second, whose hand he cured. The king was so highly satisfied with his conduct that he gave him a suite of apartments at Whitehall for his residence, that he might always be near the royal person. He died in 1761, at a very advanced age.' (Tooke.)

[54] Sir John Hill. (See note on ' The Rosciad,' line 107.)

[60] Warwick Lane, Newgate Street, where the College of Physicians was situated. The College was empowered to examine those who wished to practise medicine in London and its immediate surroundings.

Thrice happy Lane, where, uncontroll'd,
In power and lethargy grown old,
Most fit to take, in this bless'd land,
The reins which fell from Wyndham's hand,
Her lawful throne great Dulness rears,
Still more herself, as more in years ;
Where she, (and who shall dare deny
Her right, when Reeves and Chauncy's by)
Calling to mind, in ancient time,
One Garth, who err'd in wit and rhyme,   70
Ordains, from henceforth, to admit
None of the rebel sons of Wit,
And makes it her peculiar care
That Schomberg never shall be there.
   Not such as those, whom Folly trains
To letters, though unbless'd with brains ;
Who, destitute of power and will
To learn, are kept to learning still ;
Whose heads, when other methods fail,
Receive instruction from the tail,   80
Because their sires, a common case

[64] Charles Wyndham (1710-1763), second Earl of Egremont, was educated at Westminster and Christ Church, Oxford. He began political life as a Tory, but gradually allied himself with the Whigs, especially the Duke of Newcastle. On the resignation of Pitt in 1761, Egremont succeeded him as Secretary of State for the Southern Department, and remained in office for the rest of his life. He was chiefly responsible for the prosecution of Wilkes.

[68] 'Dr. Reeves was a physician of considerable practice in the city.' (Tooke.)

[68] Dr. Charles Chauncey (1706-1777) was a physician, but more famous as an antiquary, collecting prints, paintings, books and coins.

[70] Sir Samuel Garth (1661-1719), physician and poet, was elected a fellow of the College of Physicians in 1693. He was a pioneer of dispensaries for the poor, and wrote a poem in support of the project. ('The Dispensary, 1699.') He was a member of the Kit-Cat Club and intimate with many contemporary men of letters. On the accession of George I he was knighted and became physician in ordinary to the king. He was painted by Kneller and drawn by Hogarth.

[74] Dr. Isaac Schomberg (1714-1780) was a German physician practising in London, and was compelled to spend many years in a struggle for recognition by the College of Physicians. He was a friend of Hogarth's and of Garrick's and was one of the doctors who attended the latter on his death-bed.

Which brings the children to disgrace,
Imagine it a certain rule
They never could beget a fool,
Must pass, or must compound for, ere
The chaplain, full of beef and prayer,
Will give his reverend permit
Announcing them for orders fit ;
So that the prelate (what's a name ?
All prelates now are much the same)   90
May, with a conscience safe and quiet,
With holy hands lay on that Fiat
Which doth all faculties dispense,
All sanctity, all faith, all sense ;
Makes Madan quite a saint appear,
And makes an oracle of Cheere.
    Not such as in that solemn seat,
Where the Nine Ladies hold retreat—
The Ladies Nine, who, as we're told,
Scorning those haunts they loved of old,   100
The banks of Isis now prefer,
Nor will one hour from Oxford stir—
Are held for form, which Balaam's ass
As well as Balaam's self might pass,
And with his master take degrees
Could he contrive to pay the fees.
    Men of sound parts, who, deeply read,
O'erload the storehouse of the head
With furniture they ne'er can use,

[95] Martin Madan (1726-1790), a cousin of the poet Cowper and,
like him, educated at Westminster School, was influenced towards
religion by Wesley, and, taking orders, became well-known as an
Evangelist. As Chaplain to the Lock Hospital his preaching obtained
such a reputation that a new chapel was built to accommodate his
congregation. In Churchill's lifetime he had no other notoriety, but
in 1780 he horrified his friends by the publication of ' Thelyphthora.'
Like others who have given their attention to the rescue of ' fallen
women ' he became convinced that the problem of prostitution was
only to be solved by permitting polygamy. This view, it need hardly
be said, brought upon him a storm of obloquy and he was compelled
to resign his chaplaincy.

[96] The present editor has no suggestion. This is obviously not a
reference to Sir Henry Cheere, the statuary. (See note on p. xxxviii.)

Cannot forgive our rambling Muse   110
This wild excursion ; cannot see
Why Physic and Divinity,
To the surprise of all beholders,
Are lugg'd in by the head and shoulders ;
Or how, in any point of view,
Oxford hath any thing to do :
But men of nice and subtle learning,
Remarkable for quick discerning,
Through spectacles of critic mould,
Without instruction, will behold   120
That we a method here have got
To shew what is, by what is not ;
And that our drift (parenthesis
For once apart) is briefly this.
    Within the brain's most secret cells
A certain Lord Chief Justice dwells,
Of sovereign power, whom, one and all,
With common voice, we Reason call,
Though, for the purposes of satire,
A name, in truth, is no great matter :   130
Jefferies or Mansfield, which you will,
It means a Lord Chief Justice still.
Here, so our great projectors say,
The senses all must homage pay ;
Hither they all must tribute bring,
And prostrate fall before their king.
Whatever unto them is brought
Is carried on the wings of thought
Before his throne, where, in full state,
He on their merits holds debate,   140
Examines, cross-examines, weighs
Their right to censure or to praise :
Nor doth his equal voice depend
On narrow views of foe and friend,
Nor can or flattery or force
Divert him from his steady course ;
The channel of inquiry's clear ;

131 Jeffreys. (See note on ' The Conference,' line 352.)
131 Mansfield. (See note on ' The Epistle to Hogarth,' line 76.)

No sham examination's here.
He, upright Justicer, no doubt
Ad libitum puts in and out,   150
Adjusts and settles in a trice
What virtue is, and what is vice ;
What is perfection, what defect ;
What we must choose, and what reject ;
He takes upon him to explain
What pleasure is, and what is pain ;
Whilst we, obedient to the whim,
And resting all our faith on him,
True members of the Stoic weal,
Must learn to think and cease to feel.   160
   This glorious system form'd for man
To practise when and how he can,
If the five senses in alliance
To Reason hurl a proud defiance,
And, though oft conquer'd, yet unbroke,
Endeavour to throw off that yoke
Which they a greater slavery hold
Than Jewish bondage was of old ;
Or if they, something touch'd with shame,
Allow him to retain the name   170
Of Royalty, and, as in sport,
To hold a mimic formal court,
Permitted (no uncommon thing)
To be a kind of puppet-king,
And suffer'd, by the way of toy,
To hold a globe, but not employ ;
Our system-mongers, struck with fear,
Prognosticate destruction near ;
All things to anarchy must run ;
The little world of man's undone.   180
   Nay, should the eye, that nicest sense,
Neglect to send intelligence

---

[148] ' Alluding to the conduct of the House of Commons, respecting one Alexander Dunn's attempt to assassinate Wilkes. Dunn was brought to the Bar, but discharged on the ground of his insanity. The friends of Mr. Wilkes denied the fact of insanity, but insisted that it was a ministerial manœuvre to screen their instrument.' (Tooke.)

Unto the brain distinct and clear,
Of all that passes in her sphere ;
Should she presumptuous joy receive
Without the understanding's leave,
They deem it rank and daring treason
Against the monarchy of Reason,
Not thinking, though they're wondrous wise,
That few have reason, most have eyes ;   190
So that the pleasures of the mind
To a small circle are confined,
Whilst those which to the senses fall
Become the property of all.
Besides, (and this is sure a case
Not much at present out of place)
Where nature reason doth deny,
No art can that defect supply ;
But if (for it is our intent
Fairly to state the argument)   200
A man shall want an eye or two,
The remedy is sure, though new ;
The cure's at hand—no need of fear—
For proof—behold the Chevalier—
As well prepared, beyond all doubt,
To put eyes in as put them out.
    But, argument apart, which tends
To embitter foes and separate friends,
(Nor, turn'd apostate from the Nine,
Would I, though bred up a divine,   210
And foe, of course, to Reason's weal,
Widen that breach I cannot heal)
By his own sense and feelings taught,
In speech as liberal as in thought,
Let every man enjoy his whim ;
What's he to me, or I to him ?

[204] John Taylor (1703-1772), commonly known as the ' Chevalier,'
was an itinerant oculist who travelled all over Europe treating diseases
of the eye. He had considerable skill as an operator, but his methods
of advertisement were those of the charlatan, and his writings were
couched in the most bombastic style. His ' History of the Travels and
Adventures of the Chevalier John Taylor, Ophthalmiater,' appeared in
London in 1761.

Might I, though never robed in ermine,
A matter of this weight determine,
No penalties should settled be
To force men to hypocrisy,   220
To make them ape an awkward zeal,
And, feeling not, pretend to feel.
I would not have, might sentence rest
Finally fix'd within my breast,
E'en Annet censured and confined,
Because we're of a different mind.
    Nature who, in her act most free,
Herself delights in liberty,
Profuse in love, and without bound,
Pours joy on every creature round ;   230
Whom yet, was every bounty shed
In double portions on our head,
We could not truly bounteous call,
If freedom did not crown them all.
    By Providence forbid to stray,
Brutes never can mistake their way ;
Determined still, they plod along
By instinct, neither right nor wrong ;
But man, had he the heart to use
His freedom, hath a right to choose ;   240
Whether he acts or well, or ill,
Depends entirely on his will.
To her last work, her favourite man,
Is given on Nature's better plan,
A privilege in power to err !
Nor let this phrase resentment stir
Amongst the grave ones, since indeed,
The little merit man can plead
In doing well, dependeth still

225 Peter Annet (1693-1769), a deistical writer, published in 1761
nine numbers of a paper entitled *The Free Enquirer* in which he threw
doubts on the Old Testament history.   In 1763 he was tried for
blasphemous libel and sentenced to a month's imprisonment in New-
gate, to stand twice in the pillory, to spend a year in Bridewell at hard
labour and to find sureties for good behaviour during the rest of his
life.   Such is the fate of writers who anticipate the opinions of bishops
by a century and a half.

Upon his power of doing ill.   250
   Opinions should be free as air ;
No man, whate'er his rank, whate'er
His qualities, a claim can found
That my opinion must be bound,
And square with his ; such slavish chains
From foes the liberal soul disdains ;
Nor can, though true to friendship, bend
To wear them even from a friend.
Let those who rigid judgment own
Submissive bow at Judgment's throne,   260
And if they of no value hold
Pleasure, till pleasure is grown cold,
Pall'd and insipid, forced to wait
For Judgment's regular debate
To give it warrant, let them find
Dull subjects suited to their mind.
Theirs be slow wisdom ; be my plan,
To live as merry as I can,
Regardless as the fashions go,
Whether there's reason for't or no :   270
Be my employment here on earth
To give a liberal scope to mirth,
Life's barren vale with flowers t'adorn,
And pluck a rose from every thorn.
   But if, by error led astray,
I chance to wander from my way,
Let no blind guide observe, in spite,
I'm wrong, who cannot set me right.
That doctor could I ne'er endure
Who found disease, and not a cure ;   280
Nor can I hold that man a friend
Whose zeal a helping hand shall lend
To open happy Folly's eyes,
And, making wretched, make me wise :
For next (a truth which can't admit
Reproof from Wisdom or from Wit)
To being happy here below,
Is to believe that we are so.
   Some few in knowledge find relief ;

I place my comfort in belief.   290
Some for reality may call ;
Fancy to me is all in all.
Imagination, through the trick
Of doctors, often makes us sick,
And why, let any sophist tell,
May it not likewise make us well ?
This I am sure, whate'er our view,
Whatever shadows we pursue—
For our pursuits, be what they will,
Are little more than shadows still—   300
Too swift they fly, too swift and strong,
For man to catch or hold them long ;
But joys which in the fancy live,
Each moment to each man may give :
True to himself, and true to ease,
He softens Fate's severe decrees,
And (can a mortal wish for more ?)
Creates, and makes himself new o'er,
Mocks boasted, vain reality,
And is whate'er he wants to be.   310
    Hail, Fancy—to thy power I owe
Deliverance from the gripe of woe ;
To thee I owe a mighty debt,
Which Gratitude shall ne'er forget,
Whilst Memory can her force employ
A large increase of every joy.
When at my doors, too strongly barr'd,
Authority had placed a guard,
A knavish guard, ordain'd by law
To keep poor Honesty in awe ;   320
Authority severe and stern,
To intercept my wish'd return ;
When foes grew proud, and friends grew cool,
And laughter seized each sober fool ;
When Candour started in amaze,
And, meaning censure, hinted praise ;
When Prudence, lifting up her eyes
And hands, thank'd Heaven that she was wise ;
When all around me, with an air

Of hopeless sorrow, look'd despair ;   330
When they or said, or seem'd to say
' There is but one, one only way :
Better, and be advised by us,
Not be at all, than to be thus ;'
When Virtue shunn'd the shock, and Pride,
Disabled, lay by Virtue's side,
Too weak my ruffled soul to cheer,
Which could not hope, yet would not fear ;—
Health in her motion, the wild grace
Of pleasure speaking in her face,   340
Dull regularity thrown by,
And comfort beaming from her eye,
Fancy, in richest robes array'd,
Came smiling forth, and brought me aid ;
Came smiling o'er that dreadful time,
And, more to bless me, came in rhyme.
   Nor is her power to me confined ;
It spreads ; it comprehends mankind.
   When (to the spirit-stirring sound
Of trumpets, breathing courage round,   350
And fifes, well-mingled to restrain
And bring that courage down again ;
Or to the melancholy knell
Of the dull, deep, and doleful bell,
Such as of late the good Saint Bride
Muffled, to mortify the pride
Of those, who, England quite forgot,
Paid their vile homage to the Scot,
Where Asgill held the foremost place,

---

[344] A reference to the financial profits of his writings.

[355] ' On the signing, under Lord Bute's administration, of the
Treaty of Paris which terminated the war which had been conducted
with such brilliant success by Pitt, an address of congratulation having
been wrung from the city of London, it was carried up to St. James's,
12th of May, 1763, by Sir Charles Asgill as locum tenens, accompanied
by other civic officers. The procession was throughout received with
hootings by the mob, and as it passed Fleet Street the great bell of
St. Bride's began to toll, and then a dumb peal struck up ; at its
return it received a similar salutation from Bow Bells.' (Tooke.)

[359] Sir Charles Asgill (died 1788) rose from a clerkship in a bank to
a partnership, was alderman in 1749-77, sheriff and knighted 1752,

Whilst my Lord figured at a race)   360
Processions ('tis not worth debate
Whether they are of stage or state)
Move on, so very, very slow,
'Tis doubtful if they move or no ;
When the performers all the while
Mechanically frown or smile,
Or, with a dull and stupid stare,
A vacancy of sense declare,
Or, with down-bending eye, seem wrought
Into a labyrinth of thought,   370
Where Reason wanders still in doubt,
And, once got in, cannot get out,
What cause sufficient can we find,
To satisfy a thinking mind
Why, duped by such vain farces, man
Descends to act on such a plan ?
Why they, who hold themselves divine,
Can in such wretched follies join,
Strutting like peacocks, or like crows,
Themselves and Nature to expose ?   380
What cause, but that (you'll understand
We have our remedy at hand,
That if perchance we start a doubt,
Ere it is fix'd, we wipe it out ;
As surgeons, when they lop a limb,
Whether for profit, fame, or whim,
Or mere experiment to try,
Must always have a styptic by)
Fancy steps in, and stamps that real,
Which, *ipso facto*, is ideal.   390
    Can none remember ? yes, I know,
All must remember that rare show
When to the country Sense went down,
And fools came flocking up to town ;
When knights (a work which all admit

Lord Mayor of London 1757, and baronet 1761. It was the soldier
son of Charles Asgill who was the subject of a dispute between Wash-
ington and Clinton, and narrowly escaped the fate of Major André.

[388] ' A styptic,' *i.e.*, an astringent.

To be for knighthood much unfit)
Built booths for hire ; when parsons play'd,
In robes canonical array'd,
And, fiddling, join'd the Smithfield dance,
The price of tickets to advance ;   400
Or, unto tapsters turn'd, dealt out,
Running from booth to booth about,
To every scoundrel, by retail,
True pennyworths of beef and ale,
Then first prepared, by bringing beer in,
For present grand electioneering ;
When heralds, running all about
To bring in order, turn'd it out ;
When, by the prudent Marshal's care,
Lest the rude populace should stare,   410
And with unhallow'd eyes profane
Gay puppets of Patrician strain,
The whole procession, as in spite,
Unheard, unseen, stole off by night ;
When our loved monarch, nothing loath,
Solemnly took that sacred oath
Whence mutual firm agreements spring
Betwixt the subject and the king ;
By which, in usual manner crown'd,
His head, his heart, his hands, he bound,   420
Against himself, should passion stir
The least propensity to err,
Against all slaves, who might prepare
Or open force, or hidden snare,
That glorious Charter to maintain,
By which we serve, and he must reign ;
Then Fancy, with unbounded sway,
Revell'd sole mistress of the day,
And wrought such wonders, as might make
Egyptian sorcerers forsake   430
Their baffled mockeries, and own
The palm of magic hers alone.

[406] ' A new parliament was summoned at the accession of George
the Third, and met in November, 1761 ; the canvassing was con-
sequently at its height at the time of the coronation.' (Tooke.)

A knight (who in the silken lap
Of lazy Peace, had lived on pap ;
Who never yet had dared to roam
'Bove ten or twenty miles from home,
Nor even that, unless a guide
Was placed to amble by his side,
And troops of slaves were spread around
To keep his Honour safe and sound ;   440
Who should not suffer, for his life,
A point to sword, or edge to knife,
And always fainted at the sight
Of blood, though 'twas not shed in fight ;
Who disinherited one son
For firing off an alder gun,
And whipt another, six years old,
Because the boy, presumptuous, bold
To madness, likely to become
A very Swiss, had beat a drum,   450
Though it appear'd an instrument
Most peaceable and innocent,
Having, from first, been in the hands
And service of the City bands)
Graced with those ensigns, which were meant
To further Honour's dread intent,
The minds of warriors to inflame,
And spur them on to deeds of fame :
With little sword, large spurs, high feather,
Fearless of every thing but weather,   460
(And all must own, who pay regard
To charity, it had been hard
That in his very first campaign
His honours should be soil'd with rain)
A hero all at once became,
And (seeing others much the same
In point of valour as himself,
Who leave their courage on a shelf
From year to year, till some such rout
In proper season calls it out)   470
Strutted, look'd big, and swagger'd more

⁴³³ See note on line 485 below.

Than ever hero did before :
Look'd up, look'd down, look'd all around,
Like Mavors, grimly smiled and frown'd ;
Seem'd heaven, and earth, and hell to call
To fight, that he might rout them all,
And personated valour's style
So long, spectators to beguile,
That passing strange, and wondrous true,
Himself at last believed it too ;   480
Nor for a time could he discern,
Till truth and darkness took their turn,
So well did Fancy play her part,
That coward still was at the heart.
   Whiffle (who knows not Whiffle's name,
By the impartial voice of Fame
Recorded first through all this land
In Vanity's illustrious band ?)
Who, by all bounteous Nature meant
For offices of hardiment,   490
A modern Hercules at least
To rid the world of each wild beast,
Of each wild beast which came in view
Whether on four legs or on two,
Degenerate, delights to prove
His force on the parade of Love,
Disclaims the joys which camps afford,
And for the distaff quits the sword ;
Who fond of women would appear
To public eye and public ear,   500
But, when in private, let's them know
How little they can trust to show ;
Who sports a woman, as of course,
Just as a jockey shews a horse,
And then returns her to the stable,
Or, vainly plants her at his table,
Where he would rather Venus find,
(So pall'd, and so depraved his mind)
Than, by some great occasion led,
To seize her panting in her bed,   510

[485] Wodhull identifies Whiffle as Sir Francis Blake Delaval, K.B.

Burning with more than mortal fires,
And melting in her own desires ;
Who, ripe in years, is yet a child,
Through fashion, not through feeling, wild ;
Whate'er in others, who proceed
As Sense and Nature have decreed,
From real passion flows, in him
Is mere effect of mode and whim ;
Who laughs, a very common way,
Because he nothing has to say,   520
As your choice spirits oaths dispense
To fill up vacancies of sense ;
Who having some small sense defies it,
Or, using, always misapplies it ;
Who now and then brings something forth
Which seems indeed of sterling worth ;
Something, by sudden start and fit,
Which at a distance looks like wit,
But, on examination near,
To his confusion will appear,   530
By truth's fair glass, to be at best
A threadbare jester's threadbare jest ;
Who frisks and dances through the street,
Sings without voice, rides without seat,
Plays o'er his tricks, like Æsop's ass,
A *gratis* fool to all who pass ;
Who riots, though he loves not waste,
Whores without lust, drinks without taste,
Acts without sense, talks without thought,
Does every thing but what he ought ;   540
Who, led by forms, without the power
Of vice, is vicious ; who one hour,
Proud without pride, the next will be
Humble without humility :
Whose vanity we all discern,
The spring on which his actions turn ;
Whose aim in erring, is to err,
So that he may be singular,
And all his utmost wishes mean
Is, though he's laugh'd at, to be seen :   550

167

Such (for when Flattery's soothing strain
Had robb'd the Muse of her disdain,
And found a method to persuade
Her art to soften every shade,
Justice, enraged, the pencil snatch'd
From her degenerate hand, and scratch'd
Out every trace, then, quick as thought,
From life this striking likeness caught)
In mind, in manners, and in mien,
Such Whiffle came, and such was seen   560
In the world's eye; but (strange to tell !)
Misled by Fancy's magic spell,
Deceived, not dreaming of deceit,
Cheated, but happy in the cheat,
Was more than human in his own.
O bow, bow all at Fancy's throne,
Whose power could make so vile an elf
With patience bear that thing *himself*.
    But, mistress of each art to please,
Creative Fancy, what are these,   570
These pageants of a trifler's pen,
To what thy power effected then ?
Familiar with the human mind,
And swift and subtle as the wind,
Which we all feel, yet no one knows
Or whence it comes, or where it goes,
Fancy at once in every part
Possess'd the eye, the head, the heart ;
And in a thousand forms array'd,
A thousand various gambols play'd.   580
    Here, in a face which well might ask
The privilege to wear a mask
In spite of law, and justice teach
For public good t'excuse the breach,
Within the furrow of a wrinkle
'Twixt eyes, which could not shine, but twinkle
Like sentinels i' th' starry way,
Who wait for the return of day,
Almost burnt out, and seem to keep
Their watch, like soldiers, in their sleep ;   590

Or like those lamps, which, by the power
Of law, must burn from hour to hour,
(Else they, without redemption, fall
Under the terrors of that Hall
Which, once notorious for a hop,
Is now become a justice shop)
Which are so managed, to go out
Just when the time comes round about,
Which yet, through emulation, strive
To keep their dying light alive,   600
And (not uncommon, as we find
Amongst the children of mankind)
As they grow weaker, would seem stronger,
And burn a little, little longer :
Fancy, betwixt such eyes enshrined,
No brush to daub, no mill to grind,
Thrice waved her wand around, whose force
Changed in an instant Nature's course,
And, hardly credible in rhyme,
Not only stopp'd, but call'd back time ;   610
The face of every wrinkle clear'd,
Smooth as the floating stream appear'd,
Down the neck ringlets spread their flame,
The neck admiring whence they came ;
On the arch'd brow the Graces play'd ;
On the full bosom Cupid laid ;
Suns, from their proper orbits sent,
Became for eyes a supplement ;
Teeth, white as ever teeth were seen,
Deliver'd from the hand of Green,   620

591 ' By an act of parliament then lately passed, for the more effec-
tually lighting, etc., the liberty of Westminster, the sitting magis-
trate at Bow Street was armed with very stringent powers for punishing
such lamplighters as neglected their duties.' (Tooke.)

594 ' The Westminster Session-house was then held at a house in
King Street, which had probably been a low place of public enter-
tainment.' (Tooke.)

620 Green is known to have been the junior partner of Samuel
Rutter who practised as a dentist in Racquet Court, Fleet Street, and
whose death was announced in the Gentleman's Magazine for 1761.
He presumably succeeded to the practice just when Churchill com-
menced author.

Started, in regular array,
Like train-bands on a grand field-day,
Into the gums, which would have fled,
But, wond'ring, turn'd from white to red ;
Quite alter'd was the whole machine,
And Lady ―― was fifteen.
Here she made lordly temples rise
Before the pious Dashwood's eyes,
Temples which, built aloft in air,
May serve for show, if not for prayer ;   630
In solemn form herself, before,
Array'd like Faith, the Bible bore :
There, over Melcombe's feather'd head,―
Who, quite a man of gingerbread,
Savour'd in talk, in dress, and phiz,
More of another world than this,
To a dwarf Muse a giant page,
The last grave fop of the last age,
In a superb and feather'd hearse,

---

[626] The present editor is unable to offer any suggestion.

[628] Sir Francis Dashwood (1708-1781) succeeded to the title of his father, the first Baronet, in 1724. While on the Grand Tour he created some scandal in foreign countries by his profligacy, even making advances to the Empress Anne of Russia. His dislike of Sir Robert Walpole led him also to coquet with the Pretender, but did not prevent him from taking his seat in Parliament in 1741. He distinguished himself by defending the unfortunate Admiral Byng, but he was scarcely heard of again, politically, until he became Chancellor of the Exchequer in Lord Bute's administration, and contributed largely to the unpopularity of the ministry by his proposal for a tax on cider. He is chiefly remembered as the founder and ' abbot ' of the Hell Fire Club, which celebrated its orgies at Medmenham Abbey. In 1763 he obtained the Barony of Le Despencer, the title having fallen into abeyance on the death of the Earl of Westmorland in 1762, and being revived in favour of Dashwood, whose mother was the daughter of the fourth Earl. Lord Le Despencer, before he died, built a church at West Wycombe, and enclosed in the ball of the spire the heart of Paul Whitehead, who had been secretary of the Hell Fire Club. (See notes on ' The Candidate,' line 696, and 700.)

[633] ' Melcombe's feather'd head ' is a strange expression, but taken in conjunction with the lines that follow, seems to be a reference to his funeral—a recent event when this poem was written. (See note on 'Gotham,' Book I, line 461.) The feathers, of course, were fixed on the corners of the hearse.

Bescutcheon'd and betagg'd with verse,   640
Which, to beholders from afar,
Appear'd like a triumphal car,
She rode, in a cast rainbow clad ;
There, throwing off the hallow'd plaid,
Naked, as when (in those drear cells
Where self-bless'd, self-cursed Madness dwells)
Pleasure, on whom, in Laughter's shape,
Frenzy had perfected a rape,
First brought her forth, before her time,
Wild witness of her shame and crime ;   650
Driving before an idol band
Of drivelling Stuarts, hand in hand ;
Some who, to curse mankind, had wore
A crown they ne'er must think of more ;
Others, whose baby brows were graced
With paper crowns, and toys of paste ;
She jigg'd, and playing on the flute,
Spread raptures o'er the soul of Bute,
   Big with vast hopes, some mighty plan,
Which wrought the busy soul of man   660
To her full bent, the Civil Law,
(Fit code to keep a world in awe)
Bound o'er his brows, fair to behold,
As Jewish frontlets were of old ;
The famous Charter of our land
Defaced, and mangled in his hand ;
As one whom deepest thoughts employ,
But deepest thoughts of truest joy,
Serious and slow he strode, he stalk'd ;
Before him troops of heroes walk'd,   670
Whom best he loved, of heroes crown'd,
By Tories guarded all around ;
Dull, solemn pleasure in his face,
He saw the honours of his race,

[640] It was the custom to affix elegiac verses to the hearse of a distinguished man.

[657] ' She,' *i.e.* Fancy, the Fancy that the Stuarts, the last two generations of whom had had only paper crowns, might be restored, brought rapture to Bute, himself a Stuart.

He saw their lineal glories rise,
And touch'd, or seem'd to touch the skies;
Not the most distant mark of fear,
No sign of axe, or scaffold near,
Not one cursed thought, to cross his will,
Of such a place as Tower Hill.   680
    Curse on this Muse, a flippant jade !
A shrew ; like every other maid
Who turns the corner of nineteen,
Devour'd with peevishness and spleen :
Her tongue, (for as when bound for life,
The husband suffers for the wife,
So if in any works of rhyme
Perchance there blunders out a crime,
Poor culprit bards must always rue it,
Although 'tis plain the Muses do it)   690
Sooner or later cannot fail
To send me headlong to a jail.
Whate'er my theme, (our themes we choose
In modern days without a Muse,
Just as a father will provide
To join a bridegroom and a bride,
As if, though they must be the players,
The game was wholly his, not theirs)
Whate'er my theme, the Muse, who still
Owns no direction but her will,   700
Flies off, and ere I could expect,
By ways oblique and indirect,
At once quite over head and ears
In fatal politics appears.
Time was, and, if I aught discern
Of fate, that time shall soon return,
When, decent and demure at least,
As grave and dull as any priest,
I could see Vice in robes array'd,
Could see the game of Folly play'd   710
Successfully in fortune's school,
Without exclaiming rogue or fool :
Time was, when nothing loth or proud,
I lackeyed with the fawning crowd

172

Scoundrels in office, and would bow
To cyphers great in place ; but now
Upright I stand, as if wise Fate,
To compliment a shatter'd state,
Had me, like Atlas, hither sent
To shoulder up the firmament,   720
And if I stoop'd, with general crack,
The heavens would tumble from my back :
Time was, when rank and situation
Secured the great ones of the nation
From all control ; satire and law
Kept only little knaves in awe ;
But now, decorum lost, I stand
Bemused, a pencil in my hand,
And, dead to every sense of shame,
Careless of safety and of fame,   730
The names of scoundrels minute down,
And libel more than half the town.
    How can a statesman be secure
In all his villanies, if poor
And dirty authors thus shall dare
To lay his rotten bosom bare ?
Muses should pass away their time
In dressing out the poet's rhyme
With bills and ribands, and array
Each line in harmless taste, though gay.   740
When the hot burning fit is on,
They should regale their restless son
With something to allay his rage,
Some cool Castalian beverage,
Or some such draught (though they, 'tis plain,
Taking the Muse's name in vain,
Know nothing of their real court,
And only fable from report)
As makes a Whitehead's ode go down,
Or slakes the feverette of Brown :   750

[744] The Castalian spring lies at the base of the precipice of Parnassus.
It was sacred to Apollo and the Muses.
[750] A feverette, or feveret, is a slight fever ; the term came into use
at the beginning of the eighteenth century. The Rev. John Brown

But who would in his senses think
Of Muses giving gall to drink,
Or that their folly should afford
To raving poets gun or sword ?
Poets were ne'er design'd by fate
To meddle with affairs of state,
Nor should (if we may speak our thought
Truly as men of honour ought)
Sound policy their rage admit,
To launch the thunderbolts of wit   760
About those heads which, when they're shot,
Can't tell if 'twas by Wit or not.
    These things well known, what devil in spite
Can have seduced me thus to write
Out of that road, which must have led
To riches, without heart or head,
Into that road, which had I more
Than ever poet had before
Of wit and virtue, in disgrace
Would keep me still, and out of place ;   770
Which, if some judge (you'll understand
One famous, famous through the land
For making law) should stand my friend,

(1715-1766) is chiefly remembered as the author of ' An Estimate of
the Manners and Principles of the Times ' (1757), but his essay on
Shaftesbury's ' Characteristics ' contains a memorable statement of
utilitarianism, and his ' Essay upon Satire ' gained him the friendship
of Warburton. This connection would in itself be sufficient to explain
Churchill's hostility : but Tooke quotes a letter from Brown to Gar-
rick in which he writes : ' I do not like your friend Churchill's third
book of the Ghost ; to talk in the grand epic style, it has neither
beginning, nor middle, nor end ; it is crammed with personal abuse,
and that thrown on people who did not deserve it for aught that
appears. It is obscure ; here and there a good line, but many of the
mediocre rank in my opinion. In short, he will scribble himself down
in spite of genius.' Such an opinion of the third book explains his
personal appearance in the fourth. He committed suicide on being
forbidden by his doctors to go to St. Petersburg at the invitation of the
Empress for the purpose of organising Russian education. Brown, in
addition to his other activities, was a dramatist, and his ' Barbarossa '
(1754) and ' Athelstane ' (1756) were produced by Garrick.
    [773] Tooke, himself a solicitor, remarks that in this passage Churchill
is ' alluding to Lord Mansfield's scheme of successive judicial deci-
sions, which now constitute a third division or code generally desig-
nated as Judge-made law.'

At last may in a pillory end ;
And all this, I myself admit,
Without one cause to lead to it ?
  For instance now—this book—the Ghost—
Methinks I hear some critic Post
Remark most gravely—' The first word
Which we about the Ghost have heard.'   780
Peace, my good Sir !—not quite so fast—
What is the first, may be the last,
Which is a point, all must agree,
Cannot depend on you or me.
Fanny, no Ghost of common mould,
Is not by forms to be controll'd
To keep her state, and shew her skill ;
She never comes but when she will.
I wrote and wrote—perhaps you doubt,
And shrewdly, what I wrote about ;   790
Believe me, much to my disgrace,
I, too, am in the self-same case ;
But still I wrote, till Fanny came
Impatient, nor could any shame
On me, with equal justice, fall,
If she had never come at all.
An underling, I could not stir
Without the cue thrown out by her,
Nor from the subject aid receive
Until she came and gave me leave.   800
So that, (ye sons of Erudition,
Mark, this is but a supposition,
Nor would I to so wise a nation
Suggest it as a revelation)
If henceforth, dully turning o'er
Page after page, ye read no more
Of Fanny, who, in sea or air,
May be departed God knows where,
Rail at jilt Fortune, but agree
No censure can be laid on me ;   810
For sure (the cause let Mansfield try)
Fanny is in the fault, not I.
  But, to return—and this I hold

175

A secret worth its weight in gold
To those who write, as I write now,
Not to mind where they go, or how,
Through ditch, through bog, o'er hedge and stile,
Make it but worth the reader's while,
And keep a passage fair and plain
Always to bring him back again.   820
Through dirt who scruples to approach,
At Pleasure's call, to take a coach?
But we should think the man a clown,
Who in the dirt should set us down.
    But, to return—If Wit, who ne'er
The shackles of restraint could bear,
In wayward humour should refuse
Her timely succour to the Muse,
And, to no rules and orders tied,
Roughly deny to be her guide,   830
She must renounce decorum's plan,
And get back when, and how she can;
As parsons, who, without pretext,
As soon as mention'd, quit their text,
And, to promote sleep's genial power,
Grope in the dark for half an hour,
Give no more reason (for we know
Reason is vulgar, mean, and low)
Why they come back (should it befal
That ever they come back at all)   840
Into the road, to end their rout,
Than they can give why they went out.
    But to return—this book—the Ghost—
A mere amusement at the most;
A trifle, fit to wear away
The horrors of a rainy day;
A slight shot silk, for summer wear,
Just as our modern statesmen are,—
If rigid honesty permit
That I for once purloin the wit   850
Of him, who, were we all to steal,
Is much too rich the theft to feel;
Yet in this book, where ease should join

With mirth to sugar every line ;
Where it should all be mere chit-chat,
Lively, good-humour'd, and all that ;
Where honest Satire, in disgrace,
Should not so much as show her face,
The shrew, o'erleaping all due bounds,
Breaks into laughter's sacred grounds,   860
And, in contempt, plays o'er her tricks
In science, trade, and politics.
  But why should the distemper'd scold
Attempt to blacken men enroll'd
In power's dread book, whose mighty skill
Can twist an empire to their will ;
Whose voice is fate, and on their tongue
Law, liberty, and life, are hung ;
Whom on inquiry, truth shall find,
With Stuarts link'd ; time out of mind   870
Superior to their country's laws,
Defenders of a tyrant's cause ;
Men, who the same damn'd maxims hold,
Darkly, which they avow'd of old ;
Who, though by different means, pursue
The end which they had first in view,
And, force found vain, now play their part
With much less honour, much more art ?
Why, at the corners of the streets,
To every patriot drudge she meets,   880
Known or unknown, with furious cry
Should she wild clamours vent ? or why,
The minds of groundlings to inflame,
A Dashwood, Bute, and Wyndham name ?
Why, having not, to our surprise,
The fear of death before her eyes,
Bearing, and that but now and then,
No other weapon but her pen,
Should she an argument afford

---

[884] Sir Francis Dashwood, Lord Le Despencer, (see note on ' The Epistle to Hogarth,' line 22) ; Bute (see note on ' The Prophecy of Famine,' line 533) ; Charles Wyndham, Earl of Egremont (see note on line 64 above).

For blood, to men who wear a sword ?　　　890
Men, who can nicely trim and pare
A point of honour to a hair ;
(Honour—a word of nice import,
A pretty trinket in a court,
Which my Lord, quite in rapture, feels
Dangling and rattling with his seals ;
Honour—a word which all the Nine
Would be much puzzled to define ;
Honour—a word which torture mocks,
And might confound a thousand Lockes ;　　900
Which (for I leave to wiser heads,
Who fields of death prefer to beds
Of down, to find out, if they can,
What Honour *is*, on their wild plan)
Is *not*,—to take it in their way,
And this we sure may dare to say
Without incurring an offence,—
Courage, law, honesty, or sense)
Men, who all spirit, life, and soul,
Neat butchers of a buttonhole,　　　　910
Having more skill, believe it true
That they must have more courage too ;
Men who, without a place or name,
Their fortunes speechless as their fame,
Would by the sword new fortunes carve,
And rather die in fight than starve.
At coronations, a vast field,
Which food of every kind might yield,
Of good, sound food, at once most fit,
For purposes of health and wit,　　　　920
Could not ambitious Satire rest,
Content with what she might digest ?
Could she not feast on things of course,
A champion, or a champion's horse ?

⁹⁰⁰ John Locke (1632-1704), author of the ' Essay concerning Human Understanding.'

⁹²⁴ Lord Talbot was High Steward, and in that capacity present at the Coronation of George III. Walpole says (Letter to George Montagu, September 24th, 1761) : ' Lord Talbot piqued himself on backing

A champion's horse—no better say,
Though better figured on that day—
A horse, which might appear to us
Who deal in rhyme, a Pegasus ;
A rider, who, when once got on,
Might pass for a Bellerophon   930
Dropt on a sudden from the skies,
To catch and fix our wondering eyes,
To witch, with wand instead of whip,
The world with noble horsemanship ;
To twist and twine, both horse and man,
On such a well-concerted plan,
That, Centaur-like, when all was done,
We scarce could think they were not one.
Could she not to our itching ears
Bring the new names of new-coin'd peers,   940
Who walk'd, nobility forgot,
With shoulders fitter for a knot
Than robes of honour ; for whose sake
Heralds, in form, were forced to make,—

his horse down the Hall ; and not turning its rump towards the King, but he had taken such pains to dress it to that duty, that it entered backwards ; and at his retreat the spectators clapped, a terrible indecorum, but suitable to such Bartholomew-fair doings.' Wilkes ridiculed Talbot very severely in No. 12 of *The North Briton*, which appeared in August, 1762. ' A politeness equal to that of Lord Talbot's horse ought not to pass unnoticed. At the coronation he paid a new, and, for a horse, singular respect to his sovereign. Caligula's horse had not half that merit. We remember how nobly he was provided for. What the exact proportion of merit was between his lordship and his horse, and how far the pension should be divided between them, I will not take it upon me to determine. The impartial and inimitable pen of Cervantes has made Rosinante immortal as well as Don Quixote. Lord Talbot's horse, like the great planet in Milton, danced about in various rounds his wandering course. At different times he was progressive, retrograde, or standing still. The progressive motion I should rather incline to think the merit of the horse ; the retrograde motion, the merit of the lord. Some of the regulations of the courtiers themselves for that day had long been settled by former lord stewards. It was reserved for Lord Talbot to settle on etiquette for their horses, etc.' The duel to which this attack led, and to which Wilkes was careful to give the utmost publicity, contributed largely to his popularity throughout the country.

[940] Alluding to the creation by Lord Bute of sixteen new peerages.

[942] The knot worn on the shoulder by lackeys in livery.

179

To make, because they could not find,—
Great predecessors to their mind ?
Could she not (though 'tis doubtful since,
Whether he plumber is, or prince)
Tell of a simple knight's advance
To be a doughty peer of France ?   950
Tell how he did a dukedom gain,
And Robinson was Aquitaine ?
Tell how her city chiefs, disgraced,
Were at an empty table placed ?
A gross neglect, which, whilst they live,
They can't forget, and won't forgive,
A gross neglect of all those rights
Which march with city appetites,
Of all those canons, which we find
By Gluttony, time out of mind   960
Established, which they ever hold
Dearer than any thing but gold.
      Thanks to my stars—I now see shore—
Of courtiers, and of courts no more—
Thus stumbling on my city friends,
Blind Chance my guide, my purpose bends
In line direct, and shall pursue
The point which I had first in view,
Nor more shall with the reader sport
Till I have seen him safe in port.   970
Hush'd be each fear—no more I bear
Through the wide regions of the air
The reader, terrified ; no more
Wild ocean's horrid paths explore.
Be the plain track from henceforth mine—

⁹⁵³ ' At the coronation of George the Third, the Duke of Normandy
(not Aquitaine) was represented by Sir Thomas Robinson, elder
brother of the first Lord Rokeby.' (Tooke.)

⁹⁵⁴ At the coronation banquet of George III there was, by some over-
sight, no table set for the Mayor and aldermen of the City of London.
' Beckford (Lord Mayor of London) told the Earl (Lord Talbot, the
Lord High Steward) it was hard to refuse a table to the City of Lon-
don, whom it would cost ten thousand pounds to banquet the King,
and that his lordship would repent it, if they had not a table in the
Hall ; they had.' (Walpole to George Montagu, September 24th, 1761.)

Cross-roads to Allen I resign ;
Allen, the honour of this nation ;
Allen, himself a corporation ;
Allen, of late notorious grown
For writings none, or all his own ;   980
Allen, the first of letter'd men,
Since the good Bishop holds his pen,
And at his elbow takes his stand
To mend his head, and guide his hand.
But hold—once more, Digression, hence !
Let us return to common sense ;
The car of Phœbus I discharge,
My carriage now a Lord Mayor's barge.
    Suppose we now (we may suppose
In verse, what would be sin in prose)   990
The sky with darkness overspread,
And every star retired to bed ;
The gewgaw robes of Pomp and Pride
In some dark corner thrown aside,
Great lords and ladies giving way
To what they seem to scorn by day,
The real feelings of the heart,
And Nature taking place of Art ;
Desire triumphant through the night,
And Beauty panting with delight ;   1000
Chastity, woman's fairest crown,
Till the return of morn laid down,
Then to be worn again as bright
As if not sullied in the night ;
Dull Ceremony, business o'er,
Dreaming in form at Cottrell's door ;
Precaution trudging all about
To see the candles safely out ;
Bearing a mighty master-key,
Habited like Economy,   1010
Stamping each lock with triple seals,
Mean Avarice creeping at her heels.

[981] Ralph Allen was the inventor and farmer of cross-posts, an extremely lucrative business. His niece married Bishop Warburton.
[1006] Sir Clement Cottrell, master of the ceremonies.

181

Suppose we too, like sheep in pen,
The Mayor and Court of Aldermen
Within their barge, which through the deep,
The rowers more than half asleep,
Moved slow, as overcharged with state ;
Thames groan'd beneath the mighty weight,
And felt that bawble heavier far
Than a whole fleet of men of war.   1020
Sleep o'er each well-known, faithful head
With liberal hand his poppies shed,
Each head, by Dulness render'd fit
Sleep and his empire to admit.
Through the whole passage not a word,
Not one faint, weak half-sound was heard ;
Sleep had prevail'd to overwhelm
The steersman nodding o'er the helm ;
The rowers, without force or skill,
Left the dull barge to drive at will ;   1030
The sluggish oars suspended hung,
And even Beardmore held his tongue.
Commerce, regardful of a freight
On which depended half her state,
Stepp'd to the helm ; with ready hand
She safely clear'd that bank of sand,
Where, stranded, our west-country fleet
Delay and danger often meet,
Till Neptune, anxious for the trade,
Comes in full tides, and brings them aid.   1040
Next (for the Muses can survey
Objects by night as well as day ;
Nothing prevents their taking aim,
Darkness and light to them the same)
They pass'd that building which of old
Queen-mothers was design'd to hold ;

1032 ' Beardmore, the under-sheriff, was an occasional writer in the
Monitor, an opposition paper, and was employed by Wilkes as his
solicitor in his contest with government.' (Tooke.)

1045 Old Somerset House was the traditional residence of the Queen
of England. The Queen Dowager, Catherine of Braganza, departed
to Portugal in 1692, and soon afterwards the Government put the

At present a mere lodging-pen,
A palace turn'd into a den,
To barracks turn'd ; and soldiers tread
Where dowagers have laid their head.   1050
Why should we mention Surrey Street,
Where every week grave judges meet
All fitted out with hum and ha,
In proper form to drawl out law,
To see all causes duly tried
'Twixt knaves who drive, and fools who ride ?
Why at the Temple should we stay ?
What of the Temple dare we say ?
A dangerous ground we tread on there,
And words perhaps may actions bear ;   1060
Where, as the brethren of the seas
For fares, the lawyers ply for fees.
What of that Bridge most wisely made

building in repair for the accommodation of the poorer nobility, per-
sons holding official positions at Court, etc. Hence Churchill's
description of it as ' a mere lodging-pen.'

[1051] ' A hackney coach office was established in 1696 in Surrey
Street, Strand, and five Commissioners were appointed to regulate the
fares and settle disputes.' (Tooke.)

[1057] The temple, on the south side of Fleet Street, consists of the
two societies of the Inner Temple and the Middle Temple, two of the
four Inns of Court established from early times for the study and prac-
tice of the law. In 1608 they were confirmed by James I in the pos-
session of the property originally granted to the Templars and then to
the Hospitallers, and said to have been made over by the latter to the
legal societies in the reign of Edward III.

[1063–1086] The following extract from an article in ' Notes and
Queries ' VIII (July 15, 1865), pp. 41 and 42, provides the best
explanation of this passage in Churchill's poem :
' It is just about a century since Blackfriars Bridge was first built,
and very nearly a quarter of a century since it began to show chronic
symptoms of failure and decay, and the skill of our eminent engineers
was required to prevent the old structure from making away with
itself. No less than ten years and three-quarters were consumed in
building it, and it cost from first to last 152,840£.
' As a curious question of longevity, is there to be found among us
one who can call to mind the battle of the arches—the elliptical of Mr.
Robert Mylne the engineer, *versus* the semicircular of Mr. Thomas
Simpson the mathematician ? *Pendente lite*, Dr. Johnson, as is well
known, engaged in the controversy in behalf of his friend, Mr.
Gwynn, one of the competitors, and wrote three letters in *The*

To serve the purposes of trade,
In the great mart of all this nation,
By stopping up the navigation,
And to that sand bank adding weight,
Which is already much too great ?
What of that Bridge, which, void of sense,
But well supplied with impudence,   1070
Englishmen, knowing not the Guild,
Thought they might have a claim to build,
Till Paterson, as white as milk,
As smooth as oil, as soft as silk,
In solemn manner had decreed
That on the other side the Tweed,

Gazetteer in opposition to the elliptical side of the question. The palm of victory was ultimately awarded to the Scotch engineer.

' The last day of October, 1865, will be the 105th anniversary of the commencement of the old Bridge, when the first stone was formally laid in the north abutment, with much state and the firing of several rounds of cannon, by Sir Thomas Chitty, the then Lord Mayor. Under the stone was deposited money in gold, silver, and copper coins of the reign of George II, namely a five-guinea piece, a two-guinea piece, and a guinea and half-guinea, a crown, a half-crown, a shilling a sixpence, a halfpenny, a farthing, together with the silver medal given to the architect, Mr. Mylne, by the Roman Academy of St. Luke. There was also inclosed in the cavity under the stone a plate of pure tin, containing the famed Latin inscription eulogising the political merits and social virtues of the great commoner, William Pitt, after whom it was originally intended the Bridge should be named. But long before it could be formally christened, it was so widely known as Blackfriars, that all attempts to alter its designation were wisely abandoned. On Wednesday, Nov. 9, 1768, the Bridge was made passable as a bridle-way, and was finally opened for traffic on Sunday, Nov. 19, 1769. It may not be generally known that Iolo Morganwg (*i.e.*, Edward Williams, the Bard, and last of the Druids), the most indefatigable of literary Welsh antiquaries, worked as a common mason on this Bridge.

' The site of the old Bridge may be considered classic ground ; for here lies embedded " in a tongue unknown to our citizens," the memorable specimen of " City Latin," the scholastic effort of that " famous citizen of credit and renown," Mr. John Paterson, nick-named by the wits of his day, Busby Birch, LL.D. The luckless solicitor to the Corporation never heard the end of his " City Latin." Churchill . . . expresses the popular feeling against Paterson as well as Mylne.

' A witty and critical dissection of this inscription also appeared in a pamphlet, entitled :

' " City Latin, or, Critical and Political Remarks on the Latin inscription on laying the first stone of the intended new Bridge at Black

184

Art, born and bred, and fully grown,
Was with one Mylne, a man unknown,
But grace, preferment, and renown
Deserving, just arrived in town ;   1080
One Mylne, an artist perfect quite
Both in his own and country's right,
As fit to make a bridge as he,
With glorious Patavinity,
To build inscriptions, worthy found
To lie for ever underground.
    Much more, worth observation too,
Was this a season to pursue
The theme, our Muse might tell in rhyme :
The will she hath, but not the time :   1090
For, swift as shaft from Indian bow,
(And when a goddess comes, we know
Surpassing Nature acts prevail,
And boats want neither oar nor sail)
The vessel pass'd, and reach'd the shore

Fryars ; proving almost every word, and every letter of it to be erron-
eous, and contrary to the practice of both Ancients and Moderns in
this kind of writing : interspersed with curious Reflections on An-
tiques and Antiquity : with a Plan or Pattern for a new Inscription.
Dedicated to the venerable Society of Antiquaries. By the Rev. Busby
Birch, LL.D., F.R.S., F.A.S., F.G.C., and M.S.E.A.M.C., *i.e.*,
Member of the Society for the Encouragement of Arts, Manufacture
and Commerce, London, 8vo., 1760, second edition, 1761."
    ' This sparkling frisky squib, from the pen of Bonnel Thornton, was
let off more in merriment than rancour. The witty author followed up
his whimsical strictures in another droll pamphlet, entitled :
    ' " Plain English, in Answer to City Latin ; or Critical and Political
Remarks on the Latin Inscription on laying the first stone of the in-
tended new Bridge at Black-Fryars : showing the several applications
made, or proposed to be made, to the Universities of Oxford, Cam-
bridge, &c., &c., the London Clergy, the Lawyers, the College of
Physicians, &c. for a proper Latin Inscription : likewise pointing out
the supposed Author of the Inscription, first in English, and the real
Translator of it afterwards in Latin. By a Deputy. London, 8vo,
1761."   J. Y.'
    Churchill's hostility may be explained by the fact that Paterson was
the leader of the anti-Wilkite party in the city, and Mylne was of
Scottish origin. He was, of course, acquainted with the satires of his
intimate friend, Bonnel Thornton.

[1084] ' Patavinity ' is defined as the dialectical characteristics of Pata-
vium or Padua, as shown in Livy's writings; hence, provincialism in style.

So quick, that thought was scarce before.
　Suppose we now our city court
Safely deliver'd at the port,
And, of their state regardless quite,
Landed, like smuggled goods, by night.　　1100
The solemn magistrate laid down,
The dignity of robe and gown,
With every other ensign gone,
Suppose the woollen nightcap on ;
The flesh-brush used, with decent state,
To make the spirits circulate,
(A form which, to the senses true,
The lickerish chaplain uses too,
Though, something to improve the plan,
He takes the maid instead of man)　　1110
Swathed, and with flannel cover'd o'er,
To shew the vigour of threescore,
The vigour of threescore and ten
Above the proof of younger men,
Suppose, the mighty Dulman led
Betwixt two slaves, and put to bed ;
Suppose, the moment he lies down,
No miracle in this great Town,
The drone as fast asleep, as he
Must in the course of nature be,　　1120
Who, truth for our foundation take,
When up, is never half awake.
　There let him sleep, whilst we survey
The preparations for the day ;
That day on which was to be shown
Court pride by City pride outdone.
　The jealous mother sends away,
As only fit for childish play,
That daughter who, to gall her pride,
Shoots up too forward by her side.　　1130
　The wretch, of God and man accurst,
Of all hell's instruments the worst,
Draws forth his pawns, and for the day

1105 The flesh-brush is a brush used for rubbing the surface of the
body to excite the circulation.

Struts in some spendthrift's vain array;
Around his awkward doxy shine
The treasures of Golconda's mine;
Each neighbour, with a jealous glare,
Beholds her folly publish'd there.
Garments well saved, (an anecdote
Which we can prove, or would not quote)   1140
Garments well saved, which first were made
When tailors, to promote their trade,
Against the Picts in arms arose,
And drove them out, or made them clothes;
Garments immortal, without end,
Like names and titles, which descend
Successively from sire to son;
Garments, unless some work is done
Of note, not suffer'd to appear
'Bove once at most in every year,   1150
Were now, in solemn form, laid bare,
To take the benefit of air,
And, ere they came to be employ'd
On this solemnity, to void
That scent, which Russia's leather gave,
From vile and impious moth to save.
Each head was busy, and each heart
In preparation bore a part;
Running together all about
The servants put each other out,   1160
Till the grave master had decreed,
The more haste, ever the worst speed.
Miss, with her little eyes half-closed,
Over a smuggled toilette dosed:
The waiting-maid, whom story notes
A very Scrub in petticoats,
Hired for one work, but doing all,
In slumbers lean'd against the wall.
Milliners, summon'd from afar,
Arrived in shoals at Temple Bar,   1170
Strictly commanded to import

[1166] Scrub, the man-of-all-work at Squire Sullen's, in Farquhar's
' The Beaux' Stratagem.'

Cart loads of foppery from court.
With labour'd, visible design
Art strove to be superbly fine ;
Nature, more pleasing, though more wild,
Taught otherwise her darling child,
And cried, with spirited disdain,
Be Hunter elegant and plain.
  Lo ! from the chambers of the East,
A welcome prelude to the feast,   1180
In saffron-colour'd robe array'd,
High in a car by Vulcan made,
Who work'd for Jove himself, each steed
High-mettled, of celestial breed,
Pawing and pacing all the way,
Aurora brought the wish'd-for day,
And held her empire, till out-run
By that brave, jolly groom the Sun.
  The trumpet—hark ! it speaks—it swells
The loud, full harmony ; it tells   1190
The time at hand when Dulman, led
By Form, his citizens must head,
And march those troops, which at his call
Were now assembled, to Guildhall,
On matters of importance great,
To court and city, church and state.
  From end to end the sound makes way,
All hear the signal and obey ;
But Dulman, who, his charge forgot,
By Morpheus fetter'd, heard it not ;   1200
Nor could, so sound he slept and fast,
Hear any trumpet, but the last.
  Crape, ever true and trusty known,
Stole from the maid's bed to his own ;
Then in the spirituals of pride,
Planted himself at Dulman's side.
Thrice did the ever-faithful slave,
With voice which might have reach'd the grave,
And broke death's adamantine chain,

1178 Kitty Hunter. (See note on ' The Ghost,' Book III, line 204.)
1203 Rev. Samuel Bruce. (See note on Book III, line 670.)

On Dulman call, but call'd in vain.   1210
Thrice with an arm, which might have made
The Theban boxer curse his trade,
The drone he shook, who rear'd the head,
And thrice fell backward on his bed.
What could be done ? Where force hath fail'd
Policy often hath prevail'd,
And what, an inference most plain,
Had been, Crape thought might be again.
    Under his pillow (still in mind
The proverb kept, Fast bind, fast find)   1220
Each blessed night the keys were laid,
Which Crape to draw away assay'd.
What not the power of voice or arm
Could do, this did, and broke the charm ;
Quick started he with stupid stare,
For all his little soul was there.
    Behold him, taken up, rubb'd down,
In elbow-chair, and morning-gown ;
Behold him, in his latter bloom,
Stripp'd, wash'd, and sprinkled with perfume ; 1230
Behold him bending with the weight
Of robes, and trumpery of state ;
Behold him (for the maxim's true,
Whate'er we by another do
We do ourselves, and chaplain paid,
Like slaves in every other trade,
Had mutter'd over God knows what,
Something which he by heart had got)
Having, as usual, said his prayers,
Go titter, totter, to the stairs :   1240
Behold him for descent prepare
With one foot trembling in the air ;
He starts, he pauses on the brink,
And, hard to credit ! seems to think ;
Through his whole train (the chaplain gave
The proper cue to every slave)
At once, as with infection caught,

1220 Shylock : ' Fast bind, fast find,
      A proverb never stale in thrifty mind.'

Each started, paused, and aim'd at thought;
He turns, and they turn; big with care,
He waddles to his elbow-chair,   1250
Squats down, and, silent for a season,
At last with Crape begins to reason:
But first of all he made a sign,
That every soul but the divine
Should quit the room; in him, he knows,
He may all confidence repose.
   ' Crape—though I'm yet not quite awake—
Before this awful step I take,
On which my future all depends,
I ought to know my foes and friends.   1260
My foes and friends—observe me still—
I mean not those who well or ill
Perhaps may wish me, but those who
Have't in their power to do it too.
Now if, attentive to the state,
In too much hurry to be great,
Or through much zeal,—a motive, Crape,
Deserving praise,—into a scrape
I, like a fool, am got, no doubt
I, like a wise man should get out: 1270
Not that (remark without replies)
I say that to get out is wise,
Or by the very self-same rule
That to get in was like a fool.
The marrow of this argument
Must wholly rest on the event;
And therefore, which is really hard,
Against events too I must guard.
   ' Should things continue as they stand,
And Bute prevail through all the land   1280
Without a rival, by his aid
My fortunes in a trice are made;
Nay, honours, on my zeal may smile,
And stamp me Earl of some great Isle:
But if, a matter of much doubt,

[1284] Like the Earls of Bute who took their title from the island in the Firth of Clyde.

The present minister goes out,
Fain would I know on what pretext
I can stand fairly with the next.
For as my aim, at every hour,
Is to be well with those in power,   1290
And my material point of view,
Whoever's in, to be in too,
I should not, like a blockhead, choose
To gain these so as those to lose :
'Tis good in every case, you know,
To have two strings unto our bow.'
    As one in wonder lost, Crape view'd
His lord, who thus his speech pursued :
    ' This, my good Crape, is my grand point ;
And as the times are out of joint,   1300
The greater caution is required
To bring about the point desired.
What I would wish to bring about
Cannot admit a moment's doubt ;
The matter in dispute, you know,
Is what we call the *quomodo*.
That be thy task '—The reverend slave
Becoming in a moment grave,
Fix'd to the ground and rooted, stood
Just like a man cut out of wood,   1310
Such as we see (without the least
Reflection glancing on the priest)
One or more, planted up and down,
Almost in every church in town ;
He stood some minutes, then, like one
Who wish'd the matter might be done,
But could not do it, shook his head,
And thus the man of sorrow said :
    ' Hard is this task, too hard I swear,
By much too hard for me to bear ;   1320
Beyond expression hard my part,
Could mighty Dulman see my heart,
When he, alas ! makes known a will
Which Crape's not able to fulfil.
Was ever my obedience barr'd

191

By any trifling, nice regard
To sense and honour ? could I reach
Thy meaning without help of speech,
At the first motion of thy eye
Did not thy faithful creature fly ?   1330
Have I not said, not what I ought,
But what my earthly master taught ?
Did I e'er weigh, through duty strong,
In thy great biddings, right and wrong ?
Did ever Interest, to whom thou
Canst not with more devotion bow,
Warp my sound faith, or will of mine
In contradiction run to thine ?
Have I not, at thy table placed,
When business call'd aloud for haste,   1340
Torn myself thence, yet never heard
To utter one complaining word,
And had, till thy great work was done,
All appetites, as having none ?
Hard is it, this great plan pursued
Of voluntary servitude,
Pursued, without or shame or fear,
Through the great circle of the year,
Now to receive, in this grand hour,
Commands which lie beyond my power,   1350
Commands which baffle all my skill,
And leave me nothing but my will :
Be that accepted ; let my Lord
Indulgence to his slave afford :
This task, for my poor strength unfit,
Will yield to none but Dulman's wit.'
    With such gross incense gratified,
And turning up the lip of pride,
' Poor Crape '—and shook his empty head—
' Poor puzzled Crape ! '—wise Dulman said,   1360
' Of judgment weak, of sense confined,
For things of lower note design'd ;
For things within the vulgar reach,
To run on errands, and to preach ;
Well hast thou judg'd that heads like mine

Cannot want help from heads like thine ;
Well hast thou judged thyself unmeet
Of such high argument to treat ;
'Twas but to try thee that I spoke,
And all I said was but a joke.   1370
   ' Nor think a joke, Crape, a disgrace
Or to my person or my place ;
The wisest of the sons of men
Have deign'd to use them now and then.
The only caution, do you see,
Demanded by our dignity,
From common use and men exempt,
Is that they may not breed contempt.
Great use they have, when in the hands
Of one like me, who understands,   1380
Who understands the time and place
The person, manner, and the grace
Which fools neglect ; so that we find,
If all the requisites are join'd
From whence a perfect joke must spring,
A joke's a very serious thing.
   ' But to our business—my design,
Which gave so rough a shock to thine,.
To my capacity is made
As ready as a fraud in trade ;   1390
Which, like broad-cloth, I can, with ease
Cut out in any shape I please.
   ' Some, in my circumstance, some few,
Aye, and those men of genius too,
Good men, who, without love or hate,
Whether they early rise or late,
With names uncrack'd, and credit sound,
Rise worth a hundred thousand pound,
By threadbare ways and means would try
To bear their point—so will not I.   1400
New methods shall my wisdom find
To suit these matters to my mind,
So that the infidels at court,

1391 The Lord Mayor had been a clothier. (See note on **Book III**, lines 627 and 1085.)

Who make our City wits their sport,
Shall hail the honours of my reign,
And own that Dulman bears a brain.
  ' Some, in my place, to gain their ends,
Would give relations up, and friends ;
Would lend a wife, who they might swear
Safely, was none the worse for wear ;   1410
Would see a daughter, yet a maid,
Into a statesman's arms betray'd ;
Nay, should the girl prove coy, nor know
What daughters to a father owe,
Sooner than schemes so nobly plann'd
Should fail, themselves would lend a hand ;
Would vote on one side, whilst a brother,
Properly taught, would vote on t'other ;
Would every petty band forget ;
To public eye be with one set,   1420
In private with a second herd,
And be by proxy with a third ;
Would (like a queen, of whom I read
The other day—her name is fled—
In a book where, together bound,
Whittington and his Cat I found—
A tale most true, and free from art,
Which all Lord Mayors should have by heart—
A queen (O might those days begin
Afresh, when queens would learn to spin)   1430
Who wrought, and wrought, but, for some plot
The cause of which I've now forgot,
During the absence of the sun
Undid what she by day had done)
While they a double visage wear,
What's sworn by day, by night unswear.
  ' Such be their arts, and such perchance,
May happily their ends advance ;
From a new system mine shall spring,
A *Locum tenens* is the thing.   1440
That's your true plan—to obligate
The present ministers of state,
My shadow shall our court approach,

And bear my power, and have my coach ;
My fine state-coach, superb to view,
A fine-state coach, and paid for too.
To curry favour, and the grace
Obtain of those who're out of place ;
In the mean time I—that's to say
I proper, I myself—here stay.   1450
  ' But hold—perhaps unto the nation,
Who hate the Scot's administration,
To lend my coach may seem to be
Declaring for the ministry ;
For where the City-coach is, there
Is the true essence of the Mayor :
Therefore (for wise men are intent
Evils at distance to prevent,
Whilst fools the evils first endure,
And then are plagued to seek a cure)   1460
No coach—a horse—and free from fear
To make our Deputy appear,
Fast on his back shall he be tied,
With two grooms marching by his side ;
Then—for a horse—through all the land,
To head our solemn city-band,
Can any one so fit be found
As he, who in Artillery ground,
Without a rider, noble sight !
Led on our bravest troops to fight ?   1470
  ' But first, Crape, for my honour's sake—
A tender point—inquiry make
About that horse, if the dispute
Is ended, or is still in suit :
For whilst a cause (observe this plan
Of justice) whether horse or man
The parties be, remains in doubt,
Till 'tis determined out and out,
That power must tyranny appear
Which should, prejudging, interfere,   1480
And weak, faint judges overawe
To bias the free course of law.
  ' You have my will—now quickly run,

And take care that my will be done.
In public, Crape, you must appear,
Whilst I in privacy sit here;
Here shall great Dulman sit alone,
Making this elbow-chair my throne,
And you, performing what I bid,
Do all, as if I nothing did.'   1490
   Crape heard, and speeded on his way;
With him to hear was to obey;
Not without trouble, be assured,
A proper proxy was procured
To serve such infamous intent,
And such a lord to represent;
Nor could one have been found at all
On t'other side of London Wall.
   The trumpet sounds—solemn and slow
Behold the grand procession go,   1500
All moving on, cat after kind,
As if for motion ne'er design'd.
   Constables, whom the laws admit
To keep the peace by breaking it;
Beadles, who hold the second place
By virtue of a silver mace,
Which every Saturday is drawn,
For use of Sunday, out of pawn;
Treasurers, who with empty key
Secure an empty treasury;   1510
Churchwardens, who their course pursue
In the same state, as to their pew
Churchwardens of St. Margaret go,
Since Peirson taught them pride and show;
Who in short, transient pomp appear,
Like almanacks changed every year;
Behind whom, with unbroken locks,

---

¹⁵¹⁴ ' Mr. Peirson was a leading man in the parish committee for
repairing and beautifying St. Margaret's Church, and the contest of
that committee with Dr. Pearce, Dean of Westminster, and Bishop of
Rochester, about the beautifully painted eastern window purchased
by them for 400 guineas, excited much attention. The Dean insisted
upon its being Popish and idolatrous, and demanded its removal, but
without effect.' (Tooke.)

Charity carries the poor's box,
Not knowing that with private keys
They ope and shut it when they please;   1520
Overseers, who by frauds ensure
The heavy curses of the poor;
Unclean came flocking, bulls and bears,
Like beasts into the ark, by pairs.
Portentous, flaming in the van,
Stalk'd the Professor Sheridan,
A man of wire, a mere pantine,
A downright animal machine;
He knows alone in proper mode
How to take vengeance on an ode,   1530
And how to butcher Ammon's son
And poor Jack Dryden both in one:
On all occasions next the chair
He stands for service of the Mayor,
And to instruct him how to use
His A's and B's, and P's and Q's:
O'er letters, into tatters worn,
O'er syllables, defaced and torn,
O'er words disjointed, and o'er sense,
Left destitute of all defence,   1540
He strides; and all the way he goes
Wades, deep in blood, o'er Criss-cross-rows:

[1523] The Stock Exchange terms, ' bulls ' and ' bears ' appear early
in the eighteenth century and were common at the time of the South
Sea Bubble.

[1526] Professor Sheridan, *i.e.*, Professor of Elocution. (See note on
' The Rosciad,' line 648.)

[1527] A pantine is a pasteboard figure of a human being, having the
neck, body and limbs jointed, so as to move when pulled by a thread or
wire. It was a fashionable toy in the middle of the eighteenth century.
The name is said to be derived from Mlle. Pantein, or Pantini, the
reputed inventor of the toy, and one of the mistresses of Marshal
Saxe, but some French etymologists refer it to Pantin, a village near
Paris.

[1530] ' Mr. Sheridan recited an ode of Dryden's at his own benefit.'
(Tooke.)

[1531] Ammon's son is Alexander the Great, who assumed divine
parentage.

[1542] Criss-cross-row: the alphabet. (See note on ' The Apology,'
line 90.)

197

Before him every consonant
In agonies is seen to pant;
Behind, in forms not to be known,
The ghosts of tortured vowels groan.
    Next Hart and Duke, well worthy grace
And City favour, came in place :
No children can their toils engage;
Their toils are turn'd to reverend age;   1550
When a court dame, to grace his brows
Resolved, is wed to City-spouse,
Their aid with Madam's aid must join,
The awkward dotard to refine,
And teach (whence truest glory flows)
Grave sixty to turn out his toes.
Each bore in hand a kit; and each—
To show how fit he was to teach
A Cit, an Alderman, a Mayor—
Led in a string a dancing bear.   1560
    Since the revival of Fingal,
Custom—and custom's all in all—
Commands that we should have regard,
On all high seasons, to the bard.
Great acts like these, by vulgar tongue
Profaned, should not be said, but sung.
This place to fill, renown'd in fame,
The high and mighty Lockman came;
And—ne'er forgot in Dulman's reign,
With proper order to maintain   1570
The uniformity of pride,—
Brought Brother Whitehead by his side.
    On horse, who proudly paw'd the ground,
And cast his fiery eyeballs round,
Snorting, and champing the rude bit,

1547 Hart and Duke were dancing-masters.

1557 A kit is a very small fiddle formerly used by dancing-masters.
The word is perhaps derived from the Greek κιθάρα.

1568 'John Lockman, secretary to the British herring fishery.'
(Tooke.) He died in 1771.

1572 William Whitehead, Poet Laureate. (See note on 'The
Ghost,' Book III, line 117.)

As if, for warlike purpose fit,
His high and generous blood disdain'd,
To be for sports and pastimes rein'd,
Great Dymoke, in his glorious station,
Paraded at the coronation.   1580
Not so our city Dymoke came,
Heavy, dispirited, and tame ;
No mark of sense, his eyes half-closed,
He on a mighty dray-horse dozed :
Fate never could a horse provide
So fit for such a man to ride,
Nor find a man with strictest care,
So fit for such a horse to bear.
Hung round with instruments of death,
The sight of him would stop the breath   1590
Of braggart Cowardice, and make
The very court Drawcansir quake ;
With dirks, which, in the hands of Spite,
Do their damn'd business in the night,
From Scotland sent, but here display'd
Only to fill up the parade ;
With swords, unflesh'd, of maiden hue,
Which rage or valour never drew ;
With blunderbusses, taught to ride
Like pocket-pistols by his side,   1600
In girdle stuck, he seem'd to be
A little moving armoury.
One thing much wanting to complete
The sight, and make a perfect treat,
Was, that the horse, (a courtesy
In horses found of high degree)
Instead of going forward on,
All the way backward should have gone.
Horses, unless they breeding lack,
Some scruple make to turn their back,   1610

1579 Dymoke, the King's champion.
1592 Drawcansir : a boasting bully in Buckingham's ' The Re-
hearsal.'
1608 A side glance at the conduct of Lord Talbot's horse at the
Coronation of George III. (See note on line 924.)

199

Though riders, which plain truth declares,
No scruple make of turning theirs.
　　Far, far apart from all the rest,
Fit only for a standing jest,
The independent, (can you get
A better suited epithet !)
The independent Amyand came,
All burning with the sacred flame
Of liberty, which well he knows
On the great stock of slavery grows.　　　　1620
Like sparrow, who, deprived of mate
Snatch'd by the cruel hand of Fate,
From spray to spray no more will hop,
But sits alone on the house-top ;
Or like himself, when all alone
At Croydon, he was heard to groan,
Lifting both hands in the defence
Of interest, and common sense ;
Both hands, for as no other man
Adopted and pursued his plan,　　　　1630
The left hand had been lonesome quite,
If he had not held up the right,—
Apart he came, and fix'd his eyes
With rapture on a distant prize,
On which, in letters worthy note,
There, twenty thousand pounds, was wrote.

[1617] ' George and Claudius Amyand were at this period among the
most eminent merchants in the city of London ; the former was M.P.
for Barnstaple, was created a baronet in 1764, and died in 1766. . . .
The Amyands uniformly gave the weight of their influence to admin-
istration.' (Tooke.)
　　[1624] Claudius Amyand was a commissioner of customs and held the
lucrative post of receiver-general of the land tax for London and
Middlesex. It is possible that this may explain the otherwise obscure
reference to Croydon.
　　[1636] A reference to the government loan floated in 1763, by the
terms of which the contractors were allowed 10% of the money sub-
scribed. *The North Briton* commented upon this in the following
terms :
　　' The whole loan amounted to £3,500,000, consequently in a period
of a very few days, the minister gave among his creatures, and the tools
of his power, £350,000, which was levied on the public ; the most
enormous sum ever divided in so short a time among any set of

False trap, for credit sapp'd is found
By getting twenty thousand pound :
Nay, look not thus on me, and stare,
Doubting the certainty—to swear   1640
In such a case I should be loath—
But Perry Cust may take his oath.
   In plain and decent garb array'd
With the prim Quaker, Fraud, came Trade ;
Connivance, to improve the plan
Habited like a juryman,
Judging as interest prevails,
Came next, with measures, weights, and scales ;
Extortion next, of hellish race,
A cub most damn'd, to shew his face   1650
Forbid by fear but not by shame,
Turn'd to a Jew, like Gideon came ;

men. A few of their names I will mention, to show in what estima-
tion they are held by the public. Messrs. Touchet, Glover, Cust
(brother to the able and impartial speaker), Amyand, Maygens,
Salvador, Colebrooke, Thornton and Muilman, had each £200,000
of the new subscription, and of course almost immediately cleared
£20,000 each, which they have, or have not shared among their
friends. Mr. Fox had £100,000, Mr. Calcraft £72,000, Mr. Drum-
mond £10,000,' etc.

[1642] Peregrine Cust, M.P., brother to the Speaker of the House of
Commons, published an affidavit in defence of his conduct. The
document concludes :

' And the deponent saith, that the assertion contained in the said
paper called *The North Briton*, that a sum of £350,000 was levied on
the public, is according to this deponent's opinion, judgment, and best
of his belief, a false and unjust misrepresentation, inasmuch as it was
in this deponent's opinion and judgment uncertain at the time . . .
whether the agreement for the public loan would or would not be
attended with benefit to the subscribers ; and there was not in this
deponent's judgment any possibility that the subscribers to the same
would derive any large, considerable or unreasonable benefit from it,
nor was the agreement itself, in this deponent's opinion, unfair or in-
equitable or inadequate to the risk run.' Tooke, from whom this note
is derived, gives a much longer extract from Cust's affidavit which the
present editor has not thought it necessary to transcribe.

[1652] ' Sampson Gideon, a Jew broker of immense wealth, who hav-
ing been a staunch supporter of Sir Robert Walpole, in all his financial
operations in the city, considered himself entitled to a baronetage,
which Sir Robert was quite willing to concede ; but strong prejudices
then existing in consequence of the Jews' naturalization bill, George
the Second declined conferring it ; it was, however, afterwards be-

Corruption, Midas-like, behold
Turning whate'er she touch'd to gold;
Impotence, led by Lust, and Pride,
Strutting with Ponton by her side ;
Hypocrisy, demure and sad,
In garments of the priesthood clad,
So well disguised, that you might swear,
Deceived, a very priest was there ;   1660
Bankruptcy, full of ease and health,
And wallowing in well-saved wealth,
Came sneering through a ruin'd band,
And bringing B—— in her hand ;
Victory, hanging down her head,
Was by a Highland stallion led ;
Peace, clothed in sables, with a face
Which witness'd sense of huge disgrace,
Which spake a deep and rooted shame
Both of herself and of her name,   1670
Mourning creeps on, and, blushing, feels
War, grim War, treading on her heels ;
Pale Credit, shaken by the arts
Of men with bad heads and worse hearts,
Taking no notice of a band
Which near her were ordain'd to stand,
Well nigh destroy'd by sickly fit,
Look'd wistful all around for Pitt ;
Freedom—at that most hallow'd name
My spirits mount into a flame,   1680
Each pulse beats high, and each nerve strains
Even to the cracking ; through my veins
The tides of life more rapid run,
And tell me I am Freedom's son—
Freedom came next, but scarce was seen,

stowed on his son, a Christian and M.P. for Worcester, whose steady
adherence to government was ultimately rewarded by an Irish peerage
under the title of Lord Eardley.' (Tooke.)

    [1656] ' David Ponton, a gentleman of fortune, who had served the
office of sheriff, and was in the magistracy for the county of Surrey.
The warmth with which Mr. Ponton supported the cause of adminis-
tration rendered him obnoxious to the opposition. He died in 1777.'
(Tooke.)

When the sky, which appear'd serene
And gay before, was overcast ;
Horror bestrode a foreign blast,
And from the prison of the North,
To Freedom deadly, storms burst forth.   1690
   A car like those, in which, we're told,
Our wild forefathers warr'd of old,
Loaded with death, six horses bear
Through the blank region of the air.
Too fierce for time or art to tame,
They pour'd forth mingled smoke and flame
From their wide nostrils ; every steed
Was of that ancient savage breed
Which fell Geryon nursed ; their food
The flesh of man, their drink his blood.   1700
   On the first horses, ill-match'd pair,
This fat and sleek, that lean and bare,
Came ill-match'd riders side by side,
And Poverty was yoked with Pride ;
Union most strange it must appear,
Till other Unions make it clear.
   Next in the gall of bitterness,
With rage, which words can ill-express,
With unforgiving rage, which springs
From a false zeal for holy things,   1710
Wearing such robes as prophets wear,
False prophets placed in Peter's chair,
On which, in characters of fire,
Shapes antic, horrible, and dire
Inwoven flamed ; where, to the view,
In groups appear'd a rabble crew
Of sainted devils ; where, all round,
Vile relics of vile men were found,
Who, worse than devils, from the birth
Perform'd the work of hell on earth,   1720
Jugglers, Inquisitors, and Popes,

[1699] Churchill's memory played him false in this line, and made him
confuse two distinct Labours of Hercules : overcoming the man-
eating horses of Diomedes and driving off the oxen of Geryon.
[1706] ' Other Unions,' *i.e.*, the Union of England and Scotland.

Pointing at axes, wheels, and ropes,
And engines, framed on horrid plan,
Which none but the destroyer, man
Could, to promote his selfish views,
Have head to make or heart to use ;
Bearing, to consecrate her tricks,
In her left hand a crucifix—
Remembrance of our dying Lord ;
And in her right a two-edged sword ;   1730
Having her brows, in impious sport,
Adorn'd with words of high import,
' On earth peace, amongst men good will ;
Love bearing, and forbearing still,'
All wrote in the heart's blood of those
Who rather death than falsehood chose ;
On her breast, (where, in days of yore,
When God loved Jews, the High Priest wore
Those oracles which were decreed
To instruct and guide the chosen seed)   1740
Having with glory clad and strength,
The Virgin pictured at full length,
Whilst at her feet, in small pourtray'd,
As scarce worth notice, Christ was laid,
Came Superstition, fierce and fell,
An imp detested, e'en in hell ;
Her eye inflamed, her face all o'er
Foully besmear'd with human gore,
O'er heaps of mangled saints she rode ;
Fast at her heels Death proudly strode,   1750
And grimly smiled, well pleased to see
Such havoc of mortality :
Close by her side, on mischief bent,
And urging on each bad intent,
To its full bearing, savage, wild,

1729   ' And on his breste a bloodie crosse he bore,
          The deare remembrance of his dying Lorde.'
                                        FAERIE QUEENE.

1738 Exodus xxviii, 13-30, describes the high-priestly ephod and the
breastplate with the Urim and Thummim. These last were used for
divination, but their precise nature is uncertain. After the death of
David no instance of their use is mentioned in the Old Testament.

The mother fit of such a child,
Striving the empire to advance
Of Sin and Death, came Ignorance.
 With looks, where dread command was placed,
And sovereign power by pride disgraced ; 1760
Where, loudly witnessing a mind
Of savage, more than human kind ;
Not choosing to be loved, but fear'd ;
Mocking at right, Misrule appear'd,
With eyeballs glaring fiery red,
Enough to strike beholders dead ;
Gnashing his teeth, and in a flood
Pouring corruption forth and blood
From his chafed jaws ; without remorse
Whipping, and spurring on his horse, 1770
Whose sides, in their own blood embay'd,
E'en to the bone were open laid,
Came Tyranny, disdaining awe,
And trampling over sense and law.
One thing, and only one, he knew,
One object only would pursue :
Though less (so low doth passion bring)
Than man, he would be more than king.
 With every argument and art
Which might corrupt the head and heart, 1780
Soothing the frenzy of his mind,
Companion meet, was Flattery join'd ;
Winning his carriage, every look
Employ'd, whilst it conceal'd, a hook ;
When simple most, most to be fear'd ;
Most crafty, when no craft appear'd ;
His tales no man like him could tell ;
His words, which melted as they fell,
Might even a hypocrite deceive,
And make an infidel believe, 1790
Wantonly cheating o'er and o'er
Those who had cheated been before.
Such Flattery came, in evil hour,
Poisoning the royal ear of power ;
And, grown by prostitution great,

Would be first minister of state.
  Within the chariot, all alone,
High seated on a kind of throne,
With pebbles graced, a figure came,
Whom Justice would, but dare not, name.   1800
Hard times when Justice without fear
Dare not bring forth to public ear
The names of those who dare offend
'Gainst justice, and pervert her end !
But, if the Muse afford me grace,
Description shall supply the place.
  In foreign garments he was clad ;
Sage ermine o'er the glossy plaid
Cast reverend honour ; on his heart,
Wrought by the curious hand of Art,   1810
In silver wrought, and brighter far
Than heavenly or than earthly star,
Shone a White Rose, the emblem dear
Of him he ever must revere,
Of that dread lord, who, with his host
Of faithful native rebels lost,
Like those black spirits doom'd to hell,
At once from power and virtue fell :
Around his clouded brows was placed
A bonnet, most superbly graced   1820
With mighty thistles, nor forgot
The sacred motto—' Touch me not.'
  In the right hand a sword he bore
Harder than adamant, and more
Fatal than winds which from the mouth
Of the rough North invade the South ;
The reeking blade to view presents
The blood of helpless innocents,
And on the hilt, as meek become
As lambs before the shearers dumb,   1830
With downcast eye, and solemn show

<hr>

[1799] 'A figure,' *i.e.*, Mansfield. (See note on ' The Epistle to Hogarth,' line 76.)
[1822] The ' sacred motto' was indeed ' Noli me tangere' ; the Scottish, ' Nemo me impune lacessit.'

Of deep, unutterable woe,
Mourning the time when Freedom reign'd,
Fast to a rock was Justice chain'd.
   In his left hand, in wax imprest,
With bells and gewgaws idly drest,
An image, cast in baby mould,
He held, and seem'd o'erjoy'd to hold :
On this he fix'd his eyes ; to this
Bowing, he gave the loyal kiss,   1840
And, for rebellion fully ripe,
Seem'd to desire the antitype.
What if to that Pretender's foes
His greatness, nay, his life, he owes ?
Shall common obligations bind,
And shake his constancy of mind ?
Scorning such weak and petty chains,
Faithful to James he still remains
Though he the friend of George appear :
Dissimulation's virtue here.   1850
   Jealous and mean, he with a frown
Would awe, and keep all merit down ;
Nor would to truth and justice bend,
Unless out-bullied by his friend :
Brave with the coward, with the brave
He is himself a coward slave :
Awed by his fears, he has no heart

[1848] Mansfield's brother was actually in the service of the Stuarts and he himself was credited with strong Jacobite sympathies. *Cf.* :

   ' The new-fangl'd Scot, who was brought up at Home,
   In the very same School as his Brother at Rome,
   Kneel'd conscious, as tho' his old comrades might urge,
   He had formerly drank to the *King* before George.'
                    ' The Processionade.'

This satire published in 1746 and ' The Causidicade ' published in 1742 on the appointment of Murray, the future Lord Mansfield, to the place of Solicitor-General, are supposed to have been written by an Irishman named Macnamara Morgan. He was a member of Lincoln's Inn and died in 1762. (See ' Notes and Queries,' 2nd Series, IV, 1857, p. 94.)

[1854] The ' friend ' is ' Bully Norton ' (see note on the ' Epistle to Hogarth,' line 75) to whose vehemence Mansfield is thought by Churchill to have yielded, for the sake of peace.

To take a great and open part :
Mines in a subtle train he springs,
And, secret, saps the ears of kings ;   1860
But not e'en there continues firm
'Gainst the resistance of a worm :
Born in a country, where the will
Of one is law to all, he still
Retain'd the infection, with full aim
To spread it wheresoe'er he came ;
Freedom he hated, law defied,
The prostitute of power and pride ;
Law he with ease explains away,
And leads bewilder'd Sense astray ;   1870
Much to the credit of his brain,
Puzzles the cause he can't maintain,
Proceeds on most familiar grounds,
And where he can't convince confounds :
Talents of rarest stamp and size,
To Nature false, he misapplies,
And turns to poison what was sent
For purposes of nourishment.
Paleness, not such as on his wings
The messenger of sickness brings,   1880
But such as takes its coward rise
From conscious baseness, conscious vice,
O'erspread his cheeks ; disdain and pride,
To upstart fortunes ever tied,
Scowl'd on his brow ; within his eye,
Insidious, lurking like a spy,
To caution principled by fear,
Not daring open to appear,
Lodged covert mischief : passion hung
On his lip quivering : on his tongue   1890
Fraud dwelt at large : within his breast
All that makes villain found a nest ;
All that, on hell's completest plan,
E'er join'd to damn the heart of man.

1863 Mansfield was born at Scone in Scotland. ' A country where the
will of one is law to all ' would seem to be a reference to the clan
system and to the powers of the chief.

Soon as the car reach'd land, he rose,
And with a look which might have froze
The heart's best blood ; which was enough
Had hearts been made of sterner stuff
In cities than elsewhere, to make
The very stoutest quail and quake,   1900
He cast his baleful eyes around :
Fix'd without motion to the ground,
Fear waiting on surprise, all stood,
And horror chill'd their curdled blood ;
No more they thought of pomp, no more
(For they had seen his face before)
Of law they thought ; the cause forgot,
Whether it was or Ghost, or plot,
Which drew them there : they all stood more
Like statues than they were before.   1910
    What could be done ? Could art, could force,
Or both, direct a proper course
To make this savage monster tame,
Or send him back the way he came ?
    What neither art, nor force, nor both,
Could do, a Lord of foreign growth,
A Lord to that base wretch allied
In country, not in vice and pride,
Effected ; from the self-same land,
(Bad news for our blaspheming band   1920
Of scribblers, but deserving note)
The poison came and antidote.
Abash'd, the monster hung his head,
And like an empty vision fled ;
His train, like virgin snows, which run,
Kiss'd by the burning, bawdy sun,
To lovesick streams, dissolved in air ;
Joy, who from absence seem'd more fair,

[1917] It was obvious to all contemporary readers that Churchill's mark in the preceding passage was Mansfield. The author, either to protect himself against the Judge (famous for his severity to libellers) or to add sarcastic point to his satire, now brings in Mansfield by name and represents him as the enemy of ' the monster ' before described.

Came smiling, freed from slavish awe ;
Loyalty, Liberty, and Law,
Impatient of the galling chain,
And yoke of power, resumed their reign ;
And, burning with the glorious flame
Of public virtue, Mansfield came.

1930

END OF VOLUME I.

THE POEMS
OF CHARLES
CHURCHILL

VOL. TWO

POEMS

OF

CHARLES
CHURCHILL

EDITED BY
JAMES LAVER

VOLUME TWO

MCMXXXIII

CHURCHILL'S POEMS

VOLUME TWO

THE PROPHECY OF FAMINE

AN EPISTLE TO WILLIAM HOGARTH

THE CONFERENCE

THE AUTHOR

THE DUELLIST

GOTHAM

THE CANDIDATE

THE FAREWELL

THE TIMES

INDEPENDENCE

THE JOURNEY

FRAGMENT OF A DEDICATION

THE PROPHECY OF FAMINE*

A SCOTS PASTORAL

INSCRIBED TO JOHN WILKES, ESQ.

Carmina tum melius, cum venerit ipse, canemus.

DR. KING, Oxon.

WHEN Cupid first instructs his darts to fly
From the sly corner of some cook-maid's eye,
The stripling raw, just enter'd in his teens,
Receives the wound, and wonders what it means ;
His heart, like dripping, melts, and new desire
Within him stirs, each time she stirs the fire ;
Trembling and blushing, he the fair one views,
And fain would speak, but can't—without a Muse.
    So to the sacred mount he takes his way,
Prunes his young wings, and tunes his infant lay ;   10
His oaten reed to rural ditties frames,
To flocks and rocks, to hills and rills, proclaims,
In simplest notes, and all unpolish'd strains,
The loves of nymphs, and eke the loves of swains.
    Clad, as your nymphs were always clad of yore,
In rustic weeds—a cook-maid now no more—
Beneath an aged oak Lardella lies,
Green moss her couch ; her canopy the skies.
From aromatic shrubs the roguish gale   19
Steals young perfumes, and wafts them through the vale.
The youth, turn'd swain, and skill'd in rustic lays,
Fast by her side his amorous descant plays.
Herds low, flocks bleat, pies chatter, ravens scream,
And the full chorus dies a-down the stream.
The streams, with music freighted, as they pass

---

* First published in January, 1763, by the Author, and sold by
G. Kearsley.

9 Churchill detested false pastoral and never lost an opportunity
of sneering at its practitioners.

17 A purposely ridiculous name.

Present the fair Lardella with a glass,
And Zephyr, to complete the love-sick plan,
Waves his light wings, and serves her for a fan.
　But when maturer Judgment takes the lead,
These childish toys on Reason's altar bleed ;　　　　30
Form'd after some great man, whose name breeds awe,
Whose every sentence Fashion makes a law ;
Who on mere credit his vain trophies rears,
And founds his merit on our servile fears ;
Then we discard the workings of the heart,
And nature's banish'd by mechanic art ;
Then, deeply read, our reading must be shown ;
Vain is that knowledge which remains unknown :
Then Ostentation marches to our aid,
And letter'd Pride stalks forth in full parade ;　　　　40
Beneath their care behold the work refine,
Pointed each sentence, polish'd every line ;
Trifles are dignified, and taught to wear
The robes of ancients with a modern air ;
Nonsense with classic ornaments is graced,
And passes current with the stamp of taste.
　Then the rude Theocrite is ransack'd o'er,
And courtly Maro call'd from Mincio's shore ;
Sicilian Muses on our mountains roam,
Easy and free as if they were at home ;　　　　50
Nymphs, Naiads, Nereids, Dryads, Satyrs, Fauns,
Sport in our floods, and trip it o'er our lawns ;
Flowers which once flourish'd fair in Greece and Rome,
More fair revive in England's meads to bloom ;
Skies without cloud exotic suns adorn,
And roses blush, but blush without a thorn ;
Landscapes unknown to dowdy Nature rise,
And new creations strike our wond'ring eyes.
　For bards like these, who neither sing nor say,

---

[47] Scarcely one half of the works of Theocritus are strictly pastoral,
but to the eighteenth century his writings were the prototype of all
' rude ' (*i.e.*, rustic) poetry.
　[48] The Mincio (Mincius) is a river in northern Italy which flows
through the Lago di Garda and falls into the Po, a little below Mantua,
near which town ' courtly Maro ' (*i.e.*, Virgil) was born in 70 B.C.

Grave without thought, and without feeling gay,   60
Whose numbers in one even tenor flow,
Attuned to pleasure, and attuned to woe ;
Who, if plain Common-sense her visit pays,
And mars one couplet in their happy lays,
As at some ghost affrighted, start and stare,
And ask the meaning of her coming there ;—
For bards like these a wreath shall Mason bring,
Lined with the softest down of Folly's wing ;
In Love's pagoda shall they ever doze,
And Gisbal kindly rock them to repose ;   70
My Lord —— to letters as to faith most true—
At once their patron and example too—
Shall quaintly fashion his love-labour'd dreams,
Sigh with sad winds, and weep with weeping streams ;
Curious in grief, (for real grief, we know,

⁶⁷ William Mason (1724-1797) made the acquaintance of Thomas
Gray while at Cambridge and by his influence was elected fellow of
Pembroke. Mason was Gray's disciple and imitator for the rest of his
life. Warburton admired some of his works, and this may account for
Churchill's hostility. Mason became one of the king's chaplains and
a canon of York, but he did not abandon literature. In 1756 he pub-
lished four odes, and in 1759 his ' Caractacus ' was revised by Gray.
Colman (the elder) and Lloyd ridiculed both Gray and Mason in their
' Odes to Obscurity and Oblivion.' At Gray's death Mason became
possessed of the poet's papers and brought out Gray's ' Life and
Letters ' in 1771.

⁷⁰ ' Gisbal, an Hyperbonean tale, translated from the fragments of
Ossian, the son of Fingal.'

⁷¹ ' My Lord,' *i.e.*, Lord Lyttelton. George Lyttelton (1709-1773),
first Baron Lyttelton, was educated at Eton and Christ Church,
Oxford. His political importance was due largely to his family con-
nections with the Temples, the Grenvilles and Pitt. Lyttelton, how-
ever, was estranged from Pitt from 1756 until about 1764, when he
became reconciled to Temple also, with whom he had quarrelled
violently in 1758. Churchill's hostility is, therefore, understandable,
although Lyttelton opposed the cider bill in 1763, which might have
been a point in his favour. Lyttelton had been friendly with Pope
and had befriended Thomson. His own compositions are somewhat
derivative, and marred by false pastoralism. On his ' Progress of
Love' in four eclogues, London, 1732, Johnson remarks : ' They cant
of shepherds and flocks, and crooks dressed with flowers.' Lyttelton's
famous poem : ' To the Memory of a Lady [*i.e.* Lucy Lyttelton, his
wife] lately deceased : A Monody,' London, 1747, was cruelly bur-
lesqued by Smollett. For the meaning of the reference to Lord
Lyttelton's ' faith,' see note on line 231.

Is curious to dress up the tale of woe)
From the green umbrage of some Druid's seat
Shall his own works in his own way repeat.
  Me, whom no Muse of heavenly birth inspires,
No judgment tempers when rash genius fires ;   80
Who boast no merit but mere knack of rhyme,
Short gleams of sense, and satire out of time ;
Who cannot follow where trim fancy leads
By prattling streams, o'er flower-empurpled meads ;
Who often, but without success, have pray'd
For apt Alliteration's artful aid ;
Who would, but cannot, with a master's skill,
Coin fine new epithets, which mean no ill ;
Me, thus uncouth, thus every way unfit
For pacing poesy, and ambling wit,   90
Taste with contempt beholds, nor deigns to place
Amongst the lowest of her favour'd race.
  Thou, Nature, art my goddess—to thy law
Myself I dedicate—hence, slavish awe,
Which bends to fashion, and obeys the rules
Imposed at first, and since observed by fools !
Hence those vile tricks which mar fair Nature's hue,
And bring the sober matron forth to view,
With all that artificial, tawdry glare
Which virtue scorns, and none but strumpets wear ! 100
Sick of those pomps, those vanities, that waste
Of toil, which critics now mistake for taste ;
Of false refinements sick, and labour'd ease,
Which art, too thinly veil'd, forbids to please,
By Nature's charms (inglorious truth !) subdued,
However plain her dress, and 'haviour rude,
To northern climes my happier course I steer,
Climes where the goddess reigns throughout the year ;
Where, undisturb'd by Art's rebellious plan,
She rules the loyal laird, and faithful clan.   110
  To that rare soil, where virtues clust'ring grow,
What mighty blessings doth not England owe !
What waggon-loads of courage, wealth, and sense,

---

[110] *I.e.*, loyal to the Pretender. The rebellion of 1745 was still
fresh in the public memory.

Doth each revolving day import from thence !
To us she gives, disinterested friend !
Faith without fraud, and Stuarts without end.
When we prosperity's rich trappings wear,
Come not her generous sons and take a share ?
And if, by some disastrous turn of fate,
Change should ensue, and ruin seize the state,   120
Shall we not find, safe in that hallow'd ground,
Such refuge as the holy martyr found?
Nor less our debt in science, though denied
By the weak slaves of prejudice and pride.
Thence came the Ramsays, names of worthy note,
Of whom one paints as well as t'other wrote;
Thence, Home, disbanded from the sons of prayer

[116] ' Stuart, the family name of Lord Bute : it was noticed by the opposition papers of the day that out of sixteen names in one list of gazette promotions there were eleven Stuarts and four M'Kenzies.' (Tooke.)

[122] A bitter taunt against the Scots for having delivered up Charles I to the English Parliament.

[125] Allan Ramsay, the portrait painter (1713-1784), was the son of Allan Ramsay, author of the pastoral drama of ' The Gentle Shepherd.' The younger Ramsay studied partly in London, partly in Italy, and on his return from that country settled for a while in Edinburgh. He set up as a painter in London about 1762 and was very successful. Bute, whose portrait he painted, introduced him to King George III, whose Painter in Ordinary he became on the death of Shackleton in 1767. Ramsay was a cultivated man and his conversational powers were highly praised by Dr. Johnson. The elder Ramsay died in 1758.

[127] John Home (1722-1808) was brought up to the church, and after some fighting on the Hanoverian side in the '45, was inducted minister of Athelstaneford in East Lothian in succession to Robert Blair, author of ' The Grave.' Home's first tragedy, ' Agis,' was taken to London in 1747 and rejected by Garrick. It was, however, admired by Lord Lyttelton and by Pitt, and William Collins prophesied Home's ultimate success in tragedy. On his return to Scotland, Archibald Campbell, Duke of Argyle, introduced him to Bute, who became his patron. Home's ' Douglas,' his most celebrated piece, was produced in Edinburgh in 1756, and at Covent Garden in February, 1757. It was very successful, and both Hume and Gray spoke highly of it, although Johnson dismissed it with contempt. Soon afterwards Home resigned from his ministry and became, first, private secretary to Bute, and then tutor to the Prince of Wales, afterwards George III. Garrick then brought out his ' Agis ' at Drury Lane (February 21st, 1758). In 1760 his ' Siege of Aquileia ' was produced, and offices and pensions were showered upon him by his now powerful patron. When

For loving plays, though no dull dean was there;
Thence issued forth, at great Macpherson's call,
That old, new, epic pastoral, Fingal;   130
Thence Malloch, friend alike of church and state,

Bute resigned Home ceased to be his secretary, and the strong public
feeling against the Scots helped to damn his next drama, ' The Fatal
Discovery.' Home was a friend of James Macpherson, of David Hume
and of Adam Smith and, in his old age, of Scott.

¹²⁸ Zachariah Pearce, was Bishop of Rochester from 1756 until his
death in 1774. He was also Dean of Westminster (in 1768, on account
of his growing infirmities he resigned the deanery and would have
resigned his bishopric, but was not permitted to do so) and in that
capacity remonstrated with Churchill for applying his talents to so
secular a subject as that treated in ' The Rosciad.' Churchill replied
with a somewhat irrelevant gibe at Pearce's translation of Longinus,
whereupon the Dean requested him to put off his new lay clothes and
resume a more clerical habit. On the complaint of the parishioners of
St. John the Evangelist Churchill was once more censured by Pearce,
and resigned his lectureship in January, 1763.

¹²⁹ James Macpherson (1736-1796) was born at Ruthven in Inver-
ness-shire of poor parents who, however, managed to give him a good
education. He had already written verses of his own when, in 1759,
he met John Home (see note on line 127) and Dr. Carlyle of Inveresk
and repeated to them certain Gaelic verses which he said he had
collected in the Highlands. They urged him to publish translations
of these and others, and in 1760 appeared his ' Fragments of Ancient
Poetry,' which were well received and established his fame. A fund
was raised to enable Macpherson to make journeys to the Highlands
for the purpose of collecting more fragments. At the instance of Bute,
Macpherson came to London and, in 1762, issued his ' Fingal.' In
the following year appeared ' Temora,' which confirmed the doubts
which had already been raised by ' Fingal.' Macpherson promised to
produce the original but made no serious effort to do so. Through
Bute's patronage Macpherson obtained a government appointment,
and used his pen on behalf of the ministry. His subsequent writings
hardly concern us here. It is enough to say that the general charge of
forgery brought against Macpherson by Johnson and others was
unjustified, although there never was a complete epic, ' Fingal ' for
Macpherson to translate. He strung together fragments of genuine
Gaelic verse, filling in the blanks with his own compositions. The
influence of the Ossian poems on the development of Romanticism
throughout Europe was immense.

¹³¹ David Mallett (c. 1705-1765), whose real name was Malloch,
was a catholic and a member of the outlawed clan of Macgregor. His
family suffered severely in the rebellion of 1715. Mallet supported
himself by private tutoring, and in 1739 ' Mustapha ' was produced
at Drury Lane and secured the patronage of Frederick Prince of Wales
by its hostility to the King and Walpole. Mallet and Thomson were
commissioned to write the masque of ' Alfred,' which was played in
1740 in the gardens of Cliefden, and Mallet, in 1742, became the

Of Christ and Liberty, by grateful Fate
Raised to rewards, which, in a pious reign,
All daring infidels should seek in vain ;
Thence simple bards, by simple prudence taught,
To this wise town by simple patrons brought,
In simple manner utter simple lays,
And take, with simple pensions, simple praise.
    Waft me, some muse, to Tweed's inspiring stream,
Where all the little Loves and Graces dream ;   140
Where, slowly winding, the dull waters creep,
And seem themselves to own the power of sleep ;
Where on the surface lead, like feathers, swims ;
There let me bathe my yet unhallow'd limbs,
As once a Syrian bathed in Jordan's flood,
Wash off my native stains, correct that blood
Which mutinies at call of English pride,
And, deaf to prudence, rolls a patriot tide.
    From solemn thought which overhangs the brow,
Of patriot care, when things are—God knows how ;   150
From nice trim points, where Honour, slave to rule,
In compliment to folly plays the fool ;
From those gay scenes, where mirth exalts his power,
And easy humour wings the laughing hour ;
From those soft, better moments, when desire
Beats high, and all the world of man's on fire ;
When mutual ardours of the melting fair
More than repay us for whole years of care,
At Friendship's summons will my Wilkes retreat,
And see, once seen before, that ancient seat,   160
That ancient seat, where majesty display'd
Her ensigns, long before the world was made !
    Mean, narrow maxims which enslave mankind,

Prince's under-secretary. Mallet was later patronised by Bolingbroke
and was allowed to print a complete edition of Bolingbroke's works
after his death.   His flattery of Bute was rewarded in 1763 by a
sinecure post which he held until his death. He was obnoxious to
Churchill not only as a Scot, but as a contributor, at Smollett's request,
to the *Critical Review*.
   [145] *I.e.*, Naaman, who on the advice of Elisha was cured of leprosy
by bathing seven times in the river Jordan. (II Kings, v.)
   [160] Possibly a reference to ' Arthur's Seat.'

Ne'er from its bias warp thy settled mind :
Not duped by party nor opinion's slave,
Those faculties which bounteous nature gave
Thy honest spirit into practice brings,
Nor courts the smile, nor dreads the frown of kings,
Let rude, licentious Englishmen comply
With tumult's voice, and curse they know not why ;   170
Unwilling to condemn, thy soul disdains
To wear vile faction's arbitrary chains,
And strictly weighs, in apprehension clear,
Things as they are, and not as they appear.
With thee good-humour tempers lively wit ;
Enthron'd with judgment, candour loves to sit,
And nature gave thee, open to distress,
A heart to pity, and a hand to bless.
　　Oft have I heard thee mourn the wretched lot
Of the poor, mean, despised, insulted Scot,   180
Who, might calm reason credit idle tales,
By rancour forged where prejudice prevails,
Or starves at home, or practises, through fear
Of starving, arts which damn all conscience here.
When scribblers, to the charge by interest led,
The fierce North Briton foaming at their head,
Pour forth invectives, deaf to candour's call,
And, injured by one alien, rail at all ;
On northern Pisgah when they take their stand,
To mark the weakness of that Holy Land,   190
With needless truths their libels to adorn,
And hang a nation up to public scorn,
Thy generous soul condemns the frantic rage,
And hates the faithful, but ill-natured page.
　　The Scots are poor, cries surly English pride ;
True is the charge, nor by themselves denied.
Are they not then in strictest reason clear,

---

[186] *The North Briton,* conducted by Wilkes, was published during
the years 1762-1763. Churchill was intimately connected with it,
and the subject of the present poem was originally drafted in prose and
intended for inclusion in its pages.

[189] Pisgah, the mountain from which Moses was permitted to view
the Promised Land he might not enter. (Deuteronomy, iii, 27.)

Who wisely come to mend their fortunes here ?
If, by low, supple arts successful grown,
They sapp'd our vigour to increase their own ; 200
If, mean in want, and insolent in power,
They only fawn'd more surely to devour,
Roused by such wrongs should reason take alarm,
And e'en the Muse for public safety arm :
But if they own ingenuous virtue's sway,
And follow where true honour points the way ;
If they revere the hand by which they're fed,
And bless the donors for their daily bread,
Or by vast debts of higher import bound,
Are always humble, always grateful found ; 210
If they, directed by Paul's holy pen,
Become discreetly all things to all men,
That all men may become all things to them,
Envy may hate, but justice can't condemn.
" Into our places, states, and beds they creep ; "
They've sense to get what we want sense to keep.
   Once, be the hour accursed, accursed the place !
I ventured to blaspheme the chosen race.
Into those traps, which men, call'd patriots, laid,
By specious arts unwarily betray'd, 220
Madly I leagued against that sacred earth,
Vile parricide ! which gave a parent birth :
But shall I meanly error's path pursue,
When heavenly truth presents her friendly clue ?
Once plunged in ill, shall I go farther in ?
To make the oath, was rash : to keep it, sin.
Backward I tread the paths I trod before,
And calm reflection hates what passion swore.
Converted, (blessed are the souls which know
Those pleasures which from true conversion flow, 230
Whether to reason, who now rules my breast,
Or to pure faith, like Lyttelton and West)

[212] ' I am made all things to all men, that I might by all means save
some.' (I. Corinthians, ix, 22.)
[222] Churchill's mother is said to have been Scotch.
[232] Gilbert West (died 1756), the translator of Pindar and the friend
of Pitt, was instrumental in converting Lord Lyttelton from the

Past crimes to expiate, be my present aim
To raise new trophies to the Scottish name ;
To make (what can the proudest Muse do more ?)
E'en faction's sons her brighter worth adore ;
To make her glories stamp'd with honest rhymes,
In fullest tide roll down to latest times.
    ' Presumptuous wretch ! and shall a Muse like thine,
An English Muse, the meanest of the nine,   240
Attempt a theme like this ? Can her weak strain
Expect indulgence from the mighty Thane ?
Should he from toils of government retire,
And for a moment fan the poet's fire ;
Should he of sciences the moral friend,
Each curious, each important search suspend,
Leave unassisted Hill of herbs to tell,
And all the wonders of a cockleshell,
Having the Lord's good grace before his eyes,
Would not the Home step forth and gain the prize ? 250
Or if this wreath of honour might adorn
The humble brows of one in England born,
Presumptuous still thy daring must appear ;
Vain all thy towering hopes whilst I am here.'
    Thus spake a form, by silken smile, and tone
Dull and unvaried, for the Laureate known,
Folly's chief friend, Decorum's eldest son,
In every party found, and yet of none.
This airy substance, this substantial shade,
Abash'd I heard, and with respect obey'd.   260
    From themes too lofty for a bard so mean,
Discretion beckons to an humbler scene ;
The restless fever of ambition laid,
Calm I retire, and seek the sylvan shade.

scepticism of his earlier years to an acceptance of Christianity.
Lyttelton's ' Observations on the Conversion and Apostleship of St.
Paul, in a letter to Gilbert West, Esq., London, 1747,' has been re-
printed many times and is frequently attached to Gilbert West's
' Observations on the History and Evidences of the Resurrection of
Jesus Christ.'
    [242] ' The Mighty Thane ' : Bute.
    [247] Hill. (See note on ' Rosciad,' line 107.)
    [250] Home. (See note on line 127.)
    [256] William Whitehead. (See note on ' Ghost,' Book III, line 117.)

Now be the Muse disrobed of all her pride,
Be all the glare of verse by truth supplied,
And if plain nature pours a simple strain,
Which Bute may praise, and Ossian not disdain,
Ossian, sublimest, simplest bard of all,
Whom English infidels, Macpherson call,   270
Then round my head shall Honour's ensigns wave,
And pensions mark me for a willing slave.
    Two boys, whose birth, beyond all question, springs
From great and glorious, though forgotten, kings,
Shepherds, of Scottish lineage, born and bred
On the same bleak and barren mountain's head,
By niggard nature doom'd on the same rocks
To spin out life, and starve themselves and flocks,
Fresh as the morning, which, enrobed in mist,
The mountain's top with usual dulness kiss'd,   280
Jockey and Sawney to their labours rose ;
Soon clad I ween, where nature needs no clothes ;
Where, from their youth enured to winter-skies,
Dress and her vain refinements they despise.
    Jockey, whose manly, high-boned cheeks to crown,
With freckles spotted, flamed the golden down,
With meikle art could on the bag-pipes play,
E'en from the rising to the setting day ;
Sawney as long without remorse could bawl
Home's madrigals, and ditties from Fingal :   290
Oft' at his strains, all natural though rude,
The Highland lass forgot her want of food,
And, whilst she scratch'd her lover into rest,
Sunk pleased, though hungry, on her Sawney's breast.
    Far as the eye could reach, no tree was seen,
Earth, clad in russet, scorn'd the lively green :
The plague of locusts they secure defy,
For in three hours a grasshopper must die :
No living thing, whate'er its food, feasts there,
But the cameleon, who can feast on air.   300
No birds, except as birds of passage, flew ;
No bee was known to hum, no dove to coo :
No streams, as amber smooth, as amber clear,

[268] Ossian. (See note on line 129.)

221

Were seen to glide, or heard to warble here :
Rebellion's spring, which through the country ran,
Furnish'd, with bitter draughts, the steady clan :
No flowers embalm'd the air, but one white rose,
Which, on the tenth of June, by instinct blows ;
By instinct blows at morn, and when the shades
Of drizzly eve prevail, by instinct fades.   310
   One, and but one poor solitary cave,
Too sparing of her favours, nature gave ;
That one alone (hard tax on Scottish pride !)
Shelter at once for man and beast supplied.
There snares without entangling briars spread,
And thistles, arm'd against the invader's head,
Stood in close ranks, all entrance to oppose ;
Thistles now held more precious than the rose.
All creatures which, on nature's earliest plan,
Were form'd to loath, and to be loath'd by man ;   320
Which owed their birth to nastiness and spite ;
Deadly to touch, and hateful to the sight ;
Creatures, which when admitted in the ark
Their saviour shunn'd, and rankled in the dark,
Found place within : marking her noisome road
With poison's trail, here crawl'd the bloated toad :
There webs were spread of more than common size,
And half-starved spiders prey'd on half-starved flies :
In quest of food, efts strove in vain to crawl ;
Slugs, pinch'd with hunger, smear'd the slimy wall :   330
The cave around with hissing serpents rung ;
On the damp roof unhealthy vapour hung ;
And Famine, by her children always known,
As proud as poor, here fix'd her native throne.
   Here, for the sullen sky was overcast,
And summer shrunk beneath a wintry blast ;
A native blast, which, arm'd with hail and rain,
Beat unrelenting on the naked swain,
The boys for shelter made ; behind, the sheep,

[307] The white rose of the Jacobites, worn on June 10th, the young Pretender's birthday.
[318] The thistle, the Scottish emblem. Its earliest undoubted use as a national badge was in the reign of James III (1460-1488).

Of which those shepherds every day *take keep*,   340
Sickly crept on, and with complainings rude,
On nature seem'd to call, and bleat for food.

JOCKEY

Sith to this cave, by tempest, we're confined,
And within *ken* our flocks, under the wind,
Safe from the pelting of this perilous storm,
Are laid *emong* yon' thistles, dry and warm,
What, Sawney, if by Shepherds' art we try
To mock the rigour of this cruel sky ?
What if we tune some merry roundelay ?
Well dost thou sing, nor ill doth Jockey play.   350

SAWNEY

Ah ! Jockey, ill advisest thou, I wis,
To think of songs at such a time as this :
Sooner shall herbage crown these barren rocks,
Sooner shall fleeces clothe these ragged flocks,
Sooner shall want seize shepherds of the south,
And we forget to live from hand to mouth,
Than Sawney, out of season, shall impart
The songs of gladness with an aching heart.

JOCKEY

Still have I known thee for a silly swain ;
Of things past help what boots it to complain ?   360
Nothing but mirth can conquer fortune's spite ;
No sky is heavy if the heart be light :
Patience is sorrow's salve : what can't be cured,
So Donald right areeds, must be endured.

SAWNEY

Full silly swain, I wot, is Jockey now.
How didst thou bear thy Maggy's falsehood ? how,
When with a foreign loon she stole away,
Didst thou forswear thy pipe and shepherd's lay !
Where was thy boasted wisdom then, when I
Applied those proverbs, which you now apply ?   370

JOCKEY

O she was bonny ! all the Highlands round
Was there a rival to my Maggy found ?
More precious (though that precious is to all)
Than the rare med'cine which we Brimstone call,
Or that choice plant, so grateful to the nose,
Which, in I know not what far country, grows,
Was Maggy unto me : dear do I rue
A lass so fair should ever prove untrue.

SAWNEY

Whether with pipe or song to charm the ear,
Through all the land did Jamie find a peer ?   380
Cursed be that year by every honest Scot,
And in the shepherd's calendar forgot,
That fatal year when Jamie, hapless swain !
In evil hour forsook the peaceful plain :
Jamie, when our young laird discreetly fled,
Was seized, and hang'd till he was dead, dead, dead.

JOCKEY

Full sorely may we all lament that day,
For all were losers in the deadly fray.
Five brothers had I ; on the Scottish plains,
Well dost thou know were none more hopeful swains; 390
Five brothers there I lost, in manhood's pride ;
Two in the field, and three on gibbets died :
Ah ! silly swains ! to follow war's alarms ;
Ah ! what hath shepherds' life to do with arms ?

SAWNEY

Mention it not—there saw I strangers clad
In all the honours of our ravish'd plaid ;
Saw the Ferrara, too, our nation's pride,
Unwilling grace the awkward victor's side.
There fell our choicest youth, and from that day
Mote never Sawney tune the merry lay ;   400

[397] Ferrara was famous not only for its fencing-masters, but for its swords.

Bless'd those which fell ! cursed those which still survive,
To mourn fifteen renew'd in forty-five.

Thus plain'd the boys, when from her throne of turf,
With boils emboss'd, and overgrown with scurf,
Vile humours, which, in life's corrupted well
Mix'd at the birth, not abstinence could quell,
Pale Famine rear'd the head ; her eager eyes,
Where hunger e'en to madness seem'd to rise,
Speaking aloud her throes and pangs of heart,
Strain'd to get loose, and from their orbs to start :   410
Her hollow cheeks were each a deep-sunk cell,
Where wretchedness and horror loved to dwell :
With double rows of useless teeth supplied,
Her mouth from ear to ear extended wide,
Which, when for want of food her entrails pined,
She oped, and cursing, swallow'd nought but wind :
All shrivell'd was her skin ; and here and there,
Making their way by force, her bones lay bare :
Such filthy sight to hide from human view,
O'er her foul limbs a tatter'd plaid she threw.   420
  'Cease,' cried the goddess, 'cease, despairing swains !
And from a parent hear what Jove ordains :
  'Pent in this barren corner of the isle,
Where partial fortune never deign'd to smile ;
Like nature's bastards, reaping for our share
What was rejected by the lawful heir ;
Unknown amongst the nations of the earth,
Or only known to raise contempt and mirth ;
Long free, because the race of Roman braves
Thought it not worth their while to make us slaves ; 430
Then into bondage by that nation brought,
Whose ruin we for ages vainly sought ;
Whom still with unslacked hate we view, and still,
The power of mischief lost, retain the will ;
Consider'd as the refuse of mankind,
A mass till the last moment left behind,
Which frugal nature doubted, as it lay,
Whether to stamp with life or throw away ;
Which, form'd in haste, was planted in this nook,

But never enter'd in creation's book ;   440
Branded as traitors who for love of gold
Would sell their God, as once their king they sold.
Long have we borne this mighty weight of ill,
These vile injurious taunts, and bear them still ;
But times of happier note are now at hand,
And the full promise of a better land :
There, like the sons of Israel, having trod,
For the fix'd term of years ordain'd by God,
A barren desert, we shall seize rich plains,
Where milk with honey flows, and plenty reigns :   450
With some few natives join'd, some pliant few,
Who worship interest and our track pursue ;
There shall we though the wretched people grieve,
Ravage at large, nor ask the owners' leave.
  ' For us, the earth shall bring forth her increase,
For us, the flocks shall wear a golden fleece ;
Fat beeves shall yield us dainties not our own,
And the grape bleed a nectar yet unknown :
For our advantage shall their harvests grow,
And Scotsmen reap what they disdain'd to sow :   460
For us, the sun shall climb the eastern hill ;
For us, the rain shall fall, the dew distil :
When to our wishes nature cannot rise,
Art shall be task'd to grant us fresh supplies ;
His brawny arm shall drudging labour strain,
And for our pleasure suffer daily pain :
Trade shall for us exert her utmost powers,
Hers all the toil, and all the profit ours :
For us, the oak shall from his native steep
Descend, and fearless travel through the deep :   470
The sail of commerce, for our use unfurl'd,
Shall waft the treasures of each distant world :
For us, sublimer heights shall science reach ;
For us, their statesmen plot, their churchmen preach :
Their noblest limbs of council we'll disjoint,
And, mocking, new ones of our own appoint :
Devouring War, imprison'd in the North,
Shall, at our call, in horrid pomp break forth,

[442] See note on line 122.

And when, his chariot-wheels with thunder hung,
Fell Discord braying with her brazen tongue,   480
Death in the van, with Anger, Hate, and Fear,
And Desolation stalking in the rear,
Revenge, by Justice guided, in his train,
He drives impetuous o'er the trembling plain,
Shall, at our bidding, quit his lawful prey,
And to meek, gentle, generous Peace give way.
   ' Think not, my Sons, that this so bless'd estate
Stands at a distance on the roll of fate ;
Already big with hopes of future sway,
E'en from this cave I scent my destined prey.   490
Think not, that this dominion o'er a race
Whose former deeds shall time's last annals grace,
In the rough face of peril must be sought,
And with the lives of thousands dearly bought :
No—fool'd by cunning, by that happy art
Which laughs to scorn the blundering hero's heart,
Into the snare shall our kind neighbours fall
With open eyes, and fondly give us all.
   ' When Rome, to prop her sinking empire, bore
Their choicest levies to a foreign shore,   500
What if we seized, like a destroying flood,
Their widow'd plains, and fill'd the realm with blood,
Gave an unbounded loose to manly rage,
And, scorning mercy, spared nor sex, nor age ?
When, for our interest too mighty grown,
Monarchs of warlike bent possess'd the throne,
What if we strove divisions to foment,
And spread the flames of civil discontent,
Assisted those who 'gainst their king made head,
And gave the traitors refuge when they fled ?   510
When restless Glory bade her sons advance,
And pitch'd her standard in the fields of France,
What if, disdaining oaths, an empty sound,
By which our nation never shall be bound,
Bravely we taught unmuzzled war to roam,
Through the weak land, and brought cheap laurels home ?
When the bold traitors leagued for the defence
Of law, religion, liberty, and sense,

227

When they against their lawful monarch rose,
And dared the Lord's anointed to oppose,   520
What if we still revered the banish'd race,
And strove the royal vagrants to replace,
With fierce rebellions shook the unsettled state,
And greatly dared, though cross'd by partial fate ?
These facts, which might, where wisdom held the sway,
Awake the very stones to bar our way,
There shall be nothing, nor one trace remain
In the dull region of an English brain ;
Bless'd with that faith which mountains can remove,
First they shall dupes, next saints, last martyrs, prove. 530
   ' Already is this game of fate begun
Under the sanction of my darling son ;
That son, of nature royal as his name,
Is destined to redeem our race from shame :
His boundless power, beyond example great,
Shall make the rough way smooth, the crooked straight ;
Shall for our ease the raging floods restrain,
And sink the mountain level to the plain.
Discord, whom in a cavern under ground
With massy fetters their late patriot bound ;   540
Where her own flesh the furious hag might tear,
And vent her curses to the vacant air ;
Where, that she never might be heard of more,
He planted Loyalty to guard the door,
For better purpose shall our chief release,
Disguise her for a time, and call her peace.

[533] John Stuart, third Earl of Bute (1713-1792) took no part in politics during his early life, but busied himself with botany and architecture.   During a shower at the races he accidentally made the acquaintance in 1747 of Frederick, Prince of Wales, at whose court he acquired great influence.   On the death of Frederick his influence with the new Prince of Wales continued and on the latter's accession to the throne as George III, Bute became practically chief minister. He was made a Secretary of State in 1761, and having rid himself of Pitt and Newcastle, became First Lord of the Treasury in 1762 and a Knight of the Garter in the same year.   The peace with France in 1763 and the cider tax made him extremely unpopular.   He resigned, weary of the torrents of abuse poured upon him, intrigued for influence for a couple of years and then retired finally from public life. It was he who gave Dr. Johnson his pension.

' Lured by that name, fine engine of deceit !
Shall the weak English help themselves to cheat ;
To gain our love, with honours shall they grace
The old adherents of the Stuart race,   550
Who, pointed out no matter by what name,
Tories or Jacobites, are still the same ;
To soothe our rage the temporising brood
Shall break the ties of truth and gratitude,
Against their saviour venom'd falsehoods frame,
And brand with calumny our William's name :
To win our grace, (rare argument of wit !)
To our untainted faith shall they commit
(Our faith which, in extremest perils tried,
Disdain'd, and still disdains to change her side)   560
That sacred Majesty they all approve,
Who most enjoys, and best deserves their love.'

[552] ' Tories or Jacobites, are still the same.' This was no longer
true, since the Tories found that the King himself was seeking an
alliance with them in order to break the power of the great Whig
families.
[556] William Pitt.

AN EPISTLE
TO
WILLIAM HOGARTH*

Ut Pictura, Poesis. HORACE

A MONGST the sons of men how few are known
Who dare be just to merit not their own !
Superior virtue and superior sense
To knaves and fools will always give offence ;
Nay, men of real worth can scarcely bear,
So nice is jealousy, a rival there.
  Be wicked as thou wilt ; do all that's base ;
Proclaim thyself the monster of thy race.
Let Vice and Folly thy black soul divide ;
Be proud with meanness, and be mean with pride.   10
Deaf to the voice of Faith and Honour, fall
From side to side, yet be of none at all :
Spurn all those charities, those sacred ties,
Which Nature, in her bounty, good as wise,
To work our safety, and ensure her plan,
Contrived to bind and rivet man to man :
Lift against Virtue Power's oppressive rod ;
Betray thy country, and deny thy God ;
And, in one general, comprehensive line
To group, which volumes scarcely could define,   20
Whate'er of sin and dulness can be said,
Join to a Fox's heart a Dashwood's head ;

---

* First published in July, 1763. 'Printed for the Author, and sold by J. Coote.'

[22] Henry Fox (1705-1774), first Baron Holland, was born at Chiswick, and was educated at Eton with Pitt, Fielding, and Sir Charles Hanbury Williams as contemporaries. He squandered his fortune by gambling and went abroad, but on his return in 1735 was elected to Parliament. He attached himself to Sir Robert Walpole, but did not fall with him, being appointed a Lord of the Treasury in the Pelham administration. It would be outside the scope of a footnote to trace his complicated parliamentary career. In 1755 he became a Secretary of State. However, two years later, he contented himself

Yet may'st thou pass unnoticed in the throng,
And, free from envy, safely sneak along :
The rigid saint, by whom no mercy's shown
To saints whose lives are better than his own,
Shall spare thy crimes ; and Wit, who never once
Forgave a brother, shall forgive a dunce.
   But should thy soul, form'd in some luckless hour,
Vile interest scorn, nor madly grasp at power ;   30
Should love of fame, in every noble mind
A brave disease, with love of virtue join'd,
Spur thee to deeds of pith, where courage, tried
In Reason's court, is amply justified ;
Or, fond of knowledge, and averse to strife,
Shouldst thou prefer the calmer walk of life ;
Shouldst thou, by pale and sickly study led,
Pursue coy Science to the fountain-head ;
Virtue thy guide, and public good thy end,
Should every thought to our improvement tend,   40
To curb the passions, to enlarge the mind,
Purge the sick weal, and humanize mankind ;
Rage in her eye, and malice in her breast,
Redoubled Horror grinning on her crest,
Fiercer each snake, and sharper every dart,
Quick from her cell shall maddening Envy start ;
Then shalt thou find, but find, alas ! too late,
How vain is worth ! how short is glory's date !
Then shalt thou find, whilst friends with foes conspire
To give more proof than virtue would desire,   50
Thy danger chiefly lies in acting well ;
No crime's so great as daring to excel.

with the subordinate post of Paymaster-General without a seat in the
Cabinet, and in this office amassed a large fortune. In 1762 he was
admitted to Bute's cabinet, and by the grossest bribery secured
majorities for the unpopular peace. He was rewarded in 1763 with a
peerage, but kept the post of Paymaster-General until 1765. In 1769
the City of London presented a petition to the King in which Fox was
referred to as ' the public defaulter of unaccounted millions,' but Fox
was able to clear himself from the charge of having taken any more
than the usual perquisites of his office. He tried in vain to obtain an
earldom, and died a disappointed and extremely unpopular man.

[22] See note on ' The Ghost,' Book IV, l. 628.

Whilst Satire thus, disdaining mean control,
Urged the free dictates of an honest soul,
Candour, who, with the charity of Paul,
Still thinks the best, whene'er she thinks at all,
With the sweet milk of human kindness bless'd,
The furious ardour of my zeal repress'd.
   ' Canst thou,' with more than usual warmth, she cried,
' Thy malice to indulge, and feed thy pride ;   60
Canst thou, severe by nature as thou art,
With all that wondrous rancour in thy heart,
Delight to torture truth ten thousand ways,
To spin detraction forth from themes of praise,
To make Vice sit, for purposes of strife,
And draw the hag much larger than the life ;
To make the good seem bad, the bad seem worse,
And represent our nature as our curse ?
   ' Doth not humanity condemn that zeal
Which tends to aggravate and not to heal ?   70
Doth not discretion warn thee of disgrace,
And danger, grinning, stare thee in the face,
Loud as the drum which, spreading terror round,
From emptiness acquires the power of sound ?
Doth not the voice of Norton strike thy ear,
And the pale Mansfield chill thy soul with fear ?
Dost thou, fond man, believe thyself secure,
Because thou'rt honest, and because thou'rt poor ?

[76] William Murray (1705-1793), first Earl of Mansfield, was born
at Scone, and was educated at Perth Grammar School, at Westminster,
and at Christ Church, Oxford. He was called to the Bar in 1730, and
was made a Bencher of Lincoln's Inn in 1743. Pope, Bolingbroke and
Warburton were among his friends. After Walpole's fall, he was made
Solicitor-General, and his ability in debate was of immense service to
successive governments. After the '45, he was occupied with the
prosecution of the rebel lords, but this did not prevent the accusation
of Jacobitism constantly brought against him by Churchill and others.
In 1754 Murray became Attorney-General in Newcastle's adminis-
tration, and in 1756 was created Baron Mansfield. He attached himself
to Bute on the latter's accession to power in 1762, and incurred great
odium by allowing a technical flaw in the information filed in respect
of *The North Briton* and the ' Essay on Woman ' to be amended during
Wilkes's absence abroad. In 1766 he was advanced to an Earldom.
He was a very distinguished lawyer, and as an orator second only to
Pitt, his life-long rival.

Dost thou on law and liberty depend ?
Turn, turn thy eyes, and view thy injured friend.   80
Art thou beyond the ruffian gripe of power,
When Wilkes, prejudged, is sentenced to the Tower ?
Dost thou by privilege exemption claim,
When privilege is little more than name ?
Or to prerogative (that glorious ground
On which state scoundrels oft have safety found)
Dost thou pretend, and there a sanction find,
Unpunish'd, thus to libel human-kind ?
  ' When poverty, the poet's constant crime,
Compell'd thee, all unfit, to trade in rhyme,   90
Had not romantic notions turn'd thy head,
Hadst thou not valued honour more than bread ;
Had Interest, pliant Interest, been thy guide,

[82] The story of Wilkes being sent to the Tower may be told in his own words :
  ' I was conducted into a great apartment fronting the park, where Lord Halifax and Lord Egremont, the two Secretaries of State, were sitting at a table covered with paper, pens and ink. Lord Egremont received me with a supercilious, insolent air ; Lord Halifax with great politeness . . . I begged both their Lordships to remember . . . that on the very first day of the ensuing session of Parliament I would stand up in my place and impeach them for the outrage they had committed in my person against the liberties of the people. Lord Halifax answered that nothing had been done but by the advice of the best lawyers, and that it was now his duty to examine me . . . I said that this was a curiosity on his lordship's part which, however laudable in the secretary, I did not find myself disposed to gratify, and that at the end of my examination all the quires of paper on their lordship's table should be as milk-white as at the beginning. . . . His lordship then asked me if I chose to be a prisoner in my own house, at the Tower, or in Newgate, for he was disposed to oblige me. I gave his lordship my thanks, but I desired to remark that I never received an obligation but from a friend ; that I demanded justice and my immediate liberty as an Englishman who had not offended the laws of his country ; that, as to the rest, it was beneath my attention. . . . Lord Halifax then told me I should be sent to the Tower, where I should be treated in a manner suitable to my rank.'
  Wilkes's friends had meanwhile applied for a writ of *habeas corpus*, but the Secretaries of State evaded this by transferring the prisoner from the custody of Robert Blackmore and James Watson, who had apprehended him under the general warrant, to that of George Collins and Thomas Ardran, who delivered him to the Deputy-Lieutenant of the Tower. Wilkes, with characteristic wit, begged to be placed in the room in which Sir W. Wyndham, Lord Egremont's father, had been confined for treason.

234

And had not Prudence been debauch'd by Pride,
In flattery's stream thou wouldst have dipp'd thy pen,
Applied to great and not to honest men ;
Nor should conviction have seduced thy heart
To take the weaker though the better part.
  'What but rank folly, for thy curse decreed,
Could into Satire's barren path mislead,   100
When, open to thy view, before thee lay
Soul-soothing Panegyric's flowery way ?
There might the Muse have saunter'd at her ease,
And, pleasing others, learn'd herself to please ;
Lords should have listen'd to the sugar'd treat,
And ladies, simpering, own'd it vastly sweet ;
Rogues, in thy prudent verse with virtue graced,
Fools mark'd by thee as prodigies of taste,
Must have forbid, pouring preferments down,
Such wit, such truth as thine to quit the gown.   110
Thy sacred brethren too (for they no less
Than laymen, bring their offerings to success)
Had hail'd thee good if great, and paid the vow
Sincere as that they pay to God ; whilst thou
In lawn hadst whisper'd to a sleeping crowd,
As dull as Rochester, and half as proud.'
  Peace, Candour—wisely hadst thou said, and well
Could Interest in this breast one moment dwell ;
Could she, with prospect of success, oppose
The firm resolves which from conviction rose.   120
I cannot truckle to a fool of state,
Nor take a favour from the man I hate :
Free leave have others by such means to shine ;
I scorn their practice ; they may laugh at mine.
  But, in this charge, forgetful of thyself,
Thou hast assumed the maxims of that elf
Whom God in wrath for man's dishonour framed,
Cunning in heaven, amongst us Prudence named,
That servile prudence, which I leave to those
Who dare not be my friends, can't be my foes.   130

[116] Dr. Zachariah Pearce, Bishop of Rochester. (See note on ' The
Prophecy of Famine,' line 128.)

Had I, with cruel and oppressive rhymes,
Pursued and turn'd misfortunes into crimes ;
Had I, when Virtue gasping lay and low,
Join'd tyrant Vice, and added woe to woe ;
Had I made Modesty in blushes speak,
And drawn the tear down beauty's sacred cheek ;
Had I (damn'd then) in thought debased my lays,
To wound that sex which honour bids me praise ;
Had I, from vengeance, by base views betray'd,
In endless night sunk injured Ayliffe's shade ;   140
Had I (which satirists of mighty name,
Renown'd in rhyme, revered for moral fame,
Have done before, whom justice shall pursue
In future verse) brought forth to public view
A noble friend, and made his foibles known,
Because his worth was greater than my own ;
Had I spared those (so Prudence had decreed)
Whom, God so help me at my greatest need,
I ne'er will spare, those vipers to their king,
Who smooth their looks, and flatter whilst they sting ;   150
Or had I not taught patriot zeal to boast
Of those who flatter least, but love him most ;
Had I thus sinn'd, my stubborn soul should bend
At Candour's voice, and take, as from a friend,
The deep rebuke ; myself should be the first
To hate myself, and stamp my Muse accurst.
     But shall my arm—forbid it, manly pride,
Forbid it, reason, warring on my side—
For vengeance lifted high, the stroke forbear,
And hang suspended in the desert air ;   160
Or to my trembling side unnerved sink down,
Palsied, forsooth, by Candour's half-made frown ?
When Justice bids me on, shall I delay,

[140] Churchill was accused of selling to Lord Holland his unpublished
satire, ' Ayliffe's Ghost.' (See Introduction, page xlvi.)

[145] The ' noble friend ' is Addison. Pope engineered the publica-
tion of his own early correspondence, while pretending to be strongly
opposed to it. He materially altered the letters which he had received
from Addison, Steele and Congreve, so as to reflect more favourably
on himself. The matter was not finally unravelled until the middle of
the nineteenth century.

Because insipid Candour bars my way ?
When she, of all alike the puling friend,
Would disappoint my satire's noblest end ;
When she to villains would a sanction give,
And shelter those who are not fit to live ;
When she would screen the guilty from a blush,
And bids me spare whom Reason bids me crush ;   170
All leagues with Candour proudly I resign;
She cannot be for Honour's turn, nor mine.
　Yet come, cold monitor ! half foe, half friend,
Whom Vice can't fear, whom Virtue can't commend ;
Come, Candour, by thy dull indifference known,
Thou equal-blooded judge, thou luke-warm drone,
Who, fashion'd without feelings, dost expect
We call that virtue which we know defect ;
Come, and observe the nature of our crimes,
The gross and rank complexion of the times ;   180
Observe it well, and then review my plan,
Praise if you will, or censure if you can.
　Whilst Vice, presumptuous, lords it as in sport,
And Piety is only known at court ;
Whilst wretched Liberty expiring lies
Beneath the fatal burthen of Excise ;
Whilst nobles act, without one touch of shame,
What men of humble rank would blush to name ;
Whilst Honour's placed in highest point of view,
Worshipp'd by those who justice never knew ;   190
Whilst bubbles of distinction waste in play
The hours of rest, and blunder through the day ;
With dice and cards opprobrious vigils keep,
Then turn to ruin empires in their sleep ;
Whilst fathers, by relentless passion led,
Doom worthy, injured sons to beg their bread,

---

[186] Excise is a tax on articles of home manufacture as opposed to
customs duties on goods imported, but this distinction is a modern
one.　The duties were first imposed by the Parliament in 1643, during
the Civil War.　Walpole's excise bill of 1733 proposed a system of
bonded warehouses in order to check frauds in the customs revenue
from tobacco.
　[195] Tooke saw in this passage a reference to Thomas Potter. (See
note on ' The Duellist,' Book III, lines 188 and 242.)　Wodhull, how-
ever, notes : ' old Wortley Montagu.'

Merely with ill-got, ill-saved wealth to grace
An alien, abject, poor, proud, upstart race ;
Whilst Martin flatters only to betray,
And Webb gives up his dirty soul for pay ;   200
Whilst titles serve to hush a villain's fears ;
Whilst peers are agents made, and agents peers ;
Whilst base betrayers are themselves betray'd,
And makers ruin'd by the thing they made ;
Whilst C——, false to God and man, for gold,
Like the old traitor who a Saviour sold,
To shame his master, friend, and father, gives ;
Whilst Bute remains in power, whilst Holland lives,
Can Satire want a subject, where Disdain,
By Virtue fired, may point her sharpest strain ?   210
Where, clothed with thunder, Truth may roll along,
And Candour justify the rage of song ?

[199] Samuel Martin, M.P. for Camelford. (See note on ' The Duellist,' Book I, line 147.)

[200] Philip Cartaret Webb (1700-1770), M.P. for Haslemere, Solicitor to the Treasury, was a distinguished lawyer who proved extremely useful to the Crown in the trial of the prisoners, after the rebellion of 1745. Having purchased the estate of Burbridge, near Haslemere in Surrey, he sat in Parliament for Haslemere from 1754 until 1761. He was Joint-Solicitor to the Treasury from 1756 until 1765, and in that capacity was a leading official in the proceedings against Wilkes. He was instrumental in seizing Wilkes' papers, and printed a pamphlet in favour of the legality of general warrants. In the action brought against Wood, Lord Egremont's secretary, for seizing Wilkes' papers, Webb, as a witness, swore that while in the house ' he had no key in his hand.' For this he was tried before Lord Mansfield, with a special jury, for perjury, on May 22nd, 1764. (*D.N.B.*) However, he was acquitted. Webb was an antiquary, and made a valuable collection of manuscripts, coins and medals, and *objets d'art.*

[205] ' Churchill,' remarks Tooke, ' occasionally threw out an initial by way of exciting the curiosity of the reader, who was at liberty to apply the cap to the head it might, in his opinion, fit. We hope, for the honour of human nature, that this character was not drawn from the life.' It seems plain, however, that the allusion is to John Calcraft, the creature, (and rumour said) the natural son of Lord Holland, with whom, in the end, he quarrelled. (See note on ' The Conference,' line 294.) This identification is supported by Wodhull.

[208] Bute's administration lasted from May 29th, 1762, to April 8th, 1763.

[208] Henry Fox, Lord Holland. (See note on lines 22 and 140. See also ' The Duellist,' Book I, line 128.)

' Such things, such men before thee, such an age,
Where Rancour, great as thine, may glut her rage,
And sicken e'en to surfeit ; where the pride
Of Satire, pouring down in fullest tide,
May spread wide vengeance round, yet all the while
Justice behold the ruin with a smile ;
Whilst I, thy foe misdeem'd, cannot condemn
Nor disapprove that rage I wish to stem,   220
Wilt thou, degenerate and corrupted, choose
To soil the credit of thy haughty Muse ?
With fallacy, most infamous, to stain
Her truth, and render all her anger vain ?
When I beheld thee, incorrect, but bold,
A various comment on the stage unfold ;
When players on players before thy satire fell,
And poor Reviews conspired thy wrath to swell ;
When states and statesmen next became thy care,
And only kings were safe if thou wast there,   230
Thy every word I weigh'd in judgment's scale,
And in thy every word found truth prevail.
Why dost thou now to falsehood meanly fly ?
Not even Candour can forgive a lie.
    Bad as men are, why should thy frantic rhymes
Traffic in slander, and invent new crimes ?
Crimes which, existing only in thy mind,
Weak spleen brings forth to blacken all mankind.
By pleasing hopes we lure the human heart
To practise virtue, and improve in art ;   240
To thwart these ends (which, proud of honest fame,
A noble Muse would cherish and inflame)
Thy drudge contrives, and in our full career
Sicklies our hopes with the pale hue of fear ;
Tells us that all our labours are in vain ;
That what we seek we never can obtain ;
That, dead to virtue, lost to Nature's plan,
Envy possesses the whole race of man ;
That worth is criminal, and danger lies,
Danger extreme, in being good and wise.   250
    'Tis a rank falsehood ; search the world around,
There cannot be so vile a monster found,

239

Not one so vile, on whom suspicions fall
Of that gross guilt which you impute to all.
Approved by those who disobey her laws,
Virtue from vice itself extorts applause :
Her very foes bear witness to her state ;
They will not love her, but they cannot hate.
Hate Virtue for herself ! with spite pursue
Merit for merit's sake ! might this be true   260
I would renounce my nature with disdain,
And with the beasts that perish graze the plain ;
Might this be true, had we so far fill'd up
The measure of our crimes, and from the cup
Of guilt so deeply drank, as not to find,
Thirsting for sin, one drop, one dreg behind,
Quick ruin must involve this flaming ball,
And Providence in justice crush us all.
None but the damn'd, and amongst them the worst,
Those who for double guilt are doubly curst,   270
Can be so lost ; nor can the worst of all
At once into such deep damnation fall ;
By painful, slow degrees they reach this crime,
Which e'en in hell must be a work of time.
   Cease, then, thy guilty rage, thou wayward son,
With the foul gall of discontent o'errun ;
List to my voice—be honest, if you can,
Nor slander Nature in her favourite, man.
But if thy spirit, resolute in ill,
Once having err'd, persists in error still,   280
Go on at large, no longer worth my care,
And freely vent those blasphemies in air,
Which I would stamp as false, tho' on the tongue
Of angels the injurious slander hung.
   Duped by thy vanity, (that cunning elf
Who snares the coxcomb to deceive himself)
Or blinded by thy rage, didst thou believe
That we too, coolly, would ourselves deceive ?
That we, as sterling, falsehood would admit,
Because 'twas season'd with some little wit ?   290
When fiction rises pleasing to the eye,
Men will believe, because they love the lie ;

240

But Truth herself, if clouded with a frown,
Must have some solemn proof to pass her down.
Hast thou, maintaining that which must disgrace
And bring into contempt the human race ;
Hast thou, or canst thou, in Truth's sacred court,
To save thy credit, and thy cause support,
Produce one proof, make out one real ground,
On which so great, so gross a charge to found ?   300
Nay, dost thou know one man (let that appear,
From wilful falsehood I'll proclaim thee clear),
One man so lost, to nature so untrue,
From whom this general charge thy rashness drew ?
On this foundation shalt thou stand or fall—
Prove that in one which you have charged on all.
Reason determines, and it must be done ;
'Mongst men or past or present name me one.'
  Hogarth.—I take thee, Candour, at thy word,
Accept thy proffer'd terms, and will be heard.   310
Thee have I heard with virulence declaim,
Nothing retain'd of Candour but the name ;
By thee have I been charged in angry strains
With that mean falsehood which my soul disdains—
Hogarth, stand forth.—Nay, hang not thus aloof—
Now, Candour, now thou shalt receive such proof,
Such damning proof, that henceforth thou shalt fear
To tax my wrath, and own my conduct clear—
Hogarth, stand forth—I dare thee to be tried
In that great court where Conscience must preside ;   320
At that most solemn bar hold up thy hand ;
Think before whom, on what account, you stand—
Speak, but consider well—from first to last
Review thy life, weigh every action past ;
Nay—you shall have no reason to complain—
Take longer time, and view them o'er again ;
Canst thou remember from thy earliest youth,
And as thy God must judge thee, speak the truth,
A single instance where, self laid aside,
And justice taking place of fear and pride,   330
Thou with an equal eye didst genius view,
And give to merit what was merit's due ?

Genius and merit are a sure offence,
And thy soul sickens at the name of sense.
Is any one so foolish to succeed,
On Envy's altar he is doom'd to bleed ;
Hogarth, a guilty pleasure in his eyes,
The place of executioner supplies :
See how he glotes, enjoys the sacred feast,
And proves himself by cruelty a priest.   340
    Whilst the weak artist, to thy whims a slave,
Would bury all those powers which nature gave ;
Would suffer blank concealment to obscure
Those rays thy jealousy could not endure ;
To feed thy vanity would rust unknown,
And to secure thy credit blast his own,
In Hogarth he was sure to find a friend ;
He could not fear, and therefore might commend :
But when his spirit, roused by honest shame,
Shook off that lethargy, and soar'd to fame ;   350
When, with the pride of man, resolved and strong,
He scorn'd those fears which did his honour wrong,
And, on himself determined to rely,
Brought forth his labours to the public eye,
No friend in thee could such a rebel know ;
He had desert, and Hogarth was his foe.
    Souls of a timorous cast, of petty name
In Envy's court, not yet quite dead to shame,
May some remorse, some qualms of conscience feel,
And suffer honour to abate their zeal ;   360
But the man truly and completely great
Allows no rule of action but his hate ;
Through every bar he bravely breaks his way,
Passion his principle, and parts his prey.
Mediums in vice and virtue speak a mind
Within the pale of temperance confined ;
The daring spirit scorns her narrow schemes,
And, good or bad, is always in extremes.
    Man's practice duly weigh'd, through every age
On the same plan hath Envy form'd her rage.   370
'Gainst those whom fortune hath our rivals made,

---

[356] Hogarth was notoriously jealous of the success of other artists.

In way of science, and in way of trade,
Stung with mean jealousy, she arms her spite,
First works, then views their ruin with delight.
Our Hogarth here a grand improver shines,
And nobly on the general plan refines ;
He like himself o'erleaps the servile bound ;
Worth is his mark, wherever worth is found.
Should painters only his vast wrath suffice ?
Genius in every walk is lawful prize :   380
'Tis a gross insult to his o'ergrown state ;
His love to merit is to feel his hate.
    When Wilkes, our countryman, our common friend,
Arose, his king, his country to defend ;
When tools of power he bared to public view,
And from their holes the sneaking cowards drew ;
When Rancour found it far beyond her reach
To soil his honour, and his truth impeach ;
What could induce thee, at a time and place
Where manly foes had blush'd to shew their face,   390
To make that effort which must damn thy name,
And sink thee deep, deep in thy grave with shame ?
Did virtue move thee ? No ; 'twas pride, rank pride,
And if thou hadst not done it, thou hadst died.
Malice (who, disappointed of her end,
Whether to work the bane of foe or friend,
Preys on herself, and, driven to the stake,
Gives Virtue that revenge she scorns to take)
Had killed thee, tottering on life's utmost verge,
Had Wilkes and Liberty escaped thy scourge.   400
    When that Great Charter, which our fathers bought
With their best blood, was into question brought ;
When, big with ruin, o'er each English head
Vile Slavery hung suspended by a thread ;
When Liberty, all trembling and aghast,
Fear'd for the future, knowing what was past ;
When every breast was chill'd with deep despair,
Till Reason pointed out that Pratt was there ;

[408] Charles Pratt, Earl Camden (1714-1794), was the contemporary at Eton of Chatham, Lyttelton and Horace Walpole. On the acces-

Lurking most ruffian-like, behind a screen,
So placed all things to see, himself unseen,   410
Virtue, with due contempt, saw Hogarth stand,
The murderous pencil in his palsied hand.
What was the cause of Liberty to him,
Or what was Honour ? let them sink or swim,
So he may gratify, without control,
The mean resentments of his selfish soul.
Let freedom perish ; if to freedom true,
In the same ruin Wilkes may perish too.
    With all the symptoms of assured decay,
With age and sickness pinch'd and worn away,   420
Pale, quivering lips, lank cheeks, and faltering tongue,

sion of Pitt to power in 1757, he became Attorney-General, and con-
ducted the prosecution of John Shebbeare. His bill for extending
the Habeas Corpus Act to civil cases was defeated in the House of
Lords. He was appointed Chief Justice of the Common Pleas in 1761
on the death of Sir John Willes. Pratt was firmly convinced of the
illegality of general warrants, and when Wilkes was committed to the
Tower he ordered his release on the ground of privilege of Parliament.
In the case of Wilkes *versus* Wood, on December 6th, 1763, Pratt
laid down the principle that general warrants were contrary to the
fundamental principles of the constitution ; and throughout the
proceedings to which the arrest of Wilkes and his printers led, he
stood forth as the champion of popular liberties, in opposition to
Lord Mansfield.

[409] ' When Mr. Wilkes was the second time brought from the Tower
to Westminster Hall, Mr. Hogarth skulked behind, in a corner of the
gallery of the Court of Common Pleas : and while the Lord Chief-
Justice Pratt, with the eloquence and courage of old Rome, was en-
forcing the great principles of Magna Charta and the English constitu-
tion, while every breast from his caught the holy flame of liberty, the
painter was employed in caricaturing the person of the man, while all
the rest of his fellow-citizens were animated in his cause ; for they
knew it to be their own cause, that of their country, and of its laws.
It was declared to be so a few hours after, by the unanimous sentence
of the judges of that court, and they were all present.
    ' The print of Mr. Wilkes was soon after published, *drawn from the
life by William Hogarth*. It must be allowed to be an excellent com-
pound caricature, or a caricature of what Nature had already carica-
tured. I know but one short apology to be made for this gentleman, or
to speak more properly, for the *person* of Mr. Wilkes ; it is, that he did
not make it himself, and that he never was solicitous about the *case* (as
Shakespeare calls it), only so far as to keep it clean and in health.'
(Wilkes.)

[412] Hogarth was now in his sixty-sixth year.

244

The spirits out of tune, the nerves unstrung,
Thy body shrivell'd up, thy dim eyes sunk
Within their sockets deep, thy weak hams shrunk,
The body's weight unable to sustain,
The stream of life scarce trembling thro' the vein,
More than half kill'd by honest truths which fell,
Thro' thy own fault, from men who wish'd thee well,
Canst thou, e'en thus, thy thoughts to vengeance give,
And, dead to all things else, to malice live?   430
Hence, Dotard, to thy closet; shut thee in;
By deep repentance wash away thy sin;
From haunts of men to shame and sorrow fly,
And, on the verge of death, learn how to die.
    Vain exhortation! wash the Ethiop white,
Discharge the leopard's spots, turn day to night,
Control the course of Nature, bid the deep
Hush at thy pigmy voice her waves to sleep,
Perform things passing strange, yet own thy art
Too weak to work a change in such a heart.   440
That envy, which was woven in the frame
At first, will to the last remain the same.
Reason may droop, may die : but Envy's rage
Improves by time, and gathers strength from age.
Some, and not few, vain triflers with the pen,
Unread, unpractised in the ways of men,
Tell us that Envy, who, with giant stride,
Stalks through the vale of life by Virtue's side,
Retreats when she hath drawn her latest breath,
And calmly hears her praises after death.   450
To such observers Hogarth gives the lie;
Worth may be hearsed, but Envy cannot die;
Within the mansion of his gloomy breast,
A mansion suited well to such a guest,
Immortal, unimpair'd, she rears her head,
And damns alike the living and the dead.
    Oft have I known thee, Hogarth, weak and vain,
Thyself the idol of thy awkward strain,
Through the dull measure of a summer's day,
In phrase most vile, prate long, long hours away,   460
Whilst friends with friends all gaping sit, and gaze

245

To hear a Hogarth babble Hogarth's praise ;
But if athwart thee Interruption came,
And mention'd with respect some ancient's name,
Some ancient's name who, in the days of yore,
The crown of art with greatest honour wore
How have I seen thy coward cheek turn pale,
And blank confusion seize thy mangled tale !
How hath thy jealousy to madness grown,
And deemed his praise injurious to thy own !   470
Then without mercy did thy wrath make way,
And arts and artists all became thy prey ;
Then didst thou trample on establish'd rules,
And proudly levell'd all the ancient schools,
Condemn'd those works, with praise through ages graced,
Which you had never seen, or could not taste ;
' But would mankind have true perfection shewn,
It must be found in labours of my own.
I dare to challenge, in one single piece,
The united force of Italy and Greece.'   480
Thy eager hand the curtain then undrew,
And brought the boasted master-piece to view.
Spare thy remarks—say not a single word—
The picture seen, why is the painter heard ?
Call not up shame and anger in our cheeks ;
Without a comment Sigismunda speaks.

[462] ' I went t'other morning to see a portrait he is painting of Mr. Fox. Hogarth told me he had promised, if Mr. Fox would sit as he liked, to make as good a picture as Vandyke or Rubens could. I was silent—" Why now," said he, " you think this very vain, but why should one not speak truth ? " This *truth* was uttered in the face of his own Sigismonda, which is exactly a maudlin whore, tearing off the trinkets that her keeper had given her, to fling at his head. She has her father's picture in a bracelet on her arm, and her fingers are bloody with the heart, as if she had just bought a sheep's pluck in St. James's Market.' (Horace Walpole, letter to George Montagu, May 5th, 1761.)

[486] Sir Richard (afterwards Lord) Grosvenor much admired Hogarth's painting of ' The Lady's Last Stake,' and pressed the artist to undertake another ' upon the same terms.' Hogarth selected the subject of Sigismunda weeping over the heart of her murdered lover Guiscardo. He took much trouble over the picture and valued it highly, but Sir Richard refused to have it, and the painting remained on Hogarth's hands. Although not one of Hogarth's happiest efforts it is astonishing that it should have aroused such violent hostility.

Poor Sigismunda ! what a fate is thine !
Dryden, the great high-priest of all the Nine,
Revived thy name, gave what a Muse could give,
And in his numbers bade thy memory live ;   490
Gave thee those soft sensations which might move
And warm the coldest anchorite to love ;
Gave thee that virtue, which could curb desire,
Refine and consecrate love's headstrong fire ;
Gave thee those griefs, which made the Stoic feel,
And call'd compassion forth from hearts of steel ;
Gave thee that firmness, which our sex may shame,
And make man bow to woman's juster claim ;
So that our tears, which from compassion flow,
Seem to debase thy dignity of woe.   500
But, O, how much unlike ! how fallen ! how changed !
How much from Nature and herself estranged !
How totally deprived of all the powers
To shew her feelings, and awaken ours,
Doth Sigismunda now devoted stand,
The helpless victim of a dauber's hand !
    But why, my Hogarth, such a progress made,
So rare a pattern for the sign-post trade ;
In the full force, and whirlwind of thy pride,
Why was heroic painting laid aside ?   510
Why is it not resumed ? thy friends at court,
Men all in place and power, crave thy support ;
Be grateful then for once, and through the field
Of politics, thy epic pencil wield ;
Maintain the cause, which they, good lack ! avow,
And would maintain too, but they know not how.
    Through every pannel let thy virtue tell
How Bute prevail'd, how Pitt and Temple fell !

(See *e.g.* Horace Walpole's opinion in note on line 462.) It was pur-
chased by Boydell in 1789 for 56 guineas, and at last came into the
possession of the National Gallery by the will of J. H. Anderdon.

[488] Dryden's ' Sigismunda and Guiscardo ' is a translation of Boc-
caccio's story. Sigismunda, daughter of Tancred of Salerno, fell in
love with her father's squire Guiscardo. The tyrant had him strangled
and sent his heart to Sigismunda in a golden goblet encrusted with
gems, whereupon the wretched princess poisoned herself.

[518] A reference to the print of ' The Times,' in which Hogarth

How England's sons (whom they conspired to bless
Against our will, with insolent success)   520
Approve their fall, and with addresses run,
How got God knows, to hail the Scottish sun ?
Point out our fame in war, when vengeance, hurl'd
From the strong arm of Justice, shook the world ;
Thine, and thy country's honour to increase,
Point out the honours of succeeding peace ;
Our moderation, Christian-like, display,
Shew what we got, and what we gave away ;
In colours, dull and heavy as the tale,
Let a state-chaos through the whole prevail.   530
   But, of events regardless, whilst the Muse,
Perhaps with too much heat, her theme pursues ;
Whilst her quick spirits rouse at Freedom's call,
And every drop of blood is turn'd to gall ;
Whilst a dear country, and an injured friend
Urge my strong anger to the bitterest end ;
Whilst honest trophies to revenge are raised,
Let not one real virtue pass unpraised ;
Justice with equal course bids Satire flow,
And loves the virtue of her greatest foe.   540
   O ! that I here could that rare virtue mean
Which scorns the rule of envy, pride, and spleen ;
Which springs not from the labour'd works of art,
But hath its rise from Nature in the heart ;
Which in itself with happiness is crown'd,
And spreads with joy the blessing all around !
But truth forbids, and in these simple lays,
Contented with a different kind of praise,
Must Hogarth stand ; that praise which genius gives,
In which to latest time the artist lives,   550
But not the man ; which, rightly understood,
May make us great, but cannot make us good :
That praise be Hogarth's ; freely let him wear

ridiculed Pitt and Temple, and so brought upon himself the bitter
hostility of Wilkes and Churchill.

  [521] Shameless bribery was employed by the Court party in order to
obtain addresses of congratulation to the King on the conclusion of
peace. The ' Scottish sun ' is, of course, Bute.

The wreath which Genius wove, and planted there :
Foe as I am, should Envy tear it down,
Myself would labour to replace the crown.
   In walks of humour, in that cast of style
Which, probing to the quick, yet makes us smile,
In comedy, thy natural road to fame,
Nor let me call it by a meaner name,   560
Where a beginning, middle, and an end,
Are aptly joined ; where parts on parts depend,
Each made for each, as bodies for their soul,
So as to form one true and perfect whole ;
Where a plain story to the eye is told,
Which we conceive the moment we behold,
Hogarth unrivall'd stands, and shall engage
Unrivall'd praise to the most distant age.
   How couldst thou then to shame perversely run,
And tread that path which Nature bade thee shun ?   570
Why did ambition overleap her rules,
And thy vast parts become the sport of fools ?
By different methods different men excel ;
But where is he who can do all things well ?
Humour thy province, for some monstrous crime
Pride struck thee with the frenzy of sublime ;
But, when the work was finish'd, could thy mind
So partial be, and to herself so blind,
What with contempt all view'd, to view with awe,
Nor see those faults which every blockhead saw ?   580
Blush, thou vain man ! and if desire of fame,
Founded on real art, thy thoughts inflame,
To quick destruction Sigismunda give,
And let her memory die, that thine may live.
But should fond Candour, for her mercy sake,
With pity view, and pardon this mistake ;
Or should Oblivion, to thy wish most kind,
Wipe off that stain, nor leave one trace behind ;
Of arts despised, of artists, by thy frown
Awed from just hopes, of rising worth kept down,   590
Of all thy meanness through this mortal race,
Canst thou the living memory erase ?
Or shall not vengeance follow to the grave,

And give back just that measure which you gave ?
With so much merit, and so much success,
With so much power to curse, so much to bless,
Would he have been man's friend, instead of foe,
Hogarth had been a little god below.
Why then, like savage giants, famed of old,
Of whom in Scripture story we are told,   600
Dost thou in cruelty that strength employ,
Which Nature meant to save, not to destroy ?
Why dost thou, all in horrid pomp array'd,
Sit grinning o'er the ruins thou hast made ?
Most rank ill-nature must applaud thy art,
But even Candour must condemn thy heart.

For me, who, warm and zealous for my friend,
In spite of railing thousands will commend,
And no less warm and zealous against my foes,
Spite of commending thousands, will oppose,   610
I dare thy worst, with scorn behold thy rage,
But with an eye of pity view thy age,
Thy feeble age ! in which, as in a glass,
We see how men to dissolution pass.
Thou wretched being, whom, on reason's plan,
So changed, so lost, I cannot call a man,
What could persuade thee, at this time of life,
To launch afresh into the sea of strife ?
Better for thee, scarce crawling on the earth,
Almost as much a child as at thy birth,   620
To have resign'd in peace thy parting breath,
And sunk unnoticed in the arms of Death.
Why would thy gray, gray hairs resentment brave,
Thus to go down with sorrow to the grave ?
Now, by my soul, it makes me blush to know
My spirits could descend to such a foe :
Whatever cause the vengeance might provoke,
It seems rank cowardice to give the stroke.

Sure 'tis a curse which angry fates impose,
To mortify man's arrogance, that those   630
Who're fashion'd of some better sort of clay,
Much sooner than the common herd decay.
What bitter pangs must humbled Genius feel,

In their last hours, to view a Swift and Steele !
How must ill-boding horrors fill her breast
When she beholds men mark'd above the rest
For qualities most dear, plunged from that height,
And sunk, deep sunk, in second childhood's night !
Are men, indeed, such things ? and are the best
More subject to this evil than the rest,   640
To drivel out whole years of idiot breath,
And sit the monuments of living death !
O, galling circumstance to human pride !
Abasing thought ! but not to be denied.
With curious art the brain, too finely wrought,
Preys on herself, and is destroy'd by thought.
Constant attention wears the active mind,
Blots out our powers, and leaves a blank behind.
But let not youth, to insolence allied,
In heat of blood, in full career of pride,   650
Possess'd of genius, with unhallow'd rage
Mock the infirmities of reverend age :
The greatest genius to this fate may bow ;
Reynolds, in time, may be like Hogarth now.

[634] Swift died mad in 1745, Steele in 1729.
Compare Johnson's ' Vanity of Human Wishes ' :

' In life's last scene what prodigies surprise,
Fears of the brave, and follies of the wise ?
From Marlb'rough's eyes the streams of dotage flow,
And Swift expires a driv'ler and a show.'

[654] Sir Joshua Reynolds died in 1792, in full possession of his faculties and his reputation.

THE CONFERENCE*

G RACE said in form, which sceptics must agree,
When they are told that grace was said by me;
The servants gone, to break the scurvy jest
On the proud landlord, and his threadbare guest;
The King gone round, my Lady too withdrawn,
My Lord, in usual taste, began to yawn,
And, lolling backward in his elbow-chair,
With an insipid kind of stupid stare,
Picking his teeth, twirling his seals about—
'Churchill, you have a poem coming out :   10
You've my best wishes; but I really fear
Your Muse, in general, is too severe;
Her spirit seems her interest to oppose,
And where she makes one friend makes twenty foes.'

CHURCHILL

Your Lordship's fears are just; I feel their force,
But only feel it as a thing of course.
The man whose hardy spirit shall engage
To lash the vices of a guilty age,
At his first setting forward ought to know
That every rogue he meets must be his foe;   20
That the rude breath of satire will provoke
Many who feel, and more who fear the stroke;
But shall the partial rage of selfish men
From stubborn justice wrench the righteous pen?
Or shall I not my settled course pursue,
Because my foes are foes to virtue too?

LORD

What is this boasted Virtue, taught in schools,
And idly drawn from antiquated rules?

* First published in November, 1763. 'Printed for G. Kearsley ....
J. Cooke .... W. Flexney .... C. Henderson .... J. Gardiner ....
and J. Almon.'

What is her use ? point out one wholesome end :
Will she hurt foes, or can she make a friend ?   30
When from long fasts fierce appetites arise,
Can this same Virtue stifle Nature's cries ?
Can she the pittance of a meal afford,
Or bid thee welcome to one great man's board ?
When northern winds the rough December arm
With frost and snow, can Virtue keep thee warm ?
Canst thou dismiss the hard unfeeling dun
Barely by saying thou art Virtue's son ?
Or by base blundering statesmen sent to jail,
Will Mansfield take this Virtue for thy bail ?   40
Believe it not, the name is in disgrace ;
Virtue and Temple now are out of place.
   Quit then this meteor, whose delusive ray
From wealth and honour leads thee far astray.
True virtue means, let Reason use her eyes,
Nothing with fools, and interest with the wise.
Wouldst thou be great, her patronage disclaim,
Nor madly triumph in so mean a name :
Let nobler wreaths thy happy brows adorn,
And leave to Virtue poverty and scorn.   50
Let Prudence be thy guide ; who doth not know
How seldom Prudence can with Virtue go ?
To be successful try thy utmost force,
And virtue follows as a thing of course.
   Hirco, who knows not Hirco ? stains the bed
Of that kind master who first gave him bread ;
Scatters the seeds of discord through the land,
Breaks every public, every private band ;
Beholds with joy a trusting friend undone ;
Betrays a brother, and would cheat a son :   60
What mortal in his senses can endure
The name of Hirco ? for the wretch is poor !
' Let him hang, drown, starve, on a dunghill rot,
By all detested live, and die forgot ;

---

[40] Mansfield. (See note on ' The Epistle to Hogarth,' line 76.)
[42] Lord Temple resigned with Pitt in 1761.
[55] It is unlikely Churchill had any definite character in view.

Let him, a poor return, in every breath
Feel all death's pains, yet be whole years in death,'
Is now the general cry we all pursue ;
Let fortune change, and Prudence changes too,
Supple and pliant, a new system feels,
Throws up her cap, and spaniels at his heels,   70
' Long live great Hirco,' cries, by interest taught,
' And let his foes, though I prove one, be nought.'

CHURCHILL

Peace to such men, if such men can have peace ;
Let their possessions, let their state, increase ;
Let their base services in courts strike root,
And in the season bring forth golden fruit ;
I envy not : let those who have the will,
And, with so little spirit, so much skill,
With such vile instruments their fortunes carve ;
Rogues may grow fat ; an honest man dares starve.   80

LORD

These stale conceits thrown off, let us advance
For once to real life, and quit romance.
Starve ! pretty talking ! but I fain would view
That man, that honest man, would do it too.
Hence to yon mountain which outbraves the sky,
And dart from pole to pole thy strengthen'd eye,
Through all that space you shall not view one man,
Not one, who dares to act on such a plan.
Cowards in calms will say what in a storm
The brave will tremble at, and not perform.   90
Thine be the proof, and, spite of all you've said
You'd give your honour for a crust of bread.

CHURCHILL

What proof might do, what hunger might effect,
What famish'd Nature, looking with neglect
On all she once held dear, what fear, at strife
With fainting virtue for the means of life,
Might make this coward flesh, in love with breath,

Shuddering at pain, and shrinking back from death,
In treason to my soul, descend to bear,
Trusting to fate, I neither know nor care.   100
    Once, at this hour those wounds afresh I feel,
Which nor prosperity nor time can heal,
Those wounds which fate severely hath decreed,
Mention'd or thought of, must for ever bleed ;
Those wounds, which humbled all that pride of man,
Which brings such mighty aid to virtue's plan ;
Once, awed by Fortune's most oppressive frown,
By legal rapine to the earth bow'd down,
My credit at last gasp, my state undone,
Trembling to meet the shock I could not shun,   110
Virtue gave ground, and blank despair prevail'd ;
Sinking beneath the storm, my spirits fail'd,
Like Peter's faith, till one, a friend indeed,—
May all distress find such in time of need,—
One kind, good man, in act, in word, in thought,
By virtue guided, and by wisdom taught,
Image of Him whom christians should adore,
Stretch'd forth his hand, and brought me safe to shore.
    Since, by good fortune into notice raised,
And for some little merit largely praised,   120
Indulged in swerving from prudential rules,
Hated by rogues, and not beloved by fools ;
Placed above want, shall abject thirst of wealth,
So fiercely war 'gainst my soul's dearest health,
That, as a boon, I should base shackles crave,
And, born to freedom, make myself a slave ?
That I should in the train of those appear
Whom honour cannot love, nor manhood fear ?
    That I no longer skulk from street to street,
Afraid lest duns assail, and bailiffs meet ;   130
That I from place to place this carcase bear ;
Walk forth at large, and wander free as air ;

---

[113] The ' friend indeed ' was Dr. Pierson Lloyd, usher at West-
minster School and father of Robert Lloyd. He induced Churchill's
creditors to accept five shillings in the pound and himself lent money
in order that it might be paid. When Churchill made a considerable
sum by ' The Rosciad ' he paid his creditors in full.

That I no longer dread the awkward friend,
Whose very obligations must offend ;
Nor, all too froward, with impatience burn
At suffering favours which I can't return ;
That, from dependence and from pride secure,
I am not placed so high to scorn the poor,
Nor yet so low, that I ' my lord ' should fear,
Or hesitate to give him sneer for sneer ;   140
That, whilst sage Prudence my pursuits confirms,
I can enjoy the world on equal terms ;
That, kind to others, to myself most true,
Feeling no want, I comfort those who do,
And with the will have power to aid distress,
These, and what other blessings I possess,
From the indulgence of the public rise ;
All private patronage my soul defies.
By candour more inclined to save, than damn,
A generous public made me what I am.   150
All that I have, they gave ; just memory bears
The grateful stamp, and what I am, is theirs.

LORD

To feign a red-hot zeal for freedom's cause,
To mouth aloud for liberties and laws,
For public good to bellow all abroad,
Serves well the purposes of private fraud.
Prudence by public good intends her own ;
If you mean otherwise, you stand alone.
What do we mean by country and by court ?
What is it to oppose ? what to support ?   160
Mere words of course ; and what is more absurd
Than to pay homage to an empty word !
Majors and minors differ but in name ;
Patriots and ministers are much the same ;
The only difference, after all their rout,
Is, that the one is in, the other out.

[145] The distress referred to is that of Robert Lloyd, the son of
Churchill's benefactor. The younger Lloyd was confined in the Fleet
prison for debt, and Churchill allowed him a guinea a week for his
expenses.

Explore the dark recesses of the mind,
In the soul's honest volume read mankind,
And own, in wise and simple, great and small,
The same grand leading principle in all.   170
Whate'er we talk of wisdom to the wise,
Of goodness to the good, of public ties
Which to our country link, of private bands
Which claim most dear attention at our hands,
For parent and for child, for wife and friend,
Our first great mover, and our last great end
Is one, and, by whatever name we call
The ruling tyrant, self is all in all.
This, which unwilling faction shall admit,
Guided in different ways a Bute and Pitt,   180
Made tyrants break, made kings observe the law,
And gave the world a Stuart and Nassau.
    Hath Nature (strange and wild conceit of pride !)
Distinguish'd thee from all her sons beside ?
Doth virtue in thy bosom brighter glow,
Or from a spring more pure doth action flow ?
Is not thy soul bound with those very chains
Which shackle us ? or is that self, which reigns
O'er kings and beggars, which in all we see
Most strong and sovereign, only weak in thee ?   190
Fond man, believe it not ; experience tells
'Tis not thy virtue, but thy pride rebels.
Think, (and for once lay by thy lawless pen)
Think, and confess thyself like other men ;
Think but one hour, and, to thy conscience led
By Reason's hand, bow down and hang thy head :
Think on thy private life, recal thy youth,
View thyself now, and own, with strictest truth,
That self hath drawn thee from fair virtue's way
Farther than folly would have dared to stray,   200
And that the talents liberal Nature gave
To make thee free, have made thee more a slave.
    Quit then, in prudence quit that idle train
Of toys, which have so long abused thy brain,
And captive led thy powers ; with boundless will
Let self maintain her state and empire still ;

257

But let her, with more worthy objects caught,
Strain all the faculties and force of thought
To things of higher daring ; let her range
Through better pastures, and learn how to change ;   210
Let her, no longer to weak faction tied,
Wisely revolt, and join our stronger side.

CHURCHILL

Ah ! what, my Lord, hath private life to do
With things of public nature ? why to view
Would you thus cruelly those scenes unfold
Which, without pain and horror to behold,
Must speak me something more, or less than man ;
Which friends may pardon, but I never can ?
Look back ! a thought which borders on despair,
Which human nature must, yet cannot bear.   220
'Tis not the babbling of a busy world,
Where praise and censure are at random hurl'd,
Which can the meanest of my thoughts control,
Or shake one settled purpose of my soul ;
Free and at large might their wild curses roam,
If all, if all, alas ! were well at home.
No—'tis the tale which angry conscience tells,
When she with more than tragic horror swells
Each circumstance of guilt ; when stern, but true,
She brings bad actions forth into review,   230
And like the dread hand-writing on the wall,
Bids late remorse awake at reason's call ;
Arm'd at all points, bids scorpion vengeance pass,
And to the mind holds up reflection's glass,
The mind which, starting, heaves the heart-felt groan,
And hates that form she knows to be her own.
Enough of this,—let private sorrows rest,—
As to the public, I dare stand the test ;
Dare proudly boast, I feel no wish above
The good of England, and my country's love.   240
Stranger to party-rage, by reason's voice,
Unerring guide, directed in my choice,
Not all the tyrant powers of earth combined,

No, nor of hell, shall make me change my mind.
What ! herd with men my honest soul disdains,
Men who, with servile zeal are forging chains
For Freedom's neck, and lend a helping hand
To spread destruction o'er my native land.
What ! shall I not, e'en to my latest breath,
In the full face of danger and of death   250
Exert that little strength which nature gave,
And boldly stem, or perish in the wave ?

LORD

When I look backward for some fifty years,
And see protesting patriots turn'd to peers ;
Hear men most loose for decency declaim,
And talk of character without a name ;
See infidels assert the cause of God,
And meek divines wield persecution's rod ;
See men transform'd to brutes, and brutes to men,
See Whitehead take a place, Ralph change his pen,   260

[254] Probably a gibe at Pitt. He did not become Earl of Chatham
until 1766, but in 1761 he accepted a pension of £3,000 a year for
three lives and the title of Baroness Chatham for his wife.

[255] An allusion to Sandwich's attack in the House of Lords on
Wilkes' ' Essay on Woman.'

[257] Tooke saw in this line a reference to ' the religious zeal of
Wharton.' It is hardly necessary to go so far afield, as the debate on
the ' Essay on Woman ' in the House of Lords took place in the very
month in which the present poem was published. It is much more
probable that Churchill intended an attack on Kidgell, who had been
instrumental in procuring a copy of the ' Essay on Woman ' by bribing
the printers, and who published a quite hysterical attack upon the
supposed author Wilkes in a pamphlet entitled : ' A Genuine and
Succinct Narrative of a scandalous, obscene and exceedingly profane
Libel Entitled " An Essay on Woman," ' . . . by the Rev. Mr. Kidgell,
A.M., Rector of Horne in Surrey ; Preacher of Berkeley Chapel, and
Chaplain to the Right Hon. the Earl of March and Ruglen, 1763.'

[258] A hit at Warburton. (See note on ' The Duellist,' Book III,
line 125.)

[260] i.e. *Paul* Whitehead, not William. (See line 272 below. See also
note on ' The Ghost,' Book III, line 95.)

[260] James Ralph (*c.* 1705-1762) was born in Pennsylvania and came
to England in 1724 in company with Benjamin Franklin. He attacked
Pope in 1728, and in 1744 and 1746 brought out a ' History of Eng-

I mock the zeal, and deem the men in sport,
Who rail at ministers and curse a court.
Thee, haughty as thou art, and proud in rhyme,
Shall some preferment, offered at a time
When virtue sleeps, some sacrifice to pride,
Or some fair victim, move to change thy side.
Thee shall these eyes behold, to health restored,
Using, as Prudence bids, bold Satire's sword,
Galling thy present friends, and praising those
Whom now thy frenzy holds thy greatest foes.   270

CHURCHILL

    May I (can worse disgrace on manhood fall ?)
Be born a Whitehead, and baptized a Paul ;
May I (though to his service deeply tied
By sacred oaths, and now by will allied)
With false, feign'd zeal an injured God defend,
And use his name for some base private end ;
May I (that thought bids double horrors roll
O'er my sick spirits, and unmans my soul)
Ruin the virtue which I held most dear,
And still must hold ; may I, through abject fear,   280
Betray my friend ; may to succeeding times,
Engraved on plates of adamant, my crimes
Stand blazing forth, whilst mark'd with envious blot,
Each little act of virtue is forgot ;
Of all those evils which, to stamp men curst,
Hell keeps in store for vengeance, may the worst
Light on my head ; and in my day of woe,
To make the cup of bitterness o'erflow,
May I be scorn'd by every man of worth,
Wander, like Cain, a vagabond on earth,   290
Bearing about a hell in my own mind,
Or be to Scotland for my life confined,

land ' for the years 1688-1727. He was employed as a pamphleteer
by Dodington on behalf of Frederick, Prince of Wales, and after the
death of the Prince his services, in opposition to the Government,
were secured by the Duke of Bedford. However, his pen was bought
by the Pelham ministry, and Ralph's career as a journalist came to an
end.

If I am one among the many known
Whom Shelburne fled, and Calcraft blush'd to own.

LORD

Do you reflect what men you make your foes ?

CHURCHILL

I do, and that's the reason I oppose.
Friends I have made, whom Envy must commend,
But not one foe whom I would wish a friend.
What if ten thousand Butes and Hollands bawl ?
One Wilkes hath made a large amends for all.   300
'Tis not the title, whether handed down
From age to age, or flowing from the crown
In copious streams on recent men, who came
From stems unknown, and sires without a name :
'Tis not the star which our great Edward gave
To mark the virtuous, and reward the brave,
Blazing without, whilst a base heart within

294 William Petty (1737-1805), Earl of Shelburne, first Marquess of Lansdowne, served as an officer under Prince Ferdinand and Lord Granby in Germany. He sat in Parliament for High Wycombe, but on the death of his father in 1761 took his seat in the House of Lords. He was employed by Bute in the negotiation with Fox, but refused to take office under him. He was sworn a Member of the Privy Council in April, 1763, but disagreed with both Halifax and Egremont on the question of the General Warrant directed against Wilkes. Soon afterwards he joined Pitt and the Opposition and spoke in favour of Wilkes. On Pitt's return to power in 1766 Shelburne was appointed Secretary of State for the Southern Department, but his subsequent political career does not here concern us. He was created Marquis of Lansdowne in 1784.

294 John Calcraft was deputy-commissary-general of musters. He was the creature (and scandal said, the natural son) of Fox, and through the latter's influence in the matter of army contracts was able to amass a considerable fortune. A detailed, if prejudiced, picture of Calcraft was given to the world in the memoirs of George Anne Bellamy, the actress, who was for many years his mistress.

299 The first edition reads ' Foxes ' instead of ' Hollands.' Henry Fox became Lord Holland in 1763.

305 The Order of the Garter, instituted by Edward III between 1344 and 1350. Among the insignia is a star of eight points, of silver, having in the middle the cross of St. George encircled by the Garter. The reference is to Bute, who became a Knight of the Garter in 1762.

Is rotten to the core with filth and sin ;
'Tis not the tinsel grandeur, taught to wait,
At custom's call, to mark a fool of state   310
From fools of lesser note, that soul can awe,
Whose pride is reason, whose defence is law.

LORD

Suppose, (a thing scarce possible in art,
Were it thy cue to play a common part)
Suppose thy writings so well fenced in law,
That Norton cannot find nor make a flaw—
Hast thou not heard, that 'mongst our ancient tribes,
By party warpt, or lull'd asleep by bribes,
Or trembling at the ruffian hand of Force,
Law hath suspended stood, or changed its course ?   320
Art thou assured, that, for destruction ripe,
Thou may'st not smart beneath the self-same gripe ?
What sanction hast thou, frantic in thy rhymes,
Thy life, thy freedom to secure ?

CHURCHILL

                                      The times.
'Tis not on law, a system great and good,
By wisdom penn'd, and bought by noblest blood,
My faith relies : by wicked men and vain
Law, once abused, may be abused again.—
No ; on our great law-giver I depend,
Who knows and guides her to her proper end ;   330
Whose royalty of nature blazes out
So fierce, 'twere sin to entertain a doubt—
Did tyrant Stuarts now the laws dispense,
(Bless'd be the hour and hand which sent them hence !)
For something, or for nothing, for a word
Or thought, I might be doom'd to death, unheard.
Life we might all resign to lawless power,
Nor think it worth the purchase of an hour ;
But envy ne'er shall fix so foul a stain
On the fair annals of a Brunswick's reign.   340
    If, slave to party, to revenge, or pride ;

[316] Sir Fletcher Norton. (See note on ' The Ghost,' Book III, line 1144.)

If, by frail human error drawn aside,
I break the law, strict rigour let her wear ;
'Tis hers to punish, and 'tis mine to bear ;
Nor, by the voice of Justice doom'd to death,
Would I ask mercy with my latest breath :
But, anxious only for my country's good,
In which my king's, of course, is understood ;
Form'd on a plan with some few patriot friends,
Whilst by just means I aim at noblest ends,   350
My spirits cannot sink : though from the tomb
Stern Jeffries should be placed in Mansfield's room ;
Though he should bring, his base designs to aid,
Some black attorney, for his purpose made,
And shove, whilst Decency and Law retreat,
The modest Norton from his maiden seat ;
Though both, in ill confederates, should agree,
In damned league, to torture law and me ;
Whilst George is king, I cannot fear endure ;
Not to be guilty, is to be secure.   360
　　But when, in after-times, (be far removed
That day !) our monarch, glorious and beloved,
Sleeps with his fathers, should imperious fate,
In vengeance, with fresh Stuarts curse our state ;
Should they, o'erleaping every fence of law,
Butcher the brave to keep tame fools in awe ;
Should they, by brutal and oppressive force,
Divert sweet Justice from her even course ;
Should they, of every other means bereft,
Make my right hand a witness 'gainst my left ;   370
Should they, abroad by inquisitions taught,
Search out my soul, and damn me for a thought ;
Still would I keep my course, still speak, still write,

[352] Judge Jeffreys (1648-1689) was called to the Bar in 1668. He
was knighted in 1677 and next year was made Recorder of London.
He became Chief Justice of Chester in 1680 and of England in 1683 ;
was created Baron Jeffreys of Wem in 1685 and became Lord Chan-
cellor of England in 1685. He has become the type of injustice and
brutality on the bench, especially for his conduct of the ' bloody
assize ' after Monmouth's rebellion. When James II fell he was
imprisoned and died in the Tower of London. For Mansfield see
note on ' Epistle to Hogarth,' line 76.

Till death had plunged me in the shades of night.
  Thou God of Truth, thou great, all-searching eye,
To whom our thoughts, our spirits, open lie,
Grant me thy strength, and in that needful hour,
(Should it e'er come) when Law submits to Power,
With firm resolve my steady bosom steel,
Bravely to suffer, though I deeply feel.   380
  Let me, as hitherto, still draw my breath
In love with life, but not in fear of death ;
And if Oppression brings me to the grave,
And marks me dead, she ne'er shall mark a slave.
Let no unworthy marks of grief be heard,
No wild laments, not one unseemly word ;
Let sober triumphs wait upon my bier ;
I won't forgive that friend who drops one tear.
Whether he's ravish'd in life's early morn,
Or in old age drops like an ear of corn,   390
Full ripe he falls, on nature's noblest plan,
Who lives to reason, and who dies a man.

THE AUTHOR*

ACCURSED the man, whom fate ordains, in spite,
And cruel parents teach, to read and write !
What need of letters ? wherefore should we spell ?
Why write our names ? a mark will do as well.
  Much are the precious hours of youth misspent
In climbing learning's rugged, steep ascent ;
When to the top the bold adventurer's got,
He reigns, vain monarch o'er a barren spot,
Whilst in the vale of ignorance below
Folly and vice to rank luxuriance grow ;   10
Honours and wealth pour in on every side,
And proud preferment rolls her golden tide.
  O'er crabbed authors life's gay prime to waste,
To clamp wild genius in the chains of taste,
To bear the slavish drudgery of schools,
And tamely stoop to every pedant's rules ;
For seven long years debarr'd of liberal ease,
To plod in college trammels to degrees ;
Beneath the weight of solemn toys to groan,
Sleep over books, and leave mankind unknown ;   20
To praise each senior blockhead's threadbare tale,
And laugh till reason blush, and spirits fail ;
Manhood with vile submission to disgrace,
And cap the fool, whose merit is his place,
Vice-Chancellors, whose knowledge is but small,
And Chancellors who nothing know at all,
Ill-brook'd the generous spirit in those days
When learning was the certain road to praise,
When nobles, with a love of science bless'd,
Approved in others what themselves possess'd.   30
  But now, when Dulness rears aloft her throne,
When lordly vassals her wide empire own ;
When Wit, seduced by Envy, starts aside,

* First published in December, 1763. 'Printed for W. Flexney . . . .
G. Kearsley . . . . J. Coote . . . . C. Henderson . . . . J. Gardiner . . . .
and J. Almon.

And basely leagues with Ignorance and Pride ;
What, now, should tempt us, by false hopes misled,
Learning's unfashionable paths to tread,
To bear those labours which our fathers bore,
That crown withheld, which they in triumph wore ?
   When with much pains this boasted learning's got,
'Tis an affront to those who have it not :   40
In some it causes hate, in others fear,
Instructs our foes to rail, our friends to sneer.
With prudent haste the worldly-minded fool
Forgets the little which he learnt at school :
The elder brother, to vast fortunes born,
Looks on all science with an eye of scorn ;
Dependent brethren the same features wear,
And younger sons are stupid as the heir,
In senates, at the bar, in church and state
Genius is vile, and learning out of date.   50
   Is this—O death to think ! is this the land
Where merit and reward went hand in hand ?
Where heroes, parent-like, the poet view'd,
By whom they saw their glorious deeds renew'd ?
Where poets, true to honour, tuned their lays,
And by their patrons sanctified their praise ?
Is this the land, where, on our Spenser's tongue,
Enamour'd of his voice, Description hung ?
Where Jonson rigid Gravity beguiled,
Whilst Reason through her critic fences smiled ?   60
Where Nature listening stood whilst Shakespeare play'd,
And wonder'd at the work herself had made ?
Is this the land, where, mindful of her charge
And office high, fair Freedom walk'd at large ?
Where, finding in our laws a sure defence,
She mock'd at all restraints, but those of sense ?
Where, Health and Honour trooping by her side,
She spread her sacred empire far and wide ;
Pointed the way, Affliction to beguile,
And bade the face of Sorrow wear a smile,   70
Bade those who dare obey the generous call,
Enjoy her blessings, which God meant for all ?
Is this the land, where, in some tyrant's reign

When a weak, wicked, ministerial train,
The tools of power, the slaves of interest, plann'd
Their country's ruin, and with bribes unmann'd
Those wretches, who, ordain'd in Freedom's cause,
Gave up our liberties, and sold our laws ;
When Power was taught by Meanness where to go,
Nor dared to love the virtue of a foe ;   80
When, like a leperous plague, from the foul head
To the foul heart her sores Corruption spread ;
Her iron arm when stern Oppression rear'd,
And Virtue, from her broad base shaken, fear'd
The scourge of Vice ; when, impotent and vain,
Poor Freedom bow'd the neck to Slavery's chain ;
Is this the land, where, in those worst of times,
The hardy poet raised his honest rhymes
To dread rebuke, and bade Controlment speak
In guilty blushes on the villain's cheek ;   90
Bade Power turn pale, kept mighty rogues in awe,
And made them fear the Muse, who fear'd not law ?
    How do I laugh, when men of narrow souls,
Whom folly guides, and prejudice controls ;
Who, one dull, drowsy track of business trod,
Worship their Mammon, and neglect their God ;
Who, breathing by one musty set of rules,
Dote from their birth, and are by system fools ;
Who, form'd to dulness from their very youth,
Lies of the day prefer to Gospel-truth ;   100
Pick up their little knowledge from Reviews,
And lay out all their stock of faith in news ;
How do I laugh, when creatures, form'd like these,
Whom Reason scorns, and I should blush to please,
Rail at all liberal arts, deem verse a crime,
And hold not truth, as truth, if told in rhyme ?
    How do I laugh, when Publius, hoary grown
In zeal for Scotland's welfare, and his own,
By slow degrees, and course of office, drawn

[88] Tooke saw in this a reference to Andrew Marvell.
[107] Smollett, whose attack on 'The Rosciad' in 'The Critical
Review' Churchill never forgave. (See note on the 'Apology,' line
298.)

In mood and figure at the helm to yawn, 110
Too mean (the worst of curses Heaven can send)
To have a foe ; too proud to have a friend ;
Erring by form, which blockheads sacred hold,
Ne'er making new faults, and ne'er mending old,
Rebukes my spirit, bids the daring Muse
Subjects more equal to her weakness choose ;
Bids her frequent the haunts of humble swains,
Nor dare to traffic in ambitious strains ;
Bids her, indulging the poetic whim
In quaint-wrought ode, or sonnet pertly trim, 120
Along the church-way path complain with Gray,
Or dance with Mason on the first of May !
' All sacred is the name and power of kings ;
All states and statesmen are those mighty things
Which, howsoe'er they out of course may roll,
Were never made for poets to control.'
    Peace, peace, thou Dotard, nor thus vilely deem
Of sacred numbers, and their power blaspheme.
I tell thee, Wretch, search all creation round,
In earth, in heaven, no subject can be found 130
(Our God alone except) above whose weight
The poet cannot rise, and hold his state.
The blessed saints above in numbers speak
The praise of God, though there all praise is weak ;
In numbers here below the bard shall teach
Virtue to soar beyond the villain's reach ;
Shall tear his labouring lungs, strain his hoarse throat,
And raise his voice beyond the trumpet's note,
Should an afflicted country, awed by men
Of slavish principles, demand his pen. 140
This is a great, a glorious point of view,
Fit for an English poet to pursue,
Undaunted to pursue, though, in return,
His writings by the common hangman burn.
    How do I laugh, when men, by fortune placed
Above their betters, and by rank disgraced,

¹²¹ Gray's ' Elegy in a Country Churchyard ' appeared in 1751.
(See note on ' Gotham,' Book II, line 20.)
¹²² See note on ' The Prophecy of Famine,' line 67.

Who found their pride on titles which they stain,
And, mean themselves, are of their fathers vain ;
Who would a bill of privilege prefer,
And treat a poet like a creditor,   150
The generous ardour of the Muse condemn,
And curse the storm they know must break on them !
' What, shall a reptile bard, a wretch unknown,
Without one badge of merit but his own,
Great nobles lash, and lords, like common men,
Smart from the vengeance of a scribbler's pen ? '
    What's in this name of Lord, that I should fear
To bring their vices to the public ear ?
Flows not the honest blood of humble swains
Quick as the tide which swells a monarch's veins ?   160
Monarchs, who wealth and titles can bestow,
Cannot make virtues in succession flow.
Wouldst thou, proud man, be safely placed above
The censure of the Muse—deserve her love :
Act as thy birth demands, as nobles ought ;
Look back, and, by thy worthy father taught,
Who earn'd those honours thou wert born to wear ;
Follow his steps, and be his virtue's heir :
But if, regardless of the road to fame,
You start aside, and tread the paths of shame ;   170
If such thy life, that should thy sire arise,
The sight of such a son would blast his eyes,
Would make him curse the hour which gave thee birth,
Would drive him, shuddering, from the face of earth,
Once more, with shame and sorrow, 'mongst the dead
In endless night to hide his reverend head ;
If such thy life, though kings had made thee more
Than ever king a scoundrel made before ;
Nay, to allow thy pride a deeper spring,
Though God in vengeance had made thee a king,   180
Taking on Virtue's wing her daring flight,
The Muse should drag thee trembling to the light,
Probe thy foul wounds, and lay thy bosom bare
To the keen question of the searching air.
    Gods ! with what pride I see the titled slave,
Who smarts beneath the stroke which Satire gave,

Aiming at ease, and with dishonest art
Striving to hide the feelings of his heart !
How do I laugh, when, with affected air,
(Scarce able through despite to keep his chair,   190
Whilst on his trembling lip pale anger speaks,
And the chafed blood flies mounting to his cheeks,)
He talks of Conscience, which good men secures
From all those evil moments guilt endures,
And seems to laugh at those who pay regard
To the wild ravings of a frantic bard.
' Satire, whilst envy and ill-humour sway
The mind of man, must always make her way ;
Nor to a bosom with discretion fraught,
Is all her malice worth a single thought.   200
The wise have not the will, nor fools the power,
To stop her headstrong course ; within the hour,
Left to herself, she dies ; opposing strife
Gives her fresh vigour, and prolongs her life.
All things her prey, and every man her aim,
I can no patent for exemption claim,
Nor would I wish to stop that harmless dart
Which plays around, but cannot wound my heart ;
Though pointed at myself, be Satire free ;
To her 'tis pleasure, and no pain to me.'   210
      Dissembling Wretch ! hence to the Stoic school,
And there amongst thy brethren play the fool ;
There, unrebuked, these wild, vain, doctrines preach :
Lives there a man whom Satire cannot reach ?
Lives there a man who calmly can stand by,
And see his conscience ripp'd with steady eye ?
When Satire flies abroad on Falsehood's wing,
Short is her life, and impotent her sting ;
But when to truth allied, the wound she gives
Sinks deep, and to remotest ages lives.   220
When in the tomb thy pamper'd flesh shall rot,
And e'en by friends thy mem'ry be forgot,
Still shalt thou live, recorded for thy crimes,
Live in her page, and stink to after-times.

218 The first edition reads : ' Short is her life indeed, and dull
her sting.'

Hast thou no feeling yet ? Come, throw off pride,
And own those passions which thou shalt not hide.
Sandwich, who from the moment of his birth
Made human nature a reproach on earth,
Who never dared, nor wish'd behind to stay,
When Folly, Vice, and Meanness led the way,   230
Would blush, should he be told, by Truth and Wit,
Those actions, which he blush'd not to commit.
Men the most infamous are fond of fame,
And those who fear not guilt, yet start at shame.
     But whither runs my zeal, whose rapid force,
Turning the brain, bears Reason from her course ;
Carries me back to times, when poets, bless'd
With courage, graced the science they profess'd ;
When they, in honour rooted, firmly stood
The bad to punish and reward the good ;   240
When, to a flame by public virtue wrought,
The foes of freedom they to justice brought,
And dared expose those slaves who dared support
A tyrant plan, and call'd themselves a Court ?
Ah ! what are poets now ? as slavish those
Who deal in verse, as those who deal in prose.
Is there an Author, search the kingdom round,
In whom true worth and real spirit's found ?
The slaves of booksellers, or (doom'd by Fate
To baser chains) vile pensioners of state,   250
Some, dead to shame, and of those shackles proud
Which Honour scorns, for slavery roar aloud ;
Others, half-palsied only, mutes become,
And what makes Smollett write makes Johnson dumb.
     Why turns yon villain pale ? why bends his eye
Inward, abash'd, when Murphy passes by ?
Dost thou sage Murphy for a blockhead take,
Who wages war with vice for virtue's sake ?

[254] Johnson's pension was conferred in July, 1762. He had some
hesitation in accepting it, as he had stated in his dictionary that a
pension was ' generally understood to mean pay given to a state
hireling for treason to his country.' Smollett had no fixed pension
but was supposed to have been paid for his writings in defence of the
Ministry.
[256] Murphy. (See note on ' The Rosciad,' line 67.)

271

No, no, like other worldlings, you will find
He shifts his sails, and catches every wind :   260
His soul the shock of interest can't endure :
Give him a pension then, and sin secure.
    With laurell'd wreaths the flatterer's brows adorn,
Bid Virtue crouch, bid Vice exalt her horn ;
Bid cowards thrive, put Honesty to flight,
Murphy shall prove, or try to prove it right.
Try, thou state-juggler, every paltry art ;
Ransack the inmost closet of my heart,
Swear thou'rt my friend ; by that base oath make way
Into my breast, and flatter to betray ;   270
Or, if those tricks are vain, if wholesome doubt
Detects the fraud, and points the villain out,
Bribe those who daily at my board are fed,
And make them take my life who eat my bread ;
On Authors for defence, for praise depend,
Pay him but well, and Murphy is thy friend :
He, he shall ready stand with venal rhymes,
To varnish guilt, and consecrate thy crimes,
To make corruption in false colours shine,
And damn his own good name, to rescue thine.   280
    But, if thy niggard hands their gifts withhold,
And Vice no longer rains down showers of gold,
Expect no mercy ; facts, well grounded, teach,
Murphy, if not rewarded, will impeach.
What though each man of nice and juster thought,
Shunning his steps, decrees, by honour taught,
He ne'er can be a friend, who stoops so low
To be the base betrayer of a foe ?
What though, with thine together link'd, his name
Must be with thine transmitted down to shame ?   290
To every manly feeling callous grown,
Rather than not blast thine, he'll blast his own.
    To ope the fountain whence sedition springs,
To slander government, and libel kings ;
With Freedom's name to serve a present hour,

---

²⁸⁴ ' He complained publicly that he was ill-paid and threatened to
produce the letters of such as had engaged him to write in the Cause
of the Ministry.' (Gray.)

Though born and bred to arbitrary power ;
To talk of William with insidious art,
Whilst a vile Stuart's lurking in his heart,
And, whilst mean Envy rears her loathsome head,
Flattering the living, to abuse the dead,   300
Where is Shebbeare ? Oh let not foul reproach,
Travelling thither in a City-coach,
The pillory dare to name : the whole intent
Of that parade was fame, not punishment :
And that old, staunch Whig, Beardmore, standing by,
Can in full court give that report the lie.
   With rude unnatural jargon to support,
Half Scotch, half English, a declining court ;
To make most glaring contraries unite,
And prove beyond dispute that black is white ;   310
To make firm Honour tamely league with Shame,
Make Vice and Virtue differ but in name ;
To prove that chains and freedom are but one,
That to be saved must mean to be undone,
Is there not Guthrie ? Who, like him, can call

---

[301] John Shebbeare (1709-1788) was apprenticed to a surgeon and afterwards set up for himself. His career as a political writer began in 1754 when he issued a novel entitled ' The Marriage Act ' in opposition to Lord Hardwicke's reform. He was imprisoned in consequence but the work was republished several times. He brought out both periodicals and pamphlets against the Ministry and violently attacked ' the influence of Hanover on the councils of England.' Early in 1758, author, printer and publisher were arrested under a general warrant, and Shebbeare was tried for libel. Among other punishments he was condemned to stand in the pillory at Charing Cross, but the sentence was interpreted very liberally by Beardmore the under-sheriff, who allowed his prisoner to stand in a position of comfort, while a chairman held an umbrella over his head. The cheers of the crowd were a foretaste of the enthusiasm for Wilkes when he too came to be arrested under a general warrant. For a moment, however, the authorities triumphed and Beardmore was punished for his lenity. Churchill, in view of his opinion of general warrants, might have been expected to be favourable to Shebbeare, but the latter was an unrepentant Tory, an advocate of peace with France and an opponent of Wilkes. Yet he loathed Scotsmen as much as either Wilkes or Churchill. Shebbeare was pensioned by the government for his defence of the American policy of George III.

[315] William Guthrie was the author of numerous pamphlets during Grenville's Ministry. The following lines are an allusion to his

273

All opposites to proof, and conquer all?
He calls forth living waters from the rock;
He calls forth children from the barren stock:
He, far beyond the springs of Nature led,
Makes women bring forth after they are dead: 320
He, on a curious, new, and happy plan,
In wedlock's sacred bands joins man to man;
And, to complete the whole, most strange, but true,
By some rare magic, makes them fruitful too,
Whilst from their loins, in the due course of years,
Flows the rich blood of Guthrie's English Peers.
    Dost thou contrive some blacker deed of shame,
Something which Nature shudders but to name,
Something which makes the soul of man retreat,
And the life-blood run backward to her seat?   330
Dost thou contrive, for some base private end,
Some selfish view, to hang a trusting friend,
To lure him on, e'en to his parting breath,
And promise life to work him surer death?
Grown old in villany, and dead to grace,
Hell in his heart, and Tyburn in his face,
Behold, a parson at thy elbow stands,
Lowering damnation, and with open hands
Ripe to betray his Saviour for reward,
The Atheist chaplain of an Atheist lord.   340
    Bred to the church, and for the gown decreed,
Ere it was known that I should learn to read—
Though that was nothing, for my friends, who knew
What mighty Dulness of itself could do,
Never design'd me for a working priest,
But hoped I should have been a Dean at least—
Condemn'd (like many more and worthier men
To whom I pledge the service of my pen)
Condemn'd (whilst proud and pamper'd sons of lawn,
Cramm'd to the throat, in lazy plenty yawn)   350
In pomp of reverend beggary to appear,

'Peerage,' an unscholarly work full of errors, published in two volumes
in 1762 and 1763.
[327–340] Written for the 'Elegy, or Ayliffe's Ghost.' (See Intro-
duction, p. xlvi.)
[340] The Rev. Philip Francis. (See note on line 356, below.)

To pray, and starve, on forty pounds a-year.
My friends, who never felt the galling load,
Lament that I forsook the packhorse road,
Whilst Virtue to my conduct witness bears,
In throwing off that gown which Francis wears.
    What creature's that, so very pert and prim,
So very full of foppery, and whim,
So gentle, yet so brisk ; so wondrous sweet,
So fit to prattle at a lady's feet ;   360
Who looks as he the Lord's rich vineyard trod,
And by his garb appears a man of God ?
Trust not to looks, nor credit outward show ;
The villain lurks beneath the cassock'd beau ;
That's an informer ; what avails the name ?
Suffice it that the wretch from Sodom came.
His tongue is deadly—from his presence run,
Unless thy rage would wish to be undone.
No ties can hold him, no affection bind,
And fear alone restrains his coward mind ;   370
Free him from that, no monster is so fell,
Nor is so sure a blood-hound found in hell.
His silken smiles, his hypocritic air,

[356] The Rev. Philip Francis (1708-1773), Lord Holland's chaplain and confidant. He published a translation of the works of Horace, which was admired by Johnson ; but the foundation of his fortune was laid by George Anne Bellamy, who introduced him to the Fox family. Francis acted as tutor to the children, and wrote political pamphlets, notably against Pitt, on his resignation. He attacked Wilkes also with great vigour, but quarrelled with Fox because he thought he had been insufficiently rewarded. Walpole declares that Francis handed over to Churchill a quantity of letters incriminating Fox, but there is no evidence that Churchill and Francis were ever other than enemies. Francis is attacked also in ' The Candidate,' (line 38).

[357] John Kidgell (1722-1766), a fashionable preacher, was rector of Horne in Surrey, and chaplain to James Douglas, Earl of March and Ruglen, (afterwards Duke of Queensberry). He spent his time in London, in company with March, and when in 1763, a copy of ' The Essay on Woman ' was wanted for the prosecution of Wilkes, Kidgell obtained one by bribery of the printers. This he handed to March who was in alliance with Bute and Sandwich, and the last named was able to read the stolen copy in the House of Lords. Kidgell published a pamphlet to defend his conduct, but was soon afterwards compelled to fly from England to escape his creditors. He is thought to have died in Flanders. What justification Churchill had for describing him as a ' wretch from Sodom ' is not known.

His meek demeanour, plausible and fair,
Are only worn to pave Fraud's easier way,
And make gull'd Virtue fall a surer prey.
Attend his church—his plan of doctrine view—
The preacher is a Christian, dull, but true ;
But when the hallow'd hour of preaching's o'er,
That plan of doctrine's never thought of more ;   380
Christ is laid by neglected on the shelf,
And the vile priest is Gospel to himself.
  By Cleland tutor'd, and with Blacow bred,
(Blacow, whom, by a brave resentment led,
Oxford, if Oxford had not sunk in fame,
Ere this, had damn'd to everlasting shame)
Their steps he follows, and their crimes partakes ;
To virtue lost, to vice alone he wakes,
Most lusciously declaims 'gainst luscious themes,
And whilst he rails at blasphemy, blasphemes.   390
  Are these the arts which policy supplies ?
Are these the steps by which grave churchmen rise ?
Forbid it, Heaven ; or, should it turn out so,

[383] John Cleland (1709-1789) was educated at Westminster School. After numerous adventures in the Near and Far East, he returned to London and attempted to retrieve his fortunes by a scandalous novel : ' Fanny Hill, or The Memoirs of a Woman of Pleasure ' (1750). The bookseller made £10,000 but Cleland only received twenty guineas, and was summoned before the Privy Council. Lord Granville procured him a pension of £100 so that he might no longer plead absolute destitution as excuse for licentious writing. Cleland produced another and better novel and some pieces for the theatre, as well as miscellaneous writings.

[383] ' In the year 1747, a riot happening at Oxford, during which some of the students cried out repeatedly in the streets, " King James for ever ! Prince Charles. God bless the great King James the Third ! " Mr. Blacow complained to the Vice-Chancellor of this, and made the most strenuous exertion against the offenders. The Vice-Chancellor, imputing their misbehaviour to intoxication, endeavoured to waive the inquiry, but at length inflicted some trifling punishment on the delinquents. At last the Duke of Newcastle took cognizance of the offence ; a prosecution was commenced in the Court of King's Bench, against Mr. Dawes and Mr. Whitmore, two of the students, who being found guilty were sentenced to walk through Westminster-hall with a paper on their foreheads stating their crime, to pay a fine of five nobles each, be imprisoned for two years, and to find security for their good behaviour for seven years more.' (Tooke.)

Let me and mine continue mean and low.
Such be their arts whom interest controls ;
Kidgell and I have free and modest souls :
We scorn preferment which is gain'd by sin,
And will, though poor without, have peace within.

THE DUELLIST*

BOOK ONE

THE clock struck twelve ; o'er half the globe
Darkness had spread her pitchy robe :
Morpheus, his feet with velvet shod,
Treading as if in fear he trod,
Gentle as dews at even-tide,
Distilled his poppies far and wide.
    Ambition, who, when waking, dreams
Of mighty, but fantastic schemes,
Who, when asleep, ne'er knows that rest
With which the humbler soul is blest,   10
Was building castles in the air,
Goodly to look upon and fair,
But on a bad foundation laid,
Doomed at return of morn to fade
    Pale Study, by the taper's light
Wearing away the watch of night,
Sat reading, but with o'ercharged head,
Remembered nothing that he read.
    Starving midst plenty, with a face
Which might the court of Famine grace,   20
Ragged, and filthy to behold,
Gray Avarice nodded o'er his gold.
    Jealousy, his quick eye half-closed
With watchings worn, reluctant dozed ;
And, mean distrust not quite forgot,
Slumbered as if he slumbered not.
    Stretched at his length on the bare ground,
His hardy offspring sleeping round,

* Probably first published in January, 1764. 'Printed for G.
Kearsley . . . . W. Flexney . . . . J. Coote . . . . C. Henderson . . . .
J. Gardiner . . . . and J. Almon.' For the occasion of the poem see
Introduction, p. xli. Wilkes always declared that Martin had behaved
as a man of honour and the antagonists had an amicable meeting in
Paris. Churchill, however, could not forgive Martin for having so
nearly put an end to his friend's life.

Snored restless Labour ; by his side
Lay Health, a coarse but comely bride.   30
   Virtue, without the doctor's aid,
In the soft arms of sleep was laid ;
Whilst Vice, within the guilty breast,
Could not be physic'd into rest.
   Thou bloody Man ! whose ruffian knife
Is drawn against thy neighbour's life,
And never scruples to descend
Into the bosom of a friend,
A firm, fast friend, by vice allied,
And to thy secret service tied :   40
In whom ten murders breed no awe,
If properly secured from law :
Thou man of Lust ! whom passion fires
To foulest deeds, whose hot desires
O'er honest bars with ease make way,
Whilst idiot Beauty falls a prey,
And to indulge thy brutal flame
A Lucreece must be brought to shame ;
Who dost, a brave, bold sinner, bear
Rank incest to the open air,   50
And rapes, full blown upon thy crown,
Enough to weigh a nation down :
Thou simular of Lust ! vain man,
Whose restless thoughts still form the plan
Of guilt, which, withered to the root,
Thy lifeless nerves can't execute,
Whilst in thy marrowless, dry bones
Desire without enjoyment groans ;
Thou perjured Wretch ! whom falsehood clothes
E'en like a garment, who with oaths   60
Dost trifle, as with brokers, meant
To serve thy every vile intent,
In the day's broad and searching eye
Making God witness to a lie,
Blaspheming heaven and earth for pelf,
And hanging friends to save thyself :

[35] *i.e.*, Lord Holland.
[66] Friends : *i.e.*, Ayliffe. (See Introduction, p. xlvi.)

Thou son of Chance ! whose glorious soul,
On the four aces doomed to roll,
Was never yet with honour caught,
Nor on poor virtue lost one thought ;   70
Who dost thy wife, thy children, set,
Thy all, upon a single bet,
Risking, the desperate stake to try,
Here and hereafter on a die ;
Who, thy own private fortune lost,
Dost game on at thy country's cost,
And, grown expert in sharping rules,
First fooled thyself, now prey'st on fools :
Thou noble Gamester ! whose high place
Gives too much credit to disgrace ;   80
Who, with the motion of a die,
Dost make a mighty island fly,
The sums, I mean, of good French gold
For which a mighty island's sold ;
Who dost betray intelligence,
Abuse the dearest confidence,
And, private fortune to create,
Most falsely play the game of state ;
Who dost within the Alley sport
Sums, which might beggar a whole court,   90
And make us bankrupts all, if Care,
With good Earl Talbot, was not there :
Thou daring Infidel ! whom pride
And sin have drawn from Reason's side ;
Who, fearing his avengeful rod,
Dost wish not to believe a God ;
Whose hope is founded on a plan
Which should distract the soul of man,
And make him curse his abject birth ;
Whose hope is, once returned to earth,   100

[89] *i.e.*, Change Alley, where the stockjobbers had founded a club in 1762 at Jonathan's Coffee House.

[92] William, first Earl Talbot, Lord Steward of the King's Household from 1761 to 1782. He proposed certain reforms tending to economy, but the interests of the court were too strong for him. Churchill's reference is, however, ironical, as Talbot was already an object of ridicule to Wilkes and his friends.

There to lie down, for worms a feast,
To rot and perish like a beast ;
Who dost, of punishment afraid,
And by thy crimes a coward made,
To every generous soul a curse
Than hell and all her torments worse,
When crawling to thy latter end,
Call on destruction as a friend ;
Choosing to crumble into dust
Rather than rise, though rise you must :   110
Thou Hypocrite ! who dost profane,
And take the patriot's name in vain ;
Then most thy country's foe when most
Of love and loyalty you boast ;
Who for the filthy love of gold
Thy friend, thy king, thy God, hast sold,
And, mocking the just claim of Hell,
Were bidders found, thyself wouldst sell.
Ye Villains ! of whatever name,
Whatever rank, to whom the claim   120
Of Hell is certain ; on whose lids
That worm which never dies forbids
Sweet sleep to fall, come, and behold,
Whilst envy makes your blood run cold,
Behold, by pitiless Conscience led,
So Justice wills, that holy bed
Where Peace her full dominion keeps,
And Innocence with Holland sleeps.
   Bid Terror, posting on the wind
Affray the spirits of mankind ;   130
Bid Earthquakes, heaving for a vent,
Rive their concealing continent,
And, forcing an untimely birth
Through the vast bowels of the earth,
Endeavour, in her monstrous womb,
At once all nature to entomb ;
Bid all that's horrible and dire,
All that man hates and fears, conspire

[128] Lord Holland's alleged peculations were a constant theme of popular clamour. (See note on the ' Epistle to Hogarth,' line 22.)

To make night hideous as they can ;
Still is thy sleep, thou virtuous Man !   140
Pure as the thoughts which in thy breast
Inhabit, and insure thy rest ;
Still shall thy Ayliffe, taught, though late,
Thy friendly justice in his fate,
Turned to a guardian angel, spread
Sweet dreams of comfort round thy head.
    Dark was the night, by Fate decreed
For the contrivance of a deed
More black than common, which might make
This land from her foundations shake,   150
Might tear up Freedom by the root,
Destroy a Wilkes, and fix a Bute.
    Deep Horror held her wide domain ;
The sky in sullen drops of rain
Forewept the morn, and through the air,
Which, opening, laid its bosom bare,
Loud thunders rolled, and lightning streamed ;
The owl at Freedom's window screamed,
The screech-owl, prophet dire, whose breath
Brings sickness, and whose note is death ;   160
The churchyard teemed, and from the tomb,
All sad and silent, through the gloom
The ghosts of men, in former times,
Whose public virtues were their crimes,
Indignant stalked ; sorrow and rage
Blanked their pale cheeks ; in his own age
The prop of Freedom, Hampden there
Felt after death the generous care ;

---

[143] Ayliffe. (See Introduction, p. xlvi.)

[147] This seems to be poetic licence. Wilkes returned to his house
early on the morning of November 16th, 1763, after the all-night
sitting of Parliament, in which Martin had insulted him. He wrote to
Martin immediately, and Martin replied the same day fixing a meeting
in Hyde Park within one hour. Even supposing that Martin did not
send his reply until the evening, the fact that the two adversaries had
to walk ' together a little while to avoid some company which seemed
coming up to them,' implies that the day was not very far advanced
when their encounter took place.

[167] John Hampden (1594-1643) resisted the payment of Ship Money
to Charles I, and was killed in a skirmish at Chalgrove Field.

Sidney, by grief, from heaven was kept,
And for his brother patriot wept :   170
All friends of Liberty, when Fate
Prepared to shorten Wilkes's date,
Heaved, deeply hurt, the heart-felt groan,
And knew that wound to be their own.
     Hail, Liberty ! a glorious word,
In other countries scarcely heard,
Or heard but as a thing of course,
Without or energy or force :
Here felt, enjoyed, adored, she springs,
Far, far beyond the reach of kings ;   180
Fresh blooming from our mother Earth,
With pride and joy she owns her birth
Derived from us, and in return
Bids in our breasts her genius burn ;
Bids us with all those blessings live
Which Liberty alone can give,
Or nobly with that spirit die
Which makes death more than victory.
     Hail those old patriots, on whose tongue
Persuasion in the senate hung,   190
Whilst they this sacred cause maintained !
Hail those old chiefs, to honour trained,
Who spread, when other methods failed,
War's bloody banner, and prevailed !
Shall men like these unmentioned sleep
Promiscuous with the common heap,
And (Gratitude forbid the crime !)
Be carried down the stream of time
In shoals, unnoticed and forgot,
On Lethe's stream, like flags, to rot ?   200
No—they shall live, and each fair name,
Recorded in the book of Fame,
Founded on honour's basis, fast
As the round earth to ages last.
Some virtues vanish with our breath ;
Virtue like this lives after death.

[169] Algernon Sidney (c. 1622-1683), Republican patriot, executed for
alleged complicity in the Rye House Plot.

Old Time himself, his scythe thrown by,
Himself lost in eternity,
An everlasting crown shall twine
To make a Wilkes and Sidney join.   210
　But should some slave-got villain dare
Chains for his country to prepare,
And, by his birth to slavery broke,
Make her, too, feel the galling yoke,
May he be evermore accurst,
Amongst bad men be ranked the worst ;
May he be still himself, and still
Go on in vice, and perfect ill ;
May his broad crimes each day increase,
Till he can't live nor die in peace ;   220
May he be plunged so deep in shame,
That Satan mayn't endure his name,
And hear, scarce crawling on the earth,
His children curse him for their birth ;
May Liberty, beyond the grave,
Ordain him to be still a slave,
Grant him what here he most requires
And damn him with his own desires !
　But should some villain, in support
And zeal for a despairing court,   230
Placing in craft his confidence,
And making honour a pretence
To do a deed of deepest shame,
Whilst filthy lucre is his aim ;
Should such a wretch, with sword or knife
Contrive to practise 'gainst the life
Of one who, honoured through the land,
For Freedom made a glorious stand ;
Whose chief, perhaps his only crime
Is, (if plain Truth at such a time   240
May dare her sentiments to tell)
That he his country loves too well ;
May he—but words are all too weak
The feelings of my heart to speak—
May he—O for a noble curse
Which might his very marrow pierce—

The general contempt engage,
And be the Martin of his age.

BOOK TWO

Deep in the bosom of a wood,
Out of the road, a temple stood ;
Ancient, and much the worse for wear,
It called aloud for quick repair,
And, tottering from side to side,
Menaced destruction far and wide,
Nor able seemed, unless made stronger,
To hold out four or five years longer.
Four hundred pillars, from the ground
Rising in order, most unsound,   10
Some rotten to the heart, aloof,
Seem to support the tottering roof,
But to inspection nearer laid,
Instead of giving, wanted aid.
    The structure, rare and curious, made
By men most famous in their trade,
A work of years, admired by all,
Was suffered into dust to fall,
Or, just to make it hang together,
And keep off the effects of weather,   20
Was patched and patched from time to time
By wretches, whom it were a crime,
A crime, which Art would treason hold
To mention with those names of old.
    Builders, who had the pile surveyed,
And those not Flitcrofts in their trade,
Doubted (the wise hand in a doubt
Merely, sometimes, to hand his out)
Whether (like churches in a brief,

² Presumably the Houses of Parliament.
²⁶ Henry Flitcroft (1697-1769) was an architect patronised by the
Earl of Burlington.   He rebuilt a number of London churches, and
designed a house in St. James's Place, for Mary Lepel, Lady Hervey.
    ²⁹ ' The system of obtaining contributions for the repair and re-
building of churches and colleges, and other public purposes, and

Taught wisely to obtain relief   30
Through Chancery, who gives her fees
To this and other charities)
It must not, in all parts unsound,
Be ripped, and pulled down to the ground ;
Whether (though after ages ne'er
Shall raise a building to compare)
Art, if they should their art employ,
Meant to preserve, might not destroy,
As human bodies, worn away,
Battered and hasting to decay,   40
Bidding the power of Art despair,
Cannot those very medicines bear
Which, and which only, can restore,
And make them healthy as before.
    To Liberty, whose gracious smile
Shed peace and plenty o'er the Isle,
Our grateful ancestors, her plain
But faithful children, raised this fane.
    Full in the front, stretched out in length,
Where Nature put forth all her strength   50
In spring eternal, lay a plain
Where our brave fathers used to train
Their sons to arms, to teach the art
Of war, and steel the infant heart ;
Labour, their hardy nurse, when young,
Their joints had knit, their nerves had strung ;
Abstinence, foe declared to death,
Had, from the time they first drew breath,
The best of doctors, with plain food,
Kept pure the channel of their blood ;   60
Health in their cheeks bade colour rise,
And Glory sparkled in their eyes.
    The instruments of husbandry,
As in contempt, were all thrown by,

occasionally for the relief of sufferers from fire, tempest and other
casualties by reading briefs in churches, was abolished in the year
1828 by act of George IV, *c.* 42. When the practice commenced is
uncertain ; probably it was in the reign of Queen Elizabeth. The
custom is mentioned in Cowper's *Charity*, line 469.' (Tooke.)

And, flattering a manly pride,
War's keener tools their place supplied.
Their arrows to the head they drew ;
Swift to the point their javelins flew ;
They grasped the sword, they shook the spear ;
Their fathers felt a pleasing fear,   70
And even Courage, standing by,
Scarcely beheld with steady eye.
Each stripling, lessoned by his sire,
Knew when to close, when to retire ;
When near at hand, when from afar
To fight, and was himself a war.
   Their wives, their mothers, all around,
Careless of order, on the ground,
Breathed forth to Heaven the pious vow,
And for a son's or husband's brow,   80
With eager fingers, laurel wove ;
Laurel which in the sacred grove,
Planted by Liberty, they find,
The brows of conquerors to bind,
To give them pride and spirits fit
To make a world in arms submit.
   What raptures did the bosom fire
Of the young, rugged, peasant sire,
When, from the toil of mimic fight,
Returning with return of night,   90
He saw his babe resign the breast,
And, smiling, stroke those arms in jest
With which hereafter he shall make
The proudest heart in Gallia quake !
   Gods ! with what joy, what honest pride,
Did each fond, wishing, rustic bride
Behold her manly swain return !
How did her love-sick bosom burn,
Though on parades he was not bred,
Nor wore the livery of red,   100
When, Pleasure heightening all her charms,
She strained her warrior in her arms,
And begged, whilst love and glory fire,
A son, a son just like his sire !

Such were the men in former times,
Ere luxury had made our crimes
Our bitter punishment, who bore
Their terrors to a foreign shore ;
Such were the men who, free from dread,
By Edwards and by Henries led,   110
Spread, like a torrent swelled with rains,
O'er haughty Gallia's trembling plains :
Such were the men, when lust of power,
To work him woe, in evil hour
Debauched the tyrant from those ways
On which a king should found his praise ;
When stern Oppression, hand in hand
With Pride, stalked proudly through the land ;
When weeping Justice was misled
From her fair course, and Mercy dead :   120
Such were the men, in virtue strong,
Who dared not see their country's wrong,
Who left the mattock and the spade,
And, in the robes of War arrayed,
In their rough arms, departing, took
Their helpless babes, and with a look
Stern and determined, swore to see
Those babes no more, or see them free :
Such were the men whom tyrant Pride
Could never fasten to his side   130
By threats or bribes ; who, freemen born,
Chains, though of gold, beheld with scorn ;
Who, free from every servile awe,
Could never be divorced from law,
From that broad, general law which Sense
Made for the general defence ;
Could never yield to partial ties
Which from dependant stations rise ;
Could never be to slavery led,
For Property was at their head :   140
Such were the men, in days of yore,
Who, called by Liberty, before
Her temple on the sacred green,
In martial pastimes oft were seen—

Now seen no longer ; in their stead,
To laziness and vermin bred,
A race who, strangers to the cause
Of Freedom, live by other laws,
On other motives fight, a prey
To interest, and slaves for pay.   150
Valour, how glorious on a plan
Of honour founded ! leads their van ;
Discretion, free from taint of fear,
Cool, but resolved, brings up their rear ;
Discretion, Valour's better half ;
Dependance holds the general's staff.
    In plain and home-spun garb arrayed,
Not for vain shew, but service, made,
In a green, flourishing old age,
Not damned yet with an equipage,   160
In rules of Porterage untaught,
Simplicity, not worth a groat,
For years had kept the temple-door ;
Full on his breast a glass he wore,
Through which his bosom open lay
To every one who passed that way :
Now turned adrift—with humbler face,
But prouder heart, his vacant place
Corruption fills, and bears the key ;
No entrance now without a fee.   170
    With belly round, and full fat face,
Which on the house reflected grace,
Full of good fare, and honest glee,
The steward Hospitality,
Old Welcome smiling by his side,
A good old servant, often tried
And faithful found, who kept in view
His lady's fame and interest too,
Who made each heart with joy rebound,
Yet never run her state aground,   180
Was turned off, or (which word I find
Is more in modern use) *resigned.*
    Half-starved, half-starving others, bred

[182] Pitt and Temple resigned in 1761, the Duke of Newcastle in 1762.

289

In beggary, with carrion fed,
Detested, and detesting all,
Made up of avarice and gall,
Boasting great thrift, yet wasting more
Than ever steward did before,
Succeeded one, who to engage
The praise of an exhausted age,   190
Assumed a name of high degree,
And called himself Economy.
　　Within the temple, full in sight,
Where without ceasing day and night
The workman toiled ; where Labour bared
His brawny arm ; where art prepared,
In regular and even rows,
Her types, a Printing press arose ;
Each workman knew his task, and each
Was honest and expert as Leach.   200
　　Hence Learning struck a deeper root,
And Science brought forth riper fruit ;
Hence Loyalty received support,
Even when banished from the court ;
Hence Government gained strength ; and hence
Religion sought and found defence ;
Hence England's fairest fame arose,
And Liberty subdued her foes.
　　On a low, simple, turf-made throne,

[188] Wilkes, against the advice of his friends, erected a private print-ing press at his house in Great George Street, Westminster, in order to re-print *The North Briton*. He also had printed there twelve copies of the ' Essay on Woman.'

[200] Dryden Leach, a printer in Crane Court, Fleet Street. He was arrested, together with his staff, under a general warrant on the charge of being concerned in the printing of *The North Briton*. His innocence was soon apparent, and the same morning Kearsly, the actual pub-lisher, was arrested. He gave information that Balfe (of the Old Bailey) was the printer, that Wilkes had given orders for the printing, and that Churchill received the profits. He refused to name the author, but Philip Carteret Webb, Solicitor to the Treasury, decided that his evidence was sufficient to incriminate Wilkes. Balfe and his men were arrested, and action taken against Wilkes, all under the same general warrant. Leach recovered heavy damages against the King's Messengers who had taken him into custody.

[205] Early editions read ' was ' instead of ' gained.'

Raised by Allegiance, scarcely known   210
From her attendants, glad to be
Pattern of that equality
She wished to all, so far as could
Safely consist with social good,
The goddess sat ; around her head
A cheerful radiance Glory spread :
Courage, a youth of royal race,
Lovelily stern, possessed a place
On her left hand ; and on her right
Sat Honour, clothed with robes of light ;   220
Before her Magna Carta lay,
Which some great lawyer, of his day
The Pratt, was officed to explain
And make the basis of her reign :
Peace, crowned with olive, to her breast
Two smiling, twin-born infants prest ;
At her feet couching, War was laid,
And with a brindled lion played :
Justice and Mercy, hand in hand,
Joint guardians of the happy land,   230
Together held their mighty charge,
And Truth walked all about at large ;
Health for the royal troop the feast
Prepared, and Virtue was high priest.
    Such was the fame our goddess bore,
Her temple such, in days of yore.
What changes ruthless Time presents !
Behold her ruined battlements,
Her walls decayed, her nodding spires,
Her altars broke, her dying fires,   240
Her name despised, her priests destroyed,
Her friends disgraced, her foes employed,
Herself (by ministerial arts
Deprived e'en of the people's hearts,
Whilst they, to work her surer woe,
Feign her to monarchy a foe)
Exiled by grief, self-doomed to dwell

[223] Charles Pratt, Lord Camden. (See note on the ' Epistle to Hogarth,' line 408.)

291

With some poor hermit in a cell ;
Or, that retirement tedious grown,
If she walks forth, she walks unknown;   250
Hooted, and pointed at with scorn
As one in some strange country born.
   Behold a rude and ruffian race,
A band of spoilers, seize her place :
With looks, which might the heart dis-seat,
And make life sound a quick retreat;
To rapine from the cradle bred,
A staunch old blood-hound at their head,
Who, free from virtue and from awe,
Knew none but the bad part of law,   260
They roved at large ; each on his breast
Marked with a greyhound, stood confest :
Controlment waited on their nod
High wielding persecution's rod ;
Confusion followed at their heels,
And a cast statesman held the seals ;
Those seals, for which he dear shall pay,
When awful Justice takes her day.
   The Printers saw—they saw and fled ;
Science, declining, hung her head ;   270
Property in despair appeared,
And for herself destruction feared
Whilst, underfoot, the rude slaves trod
The works of men, and word of God ;
Whilst, close behind, on many a book,
In which he never deigns to look,
Which he did not, nay—could not read,
A bold, bad man (by pow'r decreed
For that bad end, who in the dark
Scorned to do mischief) set his mark   280

[253] Nathan Carrington and his King's Messengers. The famous General Warrant against the authors, printers and publishers of No. 45 of *The North Briton*, was issued to ' Nathan Carrington, John Money, James Watson and Robert Blackmore, four of His Majesty's Messengers-in-Ordinary.'

[262] The Messengers wore a silver greyhound as an emblem of dispatch.

[266] Lord Egremont or Lord Halifax, both Secretaries of State.

In the full day, the mark of Hell,
And on the Gospel stamped an L.
   Liberty fled, her friends withdrew ;
Her friends, a faithful, chosen few ;
Honour in grief threw up, and Shame,
Clothing herself with Honour's name,
Usurped his station ; on the throne
Which Liberty once called her own,
(Gods ! that such mighty ills should spring
Under so great, so good a king,   290
So loved, so loving, through the arts
Of statesmen, cursed with wicked hearts !)
For every darker purpose fit,
Behold in triumph State-craft sit.

BOOK THREE

Ah me ! what mighty perils wait
The man who meddles with a state,
Whether to strengthen, or oppose !
False are his friends, and firm his foes :
How must his soul, once ventured in,
Plunge blindly on from sin to sin !
What toils he suffers, what disgrace,
To get, and then to keep, a place !
How often, whether wrong or right,
Must he in jest or earnest fight,   10
Risking for those both life and limb
Who would not risk one groat for him !
   Under the temple lay a cave,
Made by some guilty, coward slave,
Whose actions feared rebuke, a maze
Of intricate and winding ways,
Not to be found without a clue ;
One passage only, known to few,
In paths direct led to a cell,
Where Fraud in secret loved to dwell,   20
With all her tools and slaves about her,

[282] ' L for Libell.' (Gray.)

Nor feared lest Honesty should rout her.
  In a dark corner, shunning sight
Of man, and shrinking from the light,
One dull, dim taper through the cell
Glimmering, to make more horrible
The face of darkness, she prepares,
Working unseen, all kinds of snares
With curious, but destructive art.
Here, through the eye to catch the heart,   30
Gay stars their tinsel beams afford,
Neat artifice to trap a lord ;
There, fit for all whom Folly bred,
Wave plumes of feathers for the head ;
Garters the hag contrives to make,
Which, as it seems, a babe might break,
But which ambitious madmen feel
More firm and sure than chains of steel ;
Which, slipped just underneath the knee,
Forbid a freeman to be free.   40
Purses she knew (did ever curse
Travel more sure than in a purse ?)
Which, by some strange and magic bands,
Enslave the soul, and tie the hands.
  Here Flattery, eldest born of Guile,
Weaves with rare skill the silken smile,
The courtly cringe, the supple bow,
The private squeeze, the levee vow,
With which, no strange or recent case,
Fools in, deceive fools out of place.   50
  Corruption (who in former times,
Through fear or shame concealed her crimes,
And what she did, contrived to do it
So that the public might not view it)
Presumptuous grown, unfit was held
For their dark councils, and expelled ;
Since in the day her business might
Be done as safe as in the night.
  Her eye down bending to the ground,
Planning some dark and deadly wound,   60
Holding a dagger, on which stood,

294

All fresh and reeking, drops of blood ;
Bearing a lanthorn, which of yore,
By Treason borrowed, Guy Fawkes bore,
By which, since they improved in trade.
Excisemen have their lanthorns made,
Assassination, her whole mind,
Blood-thirsting, on her arm reclined :
Death, grinning, at her elbow stood,
And held forth instruments of blood,   70
Vile instruments, which cowards choose,
But men of honour dare not use.
Around, his Lordship and his Grace,
Both qualified for such a place,
With many a Forbes, and many a Dun,
Each a resolved, and pious son,
Wait her high bidding ; each prepared
As she around her orders shared,
Proof 'gainst remorse, to run, to fly,
And bid the destined victim die,   80
Posting on Villainy's black wing,
Whether he patriot is, or king.
　　Oppression, willing to appear
An object of our love, not fear,
Or, at the most, a reverend awe
To breed, usurped the garb of Law ;
A book she held, on which her eyes

⁶⁶ ' Excisemen.' (See note on ' Epistle to Hogarth,' line 186.)

⁷⁵ Captain Forbes, a Scottish Officer in the French service, met
Wilkes in Paris, and challenged him for his insults to Scotland.
Wilkes declined on the ground that he had already challenged Lord
Egremont, and that that nobleman must take precedence, but pro-
mised to fight Forbes immediately afterwards. The French authorities
intervened and Forbes disappeared. However, Lord Egremont dying
suddenly, Wilkes remembered his promise, and spent three weeks
searching for the Scottish Captain. Failing to find him, he wrote to
Forbes' second, Murray, offering to meet his challenger at Menin, ' the
first town in Austrian Flanders.' Wilkes waited one day at Menin,
but no one came. He thereupon set off ' to Dunkerque, to Calais, to
London, and to Churchill.' Forbes followed him to London, but was
again frustrated.

⁷⁵ Alexander Dun was a mad Scotsman who, in 1763, attempted
to force his way into Wilkes's house in George Street in order to murder
him. His friends undertook to put him under restraint.

Were deeply fixed, whence seemed to rise
Joy in her breast ; a book of might
Most wonderful, which black to white   90
Could turn, and without help of laws,
Could make the worse the better cause.
She read, by flattering hopes deceived ;
She wished, and what she wished, believed,
To make that book for ever stand
The rule of wrong through all the land ;
On the back, fair and worthy note,
At large was Magna Charta wrote,
But turn your eye within, and read,
A bitter lesson, Norton's Creed.   100
Ready, e'en with a look, to run,
Fast as the coursers of the sun,
To worry Virtue, at her hand
Two half-starved greyhounds took their stand.
A curious model, cut in wood,
Of a most ancient castle stood
Full in her view ; the gates were barr'd,
And soldiers on the watch kept guard ;
In the front openly, in black
Was wrote, The Tower ; but on the back,   110
Marked with a Secretary's seal,
In bloody letters, The Bastile.
    Around a table, fully bent
On mischief of most black intent,
Deeply determined, that their reign
Might longer last, to work the bane
Of one firm patriot, whose heart, tied
To honour, all their power defied,
And brought those actions into light
They wished to have concealed in night,   120
Begot, born, bred to infamy,
A privy council sat of three:
Great were their names, of high repute

---

[100] See note on the ' Epistle to Hogarth,' line 75.
[112] The Bastile, founded in 1370, was taken by the Revolutionaries in 1789, and demolished in 1790 as the very symbol of arbitrary imprisonment.

And favour through the land of Bute,
  The first (entitled to the place
Of honour both by gown and grace,
Who never let occasion slip
To take right hand of fellowship,
And was so proud, that should he meet
The Twelve Apostles in the street,   130
He'd turn his nose up at them all,
And shove his Saviour from the wall ;
Who was so mean (Meanness and Pride
Still go together side to side)
That he would cringe, and creep, be civil,
And hold a stirrup for the devil,
If in a journey to his mind,
He'd let him mount and ride behind ;
Who basely fawned through all his life,

[125] William Warburton (1698-1779), Bishop of Gloucester and Dean of Bristol, was born at Newark, and was chiefly educated there. In 1714 he was articled to an attorney for five years, but decided to take orders, and at the end of 1723 was ordained deacon. Sir Robert Sutton obtained for him the living of Greaseley in Nottinghamshire, and in 1728 presented him to that of Brant Broughton, near Newark, then worth £560 a year. Warburton applied himself to intensive study, and gradually made the acquaintance of literary men. In 1736 appeared his ' Alliance Between Church and State,' and in the following year the first part of his ' Divine Legation of Moses Demonstrated.' This was marked by the dogmatic arrogance, paradoxical arguments and curious learning characteristic of all his later work. He soon became involved in innumerable controversies, but struck up an unexpected alliance with Pope, whose authorised commentator he became. Pope introduced him to Ralph Allen, of Prior Park, near Bath, and on September 5th, 1745, he married Allen's favourite niece, Gertrude Tucker. Pope having died in 1744, Warburton brought out an edition of the ' Dunciad ' and in 1751 one of the ' Works,' using the notes as an opportunity for attacking his own enemies. In 1747 he edited the works of Shakespeare, and when the incompetence of this performance was exposed by Thomas Edwards, he attacked the latter in a new edition of Pope. Through the influence of powerful friends, Warburton became Bishop of Gloucester at the end of 1759. In 1763 he spoke in the House of Lords against ' The Essay on Woman,' the notes to which had been ironically attributed to him. In 1764 Ralph Allen died, leaving £5,000 each to Warburton and his wife. A further £3000 a year came to them two years later on the death of Mrs. Allen. Warburton's latter years were saddened by the fate of his only son, who died of consumption four years before the Bishop. His wife married again and lived until 1796.

For patrons first, then for a wife ;   140
Wrote Dedications which must make
The heart of every Christian quake ;
Made one man equal to, or more
Than God, then left him, as before
His God he left, and, drawn by pride,
Shifted about to t'other side ;)
Was by his sire a parson made,
Merely to give the boy a trade ;
But he himself was thereto drawn
By some faint omens of the lawn,   150
And on the truly Christian plan
To make himself a gentleman,
A title in which form arrayed him,
Though Fate ne'er thought on't when she made him.
   The oaths he took, 'tis very true,
But took them as all wise men do,
With an intent, if things should turn,
Rather to temporize, than burn.
Gospel and loyalty were made
To serve the purposes of trade :   160
Religion's are but paper ties,
Which bind the fool, but which the wise,
Such idle notions far above,
Draw on and off, just like a glove :
All gods, all kings, (let his great aim
Be answered) were to him the same.
   A curate first, he read and read,
And laid in, whilst he should have fed
The souls of his neglected flock,
Of reading such a mighty stock,   170
That he o'ercharged the weary brain
With more than she could well contain ;

---

140 ' He first made his court to Mr. Pope, and was introduced by
him to Mr. Allen of Bath, whose niece, Miss Tucker, he married. On
Allen's death, he succeeded to the greatest part of his fortune.' (Gray.)

143 ' Mr. Pitt.' (Gray.)

147 ' A mistake. He was not bred to the Church but to the Law.'
(Gray.) Churchill corrected this mistake in later writings. (See the
' Dedication to Warburton,' line 158.)

More than she was with spirits fraught
To turn and methodize to thought,
And which, like ill-digested food,
To humours turned, and not to blood.
Brought up to London, from the plow
And pulpit, how to make a bow
He tried to learn ; he grew polite,
And was the poet's parasite.   180
With wits conversing (and wits then
Were to be found 'mongst noblemen)
He caught, or would have caught, the flame,
And would be nothing, or the same.
He drank with drunkards, lived with sinners,
Herded with infidels for dinners ;
With such an emphasis and grace
Blasphemed, that Potter kept not pace :
He, in the highest reign of noon,
Bawled bawdy songs to a psalm tune ;   190
Lived with men infamous and vile,
Trucked his salvation for a smile ;
To catch their humour caught their plan,
And laughed at God to laugh with man ;
Praised them, when living, in each breath,
And damned their memories after death.

[188] Thomas Potter (1718-1759) was the second son of John Potter, Archbishop of Canterbury. Owing to the marriage of his elder brother with a bedmaker at Oxford, and consequent disinheritance by his father, the younger brother was wealthy and influential. He had brilliant talents, but was of dissolute character, and he is usually regarded as the evil genius of Wilkes. From 1747 until 1754 he sat in Parliament for the Cornish borough of St. Germain, and from 1754 until 1757 for Aylesbury. He allied himself with Pitt, and in the latter year he arranged for Wilkes to have his seat at Aylesbury, while he stood for Okehampden, which Pitt exchanged for Bath. The transaction cost Wilkes £7000, and was responsible for many of his subsequent embarrassments. Potter introduced him to money-lenders and also to the Medmenham Abbey set. It is now generally admitted (see ' Notes and Queries,' 2nd series IV, pp. 1-2, 41-43) that Potter was the author of the 'Essay on Woman' printed on Wilkes' private press. The character of the burlesque notes attributed to Warburton points to the same conclusion. Potter had met Warburton at the house of Ralph Allen, near Bath, and Walpole calls Potter ' the gallant of Warburton's wife.' Wilkes and Churchill repeat the same scandal, *ad nauseam*. (See note on line 242 below.)

To prove his faith, which all admit
Is at least equal to his wit,
And make himself a man of note,
He in defence of Scripture wrote :   200
So long he wrote, and long about it,
That e'en believers 'gan to doubt it :
He wrote, too, of the inward light,
Though no one knew how he came by't,
And of that influencing grace
Which in his life ne'er found a place :
He wrote, too, of the Holy Ghost,
Of whom no more than doth a post
He knew, nor, should an angel shew him,
Would he or know, or choose to know him.   210
    Next (for he knew 'twixt every science
There was a natural alliance)
He wrote, to advance his Maker's praise,
Comments on rhymes, and notes on plays,
And with an all-sufficient air
Placed himself in the critic's chair,
Usurped o'er reason full dominion,
And governed merely by opinion.
At length dethroned, and kept in awe
By one plain, simple man of law,   220
He armed dead friends, to vengeance true,
To abuse the man they never knew.
    Examine strictly all mankind,
Most characters are mixed we find,
And vice and virtue take their turn
In the same breast to beat and burn.
Our priest was an exception here,
Nor did one spark of grace appear,

200 An allusion to Warburton's ' Divine Legation of Moses.'

212 A reference to Warburton's ' The Alliance Between Church and State, or the necessity of an established religion and a Test Act,' 1736.

214 *i.e.*, comments on Pope and notes on Shakespeare.

220 Thomas Edwards, of Lincoln's Inn, attacked Warburton in a work entitled ' Canons of Criticism.' Warburton replied, very roughly, in a note in the next edition of ' The Dunciad ' and thus ' armed dead friends . . . to abuse the man they never knew.'

Not one dull, dim spark in his soul ;
Vice, glorious vice possessed the whole,   230
And, in her service truly warm,
He was in sin most uniform.
    Injurious Satire, own at least
One snivelling virtue in the priest,
One snivelling virtue, which is placed
They say, in or about the waist,
Called Chastity ; the prudish dame,
Knows it at large by Virtue's name.
To this his wife, (and in these days
Wives seldom without reason praise)   240
Bears evidence—then calls her child,
And swears that Tom was vastly wild.
    Ripened by a long course of years,
He great and perfect now appears.
In shape scarce of the human kind,
A man, without a manly mind ;
No husband, though he's truly wed ;
Though on his knees a child is bred,
No father ; injured, without end
A foe ; and though obliged, no friend ;   250
A heart, which virtue ne'er disgraced ;
A head, where learning runs to waste ;
A gentleman well-bred, if breeding
Rests in the article of reading ;
A man of this world, for the next
Was ne'er included in his text ;
A judge of genius, though confessed
With not one spark of genius blessed ;
Amongst the first of critics placed,
Though free from every taint of taste ;   260
A Christian without faith or works,
As he would be a Turk 'mongst Turks ;
A great divine, as lords agree,
Without the least divinity.
To crown all in declining age,

---

[242] A bitter sneer at Warburton. ' Tom ' is Thomas Potter (see note
on line 188 above), and Churchill here implies that Potter was the
father of Mrs. Warburton's only son.

Inflamed with church and party rage,
Behold him, full and perfect quite,
A false saint, and true hypocrite.
    Next sat a lawyer, often tried
In perilous extremes ; when Pride   270
And Power, all wild and trembling, stood,
Nor dared to tempt the raging flood,
This bold, bad man arose to view,
And gave his hand to help them through :
Steeled 'gainst compassion, as they past
He saw poor Freedom breathe her last ;
He saw her struggle, heard her groan ;
He saw her helpless and alone,
Whelmed in that storm, which, feared, and praised
By slaves less bold, himself had raised.   280
    Bred to the law, he from the first
Of all bad lawyers was the worst.
Perfection (for bad men maintain
In ill we may perfection gain)
In others is a work of time,
And they creep on from crime to crime ;
He, for a prodigy designed
To spread amazement o'er mankind,
Started full ripened all at once
A perfect knave, and perfect dunce.   290
    Who will, for him, may boast of sense,
His better guard is impudence ;
His front, with tenfold plates of brass
Secured, Shame never yet could pass ;
Nor on the surface of his skin
Blush for that guilt which dwelt within.
How often, in contempt of laws,
To sound the bottom of a cause,
To search out every rotten part,
And worm into its very heart,   300
Hath he ta'en briefs on false pretence,
And undertaken the defence
Of trusting fools, whom in the end

269 Sir Fletcher Norton. (See note on 'The Ghost,' Book III,
line 1144.)

302

He meant to ruin, not defend !
How often, e'en in open court,
Hath the wretch made his shame his sport,
And laughed off, with a villain's ease,
Throwing up briefs, and keeping fees !
Such things as, though to roguery bred,
Had struck a little villain dead.   310
    Causes, whatever their import,
He undertakes, to serve a court ;
For he by heart this rule had got,—
Power can effect what law cannot.
    Fools he forgives, but rogues he fears ;
If Genius, yoked with Worth, appears,
His weak soul sickens at the sight
And strives to plunge them down in night.
So loud he talks, so very loud,
He is an angel with the crowd,   320
Whilst he makes Justice hang her head,
And judges turn from pale to red.
    Bid all that Nature, on a plan
Most intimate, makes dear to man,
All that with grand and general ties
Binds good and bad, the fool and wise,
Knock at his heart ; they knock in vain ;
No entrance there such suitors gain ;
Bid kneeling kings forsake the throne,
Bid at his feet his country groan ;   330
Bid Liberty stretch out her hands,
Religion plead her stronger bands ;
Bid parents, children, wife, and friends ;
If they come thwart his private ends,
Unmoved he hears the general call,
And bravely tramples on them all.
    Who will, for him, may cant and whine,
And let weak Conscience with her line
Chalk out their ways ; such starving rules
Are only fit for coward fools ;   340
Fellows who credit what priests tell,
And tremble at the thoughts of hell ;
His spirit dares contend with Grace,

303

And meets Damnation face to face.
　Such was our lawyer ; by his side,
In all bad qualities allied,
In all bad counsels, sat a third,
By birth a lord ; O sacred word !
O word most sacred, whence men get
A privilege to run in debt ;　　　　　　　　　　　　350
Whence they at large exemption claim
From Satire, and her servant Shame ;
Whence they, deprived of all her force,
Forbid bold Truth to hold her course.
　Consult his person, dress, and air,
He seems, which strangers well might swear,
The master, or, by courtesy,
The captain of a colliery.
Look at his visage, and agree
Half-hanged he seems, just from the tree　　　　　360
Escaped ; a rope may sometimes break,
Or men be cut down by mistake.
　He hath not virtue (in the school
Of Vice bred up) to live by rule ;
Nor hath he sense (which none can doubt
Who know the man) to live without.
His life is a continued scene
Of all that's infamous and mean ;
He knows not change, unless grown nice
And delicate, from vice to vice ;　　　　　　　　370
Nature designed him, in a rage,
To be the Wharton of his age,

347 Lord Sandwich. (See note on ' Gotham,' Book I, line 464.)

355 Sandwich's personal appearance was certainly unprepossessing.
He had an awkward, shambling gait, and a hang-dog expression,
although perhaps the portrait by Gainsborough in the Painted Hall at
Greenwich does him less than justice, owing to the fading of the flesh-
tints.

372 Philip, Duke of Wharton (1698-1731), made a Fleet marriage, at
the age of 16, with the daughter of Major-General Richard Holmes,
but deserted her almost immediately. A year later he succeeded to
the Marquisate and £14,000 a year. In 1716 he went abroad with a
tutor in order to be educated in Protestant principles at Geneva, but
he broke away from his mentor, went to Lyons and began to intrigue
with the Pretender. He visited the widow of James II at St. Germains,

But having given all the sin,
Forgot to put the virtues in.
To run a horse, to make a match,
To revel deep, to roar a catch ;
To knock a tottering watchman down,
To sweat a woman of the Town ;
By fits to keep the peace, or break it,
In turn to give a pox, or take it,   380
He is, in faith, most excellent,
And, in the word's most full intent,
A true Choice Spirit we admit.
With wits a fool, with fools a wit,
Hear him but talk, and you would swear
Obscenity herself was there ;
And that Profaneness had made choice,
By way of trump, to use his voice ;
That, in all mean and low things great,
He had been bred at Billingsgate ;   390
And that, ascending to the earth
Before the season of his birth,
Blasphemy, making way and room,
Had marked him in his mother's womb.
Too honest (for the worst of men
In forms are honest now and then)
Not to have, in the usual way,
His bills sent in ; too great to pay ;
Too proud to speak to, if he meets

and borrowed £2,000 to promote the Jacobite cause, but on his return
to England he abandoned the Pretender's interests entirely. In 1717
he was allowed to take his seat in the Irish House of Peers, where he
supported the government, and early in the following year was created
a duke. In 1719 he took his seat in the House of Lords, and threw
himself into violent opposition. In private life he was dissipated to a
degree, becoming notorious as the president of the ' Hell Fire Club,'
and squandering the last fragments of his estate. He made, however,
a very able speech in favour of Atterbury. In 1725 he went to Vienna
and supported the cause of ' James III,' from whom he received the
Garter and a patent as Duke of Northumberland. He was converted
to Catholicism, and served in the Spanish army at the siege of Gibral-
tar. For this he was outlawed by the House of Lords on April 3rd,
1729. His last few years were spent in drunkenness and destitution,
and he died, aged 32, in the Franciscan Monastery at Poblet, in Spain,
when all his titles became extinct.

The honest tradesman whom he cheats ;   400
Too infamous to have a friend ;
Too bad for bad men to commend,
Or good to name ; beneath whose weight
Earth groans ; who hath been spared by Fate
Only to shew, on mercy's plan,
How far and long God bears with man.
　　Such were the three who, mocking sleep,
At midnight sat, in counsel deep,
Plotting destruction 'gainst a head
Whose wisdom could not be misled ;   410
Plotting destruction 'gainst a heart
Which ne'er from honour would depart.
　　' Is he not ranked amongst our foes ?
Hath not his spirit dared oppose
Our dearest measures, made our name
Stand forward on the roll of shame ?
Hath he not won the vulgar tribes,
By scorning menaces and bribes,
And proving, that his darling cause
Is of their liberties and laws   420
To stand the champion ? In a word,
Nor need one argument be heard
Beyond this to awake our zeal,
To quicken our resolves, and steel
Our steady souls to bloody bent,
(Sure ruin to each dear intent,
Each flattering hope) he, without fear,
Hath dared to make the truth appear.'
　　They said, and, by resentment taught,
Each on revenge employed his thought ;   430
Each, bent on mischief, racked his brain
To her full stretch, but racked in vain ;
Scheme after scheme they brought to view ;
All were examined ; none would do :
When Fraud, with pleasure in her face,
Forth issued from her hiding place,
And at the table where they meet,
First having blest them, took her seat.
' No trifling cause, my darling Boys !

Your present thoughts and cares employs ;   440
No common snare, no random blow,
Can work the bane of such a foe ;
By Nature cautious as he's brave,
To honour only he's a slave ;
In that weak part without defence,
We must to honour make pretence ;
That lure shall to his ruin draw
The wretch, who stands secure in law :
Nor think that I have idly planned
This full-ripe scheme ; behold at hand   450
With three months' training on his head,
An instrument, whom I have bred,
Born of these bowels, far from sight
Of virtue's false, but glaring light,
My youngest born, my dearest joy,
Most like myself, my darling boy :
He, never touched with vile remorse,
Resolved and crafty in his course,
Shall work our ends, complete our schemes,
Most mine, when most he Honour's seems ;   460
Nor can be found, at home, abroad,
So firm and full a slave of Fraud.'
    She said, and from each envious son
A discontented murmur run
Around the table ; all in place
Thought his full praise their own disgrace,
Wondering what stranger she had got,
Who had one vice that they had not ;
When straight the portals open flew,
And, clad in armour, to their view   470
Martin, the Duellist, came forth ;
All knew, and all confessed his worth ;
All justified, with smiles arrayed,
The happy choice their dam had made.

GOTHAM

BOOK ONE *

FAR off (no matter whether east or west,
A real country, or one made in jest),
Not yet by modern Mandevilles disgraced,
Nor by map-jobbers wretchedly misplaced,
There lies an island, neither great nor small,
Which, for distinction sake, I Gotham call.
The man who finds an unknown country out,
By giving it a name, acquires, no doubt,
A Gospel title, though the people there
The pious Christian thinks not worth his care ;   10
Bar this pretence, and into air is hurl'd
The claim of Europe to the Western world.
Cast by a tempest on the savage coast,
Some roving buccaneer set up a post ;
A beam, in proper form transversely laid,
Of his Redeemer's cross the figure made,
Of that Redeemer, with whose laws his life,
From first to last, had been one scene of strife ;
His royal master's name thereon engraved,
Without more process, the whole race enslaved,   20
Cut off that charter they from Nature drew,
And made them slaves to men they never knew.

* First published on February 21st, 1764. 'Printed for the Author
and sold by W. Flexney .... G. Kearsley .... C. Henderson ....
J. Coote .... J. Gardiner .... and J. Almon.' The Second Book was
published on March 28th.

³ Sir John Mandeville, the reputed author of a 14th century book
of travels.

⁶ Gotham is a parish six miles south of Nottingham, proverbial for
the simplicity of its inhabitants, a simplicity which is said to have been
simulated in order to avert the anger of a king. 'The Towneley
Mysteries' mention the 'foles of Gotham' and a collection of stories
about Gotham was made at the beginning of the 16th century. 'A
Knacke to know a Knave' (1594) contains a reference to Gotham, and
Mrs. Centlivre's farce, 'Gotham Election,' was produced in 1715.
Churchill uses the word rather in the sense of Utopia, an imaginary
land of which he himself is king.

Search ancient histories, consult records,
Under this title the most Christian lords
Hold (thanks to conscience) more than half the ball ;
O'erthrow this title, they have none at all ;
For never yet might any monarch dare,
Who lived to truth, and breathed a Christian air,
Pretend that Christ, (who came, we all agree,
To bless his people, and to set them free)   30
To make a convert ever one law gave
By which converters made him first a slave.
   Spite of the glosses of a canting priest,
Who talks of charity, but means a feast ;
Who recommends it (whilst he seems to feel
The holy glowings of a real zeal)
To all his hearers, as a deed of worth,
To give them heaven, whom they have robb'd of earth,
Never shall one, one truly honest man,
Who, bless'd with Liberty, reveres her plan,   40
Allow one moment, that a savage sire
Could from his wretched race, for childish hire,
By a wild grant, their all, their freedom pass,
And sell his country for a bit of glass.
   Or grant this barbarous right, let Spain and France,
In slavery bred, as purchasers advance ;
Let them, whilst conscience is at distance hurl'd,
With some gay bauble buy a golden world :
An Englishman, in charter'd freedom born,
Shall spurn the slavish merchandize, shall scorn   50
To take from others, through base private views,
What he himself would rather die, than lose.
   Happy the savage of those early times,
Ere Europe's sons were known, and Europe's crimes !
Gold, cursed gold ! slept in the womb of earth,
Unfelt its mischiefs, as unknown its worth ;
In full content he found the truest wealth ;
In toil he found diversion, food, and health ;
Stranger to ease and luxury of courts,
His sports were labours, and his labours sports   60
His youth was hardy, and his old age green ;
Life's morn was vigorous, and her eve serene ;

No rules he held, but what were made for use,
No arts he learn'd, nor ills which arts produce ;
False lights he follow'd, but believed them true ;
He knew not much, but lived to what he knew.
Happy, thrice happy, now the savage race,
Since Europe took their gold, and gave them grace !
Pastors she sends to help them in their need,
Some who can't write, with others who can't read ;   70
And on sure grounds the Gospel pile to rear,
Sends missionary felons every year ;
Our vices, with more zeal than holy prayers,
She teaches them, and in return takes theirs :
Her rank oppressions give them cause to rise ;
Her want of prudence, means and arms supplies,
Whilst her brave rage, not satisfied with life,
Rising in blood, adopts the scalping-knife :
Knowledge she gives, enough to make them know
How abject is their state, how deep their woe ;   80
The worth of freedom strongly she explains,
Whilst she bows down and loads their necks with chains:
Faith, too, she plants, for her own ends imprest,
To make them bear the worst and hope the best ;
And whilst she teaches, on vile interest's plan,
As laws of God, the wild decrees of man,
Like Pharisees, of whom the Scriptures tell,
She makes them ten times more the sons of Hell.
But whither do these grave reflections tend ?
Are they design'd for any, or no end ?   90
Briefly but this—to prove, that by no act
Which Nature made, that by no equal pact
'Twixt man and man, which might, if Justice heard,
Stand good ; that by no benefits conferr'd,
Or purchase made, Europe in chains can hold
The sons of India, and her mines of gold.
Chance led her there in an accursèd hour ;
She saw, and made the country hers by power ;
Nor drawn by virtue's love from love of fame,
Shall my rash folly controvert the claim,   100
Or wish in thought that title overthrown

[72] ' Missionary felons,' *i.e.*, transported criminals.

Which coincides with, and involves my own.
   Europe discover'd India first ; I found
My right to Gotham on the self-same ground ;
I first discover'd it, nor shall that plea
To her be granted, and denied to me ;
I plead possession, and, till one more bold
Shall drive me out will that possession hold.
With Europe's rights my kindred rights I twine ;
Hers be the Western world, be Gotham mine.   110

   Rejoice, ye happy Gothamites, rejoice ;
Lift up your voice on high, a mighty voice,
The voice of gladness ; and on every tongue,
In strains of gratitude, be praises hung,
The praises of so great and good a king ;
Shall Churchill reign, and shall not Gotham sing ?

   As on a day, a high and holy day,
Let every instrument of music play,
Ancient and modern ; those which drew their birth
(Punctilios laid aside) from Pagan earth,   120
As well as those by Christian made and Jew,
Those known to many, and those known to few ;
Those which in whim and frolic lightly float,
And those which swell the slow and solemn note ;
Those which (whilst Reason stands in wonder by)
Make some complexions laugh and others cry ;
Those which, by some strange faculty of sound,
Can build walls up, and raze them to the ground ;
Those, which can tear up forests by the roots,
And make brutes dance like men, and men like brutes ;
Those which, whilst Ridicule leads up the dance,   131
Make clowns of Monmouth ape the fops of France ;
Those which, where Lady Dulness with Lord Mayors
Presides, disdaining light and trifling airs,
Hallow the feast with psalmody, and those
Which, planted in our churches to dispose

---

[120] In the first edition ' aside ' was misprinted ' wide.'

[132] Churchill on a tour with his mistress spent some time at Monmouth and seems to have been unfavourably impressed by the place.

And lift the mind to Heaven, are disgraced
With what a foppish organist calls Taste :
All, from the fiddle (on which every fool,
The pert son of dull sire, discharged from school,   140
Serves an apprenticeship in college ease,
And rises through the gamut to degrees)
To those which (though less common, not less sweet)
From famed Saint Giles's, and more famed Vine Street,
(Where Heaven, the utmost wish of Man to grant,
Gave me an old house, and an older aunt)
Thornton, whilst Humour pointed out the road
To her arch-cub, hath hitch'd into an ode ;
All instruments, (attend, ye listening Spheres,
Attend, ye sons of men, and hear with ears)   150
All instruments, (nor shall they seek one hand
Impress'd from modern Music's coxcomb band)
All instruments, self-acted, at my name
Shall pour forth harmony, and loud proclaim,
Loud but yet sweet, to the according globe,
My praises, whilst gay nature, in a robe,
A coxcomb doctor's robe, to the full sound
Keeps time, like Boyce, and the world dances round.

Rejoice, ye happy Gothamites ! rejoice ;

[144] Churchill was born in Vine Street, Westminster.

[147] Bonnell Thornton (1724-1768) was educated at Westminster School with Cowper, and through him became a friend, later, of Robert Lloyd and of George Colman the elder. In partnership with the latter he conducted a paper called *The Connoisseur*, and another called *The St. James's Chronicle*. Lloyd addressed to him in 1760 the poem ' The Actor.' His burlesque ' Ode on St. Cecilia's Day ' was set to music and performed at Ranelagh in 1763. This is the ' Ode ' referred to by Churchill. Thornton was a convivial soul and one of the members of the ' Nonsense Club.' He was buried in the east cloister of Westminster Abbey.

[158] William Boyce (1710-1779), one of the greatest English composers, is remembered not only for his own works, but for his editing of ' Cathedral Music,' (1st Vol. 1760). He occupies something of the same position in sacred music as that occupied by Arne in secular. However, he did a certain amount of work for the stage, notably, for Garrick's pantomime, ' Harlequin's Invasion,' which contains the still popular song ' Hearts of Oak.' Boyce also wrote music for ' The Tempest,' ' Cymbeline,' ' Winter's Tale,' and ' Romeo and Juliet.'

Lift up your voice on high, a mighty voice,   160
The voice of gladness ; and on every tongue,
In strains of gratitude, be praises hung,
The praises of so great and good a king :
Shall Churchill reign, and shall not Gotham sing ?

   Infancy, straining backward from the breast
Tetchy and wayward, what he loveth best
Refusing in his fits, whilst all the while
The mother eyes the wrangler with a smile,
And the fond father sits on t'other side,
Laughs at his moods, and views his spleen with pride, 170
Shall murmur forth my name, whilst at his hand
Nurse stands interpreter through Gotham's land.
   Childhood, who like an April morn appears,
Sunshine and rain, hopes clouded o'er with fears,
Pleased and displeased by starts, in passion warm,
In reason weak ; who wrought into a storm,
Like to the fretful billows of the deep,
Soon spends his rage, and cries himself asleep ;
Who, with a feverish appetite oppress'd,
For trifles sighs, but hates them when possess'd,   180
His trembling lash suspended in the air,
Half-bent, and stroking back his long, lank hair,
Shall to his mates look up with eager glee,
And let his top go down to prate of me.
   Youth, who, fierce, fickle, insolent and vain,
Impatient urges on to Manhood's reign,
Impatient urges on, yet, with a cast
Of dear regard, looks back on Childhood past,
In the mid-chase, when the hot blood runs high,
And the quick spirits mount into his eye ;   190
When pleasure, which he deems his greatest wealth,
Beats in his heart, and paints his cheeks with health ;
When the chafed steed tugs proudly at the rein,
And, ere he starts, hath run o'er half the plain ;
When, wing'd with fear, the stag flies full in view,
And in full cry the eager hounds pursue,
Shall shout my praise to hills which shout again,
And e'en the huntsman stop to cry Amen.

Manhood, of form erect, who would not bow
Though worlds should crack around him ; on his brow
Wisdom serene, to passion giving law,   201
Bespeaking love, and yet commanding awe ;
Dignity into grace by mildness wrought ;
Courage attemper'd, and refined by thought :
Virtue supreme enthroned, within his breast
The image of his Maker deep imprest ;
Lord of this earth, which trembles at his nod,
With reason bless'd, and only less than God :
Manhood, though weeping Beauty kneels for aid,
Though Honour calls, in Danger's form array'd,   210
Though clothed with sackcloth, Justice in the gates,
By wicked elders chain'd, Redemption waits,
Manhood shall steal an hour, a little hour,
(Is't not a little one ?) to hail my power.
Old Age, a second child, by Nature curst
With more and greater evils than the first :
Weak, sickly, full of pains, in every breath
Railing at life, and yet afraid of death ;
Putting things off, with sage and solemn air,
From day to day, without one day to spare ;   220
Without enjoyment covetous of pelf,
Tiresome to friends, and tiresome to himself ;
His faculties impair'd, his temper sour'd,
His memory of recent things devour'd
E'en with the acting, on his shatter'd brain,
Though the false registers of youth remain ;
From morn to evening babbling forth vain praise
Of those rare men, who lived in those rare days,
When he, the hero of his tale, was young ;
Dull repetitions faltering on his tongue ;   230
Praising gray hairs, sure mark of Wisdom's sway,
E'en whilst he curses Time, which made him gray ;
Scoffing at youth, e'en whilst he would afford
All but his gold to have his youth restored,
Shall for a moment, from himself set free,
Lean on his crutch, and pipe forth praise to me.

[226] The first edition reads ' stale register.'

Rejoice, ye happy Gothamites ! rejoice ;
Lift up your voice on high, a mighty voice,
The voice of gladness ; and on every tongue,
In strains of gratitude, be praises hung,   240
The praises of so great and good a king ;
Shall Churchill reign, and shall not Gotham sing ?

 Things without life shall in this chorus join,
And, dumb to others' praise, be loud in mine.
 The snow-drop, who in habit white and plain,
Comes on, the herald of fair Flora's train ;
The coxcomb crocus, flower of simple note,
Who, by her side struts in a herald's coat ;
The tulip, idly glaring to the view,
Who, though no clown, his birth from Holland drew ; 250
Who, once full-dress'd, fears from his place to stir,
The fop of flowers, the More of a parterre ;
The woodbine, who her elm in marriage meets,
And brings her dowry in surrounding sweets ;
The lily, silver mistress of the vale,
The rose of Sharon, which perfumes the gale ;
The jessamine, with which the queen of flowers
To charm her god adorns his favourite bowers,
Which brides, by the plain hand of Neatness drest,
Unenvied rival, wear upon their breast,   260
Sweet as the incense of the morn, and chaste
As the pure zone which circles Dian's waist ;
All flowers of various names, and various forms,
Which the sun into strength and beauty warms,
From the dwarf daisy, which, like infants, clings,
And fears to leave the earth from whence it springs,
To the proud giant of the garden race,
Who, madly rushing to the sun's embrace,
O'ertops her fellows with aspiring aim,
Demands his wedded love, and bears his name ; 270
All, one and all, shall in this chorus join,
And, dumb to others' praise, be loud in mine.

 Rejoice, ye happy Gothamites ! rejoice ;
[252] More ; an unidentified dandy of the period.

315

Lift up your voice on high, a mighty voice,
The voice of gladness ; and on every tongue,
In strains of gratitude, be praises hung,
The praises of so great and good a king ;
Shall Churchill reign, and shall not Gotham sing ?

Forming a gloom, through which, to spleen-struck
    minds,
Religion, horror stamp'd, a passage finds,   280
The ivy crawling o'er the hallow'd cell
Where some old hermit's wont his beads to tell
By day, by night ; the myrtle ever green,
Beneath whose shade Love holds his rites unseen ;
The willow, weeping o'er the fatal wave
Where many a lover finds a watery grave ;
The cypress, sacred held when lovers mourn
Their true love snatch'd away ; the laurel worn
By poets in old time, but destined now,
In grief to wither on a Whitehead's brow ;   290
The fig, which, large as what in India grows,
Itself a grove, gave our first parents clothes ;
The vine, which, like a blushing, new-made bride,
Clustering, empurples all the mountain's side ;
The yew, which in the place of sculptured stone,
Marks out the resting-place of men unknown ;
The hedge-row elm, the pine, of mountain race ;
The fir, the Scotch fir, never out of place ;
The cedar, whose top mates the highest cloud,
Whilst his old father Lebanon grows proud   300
Of such a child, and his vast body laid
Out many a mile, enjoys the filial shade ;
The oak, when living, monarch of the wood ;
The English oak, which, dead, commands the flood ;
All, one and all, shall in this chorus join,
And dumb to others' praise, be loud in mine.

Rejoice, ye happy Gothamites ! rejoice ;
Lift up your voice on high, a mighty voice,

[290] William Whitehead, Poet Laureate. (See note on ' The Ghost,'
Book III, line 117.)

The voice of gladness ; and on every tongue,
In strains of gratitude, be praises hung,   310
The praises of so great and good a king ;
Shall Churchill reign, and shall not Gotham sing ?

  The showers, which make the young hills, like **young**
      lambs,
Bound and rebound ; the old hills, like old rams,
Unwieldy, jump for joy ; the streams, which glide,
Whilst Plenty marches smiling by their side,
And from their bosom rising Commerce springs ;
The winds, which rise with healing on their wings,
Before whose cleansing breath Contagion flies ;
The sun, who, travelling in eastern skies,   320
Fresh, full of strength, just risen from his bed,
Though in Jove's pastures they were born and bred,
With voice and whip can scarce make his steeds stir,
Step by step, up the perpendicular ;
Who, at the hour of eve, panting for rest,
Rolls on amain, and gallops down the west
As fast as Jehu, oil'd for Ahab's sin,
Drove for a crown, or postboys for an inn ;
The moon, who holds o'er night her silver reign,
Regent of tides, and mistress of the brain ;   330
Who to her sons, those sons who own her power
And do her homage at the midnight hour,
Gives madness as a blessing, but dispenses
Wisdom to fools, and damns them with their senses ;
The stars, who, by I know not what strange right,
Preside o'er mortals in their own despite,
Who, without reason, govern those who most
(How truly, judge from thence !) of reason boast,
And, by some mighty magic yet unknown,
Our actions guide, yet cannot guide their own ;   340
All, one and all, shall in this chorus join,
And, dumb to others' praise, be loud in mine.

  Rejoice, ye happy Gothamites ! rejoice ;
Lift up your voice on high, a mighty voice,
The voice of gladness ; and on every tongue,

In strains of gratitude, be praises hung,
The praises of so great and good a king ;
Shall Churchill reign, and shall not Gotham sing ?

The moment, minute, hour, day, week, month, year,
Morning and eve, as they in turn appear ;   350
Moments and minutes, which, without a crime,
Can't be omitted in accounts of time,
Or, if omitted, (proof we might afford)
Worthy by parliaments to be restored ;
The hours, which, dress'd by turns in black and white,
Ordain'd as handmaids, wait on day and night ;
The day, those hours, I mean, when light presides,
And Business in a cart with Prudence rides ;
The night, those hours, I mean, with darkness hung,
When Sense speaks free, and Folly holds her tongue ;
The morn, when Nature, rousing from her strife   361
With death-like sleep, awakes to second life ;
The eve, when, as unequal to the task,
She mercy from her foe descends to ask ;
The week, in which six days are kindly given
To think of earth, and one to think of heaven ;
The months, twelve sisters, all of different hue,
Though there appears in all a likeness too ;
Not such a likeness as, through Hayman's works,
Dull Mannerist ! in Christians, Jews, and Turks,   370
Cloys with a sameness in each female face ;
But a strange something, born of Art and Grace,
Which speaks them all, to vary and adorn,
At different times of the same parents born ;
All, one and all, shall in this chorus join,
And, dumb to others' praise, be loud in mine.

Rejoice, ye happy Gothamites ! rejoice ;
Lift up your voice on high, a mighty voice,

[369] Francis Hayman (1708-1776) was a pupil of Robert Brown, and
after leaving him was employed by the booksellers to illustrate Shake-
speare, Milton, Pope, etc. He painted the decorations at Vauxhall,
where his illustrations to ' Henry IV ' in the Prince's pavilion were
particularly admired. He was occasionally employed by Fleetwood
as a scene painter at Drury Lane.

The voice of gladness ; and on every tongue,
In strains of gratitude, be praises hung,   380
The praises of so great and good a king ;
Shall Churchill reign, and shall not Gotham sing ?

Frore January, leader of the year,
Minced-pies in van and calves' heads in the rear ;
Dull February, in whose leaden reign
My mother bore a bard without a brain ;
March, various, fierce, and wild, with wind-crack'd cheeks,
By wilder Welshmen led, and crown'd with leeks ;
April, with fools, and May, with bastards blest ;
June, with White Roses on her rebel breast ;   390
July, to whom, the Dog-star in her train,

³⁸³ Frore, *i.e.*, frozen.

³⁸⁴ ' Roundheads used to celebrate the anniversary of Charles the
First's execution by having a calf's head on table.' (Tooke.)   Charles
was executed on January 30th, 1649.

³⁸⁶ Churchill was born in February, 1731.

³⁸⁸ On March 1st, St. David's Day, Welshmen eat leeks.

³⁸⁹ The licence practised at May Day celebrations was one of the
reasons for Puritan hostility.   The bastards referred to would pre-
sumably be conceived and not born in May.   If this seems a little far-
fetched, the reader may see in the line an allusion to Bute, who was
born on May 25th, 1713, and although not himself a bastard, was the
representative of the illegitimate Stuart line, the founder of his family
being John Steuart, natural son of King Robert II of Scotland.

³⁹⁰ June 10th was the Young Pretender's birthday, on which day
Jacobite sympathisers wore a white rose.

³⁹¹ The greater dog-star is Sirius, the lesser Procyon, and the dog-
days, calculated as depending on one or the other are variously reck-
oned at from thirty to fifty-four days.   In the latitude of Greenwich,
the cosmical rising of Procyon now takes place about July 27, that of
Sirius about August 11 ; in Mediterranean latitudes, the former is
somewhat later, the latter earlier.   The heliacal rising is some days
later than the cosmical; and all the phenomena now take place
later in the year than in ancient times, owing to the precession of the
equinoxes.   Thus very different dates have been assigned for the dog-
days, their beginning ranging from July 3rd to August 15th.   In cur-
rent almanacs they are said to begin on July 3rd and to end on August
11th, (*i.e.*, to be the forty days preceding the cosmical rising of Sirius).
The name arose from the pernicious qualities of the season being
attributed to the ' influence ' of the Dog-star, but it has long been
popularly associated with the belief that at this season dogs are most
apt to run mad.

Saint James gives oysters, and Saint Swithin rain ;
August, who, banish'd from her Smithfield stand,
To Chelsea flies, with Doggett in her hand ;
September, when by custom (right divine)
Geese are ordain'd to bleed at Michael's shrine,
Whilst the priest, not so full of grace as wit,
Falls to unbless'd, nor gives the saint a bit ;
October, who the cause of freedom join'd,
And gave a second George to bless mankind ;   400
November, who, at once to grace our earth,
Saint Andrew boasts, and our Augusta's birth ;
December, last of months, but best, who gave
A Christ to man, a Saviour to the slave,
Whilst, falsely grateful, man, at the full feast,
To do God honour makes himself a beast ;
All, one and all, shall in this chorus join,
And, dumb to others' praise, be loud in mine.

Rejoice, ye happy Gothamites ! rejoice ;
Lift up your voice on high, a mighty voice,   410

[392] July 25th is the feast of St. James the Apostle, who is usually
represented as a pilgrim with staff and shell. July 15th is St. Swithin's
Day ; it is popularly supposed that if it rains on this day it will rain
for forty days after.

[393] Bartholomew Fair opened on the eve of the Saint's festival—24th
August. (See note on ' The Rosciad,' line 31.)

[394] Thomas Doggett was born in Dublin and died in 1721. He was
an actor from 1691 to 1713 and in 1716 established a rowing match on
the Thames every 1st August, the prize being an orange-coloured
livery and a badge, in honour of George I. The contest is still held
under the auspices of the Fishmongers' Company.

[396] The feast of St. Michael and All Angels, commonly called
Michaelmas Day (29th September), is a festival in both the Roman and
the Anglican Churches. In England it is one of the Quarter Days on
which rents are paid, and on which it was customary to eat a goose at
dinner.

[400] George II was born on October 30th, 1683.

[402] St. Andrew's day is November 30th.

[402] Augusta, daughter of Frederick, Duke of Saxe-Gotha, and wife
of Frederick, Prince of Wales, was born on November 30th, 1719. It
is strange that Churchill should speak of her so favourably, seeing that
she was the close friend of Bute. Scandal even accused her of being
his mistress, hence the petticoat and jack-boot placed on poles by the
mob in the London streets. She died on January 8th, 1772.

The voice of gladness ; and on every tongue,
In strains of gratitude, be praises hung,
The praises of so great and good a king ;
Shall Churchill reign, and shall not Gotham sing ?

The seasons as they roll ; Spring, by her side
Lechery and Lent, lay-folly and church-pride,
By a rank monk to copulation led,
A tub of sainted salt-fish on her head ;
Summer, in light, transparent gauze array'd,
Like maids of honour at a masquerade,   420
In bawdry gauze, for which our daughters leave
The fig, more modest, first brought up by Eve,
Panting for breath, inflamed with lustful fires,
Yet wanting strength to perfect her desires,
Leaning on Sloth, who, fainting with the heat,
Stops at each step, and slumbers on his feet ;
Autumn, when Nature, who with sorrow feels
Her dread foe Winter treading on her heels,
Makes up in value what she wants in length,
Exerts her powers, and puts forth all her strength,   430
Bids corn and fruits in full perfection rise,
Corn fairly tax'd, and fruits without excise ;
Winter, benumb'd with cold, no longer known

[420] Elizabeth Chudleigh (1720-1788), Countess of Bristol, calling
herself Duchess of Kingston, was a beautiful girl who, in 1743,
through the influence of William Pulteney, was appointed maid of
honour to Augusta, Princess of Wales. In 1744 she was married
privately to the Hon. Augustus John Hervey, grandson of the Earl of
Bristol. She soon quarrelled with him and continued to be known as
Miss Chudleigh. At the court of Leicester House she became notorious
for her loose behaviour, appearing in 1749 at a masked ball as Iphi-
genia, so naked (says Horace Walpole) that you would have taken her
for Andromeda. About 1760 she became the mistress of Evelyn
Pierrepont, second Duke of Kingston, and in the same year gave a
magnificent ball in honour of the birthday of the Princess of Wales. In
Churchill's time she was at the height of her notoriety and splendour.
In 1769 she contracted a bigamous marriage with the Duke of King-
ston, for which she was tried in 1776, and convicted, but left in pos-
session of her fortune. The rest of her life she spent on the continent,
and she died in Paris on August 26th, 1788.

[432] A reference to the tax on cider and perry imposed in 1763. It
was repealed, in deference to popular clamour, in 1766.

By robes of fur, since furs became our own ;
A hag, who, loathing all, by all is loath'd,
With weekly, daily, hourly, libels clothed,
Vile Faction at her heels, who, mighty grown,
Would rule the ruler, and foreclose the throne,
Would turn all state affairs into a trade,
Make laws one day, the next to be unmade,   440
Beggar at home a people fear'd abroad,
And, force defeated, make them slaves by fraud ;
All, one and all, shall in this chorus join,
And, dumb to others' praise, be loud in mine.

Rejoice, ye happy Gothamites ! rejoice ;
Lift up your voice on high, a mighty voice,
The voice of gladness ; and on every tongue,
In strains of gratitude, be praises hung,
The praises of so great and good a king ;
Shall Churchill reign, and shall not Gotham sing ?   450

The year, grand circle ! in whose ample round
The seasons regular and fix'd are bound,
Who, in his course repeated o'er and o'er,
Sees the same things which he had seen before ;
(The same stars keep their watch, and the same sun
Runs in the track where he from first hath run ;
The same moon rules the night ; tides ebb and flow,
Man is a puppet and this world a show ;
Their old, dull follies, old, dull fools pursue,
And vice in nothing, but in mode, is new ;   460
He, —— a lord (now fair befal that pride,

⁴³⁴ Canada was ceded to Great Britain in 1763, but the price of
furs in London remained high.
⁴⁶¹ There is only space for one syllable and it is almost certain that
the missing name is Bubb, *i.e.*, George Bubb-Dodington, Lord
Melcombe (1691-1762), famous for his wealth, ostentation and the
readiness with which he supported first one political party, then
another. He took his seat in Parliament in 1715, was made Lord
Lieutenant of Somersetshire in 1721 and became a Lord of the
Treasury, in succession to Henry Pelham, in 1724. His influence lay
largely in the Parliamentary boroughs he controlled. He patronized
literary men, including Fielding, Thomson, Mallet, and Paul White-
head. The last two names are sufficient to explain Churchill's hostility,

He lived a villain, but a lord he died)
Dashwood is pious, Berkeley fix'd as Fate,
Sandwich (thank Heaven !) first Minister of State,
And, though by fools despised, by saints unbless'd,
By friends neglected, and by foes oppress'd,
Scorning the servile arts of each court elf,
Founded on honour, Wilkes is still himself)
The year, encircled with the various train
Which waits, and fills the glories of his reign,   470
Shall, taking up this theme, in chorus join,
And, dumb to others' praise, be loud in mine.

  Rejoice, ye happy Gothamites ! rejoice ;
Lift up your voice on high, a mighty voice,
The voice of gladness ; and on every tongue,
In strains of gratitude, be praises hung,

although Dodington was a tempting mark for any satirist. Before
correcting the final proof the present editor had the opportunity of
consulting Mr. Iolo Williams' copy of the 'Works' of Churchill for-
merly in the Wodhull collection, and was glad to note that Wodhull
agrees in filling up this blank with the name Bubb.

  [463] Sir Francis Dashwood, Lord Le Despencer. (See note on ' The
Ghost,' Book IV, line 628.)

  [463] ' Colonel Norbone Berkeley, in whose favour the extinct barony
of Bottetourt was revived. . . . The Colonel was second to Lord
Talbot in his duel with Mr. Wilkes. The words in the text allude to
the expression contained in the following letter addressed by the
Colonel to the Freeholders of Gloucestershire.
                                              ' April 4, 1763.
' Gentlemen, Though I am fixed as fate to abide by the determination
of the General Meeting of April 13, permit me to declare my wishes
that Lord Coleraine may be the object of your choice, as I know him
to be a man of honour and principle ' . . . etc. (Tooke.)

  [464] John Montagu (1718-1792), fourth Earl of Sandwich, succeeded
to the peerage at the age of eleven, and after some years at Eton and
Trinity College, Cambridge, started on a prolonged ' grand tour ' in
1737. On his return to England he plunged into politics, and in 1744
became a Lord Commissioner of the Admiralty. He was dismissed in
1751, but in 1755 became a joint Vice-Treasurer of Ireland, and in
1763 Ambassador Extraordinary to the Court of Madrid. Before he
could sail, however, he was nominated First Lord of the Admiralty,
and in August of the same year one of the principal Secretaries of
State. He had been a Medmenham monk in company with Wilkes,
and therefore his denunciation of the latter in the House of Lords as
the author of the ' Essay on Woman ' astonished the public by its
hypocrisy and disloyalty.

The praises of so great and good a king ;
Shall Churchill reign, and shall not Gotham sing ?

Thus far in sport—nor let our critics hence,
Who sell out Monthly trash, and call it Sense,   480
Too lightly of our present labours deem,
Or judge at random of so high a theme ;
High is our theme, and worthy are the men
To feel the sharpest stroke of Satire's pen ;
But when kind Time a proper season brings,
In serious mood to treat of serious things,
Then shall they find, disdaining idle play,
That I can be as grave and dull as they.
Thus far in sport—nor let half patriots, (those
Who shrink from every blast of Power which blows,   490
Who, with tame cowardice familiar grown,
Would hear my thoughts, but fear to speak their own ;
Who, lest bold truths, to do sage Prudence spite,
Should burst the portals of their lips by night,
Tremble to trust themselves one hour in sleep)
Condemn our course, and hold our caution cheap ;
When brave Occasion bids, for some great end,
When honour calls the poet as a friend,
Then shall they find that, e'en on danger's brink,
He dares to speak what they scarce dare to think.

BOOK TWO *

How much mistaken are the men who think
That all who will without restraint may drink ;
May largely drink, e'en till their bowels burst,
Pleading no right but merely that of thirst,
At the pure waters of the living well,
Beside whose streams the Muses love to dwell !
Verse is with them a knack, an idle toy,
A rattle gilded o'er, on which a boy

* First published 28th March, 1764. 'Printed for the Author, and
sold by G. Kearsley .... W. Flexney .... C. Henderson .... J. Coote
.... and J. Almon.'

May play untaught; whilst, without art or force,
Make it but jingle, music comes of course.   10
    Little do such men know the toil, the pains,
The daily, nightly racking of the brains,
To range the thoughts, the matter to digest,
To cull fit phrases, and reject the rest;
To know the times when Humour on the cheek
Of Mirth may hold her sports; when Wit should speak,
And when be silent; when to use the powers
Of ornament, and how to place the flowers,
So that they neither give a tawdry glare,
' Nor waste their sweetness in the desert air; '   20
To form, (which few can do, and scarcely one,
One critic in an age, can find when done)
To form a plan, to strike a grand outline,
To fill it up, and make the picture shine
A full and perfect piece; to make coy Rhyme
Renounce her follies, and with Sense keep time;
To make proud Sense against her nature bend,
And wear the chains of Rhyme, yet call her friend.
    Some fops there are, amongst the scribbling tribe,
Who make it all their business to describe,   30
No matter whether in or out of place;
Studious of finery, and fond of lace,
Alike they trim, as coxcomb fancy brings,
The rags of beggars, and the robes of kings.
Let dull Propriety in state preside
O'er her dull children; Nature is their guide,
Wild Nature, who at random breaks the fence
Of those tame drudges, Judgment, Taste, and Sense,
Nor would forgive herself the mighty crime
Of keeping terms with person, place, and time.   40
    Let liquid gold emblaze the sun at noon,
With borrow'd beams let silver pale the moon;
Let surges hoarse lash the resounding shore,
Let streams meander, and let torrents roar;

[20] Churchill, although he here quotes the ' Elegy,' did not like Gray.
(See ' The Ghost,' Book II, line 518, and ' The Author,' line 121.)
The new ' sentiment ' represented by Gray and his school was repug-
nant to Churchill's somewhat brutal commonsense.

Let them breed up the melancholy breeze
To sigh with sighing, sob with sobbing trees ;
Let vales embroidery wear ; let flowers be tinged
With various tints ; let clouds be laced or fringed,
They have their wish ; like idle monarch boys,
Neglecting things of weight, they sigh for toys ;   50
Give them the crown, the sceptre, and the robe,
Who will may take the power, and rule the globe.
    Others there are who, in one solemn pace,
With as much zeal as Quakers rail at lace,
Railing at needful ornament, depend
On sense to bring them to their journey's end :
They would not (Heaven forbid !) their course delay,
Nor for a moment step out of the way,
To make the barren road those graces wear
Which Nature would, if pleased, have planted there.   60
    Vain Men ! who blindly thwarting Nature's plan,
Ne'er find a passage to the heart of man ;
Who, bred 'mongst fogs in academic land,
Scorn every thing they do not understand ;
Who, destitute of humour, wit, and taste,
Let all their little knowledge run to waste,
And frustrate each good purpose, whilst they wear
The robes of Learning with a sloven's air.
Though solid Reasoning arms each sterling line,
Though Truth declares aloud, ' This work is mine,'   70
Vice, whilst from page to page dull morals creep,
Throws by the book, and Virtue falls asleep.
    Sense, mere dull, formal Sense, in this gay town,
Must have some vehicle to pass her down ;
Nor can she for an hour insure her reign,
Unless she brings fair Pleasure in her train.
Let her from day to day, from year to year,
In all her grave solemnities appear,
And, with the voice of trumpets, through the streets,
Deal lectures out to every one she meets ;   80
Half who pass by are deaf, and t'other half
Can hear indeed, but only hear to laugh.
    Quit then, ye graver sons of letter'd Pride,
Taking for once Experience as a guide,

326

Quit this grand error, this dull college mode ;
Be your pursuits the same, but change the road ;
Write, or at least appear to write, with ease,
' And if you mean to profit, learn to please.'
In vain for such mistakes they pardon claim,
Because they wield the pen in Virtue's name :   90
Thrice sacred is that name, thrice bless'd the man
Who thinks, speaks, writes, and lives on such a plan !
This, in himself, himself of course must bless,
But cannot with the world promote success.
He may be strong, but, with effect to speak,
Should recollect his readers may be weak :
Plain rigid truths, which saints with comfort bear,
Will make the sinner tremble and despair.
True Virtue acts from love, and the great end
At which she nobly aims, is to amend ;   100
How then do those mistake, who arm her laws
With rigour not their own, and hurt the cause
They mean to help, whilst with a zealot rage
They make that goddess, whom they'd have engage
Our dearest love, in hideous terror rise !
Such may be honest, but they can't be wise.
   In her own full and perfect blaze of light
Virtue breaks forth too strong for human sight ;
The dazzled eye, that nice but weaker sense,
Shuts herself up in darkness for defence :   110
But to make strong conviction deeper sink,
To make the callous feel, the thoughtless think,
Like God made man, she lays her glory by,
And beams mild comfort on the ravish'd eye :
In earnest most when most she seems in jest,
She worms into, and winds around, the breast ;
To conquer vice, of vice appears the friend,
And seems unlike herself to gain her end.
The sons of Sin, to while away the time
Which lingers on their hands, of each black crime   120
To hush the painful memory, and keep
The tyrant Conscience in delusive sleep,
Read on at random, nor suspect the dart
Until they find it rooted in their heart.

'Gainst vice they give their vote, nor know at first
That, cursing that, themselves too they have curst ;
They see not till they fall into the snares—
Deluded into virtue unawares.
Thus the shrewd doctor, in the spleen-struck mind
When pregnant horror sits and broods o'er wind,   130
Discarding drugs, and striving how to please,
Lures on insensibly, by slow degrees,
The patient to those manly sports which bind
The slacken'd sinews, and relieve the mind ;
The patient feels a change as wrought by stealth,
And wonders on demand to find it health.

   Some few—whom Fate ordain'd to deal in rhymes
In other lands, and here, in other times ;
Whom, waiting at their birth, the midwife Muse
Sprinkled all over with Castalian dews ;   140
To whom true Genius gave his magic pen,
Whom Art by just degrees led up to men—
Some few, extremes well shunn'd, have steer'd between
These dangerous rocks, and held the golden mean :
Sense in their works maintains her proper state,
But never sleeps, or labours with her weight ;
Grace makes the whole look elegant and gay,
But never dares from Sense to run astray :
So nice the master's touch, so great his care,
The colours boldly glow, not idly glare ;   150
Mutually giving, and receiving aid,
They set each other off like light and shade,
And, as by stealth, with so much softness blend,
'Tis hard to say where they begin or end.
Both give us charms, and neither gives offence :
Sense perfects grace, and grace enlivens sense.

   Peace to the men who these high honours claim,
Health to their souls, and to their memories fame :
Be it my task, and no mean task, to teach
A reverence for that worth I cannot reach :   160
Let me at distance, with a steady eye,
Observe and mark their passage to the sky ;
From envy free, applaud such rising worth,
And praise their heaven though pinion'd down to earth.

Had I the power I could not have the time,
Whilst spirits flow, and life is in her prime,
Without a sin 'gainst pleasure, to design
A plan, to methodize each thought, each line,
Highly to finish, and make every grace,
In itself charming, take new charms from place.   170
Nothing of books, and little known of men,
When the mad fit comes on, I seize the pen,
Rough as they run, the rapid thoughts set down,
Rough as they run, discharge them on the town ;
Hence rude, unfinish'd brats, before their time,
Are born into this idle world of Rhyme,
And the poor slattern Muse is brought to bed
' With all her imperfections on her head.'
Some, as no life appears, no pulses play,
Through the dull dubious mass no breath makes way,
Doubt, greatly doubt, till for a glass they call,   181
Whether the child can be baptized at all.
Others, on other grounds objections frame,
And, granting that the child may have a name,
Doubt, as the sex might well a midwife pose,
Whether they should baptize it Verse or Prose.
    E'en what my masters please ; bards, mild, meek men,
In love to critics stumble now and then.
Something I do myself, and something too,
If they can do it, leave for them to do.   190
In the small compass of my careless page
Critics may find employment for an age :
Without my blunders they were all undone ;
I twenty feed where Mason can feed one.
    When Satire stoops, unmindful of her state,
To praise the man I love, curse him I hate ;
When sense, in tides of passion borne along,
Sinking to prose, degrades the name of song,
The censor smiles, and whilst my credit bleeds,
With as high relish on the carrion feeds   200
As the proud Earl fed at a turtle feast,
Who turn'd by gluttony to worse than beast,
Ate till his bowels gush'd upon the floor,
Yet still ate on, and dying call'd for more.

329

When loose Digression, like a colt unbroke,
Spurning connexion and her formal yoke,
Bounds through the forest, wanders far astray
From the known path, and loves to lose her way,
'Tis a full feast to all the mongrel pack
To run the rambler down and bring her back.   210
   When gay Description, Fancy's fairy child,
Wild without art, and yet with pleasure wild,
Waking with Nature at the morning hour
To the lark's call, walks o'er the opening flower
Which largely drank all night of heaven's fresh dew,
And, like a mountain nymph of Dian's crew,
So lightly walks she not one mark imprints,
Nor brushes off the dews, nor soils the tints ;
When thus Description sports, even at the time
That drums should beat and cannons roar in rhyme, 220
Critics can live on such a fault as that
From one month to the other and grow fat.
   Ye mighty Monthly Judges ! in a dearth
Of letter'd blockheads, conscious of the worth
Of my materials, which against your will
Oft you've confess'd, and shall confess it still ;
Materials rich, though rude, inflamed with thought,
Though more by fancy than by judgment wrought ;
Take, use them as your own, a work begin,
Which suits your genius well, and weave them in,   230
Framed for the critic loom with critic art,
Till thread on thread depending, part on part,
Colour with colour mingling, light with shade,
To your dull taste a formal work is made,
And, having wrought them into one grand piece,
Swear it surpasses Rome, and rivals Greece.
   Nor think this much, for at one single word,
Soon as the mighty critic fiat's heard,
Science attends their call ; their power is own'd ;
Order takes place, and Genius is dethroned ;   240
Letters dance into books, defiance hurl'd
At means, as atoms danced into a world.
   Me higher business calls, a greater plan,
Worthy man's whole employ, the good of man,

330

The good of man committed to my charge ;
If idle Fancy rambles forth at large,
Careless of such a trust, these harmless lays
May Friendship envy, and may Folly praise ;
The crown of Gotham may some Scot assume,
And vagrant Stuarts reign in Churchill's room.   250
    O my poor People ! O thou wretched Earth !
To whose dear love, though not engaged by birth,
My heart is fix'd, my service deeply sworn,
How, (by thy father can that thought be borne ?
For monarchs, would they all but think like me,
Are only fathers in the best degree)
How must thy glories fade, in every land
Thy name be laugh'd to scorn, thy mighty hand
Be shorten'd, and thy zeal, by foes confess'd,
Bless'd in thyself, to make thy neighbours bless'd,   260
Be robb'd of vigour ; how must Freedom's pile,
The boast of ages, which adorns the Isle,
And makes it great and glorious, fear'd abroad,
Happy at home, secure from force and fraud ;
How must that pile, by ancient Wisdom raised
On a firm rock, by friends admired and praised,
Envied by foes, and wonder'd at by all,
In one short moment into ruins fall,
Should any slip of Stuart's tyrant race,
Or bastard or legitimate, disgrace   270
Thy royal seat of empire ! but what care,
What sorrow, must be mine, what deep despair
And self-reproaches, should that hated line
Admittance gain through any fault of mine !
Cursed be the cause whence Gotham's evils spring,
Though that cursed cause be found in Gotham's king.
    Let war, with all his needy ruffian band,
In pomp of horror stalk through Gotham's land
Knee-deep in blood ; let all her stately towers
Sink in the dust ; that court which now is ours   280
Become a den, where beasts may, if they can,
A lodging find, nor fear rebuke from man ;
Where yellow harvests rise be brambles found ;

[270] Bute was the representative of the illegitimate Stuart line.

331

Where vines now creep let thistles curse the ground;
Dry in her thousand valleys be the rills;
Barren the cattle on her thousand hills:
Where Power is placed let tigers prowl for prey;
Where Justice lodges let wild asses bray;
Let cormorants in churches make their nest,
And on the sails of commerce bitterns rest;   290
Be all, though princes in the earth before,
Her merchants bankrupts, and her marts no more;
Much rather would I, might the will of Fate
Give me to choose, see Gotham's ruin'd state,
By ills on ills thus to the earth weigh'd down,
Than live to see a Stuart wear her crown.
　　Let Heaven in vengeance arm all Nature's host,
Those servants who their Maker know, who boast
Obedience as their glory, and fulfil,
Unquestion'd, their great Master's sacred will;   300
Let raging winds root up the boiling deep,
And, with destruction big, o'er Gotham sweep;
Let rains rush down, till Faith, with doubtful eye,
Looks for the sign of mercy in the sky;
Let Pestilence in all her horrors rise;
Where'er I turn, let Famine blast my eyes;
Let the earth yawn, and, ere they've time to think,
In the deep gulf let all my subjects sink
Before my eyes, whilst on the verge I reel;
Feeling, but as a monarch ought to feel,   310
Not for myself, but them,—I'll kiss the rod,
And, having own'd the justice of my God,
Myself with firmness to the ruin give,
And die with those for whom I wish to live.
　　This, (but may Heaven's more merciful decrees
Ne'er tempt his servant with such ills as these)
This, or my soul deceives me, I could bear;
But that the Stuart race my crown should wear,
That crown, where, highly cherish'd, Freedom shone
Bright as the glories of the mid-day sun;   320
Born and bred slaves, that they, with proud misrule,
Should make brave, freeborn men, like boys at school,
To the whip crouch and tremble—O, that thought!

332

The labouring brain is e'en to madness brought
By the dread vision ; at the mere surmise
The thronging spirits, as in tumult, rise ;
My heart as for a passage, loudly beats,
And turn me where I will, distraction meets.
 O, my brave fellows ! great in arts and arms,
The wonder of the earth, whom glory warms   330
To high achievements ; can your spirits bend,
Through base control (ye never can descend
So low by choice) to wear a tyrant's chain,
Or let in Freedom's seat a Stuart reign ?
If Fame, who hath for ages, far and wide,
Spread in all realms the cowardice, the pride,
The tyranny and falsehood of those lords,
Contents you not, search England's fair records ;
England, where first the breath of life I drew,
Where next to Gotham, my best love is due ; 340
There once they ruled ; though crush'd by William's
  hand,
They rule no more to curse that happy land.
 The first, who, from his native soil removed,
Held England's sceptre, a tame tyrant proved :
Virtue he lack'd, cursed with those thoughts which spring
In souls of vulgar stamp, to be a king :
Spirit he had not, though he laugh'd at laws,
To play the bold-faced tyrant with applause ;
On practices most mean he raised his pride,
And Craft oft gave what Wisdom oft denied. 350
 Ne'er could he feel how truly man is blest
In blessing those around him ; in his breast,
Crowded with follies, Honour found no room ;
Mark'd for a coward in his mother's womb,
He was too proud without affronts to live,
Too timorous to punish or forgive.
 To gain a crown, which had in course of time,
By fair descent been his without a crime,
He bore a mother's exile ; to secure
A greater crown, he basely could endure 360

[350] James I, ' the wisest fool in Christendom,' was inordinately proud of what he termed king-craft.

333

The spilling of her blood by foreign knife ;
Nor dared revenge her death, who gave him life ;
Nay, by fond Fear, and fond Ambition led,
Struck hands with those by whom her blood was shed.
Call'd up to power, scarce warm on England's throne,
He fill'd her court with beggars from his own :
Turn where you would the eye with Scots was caught,
Or English knaves, who would be Scotsmen thought.
To vain expense unbounded loose he gave,
The dupe of minions, and of slaves the slave ;   370
On false pretences mighty sums he raised,
And damn'd those senates rich, whom poor he praised :
From empire thrown, and doom'd to beg her bread,
On foreign bounty whilst a daughter fed,
He lavish'd sums, for her received, on men
Whose names would fix dishonour on my pen.
Lies were his playthings, parliaments his sport ;
Book-worms and catamites engross'd the court :
Vain of the scholar, like all Scotsmen since
The pedant scholar, he forgot the prince ;   380
And having with some trifles stored his brain,
Ne'er learn'd, nor wish'd to learn, the arts to reign.
Enough he knew to make him vain and proud,
Mock'd by the wise, the wonder of the crowd ;
False friend, false son, false father, and false king,
False wit, false statesman, and false everything :
When he should act he idly chose to prate,
And pamphlets wrote when he should save the state.
Religious, if religion holds in whim
To talk with all, he let all talk with him ;   390
Not on God's honour, but his own intent,

---

[374] James's daughter, Elizabeth, was married to Frederick, Elector Palatine, in 1613. Robert Carr, the favourite, was then at the height of his influence, but can hardly have secured any of the Princess's dowry. However, the benevolence which James exacted for the purpose of assisting Protestants in Cleves and Juliers was diverted to other purposes.

[388] James I wrote a number of pamphlets, e.g., ' A Discourse of the Manner of the Discovery of the Powder Treason ' (1605), ' An Apology for the Oath of Allegiance ' (1607), etc., in addition to his ' Demonology ' (1597) and ' Basilikon Doron ' (1599).

334

Not for religion's sake, but argument ;
More vain if some sly, artful, High-Dutch slave,
Or, from the Jesuit school, some precious knave
Conviction feign'd, than if, to peace restored
By his full soldiership, worlds hail'd him Lord.
   Power was his wish, unbounded as his will,
The power, without control, of doing ill ;
But what he wish'd, what he made bishops preach,
And statesmen warrant, hung within his reach,   400
He dared not seize ; fear gave, to gall his pride,
That freedom to the realm his will denied.
   Of treaties fond, o'erweening of his parts,
In every treaty, of his own mean arts
He fell the dupe : peace was his coward care,
E'en at a time when justice call'd for war:
His pen he'd draw to prove his lack of wit,
But rather than unsheath the sword, submit.
Truth fairly must record ; and, pleased to live
In league with mercy, justice may forgive   410
Kingdoms betray'd, and worlds resign'd to Spain,
But never can forgive a Raleigh slain.
   At length, (with white let Freedom mark that year)
Not fear'd by those whom most he wish'd to fear,
Nor loved by those whom most he wish'd to love,
He went to answer for his faults above,
To answer to that God from whom alone
He claim'd to hold and to abuse the throne,
Leaving behind, a curse to all his line,
The bloody legacy of Right Divine.   420
   With many virtues which a radiance fling
Round private men ; with few which grace a king,
And speak the monarch, at that time of life
When passion holds with reason doubtful strife,
Succeeded Charles, by a mean sire undone,
Who envied virtue even in a son.
   His youth was froward, turbulent, and wild ;
He took the man up ere he left the child ;
His soul was eager for imperial sway
Ere he had learn'd the lesson to obey.   430

[411] James I made peace with Spain in 1604.

335

Surrounded by a fawning, flattering throng,
Judgment each day grew weak, and humour strong ;
Wisdom was treated as a noisome weed,
And all his follies let to run to seed.
    What ills from such beginnings needs must spring !
What ills to such a land from such a king !
What could she hope ! what had she not to fear !
Base Buckingham possess'd his youthful ear ;
Strafford and Laud, when mounted on the throne,
Engross'd his love, and made him all their own ;   440
Strafford and Laud, who boldly dared avow
The traitorous doctrine taught by Tories now ;
Each strove t' undo him in his turn and hour,
The first with pleasure, and the last with power.
    Thinking (vain thought, disgraceful to the throne !)
That all mankind were made for kings alone,
That subjects were but slaves, and what was whim,
Or worse, in common men, was law in him ;
Drunk with Prerogative, which Fate decreed
To guard good kings, and tyrants to mislead,   450
Which in a fair proportion to deny
Allegiance dares not, which to hold too high
No good can wish, no coward king can dare,
And held too high no English subject bear ;
Besieged by men of deep and subtle arts,
Men void of principle, and damn'd with parts,
Who saw his weakness, made their king their tool,
Then most a slave when most he seem'd to rule ;
Taking all public steps for private ends,

---

[438] George Villiers supplanted Carr in the favour of the King, and in 1623 became Duke of Buckingham.

[439] Thomas Wentworth, Earl of Strafford (1593-1641) was opposed to the policy of James I and, until 1628-29, to that of Charles I. In 1628 he was raised to the peerage, and soon became Charles's chief adviser. In 1640 he was made Earl of Strafford and Lord Lieutenant of Ireland. He was impeached by the Long Parliament and condemned by a Bill of Attainder.

[439] William Laud (1573-1645), Archbishop of Canterbury in 1633. He supported Charles in his opposition to the Commons. He was impeached by the Long Parliament in December, 1640, and committed to the Tower in March, 1641, but his trial did not begin until 1644 and he was not executed until January, 1645.

Deceived by favourites, whom he call'd friends, 460
He had not strength enough of soul to find
That monarchs, meant as blessings to mankind,
Sink their great state, and stamp their fame undone,
When what was meant for all, they give to one.
Listening uxorious whilst a woman's prate
Modell'd the church and parcell'd out the state,
Whilst (in the state not more than women read)
High-churchmen preach'd, and turn'd his pious head ;
Tutor'd to see with ministerial eyes ;
Forbid to hear a loyal nation's cries ; 470
Made to believe (what can't a favourite do ?)
He heard a nation, hearing one or two ;
Taught by state-quacks himself secure to think,
And out of danger e'en on danger's brink ;
Whilst power was daily crumbling from his hand,
Whilst murmurs ran through an insulted land,
As if to sanction tyrants Heaven was bound,
He proudly sought the ruin which he found.
Twelve years, twelve tedious and inglorious years,
Did England, crush'd by power, and awed by fears, 480
Whilst proud Oppression struck at Freedom's root,
Lament her senates lost, her Hampden mute :
Illegal taxes and oppressive loans,
In spite of all her pride, call'd forth her groans ;
Patience was heard her griefs aloud to tell,
And Loyalty was tempted to rebel.
　　Each day new acts of outrage shook the state,
New courts were raised to give new doctrines weight ;

465 A reference to the influence of Henrietta Maria. Hume re-
marks : ' It is allowed that, being of a passionate temper, she precipi-
tated him into hasty and imprudent counsels. Her religion likewise,
to which she was much addicted, must be regarded as a great mis-
fortune, since it augmented the jealousy which prevailed against the
Court, and engaged her to procure for the Catholics some indulgences
which were generally distasteful to the nation.'

479 Charles I contrived to rule without a parliament from March,
1628, to April, 1640.

487 ' Arbitrary courts were erected, and the power of others en-
larged ; such were the high commission court, the star-chamber, the
court of honour, the court of wards, the court of requests, etc. Patents
and monopolies of almost every article were sold to individuals to the

State-Inquisitions kept the realm in awe,
And cursed Star-Chambers made or ruled the law ;   490
Juries were pack'd, and judges were unsound ;
Through the whole kingdom not one Pratt was found.
   From the first moments of his giddy youth
He hated senates, for they told him truth :
At length against his will compell'd to treat,
Those whom he could not fright he strove to cheat ;
With base dissembling every grievance heard,
And often giving, often broke his word.
Oh where shall hapless Truth for refuge fly,
If kings, who should protect her, dare to lie ?   500
   Those who, the general good their real aim,
Sought in their country's good their monarch's fame ;
Those who were anxious for his safety ; those
Who were induced by duty to oppose,
Their truth suspected, and their worth unknown,
He held as foes and traitors to his throne,
Nor found his fatal error till the hour
Of saving him was gone and past ; till power
Had shifted hands, to blast his hapless reign,
Making their faith and his repentance vain.   510
   Hence (be that curse confined to Gotham's foes)
War, dread to mention, civil war arose ;
All acts of outrage and all acts of shame
Stalk'd forth at large, disguised with honour's name ;
Rebellion, raising high her bloody hand,
Spread universal havoc through the land ;
With zeal for party, and with passion drunk,
In public rage all private love was sunk ;
Friend against friend, brother 'gainst brother stood,
And the son's weapon drank the father's blood ;   520
Nature, aghast, and fearful lest her reign
Should last no longer, bled in every vein.
   Unhappy Stuart ! harshly though that name

great injury of the public ; knighthood, coat and conduct money,
forced loans, benevolences, arbitrary imprisonments, billeting of
soldiers, martial law, and many other illegal methods were revived or
invented to extort money from the people, in order to support the pro-
fusion of the Court ! ' (Tooke.)

Grates on my ear, I should have died with shame
To see my king before his subjects stand,
And at their bar hold up his royal hand;
At their commands to hear the monarch plead,
By their decrees to see that monarch bleed.
What though thy faults were many and were great?
What though they shook the basis of the state?   530
In royalty secure thy person stood,
And sacred was the fountain of thy blood.
Vile ministers, who dared abuse their trust,
Who dared seduce a king to be unjust,
Vengeance, with justice leagued, with power made strong,
Had nobly crush'd; ' The king could do no wrong.'
     Yet grieve not, Charles, nor thy hard fortunes blame;
They took thy life, but they secured thy fame.
Their greater crimes made thine like specks appear,
From which the sun in glory is not clear.   540
Hadst thou in peace and years resign'd thy breath
At Nature's call; hadst thou laid down in death
As in a sleep, thy name by Justice borne
On the four winds, had been in pieces torn.
Pity, the virtue of a generous soul,
Sometimes the vice, hath made thy memory whole.
Misfortunes gave what virtue could not give,
And bade, the tyrant slain, the martyr live.
     Ye Princes of the earth! ye mighty few!
Who worlds subduing, can't yourselves subdue;   550
Who, goodness scorn'd, wish only to be great,
Whose breath is blasting, and whose voice is fate;
Who own no law, no reason, but your will,
And scorn restraint, though 'tis from doing ill;

---

548 Churchill, in spite of his political opinions, regarded Charles I
as a martyr. Wilkes did not. In a note on this passage he says: ' It
was the favourite maxim of Brutus, that those who live in defiance of
the laws, and cannot be brought to a trial, ought to be taken off without
a trial. He, therefore, first planned, executed and justified the death
of Caesar. The conduct of the English nation with regard to Charles I
is still clearer. His death can never be pretended to be an assassination.
Our genius shudders at a practice too frequent among our polite
neighbours. The king had a legal solemn trial, attended with all the
fairness, and even candour, which the circumstances of a people, still
in arms for their liberties, could permit.'

Who of all passions groan beneath the worst,
Then only bless'd when they make others curst ;
Think not, for wrongs like these, unscourged to live ;
Long may ye sin, and long may Heaven forgive ;
But when ye least expect, in sorrow's day,
Vengeance shall fall more heavy for delay ;   560
Nor think, that vengeance heap'd on you alone
Shall (poor amends) for injured worlds atone ;
No, like some base distemper, which remains,
Transmitted from the tainted father's veins
In the son's blood, such broad and general crimes
Shall call down vengeance e'en to latest times,
Call vengeance down on all who bear your name,
And make their portion bitterness and shame.
     From land to land for years compell'd to roam,
Whilst Usurpation lorded it at home ;   570
Of majesty unmindful, forced to fly,
Not daring, like a king, to reign or die ;
Recall'd to repossess his lawful throne
More at his people's seeking than his own,
Another Charles succeeded. In the school
Of travel he had learn'd to play the fool,
And like pert pupils with dull tutors sent
To shame their country on the Continent,
From love of England by long absence wean'd,
From every court he every folly glean'd,   580
And was, so close do evil habits cling,
Till crown'd a beggar, and when crown'd, no king.
     Those grand and general powers which Heaven design'd
An instance of his mercy to mankind
Were lost, in storms of dissipation hurl'd,
Nor would he give one hour to bless a world.
Lighter than Levity which strides the blast,
And of the present fond, forgets the past,
He changed and changed, but, every hope to curse,
Changed only from one folly to a worse :   590
State he resigned to those whom state could please ;
Careless of majesty, his wish was ease ;
Pleasure, and pleasure only, was his aim ;
Kings of less wit might hunt the bubble fame ;

Dignity through his reign was made a sport,
Nor dared Decorum shew her face at court :
Morality, was held a standing jest,
And faith, a necessary fraud at best :
Courtiers, their monarch ever in their view,
Possess'd great talents, and abused them too :   600
Whate'er was light, impertinent, and vain,
Whate'er was loose, indecent, and profane,
(So ripe was folly, folly to acquit)
Stood all absolved in that poor bauble, wit.
   In gratitude, alas ! but little read,
He let his father's servants beg their bread,
His father's faithful servants and his own,
To place the foes of both around his throne.
   Bad counsels he embraced through indolence,
Through love of ease, and not through want of sense ;
He saw them wrong, but rather let them go   611
As right, than take the pains to make them so.
   Women ruled all, and ministers of state
Were for commands at toilets forced to wait :
Women, who have as monarchs graced the land,
But never govern'd well at second hand.
   To make all other errors slight appear,
In memory fix'd stand Dunkirk and Tangier ;
In memory fix'd so deep, that time in vain
Shall strive to wipe those records from the brain,   620
Amboyna stands—Gods ! that a king could hold

---

[613] The most influential of Charles's mistresses was Louise de Kéroualle (Madam Carwell), afterwards Duchess of Portsmouth.

[618] Dunkirk was ceded to England in 1658, after the Battle of the Dunes, but was sold to the French by Charles II for £400,000.

[618] Tangier was part of the dowry brought by Catherine of Braganza to Charles II. The English garrison was recalled in 1684 in order to save the expense of keeping up the fortifications.

[621] Amboyna is an island in the Dutch East Indies. About 1615 the British formed a settlement on the island, which they retained until 1623 when it was destroyed by the Dutch, who inflicted frightful tortures on the unhappy settlers. In 1654, after many fruitless negotiations, Cromwell compelled the United Provinces to give the sum of £300,000, together with a small island, as compensation to the descendants of those who had suffered. In 1673 Dryden produced his tragedy of ' Amboyna, or the Cruelties of the Dutch to the English Merchants.'

In such high estimate vile, paltry gold,
And of his duty be so careless found,
That when the blood of subjects from the ground
For vengeance call'd, he should reject their cry,
And, bribed from honour, lay his thunders by,
Give Holland peace, whilst English victims groan'd,
And butcher'd subjects wander'd unatoned !
O dear, deep injury to England's fame,
To them, to us, to all ! to him deep shame !   630
Of all the passions which from frailty spring,
Avarice is that which least becomes a king.

To crown the whole, scorning the public good,
Which through his reign he little understood
Or little heeded, with too narrow aim
He reassumed a bigot brother's claim,
And having made time-serving senates bow,
Suddenly died, that brother best knew how.

No matter how—he slept amongst the dead,
And James his brother reignèd in his stead :   640
But such a reign—so glaring an offence
In every step 'gainst freedom, law, and sense,
'Gainst all the rights of Nature's general plan,
'Gainst all which constitutes an Englishman,
That the relation would mere fiction seem,
The mock creation of a poet's dream ;
And the poor bard's would, in this sceptic age,
Appear as false as *their* historian's page.

Ambitious folly seized the seat of wit,
Christians were forced by bigots to submit ;   650
Pride without sense, without religion zeal
Made daring inroads on the commonweal ;
Stern Persecution raised her iron rod,
And call'd the pride of kings the power of God ;

636 The first edition reads ' reassured.' The attempts of the Commons to exclude James from the throne on the ground of his Catholicism were successfully defeated by the manœuvres of Charles.

638 *i.e.*, Charles was poisoned by James—an accusation for which there is not one jot of evidence.

653 The penal laws were rigorously enforced against Protestant Nonconformists during James II's reign, although the king himself was willing to relax them as a cover for concessions to Catholics.

Conscience and fame were sacrificed to Rome,
And England wept at Freedom's sacred tomb.
   Her laws despised, her constitution wrench'd
From its due, natural frame, her rights retrench'd
Beyond a coward's sufferance ; conscience forced,
And healing justice from the crown divorced ;   660
Each moment pregnant with vile acts of power ;
Her patriot Bishops sentenced to the Tower ;
Her Oxford (who yet loves the Stuart name)
Branded with arbitrary marks of shame,
She wept—but wept not long ; to arms she flew,
At Honour's call the avenging sword she drew,
Turn'd all her terrors on the tyrant's head,
And sent him in despair to beg his bread ;
Whilst she, (may every state in such distress
Dare with such zeal, and meet with such success)   670
Whilst she, (may Gotham, should my abject mind
Choose to enslave rather than free mankind,
Pursue her steps, tear the proud tyrant down,
Nor let me wear if I abuse the crown)
Whilst she, (through every age in every land,
Written in gold, let Revolution stand)
Whilst she, secured in liberty and law,
Found what she sought, a saviour in Nassau.

[662] William Sancroft, Archbishop of Canterbury, Francis Turner,
Bishop of Ely, William Lloyd, Bishop of St. Asaph, Thomas Kenn,
Bishop of Bath and Wells, John Lake, Bishop of Chichester, Sir
Jonathan Trelawney, Bishop of Bristol, and Thomas White, Bishop of
Peterborough, protested against the king's second Declaration of
Indulgence (April 27th, 1688). They were confined to the Tower,
but acquitted on June 30th, 1688.

[663] In December, 1687, the Fellows of Magdalen, Oxford, were
expelled and the college converted into a Catholic seminary.

[678] *i.e.*, William of Orange-Nassau. He was the son of William II,
Stadholder of the United Netherlands, and Mary, daughter of Charles
I of England, and was styled Prince of Orange before his accession to
the English throne as William III.

BOOK THREE *

Can the fond mother from herself depart ?
Can she forget the darling of her heart,
The little darling whom she bore and bred,
Nursed on her knees, and at her bosom fed,
To whom she seem'd her every thought to give,
And in whose life alone she seem'd to live ?
Yes, from herself the mother may depart,
She may forget the darling of her heart,
The little darling whom she bore and bred,
Nursed on her knees, and at her bosom fed,   10
To whom she seem'd her every thought to give,
And in whose life, alone she seem'd to live ;
But I cannot forget, whilst life remains,
And pours her current through these swelling veins,
Whilst Memory offers up at Reason's shrine ;
But I cannot forget that Gotham's mine.
Can the stern mother, than the brutes more wild,
From her disnatured breast tear her young child,
Flesh of her flesh, and of her bone the bone,
And dash the smiling babe against a stone ?   20
Yes, the stern mother, than the brutes more wild,
From her disnatured breast may tear her child,
Flesh of her flesh, and of her bone the bone,
And dash the smiling babe against a stone ;
But I, (forbid it, Heav'n !) but I can ne'er
The love of Gotham from this bosom tear ;
Can ne'er so far true royalty pervert
From its fair course, to do my people hurt.
With how much ease, with how much confidence,
As if, superior to each grosser sense   30
Reason had only, in full power array'd,
To manifest her will, and be obey'd,

* First published on 10th August, 1764. 'Printed for the Author;
and sold by J. Almon.... J. Coote.... W. Flexney.... C.
Henderson.... J. Gardiner.... and C. Moran.'

[1] Cf. 'Can a woman forget her sucking child, that she should not
have compassion on the son of her womb ? yea, they may forget, yet
will I not forget thee.' (Isaiah, xlix, 15.)

344

Men make resolves, and pass into decrees
The motions of the mind ! with how much ease,
In such resolves, doth passion make a flaw,
And bring to nothing what was raised to law !
   In empire young, scarce warm on Gotham's throne,
The dangers and the sweets of power unknown,
Pleased, though I scarce know why, like some young child,
Whose little senses each new toy turns wild,   40
How do I hold sweet dalliance with my crown,
And wanton with dominion ; how lay down,
Without the sanction of a precedent,
Rules of most large and absolute extent ;
Rules, which from sense of public virtue spring,
And all at once commence a patriot king !
   But, for the day of trial is at hand,
And the whole fortunes of a mighty land
Are staked on me, and all their weal or woe
Must from my good or evil conduct flow,   50
Will I, or can I, on a fair review,
As I assume that name, deserve it too ?
Have I well weigh'd the great, the noble part
I'm now to play ? have I explored my heart,
That labyrinth of fraud, that deep, dark cell,
Where, unsuspected, e'en by me, may dwell
Ten thousand follies ? have I found out there
What I am fit to do, and what to bear ?
Have I traced every passion to its rise,
Nor spared one lurking seed of treach'rous vice ?   60
Have I familiar with my nature grown ?
And am I fairly to myself made known ?
   A patriot king—why, 'tis a name which bears
The more immediate stamp of Heaven ; which wears
The nearest, best resemblance we can shew
Of God above, through all his works below.
   To still the voice of discord in the land,
To make weak Faction's discontented band,
Detected, weak, and crumbling to decay,
With hunger pinch'd, on their own vitals prey ;   70
Like brethren, in the selfsame interests warm'd,

[63] Bolingbroke's ' Idea of a Patriot King ' was published in 1749.

345

Like different bodies with one soul inform'd,
To make a nation, nobly raised above
All meaner thought, grow up in common love ;
To give the laws due vigour, and to hold
That secret balance, temperate, yet bold,
With such an equal hand, that those who fear
May yet approve, and own my justice clear ;
To be a common father, to secure
The weak from violence, from pride the poor ;   80
Vice and her sons to banish in disgrace,
To make Corruption dread to shew her face ;
To bid afflicted Virtue take new state
And be, at last, acquainted with the great ;
Of all religions to elect the best,
Nor let her priests be made a standing jest ;
Rewards for worth with liberal hand to carve,
To love the arts, nor let the artists starve ;
To make fair plenty through the realm increase,
Give fame in war, and happiness in peace ;   90
To see my people virtuous, great and free,
And know that all those blessings flow from me ;
O ! 'tis a joy too exquisite, a thought
Which flatters Nature more than flattery ought ;
'Tis a great, glorious task, for man too hard,
But no less great, less glorious, the reward ;
The best reward which here to man is given,
'Tis more than earth, and little short of heaven ;
A task (if such comparison may be)
The same in nature, differing in degree,   100
Like that which God, on whom for aid I call,
Performs with ease, and yet performs to all.
    How much do they mistake, how little know
Of kings, of kingdoms, and the pains which flow
From royalty, who fancy that a crown,
Because it glistens, must be lined with down !
With outside shew, and vain appearance caught,
They look no farther, and, by Folly taught,
Prize high the toys of thrones, but never find
One of the many cares which lurk behind.   110
The gem they worship which a crown adorns,

Nor once suspect that crown is lined with thorns.
Oh, might reflection folly's place supply !
Would we one moment use her piercing eye,
Then should we find what woe from grandeur springs,
And learn to pity, not to envy kings.
   The villager, born humbly and bred hard,
Content his wealth, and Poverty his guard,
In action simply just, in conscience clear,
By guilt untainted, undisturb'd by fear,   120
His means but scanty, and his wants but few,
Labour his business, and his pleasure too,
Enjoys more comforts in a single hour
Than ages give the wretch condemn'd to power.
   Call'd up by health he rises with the day,
And goes to work, as if he went to play,
Whistling off toils, one half of which might make
The stoutest Atlas of a palace quake ;
'Gainst heat and cold, which make us cowards faint,
Harden'd by constant use, without complaint   130
He bears what we should think it death to bear :
Short are his meals, and homely is his fare ;
His thirst he slakes at some pure neighbouring brook,
Nor asks for sauce where Appetite stands cook.
When the dews fall, and when the sun retires
Behind the mountains, when the village fires,
Which, waken'd all at once, speak supper nigh,
At distance catch, and fix his longing eye,
Homeward he hies, and with his manly brood
Of raw-boned cubs enjoys that clean, coarse food   140
Which, season'd with good humour, his fond bride
'Gainst his return is happy to provide.
Then, free from care, and free from thought, he creeps
Into his straw, and till the morning sleeps.
   Not so the king—with anxious cares opprest
His bosom labours, and admits not rest :
A glorious wretch, he sweats beneath the weight
Of majesty, and gives up ease for state :
E'en when his smiles, which by the fools of pride
Are treasured and preserved, from side to side   150
Fly round the court, e'en when compell'd by form,

347

He seems most calm, his soul is in a storm ;
Care, like a spectre seen by him alone,
With all her nest of vipers, round his throne
By day crawls full in view ; when night bids sleep,
Sweet nurse of Nature, o'er the senses creep ;
When Misery herself no more complains,
And slaves, if possible, forget their chains,
Though his sense weakens, though his eyes grow dim,
That rest, which comes to all, comes not to him.   160
E'en at that hour, Care, tyrant Care, forbids
The dew of sleep to fall upon his lids ;
From night to night she watches at his bed ;
Now, as one moped, sits brooding o'er his head ;
Anon she starts, and, borne on raven's wings,
Croaks forth aloud—Sleep was not made for kings.
   Thrice hath the moon, who governs this vast ball,
Who rules most absolute o'er me and all ;
To whom, by full conviction taught to bow,
At new, at full, I pay the duteous vow ;   170
Thrice hath the moon her wonted course pursued,
Thrice hath she lost her form, and thrice renew'd,
Since, (blessed be that season, for before
I was a mere, mere mortal, and no more,
One of the herd, a lump of common clay,
Inform'd with life, to die and pass away)
Since I became a king, and Gotham's throne,
With full and ample power, became my own ;
Thrice hath the moon her wonted course pursued,
Thrice hath she lost her form, and thrice renew'd,   180
Since sleep, kind sleep, who like a friend supplies
New vigour for new toil, hath closed these eyes :
Nor, if my toils are answer'd with success,
And I am made an instrument to bless
The people whom I love, shall I repine ;
Theirs be the benefit, the labour mine.
   Mindful of that high rank in which I stand,
Of millions lord, sole ruler in the land,
Let me, and Reason shall her aid afford,
Rule my own spirit, of myself be lord.   190
With an ill grace that monarch wears his crown,

Who, stern and hard of nature, wears a frown
'Gainst faults in other men, yet all the while
Meets his own vices with a partial smile.
How can a king (yet on record we find
Such kings have been, such curses of mankind)
Enforce that law 'gainst some poor subject elf
Which Conscience tells him he hath broke himself?
Can he some petty rogue to justice call
For robbing one, when he himself robs all?   200
Must not, unless extinguish'd, conscience fly
Into his cheek, and blast his fading eye,
To scourge the oppressor, when the state, distress'd
And sunk to ruin, is by him oppress'd?
Against himself doth he not sentence give?
If one must die, t' other's not fit to live.
   Weak is that throne, and in itself unsound,
Which takes not solid virtue for its ground.
All envy power in others, and complain
Of that which they would perish to obtain.   210
Nor can those spirits, turbulent and bold,
Not to be awed by threats, nor bought with gold,
Be hush'd to peace but when fair, legal sway
Makes it their real interest to obey,
When kings,—and none but fools can then rebel,—
Not less in virtue, than in power, excel.
   Be that my object, that my constant care,
And may my soul's best wishes centre there;
Be it my task to seek, nor seek in vain,
Not only how to live, but how to reign,   220
And to those virtues which from reason spring,
And grace the man, join those which grace the king.
   First, (for strict duty bids my care extend
And reach to all, who on that care depend;
Bids me with servants keep a steady hand,
And watch o'er all my proxies in the land)
First, (and that method reason shall support)
Before I look into and purge my court,
Before I cleanse the stable of the state
Let me fix things which to myself relate: 230
That done, and all accounts well settled here,

349

In resolution firm, in honour clear,
Tremble, ye slaves ! who dare abuse your trust,
Who dare be villains when your king is just.
   Are there, amongst those officers of state
To whom our sacred power we delegate,
Who hold our place and office in the realm,
Who, in our name commissioned, guide the helm ;
Are there who, trusting to our love of ease,
Oppress our subjects, wrest our just decrees,   240
And make the laws, warped from their fair intent,
To speak a language which they never meant ;
Are there such men, and can the fools depend
On holding out in safety to their end ?
Can they so much, from thoughts of danger free,
Deceive themselves, so much misdeem of me,
To think that I will prove a statesman's tool,
And live a stranger where I ought to rule ?
What ! to myself and to my state unjust,
Shall I from ministers take things on trust,   250
And, sinking low the credit of my throne,
Depend upon dependents of my own ?
Shall I, most certain source of future cares,
Not use my judgment, but depend on theirs ?
Shall I, true puppet-like, be mocked with state,
Have nothing but the name of being great ;
Attend at councils which I must not weigh,
Do what they bid, and what they dictate, say,
Enrobed, and hoisted up into my chair,
Only to be a royal cipher there ?   260
Perish the thought—'tis treason to my throne—
And who but thinks it, could his thoughts be known,
Insults me more than he, who leagued with Hell,
Shall rise in arms, and 'gainst my crown rebel.
   The wicked statesman, whose false heart pursues
A train of guilt, who acts with double views,
And wears a double face ; whose base designs
Strike at his monarch's throne ; who undermines
E'en whilst he seems his wishes to support ;
Who seizes all departments ; packs a court ;   270
Maintains an agent on the judgment-seat

To screen his crimes, and make his frauds complete ;
New-models armies, and around the throne
Will suffer none but creatures of his own,
Conscious of such his baseness, well may try
Against the light to shut his master's eye,
To keep him coop'd, and far removed from those
Who, brave and honest, dare his crimes disclose,
Nor ever let him in one place appear,
Where truth, unwelcome truth, may wound his ear. 280
  Attempts like these, well-weigh'd, themselves proclaim,
And, whilst they publish, baulk their author's aim.
Kings must be blind into such snares to run,
Or, worse, with open eyes must be undone.
The minister of honesty and worth
Demands the day to bring his actions forth ;
Calls on the sun to shine with fiercer rays,
And braves that trial which must end in praise.
None fly the day, and seek the shades of night,
But those whose actions cannot bear the light ; 290
None wish their king in ignorance to hold
But those who feel that knowledge must unfold
Their hidden guilt ; and, that dark mist dispell'd
By which their places and their lives are held,
Confusion wait them, and, by justice led,
In vengeance fall on every traitor's head.
  Aware of this, and caution'd 'gainst the pit
Where kings have oft been lost, shall I submit,
And rust in chains like these ? Shall I give way,
And whilst my helpless subjects fall a prey 300
To power abused, in ignorance sit down,
Nor dare assert the honour of my crown ?
When stern Rebellion, (if that odious name
Justly belongs to those whose only aim,
Is to preserve their country ; who oppose,
In honour leagued, none but their country's foes ;
Who only seek their own, and found their cause
In due regard for violated laws)
When stern Rebellion, who no longer feels
Nor fears rebuke, a nation at her heels, 310
A nation up in arms, though strong not proud,

351

Knocks at the palace gate, and, calling loud
For due redress, presents, from Truth's fair pen,
A list of wrongs, not to be borne by men :
How must that king be humbled, how disgrace
All that is royal in his name and place,
Who, thus call'd forth to answer, can advance
No other plea but that of ignorance !
A vile defence, which, was his all at stake,
The meanest subject well might blush to make ;   320
A filthy source from whence shame ever springs ;
A stain to all, but most a stain to kings.
The soul, with great and manly feelings warm'd,
Panting for knowledge, rests not till inform'd ;
And shall not I, fired with the glorious zeal,
Feel those brave passions which my subjects feel ?
Or can a just excuse from ignorance flow
To me, whose first great duty is—to know ?
    Hence, Ignorance :—thy settled, dull, blank eye,
Would hurt me, though I knew no reason why—   330
Hence, Ignorance !—thy slavish shackles bind
The free-born soul, and lethargise the mind—
Of thee, begot by Pride, who look'd with scorn
On every meaner match, of thee was born
That grave inflexibility of soul
Which Reason can't convince, nor fear control ;
Which neither arguments, nor prayers can reach,
And nothing less than utter ruin teach—
Hence, Ignorance !—hence to that depth of night
Where thou wast born, where not one gleam of light   340
May wound thine eye—hence to some dreary cell
Where monks with superstition love to dwell ;
Or in some college soothe thy lazy pride,
And with the heads of colleges reside ;
Fit mate for Royalty thou canst not be,
And if no mate for kings, no mate for me.
    Come, Study ! like a torrent swell'd with rains,
Which, rushing down the mountains, o'er the plains
Spreads horror wide, and yet, in horror kind,
Leaves seeds of future fruitfulness behind ;   350
Come, Study !—painful though thy course, and slow,

Thy real worth by thy effects we know—
Parent of Knowledge, come—not thee I call
Who, grave and dull, in college or in hall
Dost sit, all solemn sad, and moping, weigh
Things which, when found, thy labours can't repay—
Nor, in one hand, fit emblem of thy trade,
A rod, in t' other, gaudily array'd,
A hornbook, gilt and letter'd, call I thee,
Who dost in form preside o'er A, B, C—   360
Nor (Siren though thou art, and thy strange charms,
As 'twere by magic, lure men to thine arms)
Do I call thee, who, through a winding maze,
A labyrinth of puzzling, pleasing ways,
Dost lead us at the last to those rich plains,
Where, in full glory, real Science reigns ;
    Fair though thou art, and lovely to mine eye,
Though full rewards in thy possession lie
To crown man's wish, and do thy favourites grace,
Though, (was I station'd in an humbler place)   370
I could be ever happy in thy sight,
Toil with thee all the day, and through the night
Toil on from watch to watch, bidding my eye,
Fast rivetted on science, sleep defy ;
Yet (such the hardships which from empire flow)
Must I thy sweet society forego,
And to some happy rival's arms resign
Those charms which can, alas ! no more be mine.
    No more from hour to hour, from day to day,
Shall I pursue thy steps, and urge my way   380
Where eager love of Science calls ; no more
Attempt those paths which man ne'er trod before ;
No more the mountain scaled, the desert cross'd,
Losing myself, nor knowing I was lost,
Travel through woods, through wilds, from morn to night,
From night to morn, yet travel with delight,
And having found thee, lay me down content,
Own all my toil well paid, my time well spent.
    Farewell, ye Muses too,—for such mean things
Must not presume to dwell with mighty kings—   390
Farewell, ye Muses ! though it cuts my heart,

353

E'en to the quick, we must for ever part.
When the fresh morn bade lusty Nature wake :
When the birds, sweetly twittering through the brake,
Tune their soft pipes ; when from the neighbouring bloom
Sipping the dew, each zephyr stole perfume ;
When all things with new vigour were inspired,
And seem'd to say they never could be tired,
How often have we stray'd, whilst sportive rhyme
Deceived the way and clipp'd the wings of Time,   400
O'er hill, o'er dale ; how often laugh'd to see,
Yourselves made visible to none but me,
The clown, his work suspended, gape and stare,
And seem'd to think that I conversed with air.
When the sun, beating on the parchèd soil,
Seem'd to proclaim an interval of toil ;
When a faint languor crept through every breast,
And things most used to labour wish'd for rest,
How often, underneath a reverend oak,
Where safe and fearless of the impious stroke,   410
Some sacred Dryad lived : or in some grove
Where, with capricious fingers, Fancy wove
Her fairy bower, whilst Nature all the while
Look'd on, and view'd her mockeries with a smile,
Have we held converse sweet ! how often laid,
Fast by the Thames, in Ham's inspiring shade,
Amongst those poets which make up your train,
And, after death, pour forth the sacred strain,
Have I, at your command, in verse grown grey,
But not impair'd, heard Dryden tune that lay   420
Which might have drawn an angel from his sphere,
And kept him from his office listening here.
When dreary Night, with Morpheus in her train,
Led on by Silence to resume her reign,
With darkness covering, as with a robe,
The scene of levity, blank'd half the globe.
How oft, enchanted with your heavenly strains,
Which stole me from myself ; which in soft chains

412 The two lines which followed were cancelled by Churchill in MS. :
' Whilst Pope with envy stung, inflamed with pride,
Piped to the vacant air on t'other side.'

Of music bound my soul ; how oft have I,
Sounds more than human floating through the sky,   430
Attentive sat, whilst Night, against her will,
Transported with the harmony, stood still !
How oft in raptures, which man scarce could bear,
Have I, when gone, still thought the Muses there,
Still heard their music, and, as mute as death,
Sat all attention, drew in every breath,
Lest, breathing all too rudely, I should wound
And mar that magic excellence of sound ;
Then, Sense returning with return of day,
Have chid the night, which fled so fast away.   440
   Such my pursuits, and such my joys of yore ;
Such were my mates, but now my mates no more.
Placed out of Envy's walk, (for Envy, sure,
Would never haunt the cottage of the poor,
Would never stoop to wound my homespun lays)
With some few friends, and some small share of praise,
Beneath oppression, undisturb'd by strife,
In peace I trod the humble vale of life.
Farewell, these scenes of ease, this tranquil state ;
Welcome the troubles which on empire wait :   450
Light toys from this day forth I disavow ;
They pleased me once, but cannot suit me now :
To common men all common things are free ;
What honours them might fix disgrace on me.
Call'd to a throne, and o'er a mighty land
Ordain'd to rule, my head, my heart, my hand
Are all engross'd, each private view withstood,
And task'd to labour for the public good :
Be this my study ; to this one great end
May every thought, may every action tend.   460
   Let me the page of history turn o'er,
The instructive page, and heedfully explore
What faithful pens of former times have wrote
Of former kings ; what they did worthy note,
What worthy blame ; and from the sacred tomb
Where righteous monarchs sleep, where laurels bloom
Unhurt by time, let me a garland twine
Which, robbing not their fame, may add to mine.

Nor let me with a vain and idle eye
Glance o'er those scenes, and in a hurry fly   470
Quick as a post which travels day and night;
Nor let me dwell there, lured by false delight;
And, into barren theory betray'd,
Forget that monarchs are for action made.
When amorous Spring, repairing all his charms,
Calls Nature forth from hoary Winter's arms,
Where, like a virgin to some lecher sold,
Three wretched months, she lay benumb'd, and cold;
When the weak flower, which, shrinking from the breath
Of the rude North, and timorous of death,   480
To its kind mother earth for shelter fled,
And on her bosom hid its tender head,
Peeps forth afresh, and, cheer'd by milder skies,
Bids in full splendour all her beauties rise,
The hive is up in arms—expert to teach,
Nor, proudly, to be taught unwilling, each
Seems from her fellow a new zeal to catch;
Strength in her limbs, and on her wings dispatch,
The bee goes forth; from herb to herb she flies,
From flower to flower, and loads her lab'ring thighs   490
With treasured sweets, robbing those flowers, which, left,
Find not themselves made poorer by the theft,
Their scents as lively, and their looks as fair,
As if the pillager had not been there.
Ne'er doth she flit on Pleasure's silken wing;
Ne'er doth she, loitering, let the bloom of Spring
Unrifled pass, and on the downy breast
Of some fair flower indulge untimely rest:
Ne'er doth she, drinking deep of those rich dews
Which chymist Night prepared, that faith abuse   500
Due to the hive, and, selfish in her toils,
To her own private use convert the spoils:
Love of the stock first call'd her forth to roam,
And to the stock she brings her booty home.
    Be this my pattern—as becomes a king,
Let me fly all abroad on Reason's wing:
Let mine eye, like the lightning, through the earth
Run to and fro, nor let one deed of worth,

In any place and time, nor let one man,
Whose actions may enrich dominion's plan,   510
Escape my note : be all, from the first day
Of Nature to this hour, be all my prey.
From those whom Time, at the desire of Fame,
Hath spared, let Virtue catch an equal flame :
From those who, not in mercy, but in rage,
Time hath reprieved to damn from age to age,
Let me take warning, lesson'd to distil,
And, imitating Heaven, draw good from ill :
Nor let these great researches in my breast
A monument of useless labour rest ;   520
No—let them spread—the effects let Gotham share,
And reap the harvest of their monarch's care :
Be other times, and other countries known,
Only to give fresh blessings to my own.
    Let me, (and may that God to whom I fly,
On whom for needful succour I rely
In this great hour, that glorious God of truth,
Through whom I reign, in mercy to my youth,
Assist my weakness, and direct me right ;
From every speck which hangs upon the sight   530
Purge my mind's eye, nor let one cloud remain
To spread the shades of error o'er my brain),
Let me, impartial, with unwearied thought,
Try men and things ; let me, as monarchs ought,
Examine well on what my power depends ;
What are the general principles, and ends
Of government ; how empire first began ;
And wherefore man was raised to reign o'er man.
    Let me consider, as from one great source
We see a thousand rivers take their course,   540
Dispersed, and into different channels led,
Yet by their parent still supplied and fed,
That government, (though branch'd out far and wide,
In various modes to various lands applied)
Howe'er it differs in its outward frame,
In the main ground-work's every where the same ;
The same her view, though different her plan,
Her grand and general view—the good of man.

357

Let me find out, by reason's sacred beams,
What system in itself most perfect seems,   550
Most worthy man, most likely to conduce
To all the purposes of general use ;
Let me find, too, where, by fair reason tried,
It fails, when to particulars applied ;
Why in that mode all nations do not join,
And, chiefly, why it cannot suit with mine.
   Let me the gradual rise of empires trace,
Till they seem founded on perfection's base ;
Then (for when human things have made their way
To excellence, they hasten to decay)   560
Let me, whilst observation lends her clue,
Step after step to their decline pursue,
Enabled by a chain of facts to tell
Not only how they rose, but why they fell.
   Let me not only the distempers know
Which in all states from common causes grow,
But likewise those, which, by the will of Fate,
On each peculiar mode of empire wait ;
Which in its very constitution lurk,
Too sure at last, to do its destined work :   570
Let me, forewarn'd, each sign, each system learn,
That I my people's danger may discern,
Ere 'tis too late wish'd health to re-assure,
And, if it can be found, find out a cure.
   Let me, (though great, grave brethren of the gown
Preach all faith up, and preach all reason down,
Making those jar, whom reason meant to join,
And vesting in themselves a right divine)
Let me, through reason's glass, with searching eye,
Into the depth of that religion pry   580
Which law hath sanction'd : let me find out there
What's form, what's essence ; what, like vagrant air,
We well may change ; and what, without a crime,
Cannot be changed to the last hour of time ;
Nor let me suffer that outrageous zeal
Which, without knowledge, furious bigots feel,
Fair in pretence, though at the heart unsound,
These separate points at random to confound.

358

The times have been, when priests have dared to tread,
Proud and insulting, on their monarch's head ;   590
When, whilst they made religion a pretence,
Out of the world they banish'd common sense ;
When some soft king, too open to deceit,
Easy and unsuspecting join'd the cheat,
Duped by mock piety, and gave his name
To serve the vilest purposes of shame.
Fear not, my People, where no cause of fear
Can justly rise—your king secures you here ;
Your king, who scorns the haughty prelate's nod,
Nor deems the voice of priests the voice of God.   600
   Let me, (though lawyers may perhaps forbid
Their monarch to behold what they wish hid,
And for the purposes of knavish gain,
Would have their trade a mystery remain)
Let me, disdaining all such slavish awe,
Dive to the very bottom of the law ;
Let me (the weak, dead letter left behind)
Search out the principles, the spirit find,
Till, from the parts, made master of the whole,
I see the Constitution's very soul.   610
   Let me, (though statesmen will no doubt resist
And to my eyes present a fearful list
Of men, whose wills are opposite to mine,
Of men, great men, determined to resign)
Let me, (with firmness, which becomes a king,
Conscious from what a source my actions spring
Determined not by worlds to be withstood,
When my grand object is my country's good)
Unravel all low ministerial scenes,
Destroy their jobs, lay bare their ways and means,   620
And track them step by step ; let me well know
How places, pensions, and preferments go ;
Why Guilt's provided for, when Worth is not,
And why one man of merit is forgot ;
Let me in peace, in war, supreme preside,
And dare to know my way without a guide.
   Let me, (though Dignity, by nature proud,

621 Some editions have, ' And *trap* them step by step.'

Retires from view, and swells behind a cloud,
As if the sun shone with less powerful ray,
Less grace, less glory, shining every day ;   630
Though when she comes forth into public sight,
Unbending as a ghost, she stalks upright,
With such an air as we have often seen,
And often laugh'd at in a tragic queen,
Nor, at her presence, though base myriads crook
The supple knee, vouchsafes a single look)
Let me, all vain parade, all empty pride,
All terrors of dominion laid aside,
All ornament, and needless helps of art,
All those big looks, which speak a little heart,   640
Know (which few kings, alas ! have ever known)
How affability becomes a throne,
Destroys all fear, bids love with reverence live,
And gives those graces pride can never give.
Let the stern tyrant keep a distant state,
And, hating all men, fear return of hate,
Conscious of guilt, retreat behind his throne,
Secure from all upbraidings but his own :
Let all my subjects have access to me,
Be my ears open as my heart is free ;   650
In full, fair tide let information flow ;
That evil is half-cured, whose cause we know.
    And thou, where'er thou art, thou wretched thing,
Who art afraid to look up to a king,
Lay by thy fears—make but thy grievance plain,
And, if I not redress thee, may my reign
Close up that very moment.—To prevent,
The course of Justice, from her fair intent,
In vain my nearest, dearest friend shall plead,
In vain my mother kneel—my soul may bleed,   660
But must not change—when Justice draws the dart,
Though it is doom'd to pierce a favourite's heart,
'Tis mine to give it force, to give it aim—
I know it duty, and I feel it fame.

THE CANDIDATE *

ENOUGH of Actors—let them play the player,
And, free from censure, fret, sweat, strut, and stare.
Garrick abroad, what motives can engage
To waste one couplet on a barren stage?
Ungrateful Garrick! when these tasty days,
In justice to themselves, allow'd thee praise;
When, at thy bidding, Sense, for twenty years
Indulged in laughter, or dissolved in tears;
When, in return for labour, time, and health,
The town had given some little share of wealth   10
Couldst thou repine at being still a slave?
Darest thou presume to enjoy that wealth she gave?
Couldst thou repine at laws ordain'd by those
Whom nothing but thy merit made thy foes?
Whom, too refined for honesty and trade,
By need made tradesmen, pride had bankrupts made;
Whom fear made drunkards, and, by modern rules,
Whom drink made wits, though Nature made them fools.
With such, beyond all pardon is thy crime,
In such a manner, and at such a time,   20
To quit the stage; but men of real sense,
Who neither lightly give, nor take offence,
Shall own thee clear, or pass an act of grace,
Since thou hast left a Powell in thy place.

* First published in June, 1764. 'Printed for the Author; and
sold by W. Flexney .... G. Kearsley .... C. Henderson .... J.
Coote .... J. Gardiner .... J. Almon .... and A. Moran.' The
occasion of the poem was the contest in March, 1764, between Lord
Sandwich and Lord Hardwicke for the High Stewardship of the
University of Cambridge. The struggle was embittered by political
animosities and the election was held amid tumult (see note on line
643). Lord Hardwicke was finally successful.

³ Garrick was out of England from September, 1763, until April,
1765. (See note on ' The Rosciad,' line 1027.)

²⁴ William Powell (1735-1769) appeared at Drury Lane in October,
1763, as Philaster, in which part he had been instructed by Garrick
before the latter's departure to the Continent. His success was im-
mediate. Walpole wrote to Sir Horace Mann (October 17th, 1763),

Enough of Authors—why, when scribblers fail,
Must other scribblers spread the hateful tale ?
Why must they pity, why contempt express,
And why insult a brother in distress ?
Let those, who boast the uncommon gift of brains,
The laurel pluck, and wear it for their pains ;   30
Fresh on their brows for ages let it bloom,
And, ages past, still flourish round their tomb.
Let those who without genius write, and write,
Versemen or prosemen, all in Nature's spite,
The pen laid down, their course of folly run
In peace, unread, unmention'd be undone.
Why should I tell, to cross the will of Fate,
That Francis once endeavour'd to translate ?
Why, sweet oblivion winding round his head,
Should I recall poor Murphy from the dead ?   40
Why may not Langhorne, simple in his lay,
Effusion on effusion pour away,
With Friendship and with Fancy trifle here,
Or sleep in Pastoral at Belvidere ?
Sleep let them all, with Dulness on her throne,
Secure from any malice but their own.
    Enough of Critics—let them, if they please,
Fond of new pomp, each month pass new decrees ;

' Have you got Mr. Garrick yet ? If you have, you may keep him ;
there is come forth within these ten days a young actor, who has turned
the heads of the whole town. The first night of his appearance the
audience, not content with clapping, stood up and shouted. His name
is Powell.' He then appeared in other characters, but with less success,
owing to the lack of Garrick's instruction. However, in 1767 he ac-
quired a fourth share of Covent Garden Theatre, and later was one
of the managers of the new theatre at Bristol. He died in that town in
July, 1769.

    [38] The Rev. Philip Francis. (See note on ' The Author,' line 346.)

    [40] It was a favourite trick of Churchill's to pretend that his enemies
were dead and that he had killed them. Murphy was not dead, indeed
he survived Churchill more than forty years, dying in 1805. (See note
on ' The Rosciad,' line 67.)

    [41] John Langhorne. (See note on ' Independence,' line 458.)

    [44] Tooke notes that Langhorne ' was on terms of intimacy with
General Crawford and Lord Eardley, and laid the scene of many of
his pastoral and other poems at Belvedere in Kent, the seat of that
nobleman.'

Wide and extensive be their infant state,
Their subjects many, and those subjects great,   50
Whilst all their mandates as sound law succeed
With fools who write, and greater fools who read.
What though they lay the realms of Genius waste,
Fetter the fancy and debauch the taste ;
Though they, like doctors, to approve their skill,
Consult not how to cure, but how to kill ;
Though by whim, envy, or resentment led,
They damn those authors whom they never read ;
Though, other rules unknown, one rule they hold,
To deal out so much praise for so much gold :   60
Though Scot with Scot, in damnèd close intrigues,
Against the commonwealth of letters leagues ;
Uncensured let them pilot at the helm,
And rule in letters, as they ruled the realm :
Ours be the curse, the mean, tame coward's curse,
(Nor could ingenious Malice make a worse,
To do our sense, and honour deep despite)
To credit what they say, read what they write.
    Enough of Scotland—let her rest in peace ;
The cause removed, effects of course should cease.   70
Why should I tell how Tweed, too mighty grown,
And proudly swell'd with waters not his own,
Burst o'er his banks, and, by destruction led,
O'er our faint England desolation spread,
Whilst, riding on his waves, Ambition, plumed
In tenfold pride, the port of Bute assumed,
Now that the river god, convinced, though late,
And yielding, though reluctantly, to Fate,
Holds his fair course, and with more humble tides,
In tribute to the sea, as usual, glides ?   80
    Enough of States, and such like trifling things ;
Enough of kinglings, and enough of kings ;
Henceforth, secure let ambush'd statesmen lie,
Spread the court web, and catch the patriot fly ;
Henceforth, unwhipt of Justice, uncontroll'd
By fear or shame, let Vice, secure and bold,

[61] A gibe at ' The Critical Review,' which was largely run by Scotsmen.

Lord it with all her sons, whilst Virtue's groan
Meets with compassion only from the throne.
   Enough of Patriots—all I ask of man
Is only to be honest as he can :   90
Some have deceived, and some may still deceive ;
'Tis the fool's curse at random to believe.
Would those, who, by opinion placed on high,
Stand fair and perfect in their country's eye,
Maintain that honour, let me in their ear
Hint this essential doctrine—Persevere.
Should they (which Heaven forbid) to win the grace
Of some proud courtier, or to gain a place,
Their king and country sell, with endless shame
The avenging Muse shall mark each trait'rous name ; 100
But if, to honour true, they scorn to bend,
And, proudly honest, hold out to the end,
Their grateful country shall their fame record,
And I myself descend to praise a lord.
   Enough of Wilkes—with good and honest men
His actions speak much stronger than my pen,
And future ages shall his name adore,
When he can act and I can write no more.
England may prove ungrateful and unjust,
But fostering France shall ne'er betray her trust :   110
'Tis a brave debt which gods on men impose,
To pay with praise the merit e'en of foes.
When the great warrior of Amilcar's race
Made Rome's wide empire tremble to her base,
To prove her virtue, though it gall'd her pride,
Rome gave that fame which Carthage had denied.
   Enough of Self—that darling, luscious theme,
O'er which philosophers in raptures dream ;

---

[110] Wilkes fled to France just before Christmas, 1763. In a letter to his friend Cotes, he says : ' Goy, (a French friend of his) felt the pulse of the French Ministers about my coming here, and Churchill's upon a former report. The answer was sent from the Duke de Praslin, by the King's orders, to Monsieur St. Foy, *premier commis des affaires étrangères*, in these words : " Les deux illustres, J. W. et C. C. peuvent venir en France et à Paris aussi souvent, et pour autant de tems, qu'ils le jugeront à propos." ' (P. Fitzgerald, ' Life and Times of John Wilkes,' I, pp. 254, 255.)

Of which with seeming disregard they write,
Then prizing most, when most they seem to slight ;   120
Vain proof of folly tinctured strong with pride !
What man can from himself himself divide ?
For me, (nor dare I lie) my leading aim
(Conscience first satisfied) is love of fame ;
Some little fame derived from some brave few,
Who prizing Honour, prize her votaries too.
Let all (nor shall resentment flush my cheek)
Who know me well, what they know, freely speak,
So those (the greatest curse I meet below)
Who know me not, may not pretend to know.   130
Let none of those, whom, bless'd with parts above
My feeble genius, still I dare to love,
Doing more mischief than a thousand foes,
Posthumous nonsense to the world expose,
And call it mine, for mine, though known,
Or which if mine, I living blush'd to own.
Know all the world, no greedy heir shall find,
Die when I will, one couplet left behind.
Let none of those, whom I despise though great,
Pretending friendship to give malice weight,   140
Publish my life ; let no false, sneaking peer,
(Some such there are) to win the public ear,
Hand me to shame with some vile anecdote,
Nor soul-gall'd bishop damn me with a note.
Let one poor sprig of bay around my head

---

[138] Churchill before his death is said to have destroyed all his papers except ' The Journey ' and the ' Dedication to Warburton,' both unfinished.

[141] John Boyle (1707-1762), fifth Earl of Cork, fifth Earl of Orrery and second Baron Marston, had literary aspirations but little talent. He made the acquaintance of Swift about 1731 and their relations were apparently cordial, although Swift may well have used some contemptuous expressions of Orrery. The latter, in his ' Remarks on the Life and Writings of Jonathan Swift ' (1751), wrote with a malice which drew an angry reply from Dr. Patrick Delany. Orrery was completely incapable of understanding either the humour or the passion of Swift. He afterwards attempted to patronise Johnson, who spoke of him kindly as one ' who would have been a liberal patron if he had been rich.'

[144] An allusion to Warburton's notes on Pope. (See note on the ' Dedication to Warburton,' line 1.)

Bloom whilst I live, and point me out when dead ;
Let it, (may Heaven, indulgent, grant that prayer)
Be planted on my grave, nor wither there ;
And when, on travel bound, some rhyming guest
Roams through the Churchyard, whilst his dinner's drest,
Let it hold up this comment to his eyes—   151
Life to the last enjoy'd, here Churchill lies ;
Whilst (O, what joy that pleasing flattery gives !)
Reading my Works, he cries—Here Churchill lives.
   Enough of Satire—in less harden'd times
Great was her force, and mighty were her rhymes.
I've read of men, beyond man's daring brave,
Who yet have trembled at the strokes she gave ;
Whose souls have felt more terrible alarms
From her one line, than from a world in arms :   160
When in her faithful and immortal page
They saw transmitted down from age to age
Recorded villains, and each spotted name
Branded with marks of everlasting shame,
Succeeding villains sought her as a friend,
And, if not really mended, feign'd to mend.
But in an age, when actions are allow'd
Which strike all honour dead, and crimes avow'd
Too terrible to suffer the report,
Avow'd and praised by men who stain a court,   170
Propp'd by the arm of Power ; when Vice, high-born,
High-bred, high-station'd, holds rebuke in scorn ;
When she is lost to every thought of fame ;
And, to all virtue dead, is dead to shame ;
When Prudence a much easier task must hold
To make a new world, than reform the old,
Satire throws by her arrows on the ground,
And if she cannot cure, she will not wound.
   Come, Panegyric—though the Muse disdains,
Founded on truth, to prostitute her strains   180
At the base instance of those men, who hold
No argument but power, no god but gold,

---

[152] This line is still to be read on Churchill's tombstone—the
original stone has been replaced by another—in the churchyard of
St. Martin's, Dover.

Yet, mindful that from heaven she drew her birth,
She scorns the narrow maxims of this earth ;
Virtuous herself, brings Virtue forth to view,
And loves to praise, where praise is justly due.
   Come, Panegyric—in a former hour,
My soul with pleasure yielding to thy power,
Thy shrine I sought ; I pray'd ; but wanton air,
Before it reach'd thy ears, dispersed my prayer ;   190
E'en at thy altars whilst I took my stand,
The pen of truth and honour in my hand,
Fate, meditating wrath 'gainst me and mine,
Chid my fond zeal, and thwarted my design,
Whilst, Hayter brought too quickly to his end,
I lost a subject and mankind a friend.
   Come, Panegyric—bending at thy throne,
Thee and thy power my soul is proud to own :
Be thou my kind protector, thou my guide,
And lead me safe through passes yet untried.   200
Broad is the road, nor difficult to find,
Which to the house of Satire leads mankind ;
Narrow, and unfrequented, are the ways,
Scarce found out in an age, which lead to Praise.
   What though no theme I choose of vulgar note,
Nor wish to write as brother bards have wrote,
So mild, so meek in praising, that they seem
Afraid to wake their patrons from a dream ?
What though a theme I choose, which might demand
The nicest touches of a master's hand ?   210
Yet, if the inward workings of my soul
Deceive me not, I shall attain the goal,
And Envy shall behold, in triumph raised,
The poet praising, and the patron praised.
   What patron shall I choose ? shall public voice,
Or private knowledge, influence my choice ?

[195] Dr. Thomas Hayter (1702-1762) received much preferment from
Lancelot Blackburne, Archbishop of York, and scandal declared him
to be the Archbishop's natural son. There was, however, no truth in
this assertion. Hayter, then Bishop of Norwich, became preceptor
to the sons of Prince Frederick in 1751, but soon resigned. In 1761, by
the influence of Lord Talbot, he was translated to the Bishopric of
London.

Shall I prefer the grand retreat of Stowe,
Or, seeking patriots, to friend Wildman's go ?
  ' To Wildman's ! ' cried Discretion, (who had heard,
Close standing at my elbow, every word)   220
' To Wildman's ! art thou mad ? canst thou be sure
One moment there to have thy head secure ?
Are they not all (let observation tell)
All mark'd in characters as black as hell ;
In Doomsday book, by ministers set down,
Who style their pride the honour of the crown ?
Make no reply—let reason stand aloof—
Presumptions here must pass as solemn proof.
That settled faith, that love which ever springs
In the best subjects, for the best of kings,   230
Must not be measured now, by what men think,
Or say, or do—by what they eat and drink ;
Where and with whom, that question's to be tried
And statesmen are the judges to decide ;
No juries call'd, or, if call'd, kept in awe ;
They, facts confess'd, in themselves vest the law.
Each dish at Wildman's of sedition smacks ;
Blasphemy may be gospel at Almack's.'
  Peace, good Discretion ! peace—thy fears are vain ;
Ne'er will I herd with Wildman's factious train ;   240
Never the vengeance of the great incur,
Nor, without might, against the mighty stir.

[217] Stowe, in Buckinghamshire, then the seat of Earl Temple, afterwards of the Duke of Buckingham, and now a public school. Both Wilkes and Churchill had enjoyed the hospitality of Stowe, and Wilkes had borrowed considerable sums of Temple.

[218] Wildman kept a coffee-house in Bedford Street, Covent Garden, where Wilkes' supporters used to meet. He also opened a tavern in Albemarle Street, where an Opposition Club was established. It is probably the second of these which is referred to here.

[238] The name ' Almack's ' is given to two distinct institutions ;

1. A gaming-club with a Tory flavour, established by William Almack in Pall Mall before 1763. The club still survives with the changed name of Brooks's.

2 The assembly rooms in King Street, St. James's, opened in 1765, and fashionable until about 1840. Almack bequeathed his premises to his niece, Mrs. Willis, and the building is still known as Willis's Rooms.

If, from long proof, my temper you distrust,
Weigh my profession, to my gown be just ;
Dost thou one parson know so void of grace
To pay his court to patrons out of place ?
    If still you doubt (though scarce a doubt remains)
Search through my alter'd heart, and try my reins ;
There, searching, find, nor deem me now in sport,
A convert made by Sandwich to the court.   250
Let madmen follow error to the end,
I, of mistakes convinced, and proud to mend,
Strive to act better, being better taught,
Nor blush to own that change which reason wrought :
For such a change as this, must justice speak ;
My heart was honest, but my head was weak.
    Bigot to no one man, or set of men,
Without one selfish view, I drew my pen ;
My country ask'd, or seem'd to ask, my aid,
Obedient to that call, I left off trade ;   260
A side I chose, and on that side was strong,
Till time hath fairly proved me in the wrong :
Convinced, I change, (can any man do more ?)
And have not greater patriots changed before ?
Changed, I at once (can any man do less ?)
Without a single blush, that change confess ;
Confess it with a manly kind of pride,
And quit the losing for the winning side,
Granting, whilst virtuous Sandwich holds the rein,
What Bute for ages might have sought in vain.   270
    Hail, Sandwich—nor shall Wilkes resentment show,
Hearing the praises of so brave a foe !
Hail, Sandwich—nor, through pride, shalt thou refuse
The grateful tribute of so mean a Muse—
Sandwich, all hail—when Bute with foreign hand,
Grown wanton with ambition, scourged the land ;
When Scots, or slaves to Scotsmen, steer'd the helm ;
When peace, inglorious peace, disgraced the realm,

---

250 Sandwich was appointed one of the principal Secretaries of State
in September, 1763, on the death of the Earl of Egremont. In spite
of his former intimacy, he became as bitter an opponent of Wilkes as
his predecessor.

Distrust, and general discontent prevail'd ;
But when, (he best knows why) his spirits fail'd ;   280
When, with a sudden panic struck, he fled,
Sneak'd out of power, and hid his miscreant head ;
When, like a Mars, (fear order'd to retreat)
We saw thee nimbly vault into his seat,
Into the seat of power, at one bold leap,
A perfect connoisseur in statesmanship ;
When, like another Machiavel, we saw
Thy fingers twisting, and untwisting law,
Straining, where godlike Reason bade, and where
She warranted thy mercy, pleased to spare ;   290
Saw thee resolved, and fix'd (come what come might)
To do thy God, thy king, thy country right ;
All things were changed ; suspense remain'd no more :
Certainty reign'd where doubt had reign'd before :
All felt thy virtues, and all knew their use ;
What virtues such as thine must needs produce.
    Thy foes (for honour ever meets with foes)
Too mean to praise, too fearful to oppose,
In sullen silence sit ; thy friends (some few,
Who, friends to thee, are friends to honour too)   300
Plaud thy brave bearing, and the Commonweal
Expects her safety from thy stubborn zeal.
A place amongst the rest the Muses claim,
And bring this free-will offering to thy fame ;
To prove their virtue, make thy virtues known,
And, holding up thy fame, secure their own.
    From his youth upwards to the present day,
When vices, more than years, have mark'd him gray ;
When riotous excess, with wasteful hand,
Shakes life's frail glass, and hastes each ebbing sand, 310
Unmindful from what stock he drew his birth,
Untainted with one deed of real worth,
Lothario, holding honour at no price,
Folly to folly added, vice to vice ;

282 Bute, weary of the unceasing abuse hurled at his head, retired to
Harrogate and to private life in September, 1763. He was still sus-
pected, however, of influencing the king.
    313 Lothario, the dissolute hero of ' The Fair Penitent.'

370

Wrought sin with greediness, and sought for shame
With greater zeal than good men seek for fame.
　Where (reason left without the least defence)
Laughter was mirth, obscenity was sense ;
Where Impudence made Decency submit ;
Where noise was humour, and where whim was wit ; 320
Where rude, untemper'd license had the merit
Of liberty, and lunacy was spirit ;
Where the best things were ever held the worst,
Lothario was, with justice, always first.
　To whip a top, to knuckle down at taw,
To swing upon a gate, to ride a straw,
To play at push-pin with dull brother peers,
To belch out catches in a porter's ears,
To reign the monarch of a midnight cell,
To be the gaping chairman's oracle,　　　　　　330
Whilst in most blessed union, rogue and whore
Clap hands, huzza, and hiccup out Encore ;
Whilst gray Authority, who slumbers there
In robes of watchman's fur, gives up his chair ;
With midnight howl to bay the affrighted moon,
To walk with torches through the streets at noon ;
To force plain nature from her usual way,
Each night a vigil, and a blank each day ;
To match for speed one feather 'gainst another,
To make one leg run races with his brother ;　　340
'Gainst all the rest to take the northern wind,
Bute to ride first, and he to ride behind ;
To coin newfangled wagers, and to lay 'em,
Laying to lose, and losing not to pay 'em,—
Lothario, on that stock which nature gives,
Without a rival stands, though March yet lives.
　When Folly, (at that name in duty bound,
Let subject myriads kneel, and kiss the ground,

---

[327] Push-pin is a child's game at which each player flicks or pushes
a pin with the object of crossing that of another player.

[346] William Douglas (1725-1810) was third Earl of March and fourth
Duke of Queensberry, to which title he succeeded in 1778.　He was
famous for his fantastic wagers, being equally ready to bet on the
deaths of his friends or on the relative speed of two drops of rain
running down a window.

Whilst they who in the presence upright stand
Are held as rebels through the loyal land)   350
Queen every where, but most a queen in courts,
Sent forth her heralds, and proclaim'd her sports ;
Bade fool with fool on her behalf engage,
And prove her right to reign from age to age,
Lothario, great above the common size,
With all engaged, and won from all the prize ;
Her cap he wears, which from his youth he wore,
And every day deserves it more and more.
   Nor in such limits rests his soul confined ;
Folly may share, but can't engross his mind ;   360
Vice, bold, substantial Vice puts in her claim,
And stamps him perfect in the books of shame.
Observe his follies well, and you would swear
Folly had been his first, his only care ;
Observe his vices, you'll that oath disown,
And swear that he was born for vice alone.
   Is the soft nature of some hapless maid,
Fond, easy, full of faith, to be betray'd ;
Must she, to virtue lost, be lost to fame,
And he who wrought her guilt declare her shame ;   370
Is some brave friend, who, men but little known,
Deems every heart as honest as his own,
And, free himself, in others fears no guile,
To be ensnared, and ruin'd with a smile ;
Is law to be perverted from her course ;
Is abject fraud to league with brutal force ;
Is freedom to be crush'd, and every son
Who dares maintain her cause, to be undone ;
Is base corruption, creeping through the land,
To plan, and work her ruin, underhand,   380
With regular approaches, sure, though slow ;
Or must she perish by a single blow ;
Are kings—who trust to servants, and depend
In servants (fond, vain thought !) to find a friend—
To be abused, and made to draw their breath
In darkness thicker than the shades of death ;
Is God's most holy name to be profaned,

367 The first edition reads ' easy maid.'

His word rejected, and his laws arraign'd,
His servants scorn'd, as men who idly dream'd,
His service laugh'd at, and his Son blasphemed ;   390
Are debauchees in morals to preside ;
Is faith to take an Atheist for her guide ;
Is Science by a blockhead to be led ;
Are states to totter on a drunkard's head ;—
To answer all these purposes, and more,
More black than ever villain plann'd before,
Search earth, search hell, the devil cannot find
An agent, like Lothario, to his mind.
   Is this nobility, which, sprung from kings,
Was meant to swell the power from whence it springs ?
Is this the glorious produce, this the fruit,   401
Which Nature hoped for from so rich a root ?
Were there but two, (search all the world around)
Were there but two such nobles to be found,
The very name would sink into a term
Of scorn, and man would rather be a worm
Than be a lord : but Nature, full of grace,
Nor meaning birth and titles to be base,
Made only one, and having made him, swore,
In mercy to mankind, to make no more :   410
Nor stopp'd she there, but, like a generous friend,
The ills which error caused, she strove to mend,
And having brought Lothario forth to view,
To save her credit, brought forth Sandwich too.
   Gods ! with what joy, what honest joy of heart,
Blunt as I am, and void of every art,
Of every art which great ones in the state
Practise on knaves they fear, and fools they hate,
To titles with reluctance taught to bend,
Nor prone to think that virtues can descend,   420
Do I behold (a sight, alas ! more rare
Than honesty could wish) the noble wear
His father's honours, when his life makes known
They're his by virtue, not by birth alone ;
When he recals his father from the grave,

---

[414] The same device as that used against Mansfield in the concluding
lines of ' The Ghost.'

And pays with interest back that fame he gave :
Cured of her splenetic and sullen fits,
To such a peer my willing soul submits,
And to such virtue is more proud to yield
Than 'gainst ten titled rogues to keep the field.   430
Such, (for that truth e'en envy shall allow)
Such Wyndham was, and such is Sandwich now.
    O gentle Montague, in blessed hour
Didst thou start up, and climb the stairs of power ;
England of all her fears at once was eased,
Nor, 'mongst her many foes was one displeased :
France heard the news, and told it cousin Spain ;
Spain heard, and told it cousin France again ;
The Hollander relinquish'd his design
Of adding spice to spice, and mine to mine ;   440
Of Indian villanies he thought no more,
Content to rob us on our native shore :
Awed by thy fame, (which winds with open mouth
Shall blow from east to west, from north to south)
The western world shall yield us her increase,
And her wild sons be soften'd into peace ;
Rich eastern monarchs shall exhaust their stores,
And pour unbounded wealth on Albion's shores ;
Unbounded wealth, which from those golden scenes,
And all acquired by honourable means,   450
Some honourable chief shall hither steer,
To pay our debts, and set the nation clear.
    Nabobs themselves, allured by thy renown,
Shall pay due homage to the English crown ;
Shall freely as their king our king receive—
Provided the Directors give them leave.
    Union at home shall mark each rising year,
Nor taxes be complain'd of, though severe ;
Envy her own destroyer shall become,
And Faction with her thousand mouths be dumb :   460
With the meek man thy meekness shall prevail,

---

    [432] Charles Wyndham, Earl of Egremont. (See note on ' The
Ghost,' Book IV, line 64.)
    [456] *i.e.*, the Directors of the East India Company. (See note on
' The Farewell,' lines 475 and 493.)

Nor with the spirited thy spirit fail :
Some to thy force of reason shall submit,
And some be converts to thy princely wit :
Reverence for thee shall still a nation's cries,
A grand concurrence crown a grand excise :
And unbelievers of the first degree,
Who have no faith in God, have faith in thee.
　　When a strange jumble, whimsical and vain,
Possess'd the region of each heated brain ;　　　470
When some were fools to censure, some to praise,
And all were mad, but mad in different ways ;
When commonwealthsmen, starting at the shade
Which in their own wild fancy had been made,
Of tyrants dream'd, who wore a thorny crown,
And with state bloodhounds hunted Freedom down ;
When others, struck with fancies not less vain,
Saw mighty kings by their own subjects slain,
And, in each friend of liberty and law,
With horror big, a future Cromwell saw,　　　480
Thy manly zeal stept forth, bade discord cease,
And sung each jarring atom into peace ;
Liberty, cheer'd by thy all-cheering eye,
Shall, waking from her trance, live and not die ;
And, patronized by thee, Prerogative
Shall, striding forth at large, not die, but live ;
Whilst Privilege, hung betwixt earth and sky,
Shall not well know whether to live or die.
　　When on a rock which overhung the flood,
And seem'd to totter, Commerce shivering stood ;　　　490
When Credit, building on a sandy shore,
Saw the sea swell, and heard the tempest roar,
Heard death in every blast, and in each wave
Or saw, or fancied that she saw her grave ;
When property, transferr'd from hand to hand,
Weaken'd by change, crawl'd sickly through the land ;
When mutual confidence was at an end,
And man no longer could on man depend ;
Oppress'd with debts of more than common weight,

[499] ' The national debt on the 5th of January, 1764, amounted to
about £130,000,000 ' (Tooke.)　It is now £7,832,000,000.

When all men fear'd a bankruptcy of state ;   500
When, certain death to honour and to trade,
A sponge was talk'd of as our only aid ;
That to be saved we must be more undone,
And pay off all our debts, by paying none ;
Like England's better genius, born to bless,
And snatch his sinking country from distress,
Didst thou step forth, and, without sail or oar,
Pilot the shatter'd vessel safe to shore :
Nor shalt thou quit, till, anchor'd firm and fast,
She rides secure, and mocks the threatening blast !   510
    Born in thy house, and in thy service bred,
Nursed in thy arms, and at thy table fed,
By thy sage councils to reflection brought,
Yet more by pattern than by precept taught,
Economy her needful aid shall join
To forward and complete thy grand design ;
And, warm to save, but yet with spirit warm,
Shall her own conduct from thy conduct form.
Let friends of prodigals say what they will,
Spendthrifts at home, abroad are spendthrifts still.   520
In vain have sly and subtle sophists tried
Private from public justice to divide ;
For credit on each other they rely ;
They live together, and together die.
'Gainst all experience 'tis a rank offence,
High treason in the eye of common sense,
To think a statesman ever can be known
To pay our debts, who will not pay his own :
But now, though late, now may we hope to see
Our debts discharged, our credit fair and free,   530
Since rigid Honesty, (fair fall that hour !)
Sits at the helm, and Sandwich is in power.
With what delight I view thee, wondrous man !
With what delight survey thy sterling plan,
That plan which all with wonder must behold,
And stamp thy age the only age of Gold !
    Nor rest thy triumphs here—that Discord fled,

502 ' A sponge was talk'd of as our only aid,' *i.e.*, repudiation of debt was advocated, not for the last time.

And sought with grief the hell where she was bred ;
That Faction, 'gainst her nature forced to yield,
Saw her rude rabble scatter'd o'er the field,   540
Saw her best friends a standing jest become,
Her fools turn'd speakers, and her wits struck dumb :
That our most bitter foes (so much depends
On men of name) are turn'd to cordial friends ;
That our offended friends (such terror flows
From men of name) dare not appear our foes ;
That Credit, gasping in the jaws of death,
And ready to expire with every breath,
Grows stronger from disease ; that thou hast saved
Thy drooping country ; that thy name, engraved   550
On plates of brass, defies the rage of time ;
Than plates of brass more firm that sacred rhyme
Embalms thy memory, bids thy glories live,
And gives thee what the muse alone can give—
These heights of virtue, these rewards of fame,
With thee in common other patriots claim.
　　But, that poor, sickly Science, who had laid
And droop'd for years beneath neglect's cold shade,
By those who knew her purposely forgot,
And made the jest of those who knew her not,   560
Whilst ignorance in power, and pamper'd pride
' Clad like a priest, pass'd by on t'other side,'
Recover'd from her wretched state, at length
Puts on new health, and clothes herself with strength,
To thee we owe, and to thy friendly hand
Which raised, and gave her to possess the land :
This praise, though in a court, and near a throne,
This praise is thine, and thine, alas ! alone.
　　With what fond rapture did the goddess smile,
What blessings doth she promise to this isle,   570
What honour to herself, and length of reign,
Soon as she heard that thou didst not disdain

---

[550] ' Thy name . . . defies the rage of time.' It is odd to reflect
that the name of Sandwich, applied to the brilliant invention which
enabled the noble lord to gamble all day without the necessity of
intervals for food, has passed into every civilised language and may
well outlive the British Empire. Wellingtons are forgotten, a brougham
is an historical curiosity but the sandwich seems to be immortal.

To be her steward ; but what grief, what shame,
What rage, what disappointment, shook her frame,
When her proud children dared her will dispute,
When youth was insolent, and age was mute !
   That young men should be fools, and some wild few
To wisdom deaf, be deaf to interest too,
Moved not her wonder ; but that men, grown gray
In search of wisdom ; men who own'd the sway   580
Of reason ; men who stubbornly kept down
Each rising passion ; men who wore the gown ;
That *they* should cross her will, that they should dare
Against the cause of Interest to declare ;
That they should be so abject and unwise,
Having no fear of loss before their eyes,
Nor hopes of gain ; scorning the ready means
Of being vicars, rectors, canons, deans,
With all those honours which on mitres wait,
And mark the virtuous favourites of state ;   590
That they should dare a Hardwicke to support,
And talk, within the hearing of a court,
Of that vile beggar Conscience, who, undone,
And starved herself, starves every wretched son ;—
This turn'd her blood to gall, this made her swear
No more to throw away her time and care
On wayward sons who scorn'd her love ; no more
To hold her courts on Cam's ungrateful shore.
Rather than bear such insults, which disgrace
Her royalty of nature, birth, and place,   600
Though Dulness there unrivall'd state doth keep,
Would she at Winchester with Burton sleep ;

<hr/>

[576] ' The younger members of the University were unanimous in
favour of Lord Hardwicke.' (Tooke.) Horace Walpole's account (in
a letter to the Earl of Hertford, April 5th, 1764) is as follows : ' The
undergraduates, who, having no votes had been left to their *real*
opinions, were very near expressing their opinions against Lord Sand-
wich's friends in the most outrageous manner : hissed they were ; and
after the election, the juniors burst into the Senate-house, elected a
fictitious Lord Hardwicke, and chaired him.'

[602] Dr. John Burton was headmaster of Winchester. Wilkes, while
stationed at Winchester with the Buckinghamshire militia, was said to
have insulted Lord Bute's schoolboy son. Wilkes wrote to Dr. Burton

Or, to exchange the mortifying scene
For something still more dull, and still more mean,
Rather than bear such insults, she would fly
Far, far beyond the search of English eye,
And reign amongst the Scots : to be a queen
Is worth ambition, though in Aberdeen.
O, stay thy flight, fair Science ; what though some,
Some base-born children, rebels are become ?   610
All are not rebels ; some are duteous still,
Attend thy precepts, and obey thy will ;
Thy interest is opposed by those alone
Who either know not, or oppose their own.
    Of stubborn virtue, marching to thy aid,
Behold in black, the livery of their trade,
Marshall'd by Form, and by Discretion led,
A grave, grave troop, and Smith is at their head,
Black Smith of Trinity ; on Christian ground
For faith in mysteries none more renown'd.   620
    Next, (for the best of causes now and then
Must beg assistance from the worst of men)
Next (if old Story lies not) sprung from Greece,
Comes Pandarus, but comes without his niece :
Her, wretched maid ! committed to his trust,
To a rank lecher's coarse and bloated lust
The arch, old, hoary hypocrite had sold,
And thought himself and her well damn'd for gold.
But (to wipe off such traces from the mind,
And make us in good humour with mankind)   630

asking for an investigation, which the schoolmaster refused. Hence
Churchill's hostility.
    [618] Dr. Robert Smith (1689-1768), Master of Trinity College, Cam-
bridge. ' He was neither grave nor discreet, and as to faith or
mysteries, he never troubled himself with them.' (Gray.) He was,
however, a very distinguished mathematician and a notable benefactor
of his college and of his university. As Master of Trinity, he supported
the candidature of Sandwich; hence Churchill's hostility.
    [624] Pandarus : ' Dr. Humphrey Sumner, Provost of King's College,
Cambridge, who had been tutor to Lord Sandwich when at Eton
School. He was neither old nor an hypocrite but mean and roguish
without disguise. His niece professed herself a common whore ;
of course she fell in Lord Sandwich's way, and was for a time in his
keeping, but not at all of the Uncle's procurement.' (Gray.)

379

Leading on men, who, in a college bred,
No woman knew, but those which made their bed ;
Who, planted virgins on Cam's virtuous shore,
Continued still male virgins at threescore,
Comes Sumner, wise, and chaste as chaste can be,
With Long, as wise, and not less chaste than he.
   Are there not friends, too, enter'd in thy cause
Who, for thy sake, defying penal laws,
Were, to support thy honourable plan,
Smuggled from Jersey, and the Isle of Man ?   640
Are there not Philomaths of high degree
Who, always dumb before, shall speak for thee ?
Are there not Proctors, faithful to thy will,

[632] It is still the custom at Cambridge to employ women ' bed-makers.' Undergraduates are convinced that they are chosen for their ugliness.

[634] Sumner had a large family.

[636] Dr. Roger Long (died 1770), Master of Pembroke College, Cambridge, and Professor of Astronomy in the University.

[640] The reference to ' Jersey and the Isle of Man ' remains obscure.

[641] A philomath is an astrologer.

[643] The Cambridge Proctors could not agree on the count.

' It is the office of the proctors of the university to collect the votes in the Regent-house, and when a division happens, each of them generally takes a different side of the house, and marks down upon a line, with his pen, the *placet* or *non placet* of every person that votes on that side of the house which belongs to him, and then both meet together and cast up the numbers and join in declaring to the house, that the Grace either *placet iis* or *non placet iis*, or that *paria sunt suffragia* ; and the house must submit to their declaration.

' But the Proctors in the present case, that there might be no room to suspect either of them of error or partiality in collecting the votes, departed from their general practice, and went together to every member of the house that voted, and each of them marked down the *placet* or *non placet* of every voter ; and when they had done this, before they had put down their own votes, there appeared in both their accounts,

Placets - - - -	107
Non Placets - - -	107

Each of the Proctors then put down his own vote without putting his brother's ; and as they voted on opposite sides, the numbers then stood in Mr. *Longmire's* account :

Placets - - - -	108
Non Placets - - -	107

In Mr. *Forster's*

Placets - - - -	107
Non Placets - - -	108

But they immediately saw their mistake, and each of them corrected it

One of full growth, others in embryo still,
Who may, perhaps, in some ten years, or more,
Be ascertain'd that two and two make four,
Or may a still more happy method find,
And, taking one from two, leave none behind ?
  With such a mighty power on foot, to yield
Were death to manhood ; better in the field   650
To leave our carcasses, and die with fame,
Than fly, and purchase life on terms of shame.
Sackvilles alone anticipate defeat,
And ere they dare the battle, sound retreat.
  But if persuasions ineffectual prove,
If arguments are vain, nor prayers can move,
Yet in thy bitterness of frantic woe
Why talk of Burton ? why to Scotland go ?
Is there not Oxford, she, with open arms,
Shall meet thy wish, and yield up all her charms ; 660
Shall for thy love her former loves resign,
And jilt the banish'd Stuarts to be thine.
  Bow'd to the yoke, and, soon as she could read,
Tutor'd to get, by heart, the despot's creed,
She, of subjection proud, shall knee thy throne,
And have no principles but thine alone ;
She shall thy will implicitly receive,
Nor act, nor speak, nor think, without thy leave.
Where is the glory of imperial sway
If subjects none but just commands obey ? 670

by putting down the other's vote, and were agreed that the Members were equal.
  ' But some friends of Lord *Hardwicke*, who knew, that an equality of votes rejected the Grace, on account of the difference which first appeared in the Proctors accounts, insisted that that difference in their computation was a sufficient reason for having another scrutiny ; and Mr. *Longmire*, joined with them in insisting on the same thing, and refused to make a return without it.
  ' Those who voted against Lord *Hardwicke* refused to admit of another scrutiny, and Mr. *Forster* refused to collect the votes again, though directed and admonished so to do by the vice-chancellor ; who then ordered a Public Notary to make an act of what each Proctor declared upon that occasion ; and afterwards, in the usual form, put an end to the congregation.' (' The Gentleman's Magazine,' April, 1764, Vol. XXXIV, p. 156.)
  [653] See note on ' The Ghost,' Book I, line 250.

Then, and then only, is obedience seen,
When by command they dare do all that's mean :
Hither then wing thy flight, here fix thy stand
Nor fail to bring thy Sandwich in thy hand.
   Gods ! with what joy, (for fancy now supplies,
And lays the future open to my eyes)
Gods ! with what joy I see the worthies meet,
And Brother Lichfield Brother Sandwich greet !
Blest be your greetings, blest each dear embrace ;
Blest to yourselves, and to the human race.   680
Sickening at virtues, which she cannot reach,
Which seem her baser nature to impeach,
Let Envy, in a whirlwind's bosom hurl'd,
Outrageous, search the corners of the world,
Ransack the present times, look back to past,
Rip up the future, and confess at last,
No times, past, present, or to come, could e'er
Produce, and bless the world with such a pair.
   Phillips, the good old Phillips, out of breath,
Escaped from Monmouth, and escaped from death,   690
Shall hail his Sandwich with that virtuous zeal,
That glorious ardour for the commonweal,
Which warm'd his loyal heart and bless'd his tongue,
When on his lips the cause of rebels hung.
   Whilst Womanhood, in habit of a nun,

[678] George Henry Lee (1718-1772), third Earl of Lichfield, Chancellor of Oxford University from 1762 until his death. Tooke remarks: ' The last Earl of Litchfield succeeded the Earl of Westmorland, as Chancellor of the University of Oxford, in 1762, after a severe contest between him and Lords Foley and Suffolk ; his success was principally owing to the interference of Lord Bute in his favour.'

[689] ' Sir John Phillips, a barrister and an active member of the House of Commons who, during the rebellion of 1745, intrenching himself behind legal forces, had at a public meeting threatened to present to the Court of King's Bench, as an illegal levying of money upon the subject, the association formed for the defence of the family upon the throne. In 1763 he was called to the privy council, and died the following year.' (Tooke.)

[695] The Medmenham monks (see below) brought in prostitutes for the purposes of their orgies, and Churchill here indicates that the women were dressed as nuns. This method of adding a supposed piquancy to lust is curiously common in eighteenth century porno-

At Mednam lies, by backward monks undone;
A nation's reckoning, like an alehouse score,
Whilst Paul, the aged, chalks behind a door,
Compell'd to hire a foe to cast it up,
Dashwood shall pour, from a communion cup,   700
Libations to the goddess without eyes,
And hob or nob in cyder and excise.

    From those deep shades, where Vanity, unknown,
Doth penance for her pride, and pines alone,
Cursed in herself, by her own thoughts undone,
Where she sees all, but can be seen by none;
Where she no longer, mistress of the schools,
Hears praise loud pealing from the mouths of fools,
Or hears it at a distance; in despair
To join the crowd, and put in for a share,   710
Twisting each thought a thousand different ways,
For his new friends new-modelling old praise;
Where frugal sense so very fine is spun,

graphic literature and is still sometimes found in the indecent post-cards thrust under the noses of continental travellers.

[696] The ruins of Mednam or Medmenham Abbey still stand on the bank of the Thames midway between Marlow and Henley. It was originally a dependency of the Cistercian Abbey of Woburn, but at the Reformation had fallen into such decay that only two monks remained within its already ruined walls. The disused Abbey was rented by Sir Francis Dashwood, who furnished it, stocked its cellar, decorated the walls of the chapel with obscene paintings and established there an order of 'Franciscans' (so called from his own name) consisting of a Superior (himself) and twelve members. The names of these are variously given, but Sandwich, Bubb-Dodington, Sir William Stanhope, Sir John Dashwood-King and George Selwyn were included. Robert Lloyd is said to have been of the fraternity; Wilkes attended the meetings several times and Churchill himself at least once. 'Over the grand entrance was the famous inscription on Rabelais's Abbey of Thelème: *Fay ce que voudras.* At the end of the passage, over the door, was: *Aude, hospes, contemnere opes!* At one end of the refectory was Harpocrates, the Egyptian god of silence; at the other end the goddess Angerona, that the same duty might be enjoined on both sexes.' (Wilkes.)

[698] Paul Whitehead. (See note on 'The Ghost,' Book III, line 95.)

[700] Dashwood. (See note on 'The Ghost,' Book IV, line 629.)

[701] The poet should have said 'the goddess without speech.' Angerona was the Roman goddess of silence; she had a statue in the temple of Volupia in which she was represented with her mouth bound up. Her festival was celebrated yearly on December 12th.

It serves twelve hours, though not enough for one,
King shall arise, and, bursting from the dead,
Shall hurl his piebald Latin at thy head.
    Burton (whilst awkward affectation's hung
In quaint and labour'd accents on his tongue ;
Who 'gainst their will makes junior blockheads speak,
Ignorant of both, new Latin and new Greek,   720
Not such as was in Greece and Latium known,
But of a modern cut, and all his own ;
Who threads, like beads, loose thoughts on such a string,
They're praise and censure ; nothing, every thing ;
Pantomime thoughts, and style so full of trick,
They even make a Merry Andrew sick ;
Thoughts all so dull, so pliant in their growth,
They're verse, they're prose, they're neither, and they're
    both)
Shall (though by nature ever loath to praise)
Thy curious worth set forth in curious phrase ;   730
Obscurely stiff, shall press poor sense to death,
Or in long periods run her out of breath ;
Shall make a babe, for which, with all his fame,
Adam could not have found a proper name,
Whilst, beating out his features to a smile,
He hugs the bastard brat, and calls it Style.

715 ' Dr. William King, LL.D., Principal of St. Mary's Hall, died at an advanced age in 1764, at which time he was the oldest head of any house in the University of Oxford, having been appointed to that situation in 1719. The composition of his celebrated Radcliffe harangue and the Tory principles it advocated afforded an ample field of controversy to critics, but it earned for him an elegant compliment from Warton in his Triumph of Isis.' (Tooke.)

717 This is not the Burton referred to at line 602, although the Christian name of each was John. This John Burton (1696-1771), scholar and philanthropist, was elected a scholar of Corpus Christi College, Oxford, in 1713, and became college tutor four years later. He taught Greek energetically and Latin only less so. There seems no justification for Churchill's jibe, but Burton had incurred his hostility by an oration delivered at Oxford in 1763 in which he attacked Wilkes.

734 ' And out of the ground the Lord God formed every beast of the field, and every fowl of the air ; and brought *them* unto Adam to see what he would call them : and whatsoever Adam called every living creature, that *was* the name thereof.' (Genesis ii, 19.)

Hush'd be all nature as the land of death ;
Let each stream sleep, and each wind hold his breath ;
Be the bells muffled, nor one sound of care,
Pressing for audience, wake the slumbering air ;   740
Browne comes—behold how cautiously he creeps—
How slow he walks, and yet how fast he sleeps—
But to thy praise in sleep he shall agree ;
He cannot wake, but he shall dream of thee.

Physic, her head with opiate poppies crown'd,
Her loins by the chaste matron Camphire bound ;
Physic, obtaining succour from the pen
Of her soft son, her gentle Heberden,
If there are men who can thy virtue know,
Yet spite of virtue treat thee as a foe,   750
Shall, like a scholar, stop their rebel breath,
And in each recipe send classic death.

So deep in knowledge, that few lines can sound
And plumb the bottom of the vast profound,
Few grave ones with such gravity can think,
Or follow half so fast as he can sink ;
With nice distinctions glossing o'er the text,
Obscure with meaning, and in words perplexed ;
With subtleties on subtleties refined,
Meant to divide and subdivide the mind,   760
Keeping the forwardness of youth in awe,
The scowling Blackstone bears the train of law.

741 ' Dr. William Browne, Lord Lichfield's Vice-Chancellor of the University of Oxford from 1759 to 1769 ; he was also provost of Queen's College.' (Tooke.) The point of Churchill's satire is now lost.

746 Camphor, until about 1800, was usually spelt ' camphire.' It was formerly in repute as an antaphrodisiac.

748 William Heberden (1710-1801), a celebrated physician and extremely charitable man. He was the friend of Cowper, Warburton and Johnson, and was present at the death-bed of Garrick.

762 Sir William Blackstone (1723-1780) entered himself at the Middle Temple in 1741 and was called to the bar in 1746. In 1758 he became the first professor of English law at Oxford. In 1763 he was made solicitor-general to the Queen, and two years later appeared the first volume of the famous ' Commentaries,' a work which went into eight editions in the author's life-time and brought him in about £14,000. In the debate on the election of Wilkes, Blackstone gave it

Divinity, enrobed in college fur,
In her right hand a New Court Kalendar
Bound like a book of prayer, thy coming waits
With all her pack, to hymn thee in the gates.
   Loyalty, fix'd on Isis' alter'd shore,
A stranger long, but stranger now no more,
Shall pitch her tabernacle, and with eyes
Brim-full of rapture, view her new allies ;   770
Shall, with much pleasure and more wonder, view
Men great at court, and great at Oxford too.
   O sacred Loyalty ! accursed be those
Who, seeming friends, turn out thy deadliest foes,
Who prostitute to kings thy honour'd name,
And sooth their passions to betray their fame ;
Nor praised be those, to whose proud nature clings
Contempt of government, and hate of kings ;
Who, willing to be free, not knowing how,
A strange intemperance of zeal avow,   780
And start at Loyalty, as at a word
Which without danger Freedom never heard.
   Vain errors of vain men—wild both extremes,
And to the state not wholesome, like the dreams,
Children of night, of indigestion bred,
Which, reason clouded, seize and turn the head ;
Loyalty without Freedom, is a chain
Which men of liberal notice can't sustain,
And Freedom without Loyalty, a name
Which nothing means, or means licentious shame.   790
   Thine be the art, my Sandwich, thine the toil,
In Oxford's stubborn and untoward soil
To rear this plant of union, till at length,
Rooted by time, and foster'd into strength,
Shooting aloft, all danger it defies,
And proudly lifts its branches to the skies ;
Whilst, Wisdom's happy son, but not her slave,
Gay with the gay, and with the grave ones grave,

as his opinion that Wilkes was disqualified by Common Law from
sitting in the House. His opponents quoted the ' Commentaries '
against him, and Blackstone, in the next edition of his book, altered
the list of disqualifications so as to include Wilkes.

Free from the dull impertinence of thought,
Beneath that shade, which thy own labours wrought   800
And fashion'd into strength, shalt thou repose
Secure of liberal praise, since Isis flows
True to her Tame, as duty hath decreed,
Nor longer, like a harlot, lusts for Tweed,
And those old wreaths, which Oxford once dared twine
To grace a Stuart brow, she plants on thine.

THE FAREWELL*

POET

FAREWELL to Europe, and at once, farewell
To all the follies which in Europe dwell;
To Eastern India now, a richer clime,
Richer, alas! in everything, but rhyme,
The Muses steer their course; and, fond of change,
At large, in other worlds, desire to range,
Resolved, at least, since they the fool must play,
To do it in a different place, and way.

FRIEND

What whim is this, what error of the brain,
What madness worse than in the dog-star's reign?   10
Why into foreign countries would you roam,
Are there not knaves and fools enough at home?
If satire be thy object, and thy lays
As yet have shown no talents fit for praise;
If satire be thy object, search all round,
Nor to thy purpose can one spot be found
Like England, where, to rampant vigour grown,
Vice chokes up every virtue; where, self-sown,
The seeds of folly shoot forth rank and bold,
And every seed brings forth a hundred-fold.   20

POET

No more of this—though Truth (the more our shame;
The more our guilt) though Truth perhaps may claim,
And justify her part in this, yet here,
For the first time, e'en Truth offends my ear.

---

* Probably published in July, 1764. 'Printed for the Author,
and sold by W. Flexney .... G. Kearsley .... C. Henderson ....
J. Coote .... J. Gardiner .... J. Almon .... and C. Moran.

[10] See note on 'Gotham,' Book I, line 391.

Declaim from morn to night, from night to morn,
Take up the theme anew, when day's new-born,
I hear, and hate—be England what she will,
With all her faults she is my country still.

FRIEND

Thy country ? and what then ? Is that mere word
Against the voice of Reason to be heard ?   30
Are prejudices, deep imbibed in youth,
To counteract, and make thee hate the truth ?
'Tis the sure symptom of a narrow soul
To draw its grand attachment from the whole,
And take up with a part ; men, not confined
Within such paltry limits, men design'd
Their nature to exalt, where'er they go,
Wherever waves can roll, and winds can blow,
Where'er the blessed sun, placed in the sky
To watch this subject world, can dart his eye,   40
Are still the same, and prejudice outgrown,
Consider every country as their own ;
At one grand view they take in Nature's plan,
Not more at home in England than Japan.

POET

My good, grave Sir of Theory, whose wit,
Grasping at shadows, ne'er caught substance yet,
'Tis mighty easy o'er a glass of wine
On vain refinements vainly to refine,
To laugh at poverty in plenty's reign,
To boast of apathy when out of pain,   50
And in each sentence, worthy of the schools,
Varnish'd with sophistry, to deal out rules
Most fit for practice, but for one poor fault,
That into practice they can ne'er be brought.
At home, and sitting in your elbow-chair,
You praise Japan, though you was never there :
But was the ship this moment under sail,
Would not your mind be changed, your spirits fail ?

389

Would you not cast one longing eye to shore,
And vow to deal in such wild schemes no more?   60
Howe'er our pride may tempt us to conceal
Those passions which we cannot choose but feel,
There's a strange something, which, without a brain,
Fools feel, and which e'en wise men can't explain,
Planted in man to bind him to that earth,
In dearest ties, from whence he drew his birth.
   If honour calls, wher'er she points the way
The sons of honour follow, and obey;
If need compels, wherever we are sent
'Tis want of courage not to be content;   70
But, if we have the liberty of choice,
And all depends on our own single voice,
To deem of every country as the same
Is rank rebellion, 'gainst the lawful claim
Of Nature, and such dull indifference
May be philosophy, but can't be sense.

FRIEND

   Weak and unjust distinction, strange design,
Most peevish, most perverse, to undermine
Philosophy, and throw her empire down
By means of sense, from whom she holds her crown!
Divine Philosophy, to thee we owe   81
All that is worth possessing here below;
Virtue and wisdom consecrate thy reign,
Doubled each joy, and pain no longer pain.
   When, like a garden, where, for want of toil
And wholesome discipline, the rich, rank soil
Teems with incumbrances; where all around,
Herbs noxious in their nature make the ground,
Like the good mother of a thankless son,
Curse her own womb, by fruitfulness undone;   90
Like such a garden, when the human soul,
Uncultured, wild, impatient of control,
Brings forth those passions of luxuriant race,
Which spread, and stifle every herb of grace;
Whilst Virtue, check'd by the cold hand of scorn,

Seems withering on the bed where she was born,
Philosophy steps in, with steady hand
She brings her aid, she clears the encumber'd land ;
Too virtuous to spare Vice one stroke, too wise
One moment to attend to Pity's cries,   100
See with what godlike, what relentless power
She roots up every weed !

POET

                       And every flower.
Philosophy, a name of meek degree,
Embraced, in token of humility,
By the proud sage, who, whilst he strove to hide,
In that vain artifice, reveal'd his pride ;
Philosophy, whom Nature had design'd
To purge all errors from the human mind,
Herself misled by the philosopher,   110
At once her priest and master made us err :
Pride, pride, like leaven in a mass of flour,
Tainted her laws, and made e'en virtue sour.
   Had she, content within her proper sphere,
Taught lessons suited to the human ear,
Which might fair Virtue's genuine fruits produce,
Made not for ornament but real use,
The heart of man, unrivall'd, she had sway'd,
Praised by the good, and by the bad obey'd ;
But when she, overturning Reason's throne,   120
Strove proudly in its place to plant her own ;
When she with apathy the breast would steel,
And teach us, deeply feeling, not to feel ; ·
When she would wildly all her force employ,
Not to correct our passions, but destroy ;
When, not content our nature to restore,
As made by God, she made it new all o'er ;
When, with a strange and criminal excess,
To make us more than men she made us less ;

[107] The ' proud sage ' intended is Diogenes. Treading upon
Plato's robe, he exclaimed : ' Thus I trample under foot the pride of
Plato.' Plato calmly replied : ' Yes, and with greater pride, Diogenes.'

The good her dwindled power with pity saw,   130
The bad with joy, and none but fools with awe.
    Truth with a simple and unvarnish'd tale,
E'en from the mouth of Norton might prevail,
Could she get there ; but Falsehood's sugar'd strain
Should pour her fatal blandishments in vain,
Nor make one convert, though the Siren hung,
Where she too often hangs, on Mansfield's tongue.
Should all the Sophs, whom in his course the sun
Hath seen, or past, or present, rise in one ;
Should *he*, whilst pleasure in each sentence flows,   140
Like Plato, give us poetry in prose ;
Should he, full orator, at once impart
The Athenian's genius with the Roman's art ;
Genius and art should in this instance fail,
Nor Rome, though join'd with Athens, here prevail,
'Tis not in man, 'tis not in more than man,
To make me find one fault in Nature's plan.
Placed low ourselves, we censure those above,
And, wanting judgment, think that she wants love ;
Blame, where we ought in reason to commend,   150
And think her most a foe, when most a friend.
Such be philosophers—their specious art,
Though Friendship pleads, shall never warp my heart ;
Ne'er make me from this breast one passion tear,
Which Nature, my best friend, hath planted there.

FRIEND

    Forgiving as a friend, what, whilst I live,
As a philosopher I can't forgive,
In this one point at last I join with you,
To Nature pay all that is Nature's due ;
But let not clouded Reason sink so low,   160
To fancy debts she does not, cannot owe :
Bear, to full manhood grown, those shackles bear
Which Nature meant us for a time to wear,
As we wear leading-strings, which, useless grown,
Are laid aside, when we can walk alone ;
But on thyself by peevish humour sway'd

Wilt thou lay burdens Nature never laid ?
Wilt thou make faults, whilst Judgment weakly errs,
And then defend, mistaking them for hers ?
Darest thou to say, in our enlighten'd age,   170
That this grand master passion, this brave rage
Which flames out for thy country, was imprest
And fix'd by Nature in the human breast ?
　　If you prefer the place where you was born,
And hold all others in contempt and scorn
On fair comparison ; if on that land
With lib'ral, and a more than equal hand,
Her gifts, as in profusion, Plenty sends ;
If Virtue meets with more and better friends ;
If Science finds a patron 'mongst the great ;   180
If Honesty is minister of state ;
If Power, the guardian of our rights design'd,
Is to that great, that only end confined ;
If riches are employ'd to bless the poor ;
If law is sacred, liberty secure ;
Let but these facts depend on proofs of weight,
Reason declares thy love can't be too great,
And, in this light could he our country view,
A very Hottentot must love it too.
　　But if by Fate's decrees, you owe your birth   190
To some most barren and penurious earth,
Where, every comfort of this life denied,
Her real wants are scantily supplied ;
Where power is reason, liberty a joke,
Laws never made, or made but to be broke ;
To fix thy love on such a wretched spot,
Because in lust's wild fever there begot ;
Because, thy weight no longer fit to bear,
By chance, not choice, thy mother dropt thee there,
Is folly, which admits not of defence ;   200
It can't be nature, for it is not sense.
By the same argument which here you hold,
(When Falsehood's insolent, let Truth be bold)
If propagation can in torments dwell,
A devil must, if born there, love his hell.

393

POET

Had Fate, to whose decrees I lowly bend,
And e'en in punishment confess a friend,
Ordain'd my birth in some place yet untried,
On purpose made to mortify my pride ;
Where the sun never gave one glimpse of day,   210
Where science never yet could dart one ray ;
Had I been born on some bleak, blasted plain
Of barren Scotland, in a Stuart's reign,
Or in some kingdom, where men, weak, or worse,
Turn'd Nature's every blessing to a curse ;
Where crowns of freedom, by the fathers won,
Dropp'd leaf by leaf from each degenerate son,
In spite of all the wisdom you display,
All you have said, and yet may have to say,
My weakness here, if weakness, I confess,   220
I as my country had not loved her less.
   Whether strict reason bears me out in this,
Let those who, always seeking, always miss
The ways of reason, doubt with precious zeal ;
Theirs be the praise to argue, mine to feel.
Wish we to trace this passion to the root,
We, like a tree, may know it by its fruit ;
From its rich stem ten thousand virtues spring,
Ten thousand blessings on its branches cling ;
Yet in the circle of revolving years   230
Not one misfortune, not one vice, appears.
Hence, then, and what you reason call adore ;
This, if not reason, must be something more.
   But (for I wish not others to confine ;
Be their opinions unrestrain'd as mine)
Whether this love's of good, or evil growth,
A vice, a virtue, or a spice of both,
Let men of nicer argument decide ;
If it is virtuous, soothe an honest pride
With liberal praise ; if vicious, be content,   240
It is a vice I never can repent ;
A vice, which, weigh'd in heaven, shall more avail
Than ten cold virtues in the other scale.

394

FRIEND

This wild, untemper'd zeal (which, after all,
We, candour unimpeach'd, might madness call)
Is it a virtue ? that you scarce pretend ;
Or can it be a vice, like virtue's friend,
Which draws us off from and dissolves the force
Of private ties, nay, stops us in our course
To that grand object of the human soul,   250
That nobler love which comprehends the whole ?
Coop'd in the limits of this petty isle,
This nook, which scarce deserves a frown or smile
Weigh'd with Creation, you, by whim undone,
Give all your thoughts to what is scarce worth one.
The generous soul, by Nature taught to soar,
Her strength confirm'd in philosophic lore,
At one grand view takes in a world with ease,
And, seeing all mankind, loves all she sees.

POET

Was it most sure, which yet a doubt endures,   260
Not found in Reason's creed, though found in yours,
That these two services, like what we're told
And know of God's and Mammon's, cannot hold
And draw together ; that, however loth,
We neither serve, attempting to serve both,
I could not doubt a moment which to choose,
And which in common reason to refuse.
    Invented oft for purposes of art,
Born of the head, though father'd on the heart,
This grand love of the world must be confest   270
A barren speculation at the best.
Not one man in a thousand, should he live
Beyond the usual term of life, could give,
So rare occasion comes, and to so few,
Proof whether his regards are feign'd, or true.
    The love we bear our country, is a root

---

[264] 'No man can serve two masters : for either he will hate the one,
and love the other ; or else he will hold to the one, and despise the other.
Ye cannot serve God and Mammon.' (S. Matthew vi, 24.)

Which never fails to bring forth golden fruit ;
'Tis in the mind an everlasting spring
Of glorious actions, which become a king,
Nor less become a subject ; 'tis a debt   280
Which bad men, though they pay not, can't forget ;
A duty which the good delight to pay,
And every man can practise every day.
   Nor, for my life (so very dim my eye,
Or dull your argument) can I descry
What you with faith assert, how that dear love
Which binds me to my country, can remove,
And make me of necessity forego,
That general love which to the world I owe.
Those ties of private nature, small extent,   290
In which the mind of narrow cast is pent,
Are only steps on which the generous soul
Mounts, by degrees, till she includes the whole.
That spring of love, which, in the human mind,
Founded on self, flows narrow and confined,
Enlarges as it rolls, and comprehends
The social charities of blood and friends,
Till smaller streams included, not o'erpast,
It rises to our country's love at last ;
And he, with liberal and enlargèd mind,   300
Who loves his country, cannot hate mankind.

FRIEND

   Friend as you would appear to common sense,
Tell me, or think no more of a defence,
Is it a proof of love by choice to run
A vagrant from your country ?

POET

                   Can the son
(Shame, shame on all such sons) with ruthless eye,
And heart more patient than the flint, stand by,
And by some ruffian, from all shame divorced,
All virtue, see his honour'd mother forced !   310

Then—no, by Him that made me, not e'en then,
Could I with patience, by the worst of men,
Behold my country plunder'd, beggar'd, lost
Beyond redemption, all her glories cross'd,
E'en when occasion made them ripe, her fame
Fled like a dream, while she awakes to shame.

FRIEND

Is it not more the office of a friend,
The office of a patron, to defend
Her sinking state, than basely to decline
So great a cause, and in despair resign ?   320

POET

Beyond my reach, alas ! the grievance lies,
And, whilst more able patriots doubt, she dies.
From a foul source, more deep than we suppose,
Fatally deep and dark, this grievance flows.
'Tis not that peace our glorious hopes defeats ;
'Tis not the voice of faction in the streets ;
'Tis not a gross attack on freedom made ;
'Tis not the arm of privilege display'd
Against the subject, whilst she wears no sting
To disappoint the purpose of a king ;   330
These are no ills, or trifles, if compared
With those which are contrived though not declared.
Tell me, Philosopher, is it a crime
To pry into the secret womb of Time,
Or, born in ignorance, must we despair
To reach events, and read the future there ?
Why, be it so—still 'tis the right of man,
Imparted by his Maker, where he can,
To former times and men his eye to cast,
And judge of what's to come, by what is past.   340
Should there be found, in some not distant year,
(O how I wish to be no prophet here)
Amongst our British Lords should there be found
Some great in power, in principles unsound,

397

Who look on freedom with an evil eye,
In whom the springs of loyalty are dry;
Who wish to soar on wild Ambition's wings,
Who hate the Commons, and who love not Kings;
Who would divide the people and the throne,
To set up separate interests of their own;   350
Who hate whatever aids their wholesome growth,
And only join with, to destroy them both;
Should there be found such men in after-times,
May Heaven, in mercy to our grievous crimes,
Allot some milder vengeance, nor to them,
And to their rage, this wretched land condemn.
   Thou God above, on whom all states depend,
Who knowest from the first their rise, and end,
If there's a day mark'd in the book of Fate,
When ruin must involve our equal state;   360
When law, alas! must be no more, and we,
To freedom born, must be no longer free,
Let not a mob of tyrants seize the helm,
Nor titled upstarts league to rob the realm;
Let not, whatever other ills assail,
A damned aristocracy prevail:
If, all too short, our course of freedom run,
'Tis Thy good pleasure we should be undone,
Let us, some comfort in our griefs to bring,
Be slaves to one, and be that one a king.   370

FRIEND

   Poets, accustom'd by their trade to feign,
Oft substitute creations of the brain
For real substance, and, themselves deceived,
Would have the fiction by mankind believed.
Such is your case—but grant, to soothe your pride,
That you know more than all the world beside,
Why deal in hints, why make a moment's doubt?
Resolved, and like a man, at once speak out;
Shew us our danger, tell us where it lies,
And, to ensure our safety, make us wise.   380

POET

Rather than bear the pain of thought, fools stray ;
The proud will rather lose than ask their way :
To men of sense what needs it to unfold,
And tell a tale which they must know untold ?
In the bad, interest warps the canker'd heart,
The good are hoodwink'd by the tricks of art ;
And, whilst arch, subtle hypocrites contrive
To keep the flames of discontent alive ;
Whilst they, with arts to honest men unknown,
Breed doubts between the people and the throne,   390
Making us fear, where reason never yet
Allow'd one fear, or could one doubt admit,
Themselves pass unsuspected in disguise,
And 'gainst our real danger seal our eyes.

FRIEND

Mark them, and let their names recorded stand
On Shame's black roll, and stink through all the land.

POET

That might some courage, but no prudence be ;
No hurt to them, and jeopardy to me.

FRIEND

Leave out their names.

POET

.For that kind caution, thanks ; 400
But may not judges sometimes fill up blanks ?

FRIEND

Your country's laws in doubt then you reject.

POET

The laws I love, the lawyers I suspect.
Amongst Twelve Judges may not one be found
(On bare, bare possibility I ground

399

This wholesome doubt) who may enlarge, retrench,
Create, and uncreate, and from the bench,
With winks, smiles, nods, and such like paltry arts,
May work and worm into a jury's hearts ?
Or, baffled there, may, turbulent of soul,   410
Cramp their high office, and their rights control ;
Who may, though judge, turn advocate at large,
And deal replies out by the way of charge,
Making interpretation all the way,
In spite of facts, his wicked will obey ;
And, leaving law without the least defence,
May damn his conscience to approve his sense ?

FRIEND

Whilst, the true guardians of this charter'd land,
In full and perfect vigour, juries stand,
A judge in vain shall awe, cajole, perplex.   420

POET

Suppose I should be tried in Middlesex ?

FRIEND

To pack a jury they will never dare.

POET

There's no occasion to pack juries there.

FRIEND

'Gainst prejudice all arguments are weak ;
Reason herself without affect must speak.
Fly then thy country, like a coward fly ;
Renounce her interest, and her laws defy.
But why, bewitch'd, to India turn thine eyes ?
Cannot our Europe thy vast wrath suffice ?
Cannot thy misbegotten Muse lay bare   430
Her brawny arm, and play the butcher there ?

[421] In the action brought against Wood, Lord Egremont's secretary,
for seizing Wilkes's papers, Webb, as a witness, swore that while in
the house he had no key in his hand. For this he was tried, by the
Middlesex petty jury, for perjury, on May 22nd, 1764, and acquitted.

POET

Thy counsel taken, what should Satire do ?
Where could she find an object that is new ?
Those travell'd youths, whom tender mothers wean,
And send abroad to see, and to be seen ;
With whom, lest they should fornicate, or worse,
A tutor's sent by way of a dry nurse ;
Each of whom just enough of spirit bears
To shew our follies, and to bring home theirs,
Have made all Europe's vices so well known,   440
They seem almost as natural as our own.

FRIEND

Will India for thy purpose better do ?

POET

In one respect at least—there's something new.

FRIEND

A harmless people, in whom Nature speaks
Free and untainted, 'mongst whom Satire seeks,
But vainly seeks, so simply plain their hearts,
One bosom where to lodge her poison'd darts.

POET

From knowledge speak you this, or doubt on doubt
Weigh'd and resolved, hath Reason found it out ?
Neither from knowledge, nor by reason taught,   450
You have faith every where, but where you ought.
India or Europe—what's there in a name ?
Propensity to vice in both the same,
Nature alike in both works for man's good,
Alike in both by man himself withstood.
Nabobs, as well as those who hunt them down,
Deserve a cord much better than a crown,

456 The word nabob is a corruption of the Hindu *nawwab*, a deputy,
originally the governor of a province or commander of an army under
the Moguls.   The word came to mean anyone who had made a
fortune in India.

And a Mogul can thrones as much debase
As any polish'd prince of Christian race.

FRIEND

Could you, a task more hard than you suppose,   460
Could you, in ridicule whilst Satire glows,
Make all their follies to the life appear,
'Tis ten to one you gain no credit here ;
Howe'er well drawn, the picture, after all,
Because we know not the original,
Would not find favour in the public eye.

POET

That, having your good leave, I mean to try :
And if your observations sterling hold,
If the piece should be heavy, tame, and cold,
To make it to the side of Nature lean,   470
And meaning nothing, something seem to mean :
To make the whole in lively colours glow,
To bring before us something that we know,
And from all honest men applause to win,
I'll group the Company and put them in.

[458] The Great Mogul was the popular name for the Sovereign of the Empire founded in Hindustan by the Mongols under Babir in the sixteenth century. The Empire came to an end in 1806.

[475] ' The Company,' *i.e.* the East India Company, was incorporated by Queen Elizabeth in 1600, and fostered by later rulers until, by the care of Charles II, who granted it five important Charters, it grew into a great Chartered Company, with the right to acquire territory, coin money, command troops, make war and peace, and exercise civil and criminal jurisdiction. So long as the chief concern of the Company was with trade its control was vested in the hands of a Governor and a Committee of twenty-four, the chairman and court of directors having complete control of their servants in India. Clive's victory at Plassey in 1757 made the responsibilities of the Company too great for such a system, but it was not until Lord North's regulating Act of 1773 and Pitt's India Bill of 1784 that matters were put upon a better footing, with due provision for control by the British Government. The affairs of the Company were very much in the public mind in 1764. While Clive was in England, dissensions broke out between the Governor and Council of Calcutta. These, and some military reverses in India, caused a sharp fall in India stock, and Clive was implored to return to India to set matters in order. This he refused to do unless his old friend, Lawrence Sullivan, with whom he had quarrelled, vacated the

FRIEND

Be that ungenerous thought by shame suppress'd ;
Add not distress to those too much distress'd.
Have they not, by blind zeal misled, laid bare,
Those sores which never might endure the air ?
Have they not brought their mysteries so low,   480
That what the wise suspected not, fools know ?
From their first rise e'en to the present hour,
Have they not proved their own abuse of power,
Made it impossible, if fairly view'd,
Ever to have that dangerous power renew'd,
Whilst unseduced by ministers, the throne
Regards our interest, and knows its own ?

POET

Should every other subject chance to fail,
Those who have sail'd, and those who wish'd to sail
In the last fleet, afford an ample field,   490
Which must beyond my hopes a harvest yield.

FRIEND

On such vile food Satire can never thrive.

POET

She cannot starve, if there was only Clive.

chair at India House. His terms having been agreed to, he sailed on
May 27th, 1764.

    493 Churchill does not seem to have approved of Clive any more
than of those Directors of the Company with whom he was at issue.
Robert Clive (1725-1774) was the son of an impoverished Shropshire
Squire. As a writer in the service of the East India Company, he
reached Madras penniless in 1744. His great bravery at the siege of
Pondicherry in 1748 laid the foundation of a military career which
culminated at Plassey. This battle broke the power of Suráj ud
Dowlah, Nawáb of Bengal ; Clive installed Mir Jaffier, his general, in
his stead, and received from him a large present and the quit-rent of
the Company's territory. Clive was Governor of the Company's
possessions in Bengal from 1757 until 1760, when he re. ned to
England. He was created Baron Clive in 1762, returned to India, and
assumed the Governorship of Bengal in 1765, returning once more to
England, in shattered health, in the following year. He committed
suicide in 1774.

THE TIMES*

THE time hath been, a boyish, blushing time,
When modesty was scarcely held a crime ;
When the most wicked had some touch of grace,
And trembled to meet Virtue face to face ;
When those, who, in the cause of Sin grown gray,
Had served her without grudging, day by day,
Were yet so weak an awkward shame to feel,
And strove that glorious service to conceal :
We, better bred, and than our sires more wise,
Such paltry narrowness of soul despise :   10
To virtue every mean pretence disclaim,
Lay bare our crimes, and glory in our shame.
     Time was, ere Temperance had fled the realm,
Ere Luxury sat guttling at the helm
From meal to meal, without one moment's space
Reserved for business, or allow'd for grace ;
Ere Vanity had so far conquer'd sense
To make us all wild rivals in expense,
To make one fool strive to outvie another,
And every coxcomb dress against his brother ;   20
Ere banish'd Industry had left our shores,
And Labour was by Pride kick'd out of doors ;
Ere idleness prevail'd sole queen in courts,
Or only yielded to a rage for sports ;
Ere each weak mind was with externals caught,
And dissipation held the place of thought ;
Ere gambling lords in vice so far were gone
To cog the die, and bid the sun look on ;
Ere a great nation, not less just than free,
Was made a beggar by Economy ;   30
Ere rugged honesty was out of vogue ;

* First published on September 4th, 1764. 'Printed for the
Author, and sold by J. Coote . . . . J. Almon . . . . W. Flexney . . . .
C. Henderson . . . . J. Gardiner . . . . and C. Moran.'

30 ' The party-cry of Lord Bute's administration was " Economy ".'
(Tooke.)

Ere fashion stamp'd her sanction on the rogue ;
Time was that men had conscience, that they made
Scruples to owe what never could be paid.
　Was one then found, however high his name,
So far above his fellows damn'd to shame,
Who dared abuse, and falsify his trust,
Who, being great, yet dared to be unjust—
Shunn'd like a plague, or but at distance view'd,
He walk'd the crowded streets in solitude ;　　　　40
Nor could his rank, and station in the land
Bribe one mean knave to take him by the hand.
Such rigid maxims (O, might such revive
To keep expiring honesty alive !)
Made rogues, all other hopes of fame denied,
Not just through principle, be just through pride.
　Our times, more polish'd, wear a different face ;
Debts are an honour, payment a disgrace.
Men of weak minds, high-placed on folly's list,
May gravely tell us trade cannot subsist,　　　　50
Nor all those thousands who're in trade employ'd,
If faith 'twixt man and man is once destroy'd.
Why—be it so—we in that point accord ;
But what are trade, and tradesmen to a lord ?
　Faber, from day to day, from year to year,
Hath had the cries of tradesmen in his ear,
Of tradesmen by his villany betray'd,
And, vainly seeking justice, bankrupts made.
What is't to Faber ?　Lordly, as before,
He sits at ease, and lives to ruin more :　　　　60
Fix'd at his door, as motionless as stone,
Begging, but only begging for their own,

---

[55] Wodhull identifies Faber as the Earl of Halifax, *i.e.*, George
Montagu (1716-1771), 2nd Earl of the third creation, who, in 1741,
married the very wealthy daughter of a clothier named Dunk, and
took his name.　As President of the Board of Trade he did much to
encourage commerce with America, and the town of Halifax, Nova
Scotia, was called after him.　He became Secretary of State for the
Northern Department under Bute, and for the Southern Department
under Bute's successor, Grenville.　With Grenville and Egremont,
Halifax formed what was called the ' triumvirate,' and he was one of
the signatories of the General Warrant against Wilkes.　Hence
Churchill's hostility.

Unheard they stand, or only heard by those,
Those slaves in livery who mock their woes.
What is't to Faber ? he continues great,
Lives on in grandeur, and runs out in state.
The helpless widow, wrung with deep despair,
In bitterness of soul pours forth her prayer,
Hugging her starving babes with streaming eyes,
And calls down vengeance, vengeance from the skies. 70
What is't to Faber ? he stands safe and clear,
Heaven can commence no legal action here ;
And on his breast a mighty plate he wears,
A plate more firm than triple brass, which bears
The name of privilege, 'gainst vulgar awe ;
He feels no conscience, and he fears no law.
   Nor think, acquainted with small knaves alone,
Who have not shame outlived, and grace outgrown,
The great world hidden from thy reptile view,
That on such men, to whom contempt is due,   80
Contempt shall fall, and their vile author's name
Recorded stand through all the land of shame.
No—to his porch, like Persians to the sun,
Behold contending crowds of courtiers run ;
See, to his aid what noble troops advance,
All sworn to keep his crimes in countenance :
Nor wonder at it—they partake the charge,
As small their conscience, and their debts as large.
   Propp'd by such clients, and without control
From all that's honest in the human soul ;   90
In grandeur mean, with insolence unjust,
Whilst none but knaves can praise, and fools will trust,
Caress'd and courted, Faber seems to stand
A mighty pillar in a guilty land.
And (a sad truth, to which succeeding times
Will scarce give credit, when 'tis told in rhymes)
Did not strict honour with a jealous eye
Watch round the throne, did not true piety
(Who, link'd with honour for the noblest ends,
Ranks none but honest men amongst her friends)   100
Forbid us to be crush'd with such a weight,
He might in time be minister of state.

406

But why enlarge I on such petty crimes ?
They might have shock'd the faith of former times,
But now are held as nothing—we begin
Where our sires ended, and improve in sin ;
Rack our invention, and leave nothing new
In vice and folly for our sons to do.
   Nor deem this censure hard ; there's not a place
Most consecrate to purposes of grace,   110
Which vice hath not polluted ; none so high,
But with bold pinion she hath dared to fly,
And build there for her pleasure ; none so low
But she hath crept into it, made it know
And feel her power ; in courts, in camps she reigns,
O'er sober citizens, and simple swains ;
E'en in our temples she hath fix'd her throne,
And 'bove God's holy altars placed her own.
   More to increase the horror of our state,
To make her empire lasting as 'tis great ;   120
To make us, in full-grown perfection feel
Curses which neither art nor time can heal ;
All shame discarded, all remains of pride,
Meanness sits crown'd, and triumphs by her side ;
Meanness, who gleans out of the human mind
Those few good seeds which vice had left behind,
Those seeds which might in time to virtue tend,
And leaves the soul without a power to mend ;
Meanness, at sight of whom, with brave disdain,
The breast of manhood swells, but swells in vain ; 130
Before whom Honour makes a forced retreat,
And Freedom is compell'd to quit her seat ;
Meanness, which, like that mark by bloody Cain
Borne in his forehead for a brother slain,
God, in his great and all-subduing rage,
Ordains the standing mark of this vile age.
   The venal hero trucks his fame for gold,
The patriot's virtue for a place is sold,
The statesman bargains for his country's shame,
And for preferment priests their God disclaim ; 140
Worn out with lust, her day of lech'ry o'er,
The mother trains the daughter which she bore

In her own paths ; the father aids the plan,
And, when the innocent is ripe for man,
Sells her to some old lecher for a wife,
And makes her an adulteress for life,
Or in the papers bids his name appear,
And advertises for a L—— :
Husband and wife, (whom avarice must applaud)
Agree to save the charge of pimp and bawd ;   150
These parts they play themselves, a frugal pair,
And share the infamy, the gain to share ;
Well pleased to find, when they the profits tell,
That they have play'd the whore and rogue so well.
   Nor are these things (which might imply a spark
Of shame still left) transacted in the dark :
No—to the public they are open laid,
And carried on like any other trade ;
Scorning to mince damnation, and too proud
To work the works of darkness in a cloud,   160
In fullest vigour Vice maintains her sway ;
Free are her marts, and open at noon-day.
Meanness, now wed to Impudence, no more
In darkness skulks, and trembles, as of yore,
When the light breaks upon her coward eye ;
Boldly she stalks on earth, and to the sky
Lifts her proud head, nor fears lest time abate,

---

[148] The rhyme makes it certain that the missing name is ' Ligonier.'
John, Earl Ligonier (1680-1770), came of French Huguenot stock,
fought as a volunteer under Marlborough in 1702, purchased a com-
pany, and was present at Blenheim, Ramillies, Oudenarde and Mal-
plaquet, (where he had twenty bullets through his clothes). In 1720
he became colonel of the 8th or ' Black ' Horse, (now the 7th Dragoon
Guards) and made it one of the finest regiments in Europe. In 1742
he commanded the second division of the army at Dettingen, and was
made a K.B. by George II on the field of battle. At Fontenoy,
Ligonier commanded the British Foot. At the battle of Lauffeldt, in
1747, he led a cavalry charge which saved the British Infantry from
the pursuing French. His horse shot, he was captured, and was pre-
sented to Louis XV by Marshal Saxe, with the words : ' Sire, I
present to your Majesty a man who, by one glorious action, has discon-
certed all my projects.' Ligonier became an English Earl and a
Field-Marshal in 1766. He had all the Frenchman's impetuosity in
battle, and presumably in love also. It should be noted that neither
here, nor in line 558, does Churchill imply that Ligonier was homo-
sexual.

And turn her husband's love to canker'd hate,
Since fate, to make them more sincerely one,
Hath crown'd their loves with Montagu their son ;   170
A son so like his dam, so like his sire,
With all the mother's craft, the father's fire,
An image so express in every part,
So like in all bad qualities of heart,
That, had they fifty children, he alone
Would stand as heir apparent to the throne.
     With our own island vices not content,
We rob our neighbours on the Continent ;
Dance Europe round, and visit every court,
To ape their follies and their crimes import :   180
To different lands for different sins we roam,
And, richly freighted, bring our cargo home,
Nobly industrious to make vice appear
In her full state, and perfect only here.
     To Holland, where politeness ever reigns,
Where primitive sincerity remains,
And makes a stand ; where Freedom in her course
Hath left her name, though she hath lost her force
In that as other lands ; where simple Trade
Was never in the garb of Fraud array'd ;   190
Where Avarice never dared to shew his head :
Where, like a smiling cherub, Mercy, led
By Reason, blesses the sweet-blooded race ;
And cruelty could never find a place ;
To Holland for that charity we roam,
Which happily begins and ends at home.
     France, in return for peace and power restored,
For all those countries, which the hero's sword
Unprofitably purchased, idly thrown
Into her lap, and made once more her own ;   200

170 John Montagu, Earl of Sandwich. (See note on ' Gotham,'
Book I, line 464.)
     194 An ironical reference to the Amboyna atrocities. (See note on
' Gotham,' Book II, line 621.)
     200 France, by the peace of 1763, arranged by Bute, recovered cer-
tain rights of fishery, and a few minor colonial possessions. Spain
recovered Havana (captured in 1762 by Sir George Pocock and the
Earl of Albemarle) in exchange for the Floridas.

409

France hath afforded large and rich supplies
Of vanities full-trimm'd ; of polish'd lies,
Of soothing flatteries, which through the ears
Steal to, and melt the heart ; of slavish fears
Which break the spirit, and of abject fraud—
For which, alas ! we need not send abroad.
   Spain gives us pride—which Spain to all the Earth
May largely give, nor fear herself a dearth—
Gives us that jealousy, which, born of fear
And mean distrust, grows not by nature here ;   210
Gives us that superstition, which pretends
By the worst means to serve the best of ends ;
That cruelty, which, stranger to the brave,
Dwells only with the coward and the slave ;
That cruelty, which led her Christian bands
With more than savage rage o'er savage lands,
Bade them, without remorse, whole countries thin,
And hold of nought, but mercy, as a sin.
   Italia, nurse of every softer art,
Who, feigning to refine, unmans the heart ;   220
Who lays the realms of Sense and Virtue waste ;
Who mars while she pretends to mend our taste ;
Italia, to complete and crown our shame,
Sends us a fiend, and Legion is his name.
The farce of greatness without being great,
Pride without power, titles without estate,
Souls without vigour, bodies without force,
Hate without cause, revenge without remorse,
Dark, mean revenge, murder without defence,
Jealousy without love, sound without sense,   230
Mirth without humour, without wit grimace,
Faith without reason, Gospel without grace,
Zeal without knowledge, without nature art,
Men without manhood, women without heart ;
Half-men, who, dry and pithless, are debarr'd

---

[235] An allusion to the castrated Italians, male sopranos who came
to England to sing in the Opera. The sensation of the season of 1764
was Giovanni Manzoli. ' Manzoli's voice,' (says Dr. Burney) ' was the
most powerful and voluminous soprano that had been heard on our
stage since the time of Farinelli.' Tenducci, another *castrato*, sang

From man's best joys—no sooner made than marr'd—
Half-men, whom many a rich and noble dame,
To serve her lust, and yet secure her fame,
Keeps on high diet, as we capons feed,
To glut our appetites at last decreed ;   240
Women, who dance in postures so obscene,
They might awaken shame in Aretine ;
Who, when, retired from the day's piercing light,
They celebrate the mysteries of Night,
Might make the Muses, in a corner placed
To view their monstrous lusts, deem Sappho chaste :
These, and a thousand follies rank as these,
A thousand faults, ten thousand fools, who please
Our pall'd and sickly taste, ten thousand knaves,
Who serve our foes as spies, and us as slaves,   250
Who, by degrees, and unperceived, prepare
Our necks for chains which they already wear,
Madly we entertain, at the expense
Of fame, of virtue, taste, and common sense.
   Nor stop we here : the soft luxurious East,
Where man, his soul degraded, from the beast
In nothing different but in shape we view—
They walk on four legs, and he walks on two—
Attracts our eye ; and flowing from that source
Sins of the blackest character, sins worse   260
Than all her plagues, which truly to unfold,
Would make the best blood in my veins run cold,
And strike all manhood dead ; which but to name,
Would call up in my cheeks the marks of shame ;
Sins, if such sins can be, which shut out grace ;
Which for the guilty leave no hope, no place,

during the same season. (See letter of Horace Walpole to the Earl
of Hertford, November 25th, 1764, in which both the singers are
mentioned.)

[241] Possibly a reference to the dancer, Mlle. Camargo, who was the
first to shorten the ballet skirt to what was afterwards recognised as
the regulation length.

[242] Pietro Aretino (1492-1556), the friend of Michelangelo and
Titian, and one of the most famous and successful poets of his time,
is now chiefly remembered for the dissoluteness of his life and the
extreme licentiousness of his verses.

E'en in God's mercy ; sins 'gainst Nature's plan
Possess the land at large ; and man for man
Burns in those fires which hell alone could raise
To make him more than damn'd ; which, in the days
Of punishment, when guilt becomes her prey,   271
With all her tortures she can scarce repay.
　　Be grace shut out, be mercy deaf, let God
With tenfold terrors arm that dreadful nod
Which speaks them lost, and sentenced to despair ;
Distending wide her jaws, let hell prepare
For those who thus offend amongst mankind,
A fire more fierce, and tortures more refined :
On earth, which groans beneath their monstrous weight,
On earth, alas ! they meet a different fate,   280
And whilst the laws, false grace, false mercy shown,
Are taught to wear a softness not their own,
Men, whom the beasts would spurn, should they appear
Amongst the honest herd, find refuge here.
　　No longer by vain fear, or shame controll'd,
From long, too long security grown bold,
Mocking rebuke, they brave it in our streets :
And Lumley e'en at noon his mistress meets :
So public in their crimes, so daring grown,
They almost take a pride to have them known,   290
And each unnatural villain scarce endures
To make a secret of his vile amours.
Go where we will, at every time and place,
Sodom confronts, and stares us in the face ;
They ply in public at our very doors,
And take the bread from much more honest whores.
Those who are mean high paramours secure,
And the rich guilty screen the guilty poor ;
The sin too proud to feel from reason awe,
And those who practise it too great for law.   300

[288] Probably the Jemmy Lumley mentioned by Walpole (letter to
George Montagu, May 14th, 1761) as having been horse-whipped in
an inn-yard at Hampstead, by a Mrs. Mackenzie, to whom he had lost
considerable sums at whist, which sums, as he considered himself
cheated, he refused to pay. He was the seventh son of the first Earl
of Scarborough, but was quite illiterate. Tovey (the Editor of Gray's
Letters) calls him ' a kind of Tony Lumpkin.'

Woman, the pride and happiness of man,
Without whose soft endearments Nature's plan
Had been a blank, and life not worth a thought ;
Woman, by all the Loves and Graces taught
With softest arts, and sure, though hidden skill,
To humanize, and mould us to her will ;
Woman, with more than common grace form'd here,
With the persuasive language of a tear
To melt the rugged temper of our isle,
Or win us to her purpose with a smile ;   310
Woman, by fate the quickest spur decreed,
The fairest, best reward of every deed
Which bears the stamp of honour ; at whose name
Our ancient heroes caught a quicker flame,
And dared beyond belief, whilst o'er the plain,
Spurning the carcases of princes slain,
Confusion proudly strode, whilst Horror blew
The fatal trump, and Death stalk'd full in view ;
Woman is out of date, a thing thrown by
As having lost its use : no more the eye,   320
With female beauty caught, in wild amaze,
Gazes entranced, and could for ever gaze ;
No more the heart, that seat where Love resides,
Each breath drawn quick and short, in fuller tides
Life posting through the veins, each pulse on fire,
And the whole body tingling with desire,
Pants for those charms, which Virtue might engage
To break his vow, and thaw the frost of Age,
Bidding each trembling nerve, each muscle strain,
And giving pleasure which is almost pain.   330
Women are kept for nothing but the breed ;
For pleasure we must have a Ganymede,
A fine, fresh Hylas, a delicious boy,
To serve our purposes of beastly joy.
    Fairest of nymphs, where every nymph is fair,
Whom Nature form'd with more than common care,
With more than common care whom Art improved,
And both declared most worthy to be loved,

[332] The favourite of Jupiter.
[333] The favourite of Hercules.

413

—— neglected wanders, whilst a crowd
Pursue and consecrate the steps of ——.   340
She, hapless maid, born in a wretched hour,
Wastes life's gay prime in vain, like some fair flower,
Sweet in its scent, and lively in its hue,
Which withers on the stalk from whence it grew,
And dies uncropp'd ; whilst he admired, caress'd,
Beloved, and every where a welcome guest,
With brutes of rank and fortune plays the whore,
For this unnatural lust a common sewer.
      Dine with Apicius ; at his sumptuous board
Find all the world of dainties can afford ;   350
And yet (so much distemper'd spirits pall
The sickly appetite) amidst them all
Apicius finds no joy, but whilst he carves
For every guest, the landlord sits and starves.
      The forest haunch, fine, fat, in flavour high,
Kept to a moment, smokes before his eye,
But smokes in vain ; his heedless eye runs o'er
And loathes what he had deified before :
The turtle, of a great and glorious size,
Worth its own weight in gold, a mighty prize,   360
For which a man of taste all risks would run,
Itself a feast, and every dish in one ;
The turtle in luxurious pomp comes in,
Kept, kill'd, cut up, prepared, and dress'd by Quin ;
In vain it comes, in vain lays full in view ;
As Quin hath dress'd it, he may eat it too ;
Apicius cannot. When the glass goes round,
Quick-circling, and the roofs with mirth resound,
Sober he sits, and silent ; all alone
Though in a crowd, and to himself scarce known :   370
On grief he feeds : nor friends can cure, nor wine
Suspend his cares, and make him cease to pine.

[339] Wilkes inserts the name ' Aynam,' presumably a woman of the town.

[340] Wilkes gives ' Stroud,' evidently a catamite.

[349] See note on line 487.

[364] James Quin, the actor, was famous for good living, and often prepared dishes with his own hands. (See note on ' The Rosciad,' line 921.)

Why mourns Apicius thus ? why runs his eye,
Heedless, o'er delicates, which from the sky
Might call down Jove ? Where now his generous wish
That, to invent a new and better dish,
The world might burn, and all mankind expire,
So he might roast a phœnix at the fire ?
Why swims that eye in tears, which, through a race
Of sixty years, ne'er shew'd one sign of grace ?   380
Why feels that heart, which never felt before ?
Why doth that pamper'd glutton eat no more,
Who only lived to eat, his stomach pall'd,
And drown'd in floods of sorrow ? hath Fate call'd
His father from the grave to second life ?
Hath Clodius on his hands return'd his wife ?
Or hath the law, by strictest justice taught,
Compell'd him to restore the dower she brought ?
Hath some bold creditor, against his will,
Brought in, and forced him to discharge, a bill,   390
Where eating had no share ? hath some vain wench
Run out his wealth, and forced him to retrench ?
Hath any rival glutton got the start,
And beat him in his own luxurious art ?
Bought cates for which Apicius could not pay,
Or dress'd old dainties in a newer way ?
Hath his cook, worthy to be slain with rods,
Spoil'd a dish fit to entertain the gods ?
Or hath some varlet, cross'd by cruel fate,
Thrown down the price of empires in a plate ?   400
    None, none of these—his servants all are tried :
So sure, they walk on ice and never slide ;
His cook, an acquisition made in France,
Might put a Chloe out of countenance ;
Nor, though old Holles still maintains his stand,
Hath he one rival glutton in the land.
Women are all the objects of his hate ;

---

386 Publius Clodius, the son-in-law of Lucullus, and famous for his
debaucheries.
    404 St. Clouet, familiarly known as ' Chloe,' the Duke of Newcastle's
chef de cuisine.
    405 Holles, the family name of the Dukes of Newcastle.

His debts are all unpaid, and yet his state
In full security and triumph held,
Unless for once a knave should be expell'd ;   410
His wife is still a whore, and in his power,
The woman gone, he still retains the dower ;
Sound in the grave (thanks to his filial care
Which mix'd the draught, and kindly sent him there)
His father sleeps, and till the last trump shake
The corners of the earth, shall not awake.
   Whence flows this sorrow, then ? Behind his chair,
Didst thou not see, deck'd with a solitaire
Which on his bare breast glittering play'd, and graced
With nicest ornaments, a stripling placed,   420
A smooth, smug stripling, in life's fairest prime ?
Didst thou not mind, too, how from time to time,
The monstrous lecher, tempted to despise
All other dainties, thither turn'd his eyes ?
How he seem'd inly to reproach us all,
Who strove his fix'd attention to recal,
And how he wish'd, e'en at the time of grace,
Like Janus, to have had a double face ?
His cause of grief behold in that fair boy.
Apicius dotes, and Corydon is coy.   430
   Vain and unthinking stripling ! when the glass
Meets thy too curious eye, and, as you pass,
Flattering, presents in smiles thy image there,
Why dost thou bless the gods, who made thee fair ?
Blame their large bounties, and with reason blame ;
Curse, curse thy beauty, for it leads to shame ;
When thy hot lord, to work thee to his end,
Bids showers of gold into thy breast descend,
Suspect his gifts, nor the vile giver trust ;
They're baits for virtue, and smell strong of lust.   440
On those gay, gaudy trappings, which adorn
The temple of thy body, look with scorn ;
View them with horror ; they pollution mean,
And deepest ruin : thou hast often seen
From 'mongst the herd, the fairest and the best
Carefully singled out, and richly drest,
With grandeur mock'd, for sacrifice decreed,

416

Only in greater pomp at last to bleed.
Be warn'd in time, the threaten'd danger shun,
To stay a moment is to be undone. 450
What though, temptation proof, thy virtue shine,
Nor bribes can move, nor arts can undermine?
All other methods failing, one resource
Is still behind, and thou must yield to force.
Paint to thyself the horrors of a rape,
Most strongly paint, and, while thou canst, escape :
Mind not his promises—they're made in sport—
Made to be broke—was he not bred at court?
Trust not his honour; he's a man of birth :
Attend not to his oaths—they're made on earth, 460
Not register'd in heaven—he mocks at grace,
And in his creed God never found a place ;
Look not for Conscience—for he knows her not,
So long a stranger, she is quite forgot ;
Nor think thyself in law secure and firm ;
Thy master is a lord, and thou a worm,
A poor, mean reptile, never meant to think,
Who, being well supplied with meat and drink,
And suffer'd just to crawl from place to place,
Must serve his lusts, and think he does thee grace. 470
    Fly, then, whilst yet 'tis in thy power to fly ;
But whither canst thou go? on whom rely
For wish'd protection? Virtue's sure to meet
An armed host of foes in every street.
What boots it, of Apicius fearful grown,
Headlong to fly into the arms of Stone?
Or why take refuge in the house of prayer
If sure to meet with an Apicius there?
Trust not old age, which will thy faith betray ;
Saint Socrates is still a goat, though grey : 480

[476] It is possible that Churchill means Andrew Stone (1703-1773),
Under Secretary of State and tutor to George III while Prince of
Wales. He is thought to have been responsible for the King's Tory
principles, and as a suspected Jacobite and a friend of Bute he was
naturally obnoxious to Churchill. There seems to be no foundation for
Churchill's attack on Stone's morals.
[480] A reference to Socrates' passion for Alcibiades. The ancients
seem to have held the connection impure, or Juvenal would not have
written :

Trust not green youth ; Florio will scarce go down,
And, at eighteen, hath surfeited the town :
Trust not to rakes—alas ! 'tis all pretence—
They take up raking only as a fence
'Gainst common fame—place H—— in thy view ;
He keeps one whore as Barrowby kept two :
Trust not to marriage—T—— took a wife,

' Inter Socraticos notissima fossa cinædos,' followed by Firmicus (vii-14) who speaks of ' Socratici pædicones.' (Sir Richard Burton, *Arabian Nights*, Terminal Essay on Pederasty.)

It is doubtful whether Churchill had any contemporary ' Saint Socrates ' in mind, or intended any personal reference in ' Florio.' (See ' Night,' line 33.)

[485] Wilkes fills up this gap with the name of Hervey. This is probably not John Hervey, Pope's ' Lord Fanny,' but Thomas Hervey (1699-1775), second son of John Hervey, first Earl of Bristol, by his second wife. He wished to become a soldier but his family compelled him to study the law, and he took to drink. He sat in parliament, however, from 1733 to 1747. He eloped with the wife of Sir Thomas Hanmer, but as she died in 1741 it is unlikely that Churchill's lines refer to her. In 1744 Hervey is said to have contracted a marriage in the Fleet Prison with his mistress, Anne, daughter of Francis Coghlan. They were unhappy and Hervey endeavoured by appeals to the Court of Delegates to have the marriage set aside, but on his deathbed he sent for his wife and acknowledged the validity of their union. Hervey's affairs were in the public mind at the time Churchill was writing, and the British Museum copy of the pamphlet, ' Mr. Hervey's Answer to a Letter he received from Dr. Samuel Johnson to dissuade him from parting with his Supposed Wife ' has a manuscript note : ' first printed and written in 1763 '.

[486] William Barrowby (1682-1751) was a physician of some eminence. In the Rawlinson MSS. (in the Bodleian) Barrowby is referred to as ' a monster of lewdness and prophaneness ' (quoted in D. N. B.) He is said to have taken part in the riots at Drury Lane in December, 1743. If this is the Barrowby intended by Churchill, he could only have known of him by repute.

[487] Wilkes has no suggestion. Tooke remarks : ' This initial applies to the nobleman so severely stigmatised under the name of Apicius. His excesses of all kinds rendering it inconvenient, if not unsafe, to continue to reside in this country, he exchanged the neighbourhood of Epping for the more congenial air of Italy.' The details given seem to imply that Tooke knew to whom the initial referred, but did not wish to say. It is possible that Lord Tylney is meant. The anonymous author of ' Sodom and Onan,' speaking of Isaac Bickerstaff, remarks that he is :

> ' For Safety flown to soft Italia's shore,
> Where Tilney, B—l, Jones and many more
> Of Britain's cast outs, revel uncontroul'd.'

So many Englishmen, during the eighteenth century and later, have

Who chaste as Dian might have pass'd her life,
Had she not, far more prudent in her aim,
(To propagate the honours of his name,   490
And save expiring titles) taken care,
Without his knowledge, to provide an heir :
Trust not to marriage, in mankind unread ;
S——'s a married man, and S—— new wed.
   Wouldst thou be safe ? society forswear,
Fly to the desert, and seek shelter there ;
Herd with the brutes—they follow Nature's plan :
There's not one brute so dangerous as man
In Afric's wilds—'mongst them that refuge find
Which lust denies thee here among mankind :   500
Renounce thy name, thy nature, and no more
Pique thy vain pride on manhood : on all four
Walk, as you see those honest creatures do,
And quite forget that once you walk'd on two.
   But, if the thought of solitude alarm,
And social life hath one remaining charm ;
If still thou art to jeopardy decreed
Amongst the monsters of Augusta's breed,
Lay by thy sex, thy safety to procure,
Put off the man, from men to live secure ;   510
Go forth a woman to the public view,
And with their garb assume their manners too.

settled in Italy, and especially in Southern Italy, in order to be more
free in the indulgence of homosexual passions that the Neapolitans
speak of the vice as ' il vizio inglese.'   John (Tylney), Earl Tylney of
Castlemaine, was baptised at Wanstead (which is in the neighbourhood
of Epping), on October 22nd, 1712. But if he ' took a wife,' Cockayne's
' Complete Peerage ' knows nothing of it, and he died without issue at
Wanstead on December 16th, 1784, when all his honours became
extinct.   He may have obtained a divorce (unmentioned by Cockayne)
which would explain lines 411, 412 in the present poem.   (See also
line 559.)
   494 Wilkes fills the two blanks with the names of Sackville and
Stroud.   Churchill was not alone in bringing this accusation against
Sackville :
      ' S(ackvill)e, both Coward and Catamite, commands
      Department hon'rable, and kisses hands.'
                              (Sodom and Onan.)
For his alleged cowardice see note on ' The Ghost,' Book I, line 250.
Stroud is glanced at before in ' The Times,' line 340.

Had the light-footed Greek of Chiron's school
Been wise enough to keep this single rule,
The maudlin hero, like a puling boy
Robb'd of his plaything, on the plains of Troy
Had never blubber'd at Patroclus' tomb,
And placed his minion in his mistress' room ;
Be not in this than catamites more nice,
Do that for virtue, which they do for vice ;   520
Thus shalt thou pass untainted life's gay bloom,
Thus stand uncourted in the drawing-room ;
At midnight, thus, untempted, walk the street,
And run no danger but of being beat.
   Where is the mother, whose officious zeal,
Discreetly judging what her daughters feel
By what she felt herself in days of yore,
Against that lecher man makes fast the door ;
Who not permits, e'en for the sake of prayer,
A priest, uncastrated, to enter there,   530
Nor (could her wishes, and her care prevail)
Would suffer in the house a fly that's male ?
Let her discharge her cares, throw wide her doors,
Her daughters cannot, if they would, be whores ;
Nor can a man be found, as times now go,
Who thinks it worth his while to make them so.
   Though they more fresh, more lively than the morn,
And brighter than the noon-day sun, adorn
The works of Nature ; though the mother's grace
Revives improved, in every daughter's face ;   540
Undisciplined in dull Discretion's rules,
Untaught and undebauch'd by boarding-schools,
Free and unguarded, let them range the town,

[513] Achilles was educated by the centaur Chiron.

[515] *i.e.*, Achilles.   It is hardly necessary to remark that Homer
implies no vicious tendency in the friendship of Achilles and Patroclus.
It was assumed, much later, by Lucian, who drew the same conclusion
from the loves of Orestes and Pylades, Theseus and Pirithous. *Cf.*
Shakespeare's ' Troilus and Cressida ' :
   ' *Thersites :* Prithee, be silent, boy . . . thou art thought to be
      Achilles' male varlet.
   Patroclus : Male varlet, you rogue ! What's that ?
   Thersites : Why, his masculine whore.'

Go forth at random, and run pleasure down,
Start where she will ; discard all taint of fear,
Nor think of danger, when no danger's near.
Watch not their steps—they're safe without thy care,
Unless, like Jennets, they conceive by air,
And every one of them may die a nun,
Unless they breed, like carrion, in the sun.   550
Men, dead to pleasure, as they're dead to grace,
Against the law of Nature set their face,
The grand primeval law, and seem combined
To stop the propagation of mankind ;
Vile pathics read the Marriage Act with pride,
And fancy that the law is on their side.
    Broke down, and strength a stranger to his bed,
Old Ligonier, though yet alive, is dead ;
T—— lives no more, or lives not to our isle ;
No longer bless'd with a Czarina's smile,   560
T—— is at Petersburg disgraced,

[548] The fleetness of Spanish jennets, owing to the admixture of Arab
blood, gave rise to the fable that they were begotten by the wind.

[554]   ' Oh ! that offended Genius wou'd inspire
    Me, with one Note from Churchill's well-strung Lyre,
    To satirize those Fiends, who unconfin'd,
    Will stop the Propagation of Mankind.'
                        (Sodom and Onan.)

[555] A pathic, *i.e.*, one upon whom sodomy is practised, a catamite.

[555] Lord Hardwicke's Marriage Act (1753) relieved England and
Wales of the scandal of clandestine marriages. Perhaps, as Churchill
had himself been married in the Fleet, he felt strongly on the subject.
It is hard to see what other point there can be in his satire, apart from
the insinuation that the Marriage Act had made marriage more difficult.

[558] ' Old Ligonier.' (See note on line 148.)

[559] See note on line 487 ; but if this is the same T——, the present
line has a syllable too many.

[561] Gray fills up this blank with the name ' Trayley.' It seems
certain that Tyrawley is meant. James O'Hara, Baron Kilmaine and
second Baron Tyrawley (1690-1773), served under Marlborough, and
was wounded at Malplaquet. In 1728 he was appointed envoy-
extraordinary to Portugal, and remained there as Ambassador until
1741. From 1743 to 1745 he was Ambassador-Extraordinary to
Russia, returned to Portugal in 1752, and was in charge at Gibraltar
until 1757. In 1760 he was President of the court-martial on Lord
George Sackville.
George Anne Bellamy in her ' Apology ' claims to be one of the

And M—— grown gray, perforce grows chaste ;
Nor to the credit of our modest race,
Rises one stallion to supply their place.
A maidenhead, which, twenty years ago,
In mid December, the rank fly would blow
Though closely kept, now, when the Dog-star's heat
Inflames the marrow, in the very street
May lie untouch'd, left for the worms, by those
Who daintily pass by, and hold their nose.   570
Poor, plain Concupiscence is in disgrace,
And simple Lechery dares not shew her face,
Lest she be sent to Bridewell ; bankrupts made,

illegitimate children of Tyrawley. That his reputation was un-savoury may be gathered from Pope :

> ' Or shall we every decency confound,
> Through taverns, stews and bagnios take our round ?
> Go dine with Chartres, in each vice outdo
> K(innou)l's lewd cargo, or Ty(rawle)y's crew.'
> (*Imitations of Horace, Sixth Epistle of Third Book.*)

However, this does not imply any homosexual tendency, nor does Churchill hint at it. Tyrawley was thought licentious both at Lisbon and at St. Petersburg (no mean feat) but in perfectly normal fashion. The Czarina referred to was the Empress Elizabeth, who was born 1709, seized the throne in 1741, and died 29th December, 1761. She was notorious for her promiscuous amours.

[562] Wilkes notes ' Montague,' *i.e.*, John Montagu, Earl of Sand-wich. (See note on ' Gotham,' Book I, line 464.)

[567] See note on ' Gotham,' Book I, line 391.

[573] ' The old palace of Bridewell formerly consisted of two square courts running back from the bank of the river. After the fire, which destroyed the two courts, Bridewell was rebuilt but not on the same foundations. The new Bridewell was completed in the year 1668, partly as a school for trades to which poor boys were apprenticed, and partly as a prison for vagrants, masterless men, prostitutes and dis-orderly persons of all kinds. Bethlehem and Bridewell were under the same Board of Governors.

' The second Bridewell consisted of one large quadrangle, one side of which was occupied by the hall ; another side by the chapel and offices ; and the third and fourth side, by the prison. When the City prison of Holloway was completed, Bridewell ceased to be a House of Correction, and the prison was cleared away. . . . In 1750 the hospital was used as a place " where all strumpets, night walkers, pickpockets, vagrants and idle persons that are taken up for their ill tricks, as also incorrigible and disobedient servants, are committed by the Mayor and Aldermen, and being so committed, are forced to beat hemp in public view with due correction of whipping according to their offence for

To save their fortunes, bawds leave off their trade,
Which first had left off them ; to Wellclose square
Fine, fresh young strumpets (for Dodd preaches there)
Throng for subsistence : pimps no longer thrive,
And pensions only keep L—— alive.
    Where is the mother, who thinks all her pain,
And all her jeopardy of travail, gain   580
When a man-child is born ; thinks every prayer
Paid to the full, and answer'd in an heir ?
Short-sighted Woman ! little doth she know
What streams of sorrow from that source may flow ;
Little suspect, while she surveys her boy,
Her young Narcissus, with an eye of joy
Too full for continence, that Fate could give
Her darling as a curse ; that she may live,
Ere sixteen winters their short course have run,
In agonies of soul, to curse that son.   590
    Pray then for daughters, ye wise Mothers, pray ;
They shall reward your love, not make ye gray
Before your time with sorrow ; they shall give

such a time as the president and court shall see cause." ' (' London
in the Eighteenth Century,' by Sir Walter Besant, 1902, p. 544.)

[575] Wellclose Square, where was at first situated the Magdalen
Hospital, of which Dr. Dodd was one of the founders and the first
Chaplain.

[576] William Dodd (1729–1777) was educated at Clare Hall, Cam-
bridge, and had already dabbled in literature and written a comedy
before he was ordained deacon in 1751, and became curate at West
Ham, Essex. He was appointed to a lectureship at West Ham in 1752,
and to another at St. James's, Garlickhythe, which he exchanged in
1754 for that of St. Olave's, Hart Street. He became an immensely
popular preacher, especially on behalf of charities, and was much in
request. He preached the inaugural sermon of the ' Magdalen Home '
in 1758, and acted as Chaplain to the institution, a regular stipend of
£100 a year being voted to him in 1763. His florid and eloquent
preaching attracted people of fashion, including Horace Walpole, and
in 1763 Dodd was appointed Chaplain to the King. Churchill, there-
fore, knew of Dodd at the height, or almost the height, of his pros-
perity. The ' macaroni parson ' as he was called, lived far beyond his
means, plunged deeply into debt, and finally forged a bond for £4,200
in the name of his patron, Lord Chesterfield. For this, in spite of the
efforts of Dr. Johnson, he was hanged on 27th June, 1777, more than
a decade after the death of Churchill.

[578] L——. The present Editor has no suggestion.

Ages of peace, and comfort ; whilst ye live
Make life most truly worth your care, and save,
In spite of death, your memories from the grave.
That sense with more than manly vigour fraught,
That fortitude of soul, that stretch of thought,
That genius, great beyond the narrow bound
Of earth's low walk, that judgment perfect found   600
When wanted most, that purity of taste
Which critics mention by the name of chaste ;
Adorn'd with elegance, that easy flow
Of ready wit, which never made a foe ;
That face, that form, that dignity, that ease,
Those powers of pleasing, with that will to please,
By which Lepel, when in her youthful days,
E'en from the currish Pope extorted praise,
We see, transmitted, in her daughter shine,
And view a new Lepel in Caroline.   610
Is a son born into this world of woe ?
In never-ceasing streams let sorrow flow ;
Be from that hour the house with sables hung,
Let lamentations dwell upon thy tongue,
E'en from the moment that he first began
To wail and whine, let him not see a man :
Lock, lock him up, far from the public eye :
Give him no opportunity to buy,
Or to be bought ; B——, though rich, was sold,
And gave his body up to shame for gold.   620
Let it be bruited all about the town,
That he is coarse, indelicate, and brown,
An antidote to lust ; his face deep scarr'd

---

[607] Lady Mary Hervey, *née* Lepell (1700-1768), was equally cele-
brated for her wit and for her beauty. She remained on good terms
with her husband in spite of his infidelities.

[608] Lady Mary Hervey numbered among her admirers, Pope, Gay,
Pulteney, Chesterfield, Voltaire and Horace Walpole, the last of whom
knew her when she was already an old woman.

[610] Caroline, youngest daughter of Lord Hervey, and his wife Mary
Lepell. She died unmarried in 1819, aged 83.

[619] The missing name is probably either Burrel or Bertie. (See
also note on line 487, above.)

With the small-pox, his body maim'd and marr'd ;
Ate up with the king's evil, and his blood
Tainted throughout, a thick and putrid flood,
Where dwells corruption, making him all o'er,
From head to foot, a rank and running sore.
Shouldst thou report him, as by nature made,
He is undone, and by thy praise betray'd :   630
Give him out fair, lechers, in number more,
More brutal, and more fierce, than throng'd the door
Of Lot in Sodom, shall to thine repair,
And force a passage, though a god is there.
    Let him not have one servant that is male ;
Where lords are baffled, servants oft prevail.
Some vices they propose, to all agree ;
H—— was guilty, but was M—— free ?
    Give him no tutor—throw him to a punk,
Rather than trust his morals to a monk ;   640
Monks we all know—we, who have lived at home,
From fair report, and travellers who roam,
More feelingly ; nor trust him to the gown ;
'Tis oft a covering in this vile town
For base designs : ourselves have lived to see
More than one parson in the pillory.
Should he have brothers, (image to thy view
A scene, which, though not public made, is true)
Let not one brother be to t'other known,
Nor let his father sit with him alone.   650

[631-634] See Genesis xix, 4-11.

[638] Wilkes fills up this gap with the name of Hervey. John Hervey,
Baron Hervey of Ickworth (1696-1743) was educated at Westminster
School. At the Court of Frederick at Richmond he met Mary Lepell
and married her in 1720. He sat in Parliament from 1725, both Wal-
pole and Pulteney anxious for his support. He engineered an attack
on Pulteney and Bolingbroke in an anonymous pamphlet, and Pul-
teney replied in such insulting terms that a duel ensued, in which
both were wounded. Hervey's value to Walpole lay in the fact that as
Vice-Chamberlain he had the ear of the Queen, and through her of
the King. In 1740 Hervey became Lord Privy Seal in place of
Godolphin. On the fall of Walpole he was dismissed, and went into
opposition. Hervey was notoriously effeminate and licentious, but
was liked by women, including both the Queen and Princess Caroline.
Pope satirised him as Lord Fanny. The present Editor has no sug-
gestion for M——.

Be all his servants female, young and fair,
And if the pride of Nature spur thy heir
To deeds of venery ; if, hot and wild,
He chance to get some score of maids with child,
Chide, but forgive him ; whoredom is a crime
Which, more at this than any other time,
Calls for indulgence, and, 'mongst such a race,
To have a bastard is some sign of grace.
   Born in such times, should I sit tamely down,
Suppress my rage, and saunter through the town   660
As one who knew not, or who shared these crimes ?
Should I at lesser evils point my rhymes,
And let this giant sin, in the full eye
Of observation, pass unwounded by ?
Though our meek wives, passive obedience taught,
Patiently bear those wrongs, for which they ought,
With the brave spirit of their dams possess'd,
To plant a dagger in each husband's breast,
To cut off male increase from this fair isle,
And turn our Thames into another Nile ;   670
Though, on his Sunday, the smug pulpiteer,
Loud 'gainst all other crimes, is silent here,
And thinks himself absolved, in the pretence
Of decency, which, meant for the defence
Of real virtue, and to raise her price,
Becomes an agent for the cause of vice ;
Though the law sleeps, and through the care they take
To drug her well, may never more awake,
Born in such times nor with that patience curst
Which saints may boast of, I must speak or burst.   680
   But if, too eager in my bold career,
Haply I wound the nice, and chaster ear ;
If, all unguarded, all too rude, I speak,
And call up blushes in the maiden's cheek,
Forgive, ye fair—my real motives view,
And to forgiveness add your praises too.
For you I write—nor wish a better plan,
The cause of woman is most worthy man ;

---

[670] An allusion apparently to the death of the firstborn—the Tenth Plague of Egypt.

426

For you I still will write, nor hold my hand
Whilst there's one slave of Sodom in the land.   690
   Let them fly far, and skulk from place to place,
Not daring to meet manhood face to face ;
Their steps I'll track, nor yield them one retreat
Where they may hide their heads, or rest their feet,
Till God, in wrath, shall let his vengeance fall,
And make a great example of them all,
Bidding in one grand pile, this town expire,
Her towers in dust, her Thames a lake of fire ;
Or they (most worth our wish) convinced though late
Of their past crimes and dangerous estate,   700
Pardon of women with repentance buy,
And learn to honour them as much as I.

INDEPENDENCE*

HAPPY the bard (though few such bards we find)
Who, 'bove controlment, dares to speak his mind ;
Dares, unabash'd, in every place appear,
And nothing fears, but what he ought to fear :
Him fashion cannot tempt, him abject need
Cannot compel, him pride cannot mislead
To be the slave of greatness, to strike sail
When, sweeping onward with her peacock's tail,
Quality in full plumage passes by ;
He views her with a fix'd, contemptuous eye,   10
And mocks the puppet, keeps his own due state,
And is above conversing with the great.
    Perish those slaves, those minions of the quill,
Who have conspired to seize that sacred hill
Where the nine sisters pour a genuine strain,
And sunk the mountain level with the plain ;
Who, with mean, private views and servile art,
No spark of virtue living in their heart,
Have basely turn'd apostates ; have debased
Their dignity of office : have disgraced,   20
Like Eli's sons, the altars where they stand,
And caused their name to stink through all the land ;
Have stoop'd to prostitute their venal pen
For the support of great, but guilty men ;
Have made the bard, of their own vile accord,
Inferior to that thing we call a lord.
    What is a lord ? Doth that plain simple word
Contain some magic spell ? As soon as heard,
Like an alarum bell on Night's dull ear,
Doth it strike louder, and more strong appear   30
Than other words ? Whether we will or no,

* First published in September, 1764. 'Printed for the Author,
and sold by J. Almon . . . . J. Coote . . . . W. Flexney . . . . C.
Henderson . . . . J. Gardiner . . . . and C. Moran.'

[21] See I Samuel ii, 12-17.

Through reason's court doth it unquestion'd go
E'en on the mention, and of course transmit
Notions of something excellent ; of wit
Pleasing, though keen ; of humour free, though chaste ;
Of sterling genius, with sound judgment graced ;
Of virtue far above temptation's reach,
And honour, which not malice can impeach ?
Believe it not—'twas nature's first intent,
Before their rank became their punishment,   40
They should have pass'd for men, nor blush'd to prize
The blessings she bestow'd—she gave them eyes,
And they could see ; she gave them ears—they heard ;
The instruments of stirring, and they stirr'd ;
Like us, they were design'd to eat, to drink,
To talk, and every now and then, to think ;
Till they, by pride corrupted, for the sake
Of singularity, disclaim'd that make :
Till they, disdaining nature's vulgar mode,
Flew off, and struck into another road,   50
More fitting Quality, and to our view
Came forth a species altogether new,
Something we had not known, and could not know,
Like nothing of God's making here below ;
Nature exclaim'd with wonder : ' Lords are things
Which, never made by me, were made by kings.'
     A lord, (nor let the honest and the brave,
The true old noble, with the fool and knave
Here mix his fame ; cursed be that thought of mine,
Which with a Bute and Fox should Grafton join)   60
A lord, (nor here let Censure rashly call
My just contempt of some, abuse of all,

[60] Augustus Henry Fitzroy, 3rd Duke of Grafton (1735-1811), was
educated at Westminster and at Peterhouse, Cambridge. He suc-
ceeded to the dukedom in 1757. He was active, with Temple, in
opposition to Bute and showed his sympathy with Wilkes by visiting
him in the Tower, but offended Temple by refusing to go bail for
Wilkes. Grafton rapidly came to the fore as a politician, being a
Secretary of State in 1765. When Wilkes returned to London in 1766
Grafton received his advances coldly, and he was at the head of affairs
when Wilkes was declared incapable of sitting in Parliament. Later he
incurred the violent hostility of ' Junius ' and it is as the butt of that
writer's invective that Grafton is chiefly remembered.

429

And, as of late, when Sodom was my theme,
Slander my purpose, and my muse blaspheme,
Because she stops not, rapid in her song,
To make exceptions as she goes along—
Though well she hopes to find, another year,
A whole minority exceptions here)
A mere, mere lord, with nothing but the name,
Wealth all his worth, and title all his fame,   70
Lives on another man, himself a blank,
Thankless he lives, or must some grandsire thank
For smuggled honours, and ill-gotten pelf;
A bard owes all to nature, and himself.
   Gods, how my soul is burnt up with disdain,
When I see men, whom Phœbus in his train
Might view with pride, lackey the heels of those
Whom genius ranks among her greatest foes !
And what's the cause ? why, these same sons of scorn,
No thanks to them, were to a title born,   80
And could not help it ; by chance hither sent,
And only deities by accident.
Had fortune on our getting chanced to shine,
Their birth right honours had been yours or mine.
'Twas a mere random stroke, and should the throne
Eye thee with favour, proud and lordly grown,
Thou, though a bard, might'st be their fellow yet :
But Felix never can be made a wit.
No, in good faith—that's one of those few things
Which fate hath placed beyond the reach of kings :   90
Bards may be lords, but 'tis not in the cards,
Play how we will, to turn lords into bards.
   A bard—a lord—why, let them, hand in hand,
Go forth as friends, and travel through the land,
Observe which word the people can digest
Most readily, which goes to market best,
Which gets most credit, whether men will trust
A bard, because they think he may be just,
Or on a lord will choose to risk their gains,
Though privilege in that point still remains.   100
   A bard—a lord—Let Reason take her scales,

[63] In the preceding poem : ' The Times.'

And fairly weigh those words, see which prevails,
Which in the balance lightly kicks the beam,
And which, by sinking, we the victor deem.
   'Tis done, and Hermes, by command of Jove,
Summons a synod in the sacred grove ;
Gods throng with gods to take their chairs on high,
And sit in state, the senate of the sky,
Whilst, in a kind of parliament below,
Men stare at those above, and want to know   110
What they're transacting : Reason takes her stand
Just in the midst, a balance in her hand,
Which o'er and o'er she tries, and finds it true :
From either side, conducted full in view,
A man comes forth, of figure strange and queer ;
We now and then see something like them here.
   The first was meagre, flimsy, void of strength,
But Nature kindly had made up in length
What she in breadth denied : erect and proud,
A head and shoulders taller than the crowd,   120
He deem'd them pigmies all : loose hung his skin
O'er his bare bones : his face so very thin,
So very narrow, and so much beat out,
That physiognomists have made a doubt,
Proportion lost, expression quite forgot,
Whether it could be call'd a face or not :
At end of it, howe'er, unbless'd with beard,
Some twenty fathom length of chin appear'd :
With legs, which we might well conceive that Fate
Meant only to support a spider's weight,   130
Firmly he strove to tread, and with a stride,
Which shew'd at once his weakness and his pride,
Shaking himself to pieces, seem'd to cry,
' Observe, good people, how I shake the sky.'
   In his right hand a paper did he hold,
On which, at large, in characters of gold,
Distinct and plain for those who run to see,
Saint Archibald had wrote L, O, R, D.

[117] ' The first,' *i.e.*, Lord Lyttelton. (See note on ' The Prophecy of Famine,' line 71.)
[138] ' Saint Archibald ' is Archibald Bower (1686-1766) who was

431

This, with an air of scorn, he from afar
Twirl'd into Reason's scales, and on that bar,   140
Which from his soul he hated, yet admired,
Quick turn'd his back, and, as he came, retired.
The judge to all around his name declared ;
Each goddess titter'd, each god laugh'd, Jove stared,
And the whole people cried, with one accord,
' Good Heaven bless us all ! is that a lord ? '
    Such was the first—the second was a man
Whom nature built on quite a diff'rent plan ;
A bear, whom, from the moment he was born,
His dam despised, and left unlick'd in scorn ;   150
A Babel, which, the power of art outdone,
She could not finish when she had begun ;
An utter Chaos, out of which no might
But that of God, could strike one spark of light.
    Broad were his shoulders, and from blade to blade,
A H—— might at full length have laid :
Vast were his bones, his muscles twisted strong ;
His face was short, but broader than 'twas long ;
His features, though by nature they were large,
Contentment had contrived to overcharge,   160
And bury meaning, save that we might spy
Sense lowering on the penthouse of his eye ;
His arms were two twin oaks ; his legs so stout
That they might bear a Mansion-house about ;

admitted to the Society of Jesus in 1706. In 1726 he fled from Italy
to England, according to his enemies, in consequence of a detected
amour with a nun, but, according to his own account, because of the
' hellish proceedings ' of a court of the inquisition. In England he
abandoned Catholicism and six years later joined the Church of Eng-
land. He was patronised by Lord Aylmer and by Lord Lyttelton,
who remained his steady friend. In 1745 Bower was re-admitted to
the Society of Jesus, but left it once more in 1747. In the following
year he began to publish a professedly Protestant ' History of the
Popes,' but was exposed by the Rev. John Douglas (afterwards Bishop
of Salisbury) as a secret Romanist. His history and his private
character were likewise impugned and the rest of his life was spent in
controversy. His wife attested that he died in the Protestant faith.

    [149] ' A bear,' i.e., Churchill himself, an allusion to Hogarth's
print.·
    [156] Wodhull fills up this blank with the name of the Earl of
Harrington.

Nor were they, look but at his body there,
Design'd by fate a much less weight to bear.
O'er a brown cassock, which had once been black,
Which hung in tatters on his brawny back,
A sight most strange, and awkward to behold,
He threw a covering of blue and gold.   170
Just at that time of life, when man by rule,
The fop laid down, takes up the graver fool,
He started up a fop, and, fond of show,
Look'd like another Hercules turn'd beau ;
A subject met with only now and then,
Much fitter for the pencil than the pen ;
Hogarth would draw him (Envy must allow)
E'en to the life, was Hogarth living now.
     With such accoutrements, with such a form,
Much like a porpoise just before a storm,   180
Onward he roll'd : a laugh prevail'd around ;
E'en Jove was seen to simper ; at the sound
(Nor was the cause unknown, for from his youth
Himself he studied by the glass of truth)
He join'd their mirth ; nor shall the gods condemn
If, whilst they laugh'd at him, he laugh'd at them.
Judge Reason view'd him with an eye of grace,
Look'd through his soul, and quite forgot his face,
And, from his hand received, with fair regard
Placed in her other scale, the name of Bard.   190
     Then, (for she did as judges ought to do ;
She nothing of the case beforehand knew,
Nor wish'd to know ; she never stretch'd the laws,
Nor, basely to anticipate a cause,
Compell'd solicitors, no longer free,

[170] After the success of ' The Rosciad ' Churchill, finding himself a
man of comparative wealth, threw off his parson's gown and appeared
in a blue coat with gold lace. *Cf.* ' Churchill Dissected. A Poem,'
London, 1764 :
> ' fearing to be known,
> The better to deceive, puts off the Gown ;
> In Blue and Gold now strutting like a Peer
> Cocks his lac'd Beaver with a martial Air.'

[178] ' Was Hogarth living now.' Hogarth did not die until October
25th, 1764, a month after the publication of ' Independence ' ; Churchill
himself died nine days later.

433

To show those briefs she had no right to see)
Then she with equal hand her scales held out,
Nor did the cause one moment hang in doubt;
She held her scales out fair to public view,
The Lord, as sparks fly upwards, upwards flew,   200
More light than air, deceitful in the weight;
The Bard, preponderating, kept his state;
Reason approved, and with a voice, whose sound
Shook earth, shook heaven, on the clearest ground
Pronouncing for the Bards a full decree,
Cried—' Those must honour them, who honour me;
They from this present day, where'er I reign,
In their own right, precedence shall obtain;
Merit rules here; be it enough that birth
Intoxicates, and sways the fools of earth.'   210
   Nor think that here, in hatred to a lord,
I've forged a tale, or alter'd a record;
Search when you will, (I am not now in sport)
You'll find it register'd in Reason's court.
   Nor think that envy here hath strung my lyre,
That I depreciate what I most admire,
And look on titles with an eye of scorn,
Because I was not to a title born.
By Him that made me, I am much more proud,
More inly satisfied, to have a crowd   220
Point at me as I pass, and cry—' That's he—
A poor but honest bard, who dares be free
Amidst corruption,' than to have a train
Of flickering levee slaves, to make me vain
Of things I ought to blush for; to run, fly,
And live but in the motion of my eye;
When I am less than man, my faults t'adore,
And make me think that I am something more.
   Recall past times, bring back the days of old,
When the great noble bore his honours bold,   230
And in the face of peril, when he dared
Things which his legal bastard, if declared,

---

[212] 'In allusion to the substitution of the word "tenor" for "purport" in the record against Mr. Wilkes, which was sanctioned by Lord Mansfield.' (Tooke.)

Might well discredit ; faithful to his trust,
In the extremest points of justice, just ;
Well knowing all, and loved by all he knew ;
True to his king, and to his country true ;
Honest at court, above the baits of gain ;
Plain in his dress, and in his manners plain ;
Moderate in wealth, generous, but not profuse,
Well worthy riches, for he knew their use ;   240
Possessing much, and yet deserving more ;
Deserving those high honours which he wore
With ease to all, and in return gain'd fame
Which all men paid, because he did not claim ;
When the grim war was placed in dread array,
Fierce as the lion roaring for his prey,
Or lioness of royal whelps foredone ;
In peace, as mild as the departing sun ;
A general blessing wheresoe'er he turn'd,
Patron of learning, nor himself unlearn'd ;   250
Ever awake at Pity's tender call,
A father of the poor, a friend to all—
Recall such times, and from the grave bring back
A worth like this, my heart shall bend, or crack,
My stubborn pride give way, my tongue proclaim,
And every Muse conspire to swell his fame,
Till Envy shall to him that praise allow
Which she cannot deny to Temple now.
    This justice claims, nor shall the bard forget,
Delighted with the task, to pay that debt,   260
To pay it like a man, and in his lays,
Sounding such worth, prove his own right to praise,
But let not pride and prejudice misdeem,
And think that empty titles are my theme ;

<hr />

[258] Richard Temple Grenville (1711-1779), afterwards Grenville-Temple, Earl Temple, was the brother of George Grenville, and M.P. for Buckingham from 1734 to 1752, in which year he succeeded to his mother's peerage. He was First Lord of the Admiralty, 1756-57, and Lord Privy Seal, 1757-61. He took up the cause of Wilkes with enthusiasm and paid his legal expenses. For this he was dismissed from the Lord-Lieutenancy of Buckinghamshire. His later political history, which was largely in opposition, need not concern us. He died of an accident.

Titles, with me, are vain, and nothing worth ;
I reverence virtue, but I laugh at birth.
Give me a lord that's honest, frank, and brave,
I am his friend, but cannot be his slave ;
Though none, indeed, but blockheads would pretend
To make a slave, where they may make a friend. 270
I love his virtues, and will make them known,
Confess his rank, but can't forget my own.
Give me a lord, who, to a title born,
Boasts nothing else, I'll pay him scorn with scorn.
What ! shall my pride (and pride is virtue here)
Tamely make way, if such a wretch appear ?
Shall I uncover'd stand, and bend my knee
To such a shadow of nobility,
A shred, a remnant ? he might rot unknown
For any real merit of his own, 280
And never had come forth to public note
Had he not worn, by chance, his father's coat.
To think a Melcombe worth my least regards
Is treason to the majesty of bards.
    By nature form'd (when, for her honour's sake
She something more than common strove to make,
When, overlooking each minute defect,
And all too eager to be quite correct,
In her full heat and vigour she imprest
Her stamp most strongly on the favour'd breast) 290
The bard, (nor think too lightly that I mean
Those little, piddling witlings, who o'erween
Of their small parts, the Murphys of the stage,
The Masons and the Whiteheads of the age,
Who all in raptures their own works rehearse,
And drawl out measured prose, which they call verse)
The real bard, whom native genius fires,

---

[283] See note on ' The Ghost,' Book III, line 928.

[293] Arthur Murphy. See note on ' The Rosciad,' line 67.

[294] William Mason. See note on ' The Prophecy of Famine,' line 67.

[294] William Whitehead. See note on ' The Ghost,' Book III, line 117.

Whom every maid of Castaly inspires,
Let him consider wherefore he was meant,
Let him but answer nature's great intent,   300
And fairly weigh himself with other men,
Would ne'er debase the glories of his pen,
Would in full state, like a true monarch, live,
Nor bate one inch of his prerogative.
    Methinks I see old Wingate frowning here,
(Wingate may in the season be a peer,
Though now, against his will, of figures sick,
He's forced to diet on arithmetic,
E'en whilst he envies every Jew he meets,
Who cries old clothes to sell about the streets)   310
Methinks (his mind with future honours big,
His Tyburn bob turn'd to a dress'd bag wig)
I hear him cry—' What doth this jargon mean ?
Was ever such a damn'd dull blockhead seen ?
Majesty—Bard—Prerogative ;—disdain
Hath got into, and turn'd the fellow's brain :
To Bethlem with him—give him whips and straw—
I'm very sensible he's mad in law.

 [298] ' Every maid of Castaly,' *i.e.*, every Muse. The Castalian spring
on the slopes of Parnassus was sacred to Apollo and the Muses.

[305] Wingate is Sir Francis Dashwood, whose claim for the Barony
of Le Despencer was allowed in 1762. The following lines are an
allusion to his incapacity as Chancellor of the Exchequer. (See note on
' The Ghost,' Book IV, line 629.)

[317] The dissolved religious house of St. Mary of Bethlehem was
granted by Henry VIII to the City as a hospital for lunatics, and the
Proctor to the hospital was licensed by Edward VI to beg within the
counties of Lincoln, Cambridge, the City of London, and the Isle of
Ely. In the reign of Elizabeth the church and chapel were taken down
and houses built in their place. The new Bethlehem was built on the
south side of what is now called Finsbury Square in the year 1675. It
was open to the public as an exhibition, and for two hundred years it
was a common practice to go to Bethlehem in order to see the lunatics,
as one of the sights of London. Payment was made for admission, and
a considerable addition—as much as £400 a year—accrued to the
revenues of the place by this entrance fee. The hospital could
accommodate 150, and when it was found in 1799 too small and too
ill-contrived, the Committee bought a site of nearly twelve acres in
St. George's Fields, Lambeth. The new building was completed in
1815. (See ' London in the Eighteenth Century,' by Sir Walter
Besant, 1902, p. 374.)

A saucy groom, who trades in reason, thus
To set himself upon a par with us ;   320
If this here's suffer'd, and if that there fool
May when he pleases send us all to school,
Why, then our only business is outright
To take our caps, and bid the world good night.
I've kept a bard myself this twenty years,
But nothing of this kind in him appears ;
He, like a thorough, true-bred spaniel, licks
The hand which cuffs him, and the foot which kicks ;
He fetches and he carries, blacks my shoes,
Nor thinks it a discredit to his muse ;   330
A creature of the right chameleon hue,
He wears my colours yellow or true blue,
Just as I wear them : 'tis all one to him
Whether I change through conscience, or through whim.
Now this is something like ; on such a plan
A bard may find a friend in a great man ;
But this proud coxcomb—Zounds, I thought that all
Of this queer tribe had been like my old Paul.'
    Injurious thought ! accursed be the tongue
On which the vile insinuation hung,   340
The heart where 'twas engender'd ! curst be those,
Those bards, who not themselves alone expose,
But me, but all, and make the very name
By which they're call'd a standing mark of shame.
    Talk not of custom—'tis the coward's plea,
Current with fools, but passes not with me ;
An old, stale trick, which guilt hath often tried
By numbers to o'er power the better side.
Why tell me then that from the birth of rhyme,
No matter when, down to the present time,   350
As by the original decree of fate,
Bards have protection sought amongst the great ;
Conscious of weakness, have applied to them
As vines to elms, and twining round their stem,
Flourish'd on high ; to gain this wish'd support
E'en Virgil to Mæcenas paid his court.

[332] The political colours of the Whigs and the Tories.
[338] Paul Whitehead. See note on ' The Ghost,' Book III, line 95.

As to the custom, 'tis a point agreed,
But 'twas a foolish diffidence, not need,
From which it rose ; had bards but truly known
That strength which is most properly their own,   360
Without a lord, unpropp'd they might have stood,
And overtopp'd those giants of the wood.
   But why, when present times my care engage,
Must I go back to the Augustan age ?
Why, anxious for the living, am I led
Into the mansions of the ancient dead ?
Can they find patrons no where but at Rome,
And must I seek Mæcenas in the tomb ?
Name but a Wingate, twenty fools of note
Start up, and from report Mæcenas quote ;   370
Under his colours lords are proud to fight,
Forgetting that Mæcenas was a knight :
They mention him, as if to use his name
Was, in some measure, to partake his fame,
Though Virgil, was he living, in the street
Might rot for them, or perish in the Fleet.
See how they redden, and the charge disclaim—
' Virgil, and in the Fleet—forbid it, Shame ! '
Hence, ye vain boasters, to the Fleet repair,
And ask, with blushes ask, if Lloyd is there.   380
   Patrons in days of yore were men of sense,
Were men of taste, and had a fair pretence
To rule in letters—some of them were heard
To read off-hand, and never spell a word ;
Some of them, too, to such a monstrous height
Was learning risen, for themselves could write,
And kept their secretaries, as the great
Do many other foolish things, for state.
   Our patrons are of quite a different strain,
With neither sense nor taste ; against the grain   390
They patronize for fashion's sake—no more—
And keep a bard, just as they keep a whore.
Melcombe (on such occasions I am loath
To name the dead) was a rare proof of both.

[380] Lloyd was confined in the Fleet prison for debt on the failure of
' The St. James's Magazine.' (See note on ' The Rosciad,' line 232.)

Some of them would be puzzled e'en to read,
Nor could deserve their clergy by their creed ;
Others can write, but such a Pagan hand,
A Willes should always at our elbow stand :
Many, if begg'd, a chancellor, of right,
Would order into keeping at first sight.   400
Those who stand fairest to the public view
Take to themselves the praise to others due ;
They rob the very 'Spital, and make free
With those, alas, who've least to spare—we see
—— hath not had a word to say,
Since winds and waves bore Singlespeech away.
    Patrons in days of yore, like patrons now,
Expected that the bard should make his bow
At coming in, and every now and then
Hint to the world that they were more than men ;   410
But, like the patrons of the present day,
They never bilk'd the poet of his pay.
Virgil loved rural ease, and, far from harm,
Mæcenas fix'd him in a neat, snug farm,
Where he might free from trouble pass his days
In his own way, and pay his rent in praise.
Horace loved wine, and, through his friend at court,
Could buy it off the quay in every port :
Horace loved mirth, Mæcenas loved it too ;
They met, they laugh'd, as Goy and I may do,   420
Nor in those moments paid the least regard
To which was minister, and which was bard.

[398] Dr. Edward Willes (died 1773), Bishop of Bath and Wells,
Decypherer to the King. He ordained Churchill deacon.

[406] William Gerard Hamilton (1729-1796), known as 'Single speech
Hamilton,' was returned to Parliament in 1754 and on November 13th,
1755, made his famous maiden speech. This was so brilliant an effort
that it eclipsed any later speeches he may have made. Some of his
contemporaries credited him with having written the 'Letters of
Junius.' In 1761 he went to Ireland as principal Secretary of State to
the Lord-Lieutenant Halifax. The present editor is unable to suggest
any name for the blank in the preceding line.

[420] Pierre Goy, a friend of Wilkes and an admirer of Churchill. The
former in a letter to the latter from Paris, dated August 29th, 1764,
says : ' You are read and admir'd here—my intimate friend Goy has
almost got you by heart.'

Not so our patrons—grave as grave can be,
They know themselves, they keep up dignity;
Bards are a forward race, nor is it fit
That men of fortune rank with men of wit:
Wit, if familiar made, will find her strength—
'Tis best to keep her weak, and at arm's length.
'Tis well enough for bards, if patrons give,
From hand to mouth, the scanty means to live.   430
Such is their language, and their practice such;
They promise little, and they give not much.
Let the weak bard, with prostituted strain,
Praise that proud Scot whom all good men disdain;
What's his reward? why, his own fame undone,
He may obtain a patent for the run
Of his lord's kitchen, and have ample time,
With offal fed, to court the cook in rhyme;
Or (if he strives true patriots to disgrace)
May at the second table get a place,   440
With somewhat greater slaves allow'd to dine,
And play at crambo o'er his gill of wine.
    And are there bards, who, on creation's file,
Stand rank'd as men, who breathe in this fair isle
The air of freedom, with so little gall,
So low a spirit, prostrate thus to fall
Before these idols, and without a groan
Bear wrongs might call forth murmurs from a stone?
Better, and much more noble, to abjure
The sight of men, and in some cave, secure   450
From all the outrages of pride, to feast
On Nature's salads, and be free at least.
Better (though that, to say the truth, is worse
Than almost any other modern curse)
Discard all sense, divorce the thankless Muse,
Critics commence, and write in the Reviews,
Write without tremor—Griffiths cannot read;
No fool can fail, where Langhorne can succeed.

[434] Bute. (See note on ' The Prophecy of Famine,' line 533.)

[442] Crambo was a rhyming game, the repetition of a rhyme involving a ' forfeit.'

[458] John Langhorne (1735-1779) was in 1764 appointed curate and

441

But (not to make a brave and honest pride,
Try those means first she must disdain when tried)   460
There are a thousand ways, a thousand arts,
By which, and fairly, men of real parts
May gain a living, gain what Nature craves ;
Let those, who pine for more, live, and be slaves.
Our real wants in a small compass lie ;
But lawless appetite, with eager eye,
Kept in a constant fever, more requires,
And we are burnt up with our own desires.
Hence our dependence, hence our slavery springs ;
Bards, if contented, are as great as kings.   470
Ourselves are to ourselves the cause of ill ;
We may be independent, if we will.
The man who suits his spirit to his state
Stands on an equal footing with the great ;
Moguls themselves are not more rich, and he
Who rules the English nation, not more free.
Chains were not forged more durable and strong
For bards than others, but they've worn them long,
And therefore wear them still ; they've quite forgot
What freedom is, and therefore prize her not.   480
Could they, though in their sleep, could they but know
The blessings which from Independence flow ;
Could they but have a short and transient gleam
Of liberty, though 'twas but in a dream,
They would no more in bondage bend their knee,
But, once made freemen, would be always free.
The Muse, if she one moment freedom gains,
Can never more submit to sing in chains.
Bred in a cage, far from the feather'd throng,
The bird repays his keeper with his song ;   490
But, if some playful child sets wide the door,
Abroad he flies, and thinks of home no more ;

lecturer at St. John's, Clerkenwell, and soon after contributed to
' The Monthly Review,' edited by Ralph Griffiths.   He succeeded
Smollett as editor of ' The Critical Review,' a publication consistently
hostile to Churchill, and the University of Edinburgh is said to have
presented him with the honorary degree of D.D. in reward for his
' Genius and Valour : A Scotch Pastoral ' in answer to Churchill's
' Prophecy of Famine.'

With love of liberty begins to burn,
And rather starves than to his cage return.
   Hail, Independence—by true reason taught,
How few have known, and prized thee as they ought !
Some give thee up for riot ; some, like boys,
Resign thee, in their childish moods, for toys ;
Ambition some, some avarice misleads,
And in both cases Independence bleeds.   500
Abroad, in quest of thee, how many roam,
Nor know they had thee in their reach at home !
Some, though about their paths, their beds about,
Have never had the sense to find thee out :
Others, who know of what they are possess'd,
Like fearful misers, lock thee in a chest,
Nor have the resolution to produce,
In these bad times, and bring thee forth for use.
Hail, Independence—though thy name's scarce known,
Though thou, alas ! art out of fashion grown,   510
Though all despise thee, I will not despise,
Nor live one moment longer than I prize
Thy presence, and enjoy : by angry fate
Bow'd down, and almost crush'd, thou cam'st, though late,
Thou cam'st upon me, like a second birth,
And made me know what life was truly worth.
Hail, Independence—never may my cot,
Till I forget thee, be by thee forgot :
Thither, O thither, oftentimes repair ;
Cotes, whom thou lovest too, shall meet thee there : 520
All thoughts but what arise from joy give o'er,
Peace dwells within, and Law shall guard the door.
   O'erweening Bard ! Law guard thy door ! what law ?
The law of England.—To control and awe
Those saucy hopes, to strike that spirit dumb,
Behold, in state, Administration come.
   Why, let her come, in all her terrors too ;
I dare to suffer all she dares to do.
I know her malice well, and know her pride,

520 Humphry Cotes, a wine merchant in St. Martin's Lane, was an ardent supporter of Wilkes. It was he who travelled to the Continent with Churchill and brought back his dead body to Dover.

443

I know her strength, but will not change my side. 530
This melting mass of flesh she may control
With iron ribs, she cannot chain my soul.
No—to the last resolved her worst to bear,
I'm still at large, and independent there.
   Where is this minister ? where is the band
Of ready slaves, who at his elbow stand
To hear, and to perform his wicked will ?
Why, for the first time, are they slow to ill ?
When some grand act 'gainst law is to be done,
Doth —— sleep ; doth blood-hound —— run 540
To L——, and worry those small deer,
When he might do more precious mischief here ?
Doth Webb turn tail ? doth he refuse to draw
Illegal warrants, and to call them Law ?·•
Doth ——, at Guilford kick'd, from Guilford run,
With that cold lump of unbaked dough, his son,
And, his more honest rival Ketch to cheat,

540-554 This is one of the most obscure passages in the whole of Churchill's writings, and Tooke makes no effort to supply the blanks. These blanks are not quite so many as at first appear, since it is obvious, after consideration, that the first blank in line 540 is the same as both blanks in line 549. The name ' Mansfield ' should probably fill all three. The second blank in line 540 probably stands for Norton, i.e., Sir Fletcher Norton, Solicitor-General, who with Charles Yorke, the Attorney-General, pronounced No. 45 of 'The North Briton' to be ' an infamous and seditious libel ; tending to inflame the minds, and alienate the affections of the people from his majesty, and excite them to traitorous insurrections against his government.' If Norton be the missing word then the blank in the next line (541) can be filled up with the word Lancaster, Norton being Attorney-General for the County Palatine. The probability is perhaps strengthened by the fact that Mansfield and Norton are mentioned together in one sentence in ' The Farewell ' (lines 132-137). The name Norton can also be inserted in line 551. There remain the blanks in lines 545 and 553, both to be filled up by the same one-syllabled name. In the first edition, line 543 contained a blank also, later filled by the name Webb. It is tempting to assume that the same name should fill all three blanks, since Webb, when the satire was written, had a comparatively young son, and his estate of Burbridge in Surrey is not far from Guildford. The precise meaning of ' from Guilford kick'd ' would still remain obscure. The other possibilities are (1) Robert Wood, Under-Secretary of State, and active in seizing Wilkes' papers, and (2) the Charles Yorke, above-mentioned. Of these two, Wood is the more likely, but he sat for the pocket-borough of Brackley in Northamptonshire and seems to have had nothing whatever to do with Guildford.

Purchase a burial-place where three ways meet ?
Believe it not ; —— is —— still,
And never sleeps, when he should wake to ill :   550
—— doth lesser mischiefs by the bye,
The great ones till the term in petto lie :
—— lives, and, to the strictest justice true,
Scorns to defraud the hangman of his due.
   O my poor Country—weak, and overpower'd
By thine own sons—ate to the bone—devour'd
By vipers, which, in thine own entrails bred,
Prey on thy life, and with thy blood are fed—
With unavailing grief thy wrongs I see,
And, for myself not feeling, feel for thee.   560
I grieve, but can't despair—for, lo, at hand
Freedom presents a choice, but faithful band
Of loyal patriots ; men who greatly dare
In such a noble cause ; men fit to bear
The weight of empires ; Fortune, Rank, and Sense,
Virtue and Knowledge, leagued with Eloquence,
March in their ranks ; Freedom from file to file
Darts her delighted eye, and with a smile
Approves her honest sons, whilst down her cheek,
As 'twere by stealth, (her heart too full to speak)   570
One tear in silence creeps, one honest tear,
And seems to say, Why is not Granby here ?
   O ye brave few, in whom we still may find
A love of virtue, freedom, and mankind,
Go forth—in majesty of woe array'd,
See at your feet your country kneels for aid,
And, (many of her children traitors grown)
Kneels to those sons she still can call her own ;
Seeming to breathe her last in every breath,

[572] John Manners, Marquis of Granby (1721-1770), served against the
Young Pretender in the '45, became a major-general in 1755, and on
the outbreak of the Seven Years' War in 1758 went to Germany in
command of a brigade of cavalry. At Minden he showed more energy
than his commander Lord George Sackville, and on the resignation
of the latter was appointed to succeed him. He was a brilliant
divisional commander and beloved by his men. He returned home,
very popular, in 1763, but his political activities soon made him
enemies, and his immense debts laid him open to the charge of chang-
ing his principles for pay.

445

She kneels for freedom, or she begs for death.   580
Fly, then, each duteous son, each English chief,
And to your drooping parent bring relief.
Go forth—nor let the Siren voice of ease
Tempt ye to sleep, whilst tempests swell the seas ;
Go forth—nor let Hypocrisy, whose tongue
With many a fair, false, fatal art is hung,
Like Bethel's fawning prophet, cross your way,
When your great errand brooks not of delay ;
Nor let vain Fear, who cries to all she meets,
Trembling and pale, ' A lion in the streets ! '   590
Damp your free spirits ; let not threats affright,
Nor bribes corrupt, nor flatteries delight :
Be as one man—concord success ensures—
There's not an English heart but what is yours.
Go forth—and Virtue, ever in your sight,
Shall be your guide by day, your guard by night.
Go forth—the champions of your native land,
And may the battle prosper in your hand.
It may, it must : ye cannot be withstood.
Be your hearts honest, as your cause is good.   600

587 See 1 Kings xiii, 1-32.

THE JOURNEY*
A FRAGMENT

SOME of my friends, (for friends I must suppose
All, who, not daring to appear my foes,
Feign great good will, and, not more full of spite
Than full of craft, under false colours fight)
Some of my friends, (so lavishly I print)
As more in sorrow than in anger, hint
(Though that indeed will scarce admit a doubt)
That I shall run my stock of genius out,
My no great stock, and, publishing so fast,
Must needs become a bankrupt at the last.   10
  ' The husbandman, to spare a thankful soil,
Which, rich in disposition, pays his toil
More than a hundredfold, which swells his store
E'en to his wish, and makes his barns run o'er,
By long experience taught, who teaches best,
Foregoes his hopes a while, and gives it rest :
The land, allow'd its losses to repair,
Refresh'd, and full in strength, delights to wear
A second youth, and to the farmer's eyes
Bids richer crops, and double harvests rise.   20
  ' Nor think this practice to the earth confined,
It reaches to the culture of the mind.
The mind of man craves rest, and cannot bear
Though next in power to God's, continual care.
Genius himself (nor here let Genius frown)
Must, to ensure his vigour, be laid down,
And fallow'd well : had Churchill known but this,
Which the most slight observer scarce could miss,
He might have flourish'd twenty years, or more,
Though now, alas ! poor man ! worn out in four.'   30
  Recover'd from the vanity of youth,

---

* First published 1765. 'Printed for John Churchill (**Executor to**
the late C. Churchill) and sold by W. Flexney.'

I feel, alas ! this melancholy truth,
Thanks to each cordial, each advising friend,
And am, if not too late, resolved to mend ;
Resolved to give some respite to my pen,
Apply myself once more to books and men,
View what is present, what is past review,
And, my old stock exhausted, lay in new.
For twice six moons, (let winds, turn'd porters, bear
This oath to heaven) for twice six moons, I swear,   40
No Muse shall tempt me with her Siren lay,
Nor draw me from improvement's thorny way.
Verse I abjure, nor will forgive that friend,
Who, in my hearing, shall a rhyme commend.
    It cannot be—whether I will, or no,
Such as they are, my thoughts in measure flow.
Convinced, determined, I in prose begin,
But ere I write one sentence, verse creeps in,
And taints me through and through ; by this good light
In verse I talk by day, I dream by night !   50
If now and then I curse, my curses chime,
Nor can I pray, unless I pray in rhyme.
E'en now I err, in spite of common sense,
And my confession doubles my offence.
    Rest then, my friends ;—spare, spare your precious
        breath,
And be your slumbers not less sound than death ;
Perturbèd spirits, rest, nor thus appear
To waste your counsels in a spendthrift's ear ;
On your grave lessons I cannot subsist,
Nor e'en in verse become economist.   60
Rest then, my friends, nor hateful to my eyes,
Let Envy, in the shape of Pity, rise
To blast me ere my time ; with patience wait,
('Tis no long interval) propitious Fate
Shall glut your pride, and every son of phlegm
Find ample room to censure and condemn.
Read some three hundred lines, (no easy task,
But probably the last that I shall ask)

    [47] This happened to the projected paper for ' The North Briton '
which turned into ' The Prophecy of Famine.'

And give me up for ever ; wait one hour—
Nay, not so much—revenge is in your power,   70
And ye may cry, ere Time hath turn'd his glass,
' Lo ! what we prophesied is come to pass.'
   Let those who poetry in poems claim,
Or not read this, or only read to blame ;
Let those who are by fiction's charms enslaved,
Return me thanks for half-a-crown well saved ;
Let those who love a little gall in rhyme
Postpone their purchase now, and call next time ;
Let those who, void of nature, look for art,
Take up their money, and in peace depart ;   80
Let those who energy of diction prize,
For Billingsgate quit Flexney, and be wise :
Here is no lie, no gall, no art, no force,
Mean are the words, and such as come of course ;
The subject not less simple than the lay ;
A plain, unlabour'd Journey of a Day.
   Far from me now be every tuneful maid ;
I neither ask, nor can receive their aid.
Pegasus turn'd into a common hack,
Alone I jog, and keep the beaten track,   90
Nor would I have the Sisters of the hill
Behold their bard in such a dishabille.
Absent, but only absent for a time,
Let them caress some dearer son of rhyme ;
Let them, as far as decency permits,
Without suspicion, play the fool with wits,
'Gainst fools be guarded ; 'tis a certain rule,
Wits are safe things ; there's danger in a fool.
   Let them, though modest, Gray, more modest, woo ;
Let them with Mason bleat, and bray, and coo ;   100
Let them with Franklin, proud of some small Greek,
Make Sophocles, disguised, in English speak ;

---

[82] Flexney was Churchill's publisher.

[99] For Churchill's feelings towards Gray, see note on ' Gotham,'
Book II, line 20.

[100] See note on ' The Prophecy of Famine,' line 67.

[101] See note on ' The Rosciad,' line 63.

449

Let them with Glover o'er Medea doze ;
Let them with Dodsley wail Cleone's woes,
Whilst he, fine-feeling creature, all in tears,
Melts as they melt, and weeps with weeping peers ;
Let them with simple Whitehead taught to creep
Silent and soft, lay Fontenelle asleep ;
Let them with Brown contrive, no vulgar trick,
To cure the dead, and make the living sick ;   110
Let them, in charity to Murphy, give
Some old French piece, that he may steal and live ;
Let them with antic Foote subscriptions get,
And advertise a summer-house of wit.
    Thus, or in any better way they please,
With these great men, or with great men like these,
Let them their appetite for laughter feed ;
I on my Journey all alone proceed.
    If fashionable grown, and fond of power,
With humorous Scots let them disport their hour ;   120
Let them dance, fairy-like, round Ossian's tomb ;
Let them forge lies and histories for Hume ;
Let them with Home, the very prince of verse,
Make something like a tragedy in Erse ;

[103] See note on ' The Ghost,' Book III, line 1032.

[104] Robert Dodsley (1703-1764) was a footman who wrote verses and in 1735 opened a bookseller's shop in Pall Mall. He was the author of several dramatic pieces, and his ' Cleone ' was produced at Covent Garden on December 2nd, 1758. It had the then successful run of sixteen nights and 2,000 copies of the work were sold at once. Dodsley is now remembered chiefly as the friend of Johnson.

[107] Whitehead's ' The School for Lovers ' was founded on Fontenelle's ' Le Testament.'

[109] Dr. Brown was a physician, and his ' Cure of Saul,' a sacred ode, was set to music and performed as an oratorio in 1763.

[111] Murphy adapted a number of plays from Voltaire, Molière, etc. (See note on the ' Rosciad,' line 67.)

[113] See note on the ' Rosciad,' line 396.

[122] David Hume's History of England in six volumes was published between 1754 and 1761. His opinions as a Tory and his prejudices as a Scot were particularly obnoxious to Churchill.

[123] An allusion to Home's ' Douglas.' (See note on ' The Prophecy of Famine,' line 127.)

Under dark allegory's flimsy veil
Let them with Ogilvie spin out a tale
Of rueful length ; let them plain things obscure,
Debase what's truly rich, and what is poor
Make poorer still by jargon most uncouth ;
With every pert, prim prettiness of youth,   130
Born of false taste ; with Fancy (like a child
Not knowing what it cries for) running wild ;
With bloated style, by affectation taught,
With much false colouring, and little thought,
With phrases strange, and dialect decreed
By reason never to have pass'd the Tweed ;
With words, which nature meant each other's foe,
Forced to compound whether they will or no ;
With such materials, let them, if they will,
To prove at once their pleasantry and skill,   140
Build up a bard to war 'gainst common sense,
By way of compliment to Providence ;
Let them with Armstrong, taking leave of sense,
Read musty lectures on Benevolence,
Or con the pages of his gaping Day,
Where all his former fame was thrown away,
Where all but barren labour was forgot,
And the vain stiffness of a letter'd Scot ;
Let them with Armstrong pass the term of light,
But not one hour of darkness : when the night   150
Suspends this mortal coil, when memory wakes,
When for our past misdoings conscience takes
A deep revenge, when, by reflection led,
She draws his curtains, and looks comfort dead,
Let every muse be gone ; in vain he turns,
And tries to pray for sleep ; an Ætna burns,
A more than Ætna, in his coward breast,
And guilt, with vengeance arm'd, forbids him rest :
Though soft as plumage from young Zephyr's wing,
His couch seems hard, and no relief can bring ;   160

[126] John Ogilvie was the author of an extremely long allegorical
poem entitled ' Providence,' published in 1764.

[143] Armstrong's ' Benevolence, an Epistle,' was published in 1751 ;
his ' Day ' in 1761. (See Introduction, p. xxv, note 2.)

451

Ingratitude hath planted daggers there
No good man can deserve, no brave man bear.
   Thus, or in any better way they please,
With these great men, or with great men like these,
Let them their appetite for laughter feed ;
I on my journey all alone proceed.

FRAGMENT OF A
DEDICATION TO
DR. W. WARBURTON*
BISHOP OF GLOUCESTER

HEALTH to great Glo'ster—from a man unknown,
Who holds thy health as dearly as his own,
Accept this greeting—nor let modest fear
Call up one maiden blush—I mean not here
To wound with flattery ; 'tis a villain's art,
And suits not with the frankness of my heart.
Truth best becomes an orthodox divine,
And, spite of hell, that character is mine :
To speak e'en bitter truths I cannot fear ;
But truth, my Lord, is panegyric here.   10
    Health to great Glo'ster—nor, through love of ease,
Which all priests love, let this address displease.

* The ' Sermons ' of Charles Churchill to which this dedication was
attached, were advertised to be published on 14th November, 1764,
but owing to the poet's death on 4th November, they did not appear
until early in 1765. ' Printed by W. Griffin ; for John Churchill
(Executor of Charles Churchill) and William Flexney.'

1 William Warburton (1698-1779) was at first articled to an attorney
in Nottinghamshire but was ordained in 1723 and in 1727 became
vicar of Greaseley. He read widely and, in 1736, published ' The
Alliance of Church and State.' ' The Divine Legation of Moses'
appeared between 1737 and 1741 and plunged Warburton into con-
troversies which lasted thirty years. In 1738 he became chaplain to
Frederick, Prince of Wales. His defence of Pope's ' Essay on Man '
won him the poet's friendship, and he became his literary executor,
bringing out a collected edition of Pope's works in 1751. In 1747 he
had published an edition of Shakespeare which was bitterly attacked
by his enemies. He rose steadily in the hierarchy to become Bishop of
Gloucester in 1759. Warburton's controversial methods were violent
and scurrilous in the extreme, and his theological arguments para-
doxical to the verge of absurdity. Part at least of his rise was due to
the friendship of Ralph Allen, the wealthy farmer of cross-posts to
whom he was introduced by Pope and whose niece, Gertrude Tucker,
he married in 1745. Allen on his death left Warburton and his wife
£5000 each with a further £3000 a year on the death of Mrs. Allen.

453

I ask no favour ; not one *note* I crave ;
And when this busy brain rests in the grave,
(For till that time it never can have rest)
I will not trouble you with one bequest.
Some humbler friend, my mortal journey done,
More near in blood, a nephew or a son,
In that dread hour executor I'll leave,
For I, alas ! have many to receive—   20
To give, but little.—To great Glo'ster health ;
Nor let thy true and proper love of wealth
Here take a false alarm—in purse though poor,
In spirit I'm right proud, nor can endure
The mention of a bribe—thy pocket's free :
I, though a dedicator, scorn a fee.
Let thy own offspring all thy fortunes share ;
I would not Allen rob, nor Allen's heir.
    Think not—a thought unworthy thy great soul,
Which pomps of this world never could control ;   30
Which never offer'd up at Power's vain shrine—
Think not that pomp and power can work on mine.
'Tis not thy name, though that indeed is great,
'Tis not the tinsel trumpery of state,
'Tis not thy title, Doctor though thou art,
'Tis not thy mitre which hath won my heart.
State is a farce ; names are but empty things ;

²⁴ Wilkes' notes : ' The reverend emissary of Lord Holland (Mr. Francis, the translator of Horace) who waited on the poet soon after the advertisement of " Ayliffe's Ghost, by C. Churchill," can best explain this passage. The untimely death of the author deprived us of that elegy ; but his lordship was convinced, at last, that every man has NOT his price.' We may readily believe that Churchill refused the bribe, yet there is some mystery in the affair. Tooke says that he destroyed all his unfinished works before his death, but when, and why, seeing that he did not expect to die in France, and it is unlikely that he had all his papers with him ? And why did he not destroy the ' Dedication to Warburton ' which is admittedly a fragment ? (For Ayliffe, see Introduction, p. xlvi.

²⁸ Warburton lived with the Allens at Prior Park near Bath, and having married Allen's niece, inherited Allen's fortune. Potter was supposed to be the father of Mrs. Warburton's children. *Cf.* ' The Duellist ' :
> ' No husband, though he's truly wed ;
> Though on his knees a child is bred,
> No father,'

Degrees are bought ; and, by mistaken kings,
Titles are oft' misplaced ; mitres, which shine
So bright in other eyes, are dull in mine,   40
Unless set off by virtue ; who deceives
Under the sacred sanction of lawn sleeves
Enhances guilt, commits a double sin,
So fair without, and yet so foul within.
'Tis not thy outward form, thy easy mien,
Thy sweet complacency, thy brow serene,
Thy open front, thy love-commanding eye,
Where fifty Cupids, as in ambush, lie,
Which can from sixty to sixteen impart
The force of Love, and point his blunted dart ;   50
'Tis not thy face, though that by nature's made
An index to thy soul ; though there display'd
We see thy mind at large, and through thy skin
Peeps out that courtesy which dwells within ;
'Tis not thy birth, for that is low as mine ;
Around our heads no lineal glories shine ;
But what is birth, when, to delight mankind,
Heralds can make those arms they cannot find ;
When thou art to thyself, thy sire unknown,
A whole Welsh genealogy alone ?   60
No ; 'tis thy inward man, thy proper worth,
Thy right just estimation here on earth,
Thy life and doctrine uniformly join'd,
And flowing from that wholesome source, thy mind ;

[45] Warburton was *not* famous either for a handsome figure or an agreeable countenance. Wilkes has a long, elaborately ironical note of which the following is a sufficient sample :
  ' His whole figure excels the most perfect Grecian forms and, in my opinion, is a superior composition to the Apollo Belvidere. . . . Among all the arts of ancient Egypt, which the bishop so much admires, I most regret that the art of embalming, in such a manner as to preserve even the minutest feature, is now totally lost. . . . This loss is the more to be lamented, because the heir to his fortunes is unhappily not the heir to his graces. It is generally allowed, that the boy does not in the least resemble him ; but seems to be of quite another mould, or *potter's* earth.'
  One cannot help feeling that Wilkes and his friends worked this old scandal to death.
  [60] The Welsh, like other Celtic races, were fond of tracing their descent back to semi-mythical beings and heroes.

Thy known contempt of persecution's rod,
Thy charity for man, thy love of God,
Thy faith in Christ, so well approved 'mongst men,
Which now give life and utterance to my pen.
Thy virtue, not thy rank, demands my lays ;
'Tis not the Bishop, but the Saint, I praise :   70
Raised by that theme, I soar on wings more strong,
And burst forth into praise withheld too long.
 Much did I wish, e'en whilst I kept those sheep
Which, for my curse, I was ordain'd to keep,
Ordain'd, alas ! to keep through need, not choice,
Those sheep which never heard their shepherd's voice ;
Which did not know, yet would not learn their way ;
Which stray'd themselves, yet grieved that I should
  stray ;
Those sheep which my good father (on his bier
Let filial duty drop the pious tear)   80
Kept well, yet starved himself ; e'en at that time
Whilst I was pure and innocent of rhyme ;
Whilst, sacred dulness ever in my view,
Sleep at my bidding crept from pew to pew,
Much did I wish, though little could I hope,
A friend in him who was the friend of Pope.
 His hand, said I, my youthful steps shall guide,
And lead me safe where thousands fall beside ;
His temper, his experience shall control,
And hush to peace the tempest of my soul ; 90
His judgment teach me, from the critic school
How not to err, and how to err by rule ;
Instruct me, mingle profit with delight,
Where Pope was wrong, where Shakspeare was not right ;

[77-78] The original version ran :
 ' Which accents of rebuke could never bear,
  Nor would have heeded Christ, had Christ been there.'
In the proof-sheets given by Churchill to Wilkes at Boulogne (now in
the British Museum) these two lines are cancelled and the present two
substituted.

[86] Warburton's notes on Pope were generally considered to have
done his dead friend an injury rather than a service.

[94] A reference to Warburton's notes on Pope and commentaries
on Shakespeare.

Where they are justly praised, and where through whim;
How little's due to them, how much to him.
Raised 'bove the slavery of common rules,
Of common-sense, of modern, ancient schools;
Those feelings banish'd which mislead us all,
Fools as we are, and which we Nature call,   100
He by his great example might impart
A better something, and baptize it Art;
He, all the feelings of my youth forgot,
Might shew me what is taste by what is not;
By him supported with a proper pride,
I might hold all mankind as fools beside;
He (should a world, perverse and peevish grown,
Explode his maxims and assert their own)
Might teach me, like himself to be content,
And let their folly be their punishment;   110
Might, like himself, teach his adopted son,
'Gainst all the world, to quote a Warburton.
     Fool that I was! could I so much deceive
My soul with lying hopes? could I believe
That he, the servant of his Maker sworn,
The servant of his Saviour, would be torn
From their embrace, and leave that dear employ,
The cure of souls, his duty and his joy,
For toys like mine, and waste his precious time,
On which so much depended, for a rhyme?   120
Should he forsake the task he undertook, ·
Desert his flock, and break his pastoral crook?
Should he (forbid it, Heaven!) so high in place,
So rich in knowledge, quit the work of grace,
And, idly wandering o'er the Muses' hill,
Let the salvation of mankind stand still?
     Far, far be that from thee—yes, far from thee
Be such revolt from grace, and far from me
The will to think it—guilt is in the thought.
Not so, not so hath Warburton been taught,   130

[111] Wilkes' notes: ' The poet does not mean the bishop's *adopted* son master Warburton; but the sense he might teach *him* [Churchill] as an " adopted son." ' ' Adopted ' is, of course, yet another sneer at the alleged infidelity of Warburton's wife.

Not so learn'd Christ—recall that day, well known,
When (to maintain God's honour—and his own)
He call'd blasphemers forth : methinks I now
See stern rebuke enthronèd on his brow,
And arm'd with tenfold terrors : from his tongue,
Where fiery zeal and Christian fury hung,
Methinks I hear the deep-toned thunders roll,
And chill with horror every sinner's soul ;
In vain they strive to fly—flight cannot save ;
And Potter trembles even in his grave ;   140
With all the conscious pride of innocence
Methinks I hear him, in his own defence,
Bear witness to himself, whilst all men knew,
By gospel rules his witness to be true.
    O glorious man ! thy zeal I must commend,
Though it deprived me of my dearest friend ;
The real motives of thy anger known,
Wilkes must the justice of that anger own ;
And, could thy bosom have been bared to view,
Pitied himself, in turn had pitied you.   150
Bred to the law, you wisely took the gown,
Which I, like Demas, foolishly laid down ;
Hence double strength our Holy Mother drew,
Me she got rid of, and made prize of you.
I, like an idle truant fond of play,
Doting on toys, and throwing gems away,
Grasping at shadows, let the substance slip ;
But you, my lord, renounced attorneyship

[131] ' that day,' *i.e.*, November 15th, 1763, when Lord Sandwich rose
in the House of Lords and denounced the ' Essay on Woman ' as a
' blasphemous, obscene and abominable libel.' Sandwich read some
passages from the work until Lord Lyttelton interposed with the
request that the ears of those present might be spared such horrible
indecencies. Warburton, in great excitement, assured the House that
he had not written any of the notes, calling God to witness. No one,
he declared, but the devil concocted such a work, and added : ' I beg
the devil's pardon, for I do not think even him capable of so infamous
a production.'
[141] This line perhaps shows that, in Churchill's opinion at least, the
author of the ' Essay on Woman ' was Potter and not Wilkes. (See
the ' Epistle to Hogarth,' line 195.)
[158] Wilkes remarks : ' The name and profession of an attorney,

With better purpose, and more noble aim,
And wisely play'd a more substantial game :   160
Nor did Law mourn, bless'd in her younger son,
For Mansfield does what Glo'ster would have done.
  Doctor ! Dean ! Bishop ! Glo'ster ! and my Lord,
If haply these high titles may accord
With thy meek spirit ; if the barren sound
Of pride delights thee, to the topmost round
Of Fortune's ladder got, despise not one
For want of smooth hypocrisy undone,
Who, far below, turns up his wondering eye,
And, without envy, sees thee placed so high :   170
Let not thy brain (as brains less potent might)
Dizzy, confounded, giddy with the height,
Turn round, and lose distinction, lose her skill
And wonted powers of knowing good from ill,
Of sifting truth from falsehood, friends from foes ;
Let Glo'ster well remember how he rose,
Nor turn his back on men who made him great ;
Let him not, gorged with power, and drunk with state,
Forget what once he was, though now so high ;
How low, how mean, and full as poor as I.   180

·   ·   ·   ·   ·   ·   ·   ·

Cœtera desunt.

my lord did indeed renounce ; but the wrangling and cavilling, the
subterfuges and mean arts of vile attorneys (as Pope calls them . . .)
may be found in all his controversial writings. He can, however, at
a pinch, still do business for himself as an attorney ; and, in the idea
of the world, Mr. Allen's will does honour to the proficiency he made
in his former trade.'

INDEX

The volumes are numbered straight through, Volume I containing pp. i-lii and 1-210, Volume II, pp. 211-460.

Ackman, —, 4 and n., 23
Actor, The (Lloyd), xviii
Addison, Joseph, 236 n.
Aldrich, Rev. Dr. Stephen, 90 n., 139
Allen, Ralph, 181 and n., 297 n., 298 n., 454 and n.
Almack, William, 368 and n.
Amyand, Cladius, 200 and n.
Annet, Peter, 159 and n.
' Apicius,' 414 *et seq.*, 418
Aretino, Pietro, 411 and n.
Armstrong, John, xxiii, xxxv n., 451 and n.
Arne, Dr. Thomas Augustine, 32 and n., 36 n.
' Arrow,' 94 and n., 120 and n.
Asgill, Sir Charles, 162 and n.
Augusta, Princess, 320 and n.
Austin, —, 23 and n.
Author's Apology, The (Lloyd), xviii
' Avaro,' *see* Pearce, Zechariah
Ayliffe, —, xlvi, 279, 282
Ayliffe's Ghost (Churchill), xlvi, 236 n., 274
Aynam, —, 414 and n.

B——, 202
B——, 424 and n.
Baker, Sir George, 85 and n.
Barrowby, William, 418 and n.
Barry, Spranger, xxii, 4 and n., 39 and n., 40 and n.
Beard, John, 9 n., 14 n., 30 n., 33 and n.
Beardmore, the under-sheriff, 182, 273
Beckford, William, 146 and n., 180 n.
Bedford, John Russell, Duke of, xxix
Bellamy, George Anne, 5 n., 29 n., 35 n., 40 n., 275 n., 421 n.
Berkeley, Col. Norbone, 323 and n.

Betterton, Thomas, 41 and n.
Blackstone, Sir William, 385 and n.
Blacow, —, 276 and n.
Blakes, —, 24 and n.
Bower, Archibald, 431 and n.
Boyce, William, 312 and n.
Bransby, —, 24 and n.
Brent, Charlotte, 33 and n., 60 and n.
Bride, Miss —, 35 and n.
Brown, Dr. —, 450 and n.
Brown, Rev. John, 173 and n.
Browne, Dr. William, 385 and n.
Bruce, Rev. Samuel, 134 and n., 145 *et seq.*, 188 *et seq.*
Burlington, Richard Boyle, Earl of, 132 n.
Burton, Dr. John, 378 and n., 381
Burton, John (of C.C.C. Oxon.), 384 and n.
Bute, John Stuart, Earl of, xxix, 6 n., 7 n., 11 and n., 25 n., 133, 149 and n., 171 and n., 177, 190, 215 n., 220-1, 228 and n., 238, 247, 261, 282, 331, 370, 404 n., 429, 441

C——, 101
Calcraft, John, 35 n., 236 and n., 261
Camargo, La, 411 n.
Camden, Charles Pratt, Earl, xxxv, 243 and n., 291 and n.
Canning, Elizabeth, 88 and n., 137
Carew, Bampfylde Moore, 74 and n.
Carr, Elizabeth, xxxi n., xxxviii and n.-xl, 94 n., 95 n.
Carrington, Nathan, 292 and n.
Charlotte, Queen, 95 and n.
Chauncey, Dr. Charles, 154 and n.
' Chloe,' 415 and n.

461

Chudleigh, Elizabeth, 321 and n.
Churchill, Charles ; birth, xiii, 319 and n. ; parentage and relatives, xiii ; education, xiii-xiv ; marriage, xiv ; ordination, xv-xvi ; *The Fortune Teller*, xv ; teaching, xvii ; separation from wife, xviii ; and Zechariah Pearce, xviii, 216 n. ; *The Bard*, xviii ; *The Conclave*, xviii ; *The Rosciad*, xix-xxii ; makes money, xxiii ; *The Apology*, xxii ; *Night*, xxii, xxvi n. ; meets Wilkes, xxv ; *The Ghost*, xv, xxvii ; with syphilis, xxxi ; *Prophecy of Famine*, xxx-xxxii ; No. 45 'North Briton,' xxxiv ; escapes arrest, xxxiv ; tours Wales, xxxv ; *Epistle to Hogarth*, xxxv ; caricatured by Hogarth, xxxv ; and Elizabeth Carr, xxxviii ; helps Lloyd, xl, 12 n.; *The Conference*, xlii ; *The Author*, xlii ; *The Duellist*, xlii ; *Gotham*, xlii ; *The Candidate*, xliii ; *The Times*, xliii ; *The Farewell*, xliv ; *The Journey*, xlv ; travels to Boulogne, xlv ; death, xlvi ; satire on Colman, xlvi ; his papers, xlvi, 365 and n. ; *Ayliffe's Ghost*, xlvi ; *Dedication to Warburton*, xlvii ; his sons, xlvii ; Walpole on, xlvii ; Johnson on, xlviii ; Cowper on, xlviii ; Letters, xxviii, xxx, xxxi, xxxv n., xxxvii
Churchill, Patty, xiii, xl, 12 n.
Cibber, Colley, 31 n., 106 and n.
Cibber, Susannah Maria, 36 and n., 40 n.
Cibber, Theophilus, 36 n.
Cleland, John, 276 and n.
Clive, Catherine, 31 and n., 33 and n.
Clive, Robert, Baron, 2, 403 and n.
Coan, John, 4 and n.
Colman, George (the elder), xiii, xx, 5 and n., 14 n., 52 and n.
Cooper, Lucy, 16 n.
Cotes, Humphrey, xxxix, xlii, xlvi, 443 and n.

Cowper, William, xiii, 5 n.
'Crape,' see Bruce, Rev. Samuel
Cumberland, William Augustus, Duke of, 25 n.
Cust, Peregrine, 201 and n.

Dashwood, Sir Francis, Bt., xxvii, 170 and n., 177, 231, 323 and n., 383, 437 and n., 439
Davies, Mrs., 15 and n.
Davies, Thomas, xxi, 15 and n., 34 n., 39 n., 45
Day (Armstrong), xxiii
Delaval, Sir Francis Blake, 166 and n.
Despencer, Baron Le, see Dashwood, Sir Francis
Dodd, Dr. William, 423 and n.
Dodsley, Robert, 450 and n.
Doggett, Thomas, 320 and n.
Douglas, John, Bp. of Salisbury, 97 and n.
Dryden, John, 60, 354
Duke, the dancing-master, 198 and n.
'Dulman,' see Fludyer, Samuel
Dunn, Alexander, 157 n., 295 and n.
Dymoke, —, 199

East India Company, 402 and n.
Edwards, Thomas, 300 n.
Egremont, Charles Wyndham, Earl of, xxxviii, 154 and n., 177, 234 n., 266 n., 295 n., 374
Elliot, Ann, 25 and n.
Essay on Woman (Wilkes-Potter), xli, 290 n., 297 n., 299 n., 458 n.

Faden, —, 85 and n.
Fielding, Henry, 52 and n.
Fisher, Catherine, 92 and n.
Fitzpatrick, —, 8 et seq.
Flexney, W.; 449
Flitcroft, Henry, 285 and n.
Fludyer, Sir Samuel, Bt., 133 and n., 136 et seq., 186 et seq.
Foote, Samuel, xxii, 3 and n., 19 and n., 20, 24 n., 450
Forbes, Capt., xxxviii, 295 and n.
Foster, Sir Michael, 13 and n.
Fox, Henry, Baron Holland, xlvi, 231 and n., 236 n., 238, 261 n., 279 and n., 281, 429

462

Francis, Rev. Philip, xlvi, 117 and n., 274-275 and n., 362 and n., 454 and n.
Franklin, Dr. Thomas, 5 and n., 449 ·

Garrick, David, xxii, xxiii ; Letter from, xxiii ; 4, 7 n., 8 n., 16 n., 28 n., 30 n., 38, 40 n., 42, 45 and n., 56 n., 361 and n.
Garth, Sir Samuel, 154 and n.
Gascoyne, Sir Crisp, 88 and n., 137
Genius and Valour (Griffiths), 442 n.
George III, 95 and n., 128 n., 263
Gideon, Sampson, 201 and n.
Glover, Richard, 144 and n., 450
Goy, Pierre, xxxviii, 364 n., 440 and n.
Grafton, Augustus Henry Fitzroy, Duke of, 429 and n.
Granby, John Manners, Marquess of, 124 and n., 445 and n.
Gray, Thomas, 106, 268, 325 and n., 449
Green, the dentist, 169 and n.
Grenville, George, xxxiv
Griffiths, Ralph, 441 and n.
Grosvenor, Sir Richard, 246 n.
Guthrie, William, 273 and n.

Halifax, George Montagu Dunk, Earl of, 234 n., 266 n., 405 and n.
Hamilton, Alexander, 49 and n.
Hamilton, William Gerard, 440 and n.
Hampden, John, 282 and n.
Hardwicke, Philip Yorke, Earl of, xliii, 378 and n.
Harrington, William Stanhope, Earl of, 432 and n.
Hart, Mrs., 35 and n.
Hart, a dancing-master, 122 and n., 150, 198
Havard, William, xxii, 15 and n.
Hayman, Francis, 318 and n.
Hayter, Thomas, Bp. of London, 367 and n.
Heberden, William, M.D., 385 and n.
Hell-Fire Club, xxvii, 382-3 and n.

Herbert, Lady Henrietta, 33 n.
Hervey, Caroline, 424 and n.
Hervey, John, Baron, 425 and n.
Hervey, Mary (Lepel), Bnss., 424 and n.
Hervey, Thomas, 418 and n.
Hill, John, 7 and n., 153, 220
Hogarth, William, xxxiii *et seq.*, 2 n., 241 *et seq.*, 432 n., 433
Holland, Charles, 15 and n.
Holland, Lord, *see* Fox, Henry
Home, John, 144 and n., 215 and n., 220, 450 and n.
Hume, David, xlii, 450
Hunter, Catherine, 120 and n., 131, 188

Idea of a Patriot King (Bolingbroke), xliii, 345 n.

Jackson, John, 21 and n.
Johnson, Samuel, xxiv-v, xlviii, 4, 90 n., 97 and n., 101 and n., 108, 110, 136 and n., 138 and n., 271 and n.

Kearsley, G., xxxiv, 289 n.
Kent, William, 90 n.
Kidgell, Rev. John, 259 n., 275 and n., 277
King, Thomas, xxii, 16 and n.
King, Dr. William, 384 and n.

Langhorne, John, 362 and n., 441 and n.
Lauder, William, 97 and n.
Leach, Dryden, 290 and n.
Lennox, Charlotte, *see* Ramsay, Charlotte
Lichfield, George Henry Lee, Earl of, 382 and n.
Ligonier, John, Earl, 408 and n., 421
Lloyd, Dr. Pierson, xiii, xvii, 255 and n.
Lloyd, Robert, xiii, xvii, xviii, xl, 5, 10, 11, 13 ; ' Ode to Oblivion,' 14 ; 52 and n., 62, 64 n., 255 n., 256, 439
Lockman, John, 198 and n.
Long, Dr. Roger, 380 and n.
Love, James, 21 and n., 22
Lumley, James, 412 and n.
' Lun,' 30 and n.

Lynes, Fanny, 90 and n., 98
Lyttelton, George, 1st Bn., 213 and n., 215 n., 219 and n., 431 and n.

M——, 425 and n.
Macklin, Charles, 28 and n., 29, 31 n., 121 n.
Macklin, Miss, 33 n.
Macpherson, James, 216 and n., 221
Madan, Martin, 155 and n.
Mallett, David, 129 n., 216 and n.
Mansfield, William Murray, 1st Earl of, 9, 13, 136, 156, 174 n., 175, 202, 207-10, 233 and n., 263, 392, 434 n., 444 and n., 459
Manzoli, Giovanni, 410 n.
March, William Douglas, Earl of, 371 and n.
Martin, Samuel, xli, 238 and n., 278 n., 285, 307
Mason, William, ' Ode to Memory,' 14 n., 213 and n., 268, 329, 436, 449
Melcombe, George Bubb Dodington, Baron, 142 and n., 170 and n., 322 and n., 436, 439
Moody, John, 8 n., 24 and n.
Moore, Rev. —, 90 n., 107 and n., 109, 113, 136 and n.
More, a dandy, 315
Morgan, Macnamara, 207 n.
Mossop, Henry, xxii, 39 and n.
Murphy, Arthur, 4 n., 5 and n., 6 n., 25 and n., 33, 34 n., 53 n., 271, 272, 362 and n., 436, 450 and n.
Murray, David, Viscount Stormont, 207 and n.
Mylne, Robert, 183 n., 185

N——, 130
Newcastle, Thomas Pelham Holles, Duke of, 149 and n., 289 and n., 415 and n.
Norris, Henry, 23 and n.
North Briton, xxvii et seq.; No. 45, xxiv; xlii, 290 n., 292, 444 n.
Norton, Sir Fletcher, 148 and n., 207 and n., 233, 262, 301, 392, 444 and n.

O'Brien, William, 20 and n.

Ogilvie, John, 451 and n.
Orrery, John Boyle, 5th Earl of, 365 n.

Palmer, John, 4 and n., 16 n.
Palmer, Mrs. (' Statira '), 28 and n., 35 n.
' Pandarus,' see Sumner, Humphrey
Parsons, Elizabeth, 90 n.
Pearce, Zechariah, Bp. of Rochester, xviii, xxiii, 104 and n., 196 n., 216 and n., 235
Peirson, —, 196 and n.
Phillips, Sir John, 382 and n.
Pitt, William, Earl of Chatham, 72 n., 123 and n., 147, 229, 247, 259 and n., 289
' Plausible,' see Sellon, Rev. William
' Pomposo,' see Johnson, Samuel
Ponton, David, 202 and n.
Pope, Alexander, 59 and n., 236 n., 297 n., 354
Pope, Jane, 32 and n.
Potter, Thomas, 237, 299 and n. et seq., 454 n., 458 and n.
Powell, William, 361 and n.
Pritchard, Hannah, 28 n., 35 n., 37 and n., 38

Quin, James, 41 and n., 43 n., 414 and n.

Ralph, James, 259 and n.
Ramsay, Allan, 215 and n.
Ramsay, Charlotte, 93 and n.
Reeves, Dr. —, 154 and n.
Reynolds, Sir Joshua, 251
Rich, Charlotte, 33 n.
Rich, John, 30 n., 152 and n.
Rigby, Richard, xxix, xxx
Robinson, Sir Thomas, 180 and n.
Rolt, Richard, 29 and n.
Ross, David, xxii, 28 and n.

Sackville, Lord George, 81 and n., 124 n., 381, 419 and n., 444 n.
Sandwich, John Montagu, Earl of, xli, xliii, 27 n., 259 and n., 304 n., 323 and n., 369 and n., 386, 409, 422 and n., 458 and n.

INDEX

Say, —, 85 and n.
Schomberg, Dr. Isaac, 154 and n.
Secker, Thomas, Abp. of Canterbury, 148 n.
Sellon, Rev. William, 65 n., 101 and n., 108, 113, 136 and n., 138
Shebbeare, John, 273 and n.
Shelburne, William Petty, Earl of, 261 and n.
Sheridan, Richard Brinsley, 45 n.
Sheridan, Thomas, 29 and n., 34 n., 44, 98 and n., 121 n., 197 and n.
Shuter, Edward, xxii, 2 and n., 3, 29
Smith, Dr. Robert, 379 and n.
Smith, William, 27 and n.
Smollett, Tobias George, xxiii, xxvi, 50 n., 52, 57 and n., 85, 267, 271
Sparks, Luke, xxii, 27 and n.
Squires, Mary, 74 and n., 88 n.
Steele, Richard, 251
Sterne, Rev. Laurence, xlv, 4, 96 and n., 143
Sternhold, Thomas, 60 and n.
Stone, Andrew, 417 and n.
Stroud, —, 414 and n., 419 and n.
Sumner, Dr. Humphrey, 379 and n., 380
Swift, Jonathan, Dean, 95, 251
Sydney, Algernon, 283 and n.

Talbot, William, Earl, xxx, 80 n., 178 n., 280 and n.
Taylor, John (the Chevalier), 158 and n.
Temple, Richard Grenville-Temple, Earl, 247, 253, 289 and n., 368 n., 435 and n.
Thornton, Bonnell, xiii, xx, xxii, 12 n., 122 n., 312 and n.
Tofts, Mary, 87 and n.
Tucker, Gertrude, (Mrs. Warburton), 297 n., 298 and n.
Tylney, John, Earl, 418 and n., 421 n.
Tyrawley, James O'Hara, Bn., 421 and n.

Vaughan, Thomas, 27 and n.

Vincent, Mrs. (also Miss Burchell and Mrs. Mills), 32 and n.
Violetti, Eva Marie, 45 n.

Waller, Edmund, 59 and n.
Warburton, William, Bp. of Gloucester, 181 and n., 259 and n., 297 and n. et seq., 365 and n., 453 et seq.
Ward, Joshua, 153 and n.
Webb, Philip Carteret, 238 and n., 290 n., 400 n., 444 and n.
Wedderburn, Alexander (Bn. Loughborough), 5 and n., 6
West, Gilbert, 219 and n.
Wharton, Philip, Duke of, 304 and n.
'Whiffle,' see Delaval, Sir Francis
Whitefield, George, 75 and n.
Whitehead, Paul, 116 and n., 170 n., 259, 260, 383, 438
Whitehead, William, 107 and n., 116 and n., 117 and n., 173, 198, 220, 436, 450 n.
Wildman, coffee-house keeper, 368 and n.
Wilkes, John; as editor of Churchill, vii-viii; meets Churchill, xxv; founds The North Briton, xxvii, 217-218; and governorship of Canada, xxix; attempted assassination of, 157; duel with Talbot, xxx; attacks Hogarth, xxxiv; arrested, xxxiv, 234 and n.; caricatured by Hogarth, xxxv, 244 n.; release, xxxv; in Paris, xxxvii; and Forbes, xxxviii, 295 and n.; No. 45, North Briton, xli; Essay on Woman, xli, 290 n.; duel with Martin, xli, 278 n., 282 and n.; in France, xli; suggests printing Hanbury-Williams' letters, xliv; destroys Churchill's papers, xlvi; other references, 323 and n., 339 n., 364 n., 369, 400 n., 429 n.
    Letters to Churchill, vii n., xxvii n., xxx n., xxxi, xxxiii, xxxvii, xxxviii, xxxix, xliv, xlv, 364 n.
Wilkinson, Tate, 3 and n., 20

465

INDEX

Wilks, Robert, 23 and n.
Willes, Dr. Edward, Bp. of Bath and Wells, 440 and n.
Wingate, *see* Dashwood, Sir Francis
Wood, Robert, 238 n., 244 n., 400 n., 444 and n.

Woodward, Henry, xxii, 7 n., 18 and n., 20, 40 n.

Yates, Mary Ann, 34 and n.
Yates, Richard, xxi, 2 and n., 3 n., 17, 25, 34 n.
Yorke, Charles, 444 and n.